ENCYCLOPEDIA
OF
THE LIBRARY OF CONGRESS:
FOR CONGRESS, THE NATION & THE WORLD

ISBN: 0-89059-971-8

Library of Congress Control Number: 2005920202

Printed by Automated Graphic Systems, Inc., White Plains, MD, on acid-free paper
that meets the American National Standards Institute Z39-48 standard.

2005 2004 4 3 2 1

To order reproductions of the images that appear in the *Encyclopedia*, please note the Library of Congress negative number provided with the image (LC-USZ6-, LCZ62-, LC-P6-, or LC-B indicates black and white negative; LC-USZC4- indicates color transparency). Where no negative exists, note the Library division and the title of the item. For pricing and ordering information, please contact the Library of Congress Photoduplication Service, Washington, D.C. 20450-4570; phone: (202) 707-5640; fax: (202) 707-1771; e-mail: photoduplication@loc.gov; Web site: www.loc.gov/preserv/pds.

BERNAN PRESS
4611-F Assembly Drive
Lanham, MD 20706
800-274-4447
email: info@bernan.com
www.bernanpress.com

ENCYCLOPEDIA
OF
THE LIBRARY OF CONGRESS:
FOR CONGRESS, THE NATION & THE WORLD

John Y. Cole and Jane Aikin, Editors

THE LIBRARY OF CONGRESS
WASHINGTON D.C.

IN ASSOCIATION WITH

BERNAN PRESS
Lanham, MD

ENCYCLOPEDIA OF THE LIBRARY OF CONGRESS: FOR CONGRESS, THE NATION & THE WORLD

Edited by John Y. Cole and Jane Aikin

TABLE OF CONTENTS

Portfolio: The Thomas Jefferson Building

The dome of the Thomas Jefferson Building, Library of Congress, capped by the torch of knowledge, shares the Capitol Hill skyline with the dome of the U.S. Capitol. *Photograph by Carol Highsmith.*

The U.S. Capitol Building

The First Location of the Library of Congress

Watercolor of the Capitol in the late 1820s by John Reubens Smith. The Library of Congress occupied the west front of the building.
Prints and Photographs Division, LC-USZC4-3579.

The Three Capitol Hill Buildings of the Library of Congress

The three sites of the modern Library of Congress: the Thomas Jefferson Building at center, the Adams Building behind it, and the James Madison Building at right. *Photograph: Carol Highsmith.*

Ten First Street Southeast

The facade of the Thomas Jefferson Building. *Photograph: Jim Higgins.*

The Neptune Fountain

The huge figure of the Roman sea god Neptune holds sway over his animated court of tritons and nymphs in the fountain by Roland H. Perry. *Photograph: Reid Baker.*

"Knowledge," a circular mural on the second floor, is one of a series of emblematic women painted by Robert Reid. The quote is from Alfred, Lord Tennyson's "Locksley Hall." *Photograph: Anne Day.*

A glass french door, framed by George W. Maynard's panels at the end of a second floor corridor, casts light onto the highly patterned terrazzo floor. *Photograph: Anne Day.*

The majestic mosaic of the goddess Minerva by Elihu Vedder, represents the triumph of civilization. She holds pride of place on the landing leading to the visitor's gallery. *Photograph: Anne Day.*

THE MAIN READING ROOM

The Jefferson Building's octagonal Reading Room is made up of massive piers with engaged columns. The arches they support create eight bays and the arches above support an entablature from which springs the room's magnificent dome. *Photograph: Anne Day*.

A winged Father Time clutching his scythe appears to float above John Flannagan's handsome and complex bronze and marble clock assemblage. *Photograph: Anne Day.*

At the apex of the dome, and beneath its lantern, is Edwin Blashfield's mural, "Human Understanding Lifting Her Veil." The veil represents ignorance and the composition celebrates the educating and civilizing power of learning. *Photograph: Anne Day.*

A reader at a desk is framed by the great dome and arches supporting the dome.
Photograph: Carol Highsmith.

THE PAVILIONS

Four circular pavilions occupy the four corners of the Jefferson Building. Each is decorated in similar fashion with lunettes and ceiling discs that depict different themes.

(room) The Northwest Pavilion: The Arts and Sciences Pavilion: the arts and sciences are the themes of the murals and ceiling disc. *Architect of the Capitol.*

The Southwest Pavilion: Pavilion of the Discoverers: the ceiling disc by George W. Maynard, depicts women exhibiting symbols of the qualities necessary in a Nation's successful development. *Architect of the Capitol.*

The Southeast Pavilion: The Pavilion of the Elements: the ceiling disc is by Robert L. Dodge, and shows Apollo, the sun god, in his chariot, surrounded by discs of the four elements. *Architect of the Capitol.*

<u>The Northeast Pavilion</u>: The Pavilion of the Seals: the disc in the dome is by Elmer E. Garnsey. At the center is the Great Seal of the United States surrounded by a circular band of stars. The outer rim holds Lincoln's immortal words: "...That government of the people, by the people, for the people, shall not perish from this earth." *Photograph: Carol Highsmith.*

PREFACE

In 1800, the United States was taking the first steps toward becoming a great democratic nation. Born out of revolution and filled with a stubborn independent spirit, the new country was guided by an extraordinary group of individuals whose ideals had been shaped by the precepts of the Enlightenment—among them, reliance on reason, belief in progress, and profound appreciation of the importance of knowledge in an ever-changing world. "Knowledge will forever govern ignorance," James Madison wrote in 1822. "And a people who mean to be their own governours, must arm themselves with the power which knowledge brings."

James H. Billington,
The Librarian of Congress.
Photograph: © Sam Kittner.

In 1800, the Congress of the United States was becoming part of this new world: it established a congressional library to help provide it with the information and knowledge required to administer this boisterous and growing land. In the nineteenth century, the Library expanded and became not only a resource for Congress but also a national library for the United States; early in the next century it became one of the world's greatest intellectual and cultural resources. The initial collection of a few hundred books and three maps has grown into diverse collections numbering nearly 128 million items—and we continue to acquire thousands more each year.

Remarkable treasures are found within the Library's three Capitol Hill buildings: 4,000-year-old clay tablets about the Sumerian economy are here, as are fifteenth-century illuminated manuscripts, sixteenth-century holograph music scores, seventeenth-century scientific treatises, eighteenth-century fine prints and political cartoons, nineteenth-century dime novels and illustrated books, and twentieth-century television shows, movies, and CD-ROMs. Reflecting America's history, as well as this country's membership in the community of nations, our collections come from around the world. Researchers from abroad are welcomed here along with the hundreds of thousands of Americans who visit our buildings—their buildings and collections—each year. Around the globe, millions more visit us each day via the Internet; currently about eight million items from our collections are accessible on our Web site, and this will increase. Beginning our third century of service to Congress, the nation, and the world, the Library of Congress continues to be guided by the belief in the power of knowledge that inspired its creation.

This *Encyclopedia of the Library of Congress* is a historically based guide to this great and complex institution, emphasizing its development but also providing current information about its collections, services, and administrative units. It records a proud history of preserving, recording, and sharing the cultural heritage of America and the world. We invite you to learn about us and visit us—in person or via the Internet: <www.loc.gov>. This priceless legacy is yours, not ours.

James H. Billington
The Librarian of Congress

INTRODUCTION

The idea of a one-volume resource emphasizing the history of the Library of Congress emerged in the mid-1990s as the Library began planning for its bicentennial in the year 2000. Our own earlier books provided a helpful outline for the task: John's *For Congress and the Nation: A Chronological History of the Library of Congress* (1979) and Jane's *The Nation's Great Library: Herbert Putnam and the Library of Congress* (1993).

Recognizing that a new, fully documented history of the Library was a worthy goal but in this instance not a practical possibility, we chose a middle ground: a wide-ranging, selective (but not comprehensive) description of the Library and its activities presented through brief overview essays, short articles, illustrations, and statistical appendices. For contributors, we sought individuals knowledgeable about the Library—mostly Library of Congress specialists.

John Y. Cole

The book's goal is to provide a general audience with insights into the historical development of the Library's principal collections, major functions, buildings, and major administrative units. A second, implicit focus is on the contributions of key Library of Congress staff members.

The opening essay in Part I summarizes the Library's historical development chronologically. While most events mentioned also are described elsewhere in the volume, our intent is to paint a broad picture of the Library's evolution for readers who prefer a connected history and who might not be using the book mostly for reference purposes.

Other essays emphasize specialized aspects of the Library's history, such as the Congressional Research Service and the Copyright Office, the Library's electronic resources and its plans for its digital future; and the development of its international and scholarly roles. Descriptions of the Library's historical relationships with the American library community and with two of its sister national institutions, the Smithsonian Institution and the National Archives and Records Service, are included.

Jane Aikin

The shorter articles in Part II, arranged alphabetically, present brief introductions to selected collections, functions, services and administrative units. The appendices in Part III provide historical information and statistics, much of it never before gathered.

We are aware that there is some overlap in and among the essays and the shorter articles; we have tried to keep such duplication to a minimum. However, the stories of the growth and development of the Library's varied collections, functions, and services are thoroughly intertwined and not easily separated. Furthermore, as in most compilations, different authors frequently use different approaches in describing their topics. Each article, however, includes basic historical information.

Because of the general nature of this volume, we have minimized technical terminology and explanations and bibliographic references. The published *Annual Reports of the Librarian of Congress* (1866–) were the most important source for this work, along with the Library of Congress *Information Bulletin* (1943–) and *The Gazette* (1990–), a weekly Library of Congress newspaper for the Library's staff. Essays and articles without any bibliographic references were compiled mostly from these sources. Part IV, Further Research and Reading, suggests additional resources.

Since this endeavor was conceived in the mid-1990s, an important new resource about the Library of Congress and its myriad activities has developed: the Library's Web site (<www.loc.gov>). The site supplements this volume with up-to-date information about the institution's services, collections, and programs—and more. We encourage you to explore the Library's constantly changing and expanding Web site.

We hope that those who use this book will enjoy learning more about a remarkable American institution—one founded by the United States Congress for itself, but with generous congressional support expanded to serve the nation, and now accessible to people everywhere.

John Y. Cole
Jane Aikin

ACKNOWLEDGMENTS

The editors wish to thank the many individuals who have supported us as this project has developed during the past decade. This *Encyclopedia of the Library of Congress* formally began in 1996, when its senior editor, John Y. Cole, Director of the Library's Center for the Book, received official approval for the publication from the Library of Congress. Knowing that this was a large project that had to be completed outside of normal working hours, he immediately recruited historian Jane Aikin as his associate and co-editor.

From 1997 to 1999, many Library of Congress subject specialists generously prepared *Encyclopedia* articles about their administrative units and the collections for which their divisions had custodial responsibility. However the project was delayed, first when the senior editor was named the co-chair of the Library's bicentennial celebration in 2000, and next, in 2001, when, in addition to his duties as director of the Center for the Book, he became program coordinator for the new National Book Festival, a joint project of the Library of Congress and First Lady Laura Bush. In order to complete the volume in accordance with a new deadline and new space limitations, the editors have condensed, revised, and updated many of the articles originally prepared by Library of Congress specialists for this volume. In a few instances, we found we could not use an article as submitted; instead, we incorporated much of the information into other articles. The staff of the Library of Congress always has been one of the major audiences the editors had in mind for this work; it is appropriate that staff members have made such a major contribution, for which we are grateful.

We owe special thanks to Maurvene D. Williams, Program Officer, Center for the Book, for her help and superb organizational skills; to W. Ralph Eubanks, head of the Library of Congress's Publishing Office, for his administrative guidance and general support; to Blaine Marshall of the Publishing Office, our skillful photo editor; to Josephus Nelson of the Manuscript Division and Clarke Allen of the Publishing Office for assistance with illustrations; to Katherine DeBrandt, Jacalyn Houston, Kara Prezocki, Mark Siegal, and Tamera Wells-Lee of Bernan Press, who capably coordinated the production of this historic publication; and to George T. Kurian, President, International Encyclopedia Society, for his patience and his faith that indeed, one day, he would receive a completed manuscript.

The authors of the signed essays and articles are identified in the "Contributors" section at the back of the volume. In the same section we are pleased to acknowledge more than a dozen current and former Library staff members who submitted ideas and early drafts of articles, or whom we called on for advice.

AMERICA'S LIBRARY: A BRIEF HISTORY OF THE LIBRARY OF CONGRESS

by John Y. Cole and Jane Aikin

An engraving of the new Library of Congress Building, or Congressional Library, as it was known when it first opened in 1897. LC/General Collections.

The Library of Congress occupies a unique place in American civilization. Established as a legislative library in 1800, it grew into a national institution in the nineteenth century. Since World War II, it has become an international resource of unparalleled dimension. In 1950, the Library's sesquicentennial year, the eminent librarian S. R. Ranganathan paid the Library and the U.S. Congress an unusual tribute:

> *The institution serving as the national library of the United States is perhaps more fortunate than its predecessors in other countries. It has the Congress as its godfather...This stroke of good fortune has made it perhaps the most influential of all the national libraries of the world.*

By 2004, the Library built and supported by the U.S. Congress had achieved an even greater degree of prominence. Since 1950, the size of its collections and staff had more than tripled, and its annual appropriation soared from $9 million to $540 million. With collections totaling approximately 128 million items, a staff of approximately 4,500 people, and services unmatched in scope by any other research library, the Library of Congress was widely recognized as one of the world's leading cultural institutions.

The diversity of the Library of Congress is startling. Simultaneously it serves as a legislative library and the major research arm of the U.S. Congress; the copyright agency of the United States; a center for scholarship that collects research materials in many media and in most subjects from throughout the world, with 460 languages represented in its collections; a public institution that is open to everyone over high school age and serves readers in 22 reading rooms; a federal library that is heavily used by the executive branch and the judiciary; a national library for the blind and physically handicapped; an outstanding law library; one of the world's largest providers of bibliographic data and products; a center for the commissioning and performance of chamber music; the home of the nation's poet laureate; the sponsor of exhibitions and of musical, literary, and cultural programs that reach across the nation and the world; a research center for the preservation and conservation of library materials; and the world's largest repository of maps, atlases, printed and recorded music, motion pictures and television programs.

The Library occupies three massive structures on Capitol Hill, near the U.S. Capitol. The elaborately decorated Jefferson Building, opened in 1897, is a grand monument to civilization, culture, and American achievement. The handsome, functional Adams Building was opened to the public in 1939. The modern Madison Building, completed in 1980, is by far the largest of the three. Currently collection storage facilities are being constructed and occupied at Fort Meade, Maryland and an National Audio-Visual Conservation Center is being built in Culpeper, Virginia. Nearly two million researchers, scholars, and tourists visit the Library of Congress each year and millions more use its services via the Internet.

Since its creation, the Library of Congress has been part of the legislative branch of the American government. Although it is recognized as the de facto national library of the United States, it does not have that official designation. Nevertheless, it performs those functions performed by national libraries elsewhere, and it has become a symbol of American democracy and faith in the power of learning.

How did a library established by the legislature for its own use become such an ambitious, multipurpose institution? Two points are clear; the expansion of the Library's functions derives from the expansion of its collections; and the growth of the institution is tied to the growth and ambitions of the United States itself. The development of the Library of Congress cannot be separated from the history of the nation it serves. Nor can it be separated from the philosophy and ideals of Thomas Jefferson (1743–1826), its principal founder.

John Adams, second president of the United States, in a lithograph after a portrait by Gilbert Stuart. In 1800, he approved legislation that appropriated funds for "such books as may be necessary for the use of the Congress," which was the birth of the Library of Congress.
LC/Prints and Photographs Division. LC-USZ62-3992.

The Library was established as the legislature of the young republic prepared to move from Philadelphia to the new capital city of Washington. On April 24, 1800, President John Adams approved legislation that appropriated $5,000 to purchase "such books as may be necessary for the use of Congress." The first books, ordered from London, arrived in 1801 and were stored in the U.S. Capitol, the Library's first home. The collection consisted of 740 volumes and three maps. On January 26, 1802, President Thomas Jefferson approved the first law defining the role and functions of the new institution. This measure created the post of Librarian of Congress and gave Congress, through a Joint Committee on the Library, the authority to establish the Library's budget and its rules and

"A view of the President's House in the City of Washington after the conflagration of the 24th August, 1814." Also destroyed in the attack against Washington were the Treasury building and the Capitol which housed the Library of Congress.
LC/Prints and Photographs Division. LC-USZ62-7578.

regulations. From the beginning, however, the institution was more than just a legislative library, for the 1802 law made the appointment of the Librarian of Congress a presidential responsibility. It also permitted the president and vice president to borrow books, a privilege that, in the next three decades, was extended to most government agencies and to the judiciary.

Three developments in the Library's early history permanently established the institution's national roots. First, the Library of Congress was created by the national legislature, which took direct responsibility for its operation. Second, the Library of Congress served as the first library of the U.S. government. Finally, in 1815, the scope of the Library's collection was permanently expanded. The ideals, intellectual curiosity, and pragmatism of Thomas Jefferson were the key to this transformation.

Jefferson believed that the power of the intellect could shape a free and democratic society. A man who once said that he could not live without books, he took a keen interest in the Library of Congress and its collection while he was president of the United States (1801–1809). Throughout his presidency, he personally recommended books for the Library, and he appointed the first two Librarians of Congress. In 1814, the British army invaded the city of Washington and burned the Capitol, including the 3,000-volume Library of Congress. By then retired to Monticello, Jefferson offered to sell his personal library, the largest and finest in the country, to the Congress to replace the destroyed collection. The purchase of Jefferson's 6,487 volumes for $23,940 was approved in 1815.

The library that Jefferson sold to Congress not only included over twice the number of volumes that had been destroyed, it expanded the scope of the

Library far beyond the bounds of a legislative library devoted primarily to legal, economic, and historical works. Jefferson was a man of encyclopedic interests, and his library included works on architecture, the arts, science, literature, and geography. It contained books in French, Spanish, German, Latin, Greek, and one three-volume statistical work in Russian. He believed that the American legislature needed ideas and information on all subjects and in many languages in order to govern a democracy. Anticipating the argument that his collection might be too comprehensive, he argued that there was "no subject to which a Member of Congress may not have occasion to refer."

The acquisition by Congress of Jefferson's library provided the base for the expansion of the Library's functions. The Jeffersonian concept of universality is the rationale for the comprehensive collecting policies of today's Library of Congress. Jefferson and his friend and successor as president, James Madison (1809–1817) believed in the power of knowledge and the direct link between knowledge and democracy. The vast collections and varied services of the Library of Congress are founded on this belief.

One congressman who favored the purchase of Jefferson's library expressed a growing cultural nationalism in the United States when he argued that it would make "a most admirable substratum for a National Library." Many Americans, aware of the cultural dependence of the United States on Europe, were anxious that their country establish its own traditions and institutions. For example, an editorial in the July 15, 1815, (Washington, D.C.) daily *National Intelligencer* pointed out: "In all civilized nations of Europe there are national libraries...In a country of such general intelligence as this, the Congressional or National Library of the United States [should] become the great repository of the literature of the world."

The Library grew slowly but steadily after the Jefferson library purchase. A separate law department was approved in 1832, along with an appropriation to purchase law books under the guidance of the chief justice of the United States. Yet even as the Library was beginning to grow, it appeared that the Smithsonian Institution might become the American national library. During the early 1850s, the Smithsonian's talented and aggressive librarian, Charles Coffin Jewett, tried to move the institution in that direction and turn it into a national bibliographical center. Jewett's efforts were opposed, however, by Smithsonian Secretary Joseph Henry, who insisted that the Smithsonian focus on scientific research and publication. In fact, the secretary favored the eventual development of a national library at the Library of Congress, which he viewed as the appropriate foundation for "a collection of books worthy of a Government whose perpetuity principally depends on the intelligence of the people." On July 10, 1854, Henry dismissed Jewett, ending any possibility that the Smithsonian might become the national library. Moreover, 12 years later, Henry readily agreed to the transfer of the entire 40,000-volume library of the Smithsonian Institution to the Library of Congress.

A selection of books from Thomas Jefferson's library, which he sold to Congress in 1815 to replace the collection of books lost in the disastrous fire of 1814. The open volume of Cicero's letters in the foreground features dual-language text and a handwritten emendation by Jefferson.
LC/Rare Book and Special Collections Division.

The Library of Congress suffered difficult times during the 1850s. The growing division between North and South hindered the growth of government institutions. Furthermore, in late 1851 the most serious fire in the Library's history destroyed about two-thirds of its 55,000 volumes, including two-thirds of Jefferson's library. Congress responded quickly and generously: in 1852 a total of $168,700 was appropriated to restore the Library's rooms in the Capitol and to replace the lost books. However, no plan was set forth for expanding the collection or the Library's services. This philosophy was in keeping with the conservative views of John Silva Meehan, Librarian of Congress from 1829 to 1861, and Senator James A. Pearce of Maryland, the chairman of the Joint Committee on the Library (1845–1862), who favored keeping strict limits on the Library's activities.

In the late 1850s, the Library lost several collection-building functions, further impeding its progress toward the comprehensive collection that Jefferson had favored. In the 1830s and 1840s, on

Ainsworth Rand Spofford as a young man before he came to Washington. Appointed Librarian of Congress by President Lincoln in 1864, he convinced Congress of the need for the Library to have its own building, separating it entirely from its severely overcrowded rooms in the Capitol.
LC Archives.

behalf of the U.S. government, the Library began distributing public documents to institutions throughout the United States and exchanging books and documents with foreign institutions. However, a joint resolution of Congress in 1857 transferred responsibility for public document distribution to the Bureau of Interior and responsibility for international exchange of books and documents to the Department of State. Moreover, in 1859 all U.S. copyright activities were centralized at the Patent Office, which meant that the Library of Congress and the Smithsonian Institution no longer received the copies of books and pamphlets deposited for copyright that had been sent to each institution since 1846.

The individual responsible for transforming the Library into an institution of national significance in the Jeffersonian spirit was Ainsworth Rand Spofford, a former Cincinnati bookseller and journalist who served as Librarian of Congress from 1864 until 1897. Spofford accomplished this task by permanently linking the legislative and national functions of the Library, first in practice and then by law, through the reorganization of the Library approved by Congress in 1897. He provided his successors as Librarian with four essential prerequisites for the development of an American national library; (1) firm, bipartisan congressional support for the notion of the Library of Congress as both a legislative and a national library; (2) the beginning of a comprehensive collection of Americana; (3) a magnificent new building, itself a national monument; and (4) a strong and independent office of Librarian of Congress. Spofford had the vision, skill, and perseverance to capitalize on the Library of Congress's claim to a national role, and each subsequent Librarian of Congress has built upon his accomplishments. Each has shaped the institution in a different way, but none has wavered from the Jeffersonian belief that the democratic form of government depends on a comprehensive base of knowledge and information.

The idea of an American national library that Spofford revived had been languishing since Jewett's departure from the Smithsonian in 1854. Spofford and Jewett shared several ideas relating to a national library; in particular, both recognized the importance of copyright deposit in developing a comprehensive collection of a nation's literature. Yet there was a major difference in their views. Spofford never envisioned the Library of Congress as the center of a network of American libraries, a focal point for providing other libraries with cataloging and bibliographic services. Instead, he viewed it as a unique, independent institution—a single, comprehensive collection of a nation's literature to be used both by Congress and the American people. Congress needed such a collection because, as Spofford paraphrased Jefferson, "there is almost no work, within the vast range of literature and science, which may not at some time prove useful to the legislature of a great nation." It was imperative, he felt, that such a great national collection be shared with all citizens, for the United States was "a Republic which rests upon the popular intelligence."

During the post-Civil War period, Spofford took full advantage of several trends to promote the Library's growth: a favorable political and cultural climate, increasing national confidence, and expansion of the federal government. He always believed that the Library of Congress was the national library and he used every conceivable argument to convince others, particularly the Joint Committee on the Library and the rest of Congress.

In the first years of his administration, Spofford obtained congressional approval of six laws or resolutions that ensured a national role for the Library of Congress. The legislative acts were: an appropriation for the expansion of the Library in the Capitol Building, approved in early 1865; the copyright amendment of 1865, which once again brought copyright deposits into the Library's collection; the Smithsonian deposit of 1866, whereby the entire library of the Smithsonian Institution, a collection especially strong in scientific materials, was transferred to the Library; the 1867 purchase, for $100,000, of the private library of historian and archivist Peter Force, establishing the foundation of the Library's Americana and incunabula collections; the international exchange resolution of 1867, providing for the

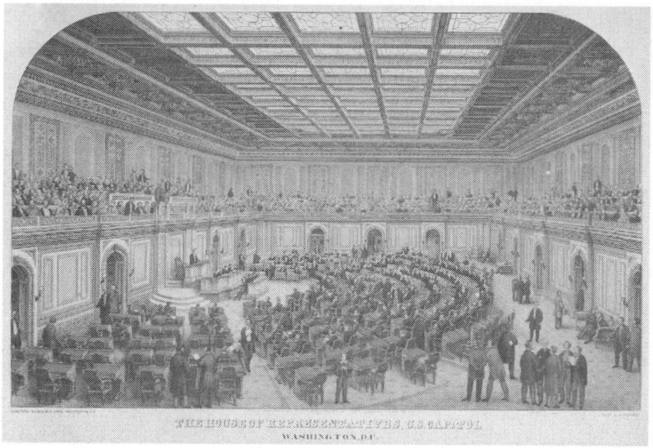

The House of Representatives in 1866 in the U.S. Capitol in a lithograph by Sachse.
LC/Prints and Photographs Division. LC-USZC4-422.

development of the Library's collection of foreign public documents; and the Copyright Act of 1870, which brought all U.S. copyright registration and deposit activities to the Library.

The centralization of copyright activities at the Library was Spofford's most impressive collection-building feat. The first U.S. copyright law was approved in 1790, but the practice of depositing items registered for copyright protection in libraries for the use of the public was not enacted until 1846, when the newly established Smithsonian Institution and the Library of Congress obtained the privilege. The Library of Congress received single copies of deposits from 1846 until 1859, and the practice started again in 1865. Enforcement was a problem, however, and Spofford decided he needed the authority that would come from centralizing all registration and deposit activities at the Library, consolidating functions then performed at the Patent Office and by the district courts. The Copyright Law of 1870 ensured the continuing development of the Library's Americana collections, for it stipulated that two copies of every book, pamphlet, map, print, photograph, and piece of music registered for copyright be deposited in the Library.

In its 1876 survey of the libraries of the United States, the U.S. Bureau of Education listed the rapidly growing Library of Congress and the Boston Public Library as the two largest libraries in the United States, with approximately 300,000 volumes apiece. By 1897, when the Library moved from its overcrowded rooms in the Capitol into its spacious new building, its collections ranked first among American libraries in size and scope. Over 40 percent of its 840,000 volumes and at least 90 percent of its map, music, and graphic arts collections had been acquired through copyright deposit. Important items deposited through copyright included Civil War photographs by Mathew Brady and what today are considered the earliest motion pictures.

The copyright privilege not only built the Library's collections, it also helped determine the direction of their growth. When the staff moved into the new building, separate custodial units were established for the special collections formed primarily through copyright deposit: maps, music and graphic arts. Spofford's successors as Librarian of Congress hired subject specialists to develop these and other collections and persuaded Congress to begin appropriating substantial funds for the purchase of research materials for all collections. Today, copyright is still one of the Library's major acquisitions sources, but between the years 1865 and 1897, it played a crucial role in the development of the Library of Congress into a national institution.

The Copyright Law of 1870 had another major effect: it forced the construction of a building for the Library. Spofford foresaw this result almost immediately. In his 1871 *Annual Report,* he suggested that a separate building might be needed because of the increased receipts resulting from the new copyright law. The next year he presented a plan for such a building, initiating an endeavor that dominated the rest of his career as Librarian. In the 25-year struggle to make the building a reality, Spofford enlisted the support of many powerful public figures: congressmen, cultural leaders, journalists, and even presidents. The speeches and statements he elicited usually endorsed not only a separate building, but also the concept of the Library of Congress as a national library.

Spofford's most dependable supporters were two senators, both personal friends and frequent Library of Congress users: Justin S. Morrill of Vermont and Daniel W. Voorhees of Indiana. In

Senators Justin S. Morrill, Republican of Vermont, left, and Daniel W. Voorhees, right, made eloquent speeches on behalf of a new building for the Library, giving Librarian Spofford moral support. Eventually, together they successfully steered the necessary legislation through Congress. LC/Prints and Photographs Division. Morrill: LC-BH82-4787. Voorhees: LC-USZ62-117814.

March 1879, Morrill delivered a major speech in which he strongly endorsed a separate Library building and Spofford's national library concept:

We must either reduce the Library to the stinted and specific wants of Congress alone, or permit it to advance to national importance, and give it room equal to the culture, wants, and resources of a great people. The higher education of our common country demands that this institution shall not be crippled for lack of room.

Senator Voorhees, chairman of the Joint Committee on the Library, was more passionate. In a May 1880 speech, he expressed his very Jeffersonian belief in the essential moral value of books and intellectual activity:

Let us therefore give this great national library our love and our care. Nothing can surpass it in importance. Knowledge is power, the power to maintain free government and preserve constitutional liberty. Without it the world grows dark and the human race takes up its backward race to the regions of barbarism. I cannot believe that the plain imperative duty of Congress on the subject of its Library will be longer neglected.

Such eloquence, plus behind-the-scenes efforts by Morrill, Voorhees, and Spofford, finally resulted in 1886 in authorization for a structure directly across the east plaza from the Capitol. After further delays, construction began in earnest in 1889 and the new building, opened to the public in 1897, was immediately hailed as a national monument. Now called the Thomas Jefferson Building, this imposing structure in the style of the Italian Renaissance, with its grand Main Reading Room at the center and exuberant interior decoration throughout, is an incomparable symbol of the universality of knowledge.

The splendid new Congressional Library, as it was called when it opened in 1897. The statue of George Washington at right is now in the Smithsonian Institution's National Museum of American History.
LC/Prints and Photographs Division. LC-P6-6534A.

To Spofford also goes primary credit for beginning the Library's tradition of broad public service. In 1865, he extended the hours of service, so that the Library was open every weekday all year. In 1869, he began advocating evening hours, but this innovation was not approved by Congress until 1898. Finally, in the mid-1880s, Spofford began lending books directly to the citizens of the District of Columbia if an appropriate sum was left on deposit, a procedure that ended in 1894, when preparations were started for the move into the new Library building.

In 1896, just before the actual move, the Joint Committee on the Library held hearings about "the condition" of the Library and its possible reorganization. The hearings provided an occasion for a detailed examination of the Library's history and present functions and for a review of what new functions the Library might perform once it occupied the spacious new building. The American Library Association sent six witnesses, including future Librarian of Congress Herbert Putnam from the Boston Public Library and Melvil Dewey from New York State Library. Members of Congress listened with great interest to the testimony of Putnam and Dewey, who argued that the national services of the Library should be greatly expanded. Dewey felt that the Library of Congress now had the opportunity to act as a true national library, which he defined as "a center to which the libraries of the whole country can turn for inspiration, guidance, and practical help, which can be rendered so economically and efficiently in no other possible way." Testimony at the 1896 hearings greatly influenced the reorganization of the Library, which was incorporated into the Legislative Appropriations Act approved February 19, 1897, and became effective on July 1, 1897. All phases of the Library's activities were expanded and new administrative units were established.

President William McKinley appointed a new Librarian of Congress to supervise the move from the Capitol and implement the new reorganization. He was John Russell Young, who held office briefly, from July 1, 1897, until his death in January 1899. A journalist and former diplomat, Young worked hard to strengthen both the comprehensiveness of the collections and the scope of the services provided to Congress. He honored Jefferson's influence on the

Library, placing Jefferson's books in a special room and commissioning a report on the Jefferson library that was published in the Library's 1898 *Annual Report.*

Librarian Young used his diplomatic ties and experience to enlarge the Library's collections. In February 1898, for example, he sent a letter to U.S. diplomatic and consular representatives throughout the world, asking them to send "to the national library" newspapers, journals, pamphlets, manuscripts, broadsides, and "documents illustrative of the history of those various nationalities now coming to our shores to blend into our national life. "He asked for a broad range of materials, in fact "whatever, in a word, would add to the sum of human knowledge." By the end of 1898, books and other materials had been received from eleven legations and seven consulates.

Young skillfully guided the administrative reorganization. He made many important professional appointments, including Thorvald Solberg, the first register of copyrights, and catalogers J. C. M. Hanson and Charles Martel, who began reclassifying the collections after nearly a century of reliance on the classification scheme Thomas Jefferson provided to the Library along with his books. He also inaugurated what today is one of the Library's best known national activities: library service for the blind and physically handicapped. In November of 1897, the Library began a program of daily readings for the blind in a special "pavilion for the blind" complete with its own library. In 1913, Congress stipulated the deposit in the Library of the embossed books produced by the American Printing House for the Blind, and in 1931 a separate appropriation was authorized for providing "books for the use of adult blind residents of the United States."

Herbert Putnam, Young's successor, was appointed by President McKinley in the spring of 1899 and served as Librarian of Congress for 40 years, until the autumn of 1939. Asked to characterize the Library as he neared the end of his long career, Putnam penned the phrase "Universal in Scope: National in Service." This apt phrase described his entire tenure, for if Spofford's major contributions were the creation of a national collection and a separate building, Putnam was the Librarian of Congress who did the most to extend the Library to the American people. He created a systematic program of widespread public use that exists to this day, opening up the collections to scholars, the public, and to other libraries. The first experienced librarian to serve as Librarian of Congress, Putnam established a working partnership between the Library of Congress and the American library movement. Rather than serving merely as a great national accumulation of books, a national library should, he felt, actively serve other libraries as well as researchers and scholars.

Herbert Putnam, head of the Boston Public Library, was the first experienced librarian to become Librarian of Congress. President McKinley appointed him in 1899.
LC/Prints and Photographs Division. LC-USZ62-6012A.

In the quarter century before Putnam took office, a new structure of scientific and scholarly activity had evolved rapidly in the United States. Professional schools and new universities offering graduate work were established; numerous professional associations and societies came into existence; and the federal government became an active supporter of education, research, and scientific activity. By 1900, the age of the great library had arrived in America, characterized by huge bookstacks, scientific cataloging and classification, and full-time professional staffs. The new Library of Congress building symbolized this age. As the largest library in the country and the first American library to reach one million volumes in size, the Library of Congress became the leader among American libraries. Putnam's imaginative and decisive actions to develop the Library's role were approved by both the Joint Library Committee and the professional library community. Under his leadership, the first volume of a completely new classification scheme, based on the Library's own collections, was published; access to the Library was extended to "scientific investigators and duly qualified individuals" throughout the United States; an interlibrary loan service was inaugurated; and the sale and distribution of Library of Congress printed catalog cards began.

The interlibrary loan system was an especially radical step, for it signaled the institution's transition from a national storehouse of books to a national laboratory or workshop, actively promoting the use of

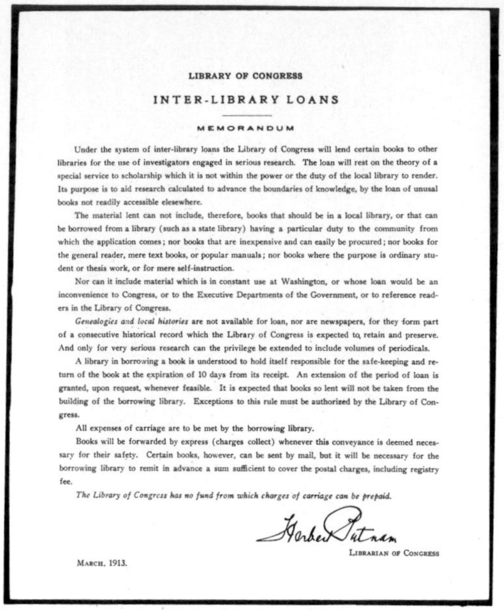

LIBRARY OF CONGRESS

INTER-LIBRARY LOANS

MEMORANDUM

Under the system of inter-library loans the Library of Congress will lend certain books to other libraries for the use of investigators engaged in serious research. The loan will rest on the theory of a special service to scholarship which it is not within the power or the duty of the local library to render. Its purpose is to aid research calculated to advance the boundaries of knowledge, by the loan of unusal books not readily accessible elesewhere.

The material lent can not include, therefore, books that should be in a local library, or that can be borrowed from a library (such as a state library) having a particular duty to the community from which the application comes; nor books that are inexpensive and can easily be procured; nor books for the general reader, mere text books, or popular manuals; nor books where the purpose is ordinary student or thesis work, or for mere self-instruction.

Nor can it include material which is in constant use at Washington, or whose loan would be an inconvenience to Congress, or to the Executive Departments of the Government, or to reference readers in the Library of Congress.

Genealogies and local histories are not available for loan, nor are newspapers, for they form part of a consecutive historical record which the Library of Congress is expected to retain and preserve. And only for very serious research can the privilege be extended to include volumes of periodicals.

A library in borrowing a book is understood to hold itself responsible for the safe-keeping and return of the book at the expiration of 10 days from its receipt. An extension of the period of loan is granted, upon request, whenever feasible. It is expected that books so lent will not be taken from the building of the borrowing library. Exceptions to this rule must be authorized by the Library of Congress.

All expenses of carriage are to be met by the borrowing library.

Books will be forwarded by express (charges collect) whenever this conveyance is deemed necessary for their safety. Certain books, however, can be sent by mail, but it will be necessary for the borrowing library to remit in advance a sum sufficient to cover the postal charges, including registry fee.

The Library of Congress has no fund from which charges of carriage can be prepaid.

Herbert Putnam
LIBRARIAN OF CONGRESS

MARCH, 1913.

This 1913 memorandum codified Putnam's 1901 decision to lend items from the Library's collections to other libraries and their users.
LC Archives.

the collections. It required special legislation by Congress and approval was by no means assured. When asked to defend his position that books should be sent outside the District of Columbia, the Librarian explained that the risk was justified because "a book used, is after all, fulfilling a higher mission than a book which is merely being preserved for possible future use." It was a telling statement about the openness of American libraries and the spirit of cooperation that would weld them into a strong community. Moreover, Librarian Putnam's extension of the Library's classification and cataloging schemes to the rest of the nation helped "democratize" knowledge, nationally and internationally, for it established bibliographic standards and encouraged cooperative endeavors among librarians and scholars. This sharing of the Library's "bibliographic apparatus" helped systematize and communicate information about intellectual activity in America and propelled the Library of Congress into a position of international leadership among research institutions.

The development of the Library's collections into a nationally useful resource took many forms. To aid historical research, Putnam felt that the national library "should be able to offer original sources" about the national life. In 1903, he persuaded his friend and supporter, President Theodore Roosevelt, to issue an executive order that transferred the papers of many of the nation's founding fathers, including George Washington, Thomas Jefferson, and James Madison, from the State Department archives to the Library's Manuscript Division. In 1904, the Library began publishing important historical texts from its collections, such as the *Journals of the Continental Congress*. Putnam felt the publication of such manuscripts was "not perhaps so much a service from us as a library as a duty from us as the custodians of original sources for American history."

As American influence and interests to expand in the twentieth century, Putnam looked abroad to build the Library's collections, boldly applying Jefferson's dictum that no subject was beyond the possible concern of Congress or the American people. The Librarian was especially farsighted in acquiring research materials about other countries and cultures. In 1904, he purchased a 4,000-volume library of Indica, explaining in the Library's *Annual Report* that he "could not ignore the opportunity to acquire a unique collection which scholarship thought worthy of prolonged, scientific, and enthusiastic research, even though the immediate use of such a collection may prove meager." In 1906, he acquired the famous 80,000-volume private library of Russian literature owned by G. V. Yudin of Siberia, even sending a staff member to Russia to supervise the packing and shipping of the books. The Schatz Collection of early opera librettos was purchased from a German collector in 1908. Large and important collections of Hebraica and Chinese and Japanese books also were acquired. By 1926, the Library had obtained appropriated funds to send a permanent representative to Europe, stationed in Paris, to assist with acquisitions by developing contacts with "dealers, collectors, scholars, and learned institutions."

In one notable instance, Congress took the initiative in building the Library's collections. In December 1929, despite the stock market crash two months earlier, Congressman Ross Collins of Mississippi proposed the purchase for $1.5 million of the 3,000-volume collection of early books assembled by collector Otto F. Vollbehr, which included one of three perfect existing vellum copies of the Gutenberg Bible. Congressman Albert Johnson of Washington, in the debate in the House of Representatives, maintained that "even if times are hard," Congress should purchase the collection because "it is all for the United States of America which is going to live we hope for thousands of years." Testifying before the Senate Library Committee, Putnam added his endorsement to the enthusiasm expressed by the House of Representatives. He reminded the committee that in 1815, the government paid Thomas Jefferson nearly $24,000 for his library, and "in proportion to the resources of the country that sum was not much short of the million and a half" asked for the Vollbehr collection. Moreover, "what was true of that purchase is certainly true of the one before you. It

Included in the Vollbehr Collection was one of three perfect copies of the Gutenberg bible in existence, (pictured) which had been purchased from a Benedictine monastery in Austria. The collection of incunabula, worth approximately $3 million, included books produced by some 635 early printing establishments, some in vernacular languages instead of the usual Latin.
LC/Rare Book and Special Collections Division.

Librarian Putnam at left, and Otto H. F. Vollbehr at right, holding onto the case, bring the 3,000 volume collection of fifteenth century books to the Library of Congress. The collection came to the Library through a congressional appropriation of $1.5 million, considered a bargain price at the time.
LC Archives.

would form a most admirable substratum for a (greater) national library." The purchase was approved in 1930.

The Library's foremost function, support for legislative activities, was strengthened in 1914 when the Legislative Reference Service was established as a separate administrative unit. Its creation occurred in response to the Progressive era advocacy of the "scientific" (and Jeffersonian) use of information to solve governmental problems. After specialized library units for legislative research were established in several states, notably Wisconsin, during the early 1900s, Putnam explained the function of a similar legislative reference bureau within the Library:

What we do not do, and what a legislative reference division in the Library would do, is to select out of this great collection—now 2,000,000 books and pamphlets—the material that may bear upon one or another of the topics under consideration by Congress or that are likely to be under consideration, or that come up under particular discussions.

In other words, the Library would begin providing the Congress a research service.

In 1915, the Librarian reported that the new legislative service was anticipating questions from Congress on: "the conservation bills, so-called," the merchant marine, the government of the Philippines, immigration, convict-made goods, railroad securities, federal aid in roadmaking, publicity in campaign contributions, and a national budget system.

While enhancing established functions Putnam also moved the Library in new directions. The Library of Congress Trust Fund Board Act of 1925, which enabled the institution to accept gifts and bequests from private citizens, was the major vehicle for the Librarian's innovations. This legislation, which created a new cultural role for the Library, was inspired by a proposal from private citizen, Elizabeth Sprague Coolidge. She offered an endowment to the Library for promoting the appreciation and understanding of music and to pay for a concert hall within the Library building that would support the commissioning of new works of music and provide the chief of the Music Division with a generous honorarium. Prominent individuals such as James B. Wilbur, Archer Huntington, John D. Rockefeller, Gertrude Clarke Whittall, and many others soon joined Mrs. Coolidge as Library of Congress benefactors. In particular, Gertrude Clarke Whittall's donation of five Stradivari instruments and the funding for concerts at which they could be played helped establish the Library as a patron of the arts. This new private funding through the Trust Fund also allowed the Library

Three Stradivari violins – The Ward (1700), the Castelbarco (1699), and the Betts (1704) – three of the Stradivari instruments donated by Mrs. Gertrude Whittall in 1935 which have been played regularly in the Coolidge Auditorium by the resident string quartet. The string quartet is supported by the Gertrude Clarke Whittall Foundation. Photograph: © Dane Penland.

to establish chairs and consultantships for scholars and a consultantship for poetry, which has evolved today into the Poet Laureate Consultant in Poetry.

Putnam was careful to define precisely appropriate uses of the support the Library received through the Trust Fund. Private funds were to serve a limited role, to "do for American scholarship and cultivation what is not likely to be done by other agencies" and most definitely supplement, not replace, the annual government appropriation. His vision for the Library's cultural and educational role and how it could be developed and funded established the precedent for the valuable private sector support that the Library of Congress receives today.

The Librarian enhanced the Library's symbolic role as a cradle of Jeffersonian democracy in 1921 when he arranged for the nation's two most precious documents, the Declaration of Independence and the Constitution, to be transferred to the Library from the State Department. In 1924, the documents went on permanent public display in a specially designed "Shrine" in the Library's Great Hall. The Library transferred both documents to the National Archives in 1952, but still holds, as one of its greatest treasures, Jefferson's handwritten draft of the Declaration of Independence. In his book *The Epic of America*, published in 1931, historian James Truslow Adams paid tribute to the Library of Congress "as a symbol of what democracy can accomplish on its own behalf...founded and built by the people, it is for the people."

The Declaration of Independence and the Constitution of the United States in the Shrine designed by Francis H. Bacon to be displayed in the magnificent Great Hall. The State Department transferred these precious documents to the Library in 1921. The Shrine was dedicated in 1924 in a ceremony consisting only of the singing of two stanzas of "America."
LC Archives.

The North Reading Room in the Adams Building, known as the Annex Building when it opened in 1939, features artist Ezra Winters's distinctive murals of the procession of Chaucer's pilgrims from "the Canterbury Tales."
LC/Prints and Photographs Division. LC-US-P6-72A.

The rapid expansion of the Library's collections and services during Putnam's 40 years as Librarian naturally required increased space. Additional bookstacks within the Jefferson Building were built in 1910 and 1927. In 1907, Putnam had assured Congress that when the shelving space in the Jefferson Building was gone, "storage shelving may be extended into plain, simple, inexpensive but appropriate buildings in the neighborhood." Legislation to acquire land for a new structure was approved in 1928, and the Annex Building (today the Adams Building) was authorized in 1930. Construction was delayed during the Depression years, but the classically simple, rectangular structure, chiefly intended for book storage, was completed in 1938 and opened to the public in 1939.

The Library of Congress as a democratic institution and repository of American cultural traditions was a concept that captured the imagination of Putnam's successor, writer, lawyer and poet Archibald MacLeish. Appointed by President Franklin Roosevelt in 1939, MacLeish served as Librarian of Congress until the end of 1944, when he became assistant secretary of state. An advocate of U.S. involvement in World War II, MacLeish used the office of Librarian of Congress imaginatively to speak out on behalf of democracy. He urged librarians to "become active and not passive agents of the democratic process," and criticized his fellow intellectuals for their failure to defend American culture against the threat of totalitarianism. He became the most publicly visible Librarian of Congress in the history of the office.

MacLeish brought the Library and its unique collections directly into the war effort. His statement in the Library's 1940 *Annual Report* regarding reference service, explained that the Library would undertake "for officers and departments of government research projects, appropriate to the Library, which can be executed by reference to its collections, and which the staffs of offices and departments are unable to execute." A Defense Section was established in the Legislative Reference Service in 1941, and expanded in the next few years to support the work of various government war agencies. Its projects were partly supported by those agencies through transferred appropriated funds.

Paying tribute to Jefferson's concept of liberty and self-government, Librarian MacLeish dedicated the South Reading Room in the Adams Building to the Library's principal founder in 1941. At MacLeish's request, artist Ezra Winter decorated the Jefferson Reading Room with four murals that drew their themes from quotations from Jefferson on the subjects of freedom, labor, the "living generation," education, and democratic government. MacLeish also established a "democracy alcove" in the Main Reading Room, where readers could find "the classic texts of the American tradition," including the Declaration of Independence, the Constitution, the Federalist Papers, and other writings of American statesmen. When in 1943, the Library commemorated the bicentennial of Jefferson's birth, MacLeish called Jefferson's definition of liberty the "greatest and the most moving, as it is the most articulate." An annotated catalog of the books in Jefferson's personal library by bibliographer E. Millicent Sowerby was undertaken; it was published in five volumes between 1952 and 1959.

Thanks to MacLeish's personal interests and contacts, during his librarianship the Library of Congress established new and enduring relationships with American writers and scholars. Other highlights of the fruitful MacLeish years were the development of Library-wide objectives; an administrative reorganization so thorough that it lasted for more than three decades; the creation of a rotating consultantship in poetry; and fellowship programs for young scholars. The Librarian extended Jefferson's rationale to foreign materials, asserting, in his "Canons of Selection" in the 1940 *Annual Report*, that the Library should acquire the "written records of those societies and peoples whose experience is of most immediate concern to the people of the United States." Indeed, World War II's most important effect on the Library was to stimulate further development of its collections about other nations.

Librarian MacLeish resigned in 1944 and, in 1945, President Truman named assistant librarian Luther H. Evans, a political scientist, as Librarian. Evans served until 1953. To justify his ambitious proposals in fiscal year 1947 to expand the Library's collections and services, Evans emphasized Jefferson's "doctrine of completeness and inclusiveness." The challenges of the post-war years meant, to Evans, that "no spot on the earth's surface is any longer alien to the interest of the American people." He felt that the major lesson of World War II was that "however large our collections may now be, they are pitifully and tragically small in comparison with the demands of the nation." He described the need for larger collections of foreign research materials in practical as well as patriotic terms, noting that in the years leading up to the war "the want of early issues of the *Voelkische Boebachter* prevented the first auguries of Naziism," while during the war, weather data on the Himalayas from the Library's collections helped the Air Force.

One answer was improved cooperation among libraries. As chief assistant librarian, in 1942 Evans and Librarian MacLeish represented the Library at the first planning meeting for the Farmington Plan, a cooperative acquisitions project among American research libraries. As Librarian of Congress, he continued to support the project.

To continue exploiting the Library's collections for national defense and security purposes, senior staff entered an agreement in 1947 to handle scientific and technical literature research for the Office of Naval Research. In 1948, Evans established the Air Research Unit in the Library's Aeronautics Division to "provide certain services to the United States Air Force in connection with the collections of the Library and with other materials available to the Library." Fifteen years later, when Librarian of Congress L. Quincy Mumford changed the name of the Air Research Division to the Defense Research Division, the Library would begin providing contract research services on a nearly global basis to the U.S. Army and Navy as well.

The acquisitions, cataloging, and bibliographic services of the Library grew during the Evans years, but not as rapidly as the Librarian desired. He believed that the Library of Congress should actively serve all libraries, but an economy-minded, post-war Congress balked at his expansionist plans. His strong personal interest in issues such as copyright and intellectual freedom strengthened the Library's involvement in each of these areas. But most of all, Evans's interests and activities shaped a new Library of Congress. The Library of Congress Mission in Europe, organized by Evans and director of acquisitions Verner W. Clapp in 1945, acquired European publications for the Library and for other American libraries. The Library soon initiated automatic book purchase agreements with foreign dealers around the world and greatly expanded its agreements for the international exchange of official publications. It organized a reference library in San Francisco in 1945 to assist the participants in the meeting that established the United Nations. In 1947, a Library of Congress Mission to Japan provided advice for the establishment of the National Diet Library.

Evans's successor as Librarian of Congress was L. Quincy Mumford, who was director of the Cleveland Public Library in 1954 when he was nominated by President Eisenhower. During his 20 years in office, he guided the Library through its most intensive period of national and international expansion. In 1957, Mumford initiated studies for a third major Library building. In the 1960s, the Library of Congress benefited from increased federal funding for education, libraries, and research. Most dramatic was the growth of the foreign acquisitions program, an expansion partially based on Evans's achievements a decade earlier. In 1958, the Library was authorized by Congress to acquire books by using U.S.-owned foreign currency under the terms of the Agricultural Trade Development and Assistance Act of 1954 (Public Law 480). The first appropriation for this purpose was made in 1961, enabling the Library to establish acquisitions centers in New Delhi and Cairo to purchase publications and distribute them to research libraries throughout the United States. This, however, was only the first step.

In 1965, President Lyndon B. Johnson approved a Higher Education Act which, through Title IIC, directed the Library of Congress to acquire, insofar as possible, all current library materials of value to scholarship published throughout the world, and to provide cataloging information for these materials promptly after they had been received. This law came closer than any other legislation to making Jefferson's concept of comprehensiveness part of the Library's official mandate. The new effort was christened the National Program for Acquisitions and Cataloging (NPAC). The first NPAC office was opened in London in 1966 and expanded rapidly. The cataloging provided by Library of Congress catalogers benefited every other library that acquired the same material. Today, the Library has six overseas offices (New Delhi, Islamabad, Cairo, Jakarta, Nairobi, Rio de Janeiro) and cooperative acquisitions arrangements with booksellers and libraries around the world.

Shared acquisitions and cataloging made international bibliographic standards imperative. The crucial development took place in the mid-1960s: the creation of the Library of Congress MARC (MAchine Readable Cataloging) format for communicating bibliographic data in machine-readable form. This new capability for converting, maintaining, and distributing bibliographic information soon became the standard format for sharing data about books and other research materials. The potential for worldwide application was immediately recognized, and the MARC format structure became an official national standard in 1971 and an international standard in 1973.

The preservation and conservation of library collections became an important concern of research libraries in the 1960s. In 1967, the Library of Congress inaugurated a pilot project to study techniques for the preservation of deteriorating or "brittle " books—volumes disintegrating because they were printed on acidic paper. Today, the Library's Preservation Office administers what has become the world's largest library research and conservation laboratory and shares techniques with the library community.

Mary Wooten in the Library's Conservation Office, treating the autograph manuscript of Arnold Schoenberg's "Pierrot Lunaire." Photograph: Jim Higgins/LC.

Amid the rapid growth of collections, computer and preservation methods, there took place the most recent serious public debate about the dual legislative and national roles of the Library of Congress. The Library of Congress has played a leadership role in the American library community since 1901; however, its first responsibility, as part of the legislative branch of the American government, always has been to support the reference and research needs of the American national legislature. In 1962, at the request of Sen. Claiborne Pell of the Joint Library Committee, Douglas Bryant, associate director of the Harvard University Library, prepared a memorandum on "what the Library of Congress does and ought to do for the Government and the Nation generally." Bryant urged further expansion of the Library's national activities and services, proposals endorsed by many professional librarians, and suggested several organizational changes. He also said it would be "desirable" to transfer the Library to the executive branch of government. Mumford replied to the Bryant memorandum in his 1962 *Annual Report*, strongly defending the Library's position in the legislative branch and stating his opposition to the suggestion that the Library's name might be altered to reflect its national role: "The Library of Congress is a venerable institution, with a proud history, and to change its name would do unspeakable violence to tradition."

The debate continued in the professional library community. However, the fiscal retrenchments of the 1970s and congressional reemphasis on the Library's legislative services under the provisions of the Legislative Reorganization Act of 1970 made increased national library aspirations impractical. The new law changed the name of the Legislative Reference Service to the Congressional Research Service and expanded its functions, placing increased emphasis on policy research and analysis and on direct services to both individual members of Congress and congressional committees.

Before he retired in 1974, Librarian Mumford witnessed the authorization by Congress of the construction of a third Library of Congress Building and, in 1971, the beginning of its construction. In 1975, President Gerald R. Ford nominated historian Daniel J. Boorstin, previous director of the Smithsonian Institution's National Museum of History and Technology (now the National Museum of American History), to be the 12th Librarian of Congress. Boorstin was confirmed by the Senate and took the oath of office on November 12, 1975, in a ceremony in the Library's Great Hall.

Boorstin immediately faced two major challenges: the need to review the Library's organization and functions and, pending the forthcoming expansion into the James Madison Memorial Building, the lack of space for both collections and staff. In 1976, he created a Task Force on Goals, Organization, and Planning, a staff group that conducted, with help from outside advisers, a one-year review of the Library and its role. Many of the task force's recommendations were incorporated into a subsequent reorganization. Legislation to establish the American Folklife Center in the Library of Congress was pending when Boorstin became Librarian of Congress; President Ford signed it into law in early 1976 and Librarian Boorstin soon thereafter convened the inaugural meeting of its Board of Trustees. Another new office was a result of Boorstin's personal initiative: the Center for the Book in the Library of Congress, which was established in 1977 to stimulate public interest in books and reading. Through his leadership, in 1979

A young James Madison portrayed in this miniature painting, would become an early advocate of the Library of Congress, the primary architect of the U.S. Constitution, and the namesake of the Library's third major building.
LC/Rare Book and Special Collections Division.

the Library of Congress and the Kennedy Center opened a jointly sponsored Performing Arts Library at the Kennedy Center.

The move into the Madison Building, which began in 1980 and was completed in 1982, relieved administrative as well as physical pressures, and enabled Librarian Boorstin to focus on what he deemed most important: the strengthening of the Library's ties to Congress, and the development of new relationships between the Library and scholars, authors, publishers, cultural leaders, and the business community.

The Library of Congress grew steadily during Boorstin's administration, with its annual appropriation increasing from $116 million in 1975 to more than $250 million in 1987. In collaboration with Architect of the Capitol George M. White, Librarian Boorstin initiated an effort that led to a $81.5 million appropriation, approved in 1984, for the renovation and restoration of the Library's two older structures, the Thomas Jefferson and John Adams Buildings. Work started in 1986 and was completed in 1995. In 1986, Boorstin confronted Congress directly regarding plans to drastically reduce the Library's budget. His eloquent plea, which earned him the sobriquet of "an intellectual Paul Revere," resulted in the restoration of a substantial part of the sum that had been cut.

Boorstin relied heavily on his professional staff in technical areas such as cataloging, automation, and library preservation. But he took a keen personal interest in collection development, copyright, book and reading promotion, and in the symbolic role of the Library of Congress in American life. He characterized the Library's comprehensive collections as "the world's greatest Multi-Media Encyclopedia." Boorstin's visibility, articulate style, and active promotion of the Library led a *New York Times* reporter, discussing Boorstin's January 1987 decision to retire as Librarian, to call the post of Librarian of Congress "perhaps the leading intellectual public position in the nation."

Boorstin's successor, historian James H. Billington, was nominated by President Reagan and took the oath of office as the 13th Librarian of Congress on September 14, 1987. Billington instituted his own one-year review of the Library's functions through an internal Management and Planning (MAP) Committee, a review that also included regional forums in nine cities. The result was a major administrative reorganization based on goals identified through the MAP study. Convinced that the Library of Congress needed to share its resources more widely throughout the nation, he instituted several projects to test new technologies that might provide for direct access by libraries and schools to the Library's collections and data bases. The experimental American Memory project, for example, provided in electronic format, selected collections of American history and culture to schools and libraries. A two-year pilot project to extend online access to the Library to the 50 state library agencies began in 1991.

Envisioning a new educational role for the Library, Billington began strengthening the Library's cultural programs and educational outreach functions. His recognition of the crucial importance of private funds in building and sustaining national outreach projects led him to create the Library's first Development Office in 1988, and two years later he established the James Madison Council, a private-sector support body consisting mostly of business executives and entrepreneurs. In fiscal 1991, Billington obtained a 12 percent budget increase for the Library to help make its collections more accessible. However, in response to a series of thefts and discoveries of vandalism, the following year the Library was forced to undertake new security measures that closed the bookstacks to the public.

In his budget presentation to Congress for fiscal year 1993, Billington emphasized that the Library of Congress is "becoming an even more important catalyst for the educational, competitive, and creative needs of our nation." The complexities of the information age were most apparent in the Librarian's discussion of new electronic technology. This new technology, "properly organized and supported" should, according to Billington, be applied to a Jeffersonian purpose: enabling the Library to "increase the knowledge available to Americans in their local communities—in schools, colleges, libraries, and private sector research enterprises." Thus, "even those Americans

Automated Reference Services Librarian Elizabeth L. Brown acquaints visitors with the Library of Congress Internet Web pages in the National Digital Library Education Center in the James Madison Memorial Building. Photograph: LC/Carol Highsmith.

far from great universities and the most affluent schools and libraries can still have access to the best of the nation's heritage and the latest in up-to-date information."

In 1994, the Library made its bibliographic records and selected items from its Americana collections available electronically, and the institution began establishing what is now a multi-tiered presence on the World Wide Web. The same year Congress approved the Library's five-year National Digital Library (NDL) program. Through a combination of private and government funding, the NDL program began digitizing historical materials from more than 70 American history and culture collections in the Library and collecting them from 33 other research institutions to make them available, free of charge, on the Library's American Memory Web site.

Thus began a new era of service and access to the Library's collections. Today the Library is a leader among large institutions making collections available via the World Wide Web. Its Web site, with sections devoted to its own collections, catalogs, and exhibitions as well as to legislation from Congress and information from the U.S. Copyright Office, is one of the most frequently used in the world. During fiscal year 2003, more than 2.6 billion transactions were recorded on all of the Library's computer systems. In testimony before Congress in January 2000, Billington told the legislative branch appropriations subcommittee that the Library of Congress had become the "leading provider of high-quality, free educational material in the revolutionary new world of the Internet." Moreover, a National Academy of Sciences report about the Library's role in the digital world, commissioned by Billington in 1998 and released in July 2000, called on the Library to greatly increase its resources and leadership capabilities to develop a digital strategy for the next century. Additional appropriations enabled the Library to announce, in 2003, a plan for a new National Digital Information Infrastructure and Preservation Program.

A historian of Russian culture, Librarian Billington has taken special interest in using the Library and its resources to encourage the development of democracy in Russia and in Central and Eastern Europe after the collapse of Communism in the early 1990s. Congressionally-approved projects included a parliamentary assistance program for Central and Eastern Europe (1990–1996) and, beginning in 1999, the Russian Leadership Program to bring young Russian civic, political, and professional leaders to the United States to observe American democracy and business firsthand.

The Library of Congress commemorated its bicentennial throughout 2000. The Bicentennial Steering Committee chose "Libraries-Creativity-Liberty" as the major theme because it encompassed the Library's ambition to promote creativity in the preservation, organization, and sharing of recorded knowledge as well as the key role all libraries play in connecting knowledge and information to citizenship in a democracy. As the year came to a close, Librarian Billington made two important announcements: the Library had achieved its bicentennial goal of mounting five million digital items on its American Memory Web site, and the Madison Council chairman, John W. Kluge, marked the bicentennial by giving the Library an unprecedented gift of $60 million to establish a Kluge center for scholars and a Kluge Prize in the Human Sciences.

In 2001, responding to a proposal by First Lady Laura Bush, Billington launched a major new Library of Congress public program: the first National Book Festival. Hosted by Mrs. Bush but organized and sponsored by the Library of Congress, the annual festival celebrates and promotes reading and is an increasingly popular Library of Congress educational initiative.

In his Sixth Annual Message as president, Thomas Jefferson proposed the creation of a national university, because "a public institution alone can supply those sciences which, though rarely called for, are yet necessary to complete the circle, all the parts of which contribute to the improvement of the country." At the beginning of a new century, when the interdependence and complementarity of all types of educational and cultural institutions is increasingly recognized, Billington's efforts to exploit new electronic technologies and educational partnerships, governmental and private, have greatly enhanced the Library's educational role. They also present the intriguing possibility of the Library of Congress, nearly two centuries after Jefferson's proposal, becoming a key partner in a new "Electronic National University."

Librarian Billington's determination to extend the reach and influence of the Library of Congress is very much in the ambitious tradition of his predecessors. Alone among the world's great libraries, the Library of Congress still attempts to be a universal library, collecting materials of research value in almost all languages and media. In the early years of its third century, it continues to be guided by Thomas Jefferson's beliefs that democracy depends on knowledge and that all topics are important to the library of the American national legislature—and therefore to the American people and indeed to all people.

Cole, John Y. *For Congress and the Nation: A Chronological History of the Library of Congress.* Washington, D.C.: Library of Congress, 1979.

Cole, John Y., ed. *Jefferson's Legacy: A Brief History of the Library of Congress.* Washington, D.C.: Library of Congress, 1993.

Johnston, William Dawson. *History of the Library of Congress, 1800–1864.* Washington, D.C.: Government Printing Office, 1904.

Lacy, Dan. "Library of Congress: A Sesquicentennial Review," *Library Quarterly* 20 (July 1950): 157–179; 20 (October 1950): 235–258.

Mearns, David C. *The Story Up to Now: The Library of Congress, 1800–1946.* Washington, D.C.: Library of Congress, 1947.

Rosenberg, Jane Aikin. *The Nation's Great Library: Herbert Putnam and the Library of Congress, 1899–1939.* Urbana, Ill.: University of Illinois Press, 1993.

THE CONGRESSIONAL RESEARCH SERVICE

by John Y. Cole

Congressional Research Service

The Library of Congress was established in 1800 in the legislative branch of the national government to provide books and information needed by the national legislature. Supporting congressional reference and research needs is still the Library's most important function. This service is performed primarily by the Congressional Research Service (CRS), the research and analytical arm of the U.S. Congress and a major Library of Congress service unit that has its own separate budget.

CRS works exclusively and directly for Congress by providing research that is reliable, timely, objective, nonpartisan, and confidential. CRS anticipates the legislative needs of Congress by providing immediate access to research and analysis on the CRS Web site, by creating or revising new products and formats to deliver the most relevant and up-to-date analysis and information on current legislative issues, and by making its staff members available for consultations and briefings.

Origins and Development

Because the Library is part of the legislative branch of the U.S. government, and because its relationship with Congress is of utmost importance, CRS (called the Legislative Reference Service from 1914–1970) has a special, "first among equals" standing within the Library. The Library grew slowly through most of the nineteenth century when it was in the U.S. Capitol (1800–1897). Here the legislative function dominated. The Jefferson Building, the Library's first separate structure, opened in 1897, and a new national role became possible. It took the better part of a decade for Librarians of Congress John Russell Young (1897–1899) and Herbert Putnam (1899–1939) to establish the institution's basic functions, roles, and services. A separate Legislative Reference Service was established in 1914. By then, under Putnam's leadership, the Library had expanded its role to take on new "national library" functions. In the succeeding decades, a new and important discussion developed: was the Library of Congress a legislative or a national institution or perhaps both? With increased expectations, how were its limited resources to be allocated? This "debate" helped shape the Library's development during the latter half of the twentieth century. Moreover, one can argue that the Library's "dual" legislative and national roles stimulated the institution's growth and helped generate and justify the generous congressional appropriations that continue to support not only its legislative and national functions but also its increasingly important international role.

The Joint Congressional Committee on the Library dominated the Library of Congress until the administration of Librarian of Congress Ainsworth Rand Spofford (1864–1897). The Library's first books and maps, ordered by the Joint Committee, arrived in 1801 and were housed in the west front of the still-being-built Capitol. In its first years, the Library slowly established itself as a resource for members of Congress—for legislative information, but also for books for recreational reading. Moreover, after 1824, when the Library moved into a spacious new room in the center of the west front of the U.S. Capitol, it became a "tourist attraction" for members of Congress and their families and friends, but also for the public.

In 1829, the new president, Andrew Jackson, chose a political supporter, John Silva Meehan, to be the new Librarian of Congress. Meehan performed a passive role during his long librarianship (1829–1861), deferring in all respects to the wishes of the Joint Committee on the Library and particularly its chairmen. It should be noted, however, that the committee generally did a satisfactory job in obtaining the books most needed by Congress for the transaction of its ever-changing legislative agenda. Surveying how congressmen used their Library during the expansionist years of 1840–1859, library historian Carl Ostrowski notes that "very few books on the West seem to have escaped the notice of the Joint Committee on the Library." Conservative Senator James A. Pearce of Maryland, who chaired the committee from 1846 until his death in 1862, was comfortable with the Library's limited legislative function. Librarian of Congress Meehan supported this role, providing the books requested by members of Congress and trying to maintain order in the Library's procedures and operations.

Spofford, who believed that the Library of Congress had a national as well as a legislative function, went much further than Meehan in providing reference services for individual members of Congress. Working daily with congressmen in the Capitol building, he actively but discreetly lobbied for the Library's expansion by impressively answering specific questions and even by making suggestions for future congressional speeches. He also served as a book purchasing agent for several Ohio congressmen, all personal friends from when he had owned a bookstore and been a newspaper editor in Cincinnati between 1845–1861; his best clients were Senator John Sherman and Congressmen James A. Garfield and Rutherford B. Hayes. Garfield, one of the Library's heaviest users, even allowed Spofford to use his personal frank for the Library's mail until the Librarian finally succeeded in obtaining the government franking privilege for the Library. In Cleveland in 1873 trying to compose a speech without Spofford's help, he lamented in his diary: "Every day I miss Spofford and our great Library of Congress."

The collections and services of the Library of Congress were not systematically organized until after 1897, when the Library moved from its by-then crowded quarters in the U.S. Capitol into the Jefferson Building, its first separate structure. The importance of Congress was clearly indicated by its two richly decorated reading rooms, the most elaborate in the new building, both for the exclusive use of members of Congress—one for senators, the other for members of the House of Representatives. Directly facing the Capitol, they were open during the sessions of Congress each day until adjournment and from 9 a.m. until 4 p.m. when Congress was not in session. When not in use by senators and representatives, the rooms

The U.S. Congress has always been the Library's most important client. This reading room for members of the House of Representatives, along with an adjacent reading room for U.S. Senators, were the most richly decorated spaces in the Jefferson Building when it opened in 1897.
LC/Prints and Photographs Division. LC-USZ62-61467.

were open to visitors. In addition, direct book service to Congress was provided by a pneumatic tube system which conveyed books through a narrow tunnel that connected the Capitol and the Jefferson Building. Early in the century the Library established a "Congressional Reference Library" (later called "Capitol Station") in the Capitol that included a collection of reference books, bibliographic aids, and a card catalog. Its staff provided members of Congress with on-the-spot reference service and guidance to the resources and experts available in the Jefferson Building.

The Library also served Congress indirectly through published bibliographies. In his *Annual Report of the Librarian of Congress* for 1898, John Russell Young took pride in the bibliographies (called "bulletins") that had been prepared both for the general public and for Congress "in the belief that Congress might value the information thus presented." In 1898, these bulletins included lists of books on topics of congressional concern such as Cuba, the Philippines, Hawaii, Alaska, and proposed routes for a canal and railroad that would connect the Caribbean Sea and the Pacific Ocean. Not only was the Library trying to "anticipate the wants of Congress upon subjects of legislation," Young noted, it was aiming "to hold the resources ever at the command of those for whom it was founded."

The Library of Congress did not pioneer in the development of a separate reference service for Congress. Melvil Dewey established a specialized information service for legislators in 1890 in the New York State Library—the first such service. Its focus, however, was on indexing current state laws, and the service provided no assessment of the information it conveyed. The Wisconsin legislative reference department, founded by Charles McCarthy in 1901 and approved by Gov. Robert M. LaFollette Sr., not only supplied all requested information, it helped the legislator assess its value. By 1915, 32 states had made arrangements to provide reference and research service to legislators.

Support for a national legislative reference service began to develop soon after U.S. Senator Robert Owen of Oklahoma introduced the notion in 1911. However it was the "Wisconsin idea" of making use of the specialized knowledge of academics and other "experts" outside the legislature, as introduced by Wisconsin legislators Representative John Nelson and Senator Robert M. La Follette that eventually succeeded at the national level. Hearings were held in the House of Representatives in February 1912 and in the U.S. Senate in February 1913. Nelson and La Follette led the effort to establish a legislative reference bureau within the Library of Congress, and the needed legislation was passed by Congress in June

Wisconsin's Senator Robert M. La Follette Sr. and Representative John Nelson cosponsored the amendment in 1914 that established the Library's Legislative Reference Service, now the Congressional Research Service. La Follette, pictured here, learned the value of such a service early in his career. In 1901, as state governor, he approved the creation of the Wisconsin legislative reference department. The service supplied needed information and helped the legislator assess its value. LC/Center for the Book.

1914 and approved by President Woodrow Wilson in July. The idea of a legislative reference service was popular among both progressives like La Follette, who hoped that reliance on independent experts would help free lawmakers from dependence on special interests, and among conservatives who looked to the experts to supplant the influence of populists and amateurs in the lawmaking function. In 1915, Congress broadened the term "legislative reference" to enable the Librarian of Congress to employ competent persons to gather data for, or bearing upon legislation, and "to render such data serviceable to Congress and Committees and Members thereof." With few changes, this language appeared annually in each appropriations act until it received permanent statutory standing in the Legislative Reorganization Act of 1946.

In 1935, Congress directed the Legislative Reference Service (LRS) to prepare and publish a digest of the bills (other than those of a private and local character) introduced into either House of Congress. The *Digest of Public General Bills and Resolutions* has been issued without interruption since that date.

The Legislative Reference Service began to grow rapidly with the outbreak of World War II in 1939. Between 1920 and 1946, the number of annual inquiries rose from 1,604 to 16,444. As part of a general administrative reorganization initiated in 1940, Librarian of Congress Archibald MacLeish moved the Legislative Reference Service into the newly created Reference Department. Its functions or responsibilities did not change, however; it remained a service to Congress that was "parallel" to the Library's public reference services. It consisted of 68 staff members, and MacLeish asked for a staffing increase because Congress "has a right to scholarly research and counsel in law and history and economics" at least equal to that of people who testify before congressional committees. The subcommittee deferred the request pending study, but further expansion soon occurred in part as a response to the growing need for information in a nation at war.

A Defense Section within the Legislative Reference Service was established in 1941 to assist in the war effort. Renamed the War Service Section in 1942, the unit eventually grew to a staff of 38. It provided services on a contractual basis for the constituent agencies of the Office for Emergency Planning, the first time Congress had asked LRS to provide assistance outside the legislative branch, and one of the first instances when funds from other agencies supported Library of Congress activities. Projects included preparation of bibliographies on topics such as camouflage, synthetic rubber, war production and strikes in the defense industries; furnishing translations and abstracts of selected foreign language publications; and digesting and circulating summaries of congressional hearings relating to the war. Prominent members of Congress were impressed by LRS's performance during World War II and called for an expansion of its scope and its services. They were joined by the American Political Science Association's Committee on Congress, which issued a report in 1945 urging Congress to provide for itself "independent research facilities and a research staff equal in quality to the staff and facilities available to the Executive Branch of government and to special interest groups." The committee also noted the disparity in salaries of the Legislative Reference staff with those experts in the executive branch.

Reorganization

The first vehicle was the Legislative Reorganization Act of 1946, a result of the work of a Joint Committee on the Organization of Congress, co-chaired by Senator Robert M. La Follette Jr. of Wisconsin, and Representative A.S. "Mike" Monroney of Oklahoma. The new law expanded the responsibilities of LRS in assisting both Congress and its committees; gave LRS permanent statutory basis as a separate Library department; and increased its appropriation to enable the service to employ nationally eminent specialists in 19 broad subject fields roughly corresponding to the jurisdictions of the new standing committees in Congress. Moreover, the pay grade of these specialists would not be less than that of their counterparts in the executive branch.

Policy and research demands on members of Congress continued to expand and grow more complicated during the next two decades, as America faced

CRS Director Gilbert Gude, second from right, presents copies of the Congressional Research Oversight Manual *to (from left to right) Majority Whip John Brademas and Speaker of the House Thomas P. O'Neill Jr., while Alfred R. Greenwood of CRS looks on.* LC/Congressional Research Service.

challenges to its leadership, new concerns about the environment, and increased racial strife and poverty in its inner cities, among other issues. A new Joint Committee on the Organization of Congress was established in 1965. After five months of hearings, it issued a final report, containing some 100 recommendations, on July 28, 1966.

Senators Everett M. Dirksen and John L. McClellan consult books and one another in the Congressional Reading Room, ca. 1955. LC/Congressional Research Service.

The Joint Committee report accepted the basic assumptions of the 1946 reorganization (that Congress should have its own separate research agency and that the use of independent experts was effective) and noted that its recommendations were meant to reinforce the guiding principles adopted in 1946 and to provide the basis for improving the efficiency and responsiveness of this organization. Basic issues were addressed in the recommendations, including the need for a name change (to the Congressional Research Service); the relationship of the Service to the Library of Congress; and how the director of the Service was to be selected. Hearings were held and the Senate approved a bill in 1967, but the House of Representatives did not. Additional hearings were held, and in 1969 a revised bill was introduced and discussed. A bill was finally passed by both Houses of Congress and approved by President Richard Nixon on October 26, 1970.

The Legislative Reorganization Act of 1970 changed the name of the Legislative Reference Service to the Congressional Research Service (CRS). It expanded the Service's duties, increasing the emphasis to be placed on policy research and analysis and on direct services to committees and to individual members of Congress. To assist the Service in performing its new functions, the act authorized the appointment of senior specialists and specialists in fields other than those specified in the statute, as well as the use of the services of other experts, consultants, and research organizations. The act gave the Congressional Research Service maximum practicable administrative independence and fiscal autonomy within the Library's administrative structure, stipulating that the Librarian of Congress shall "in every possible way, encourage, assist, and promote the

Congressional Research Service," according it "complete research independence." The salary of the director of the Service was raised above that of other Library of Congress department heads. The act also stated that the director would be appointed by the Librarian of Congress "after consultation with the Joint Committee on the Library."

In accordance with the wishes of Congress expressed during the debates on the Legislative Reorganization Act of 1970, the Congressional Research Service was rapidly expanded between 1970, when the Service had 323 budgeted positions, and 1975, when it reached 703 positions.

The dramatic and sudden collapse of Communist regimes in Central and Eastern Europe prompted a congressional response that led to an additional mission for the Congressional Research Service for a period of time. Between 1990 and 1996, the Congress established parliamentary assistance programs in 12 emerging countries in Central and Eastern Europe and the former Soviet Union, providing information about the structure and organization of democratic institutions and societies. The Service was asked to administer and implement the overall program, with the House of Representatives Information Systems Office providing the automation experts needed to carry out the program. Direction was provided by a special House of Representatives Task Force on the Development of Parliamentary Institutions in Eastern Europe. These parliamentary development programs were envisioned as short-term "jump start" efforts. Thus when faced in 1995 with difficult fiscal choices in a tight budget environment, Congress decided to end the involvement of the Congressional Research Service in activities that were outside its mission of direct support to the national legislature. The fiscal year 1996 Legislative Appropriations Act mandated that the Service complete all approved programs by the end of 1996 and not provide assistance to foreign parliaments in the future.

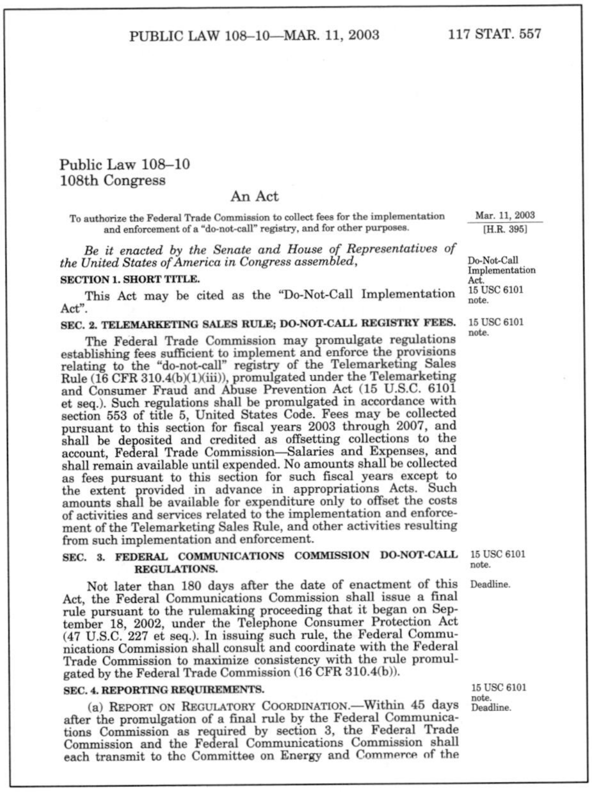
PUBLIC LAW 108–10—MAR. 11, 2003 117 STAT. 557

Public Law 108–10
108th Congress

An Act

To authorize the Federal Trade Commission to collect fees for the implementation and enforcement of a "do-not-call" registry, and for other purposes.

Mar. 11, 2003 [H.R. 395]

Be it enacted by the Senate and House of Representatives of the United States of America in Congress assembled,

Do-Not-Call Implementation Act. 15 USC 6101 note.

SECTION 1. SHORT TITLE.

This Act may be cited as the "Do-Not-Call Implementation Act".

SEC. 2. TELEMARKETING SALES RULE; DO-NOT-CALL REGISTRY FEES. 15 USC 6101 note.

The Federal Trade Commission may promulgate regulations establishing fees sufficient to implement and enforce the provisions relating to the "do-not-call" registry of the Telemarketing Sales Rule (16 CFR 310.4(b)(1)(iii)), promulgated under the Telemarketing and Consumer Fraud and Abuse Prevention Act (15 U.S.C. 6101 et seq.). Such regulations shall be promulgated in accordance with section 553 of title 5, United States Code. Fees may be collected pursuant to this section for fiscal years 2003 through 2007, and shall be deposited and credited as offsetting collections to the account, Federal Trade Commission—Salaries and Expenses, and shall remain available until expended. No amounts shall be collected as fees pursuant to this section for such fiscal years except to the extent provided in advance in appropriations Acts. Such amounts shall be available for expenditure only to offset the costs of activities and services related to the implementation and enforcement of the Telemarketing Sales Rule, and other activities resulting from such implementation and enforcement.

SEC. 3. FEDERAL COMMUNICATIONS COMMISSION DO-NOT-CALL REGULATIONS. 15 USC 6101 note.

Deadline. Not later than 180 days after the date of enactment of this Act, the Federal Communications Commission shall issue a final rule pursuant to the rulemaking proceeding that it began on September 18, 2002, under the Telephone Consumer Protection Act (47 U.S.C. 227 et seq.). In issuing such rule, the Federal Communications Commission shall consult and coordinate with the Federal Trade Commission to maximize consistency with the rule promulgated by the Federal Trade Commission (16 CFR 310.4(b)).

SEC. 4. REPORTING REQUIREMENTS. 15 USC 6101 note.

Deadline. (a) REPORT ON REGULATORY COORDINATION.—Within 45 days after the promulgation of a final rule by the Federal Communications Commission as required by section 3, the Federal Trade Commission and the Federal Communications Commission shall each transmit to the Committee on Energy and Commerce of the

The Congress directed the Legislative Reference Service in 1935 to prepare and publish a digest of the bills (other than those of private and local character), and the Digest of Public General Bills and Resolutions *has been issued ever since. Public Law 108-10 of the 108th Congress is an example of one General Public Bill.*
The Digest of Public Bills and Resolutions. LC/General Collections.

The Congressional Research Service Today

At the end of fiscal year 2003, the Congressional Research Service's staff numbered 707. In mid-2004, CRS was organized into six administrative offices and seven subject divisions: the offices of the Director, Congressional Affairs and Counselor to the Director, Finance and Administration, Information Research Management, Legislative Information, and Workforce Development, and divisions covering the topics of American Law; Domestic Social Policy; Foreign Affairs, Defense, and Trade; Government and Finance; Information Research; and Resources, Science, and Industry. In 2003, CRS prepared approximately 800,000 responses to congressional inquiries. Its services to Congress included policy analysis; comparison of various bills introduced before Congress; individual memoranda tailored to the specific concerns of individual members of Congress, and in-person briefings for those members; telephone consultations, database searches, and information and reference services; making online electronic research products available to congressional offices and committees on a 24-hour basis; and comprehensive training in legislative and budget processes for congressional staff.

CRS provides Congress with legislative assistance while implementing new technology and management initiatives, including improving its Web services, recruiting staff, and enhancing its technology to make it more secure, sophisticated, and efficient.

The CRS Web site is a valuable tool for Congress, offering a wide range of services, including the full text of all CRS reports; the status of appropriations bills with links to CRS appropriations reports, bills, and committee reports; and links to reference sources needed by legislative staff. In fiscal year 2003, the CRS Current Legislative Issues (CLI) system supported immediate analytical and information needs of the 108th Congress in 160 policy areas identified by CRS research staff as of particular importance. Reflecting the growing use of video over the Web, recently CRS has produced live Web cast as well as video recordings of seminars on a variety of key legislative issues, including the war in Iraq, the effect of tax reform, and the military personnel system. Use of the Legislative Information System (LIS), the online retrieval system that provides Congress with accurate and timely information about pending legislation, increases each year.

The accessibility of the CRS research and published reports prepared for Congress to the general public is a topic of continuing debate. Members of Congress can make the information available if they so desire. Generally speaking, however, the results of CRS research are not widely available.

Each year the CRS provides information and assistance to Congress on a wide range of domestic and international issues, in most cases relating directly to potential or pending legislation. Since the September 11, 2001 attacks on the United States, many of the issues have pertained to terrorism and national security. Examples include: the war with Iraq, the post-war needs of Iraq for humanitarian and reconstruction assistance and the roles of the international community and the United Nations in the reconstruction; homeland security and terrorism; bioterrorism and public health; border and transportation security; the continuity of Congress, focusing on proposed legislation requiring expedited conduct of special elections in the event of the death or incapacitation of large numbers of members of Congress; immigration and the Department of Homeland Security; and the legal ramifications of antiterrorism enforcement.

Other examples reflect continuing CRS information and research support for domestic and international topics of concern to Congress, such as federal food and farm policy; the state of the economy, including customized briefings for congressional staff in preparation for the semi-annual monetary policy hearing with the chairman of the Federal Reserve Board; omnibus energy legislation and the security and reliability of the nation's energy infrastructure; medical malpractice insurance and liability; medicare and prescription drug legislative proposals; the space program, particularly in the aftermath of the space shuttle Columbia tragedy; U.S. trade and labor policy, including free trade agreements.

In response to the September 11, 2001 attacks on the United States, CRS provided information and analysis to Congress on a wide range of international and domestic issues. Homeland Security Secretary Tom Ridge testifies at a Senate hearing at the U.S. Capitol on January 17, 2003, showing the cooperation displayed by the Congress and Senate together to respond to the situation.
Photograph: Tina Hager, White House Photo.

Cole, John Y. "For Congress & the Nation: The Dual Nature of the Library of Congress," *The Quarterly Journal of the Library of Congress* 32 (April 1975): 119–138.

Putnam, Herbert. "Legislative Reference for Congress," *The American Political Science Review* 9 (August 1915): 542–549.

THE LAW LIBRARY AND COLLECTIONS

by Donald R. DeGlopper

A librarian examines a book in the stacks of the Law Library in the Madison Building. The Law Library holds some 2.5 million volumes occupying 59 miles of shelving. Photograph: David Doyle.

The Law Library

The Law Library maintains and develops the world's largest collection of legal information, with some 2.5 million volumes occupying more than 59 miles of shelving. More than half the collection is in languages other than English. The goal of the Library is to collect primary legal material from every jurisdiction in the world. Because "the law" can change from day to day, a very high priority is put on providing the most timely and therefore accurate and authoritative information possible.

The collection is used by a staff of specialists in foreign and international law to provide research and reference services to the United States Congress, the Supreme Court, Executive Branch Agencies, the legal profession, the academic community and the general public. The Law Library operates a reading room that provides reference service in the law of the United States to all users, although priority goes to congressional requests. The Law Library's Research Directorate provides research in foreign, comparative and international law to congressional and government requesters, and reference service to all. The collection also supports the work of the Congressional Research Service's American Law Division. The Law Library has been producing guides to and indexes of foreign law since 1912, and is currently playing a leading role in an international cooperative network to index and abstract law and make the database available through the Internet.

During recent global crises, legal specialists in the Law Library were increasingly called upon to provide Congress with critical information and analyses concerning the legislative actions of the world's governing bodies. In fiscal 2003, Law Library legal specialists and analysts wrote more than 1,100 research reports and special studies on the legal aspects of headline issues of concern to Congress and other federal agencies. The Law Library's foreign and international research and reference staff also wrote more than 600 reports, studies, and memoranda in response to congressional inquiries.

Law Collections and Services in the Early Years of the Library of Congress

Law books made up nearly 20 percent of the initial Library of Congress collection. These were for the most part publications in English and international law. The purchase of Thomas Jefferson's library in 1815 brought 475 law titles, 318 of which were published in England. It included Virginia laws and court decisions, but material from other states (which Jefferson had classified as "foreign law") remained limited. Although the Library received copies of all federal laws and Supreme Court decisions, obtaining state laws and decisions of state courts remained a problem for decades.

Although the early Library of Congress served primarily as an in-house reference collection for members of Congress, there were repeated efforts

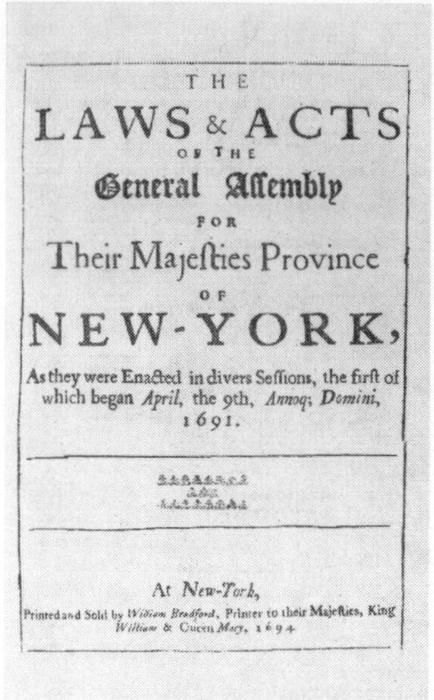
THE
LAWS & ACTS
OF THE
General Aſſembly
FOR
Their Majeſties Province
OF
NEW-YORK,
As they were Enacted in divers Seſſions, the firſt of which began *April*, the 9th, *Annoq; Domini*, 1691.

At *New-York*,
Printed and Sold by *William Bradford*, Printer to their Majeſties, King *William* & Queen *Mary*, 1694.

A volume of The Laws and Acts of the General Assembly for Their Majesties Province of New York as They were Enacted in Divers Sessions, the First of which began April 9, 1691. LC/Prints and Photographs Division. LC-USZ62-61140.

to extend its use to other government officials and especially to the federal judiciary. The two sides of the issue were expressed in a December 1801 debate in Congress on the act establishing the Library. One member moved to extend borrowing privileges not only to the Supreme Court but to the judges of the District of Columbia as well, because of "the great expense and extreme scarcity of some of the most valuable and necessary law books." Countering this with the need for ensuring the security of the collection, Representative James Bayard of Delaware expressed the hope that "the Congressional Library would never be subjected to the abuse which books used in courts of justice were too liable." As it became apparent that extending borrowing privileges might necessitate a larger appropriation, the clause permitting wider use was deleted.

The Supreme Court sat in the United States Capitol Building from 1801 to 1935. For the first decade of the nineteenth century its justices could not formally use the Library of Congress, although they may have been able to consult the books with a letter of introduction from a member of Congress. On March 2, 1812, a Joint Resolution of both Houses of Congress authorized use of the Library by the justices of the Supreme Court, on whose behalf Chief Justice John Marshall (served 1801–1835) wrote a polite letter thanking Congress for the favor.

In the early years of the nineteenth century the books for the Library of Congress were generally selected by the Congressional Joint Committee on the Library, which seems often to have included those members of Congress with scholarly or literary interests. Any year's selection reflected the particular composition and expertise of the committee. In 1826, the Honorable Edward Everett, former professor of Greek at Harvard and a future president of Harvard, discussed law books with Associate Justice of the Supreme Court Joseph Story (served 1812–1845). Justice Story wrote "I entirely agree with you respecting the civil-law books to be placed in the Congress Library. It would be a sad dishonor of a national library not to contain the works of Cojacius, Vinnius ...etc. How could one be sure of some nice doctrine in the civil law of Louisiana without possessing and consulting them? What is to become of the laws of Florida without them?" As early as 1826 then, the need to expand the collection beyond Anglo-American common law, which was to become a major theme in the next century, was already becoming apparent.

Establishment of the Law Library

The first three decades of the nineteenth century saw repeated unsuccessful attempts to establish a separate Law Library to serve both Congress and the Supreme Court. The initiative came from those members of Congress who had distinguished legal or judicial careers. Congressman Wickliffe, who had won great distinction in the law in his native Kentucky, introduced resolutions calling for the establishment of a separate Law Library in 1826, 1828, and 1830. Finally, in December 1831, Senator Felix Grundy, a former Chief Justice of the Tennessee Court of Appeals and a famous trial lawyer, introduced a motion instructing the Senate Judiciary Committee to look into the creation of a separate Law Library, which would be under the supervision of the Supreme Court. On January 20, 1832, his colleague on the Judiciary Committee, New York Senator William Marcy, a sometime Associate Judge of the Supreme Court of New York, introduced a bill to "Increase and Improve the Law Department of the Library of Congress." This time, the bill passed both Houses of Congress and was signed by President Andrew Jackson on July 14, 1832.

The act directed the Librarian to prepare an "apartment" for the purpose of a Law Library and to remove the law books from the library into the apartment. The justices of the Supreme Court were authorized to make rules and regulations for the use of the Law Library during the sitting of the court. The Law Library, however, remained a part of the Library of Congress, which was responsible for its incidental expenses. A sum of $5,000 was appropriated "for the present year" to purchase law books, with $1,000 for each of the next five years. The books would be selected by the chief justice, which provided more consistent selection than that resulting from the changing membership of the Joint Committee on the Library. Some 2,011 law books were transferred from the general collection, and became the nucleus of a collection that now exceeds two million volumes. The Law Library thus acquired its own appropriation and budget line, as well as a statutory relationship with the Supreme Court that would endure until 1935.

Locations of the Law Library

The first Law Library occupied a room adjacent to the main Library on the west front of the main (second) floor of the Capitol. In 1842, the collection was moved to a room across the hall from the Supreme Court chamber in the basement (first) floor on the east front of the Capitol. A small collection of duplicate law books was placed in a Court Conference Room, for the exclusive use of the justices. In 1859, the Supreme Court moved up one floor to occupy the former Senate Chamber, and in 1860 the Law Library was moved into the former Court Chamber. A spiral staircase connected this with the Court above, and the Custodian of Law climbed the stair to deliver materials requested by the Justices. With the opening of the new Library of Congress

The Law Library in the U.S. Capitol, ca. 1895. The Supreme Court Chamber until 1860, the Law Library occupied this space from 1860 to 1950. Samuel Morse sent his first telegram from this room on May 24, 1844.
LC/Prints and Photographs Division. LC-USZ62-61137.

Building in 1897, the collection was gradually transferred to that building, coming to occupy several sites there, which relieved the overcrowding in the Capitol Law Library but created problems of controlling and accessing the collections. By 1917, the bulk of the collection was in the main Library building, with administrative offices in the Northeast Pavilion on the second floor. The Law Library in the Capitol became an annex, serving the reference needs of the court and Congress until moved to new quarters in 1950. That collection and its reference librarian was maintained in the Capitol Building until 1988. By the 1940s, the law collections, offices and two reading rooms (American Law and Foreign Law) were concentrated on the second floor of the Main (now Jefferson) Building on the north side. In 1981, the collections were moved to the sub-basement of the new Madison Building, with the Law Reading Room and offices on the second floor.

Expansion of Scope and Staff

The 1909 publication of the index to the United States federal statutes, which immediately became a standard reference work for law libraries, marked the beginning of the Law Library's transition from a purely local reference library to a major center for legal research. Law Librarian Borchard began the production of bibliographic guides to the law of foreign countries with the 1912 publication of a guide to the law of Germany, followed in 1913 by Borchard's own *Bibliography of International Law and Continental Law*. For the next several decades major publications on the laws of Spain, France, the larger Latin American countries, Eastern Europe and East Asia were produced, usually with support from various foundations or government agencies. Initially the work was done by temporary staff or outside experts, but after the mid-1930s the Law Library gradually began adding permanent staff whose primary qualifications were in foreign rather than U.S. law.

By the early 1940s, there was an American and British Law Section and a Foreign Law Section, each associated with its own Reading Room. In 1943, the Latin American (later Hispanic) Law Section was founded. The Foreign Law Section eventually divided into a Far Eastern, a European and a Near Eastern and African Law Section. The staff of the Law Library grew from five in 1901 to six in 1910, stayed at seven from 1911 through 1921, and numbered 10 when Vance became Law Librarian in 1924. By 1946, it stood at 30, and the Law Library requested 30 additional positions to relieve the overburdened staff. In 2003, the Law Library had 107 appropriated positions, with this staff supplemented by various contract positions.

Funding from outside bodies supported the expansion of the Law Library's foreign research capabilities after the Second World War. From 1949 to 1960, the National Committee for a Free Europe supported a staff of 12 lawyers from Eastern European and Baltic countries, then under Communist rule. In 1951, the Department of State began a Far Eastern Law Project, under which refugee scholars from China collected and translated legal material from the newly established People's Republic of China. By

1960, the pattern of a Reading Room providing reference service in U.S. federal and state law and a foreign legal research and reference wing organized into five geographically distinct divisions was set.

Institutional Differentiation

After about 1900, as the volume of acquisitions and the percentage of foreign language materials both increased and the workload of the Supreme Court also increased, the justices played a diminishing role in the selection of books for the Law Library. The move of the Supreme Court to its own building in 1935, and the establishment of a separate Supreme Court Library of American and British law brought the close institutional relations between the Law Library and the court to an end. The Law Library continues to support the Supreme Court's needs for information on foreign and international law.

Congress established the Legislative Reference Service (the organizational ancestor of the present Congressional Research Service) in 1914, but for its first decade the LRS was headed by the Law Librarian and much of its work consisted of legal indexing, for both American and foreign law, and responses to congressional requests about American, international and foreign law. By the late 1920s, the division of labor that endures to the present was established. The LRS (later CRS) contains an American Law Section (now Division) working exclusively for Congress and depending on the collection maintained by the Law Library. The Law Library operates the Reading Room, provides reference service in U.S. law to Congress on a priority basis, and is responsible for all reference and research service in foreign comparative and international law. The Law Library provides Congress with services that parallel those of CRS and maintains close ties with CRS.

Readers at tables make use of some of the items in the world's largest collection of legal material in the spacious reading room on the second floor of the James Madison Memorial Building.
Photograph: David Doyle.

Many requests come to the Law Library through CRS, and Law Library publications are listed in the *Guide to CRS Products* that goes to congressional offices every month.

Service to Congress

Since its establishment in 1832, the Law Library's first priority has been service to Congress. The Research Directorate, staffed by foreign-trained attorneys and by research analysts with foreign language and area qualifications, responds to Congressional inquiries on all aspects of foreign and international law. Apart from immediate telephone reference, it produces several hundred written reports every year; in 2002, for example, the total was 874. These range from one to two-page summaries to multi-author, multi-jurisdictional reports on such matters as foreign laws on campaign finance, gun control, status of refugees and asylum seekers, terrorism, organ donation, and dual nationality. Single-country reports have included proxy divorce in Iran, European Union anti-dumping measures, Russia's law restricting religious proselytization, the legal status of the Palestinian Authority, and Hong Kong's courts. The Directorate also produces for Congress a monthly *World Law Bulletin*, which includes brief notices of recent developments in foreign nations and multinational organizations, and essays on special topics of interest to Congress, such as drug laws or taxation systems.

Congressional inquiries cover a wider range of topics than requests from any other source. Congress is interested in broad political and constitutional questions, including the structure of foreign governments and courts, procedures for elections, parliamentary immunity, and international law and treaties. It is also interested in commercial and financial matters, such as intellectual property protection, taxation, regulation of commercial activity, or international agreements on fisheries or maritime shipping. It is also interested in such matters as human rights, criminal procedure, citizenship and nationality of individuals, and refugee and immigration law, as well as questions involving the foreign marriages, divorces, inheritances or civil suits of their constituents. Staff responding to congressional requests must be able to produce cogent responses to broad and generally-phrased questions as well as to requests for specific items or bits of information.

As mandated by law (2 USC § 138) the Law Library Reading Room is staffed by at least one attorney/librarian qualified in U.S. law whenever and for as long as either House of Congress is in session, which occasionally makes for late nights. Since the 1988 closing of the Law Library annex in the Capitol Building, the Reading Room has provided a special telephone line exclusively for congressional requests, and received some 2,100 such requests in 2002. The Reading Room is staffed by reference librarians who provide Congress with several hundred written responses to questions on U.S. federal and state law each year. The Reading Room staff offer several brief classes in legal research for congressional staffers, serving 400 to 500 staffers each year.

Service to Government and Private Requesters

Research services, especially in foreign, comparative and international law, are also provided to the judiciary and a wide variety of U.S. government bodies. Law Library legal research specialists qualified to practice law in foreign countries have on occasion served as expert witnesses on foreign law in U.S. federal courts. Offices of the Justice Department have been interested in foreign statutes on money-laundering; the Internal Revenue Service has inquired about taxation of corporations; the Navy has been interested in foreign maritime claims; and the Arms Control and Disarmament Agency has required information on ratification of treaties by foreign governments. The Law Library was responding to so many requests from the Immigration and Naturalization Service that in 1992 an Interagency Agreement was made with that Service. Most INS inquiries involve determination of the legality of claimed foreign marriages, divorces, adoptions, or nationality. For all U.S. government bodies the Law Library provides research services, writing often lengthy reports and on some occasions providing interpretation of foreign law. Requests from government agencies tend to be narrowly focused and to refer to specific bodies of legal information.

Private requesters, many of whom are domestic law firms, receive reference service—that is to say, assistance in locating domestic or foreign law, but absolutely no interpretation. Private requesters come last in the priority scheme, while Congress comes first and the U.S. Courts and executive branch agencies come after Congress. The Law Reading Room provides terminals that allow readers to access the Library of Congress catalogs as well as any private legal database on which they already have an account. Requests cover the gamut of American law, and for foreign law tend to concentrate on business and commercial issues.

General Research Methods

For all research and reference work, the Law Library strives to use primary legal materials, such as official gazettes, annual compilations of laws, court reports, or administrative regulations. One of the peculiar qualities of legal information is that it changes constantly, as new laws are passed, old ones are amended or repealed, and court decisions provide authoritative interpretations. "The Law" is both a Platonic Ideal and a moving target, and any legal research organization must strive to keep up with it and provide information that is as current and therefore accurate as possible. The endless cycle of updates, amendments and judicial decisions dictates needs for special modes of processing incoming materials and

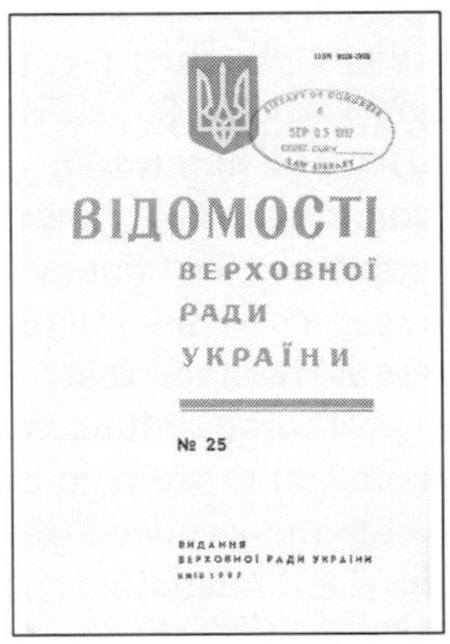

Four covers from a large and unique collection of legal gazettes from around the world: the four represented here are from Kuwait, Uruguay, the Ukraine, and the Republic of Korea. LC/Law Library.

accessing the most current information. For the laws of the United States, a sophisticated set of periodical reporting publications and online databases is available and heavily used by the Reading Room reference librarians.

Foreign law presents its own challenges. Apart from more often than not being available only in foreign languages, it is frequently organized differently from the American law that most requesters have in mind. Legal research specialists and research analysts devote much effort to translation of concepts and categories. The Law Library's solution to the manifold problems of trying to find, much less interpret, foreign legal information is to, whenever possible, employ individuals trained in the law of the country in question and able to provide authoritative answers in English. The staff of foreign-trained attorneys has, over the years since the late 1940s, included former judges, private practitioners, diplomats, and legislative drafters. The basic method is to combine the expert with the collection. In fact, the foreign attorneys play a significant role in developing the collection, selecting the most relevant texts and serials for the jurisdictions they cover. The books alone or the expert without the books would be of little use to most requesters, but in combination they make a powerful instrument. The work of the foreign-trained attorneys is complemented by various editors and research analysts who bring expertise in public policy research and publication.

Indexing Foreign Law

Indexes and other finding aids are indispensable tools for legal research, but the laws of many countries are not well-indexed or available in authoritative or up-to-date codes or collections. The first major project of the Law Library was the 1907–1910 preparation of an index to U.S. federal statutes, an endeavor funded by a special congressional appropriation. In 1902, Librarian of Congress Herbert Putnam proposed a comprehensive index to current legislation from all the countries of the world. He noted that "If accompanied by a reference to preceding statutes or by brief abstracts ... it may become an instrument of the highest value not merely to the theoretic investigator, but to the practical legislator." Although there were far fewer sovereign countries in 1902 than today, Congress's practical legislators refused to fund so ambitious a project. The idea did not die though, and various guides to the legislation of foreign countries were produced as funding permitted. Legislative indexing was a major activity of the Legislative Reference Service during its first 10 years (1916–1924), and the staff of the Law Library began keeping a card index to Latin American laws sometime during the late 1920s. This was eventually published as the *Index to Latin American Legislation* in a two-volume set in 1961, with two supplements—in 1973 and 1978—covering the years from 1961 through 1975. The indexing of Latin American legislation continued, being adapted to existing information-processing technology as it developed from the 1970s through the 1990s.

By the 1990s, it was increasingly clear that the solution to the problem of control of a rapidly expanding body of legal information from a growing number of jurisdictions depended on harnessing information technology. It was also clear that no single body, even the world's largest law library, would be able to act on its own as a master indexer. The magnitude of the task made cooperation between institutions and countries a necessity. After several international conferences on common problems of access to legal information, the institutional solution arrived at was an international, cooperative network that makes indexes, abstracts and the complete text of new laws available over the Internet. This, the Global Legal Information Network (GLIN) is centered on the Law Library of Congress.

The Global Legal Information Network (GLIN)

GLIN is an online parliament-to-parliament cooperative exchange of laws and legal materials from more than 40 countries and institutions, which began in 1996. It combines the Law Library's extensive experience in indexing and abstracting law from many jurisdictions with available communications technology. In formal terms GLIN is a not-for-profit federation of government agencies, such as Parliamentary Libraries or Ministries of Justice or their designees, who contribute authentic texts of laws, regulations and related material to an automated database. As of 2004, GLIN had 25 member nations, which were both nations and international organizations such as the Organization of American States (OAS) or the United Nations, and offered access to the laws of some 40 nations. The Law Library of Congress provided an initial model and set standards for the indexing and abstracting work. It has organized training sessions for foreign participants and hosted four annual Project Directors Conferences. The Project has attracted support from such agencies as the World Bank and the Inter-American Development Bank, and the Library of Congress (on behalf of GLIN) has signed an Interagency Agreement with NASA for joint development of satellite communications and a data management system. In fiscal year 2003, there were about 1.7 million transactions on the GLIN database.

There is of course much legal information available over the Internet, but much of it is incomplete, outdated, of dubious reliability, or available only at high commercial rates. GLIN, reflecting long-standing Library of Congress operating principles, makes a point of offering only authentic texts with a consistent and limited set of index terms. Dates are unambiguous, and the relation of the text in question to other legal instruments (amends, repeals, expands on, etc.) is made clear. In the initial years, all abstracts and index terms are in English, while the text is in its original language. As the system matures, greater use of other languages along with English is likely. GLIN relies on official gazettes, administrative regulations, and judicial decisions from the government bodies authorized to publish them.

The Road Ahead

The GLIN Project, involving as it does participants from a growing number of nations and relations with an increasing number of financial and technical supporting bodies, presents daunting managerial challenges. It is very much a work in progress and can be expected to develop in unexpected ways. Whatever mature form it comes to take, it will doubtless bear the impress of its intellectual progenitor—the Law Library of Congress.

The Library of Congress's legal collection and its human caretakers and users can be seen, in retrospect, to have spent their first century within one building and at the service of two institutions —the United States Congress and the Supreme Court. The second century saw a much expanded range of institutional and human relations, exchanges and activities, but still centered in one city and mediated by the exchange of paper. With its third century, the Law Library contemplates a further expansion to a truly global role and one involving an increasing proportion of electronic transactions.

The Law Collection

Legal materials have been a central component of the Library of Congress collections since 1800. In 1832, the Law Library was established as a separate entity within the Library of Congress with a distinct collection to be housed in separate quarters and with its own budget line for acquisitions. At the time 2,011 law books, 639 of which had belonged to Thomas Jefferson, were removed from the Library's general collection. These formed the nucleus for what is today the world's largest collection of legal materials, consisting in 2004 of about 2.5 million items that occupy 59 miles of shelving in the sub-basement of the Library's Madison Building. The stacks in the Madison Building are essentially full. Between December 2002 and September 2003, 105,000 volumes of the law collection were transferred to the Library's new high-density storage facility at Fort Meade, Maryland.

The collection is notable not only for its sheer size, but for its diversity. It includes American law and foreign law; primary materials and commentaries, reporting series, and other secondary sources; treaties and treatises; rare medieval codices and annual editions of state laws; decisions from U.S. federal and state courts, as well as many foreign courts; religious and customary law; and more complete collections of the past laws of some countries than can be had in their national capitals. About one-third of the collection consists of U.S. federal and state law; the rest is foreign and international material. While the goal is to collect primary legal material from every jurisdiction in the world, the combination of close association with the Congress and copyright deposits have made the Law Library preeminent in American law.

A wood block print from one of the Law Library's rare 300 incunabula, the Landrechtbuch Schwabenspiegel, *a vernacular text, treating feudal law and land law. Printed in 1480 in Augsberg by Anton Sorg.*
LC/Prints and Photographs Division. LC-USZ62-61142.

Growth and Development

Before the establishment of the Library of Congress in 1800 the Congress had acquired a number of law books, which included English Statutes-at-Large, Journals of the House of Commons, standard commentaries on English law by Blackstone and others, as well as collections of treaties and material on the Law of Nations. British and international law, leavened by some Roman Law, continued to be the bulk of the collection through the first few decades of the nineteenth century, although the proportion of United States federal laws and court decisions gradually increased.

Throughout the nineteenth century the Law Library attempted to collect laws and court decisions from the states, but it was not until the end of the century that relatively complete sets were available, and historical material continues to be added. In 1829, the Congressional Joint Committee on the Library of Congress responded to a resolution of the House asking it to inquire into "more effectual means of obtaining copies of the laws of the several states" by pointing out that the federal government had no authority to direct any state to supply its laws and that the state session laws usually were not made available for purchase. The development of the legal profession and the legal publishing business, which provided copyright donations, eventually solved the problem. The twentieth century efforts to collect laws of foreign nations repeated the problem at a higher level of complexity.

The acquisition of the Louisiana territory and of Florida, which brought property and inheritance systems based on French and Spanish law, provided some incentive for the acquisition of books from the civil law tradition. The first systematic effort to collect foreign law came in 1848 soon after the conclusion of the Mexican War, when Congress directed the Library to obtain all available laws of Mexico. In 1854, Congress made a special appropriation of $1,700 to purchase additional Spanish and Mexican law books, and in the second half of the nineteenth century collections of laws of the major European nations were added. Although the Law Library benefited from its own distinct appropriation for book purchases, the amounts so appropriated were relatively modest, remaining at $1,000/year from 1832 to 1850, and at $3,000 from 1900 to 1930, when it was increased to $50,000. The annual appropriation was occasionally supplemented by special one-time appropriations, to purchase laws from a particular country or a special collection that was available.

In 1899, the law collection consisted of 103,000 volumes (including 15,000 duplicates), of which about 10,000 were in foreign languages. By 1950, 150,000 of 750,000 volumes were in foreign languages. The major acquisition of foreign language material came after World War II and reflected the great increase in the absolute number of jurisdictions in the world, the changing position of the United States in world affairs and the deliberate policy of attempting to collect legal material from all jurisdictions.

The American Law Collection

The first priority for the Law Library has always been the collection of as complete a record of American federal and state law as possible. It possesses the largest and most complete general collection of American law, although larger collections in some specialized areas may be found in some major research libraries. The American material includes original editions of colonial, state and territorial session laws,

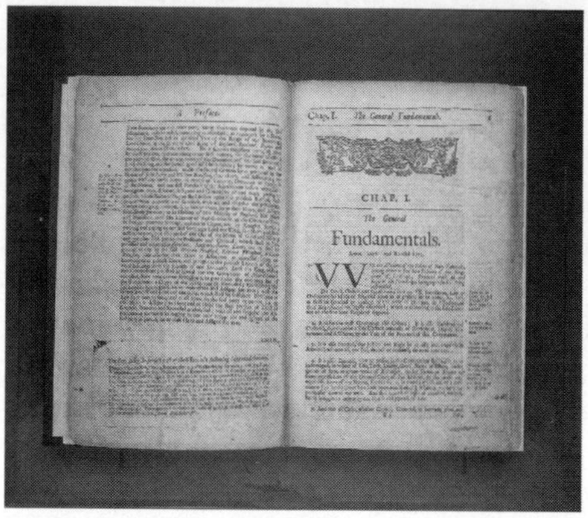

The Book of the General Laws of the Inhabitants of the Jurisdiction of New-Plimouth *is one of the oldest items in the Library's collections of American laws. This 1685 book reproduces a 1671 volume, which was the first edition of the laws to be printed.* Law Library. Photograph: Roger Foley.

codes, and compilations. The holdings of congressional publications are surpassed only by the collections of the House of Representatives and Senate themselves. Congressional holdings begin with the September 5, 1774 issue of the *Journals of the Continental Congress.* Law Library policy is to keep two copies of almost all commercial legal publications at the federal and state level, and no other research library holds so many treatises. The Law Library is one of three libraries in the United States to have a complete set of the records and briefs of the Supreme Court. The records go back to 1832; the briefs to 1854. It also has partial collections of the records and briefs of the thirteen Circuit Courts.

The Law Library's Special Collections include an extensive English and American Trials Collection, with murder trials and those involving prominent political figures well-represented. From the early 1900s, a special effort was made to collect colonial and pre-Civil War statutory law, and this collection is the largest of any library in the United States. It is supplemented by holdings of laws from the Confederate States of America (1861–1865) and of constitutions and laws of Native American groups, going back to the Cherokee Constitution of 1827. A Special Collection of Legal Americana consists of unofficial publications from the seventeenth, eighteenth and

The trial of Charles I, as depicted in the book Celebrated Trials and Remarkable Cases of Criminal Jurisprudence, from the earliest records to the year 1825, *volume one. The person in a hat with his back to us, sitting facing two men at a table is King Charles on trial for his life.*
LC/Prints and Photographs Division. LC-USZ62-61139.

early nineteenth centuries, which includes abridgements of laws, guides for justices of the peace and constables, model contracts, deeds and wills and the first legal periodical published in the United States, in Philadelphia in 1808.

The Foreign and International Law Collection

The Law Library attempts to collect primary legal material for every national-level jurisdiction in the world, as well as for some dependent areas such as Bermuda, Greenland, or the former colony of Hong Kong. This comes to about 200 jurisdictions. It also makes efforts to obtain official publications of state or provincial-level units of several large or federated nations, such as Australia, Canada, Germany, India, and Mexico. The materials include official gazettes, constitutions, session laws, administrative regulations and court decisions and reports. Commentaries and indexes to laws are also collected, as are digests and reports of court decisions, treatises and legal periodicals. Translations and reference materials such as *Tax Laws of the World* or *International Computer Law* are also acquired. These are generally obtained through purchase or exchange.

The Law Library is the repository for collections of treaties. It has an extensive collection of works on international law and the decisions of various international courts. However, the location within the Library of Congress of publications of various international or supra-national bodies is not easily predictable. Publications of the European Union, for instance, are held by the Law Library, but those of the United Nations are part of the collection of the Serials and Government Publications Division. Locating material produced by various international bodies often requires the services of reference librarians who have special knowledge of the Library of Congress collections.

The collection is especially strong in British law, which reflects the historical relations between the two countries. It holds, for example, complete records of appeals to the House of Lords, the highest court of the United Kingdom, since 1900, and of appeals since 1934 to the Judicial Committee of the Privy Council, the final court of appeal for some colonies and Commonwealth countries. The holdings of former British colonies are extensive, and sometimes more complete than those available in the countries themselves.

Congressional, government and private requesters make Canada and Mexico among the most frequently requested foreign jurisdictions year in and year out. The collections for both countries are extensive and include material from Provincial and State governments and courts. Collections from western European countries are strong, and the Law Library holds one of the largest bodies of Russian legal material outside Russia, including 13,000 volumes, many of them quite rare, from before the 1917 Revolution. The official gazettes of all the Latin American countries are microfilmed by the Law Library and have been indexed since about 1950, with this information available over the Internet to the public on the Law Library's GLIN (Global Legal Information Network) homepage, which can be accessed from the main Library of Congress homepage. Other highlights of the foreign collections include exceptionally comprehensive holdings of official gazettes and statutes of the Ottoman Empire, of Japanese legal periodicals, and rare material from areas governed by the Chinese Communist Party before the establishment of the People's Republic of China in 1949.

Special Collections

Detailed accounts of several of the special collections of the Law Library are to be found in *Special Collections in the Library of Congress: A Selective Guide* (1980), compiled by Annette Melville. Major holdings in the special collections include the 15,000-volume Roman Law collection, the core of which consists of the personal library and manuscripts of the German legal scholar Paul Krüger (1840–1926); portions of the Russian Imperial Collection (books from the personal library of the Romanov Dynasty) dealing with eighteenth and nineteenth century Russian civil and criminal law, military law, the abolition of serfdom and other special topics; and the *Coutume* Collection, some 800 volumes on the customary law of regions of France and of the modern states of Belgium, the Netherlands, Switzerland, and

Italy. Most of this collection consists of volumes printed in the sixteenth and seventeenth centuries, but there are some earlier manuscripts, such as the illustrated *Grand Coutumier de Normandie*, dated to 1450–1470. Some 3,000 volumes, half of them in Latin, make up the Canon Law collection. The English Yearbook collection of 500 volumes contains reports of pleadings in the English courts from the reigns of Edward I (1271–1307) through Henry VIII (1509–1547). Written in Anglo-Norman, these complement the Latin court decisions and illustrate the formative period of English common law. Examples of the many rare and significant volumes in the collection are provided by the 1482 German-language version of *Super Arbor Consanguinatas*, a famous treatise on succession and impediments to marriage in Roman Law; the 1491 *Las Siete Partidas*, the most important medieval Spanish code, which served as the foundation for legislation in the Spanish colonies of the New World; and the 1625 *De Jure Belli ac Pacis in Libri Tres* [On the Law of War and Peace in Three Volumes], the first edition of Grotius's famous treatise in the law of nations; and much more.

Law Library, 1832–1982: A Brief History of the First Hundred and Fifty Years. Washington, D.C.: Library of Congress, 1982.

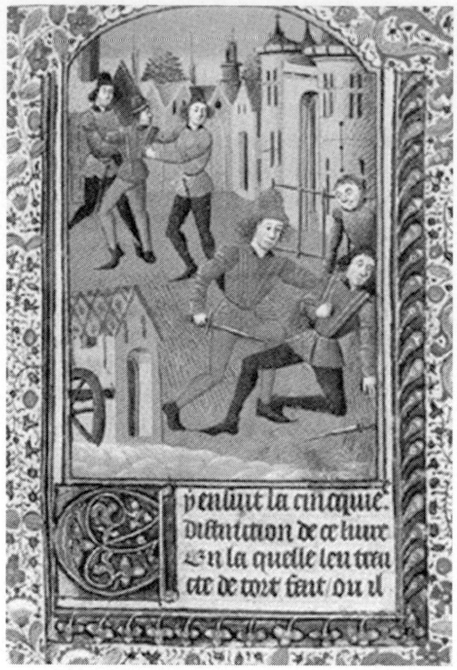

Le grande coutumier de Normandie, *an important fifteenth-century illuminated French manuscript, is significant because it contributed directly to the development of both English common law and modern French law. One of the manuscript's seven illuminations,* Judicial duel, *illustrates the consequence of a plaintiff's accusations being denied by the defendant. If the defendant could duel and stay alive from noon until the evening stars appeared, he would be declared the winner.* LC/Law Library.

THE COPYRIGHT OFFICE

by Jane Aikin and John Y. Cole

Copyright is a form of protection provided by the laws of the United States for "original works of authorship" including literary, dramatic, musical, architectural, cartographic, choreographic, pantomimic, pictorial, graphic, sculptural, and audiovisual creations. The owner of copyright has the exclusive right to reproduce, distribute, and in the case of certain works, publicly perform or display the work; to prepare derivative works; in the case of sound recordings, to perform the work publicly by means of a digital audio transmission; or to license others to engage in the same acts under specific terms and conditions. Copyright protection does not, however, extend to ideas, procedures, processes, slogans, principles or discoveries.

The copyright system has been a primary source of acquisitions for the Library of Congress collections since the U.S. copyright function was centralized at the Library of Congress in 1870, and it is especially credited with building the Library's preeminent collections of Americana. The U.S. copyright law obligates the owner of copyright in a published work to deposit two free copies with the Copyright Office for the Library's collections. The primary purpose of this mandatory deposit is to build and preserve a comprehensive collection of American publications as a record of the nation's cultural heritage, thus creating in effect a library of last resort for all works published domestically. It also applies to works first published abroad and later published in the United States, either by the importation of copies in significant numbers or by the publication of an American edition.

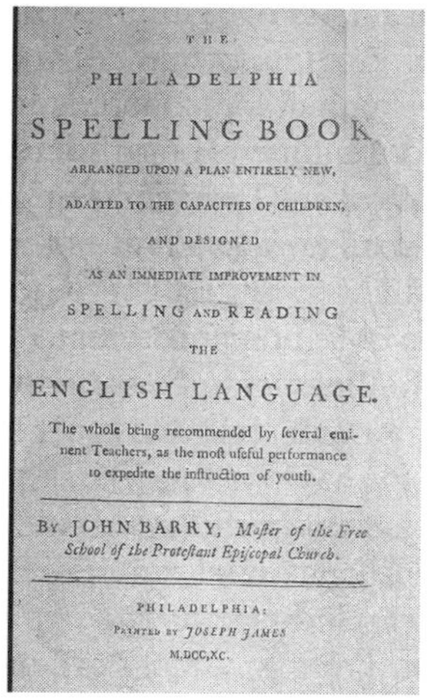
THE
PHILADELPHIA
SPELLING BOOK,
ARRANGED UPON A PLAN ENTIRELY NEW,
ADAPTED TO THE CAPACITIES OF CHILDREN,
AND DESIGNED
AS AN IMMEDIATE IMPROVEMENT IN
SPELLING AND READING
THE
ENGLISH LANGUAGE.
The whole being recommended by feveral eminent Teachers, as the moft ufeful performance to expedite the inftruction of youth.

BY JOHN BARRY, *Mafter of the Free School of the Proteftant Epifcopal Church.*

PHILADELPHIA:
PRINTED BY *JOSEPH JAMES*
M,DCC,XC.

On May 31, 1790, President George Washington signed the first federal copyright law, protecting books, maps, and charts. The first copyright certificate was issued to John Barry's The Philadelphia Spelling Book *on June 9, 1790.*
LC/Rare Book and Special Collections Division.

Copyright and the Copyright Office

The U.S. Constitution gave Congress the power "To promote the Progress of Science and useful Arts by securing for limited times to Authors and Inventors the exclusive Right to their respective Writings and Discoveries." Congress enacted the first federal copyright law in May 1790, specifying that the U. S. District Courts handle registration. The first work was registered within two weeks: John Barry's *The Philadelphia Spelling Book*, in the U.S. District Court of Pennsylvania. Barry received copyright protection, or the right to print, reprint, publish or vend his work, for a term of 14 years, renewable for another 14. The original copyright act also required a single copy of each registered work to be delivered within six months to the U.S. secretary of state. Gradually during the nineteenth-century prints, music, dramatic compositions and photographs were added to the originally protected books, maps and charts, and the term of copyright was extended to 28 years with the privilege of renewal for 14 years.

When the Smithsonian Institution was established in 1846, Congress included a copyright deposit provision authorizing the Smithsonian and the Library of Congress each to receive a copy of every work copyrighted. However, this provision proved ineffective because there was no means of enforcement, and it was repealed in 1859. Copyright deposits were sent to the Patent Office in the Department of the Interior from 1859 to 1870.

In 1865, at the urging of Librarian of Congress Ainsworth Rand Spofford, Congress again required the deposit of copyrighted materials in the Library of Congress. In 1866, Librarian Spofford called on Congress to compel publishers to deposit their books, and the following year a new law imposed a penalty of $25 for failure to comply with copyright deposit. Three years later, Spofford decided to try to obtain new legislation that transferred all copyright business to the Library. On April 9, 1870, he wrote a 1,600-word letter to Representative Thomas A. Jenckes of Rhode Island, the chairman of the Patent Committee, outlining "some leading reasons why the transfer of the entire copyright business and books to the care of the Library of Congress would promote the public interest." Congress agreed, and President Ulysses S. Grant approved the law on July 8, 1870.

Spofford viewed copyright deposit as the most practical method of acquiring a comprehensive collection of American publications; his primary objective was to build the Library's collections so that the national library would hold the collection of record for American materials. The 1870 statute centralized both registration and deposit of two copies of each work at the Library and named the Librarian as the responsible official. The U.S. law is nearly unique among nations, since most statutes do not combine copyright protection with registration and deposit.

However, the 1870 law resulted in such a flood of material that for the next 30 years and more the small staff was increasingly preoccupied with keeping up with the copyright business. In 1874, for the first time, the copyright law brought in more books than were obtained that year through purchase; by 1880, the total receipts doubled. The rapidly growing collections and Spofford's constant pressure persuaded Congress to approve a new building for the Library. Even before it was ready, the members

A photograph taken in the copyright work area of the Library of Congress, ca. 1896, when the Library was still in the U.S. Capitol. From left to right, the employees pictured are: Hamilton Rucker, Samuel M. Croft, George A. Mark, Justus S. Burlingame, J. Van Ness Ingram, and Henry S. Finkelstein. LC/Copyright Office.

These copyright deposits await sorting after being moved from the overcrowded Library rooms in the U.S. Capitol to the newly built Congressional Library in 1897.
LC/Prints and Photographs Division. LC-USZ62-38245.

responded to the pleas of authors such as Charles Dickens, whose works were being pirated by foreign publishers. They passed legislation that extended U. S. protection also to works of foreign origin if such works were deposited at the Library. This 1891 statute also specified that the Library prepare a weekly *Catalogue of Title-Entries* for copyright deposits. Several years later, in 1894, Congress expanded the staff slightly. But with these additional tasks, by 1896 the administration of the copyright law required more than three-fourths of Spofford's time and the undivided attention of 26 of the Library's 42 employees.

When the Library moved from its crowded rooms in the Capitol Building, of the 840,000 items in its collections, nearly 40 percent had been acquired by copyright deposit. Some of the Library's collections were literally created by copyright: over 90 percent of the maps, music, and graphic arts materials arrived as deposits. The accumulated photographs, engravings, etchings, lithographs, and chromolithographs, in particular, provided the Library with a collection of pictorial Americana that no other library could ever rival. Because the domestic publishing industry also rapidly increased output during the late nineteenth century, Spofford's early prediction that legal deposit would create the collection of record at the Library of Congress was quickly fulfilled.

In 1897, Congress passed legislation organizing separate departments in the Library, including establishing the position of Register of Copyrights to serve under the Librarian's direction. Located on the south side of the ground floor of the Jefferson Building, the Copyright Office had a staff of 49 by 1901, and it grew steadily as deposits continued to increase. Thovald Solberg, who had worked in the Library from 1876 to 1889 and who was by the mid-1890s a well-known authority on copyright, became the first Register. As Solberg developed the organization, the Office consisted of an Application Division, to receive applications for copyright registration; the Bookkeeping Division, which was responsible for recording and processing the fees; the Correspondence Division to deal with mail; the Deposit Division, which received the materials; the Index and Catalogue Division, responsible for indexing the applications and cataloging the articles deposited; and the Record Division, responsible for

Thorvald Solberg, an acknowledged authority on copyright in the 1890s, became the Library's first Register of Copyrights.
Photograph: Underwood and Underwood. LC Archives.

issuing copyright certificates. When the Library's John Adams Building was completed in 1938, the Copyright Office moved from the Jefferson Building into the new building. By 1969, it had outgrown the Adams offices and 325 staff members moved to Building No. 2 of the Crystal City Mall in Arlington, Virginia, returning to Capitol Hill in 1980 to occupy space on the fourth and fifth floors of the new James Madison Memorial Building.

In a general revision of the copyright statutes, a 1909 copyright law admitted some unpublished works to copyright protection and extended the renewal term of copyright from 14 to 28 years. Three years later, motion pictures, which had been registered as photographs, were added to the classes of protected works. Choreography, in the form of dance notation,

In the James Madison Building, Senior Copyright Office Specialist Frank Evina helps patron Joy Mansfield with a copyright registration, as Senior Copyright Information Office Specialist Althea Harley (right) provides information by phone.
Photograph: Carol Highsmith.

received protection in 1952 and television scripts began to arrive; but sound recordings were not protected until 1972. Another general revision of the statutes became effective in 1978, extending copyright protection for works created on or after January 1, 1978 to the life of the author and 50 years following the author's death; an act of 1998 extended the 50 years period to 70 years. Copyright registration was extended to computer programs in 1980 and to architectural works in 1990, and an agreement regarding the deposit of CD-ROM publications was reached in 1993. As each new class of material received protection, the deposit requirements have fed new special collections into the Library of Congress, thereby broadening its scope.

The Copyright Office took steps to computerize procedures at an early date, initiating the first online cataloging system in the Library, COPICS I (Copyright Office Publication and Interactive Cataloging System) in 1974 and implementing online access to the record of copyright registrations in 1982. With online access in operation, the manual filing of cards in the Copyright Catalog was discontinued, ending 112 years of filing operations in one of the oldest and largest (with 45 million cards) active card catalogs. Meanwhile, the staff was also developing the COINS system (Copyright Office In-Process System; 1978) to track claims, fees, and fee services. An optical storage system became available in 1992 to eliminate the hand stamping of copyright registration numbers on certificates by employing bar code labels. Application forms, regulations, new procedures, and announcements of policy decisions went on display on the Internet in 1995, and by 1996 the Office had developed the Electronic Registration, Recordation and Deposit System (CORDS), allowing applications and copies of works from specific submitters to be transmitted in digital form over communications networks. In 1997, to broaden its assistance to both the domestic and international copyright communities, the Office announced the U.S. Copyright Office *News/Net*, a free electronic mailing list for people involved in the field of copyright.

In 2001, the Copyright Office began a major Reengineering Program to improve the timeliness of its public services and to make several of these services, including registration, publicly available online. The program is expected to be fully implemented in 2006.

The Copyright Office: Functions and Administration

The Copyright Office's principal task is to administer and sustain an effective national copyright system, principally through the registration of works, the deposit of copyrighted works published in the

United States, and the recording of documents concerning copyrighted works. It also provides legal and policy assistance for Congress and the executive branch to ensure that the nation maintains a strong copyright system. In fiscal year 2003, the Copyright Office provided testimony to Congress on significant legislative issues, including several relating to digital technologies and the Internet, such as piracy in peer-to-peer networks and database protection.

Administratively, the Copyright Office is a major Library of Congress service unit that has its own budget and publishes its own separate annual report. Whereas in 1897, 24 administrative clerks handled about 75,000 submissions for copyright, in fiscal 2003 the staff of 503 received 607,492 claims to copyright covering more than a million works. Of these, 534,122 claims were registered. The Copyright Office cooperates closely with the Library itself. As copyright deposits are received, the Library's selection and recommending officers select appropriate items for the permanent collections. Copyright deposits are the Library's primary source of books, serials, and other works published in the United States, and nearly all U. S. newspapers are received by the Library on microfilm via copyright deposit. The Library's motion picture and sound recording collections are also heavily dependent on deposits. Extra copies or unneeded items are transferred to the Library's broad-ranging foreign exchange programs, where exchange experts send them abroad in return for important foreign publications, thus building the Library's collections without cost to U.S. taxpayers.

In addition to cooperation with the Library, the Copyright Office provides expert assistance to Congress on intellectual property matters; advises Congress on anticipated changes in U.S. copyright law; analyzes and assists in the drafting of copyright legislation and legislative reports and provides and undertakes studies for Congress; offers advice to Congress on compliance with multilateral agreements such as the Berne Convention for the Protection of Literary and Artistic Works; works with the State Department, the U.S. Trade Representative's Office, and the Patent and Trademark Office in providing technical expertise in negotiations for international intellectual property agreements; provides technical assistance to other countries in developing their own copyright laws; and through its International Copyright Institute promotes worldwide understanding and cooperation in providing protection for intellectual property.

The Copyright Office is also an office of record, a place where claims to copyright are registered and where documents relating to copyright may be recorded when the requirements of the copyright laws are met. The Office furnishes information about the provisions of the copyright law and the procedures for making registration, explains its operations and practices to the public, and reports facts found in its public records. It also administers various compulsory licensing provisions of the law, which includes collecting royalties. The Copyright Office and the Library of Congress administer the Copyright Arbitration Royalty Panels, which meet for limited times for the purpose of adjusting rates and distributing royalties.

The Copyright Office includes the Office of the Register of Copyrights and six divisions. The Office of the Register consists of the Associate Register for Policy and International Affairs, the General Counsel, the Copyright Automation Group, and the Administrative Services Office.

The Receiving and Processing Division deals with incoming and outgoing mail, creates records for all claims and fees, deposits fees, establishes and

Copyright submissions grow steadily every year; here are carts filled to overflowing with copyright receipts in 1980. Photograph: LC Archives. LC-USP6-8836m-12A.

maintains deposit accounts, routes applications for registration of copyright, handles incomplete claims, assigns copyright registration numbers and creates and mails certifications of registration. The Examining Division scrutinizes all applications and material presented to the Copyright Office for the registration of original and renewal copyright to determine their acceptability. It resolves problems with claims, provides guidance to the public, and develops policies and practices to administer the copyright laws. The Cataloging Division records bibliographic descriptions and copyright facts of all works deposited. The Information and Reference Division provides assistance to the public, produces and supplies forms and publications, furnishes search reports, prepares certifications and other legal documents, provides for the inspection of works submitted for registration and preserves, maintains and services records. The Copyright Acquisitions Division administers the mandatory deposit provisions of the copyright law.

The Licensing Division administers compulsory and statutory licenses. These licenses are issued for secondary transmissions by cable systems; for making and distributing phonorecords; for the use of certain works in connection with noncommercial broadcasting; for secondary transmissions by satellite carriers for private home viewing; and for the distribution of digital audio recording devices or media. The Division collects royalty fees from cable operators for retransmitting television and radio broadcasts; from satellite carriers for retransmitting "superstations" and network signals; and from importers or manufacturers who distribute digital audio recording devices or media in the United States. After deducting its full operating costs the Division invests the balance in interest-bearing securities with the U.S. Treasury for later distribution to copyright owners.

Copyright Records

The archives maintained by the Copyright Office constitute an important record of the American cultural and historical heritage. Since the Library does not select all copyright deposits for its collections nor does it fully catalog all works selected, copyright records often provide the only existing bibliographic records of individual creative works. These records are particularly valuable for researchers exploring, for example, pamphlets, unpublished music or dramas, lectures, and visual arts material.

Containing nearly 45 million cards, the Copyright Card Catalog housed in the Madison Building comprises an index to copyright registrations in the United States from 1870 through 1977. The Copyright Card Catalog plus post-1977 automated files provide an index of all copyright registrations to the present. The *Catalog of Copyright Entries* was published in book format from July 1, 1891 through 1978 and on microfiche from 1979 through 1982. The records from 1978 forward are available for searching on the Internet. Approximately 150,000 copyright registrations from 1790 through 1870 were kept in the Office of the Clerk of each U.S. District Court, and most of these are available on microfilm in the Copyright Office. Researchers may also investigate

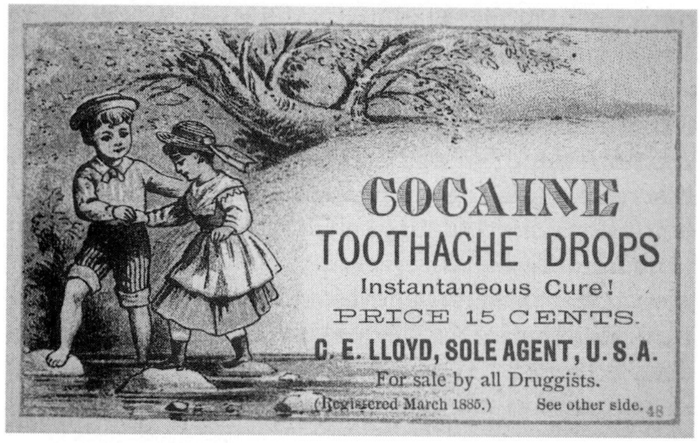

An advertisement for "Cocaine Toothache Drops" boasts an instantaneous cure. The date of copyright registration is 1885. LC/Copyright Office.

the ownership of a copyright by examining the Assignment and Related Documents Index and the Copyright Office History Documents, an online file.

The Licensing Division maintains public records of transactions related to the licenses it administers, including the secondary transmission of copyrighted works on cable television stations and by satellite carriers for private home viewing; the making and distribution of phonorecords; the use of certain works in connection with noncommercial broadcasting; public performance of copyrighted music on jukeboxes from 1978 through 1898; and initial notices of distribution filed by importers or manufacturers of digital audio recording devices or media.

The staff assists the public in using the public records of the Office. Users may conduct their own searches if they wish. For a fee, members of the public may obtain certificates of registration and certified copies of Office records. Copies of deposits may be obtained upon the request of the owner of the copyright in the deposit, by an attorney in connection with any litigation involving the copyrighted work, and through a court order issued by a court having jurisdiction in a case in which the copy is to be submitted as evidence. For a fee, the Office will conduct searches of the records and prepare reports on the copyright facts of registrations and recordations.

Assistance to the Domestic and International Communities

The Copyright Office promotes improved copyright protection for U.S. creative works abroad by actively working with the executive branch of government. The Department of State, the Department of Commerce, and the Office of the U.S. Trade Representative negotiate with foreign countries to improve the copyright protection afforded U.S. authors in these countries, either via bilateral copyright treaties or trade agreements or in multilateral efforts. In addition, the International Copyright Institute created within the Copyright Office in 1988 provides training for officials from developing and new industrialized countries and encourages development of effective intellectual property laws and enforcement overseas.

Cole, John Y. "Of Copyright, Men & A National Library," *The Quarterly Journal of the Library of Congress* 28 (April 1971): 114–136.

Foundation for a Creative America. *Patent and Copyright History Handbook Through the Year 1990*. Washington, D.C., 1991.

Rudd, Benjamin W., comp. "Notable Dates in American Copyright, 1783–1969," *The Quarterly Journal of the Library of Congress* 28 (April 1971): 137–143.

U.S. Copyright Office. *Annual Report of the Register of Copyrights for the Fiscal Year Ending September 30, 2003*. Washington, D.C., 2004.

THE NATIONAL LIBRARY SERVICE FOR THE BLIND AND PHYSICALLY HANDICAPPED

by Stephen Prine and George F. Thuronyi

The Library of Congress administers a free national library program of braille and recorded materials for blind and physically handicapped persons through the National Library Service for the Blind and Physically Handicapped (NLS). The Service selects and produces full length books and magazines in braille and on recorded disc and cassette. More than 23 million recorded and braille books and magazines were circulated to a readership of 766,137 in 2003.

Reading materials are distributed to a cooperating network of regional and subregional (local) libraries where they are circulated to eligible borrowers. The NLS program is funded annually by Congress. In fiscal year 2004, the appropriation was $50,401,000. Through an additional federal appropriation to the U.S. Postal Service, books and materials are mailed as "Free Matter for the Blind or Handicapped."

History

Library of Congress service to the blind began when Librarian John Russell Young opened in 1897 a special reading room in the Northwest Pavilion on the ground floor of the Jefferson Building.

One of the new services inaugurated by Librarian John Russell Young in 1897 was a reading program for the blind. This special reading room was opened on the ground floor in the new Thomas Jefferson Building.
LC/Prints and Photographs Division. LC-BH836-215.

Furnished with mahogany and walnut pieces from the Capitol, the reading room contained about 200 books and music items in raised characters. A special program of readings was begun: one of the first public programs featured the poet Paul Laurence Dunbar, a Library staff member, who read from his works. Material for the reading room was acquired by both gift and purchase, and acquisitions were significantly supplemented when Congress passed a law in 1913 providing that one copy of each raised type book produced for educational purposes be deposited at the Library.

Service for the blind was briefly transferred from the Library to the District of Columbia Public Library in October 1910, but it returned to its original location on January 8, 1912. As the collection grew, book stacks for braille and music items were established on deck 35 in the southeast stack in 1927, and room F on the top floor began to be used for shellacking braille manuscripts in 1935–1936. During the period of Library reorganization in the 1940s, the service moved several times. Administrative work was transferred first by January 1940 to the Southwest Pavilion and then in 1944 to the attic floor. Also in 1940, the collections moved to the Adams Building, where they occupied deck 11 south. The reading room itself moved to the third floor of that building in May 1943. But in 1948–1949 administrative service returned to the Jefferson Building, occupying room G152 while talking-book distribution, volunteer services and a regional library operated from the Adams Building's deck 11 south. Finally, in 1967 the National Library Service moved to 1291 Taylor Street NW, bringing together the entire staff and collections.

During the late 1920s, three major organizations serving the blind—the American Foundation for the Blind in New York, the American Printing House for the Blind in Louisville, Kentucky, and the Braille Institute of America in Los Angeles—urged Congress to establish a federal program of library service for the blind that would standardize the materials offered and make them available throughout the United States. In 1930, Representative Ruth Pratt (New York), and Senator Reed Smoot (Utah) introduced bills into the House and Senate authorizing an appropriation for a national library for blind adults. President Herbert Hoover signed the Pratt-Smoot Act, as it became known, into law on March 3, 1931. (Twenty-one years later, Congress removed the word "adult" from the law, thereby extending the service to children.) Thus beginning in 1931, the Library began producing and distributing reading materials for blind readers to regional libraries for circulation.

The Library's various services to the blind were consolidated into a single administrative unit, the Division for the Blind, in 1946. In 1962, Congress authorized the Library to purchase and circulate music material of an educational nature in braille, large print, and recorded formats for use by blind students and musicians. Four years later, Congress further amended the Pratt-Smoot Act to include material for persons who could not read printed books because of a physical disability. In 1978, the Division became the National Library for the Blind and Physically Handicapped.

A computer station for the handicapped in the Computer Catalog Center in the Jefferson Building. The center has 58 research stations and is conveniently located directly across the hall from the Main Reading Room.
Photograph: Public Affairs Office.

Collection Development

The National Library Service was conceived as a public library specifically for use by blind and physically handicapped individuals, thus the scope of the collections is similar to that of a public library. From its inception, librarians serving blind readers suggested titles to be embossed in braille. Their suggestions were reviewed by the Librarian of Congress. The first book ordered for the program was Woodrow Wilson's *George Washington*, in honor of the bicentennial anniversary of Washington's birth. Other works selected included Homer's *The Iliad* and *The Odyssey*, Pearl Buck's The Good Earth, and Victor Hugo's Les Miserables. In 1934, the introduction of talking books brought Shakespeare's *As You Like It* and Samuel Taylor Coleridge's *Rime of the Ancient Mariner* into the hands of blind readers.

Today the commitment to providing a public library in special formats remains the same. Books selected are primarily for leisure reading and aimed at a general audience rather than the scholarly works intended for subject specialists. With more than 50,000 books published annually in the United States, the pool of print titles is enormous. Each year the Service's staff selects approximately 2,000 titles to add to the collection.

In order to meet the varied needs of readers and to provide a balanced collection, selections are made in 15 fiction categories, such as adventure, historical fiction, and westerns; in 19 Dewey Decimal Classification categories; in seven grade levels for juvenile fiction and nonfiction; and in a few selected

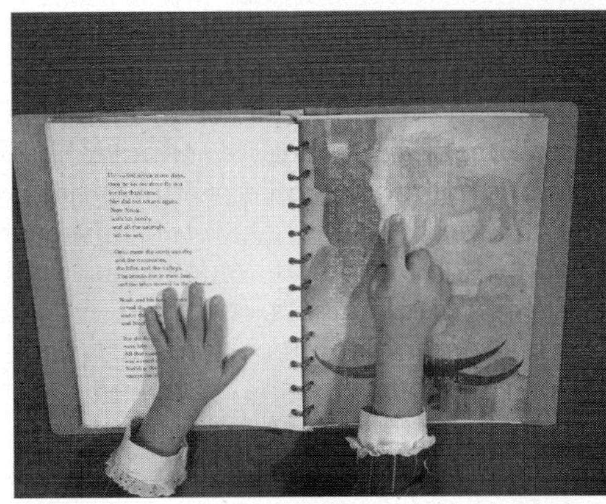

A young girl reads Noah's Ark *in braille.* LC/National Library Service for the Blind and Physically Handicapped.

languages other than English. Of the 2,000 selections in any given year, 80 percent are adult and young adult titles, 20 percent are juvenile; 45 percent are nonfiction, 50 percent are fiction; 70 percent are current and 30 percent are retrospective works.

A vital element in the collection development process is user involvement. Each year the National Advisory Group on Collection Building Activities provides a forum for obtaining patrons' advice nationwide. The group comprises four librarians from network libraries, four readers-at-large, a representative from each of three consumer organizations (American Council of the Blind, Blinded Veterans Association, National Federation of the Blind), and a librarian who serves as a children's and young adults' consultant. In addition to acting on recommendations from the advisory group, NLS responds regularly to letters and phone calls from network librarians and patrons. NLS staff consider the titles they suggest, seeking to balance the acquisition of a relatively small number of titles per year against the reading needs of a large and diverse audience.

More than 70 magazines on audio cassette and disc and in braille are offered through the program. Readers may request free subscriptions to *U.S. News and World Report, National Geographic, Consumer Reports, Good Housekeeping, Sports Illustrated for Kids*, and many other popular magazines. Current issues are mailed to readers at the same time the printed issues appear or shortly thereafter. Magazines are selected for the program in response to demonstrated reader interest.

Network of Cooperating Libraries

Prior to 1931, public libraries in several major cities began developing services for blind patrons. The Boston Public Library initiated its service in 1868, the Chicago Public Library in 1894, the Detroit Public Library in 1896, and the Free Library of Philadelphia in 1899. The State Library of New York was the first state library to develop a program in 1895. These programs were local in nature, relying on walk-in service and free-matter mailing within the city or county service area. The format of the materials offered was not standardized because prior to the selection of the Louis Braille code as the standard embossed format for English-speaking countries in 1932, braille was only one of several embossed codes used for transcription of materials for blind individuals.

The Pratt-Smoot Act directed the Librarian of Congress to provide a free library service to blind adults, and authorized the establishment of regional libraries as necessary to carry out this task. Eighteen regional libraries were developed that year; they formed one of the first library networks in the country and a unique one in that it was, and is, a network of cooperating libraries at the federal (Library of Congress), state (regional libraries), and local (subregional libraries, where applicable) levels. The network was established with handshake agreements among the first director of the National Library Service and the state librarians and public libraries. The cooperative, informal nature of the network continues today. There are no contracts for service between the National Library Service and the states, although all have agreed to work toward meeting the 1995 *Revised Standards and Guidelines for Service for the Library of Congress Network of Libraries for the Blind and Physically Handicapped* promulgated by the Association of Specialized and Cooperative Library Agencies, a division of the American Library Association.

As the talking-book program began in 1934, the network grew to 26 regional libraries. No more libraries were added until a regional library was established in Florida in 1950, but thereafter growth continued until 1976 when the establishment of the Puerto Rico and Virgin Island regional libraries increased the number to 56. Twenty years later, with the opening of the North Dakota regional library in 1995, the network had a regional library in every state, except Wyoming. Five states— California, Michigan, New York, Ohio, and Pennsylvania—have two regional libraries, and there are regional libraries in the District of Columbia, Puerto Rico, and the Virgin Islands.

Subregional libraries appeared in the 1960s. Initiated in the Midwest, subregionals spread throughout the country to a high of 104 in the 1980s, but by 2003 this number had dropped to 77. Housed and administered by county or multicounty public library systems, a subregional library serves a minimum of 200 readers with the most current books, contacting the regional library for older titles. States like Illinois, Georgia, Kansas, and Michigan established subregionals in public library systems serving the majority of, if not all, eligible readers in the state. Other states, such as Florida, Maryland, Nevada, and Indiana, established subregionals in population centers, and the regional library continues to serve patrons in the rest of the state.

Talking Books

The history of talking-book machines goes hand-in-hand with the development of the commercial recording industry. Thomas Edison envisioned recorded books for blind people as a potential use for the phonograph machine he invented. It was not until the 1930s, however, that research caught up with the idea. Technological developments made possible the recording of sound at a speed acceptable for speech, and in 1934 the talking-book program was born. Books were produced on 33-1/3 rpm records and played on phonograph machines nearly the size of a suitcase and weighing almost 50 pounds. The 12-inch records played only 12-1/2 minutes on a side, and they were heavy and brittle. These books were mailed in heavy cartons with up to 22 records per container. A book such as *Gone with the Wind* required 80 records in four containers. Record size was reduced to 10 inches in 1963, and the speed decreased to 16-2/3 rpm so that 45 minutes of reading time could be contained on a smaller record. In 1968, the speed was reduced again to 8-1/3 rpm for recorded magazines and, later, for books. That year also saw the introduction of flexible audio records, which were for a time used for both books and magazines.

An important development was the invention of cassette tape systems in the 1950s and 1960s. Two-track cassettes that played at 1-7/8 inches per second (ips) were introduced into the program in 1969. By 1974, the Service began duplicating books at the slower speed of 15/16 ips, and in 1977 began using four-track cassettes. A single cassette can now provide up to six hours of playing time, the equivalent of about 200 pages of text.

The National Library Service makes available several types of playback machines and special accessories. The standard talking-book machine plays recorded audio discs at 8-1/3 rpm, 16-2/3 rpm, and at the standard commercial speed of 33-1/3 rpm. The cassette machine plays audio cassettes at 15/16 ips and 1-7/8 ips, both two-track and four-track. A specially designed player, called the easy cassette machine, is available for readers who are unable to operate a standard player or find it difficult. A combination machine allows patrons to play both audio discs and cassettes. Readers with very limited mobility may request a remote-control unit or extension levers, and hearing impaired readers may be eligible for an auxiliary amplifier for use with headphones.

Narration for talking books is provided by professionals and volunteers in several studios around the country. Each year, the Service solicits bids from producers who are awarded contracts to perform the narration, monitoring, and reviewing of audio recording. Books are recorded in their entirety, and read at a speed that conveys the story without overly dramatic changes in voice or pitch.

Copyright

From the beginning of the program, authors and publishers have provided support by giving copyright permission for their works to be transcribed into braille and recorded, initially for the use of the blind and later the physically handicapped, without the requirement of paid royalties. In return, the National Library Service and its network of cooperating libraries ensure that the materials are used only by individuals eligible for the program. For sound recordings this is guaranteed by producing the recordings at a special speed playable only on special equipment. NLS provides the equipment to cooperating libraries, which then loan the machines to eligible readers.

From the 1930s until the fall of 1996, the Service requested copyright permission in writing prior to transcribing or recording a book or magazine. In 1996, Senator John H. Chafee sponsored legislation stipulating that NLS and its network libraries no longer seek copyright permission to record braille books, provided they are produced in a special format for the blind, are published in the United States, and are considered literary works. The bill was signed into law September 16, 1996, enabling the staff to produce books more quickly by eliminating the delays inherent in requesting copyright permissions.

Free Matter

Congress first approved the Free Matter mailing privilege in 1899 and has modified how it is implemented several times since. Free Matter is part of the

On a 1998 Madison Council tour of the National Library Service for the Blind and Physically Handicapped, Joan Wegner and Julienne Krasnoff review catalogs of braille books and acquaint themselves with some of the braille books in the Library's collection. Photograph: © N. Alicia Beyers.

Foregone Subsidy by which Congress provides funding to the United States Postal Service to underwrite the costs of bulk-mailing rates and Free Matter. What this means for NLS and its network of cooperating libraries is that all books, magazines, playback equipment, catalogs, and order forms can be sent and returned to the libraries without paying postage. This ensures that eligible patrons can use the service at no cost no matter where they reside. As long as they have a mailing address, the library can send materials as Free Matter that can then be returned the same way.

Support Services

Since its beginning, the National Library Service has played a major role in braille development, with the Library of Congress providing braille transcription learning materials, grading braille transcription lessons and manuscripts, and certifying braille transcribers. In the mid-1980s, the service received suggestions from consumer organizations and braille transcription groups to begin development of a national braille competency test. This test provides a benchmark by which knowledge of braille transcription can be measured.

Although prohibited from serving non-U.S. citizens living outside the United States, NLS is permitted to have reciprocal international interlibrary loan agreements with agencies serving the blind in other countries.

As the Service has produced titles in braille and recorded formats over the years, it has developed various means of helping users to gain access to the collections. On a bimonthly basis, each eligible patron and network library receives *Talking Book Topics* or *Braille Book Review,* publications that list new titles added to the collection during the previous two months. These listings are available in braille, large print, on flexible disc, cassette, and computer diskette. The bimonthly catalogs are cumulated annually. In 1977, a union catalog on microfiche was introduced that was sent quarterly to each network library. By the mid-1990s, the microfiche was replaced by versions of the catalog on CD and the Internet. In 2003, the catalog was migrated to the Library of Congress Voyager system. Catalogs, bibliographies, reference circulars, fact sheets, newsletters, and other information are also available online in a format that is accessible through text-based and graphical Web browsers. Links to network library home pages allow patrons to find information about their local cooperating libraries.

Another project initiated in the early 1980s was the development of automated circulation system software for small regional libraries and subregionals. Named READS (for Reader Enrollment and Delivery System) the software is controlled and maintained by the National Library Service and is available at no charge to network libraries willing to acquire the hardware needed to run it.

Volunteers

Volunteers nationwide make significant contributions to providing reading materials for blind and physically handicapped individuals. Volunteer activity is an essential program element in both the National Library Service and network libraries, and it includes production of materials, repair of equipment, circulation and maintenance, reader services, outreach, and administration. Each year, for example, volunteers contribute an effort representing $8 million in high-quality machine repairs. The Service provides technical training, support, and guidance to individuals and groups and offers network libraries technical assistance in areas such as machine maintenance and reconditioning and establishing and operating recording studios. A directory of volunteer groups that produce books for libraries and individuals is updated frequently.

Future Goals

The National Library Service's research program is directed toward improving the quality of reading materials and playback equipment, controlling program costs, and reducing the time required to deliver services to users. Current research focuses on the development of a standard for digital talking books and the application of digital techniques to recorded materials. A first step was the development of a digital standard that addresses the changing technical environment for audio reproduction of books. Written under the auspices of the National Information Standards Organization and approved in March 2002, the standard codifies the performance requirements for a digital talking book player. It addresses control, audio quality, media compatibility, copyright protection, ease of international interlibrary loan, and affordability.

Digital Talking Books: The Progress to Date. Washington, D.C.: National Library Service for the Blind and Physically Handicapped, 2002.

That All May Read: Library Service for Blind and Physically Handicapped People. Washington, D.C.: National Library Service for the Blind and Physically Handicapped, 1988.

THE INTERNATIONAL ROLE OF THE LIBRARY OF CONGRESS

by John Y. Cole

Today the Library of Congress is an unparalleled international resource. The scope of its collections is universal, and not limited by subject, format, or national boundary. More than half of its book and serial collections are in languages other than English, and approximately 460 languages are represented. The Library's collections of books, pamphlets, manuscripts, music, maps, newspapers, microforms and

CORANT OR VVEEKLY NEVVES, from Italy, Germany, Hungaria, Polonia, Bohemia, France, and the Low-Countries.

Front page of Courant or Weekly Newes, from Italy, Germany, Hungaria, Polonia, Bohemia, France and the Low-Countries, *published in London on October 11, 1621. Acquired with the Feleky Collection of Hungarica in 1953, it is one of the oldest extant copies of an English-language newspaper.*
LC/Rare Book and Special Collections Division.

graphic arts and other research materials number nearly 128 million items. This huge and diverse accumulation includes larger Hispanic American and Arabic collections than exist in Latin America or the Arabic world, and the largest Chinese, Japanese, Korean, Polish, and Russian collections outside of these respective countries.

The services provided by the Library of Congress to its congressional, public, scholarly, library, and international users are based on these collections. In the twentieth century, as its collections expanded in scope, size, and influence, so did its area studies divisions and its technical services to libraries and librarians around the world. For example, the Library played a key role in the development and continuing revision throughout the century of the *Anglo-American Cataloging Rules*. Moreover, its cataloging, classification, subject headings and other bibliographic and technical services, including the MARC (MAchine Readable Cataloging) format became known and widely used. After the 1960s, so did its preservation and conservation techniques. Since the 1990s, the World Wide Web has greatly increased knowledge of the Library's resources and enhanced their accessibility; moreover through its Web site, the Library's Global Gateway Web page provides an international perspective on those resources. Today the Library of Congress is a unique reservoir of knowledge and information for understanding the entire world.

Nineteenth-Century Origins

Thomas Jefferson's belief that a democratic legislature needed information and ideas in all subjects and from all parts of the world was the rationale for the eventual development of the Library of Congress into a world library. Jefferson's personal library, which he sold to Congress in 1815, covered many subjects and included books in French, German, Greek, Russian, and Latin. The Jeffersonian concept of universality, that all subjects were important and should be collected and then made available to both the American national legislature and the people they serve, is still the basic rationale for the Library's comprehensive collecting policies.

An Italian architecture book, an anatomy book, and a music book in the Rare Book and Special Collections Reading Room are part of Thomas Jefferson's personal and very international collection of books.
LC/Rare Book and Special Collections Division.

Although Jefferson provided the Library with the framework for its future expansion, the institution's real growth did not begin until after the Civil War. Until then, most members of Congress felt that the congressional library should play a limited role on the national scene and that its collections, by and large, should focus on American materials of obvious use to the U.S. Congress.

Yet as the official library of the national government, in the 1830s the Library began to receive documents and other publications obtained through official exchanges with other countries. The first such formal exchange took place in 1837, when the Joint Committee on the Library authorized the Librarian to "exchange Gales and Seaton's State Papers. . .and other public documents with the French government."

Between 1840 and 1852 a French citizen, Alexandre Vattemare, encouraged the exchange of documents between the French government and the Library of Congress. However, he never managed to establish a strong central exchange agency in France, and the experiment eventually failed. Moreover, in 1857 Congress transferred the Library's international exchange functions to the Department of State.

The Library's role as the recipient of documents from other countries in return for U.S. government publications was revived in 1867 by Librarian of Congress Ainsworth Rand Spofford, who obtained approval of a joint congressional resolution that would use "the already organized agency for exchanges of the Smithsonian Institution." The foreign publications received in return for the 50 extra copies of each U.S. government publication authorized by the resolution were deposited in the Library of Congress. The previous year Spofford had acquired the Smithsonian Institution's entire library, which already contained an outstanding collection of foreign scientific and official publications, and he continued to solicit material on exchange. Thus, Spofford began his work of transforming the Library of Congress into an institution of national significance, a change greatly enhanced by his centralization of all U.S. copyright activities at the Library in 1870. Spofford's view of a national library followed the European model: it was to be a comprehensive collection of a nation's literature. He successfully used Jeffersonian and nationalistic arguments to obtain the congressional approvals he needed; for example, in several annual reports he reminded Congress that "there is almost no work, within the vast range of literature and science, which may not at some time prove useful to the legislature of a great nation."

In 1897, the Library of Congress moved from the overcrowded U.S. Capitol Building into its own monumental structure, the Thomas Jefferson Building. Spofford's successor as Librarian of Congress, John Russell Young, shared Spofford's view that a national library was basically an accumulation of a nation's literature. A journalist and former diplomat, Young had an international outlook, and during his brief 18-month tenure the Library of Congress began systematically to acquire research materials from and about other countries and cultures. On February 16, 1898, for example, Young addressed a circular letter to U.S. diplomatic and consular representatives throughout the world. Invoking Jefferson's contemplation of "a National Library, universal and representative in its character, with all knowledge for its province," he asked them to send to the Library of Congress documents and research materials of all kinds, including "publications illustrative of the manners, customs, resources, and traditions of communities to which our foreign representatives are accredited." These materials were important for the "National Library," he explained, because they illustrated "the history of those various nationalities now coming to our shores to blend into our national life."

Herbert Putnam, who became Librarian of Congress in 1899, extended the Jeffersonian concept even further. To Putnam the national library was much more than a comprehensive library in the nation's capital. It was "a collection universal in scope which has a duty to the country as a whole." Moreover, Putnam defined that duty as service to scholarship, both directly and through other libraries. He was especially far-sighted in acquiring research collections about other cultures. As early as 1901, he told a group of scholars that the national library "had a duty" to gather and make available the records and publications of the other countries in the Western hemisphere. A few years later he expanded its interests throughout the world. In 1904, he purchased a

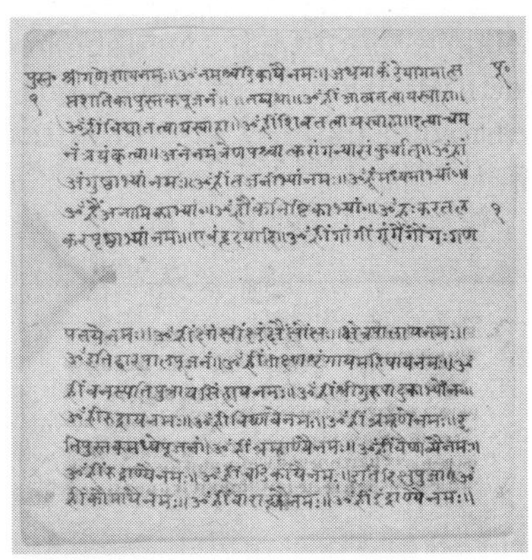

Pustakapj, *Book of Worship, Maharashira, nineteenth or early twentieth century. Part of the Southern Asian Section begun in 1904 when Librarian Herbert Putnam purchased a 4,000-volume collection of Indica from a professor of Sanskrit at the University of Berlin.* LC/Southern Asian Division.

4,000-volume library of Indica owned by a professor of Sanskrit at the University of Berlin. In 1906, he boldly acquired the 80,000-volume private library of Russian literature owned by G.V. Yudin of Siberia, even sending a Library of Congress staff member to Siberia to supervise the packing and shipping of the books. A 10,000-volume private collection of Hebraica was donated in 1912. During his 40-year tenure as Librarian, Putnam aggressively acquired official publications, even sending Library employees overseas to seek publications and new exchange agreements. In 1926, for example, James B. Childs, chief of the Documents Division, visited Germany, Russia, Lithuania, and Latvia; the next year he went to Bulgaria, Greece, Rumania, and Yugoslavia.

The close involvement of the Library of Congress with the Hispanic world began in 1927 when Archer M. Huntington presented the Library of Congress Trust Fund Board with funds to establish an endowment for the purchase of books relating "to Spanish, Portuguese, and South American arts, crafts, literature, and history." The next year Huntington donated funds to create a chair of Spanish and Portuguese literature, providing Putnam with a precedent to encourage similar endowments for other languages and literatures. The Librarian also obtained significant collections of Chinese and Japanese books. In 1928, he took pride in establishing a division of Chinese literature, which he planned to make into "the center in this hemisphere for the pursuit of oriental studies."

Through Putnam's activities and initiatives, the Library of Congress also established a reputation as a world-wide leader in librarianship. He regarded international library relations as the unique responsibility of the national library and from the early years of his tenure worked to expand the Library's involvement with other libraries worldwide. For many years, Putnam was either chairman or a member of the American Library Association's International Relations Committee, and when he became association president in 1903–1904, he planned its 1904 conference as an international library meeting. The Library of Congress also began to be involved, for the first time, with other national libraries. In 1928, at the urging of a former Library of Congress colleague, William Warner Bishop, Putnam "loaned" Charles Martel, chief of the Catalog Division, to the Vatican for a special project. In Rome, Martel joined Bishop and another former Library of Congress division chief, J.C.M. Hanson, to install in the Vatican Library "the methods of cataloging in vogue in American libraries." In describing this project, Putnam noted that there were three other foreign libraries with which the Library of Congress "would gladly develop cooperative relations: the British Museum, the Bibliothèque Nationale, and the State Library in Berlin."

The ongoing expansion of the Library's collections to include research materials in other languages and from other cultures was crucial to the eventual expansion of the Library's international role. New acquisitions were dutifully reported each year in his annual reports, yet Librarian Putnam was reluctant to formulate or at least announce any Library of Congress acquisitions policy—for U.S. or foreign materials. It was left to his successor, Librarian of Congress Archibald MacLeish, a writer and poet, to articulate officially the Jeffersonian acquisitions rationale as it applied to foreign materials.

In 1940, MacLeish announced three "canons of selection," which would become the Library's objectives "with regard to the character of the collections." The third canon states: "The Library of Congress should possess, in some useful form, the material parts of the records of other societies, past and present, and should accumulate, in original or in copy, full and representative collections of written records of those societies and peoples whose experience is of most immediate concern to the people of the United States."

A wartime librarian, MacLeish felt strongly that libraries and librarians were essential to preserving the world's cultural heritage. During his tenure, in particular he greatly strengthened the Library's newly established Hispanic Foundation. On October 12, 1939, only 10 days after he had assumed his duties as Librarian, he dedicated the new Hispanic Room to "the preservation and the study and the honor of the literature and scholarship of those other republics which share with ours the word American." A $22,000 two-year grant to the Foundation from the Rockefeller Foundation soon followed. Two years later MacLeish initiated a Hispanic Exchange Project through the Department of State, and before the end of World War II representatives of the Foreign Service and the Office of War Information were authorized to transact business on the Library's behalf, an effort that benefitted the Library's collections enormously and served as a forerunner to the Library of Congress Mission in Europe.

Facing A New World

World War II's most important effect on the Library was to stimulate the development of its collections about other countries and cultures. MacLeish's successor, Luther H. Evans, succinctly described the new era in December 1945, six months after he had taken office: "It is necessary to remember that the destruction (of civilization) has been avoided only through an unprecedented mobilization of man's knowledge of himself and his environment. . .

no spot on the earth's surface is any longer alien to the interest of the American people. No particle of knowledge should remain unavailable to them."

For Evans, "the interest of the American people" meant the interest of the Library of Congress, and he planned to revitalize and augment the Library's foreign acquisitions program and to engage the Library in cooperative international activities. During his librarianship, he failed to expand the Library's national services as he wished. Nevertheless, through his vision and persistence, he shaped the basic direction of the Library's international role for the rest of the century, involving the institution for the first time as an active participant and leader in international organizations and activities. For Luther Evans, the Library of Congress, "a universal library with a national duty," was also "an international servant of enlightenment."

Evans pushed hard to build the Library's collections of research materials about other areas of the world and never hesitated to point to specific examples that might have helped the Allies fight World War II. The Library of Congress Mission in Europe, organized in 1945 by Evans and his Library of Congress colleague Verner W. Clapp, acquired European publications for the Library and for other American libraries. The Library placed automatic purchase agreements ("blanket orders") with foreign dealers around the world, and initiated exchange agreements for the international exchange of official publications. As the major U.S. government library, the Library of Congress also received large quantities of confiscated wartime materials from the U.S. military and from other federal agencies.

In addition, Evans believed the new technology of microfilming could be an important acquisitions tool, and he used it imaginatively in cooperative projects to benefit the Library of Congress and other institutions. In 1949, for example, in cooperation with the American School of Oriental Research in Jerusalem, a Library of Congress team microfilmed significant manuscripts in St. Catherine's Monastery on Mount Sinai and in the Greek Orthodox and Armenian Patriarchate Libraries in Jerusalem. A microfilming program for official gazettes from the Mexican states was started and selected records in the Japanese Foreign Office were filmed. Evans also strengthened area studies within the Library. He established the European Affairs Division in 1948, and organized new European, British, Orientalia, and Hispanic sections in the Exchange and Gift Division. In spite of budget cuts, he added a Korean specialist to the staff of the Orientalia Division. He also supported several unique gatherings of scholars and librarians, including the First Assembly of Librarians of the Americas in 1947, the first conference of Mexican and North American historians in 1949, the first international colloquium on Luso-American Studies in 1950, and a Near Eastern colloquium in 1950. New publications started by Evans, chiefly with outside funding, included accessions lists from Russia, Eastern Europe, and Southern Asia. All of these efforts strengthened American research collections nationwide by spreading information about what materials were being published abroad.

Convent of St. Catherine, Mount Sinai. *Scottish artist David Roberts created this work February 21, 1839, on-site in the Holy Land. His works were reproduced as tinted lithographs throughout the 1840s. In 1949, the Library microfilmed manuscripts at Mount Sinai.*
LC/Prints and Photographs Division. LC-USZC4-3526.

Luther Evans extended the international role of the Library of Congress far beyond acquisitions and area studies. In 1945, he was a United States delegate to the London conference that established UNESCO as an important part of the fledgling United Nations structure. He continued his close involvement with UNESCO in the early 1950s in spite of criticism from several congressmen who complained that Evans was devoting more time to UNESCO matters than he was to the Library. In fact, Evans believed that the program and purposes of UNESCO and the Library paralleled each other, and indeed he brought the organizations together in several activities, particularly the development of the Universal Copyright Convention (1954) and promoting standardized procedures for bibliographical control of library materials.

Through the leadership of Librarian Evans, the Library of Congress became committed to international library and cultural cooperation. Evans and his associates, particularly Chief Assistant Librarian Verner Clapp, believed the Library could contribute to international affairs both by deed and example. The Library organized a reference library to assist participants in the 1945 San Francisco conference that established the United Nations. And in 1947, a Library of Congress Mission to Japan, headed by

Clapp, provided assistance in the establishment of a new Japanese national library, the National Diet Library. Evans also used the Library's exhibitions program to promote international understanding, sending Library of Congress materials abroad for display and featuring exhibitions about other cultures at the Library. His strong belief that original source materials should reside in the countries of their creation resulted several times in the repatriation of materials seized in wartime or acquired under questionable circumstances.

Sharing Information And Ideas

When Evans resigned in 1953 to become Director-General of UNESCO, his successor was L. Quincy Mumford, director of the Cleveland Public Library. Eventually Mumford guided the Library through its greatest period of national and international expansion, beginning in the late 1950s when the Library began to benefit from increased federal funding for education, libraries, and research. Most dramatic was the growth of the foreign acquisitions program, an expansion based on Evans's accomplishments a decade earlier. In 1958, the Library was authorized by Congress to acquire books and research publications by using U.S.-owned foreign currency under the terms of the Agricultural Trade Development and Assistance Act of 1954 (Public Law 480). Four years later, an appropriation allowed the Library to establish acquisitions centers in New Delhi and Cairo.

In 1965, President Lyndon B. Johnson approved the Higher Education Act of 1965. Title IIC of the new law had great significance for the Library of Congress and for all American academic and research libraries, because it provided funds to the Library for the ambitious purposes of 1) acquiring, insofar as possible, all library materials currently published throughout the world that were of value to scholarship; and 2) providing cataloging information for these materials promptly after they had been received. This law came closer than any other legislation affecting the Library of Congress to making Jefferson's concept of comprehensiveness part of the institution's official mandate and to legislating "national library" status for the institution. The new program, a major achievement of the Mumford administration, was called the National Program for Acquisitions and Cataloging (NPAC). The first NPAC office was opened in London in 1966. By 1971, the Library of Congress had 13 overseas offices—and its acquisitions program had expanded around the world in dramatic fashion.

By 1970, the development of international bibliographical standards was recognized as an important concern. The general problem had been addressed in the UNESCO conferences of 1946 and 1949 in which Luther Evans and his colleagues participated, and at an international conference on cataloging held in Paris in 1961, but by 1970 the age of automation had arrived. Computers were beginning to be used for library cataloging and for creating data banks of shared information. The crucial development had taken place at the Library in the mid-1960s: the creation of the Library of Congress MARC (MAchine Readable Cataloging) format for communicating bibliographic data in machine-readable form. The possibility and desirability of worldwide application was immediately recognized, and the MARC format became an international standard in 1973, only two years after it became the official U.S. national standard.

Today the Library of Congress, still a major world producer of bibliographic data, continues to play an important role in shaping the international standards that make the worldwide sharing of information possible. Much of this work takes place through the Library's active participation in international organizations, particularly the International Federation of Library Associations and Institutions (IFLA). Through IFLA the Library of Congress shares information and participates in many areas of world librarianship, including cataloging, classification, the recording of serial publications, document exchanges, preservation and conservation, library services to the blind and physically handicapped, library services to legislatures, map librarianship, rare books, children's literature, and reading and literacy promotion.

There are many other ways in which today's Library of Congress operates as an international institution. Through its Copyright Office, the Library administers the U.S. copyright law which, in the electronic age, increasingly is concerned with the protection of intellectual property worldwide. The Copyright Office also is responsible for developing and implementing copyright relations with other countries at both bilateral and multilateral levels. The Library's Center for the Book, established in 1977, is another example. It is a focal point for stimulating public interest in books, reading, and libraries, nationally and internationally. Its success has helped inspire the creation of book centers in several other countries, including England, Scotland, Wales, Australia, Russia, and South Africa.

Historian Daniel J. Boorstin, Librarian of Congress 1975–1987, explained the importance of the Library's international role in this way: "Our country has been peopled with immigrants from all over the world. How could we pretend to make a truly national library for our United States unless we collected in the languages that millions spoke when they arrived—

and still arrive—on our shores? In the United States, of all the nations on earth, our *national* library (like our people) must be *international*."

James H. Billington, who took office in 1987 as the 13th Librarian of Congress, is a historian of Russia and the former Soviet Union and a scholar with a deep interest in international affairs. In his activities and statements as Librarian of Congress, he has emphasized the importance of maintaining and strengthening the Library's role internationally. In the early 1990s, Billington inaugurated a series of major exhibitions of treasures from "Great Libraries" around the world, resulting in exhibitions about treasures from the Vatican Library (1993) and the Bibliotheque nationale (1995). As part of the 13-year renovation and restoration of the Library's Thomas Jefferson Building (1984–1997), he relocated all of the Library's area studies reading rooms to that building. Thus when it reopened to the public in 1997 it became, in Billington's words, "a living, universal museum of the written word—the closest thing anywhere to the world's memory, the place to find out what is unique about other people."

"Delphic Sibyl," an image from the Sistine Chapel by Giorgio Ghisi from the 1993 exhibit and catalog Rome Reborn: The Vatican Library and Renaissance Culture. *This exhibition was one of a series from great national libraries of the world inaugurated by Librarian James Billington, including those of the Bibliotheque National and the Saxon State Library.*
Photograph: The Vatican Library.

The move of the area studies reading rooms to the Jefferson Building stimulated a revival of interest within the Library not only in area studies but also in special cooperative projects with other countries. Because of Billington's personal interests and contacts, the initial emphasis was on countries of the former Soviet Union. In January 1991, for example, he led a 10-person Library of Congress delegation to Moscow for a three day conference, "The National Library in the Life of the Nation: The Lenin State Library and the Library of Congress."

Between 1990 and 1996, with support from the U.S. Congress, through its Congressional Research Service, the Library provided training and technical assistance to the newly democratic legislatures of Central and Eastern Europe. In addition, throughout the 1990s, the Library of Congress - Soros Foundation Fellowship Program brought librarians and information specialists from Russia and Central and Eastern Europe to the United States to participate in a three-month program designed to introduce foreign librarians to libraries and librarianship in America.

European materials abound in the Library of Congress divisions. This depiction of the Church of Vassili Blagennoi in Moscow built by Ivan Vassilievitch (the Terrible) in the sixteenth century is one of 60 hand-colored plates in the 1842 Excursions Daguerriennes: Vues et Momuments les plus Remarkables du Globe.
LC/Prints and Photographs Division.

In May 1999, Congress authorized the creation of a pilot exchange program for Russian decision makers—the Russian Leadership Program—and charged the Library of Congress with administrating it. The new program brought emerging Russian political and civic leaders to the United States to meet their American counterparts and see American style democracy and free enterprise in action. In late 2000, Congress established the Open World Leadership Center to provide a permanent home for the exchange, which was renamed the Open World Program. The Center is an independent entity but housed at the Library of Congress; Librarian of

Congress Billington, one of the Open World Program's founders, is Chairman of its Board of Trustees. Total funding appropriated by Congress for the Open World Program from 1999 through fiscal year 2004 was $64.5 million. In 2003, the Open World Leadership Center hosted its 7,500th participant and welcomed its highest percentage of Russian women ever (58 percent). The year 2003 also saw Congress expand eligibility for Open World to Russian cultural leaders and to 14 other countries in the region. At the Board's recommendation, Open World launched pilot expansion programs in Ukraine, Uzbekistan, and Lithuania. The cultural leaders program, which includes professional librarians, aims to forge better understanding between the United States and Russia by enabling participants to observe and experience American cultural and community life firsthand.

In other projects, new cooperative arrangements enabled the Japanese and Chinese governments to provide assistance for the cataloging of valuable Japanese and Chinese rare books in the Library's collections. New fellowship programs brought young scholars to the Library to use the foreign language collections and reading rooms. In the mid-1990s, through digitization projects with Russia, Spain, and the European Union, the Library of Congress began close cooperation with other national libraries and foreign governments to develop digital collaborations that would make available unique documents that related to their common histories with the United States.

To mark its bicentennial in 2000, on October 23–26, the Library hosted historians and directors of libraries from throughout the United States and the world for a symposium, "National Libraries of the World: Interpreting the Past, Shaping the Future." The 150 participants included 32 national library directors.

The John W. Kluge Center, established in 2000 through an endowment of $60 million from Mr. Kluge, the chairman of the Library's Madison Council, created more international opportunities for the Library. The center especially encourages humanistic and social science research that makes use of the Library's large and varied collections, welcoming in particular scholars interested in interdisciplinary, cross-cultural, and multi-lingual research. Four of the initial programs were, for example: the Library of Congress Rockefeller Fellows in Islamic Studies; the Library of Congress International Studies Fellows; the Henry Alfred Kissinger Chair in Foreign Policy and International Relations; and the Coca-Cola Fellowship for the Study of Advertising and World Cultures.

In the summer of 2001, the Library opened "World Treasures of the Library of Congress," an ongoing, rotating exhibition of the Library's rarest and most significant international items from many ages and in a variety of formats. "Beginnings"was the first of these exhibitions, showing how common themes have been treated in different cultures and exploring how world cultures have dealt with the creation of the universe and explained the heavens and the earth. In the booklet published with "Beginnings," Librarian Billington stated: "We at the Library of Congress are as proud of our international collections as we are of our American collection. . . The Library of Congress is the largest and most inclusive library in the world, and it is truly an international institution. Alone among the world's great libraries, the Library of Congress still attempts to be a universal library, collecting materials of research value in almost all languages and media. It still is guided by Thomas Jefferson's belief that democracy depends on knowledge—and that all topics are of interest to the national legislature and to the American people."

Cole, John Y. "The International Role of the Library of Congress: A Brief History," *Library of Congress Information Bulletin* 49 (January 15, 1990): 15–18, 45.

Feinberg, Gail and Tracy Arcaro. "Interpreting the Past, Shaping the Future: Library Hosts Symposium on National Libraries," *Library of Congress Information Bulletin* 59 (December 2000): 290–292, 307; "Library History Seminar X Convenes," *Library of Congress Information Bulletin* 60 (February 2001): 50–51.

Lorenz, John G., et al. "The Library of Congress Abroad." *Library Trends* 20 (January 1972): 548–576.

THE NATIONAL DIGITAL LIBRARY AND THE LIBRARY'S ELECTRONIC RESOURCES

by Guy Lamolinara

For more than 200 years, the Library of Congress has collected, preserved, and made freely available the intellectual and creative achievements of individual Americans. In fulfilling its mission to "sustain and preserve a universal collection of knowledge and creativity for future generations," it has assembled an unparalleled record of the nation's collective memory.

The Library's ever-growing electronic resources help the institution fulfill another part of its mission: sharing these collections with Congress, the nation, and the world. A beginning was made in the mid-1960s, when the Library began to distribute machine-readable cataloging information. However, it was not until the 1990s, with the advent of the Internet, that the collections of the Library could be made available to anyone who could access the World Wide Web.

When James H. Billington was sworn in as the 13th Librarian of Congress on September 14, 1987, he spoke of making the riches of the Library "even more broadly available to ever-wider circles of our multiethnic society ... using new technologies to share the substantive content, and not merely the descriptive catalog, of the nation's memory." Billington has been the driving force behind the expansion of the Library's electronic resources as a means of sharing the Library's collections. At his urging and with his full support, in 1990 the Library offered selected primary source materials from its Americana collections to schools and libraries through a five-year CD-ROM pilot project called American Memory. Its success eventually led to a proposal to Congress for the development of a more comprehensive, five-year National Digital Library Program.

During the American Memory pilot project, the Library also began experimenting with electronic technology to bring other resources to users remotely. In 1992, for example, it began making selected images and accompanying text from its major exhibitions available on the Internet; the first two exhibitions were "Revelations from the Russian Archives" and "1492: An Ongoing Voyage." For the first time those who were unable to visit the Library to view its exhibitions could still see them from anywhere in the world, and they could view them long after the physical exhibition had closed. By spring 2004, more than 40 exhibitions covering a diverse range of subjects and media, could be accessed online by users of the Library's Web site.

Before that, the Library of Congress Information System (LOCIS) became available to the public on the Internet in 1993. LOCIS included access to the Library's catalog, the status of legislation since 1973, abstracts of laws from several Hispanic-speaking countries, braille and audio materials and copyright registration records since 1978. (LOCIS has since been superceded by the Library's Integrated Library System.)

LC MARVEL (Machine-Assisted Realization of the Virtual Electronic Library) also came online in 1993. A bulletin board service, LC MARVEL provided a wide variety of information about the Library, including information about events and jobs as well as images and text from the Library's exhibitions and links to a vast collection of Internet resources worldwide. Eventually, the content of MARVEL was migrated to HTML Web pages and the service was officially retired in early 2003.

The Library's electronic resources have always been of special interest to members of the legislative and executive branches of government. Librarian Billington has testified before Congress many times about the importance of new technologies in shaping the Library's future. In April 1993, for example, he discussed the effect that the "first waves of the new electronic technology" were having both on society and the Library of Congress; he also asserted his view that this technology, in its expanding and ever-changing role, would always supplement—and never supplant—books, reading, and libraries. On July 14, 1993, Billington and Vice-President Albert Gore co-chaired the Library's first major conference on electronic library resources, "Delivering Electronic Information in a Knowledge-Based Democracy."

Partnerships with the private sector have played a vital role in the development of the Library's electronic resources. For example, pilot projects in 1993 included one in which the Library and a cable company demonstrated the new use of cable television technology for interactive access to American Memory materials in schools in Colorado, and the Library and a telephone company joined in a project in Union City, N.J., to test the use of a telephone network delivery system for disseminating unique research materials from the Library's collections.

Librarian Billington continued to make his case for the important role libraries would play in the emerging "electronic superhighway." In his Winter 1994 article in *Media Studies Journal,* he stated his belief that "if the new electronic superhighways are truly to serve America, they must do more than offer entertainment and high-priced information on demand to the well-to-do at home or in the office. Such a strategy would forfeit the technology's great potential for national progress and create information 'haves' and 'have-nots." In April 1994, he testified with other distinguished representatives from the library community before the Senate Subcommittee on Education, Arts and Humanities. "If in creating the [information] superhighway we do not include public libraries, the superhighway will bypass and shut out many of our citizens. We will have created information 'haves' and 'have nots,'" he said, echoing his article in *Media Studies*.

As the American Memory pilot project drew to a close, the Library surveyed the 44 selected schools and libraries that had participated. The response was enthusiastic, especially from teachers and students in middle and high schools. But distributing these materials in CD-ROM format was both inefficient and prohibitively expensive.

Fortunately, by 1994 technology had caught up with the Library's vision of its new educational outreach role: the World Wide Web could be used by anyone with access to the Internet. The Library took advantage of the opportunity and, on October 13, 1994, announced that it had received $13 million in private sector donations to establish the National Digital Library (NDL) program. Thanks to this fortuitous convergence of technology and vision, the National Digital Library would begin placing digital materials from the Library's collections on the newly emerging World Wide Web. The National Digital Library made its debut with a commitment to placing online five million items from the collections of the Library and other institutions by 2000. The materials would be presented as part of American Memory which on that day lost its status as a pilot and became a full-fledged program, one of the first large-scale efforts to use the Internet to disseminate high quality educational and cultural content—digital versions of vast riches of the American collections of the Library of Congress.

From the beginning, the National Digital Library Program was envisioned as a public-private partnership. The U.S. Congress agreed to appropriate $15 million for the program over its first five years and asked the Library to raise an additional $45 million in private funds, for a total of $60 million. The Library exceeded that goal by raising more than $48 million from the private sector and making available

American Memory is an electronic gateway to rich primary source materials relating to the history and culture of the United States. The site offers more than eight million digital items from more than 100 historical collections.

more than five million items by 2000. By 2004, there were more than 8.5 million items available, ranging from papers of the U.S. presidents, Civil War photographs and early films of Thomas Edison to documents from the women's suffrage and civil rights movements, Jazz Age photographs and the first baseball cards. To make the National Digital Library Program a truly national effort, the American Memory site includes important collections from more than 30 other institutions nationwide. It is the largest body of freely available educational content on the Internet.

American Memory focuses not on materials that are often available locally, but on materials that can only be accessed at the Library of Congress—iconic items from our nation's past as well as present, such as Abraham Lincoln's draft of the Gettysburg Address; personal narratives of slaves; notebooks of Walt Whitman; Alexander Graham Bell's drawing of a telephone; photographs of baseball legend Jackie Robinson, who broke the color barrier in major league baseball in 1942; the music of Aaron Copland and Leonard Bernstein; films documenting the origins of American animation; papers of Samuel F. B. Morse and an image of the first telegram ever transmitted; railroad maps; and images of U.S. presidential inaugurations, from George Washington to George W. Bush.

By April 2004, American Memory, which was offering 125 thematic collections, was handling more than 47 million transactions a month.

The growing American Memory site has spawned other online projects geared to specific audiences; the Learning Page Web site, for example, is aimed at schools. From the start, American Memory

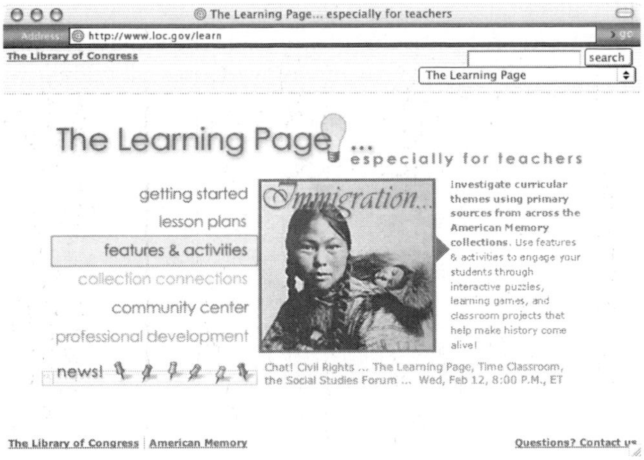

The Learning Page is created for teachers with lessons, features and activities, collection connections, a community center, and professional development suggestions.

was seen as a way to deliver primary resource materials from the Library's collections to teachers and their students. As Laura Campbell, director of the National Digital Library and Associate Librarian for Strategic Initiatives, said when the NDL Program debuted, "We will find a synergy between the Library's digitization project and the needs of elementary and secondary school teachers. We will be learning from teachers how best they want to use our digitized primary source materials in the classroom." Introduced in 1996 as a companion to the American Memory collections, the Learning Page Web site is a key component of the Library's educational outreach effort. Specifically designed for K–12 educators and their students, the site offers teachers an easy-to-use guide to using the Library's online resources in the classroom. The content of the digital collections is presented in an appropriate context—lessons, curriculum guides, "how-to" projects, and other learning activities. In addition, the Learning Page presents guides to other electronic resources, professional development workshops, and a "community center" offering online chats.

Another program to reach educators has been the American Memory Fellows Institute. Two hundred and fifty teachers have participated in these summer institutes at the Library, and in turn they have introduced the American Memory collections to other educators across the country and the world.

In 2000, the America's Library Web site for children and families was launched during the celebration of the 200th birthday of the Library of Congress. This interactive site draws on materials from American Memory and presents them in stories that are especially appealing to a younger audience. After American Memory, it is the Library's second most popular Web site, logging more than 18 million transactions per month during fiscal year 2003.

Launched on the Library's bicentennial, April 24, 2000, America's Library is for children and families. It is an easy-to-use, colorful and interactive Web site designed to make learning history fun. Often using rare and sometimes unusual items from the collections of the Library, the site introduces children to many fascinating historical items and the stories surrounding them.

In 2002, the Library launched a new online monthly magazine called "Wise Guide" to introduce newcomers to many useful educational resources on the Library's Web site in a comprehensive and visually appealing way. Each monthly magazine features seven "articles" linked to Web pages containing online materials from throughout the Library. America's Library and Wise Guide are being advertised in cooperation with the Ad Council. "There's a better way to have fun with history. Log on. Play around. Learn something" beckons users to America's Library, while "It's fun to know history" draws visitors to the Wise Guide.

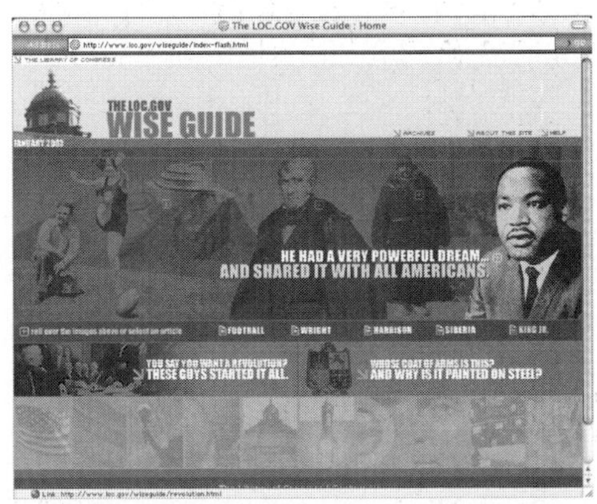

The Wise Guide portal was designed to introduce users to the many educational and useful resources available from the nation's library and one of the most popular sites of the federal government. A monthly e-zine, the site offers links to the best of the online materials.

During fiscal year 2003, more than 2.6 billion transactions were recorded on all of the Library's computer systems. Here are selected resources available on the Library's Web site not mentioned previously.

Online Catalog. The Library continues to provide free global access to its online public catalog. The catalog recorded more than 361 million transactions during fiscal year 2003—an average of more than 30 million transactions a month.

THOMAS. A new online resource for congressional information about the workings of the U.S. Congress debuted on January 5, 1995. The system was named THOMAS in honor of Thomas Jefferson, who embodied the ideals of representative democracy and was one of the Library's principal founders. A World Wide Web server administered by the Library, THOMAS is public legislative information system initiated by the leadership of the 104th Congress to bring together much of the congressional information available online in disparate places on the Internet.

THOMAS initially included the full text of bills from the 103rd and 104th Congresses, *The Congressional Record*, and links to House and Senate Web sites. Today its greatly expanded features include: Status of Appropriations; Bill Summary and Status Records; Quick Search of Text of Bills; House Floor This Week, which includes legislation expected to be considered by the House of Representatives during the current week; Roll-call Votes; Texts of Bills; Texts of Laws; *The Congressional Record* from 1989–present; Committee Reports; Presidential Nominations; Treaties; "How Our Laws Are Made;" and historical documents such as the Federalist papers, the Declaration of Independence, and the U.S. Constitution. The site is updated daily when Congress is in session. THOMAS is one of the Library's most popular resources, with 10 million transactions logged each month.

Global Gateway. The Global Gateway Web site highlights the Library's extraordinary international collections. A project that fosters international collaboration for joint digitization efforts and access to the Library's global resources, it focuses on collabora-

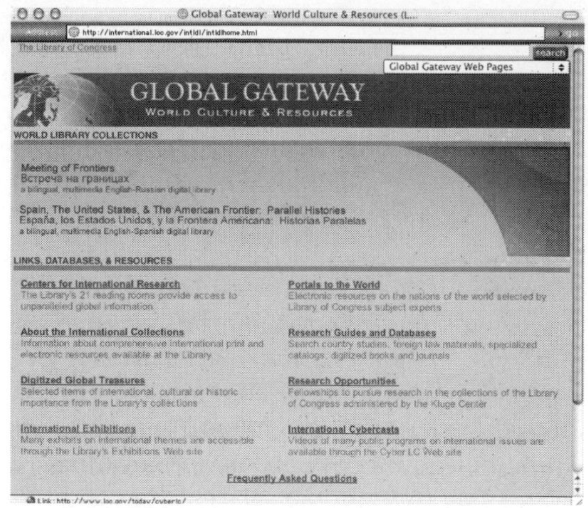

The Global Gateway consists of international collaborative digital libraries. Included is a listing of the searchable Library of Congress collections that focus on cultures and history around the world. Links, databases, and resources are provided for centers for international research. Also included are research opportunities, international collections, cybercasts, and exhibitions as well as research guides.

tive efforts with national libraries in Russia, Spain, Brazil and the Netherlands. For example, the "Meeting of Frontiers" section of Global Gateway is a bilingual, multimedia English–Russian online library that tells the story of the parallel exploration of the American and Russian frontiers, culminating in their combined settlement of Alaska and the Pacific Northwest. The Web site features thousands of images, including photographs, albums, maps, and postcards from the Russian State Library in Moscow, the National Library of Russia in St. Petersburg, the University of Alaska in Fairbanks, and of course the Library of Congress.

THE LIBRARY OF CONGRESS AND ITS DIGITAL FUTURE

by Laura E. Campbell and Amy Friedlander

The Library of Congress occupies imposing buildings on Capitol Hill in Washington, D.C., where its architecture bespeaks permanence, reliability, and the value of history and scholarship to the nation. The Library of Congress also maintains an award-winning Web site that partially reflects its embrace of digital information and communication technologies at the very end of the twentieth century. As the Library looks to the digital future, like other major libraries, it faces a fundamental tension: On the one hand, we expect our major libraries to function as stewards of heritage—a conservative role which they have successfully occupied for over a century and which will not vanish because creative expression employs digital means. On the other hand, that digital expression is fragile. The technological landscape in which the information is created evolves rapidly, sometimes in fits and starts rather than in smooth upgrades. Therefore, institutions that collect and preserve that information must transform themselves into adaptive, nimble, and forward-looking organizations. In short, as a nation, we ask our libraries, museums, and archives to embrace competing values, to be both culturally conservative and technologically innovative.

Identity, Mission, and Values

The Library of Congress is among a handful of major libraries that exert influence and leadership by example. Its stated mission is to "make its resources available and useful to the Congress and the American people and to sustain and preserve a universal collection of knowledge and creativity for future generations." In its service to the U.S. Congress, and as the home of the U.S. Copyright Office, it has a unique mandate and enjoys unique status among U.S. libraries. The Library's Digital Strategic Plan of December 2002 articulates a vision that acknowledges its national and international role and confirms the importance of acquiring, preserving and providing access to digital works. The plan describes seven current major digital initiatives (Copyright Office Re-engineering; Congressional Research Service Products, Digital Future, Global Legal Information Network, Integrated Library System, Legislative Information System/THOMAS, and the National Digital Information Infrastructure and Preservation Program [NDIIPP]), and posits four goals:

1. Expand, manage, and communicate the Library's digital strategies and roles
2. Manage and sustain digital content
3. Manage and sustain mission-critical digital programs
4. Obtain, develop, and sustain specialized expertise and resources.

The Library's collections are vast and diverse, ranging from books and other printed materials, to audio recordings and motion pictures, to computer programs and rare artifacts as well as more than 7.5 million digital items made available online through the National Digital Library Program (NDLP) and the Web sites included in the Election 2000 Collection. Between 1997 and 2001, the Library's collections in all formats increased by just under 10 (9.9) percent; more than two million items are acquired annually. As digital works become more ubiquitous, we can expect them to form an increasingly large component of the Library's collections but not to exclude ongoing collection of items in other formats.

Digital works encompass roughly three classes of materials: First, a digital work may represent a digitized version of an analogue item, for example, a digitized version of the works of William Shakespeare that can be made accessible over the Internet, by CD-ROM, or in another electronic medium. Second, a digital item may be the digital version of a work that is released in parallel formats as are many scholarly journals and newspapers. Finally, a digital work may exist exclusively in electronic form for which there is no physical analogue, the so-called "born digital" materials; the obvious example is a Web site which may appear to be a seamless display on a screen but may actually consist of several files and routines "served up" over the Internet from several computers. Adding all of these works to the Library's collections, as well as continuing to acquire books, manuscripts, films, recordings, and so on, does not alter the substance of the Library's mission. But the new technologies and the kinds of objects that can be created in the digital medium have altered—and will continue to alter—the ways in which the Library goes about executing its stewardship mission and the environment in which it does so.

Service to the U.S. Congress is central, both directly through the analyses conducted by the

Congressional Research Service and more indirectly through the acquisition, maintenance, and preservation of the collections. Over the years, the Library has also provided services for other libraries, such as Cataloging Distribution Service, and has fostered decentralized yet nation-wide programs, such as the Center for the Book and international collaborations, such as the Global Legal Information Network (GLIN). In addition, the Library has accredited functions associated with major research libraries. Its collections were used on-site, primarily by scholars, and it has been tacitly assumed by many to be the "library of last resort," which meant that the Library would acquire and retain what other libraries could not. But the American Memory pilot and subsequently the NDLP expanded on the institution's historical relationships with Congress, other libraries, and scholars at home and abroad to use the World Wide Web to bring reliable, digital versions of the Library's primary source material directly to the public with special attention to teachers and children.

As a result, the Library's pursuit of its mission to serve Congress and the public through its collections and services now reaches directly—albeit remotely—to broader and more eclectic base of users, many of whom may be unfamiliar with the traditions of a major research library. As the National Initiative for a Networked Cultural Heritage (NINCH) *Guide to Good Practice in the Digital Representation and Management of Cultural Heritage Materials* observes, digitization of rare and unique materials expands the audiences for those materials and multiplies expectations for performance, display, and use of digitized works. But these audiences may have different expectations and values so that displaying elaborate text mark-up that may be important to a literary scholar, for example, may seem to impede casual browsing by an avocational reader.

A Revolution in Information and Expectations

Information technology (IT) has fundamentally transformed the Library's relationship with the public. The technologies inform almost all the workings of the Library from systems and services to new kinds of digital works. The Library began to automate aspects of its internal business processes in the 1940s. In the 1960s, innovations in formats and systems (for example, the MARC record) became important to the development of shared information, enabling standardization, cost savings and delivery of authoritative catalog records among libraries on a broad scale. The burst of creativity in the mid-1990s associated with the expansion of the Internet and the World Wide Web represented something different from the business process/library automation systems that preceded it. Separate streams of development in computer networking and communications engineering converged with developments in digital information creation and management (for example, text mark-up, image compression, indexing, search, retrieval, and so on), so that in a very short time, a substantial segment of the population seemed to enjoy access to an enormous amount of information in digital form delivered to them on their home computers via home telephone connections.

Digital transmission, or communications, means that information in digital form can be conveyed around quickly and easily, reducing barriers of space and time and increasing efficiencies. For example, the Legislative Information System (LIS) improves access to legislative information for Congress and its staff, and its public version, THOMAS, allows citizens to follow the legislative process remotely as well as read the bills and conference reports themselves. Moreover, curators and reference staff in the different units of the Library are beginning to re-think access to their collections, recognizing that there is great diversity among remote users.

One consequence of greater transparency and access is that expectations may escalate faster than policies to address them can be articulated. For example, recent college graduates who come to work for Congress or within the Library may expect relatively easy online access to databases of aggregated journal articles to which they had become accustomed while in the university. Library of Congress offices may, in fact, subscribe to these services but procedures may not yet be in place to facilitate broader use by authorized users.

Expectations of the public will also continue to change. New questions arise when access to a work is no longer constrained by its physicality. In the past, relatively few citizens other than members of Congress, their staff, and scholars who came to Washington thought of treating the Library of Congress like a local public library from which they might conveniently find material. But more people *are* in touch and digital reference services as well as the Web site reinforce the sense that the Library truly belongs to the nation. Citizens with relatively slow connections can already download the front pages of the world's major newspapers to their home computers or listen to radio feeds from international stations. Why will they not soon come to expect similar access to animated features, like *Shrek* or *Antz*, which employed ambitious computational techniques, or to still-copyright-protected classics like *Gone With the Wind*, *Casablanca*, or National Geographic television specials that they assume exist in the Library's vast holdings? Whether and how the Library collects, retains, and can, indeed, make such works available on demand to a user is a challenging set of questions. Some of these questions concern relationships with other libraries and archives while others fall under the rubric of the much-contested and unresolved questions of intellectual property rights in the digital environment.

To date, the Library's internal digitization projects have tended to focus on primary source material and on works in the public domain. But as the scope of collecting expands to works in parallel formats and to so-called "born digital" material (that is, material experienced in an online context and for which no physical analogue exists) and as public expectations evolve, the Library can expect to reassess what it makes available, how and to whom. In addition to requirements for rights-protected access, digital works pose a set of concerns that arise from the medium itself. They may appear compact and easily searched and used—for example, the frequently cited image of the Library of Congress "on a disk." But digital works can also be voluminous, highly heterogeneous, easily corrupted, frequently ephemeral, and subject to change and updates. A Web site, for example, may not be as well-defined and self-contained as a book or a map, and electronic book may consist of a hand-held device with connection to a Web site from which content is then downloaded. Works may be displayed on multiple platforms, creating questions about which representation is the "authentic" work and leading to concerns about long- term preservation.

Preservation of digital materials for future use poses a series of questions that librarians and archivists now believe must be faced at the creation of the work as well as over its life cycle. Some of the issues are primarily technological; others require organizational solutions. Will future users have the necessary tools to access and render the work? (This is the "playback" problem, which anyone who has tried to read an old disk or a file saved in an obsolete format has already encountered.) The storage media degrade, and recent estimates suggest that about half of the world's film collections, stored on digital video disks (DVDs), may become unreadable in 10 to 15 years. Digital materials are more secure when they are redundant. Unlike rare analog works, which can be protected through restrictive physical controls, digital materials are more vulnerable when they are locked away. Bugs, viruses, damage, and mischief are detected when digital collections are used. But use also increases the likelihood that a work may be damaged. Thus, libraries and archives must simultaneously enable patrons to use these materials, safeguard the works from inadvertent damage, and protect the legitimate rights of rights holders.

Internal discussions about the life cycle of information examine the technical, managerial and legal dimensions inherent in acquiring, describing and preparing sustainable collections that can be made available now and in the future. There is wide recognition that these issues are complex and engage expertise not traditionally associated with libraries and archives. Indeed, current discussions involve a shifting mosaic of publishers, artists, film studios, engineers, computer scientists, lawyers, and scholars in many academic disciplines as well as librarians and archivists. Debates revolve around topics from the appropriate archiving of the World Wide Web, to intellectual property, to technical issues of obsolescence, large scale system design and standards, to personal privacy and national security.

Institutional Change: Decision Making, Organization and Management

In the late 1990s, the Library began to plan for the institutional changes associated with digital information and communication technologies. In 1998, the Librarian of Congress commissioned a study by the Computer Science and Telecommunications Board (CSTB) of the National Research Council (NRC) to "provide strategic advice concerning the information technology path that LC should traverse," specifically requesting attention to ways to integrate digital and analog collections and to interact with then-emerging digital library technologies, systems and projects funded by federal and state agencies and philanthropic organizations. At roughly the same time, the Library also formed the internal Digital Futures Committee, which departed from existing practice to draw broadly across units within the Library to engage in institution-wide planning.

The committee's immediate task was to consider ways to maintain the NDLP, which was then a five-year experimental program. (The staff and the digital conversion activities were placed on a permanent basis in FY 2001.) As the deliberations continued, the work of the group expanded to begin to grapple with the implications of providing digital content via the Internet. Discussion of so-called "born digital" material was deferred. Very importantly, digital information was not seen as a separate format that might be encapsulated in an organizationally distinct unit (like Manuscripts, Rare Books, Prints and Photographs, Geography and Maps, and so on) or that might be subsumed into the Information Technology Services unit, which had historically overseen technological systems and infrastructure. Rather, the structure of the committee and its scope signified recognition that works and therefore services in digital form would permeate the Library's divisions. As one observer within the Library has said, "This is ultimately a question of information management, not format."

While the Library was conducting its internal planning, the study committee assembled by CSTB met for the first time in February 1999, in what was then the height of the "dot.com" boom. The excitement of the times coupled with the success of the federal interagency Digital Libraries Initiative, led by the National Science Foundation, formed the context in which the committee reached its recommendations. Many were constructively critical of the Library although the committee also recognized its broad cultural mission, the challenges of executing that mission given the enormity and diversity of the Library's collections, the achievements of American Memory and NDLP, and the efforts of Digital Futures to initiate a broad strategic planning process. Nevertheless, the report, *LC21: A Digital Strategy for the Library of Congress* (2000), characterized the institution as having become "insular" and largely out of touch with developments in information technology. As a result, the report's authors cautioned, the leadership that the Library had historically exercised in such areas as cataloging and preservation of analog objects was not being replicated for digital and its historic primacy among the major libraries was in jeopardy.

LC21 called for a more agile Library of Congress and made many general and specific recommendations about management and personnel, finances, information technology infrastructure, collections and preservation. The authors also recommended a strategic planning approach for information technology that was both integrative and transparent and for creation of a new position of deputy librarian for strategic initiatives. As a direct outcome of the report, the Office of Strategic Initiatives was organized and Laura E. Campbell appointed to the position of Associate Librarian for Strategic Initiatives in October 2000. Recommendations in the report also led to the National Digital Information Infrastructure and Preservation Program (NDIIPP), created by Congressional legislation in December 2000 (PL 106-554). NDIIPP complements internal Library efforts confronted by the Digital Futures effort to deal with challenges inherent in long-term preservation of digital content as well as the implications of broad, distributed collaborations across many public and private entities and interests.

The Digital Futures committee has evolved into the Digital Executive Oversight Group (DEOG). Its October 23, 2002 charter sets forth its purpose: "to provide a coordinated approach to achieving the LC digital vision and meeting the digital policy and technology requirements of individual service unit and cross-service unit missions." The group is convened by the Associate Librarian for Strategic Initiatives and has representatives from each of the five service units (Copyright Office, Congressional Research Service, Library Services, Law Library, and Office of Strategic Initiatives); decisions are reached by planning, analysis, and consensus. Thus, the Library has begun to put in place management structures that recognize both local autonomy within the units, where subject and other specialists do, indeed, understand the considerations implicit in their disciplines, while achieving overall coordination and integrated support.

Old and New Partners

Librarians have been quick to recognize the networking potential of the Internet and were active partners in its early diffusion. Within the Library, an early example of a distributed virtual collection is the Law Library's Global Legal Information Network GLIN, which consists of an electronic system of shared information among a series of partners who represent many of the world's major law libraries as well as institutional partners such as NASA, and the NDLP is itself a collaborative enterprise. Moreover, as other libraries develop portals to other sites and virtual collections, material from the Library's collections become visible through venues it does not control and of which it may not necessarily be aware. Creating collections and providing access to them represents one set of challenges; long-term preservation of digital content, an historic function of the major libraries and archives, is a second. The latter currently engages broad attention, including initiatives at the National Archives and Records Administration (NARA), the National Science Foundation (NSF), and several executive agencies.

The Library's approach to long-term preservation of digital content is set forth in *Preserving Our Digital Heritage: Plan for the National Digital Information Infrastructure and Preservation Program* (NDIIPP), issued in the fall of 2002 and approved by Congress in December of that year. The plan describes a collaborative vision that ensures "the access over time to a rich body of digital content through the establishment of a national network of committed partners, collaborating in a digital preservation architecture with defined roles and responsibilities." As part of the process of developing the plan, the Library listened to the concerns of many stakeholder communities, and was encouraged to learn that there is wide public support for the basic goals of preservation, a reservoir of good will, and trust in the Library itself as an honest broker.

Digital information is distinguished from other media in quantity, heterogeneity, and vulnerability to external technological changes that may render a format obsolete relatively rapidly. For example, during the background interviews conducted during the NDIIPP planning phase, anecdotes surfaced again and again, describing careful construction of a cutting edge Web site in one format, only to discover that it had become superceded before or shortly after the Web site was launched. Data compiled in 2002 by a team at the University of California at Berkeley supported estimates that print, film, magnetic, and optical storage media produced about five exabytes of new information; over 90 percent of this was stored on magnetic media, mostly hard disks. Five exabytes of information is equivalent in size, the investigators state in their Executive Summary, to the information contain in half a million new libraries the size of the Library of Congress." No single institution can be expected to manage the full range of works from databases of scientific and socio-economic information to new forms of creative expression that may possess commercial value and may be protected by copyright for the several decades.

Coordinated and collaborative collection development to ensure redundancy without unnecessary duplication while protecting legitimate rights and reasonable access seems the only viable strategy. But working out ways in which to partition the responsibilities and sustain accountability is challenging. Within the Library, the collecting and custodial responsibilities of the various administrative units have been worked out over the years, so for example, historic musical scores are preserved in Manuscripts Division but historic recordings by different artists are held in Motion Pictures/Broadcasting/Recorded Sound Division. Similar compromises will be worked out for digital materials, and units in the Library have actively discussed how division of responsibilities might be achieved and what the implications are for the organization, including the technical requirements to ensure long- term sustainability of the collections, given the fragility of the medium and rapidly advancing technologies.

The challenges are equally great among institutions. In the past, the Library of Congress has worked out complementary and collaborative collection development policies with other major federal libraries (the National Library of Medicine [NLM] and the National Agricultural Library [NAL]) and cultural institutions like the American Film Institute, the Museum of Modern Art, the Film Preservation Board. More recently, the Library has begun to experiment with third party agreements to cover dissertations and scholarly journals. More of these agreements about responsibility for collections can be imagined not only among the national libraries but also among the major universities, public libraries, state libraries and historical societies, and private collecting institutions like the J.P. Morgan Library and the Huntington Library. Little remains fixed in the digital world, however, and NLM has found that its agreement with NAL must be periodically re-visited as the underlying science evolves so that notions of their respective areas of responsibility adequately capture important material. These agreements will require ongoing monitoring to ensure that the coverage is sufficient, and effective execution of these contracts will require new kinds of tools, for example, registers of current and obsolete formats, inventories of collections, and so on. As Lynne Brindley of the British Library has observed, librarians do have a tradition of cooperating in a general sense, but managing the new digital information across a number of institutions will require mechanisms for tighter collaboration.

Finally, there will be wholly new kinds of works, or "digital objects," as they are known, as well as extensive legacy information. Publishers of scholarly journals are now converting their back files into digital form, and as new uses are found for this legacy material among scholars, new services will continue to be built for accessing and using them. Whether the Library itself maintains sophisticated end-user services or employs third parties who, in turn, rely on the Library's collections for authoritative versions of the material remains to be seen. But a range of end-user services, from the ubiquitous keyword searching to elaborate visualization tools will characterize *users'* future landscape.

Many well-informed observers believe we are on the brink of new forms of scholarly analysis and expression. A report to the National Science Foundation by a Blue Ribbon Advisory Panel on Cyberinfrastructure released in January 2003 described a broad vision of science, enabled by "exponential" advances in computation, storage, and networking. In the arts and humanities, NINCH has completed the previously mentioned guide for good practice for cultural heritage materials in digital form, and the Coalition for Networked Information (CNI) and Internet2 sponsored a study of "best practices" for managing dissertations in the performing arts that employed telepresence and other highly advanced tools to create works that can be displayed in the cyber-environment. In mediaeval studies, the Beowulf project employed different technologies to enable a new analysis of the early text, displaying characters and alterations that had not been visible. Another classic example of detective work is the L'Enfant plan of Washington, D.C., held by the Library's Geography and Map Division. Jefferson made pencil annotations on L'Enfant's manuscript map, and those changes were incorporated into the final printed map. Because of the extensive deterioration of the original manuscript, Jefferson's annotations were basically invisible and had been forgotten. Richard W. Stephenson, formerly of the division's staff, made the connection between comments in Jefferson's letters and the changes between the manuscript and printed version's of L'Enfant's map. When he examined the manuscript carefully under special lighting conditions, he discovered Jefferson's annotations. In the late 1980s and early 1990s, the U.S. Geological Survey (USGS) scanned extremely detailed reproductions and, using image enhancement software, was able to remove the general darkening of the map and bring out Jefferson's annotations. A facsimile was then reproduced which clearly showed Jefferson's comments. Unfortunately, the software used by the USGS became obsolete, and the 30 some digital tapes on which this detective work was done can no longer be read.

Over the next decades, we can expect a mix of legacy information, scientific data, and contemporary works for which the users' demands will be both unpredictable and varied. It is an exciting vision for scholars but perhaps a bit daunting for librarians and archivists. Even more challenging is the need to develop similar relationships with private, commercial entities that create and control culturally valuable content. We have learned through historical experience that preservation requires cooperation across many communities, some of them focused on the current value of the information and others on its future cultural value. For example, the failure to collect early film reflected both a failure of imagination and a fear of new media—the nitrate film—not just at the Library but also by the studios and production companies. It is now believed that as much as 80 percent of the early output of the motion picture industry has been lost. Much the same can be said of early radio broadcasts, which were as ephemeral in their day as the World Wide Web seems now but which gave rise to many staples of contemporary mass media from soap operas to newscasts. Through private donation, acquisitions, and copyright deposit, the Motion Pictures/Broadcast/Recorded Sound collections are now very extensive and are used by commercial as well as educational and scholarly interests all of whom appreciate the importance of reliable and well-maintained collections.

We can expect the creative communities to continue to explore the limits of what is technologically feasible. But these kinds of experimental works are most difficult to manage from the point of view of identification, acquisition, and preservation because they are hard to find and least likely to conform to mainstream practice. Yet they may embody experimental techniques for new media that may one day become mainstream and perhaps representing the young work of a future master.

To recognize the long-term value of such materials, we must first make it easy for content creators to store their work, at least temporarily, and then we must establish ways to know about these works. Finally, we must build teams of specialists who can make educated appraisals about what to collect and how best to sustain the collections, and these capabilities must be diffused throughout libraries, museums and archives. This is not to say that old values and strategies for analog materials will be discarded unexamined. But they will be augmented and perhaps transformed. Professional development and retraining for existing staff become paramount and over the long run a new kind of librarian will be required. Thus, the Library is working with the American Library Association (ALA) to examine changes to professional education. In the meantime, teams within Cataloging Directorate, for example, are developing necessary competencies, enabling the expertise to begin to percolate through the staff, and NDLP employed a mix of professional capabilities: librarians, historians, subject specialists, employees for whom this was their first job, and an assortment of graphic designers, computer scientists, business managers, and editors.

In its current digital preservation efforts, the Library has begun to explore ways in which collections may be physically distributed but accessible in a virtual sense. Based on substantial research into relevant technical systems conducted by other federal agencies and commercial interests, a national network of repositories, where data are stored and managed, can be imagined that may "know" about one another. These repositories might be individually managed according to the needs of the custodial organization or they might be maintained by communities of interest to serve the needs of the member organizations. For example, major content owners might manage "certified" repositories where access to commercially valuable, copyright-protected material might be restricted. University libraries might assume responsibility for the work of their faculties, while the performing arts organizations might jointly sponsor a certified repository. The rise of institutional repositories, such as those undertaken by some of the major universities (for example, the California Digital Library and MIT, among others), suggest that these kinds of initiatives are already in progress.

Outside of higher education, interests as diverse as motion picture studios, the music industry, leading universities, the Cable Center, C-SPAN and the WGBH Educational Foundation have already begun to examine problems of long-term archiving of digital content. Scenarios can be imagined where the Library helps knit these separate initiatives together through common standards, shared information, and best practices to foster a system that achieves large scale coherence while enabling local decision-making and control. Within this scenario, we might imagine that the Library continues to collect in certain areas and also makes copyright-protected works directly available to Congress and to patrons who use the Library's facilities in Washington. These works might also be made more generally available through third parties or public libraries that may have agreements or broad arrangements with the concerned rights holders. At the same time, the Library of Congress and other major libraries might act as fail-safe protectors for the archival versions of protected works so that should all other systems fail, future use might be sustained. Thus, the Library of Congress would continue to serve as the library *for* Congress, its historical constituency; provide preservation and archival services for other libraries in concert with major cultural institutions around the world; and also offer a degree of public access, perhaps to highly specialized information for which it has major responsibility.

National Research Council. *LC21: A Digital Strategy for the Library of Congress.* Washington, D.C.: National Academy Press, 2000.

THE LIBRARY OF CONGRESS AND SCHOLARSHIP

by Jane Aikin

The Library's alliance with scholarship began with the purchase of Thomas Jefferson's personal library in 1815. "It is the choicest collection of books in the United States," wrote Jefferson, "and I hope it will not be without some general effect on the literature of the country." Jefferson's hope was realized. Since his library reached far beyond the legal and political literature that had dominated the Library of Congress's collection, its acquisition set the precedent for developing the comprehensive collections that would attract broad scholarly interest. However, scholars did not have ready access to the Library during the early 1800s. Only congressmen and senators could grant reading privileges to outsiders; and while they were generous, the result was that the Library was more a social center than a scholarly retreat during its first several decades. Researchers' interest in the Library grew as its collections increased and its scope expanded to include material in every language and from every corner of the world.

Scholars have served the Library of Congress as members of the staff, as consultants, and as members of advisory committees. They have visited the Library to lecture or to read from their works to an audience as well as to do their own research. Scholarly organizations frequently meet at the Library, and these organizations have often originated projects, funded bibliographic or research activities, and served as the Library's partners in developing the collections. Foundations have provided support for conferences intended to advance knowledge in particular fields. On occasion scholars and researchers have testified before Congress about the significance and value of the Library's collections and activities, and they have written articles about the Library for both popular and scholarly periodicals. When traveling abroad, they have selected material for the collections, copied documents in foreign archives or libraries to add to materials already held, and served as the Library's emissaries in dealing with dealers, librarians, and archivists.

Prominent American historian George Bancroft helped the Library of Congress in the nineteenth century by recommending books for its collection in the 1840s and in 1866 by endorsing Librarian Spofford's request to Congress to purchase Peter Force's personal library of Americana, telling Congress that it "will never again have such an opportunity."
LC/General Collections.

Scholars and the Collections

One of the earliest acknowledgments that the scholarly world was important to the Library occurred in 1842, when William C. Preston, as chairman of the Joint Committee on the Library, asked historian George Bancroft to recommend titles to be purchased for the collection. Whether Congress purchased what Bancroft recommended is uncertain, but with 50,000 volumes by the middle of the nineteenth century, the Library's holdings seemed substantial, at least at first glance. However, they were also uneven in coverage. Even 10 years later there was no encyclopedia newer than 1842 and no complete file of even one American newspaper. Up to one-third of the collection consisted of duplicate volumes, notwithstanding the fact that by 1863 the Library's approximately 79,000 volumes made it the fourth largest library in the United States. An 1867 tally of the borrowers' registers revealed that only 19 authors and eight scientists had ever borrowed books. However, the number of readers in the Library certainly included far more scholars than borrowing records indicate.

Ainsworth Rand Spofford, named Librarian of Congress in 1864, began transforming the Library into an international collection and an attraction for scholars. He opened it to public use, pursued foreign exchanges, and acquired both the Smithsonian's exchange collection of scientific publications and the spectacular personal library of the Washington, D.C., archivist and historian, Peter Force. Most important of all, the Copyright Act of 1870 made the Library responsible for the registration of copyrighted works and thereby through copyright deposit secured its

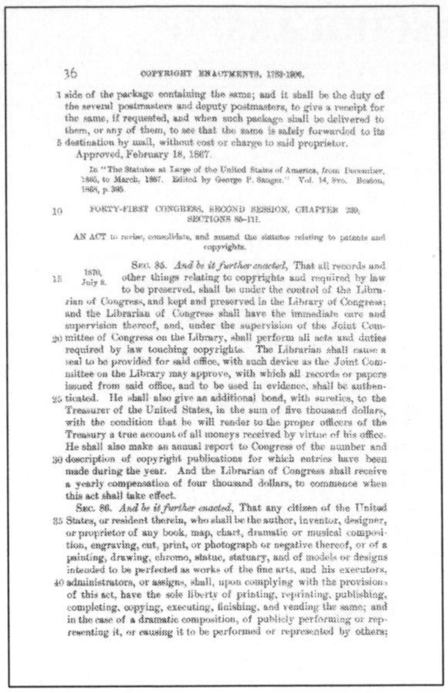

36 COPYRIGHT ENACTMENTS, 1783-1906.

side of the package containing the same; and it shall be the duty of the several postmasters and deputy postmasters, to give a receipt for the same, if requested, and when such package shall be delivered to them, or any of them, to see that the same is safely forwarded to its destination by mail, without cost or charge to said proprietor.

Approved, February 18, 1867.

In "The Statutes at Large of the United States of America, from December, 1865, to March, 1867. Edited by George P. Sanger." Vol. 14, 8vo. Boston, 1868, p. 395.

FORTY-FIRST CONGRESS, SECOND SESSION, CHAPTER 230, SECTIONS 85-111.

AN ACT to revise, consolidate, and amend the statutes relating to patents and copyrights.

1870, July 8.

SEC. 85. *And be it further enacted*, That all records and other things relating to copyrights and required by law to be preserved, shall be under the control of the Librarian of Congress, and kept and preserved in the Library of Congress; and the Librarian of Congress shall have the immediate care and supervision thereof, and, under the supervision of the Joint Committee of Congress on the Library, shall perform all acts and duties required by law touching copyrights. The Librarian shall cause a seal to be provided for said office, with such device as the Joint Committee on the Library may approve, with which all records or papers issued from said office, and to be used in evidence, shall be authenticated. He shall also give an additional bond, with sureties, to the Treasurer of the United States, in the sum of five thousand dollars, with the condition that he will render to the proper officers of the Treasury a true account of all moneys received by virtue of his office. He shall also make an annual report to Congress of the number and description of copyright publications for which entries have been made during the year. And the Librarian of Congress shall receive a yearly compensation of four thousand dollars, to commence when this act shall take effect.

SEC. 86. *And be it further enacted*, That any citizen of the United States, or resident therein, who shall be the author, inventor, designer, or proprietor of any book, map, chart, dramatic or musical composition, engraving, cut, print, or photograph or negative thereof, or of a painting, drawing, chromo, statue, statuary, and of models or designs intended to be perfected as works of the fine arts, and his executors, administrators, or assigns, shall, upon complying with the provisions of this act, have the sole liberty of printing, reprinting, publishing, completing, copying, executing, finishing, and vending the same; and in the case of a dramatic composition, of publicly performing or representing it, or causing it to be performed or represented by others;

Ainsworth R. Spofford, named Librarian in 1864, began the Library's transformation into a scholarly institution. He acquired historical collections, particularly the Smithsonian Institution's library of scientific works and documents from learned societies, and archivist Peter Force's library of books, manuscripts, and maps relating to America. Most important, through the 1870 copyright law (above), he brought copyright deposits into the Library, dramatically expanding its Americana collections in both size and scope. Photograph: Copyright Enactments. Laws Passed in the United States Since 1783 Relating to Copyright. Copyright Office Bulletin No. 8 (Revised).

Two librarians, Spofford and Putnam, in turn made decisions concerning gift policy that greatly strengthened the Library's scholarly collections. Ainsworth Spofford established the precedent for accepting gifts with the acquisition in 1882 of the 40,000-volume private library of Washington, D.C. physician Joseph M. Toner, shown here. The collection contained medical and scientific works and source material as well as writings by and about George Washington. Smithsonian Institution Archives.

future as a comprehensive collection of Americana. Spofford also established a precedent for accepting gifts with the acquisition of the 40,000-volume private library of Washington physician Joseph M. Toner. However, it was the opening of the Thomas Jefferson Building in 1897 that provided the real inspiration for increasing the Library's budget and broadening its role. The grand scale and ornate design of the new building elevated the Library of Congress to a palace of scholarship, creating a virtual mandate to fill its shelves.

Herbert Putnam, who became Librarian in 1899, was determined that the Library should collect comprehensively because he planned "the nationalization of the Library of Congress by developing its resources for service to scholarship and by extending the benefits of its collections and of its technical processes to the country at large." Under his direction, the Library's role would be to provide special service to the Congress and the federal government; serve as a library of record for the United States; provide collections and facilities to supplement other research libraries; and respond to demands from all parts of the country; "and thus equalize opportunities for research now very unequally distributed." Stating that other libraries should maintain their own collections of specialized material—local history, state and municipal materials—he declared that the Library of Congress would become the library of last resort for scholars as well as the chief repository for the literature of national history and government. It would be "a library which stands foremost as a model and example of assisting forward the work of scholarship in the United States."

While the modest appropriations of the early twentieth century seldom allowed the Library to acquire high-priced European rarities, Putnam was intent on expanding the Library's foreign holdings. He began to purchase rich but less expensive foreign collections; for example, a 4,000-volume library of Indica in 1904 and G. V. Yudin's 80,000-volume private library of Russian materials in 1906. The beginnings of a comprehensive Hebraic collection appeared with a 1912 gift of 10,000 volumes; collections of Chinese and Japanese books were established and additions made inexpensively. As these collections gradually expanded, specialized units, then divisions and reading rooms appeared with language specialists to handle both the technical work of cataloging and bibliography and assistance to scholars and other users. By the 1920s, for many areas the Library of Congress had the largest collections outside the countries of origin and continued to expand its foreign holdings to the fullest extent.

The Library had long since recognized the Army Medical Library (later the National Library of Medicine) and the Department of Agriculture Library (later the National Agricultural Library) as peers in their special fields and left to those libraries the accumulation of a definitive record of scholarship in medicine and agriculture. Putnam similarly decided that it was not possible for the Library to collect federal

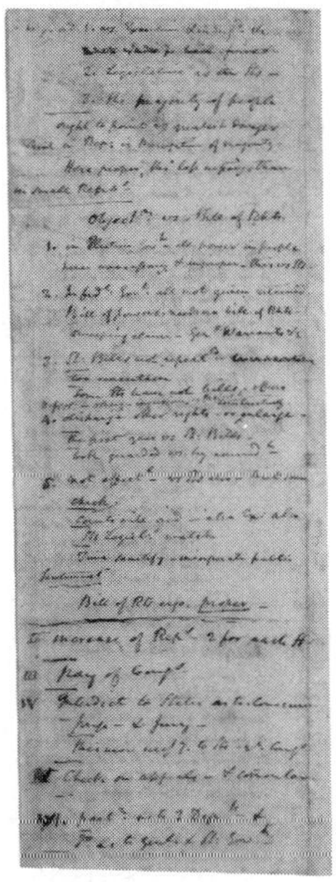

In 1903, Librarian Herbert Putnam convinced President Theodore Roosevelt to transfer the personal papers of most of the Founding Fathers from the Department of State to the Library, along with records and papers of the Continental Congress. Putnam explained that the transfer was necessary in order to build at the the Library of Congress "a library which stands foremost as a model and example of assisting forward the work of scholarship." Above, a page from James Madison's notes from the first Federal Congress in 1789, part of the transfer from the Department of State.
LC/Manuscript Division.

archives and consequently advocated the establishment of the National Archives, which occurred in 1934. This recognition of the responsibilities of other federal agencies allowed the Library of Congress to concentrate on the other sciences, the social sciences and the humanities, with building and maintaining the national collection of materials in all formats relating to the United States as the top priority. As a step toward strengthening the Americana collections, Putnam asked President Theodore Roosevelt in 1903 to order the transfer of the papers of the Founding Fathers from the State Department to the Library, including those of the first presidents. The transfer made the Library's Manuscript Division the principal center for research in American national history and culture; simultaneously Putnam and Oscar Sonneck began building the Music Division into the major collecting center for American music. By the end of 1905, the Librarian had inaugurated a program in cooperation with the American Historical Association and the Carnegie Institution to copy foreign manuscripts relating to American history that were held by overseas repositories. With about 300,000 pages already copied, in 1926 James B. Wilbur established an endowment to support the work, and two years later John D. Rockefeller provided a $450,000 grant to continue the program another five years. Under the leadership of historian Samuel Flagg Bemis, extensive copying of archival material in the Netherlands, Italy, Spain, Canada, and England enriched the growing collections.

Putnam was instrumental in the founding of the Library of Congress Trust Fund Board in 1925, the quasi-corporation established to serve as trustee for endowments given to the Library. The Board itself was an important innovation in federal governance, and the impetus to its founding was just as remarkable: Elizabeth Sprague Coolidge offered an endowment for continuing concerts and support for the Music Division. Separately she also offered funds to construct an auditorium in the Library. Congressional acceptance of her gifts involved the federal government for the first time in the support of the arts. The Board has ever since administered the private gifts that have allowed the Library to acquire rare items, enlarge the collections, and provide cultural programs. Such gifts have provided for many of the important acquisitions that during the twentieth century

Encouraged by an endowment for music from philanthropist Elizabeth Sprague Coolidge (above), in 1925 Librarian Herbert Putnam established the Library of Congress Trust Fund Board. Subsequently, the Board has administered private gifts and bequests to the Library. LC/Music Division.

The new technology of microfilming in the 1930s soon made the Library's copying programs more productive. As early as 1941 the American Council of Learned Societies began cooperating with the Library and the Rockefeller Foundation to begin filming British manuscripts and early records—only one of many filming projects undertaken in cooperation with scholarly societies. One new project was to copy valuable cultural resources such as the manuscript collections in St. Catherine's Monastery on Mt. Sinai, here shown in a lithograph after sketches drawn on-site in 1838–1839 by British travel artist David Roberts.

LC/Prints and Photographs Division. LC-USZC4-3536.

immensely enhanced the Library's value for scholarship. Gifts provided in the 1920s and early 1930s also supported the Library's first endowed chairs: William Evarts Benjamin's donation for a chair of American history, the Carnegie Corporation's endowment for a chair in the fine arts, Archer M. Huntington's gift for a chair of Spanish and Portuguese literature, Harry F. Guggenheim's endowment for a chair of aeronautics, and James B. Wilbur's gift for a chair of geography.

The introduction of microfilming technology in the 1930s made the Library's copying programs even more productive. As early as 1941, the American Council of Learned Societies and the Rockefeller Foundation began cooperating with the Library to film British manuscripts and early records. This was only one of many filming projects undertaken in cooperation with scholarly associations, and after World War II, the Library staff initiated additional projects to copy valuable historical and cultural resources; for example, the manuscript collections in St. Catherine's Monastery on Mt. Sinai, captured German and Japanese records, and Mexican official gazettes. A Center for the Coordination of Foreign Manuscript Copying was established with a grant from the Council on Library Resources, Inc. (CLR) in 1966. With a 10-member advisory board made up of scholars, representatives of learned societies, and research libraries, the Center undertook a variety of activities in locating collections to be copied, identifying projects in progress and work completed.

The Library of Congress's collections were formed at a relatively late date compared with those of the European national libraries, but its acquisitions program was aggressive from Spofford's mid-nineteenth-century initiatives forward. Collections have been acquired through purchase, gift, exchange, or by copying. However, the Library does not purchase or accept as a gift any item that might have been removed from a country contrary to the laws protecting cultural property. In a particularly telling example of this principle, on Columbus Day 1952, Librarian Luther Evans returned a 1504 letter written by Christopher Columbus to the Library of the Real Academia de la Historia in Madrid, from which it had disappeared during the Spanish Civil War. The observance of cultural property laws have made the Library's copying programs important to the advancement of American scholarship, since only through such copying could facsimile materials be supplied for research use.

By the mid-1930s, the Library of Congress had become the largest library in the world, and its extensive collections in foreign languages made it an international resource. Continuing Putnam's collecting initiatives, Librarian Archibald MacLeish's codification of the Library's collecting objectives, as the "Canons of Selection" (1940) included the acquisition of records of other societies and countries "whose experience is of most immediate concern to the people of the United States." His words proved prophetic, as World War II prompted unprecedented demand for material about countries and cultures worldwide. The war revealed how poorly prepared American research libraries were to meet scholars' and researchers' fast-expanding needs. With the help of the military, the State Department, and other government agencies, the Library succeeded in maintaining a flow of wartime acquisitions from abroad, but like other libraries, it could not gather in all the publications produced in war-torn countries. In 1945, Librarian Luther Evans and Director of Acquisitions Verner Clapp organized a cooperative acquisitions program to acquire wartime European publications for U.S. libraries, and several years later the Library joined with other research libraries to implement the Farmington Plan, which divided acquisitions responsibilities for current foreign publications among the nation's research libraries.

During Evans's administration, the Library's book and pamphlet collections increased by over 28 percent, while readership nearly doubled. The increases were in part due to post-war acquisitions initiatives and to an influx of material that federal agencies had collected during wartime for their own intelligence needs, but there was also a flow of gifts. But while Evans and the senior staff determined that

Verner Clapp, fourth from left, and colleagues pose in early post-World War II Germany. They were on a Library of Congress "Mission to Europe," sent by Librarian Luther Evans to acquire wartime European publications for the entire library community. One result was the immediate strengthening of the Library's own foreign language research collections.
LC/Prints and Photographs Division. LC-USZ62-123570.

appropriated funds would in future have to be spent mostly on contemporary material, they also decided that collection additions would not be limited by time or place. The Library of Congress would continue to be a workshop for scholars of all periods and cultures.

An increasing emphasis on science, technology, technical publications, and area studies characterized the post-war period. As wartime agencies divested themselves of flourishing technical reports collections, materials gathered abroad, and collections assembled to meet war needs, they sent material to the Library. Numerous agencies contracted with the Library for research and documentation services to meet post-war needs, with ever-mounting pressures to augment the scientific and technical materials in the collection. Between 1950 and the mid-1970s, too, rapid increases in publishing and changes in the storage, retrieval, and dissemination of information significantly affected both acquisitions and cataloging. Librarian L. Quincy Mumford received important support from the library and scholarly communities for two important collection development initiatives. The ACLS was instrumental in formulating the program funded by the Agricultural Trade Development and Assistance Act Amendments (Public Law 480, 1958), which enabled the Library to use U.S.-owned foreign currency to purchase material abroad. Title IIC of the Higher Education Act of 1965 authorized the Office of Education to transfer to the Library of Congress funds to acquire all current library materials of value to scholarship published worldwide and to provide cataloging information for them, under the title "National Program for Acquisitions and Cataloging." Under these programs, the Library was able to open offices abroad to acquire and ship publications both for its own collections and for research libraries nationwide. The programs filled important needs as area studies programs were established at the nation's colleges and universities: they provided the collections of current vernacular language materials that the scholars working on remote areas required, and did so through daily collecting in both developed and less-developed countries. The assumption of this national role in providing for research needs made the Library the major supplier of foreign materials and cataloging for the scholarly community at large.

Simultaneously, Library staff and contractors began to develop electronic databases for recording bibliographic and other data, initially in the Congressional Research Service and through the development of the (MARC) MAchine-Readable Cataloging format. From the mid-1970s on, database searching services were open to the public, and gradually the Library added subscriptions to the most important vendor database and full-text online services. A wave of new applications of electronic technology also provided the means of reproducing visual materials, resulting in the mid-1980s in the appearance of a series of videodiscs in the Prints and Photographs Reading Room. The development of

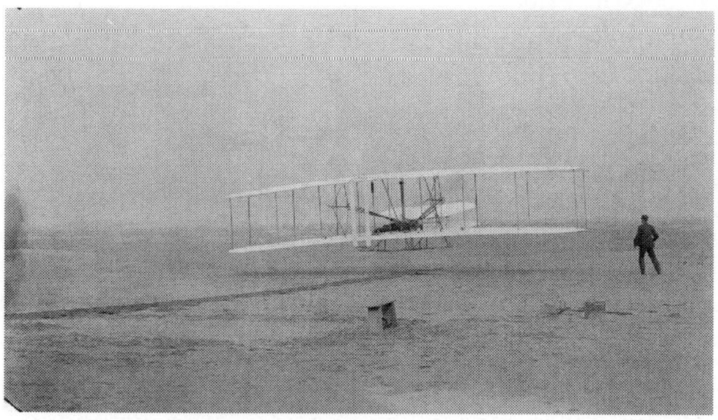

The enormous growth of the collections and readership under Evans's stewardship of the Library, was in part due to vigorous postwar acquisitions as well as a flow of gifts—like those of the collections of Orville and Wilbur Wright, shown here at the first flight, George and Ira Gershwin, Mary Pickford and Woodrow Wilson. Some of the most outstanding cultural treasures also came to the Library at that time: the Giant Bible of Mainz, the Hans Christian Andersen manuscripts and the Rachmaninoff Archives. The Library sent the signal that it intended to be a workshop for scholars of all periods and all places.
LC/Prints and Photographs Division. LC-USZ62-6166A.

Library of Congress collections since that time has included continued comprehensive collecting with new technologies increasingly employed to facilitate dissemination. Such dissemination has been a specific goal of Librarian James Billington, who in the late 1980s began the American Memory project to explore the electronic dissemination of the Library's collections. American Memory was followed by the National Digital Library initiative, so that from the mid-1990s, selected materials from the Library's collections have been made available on the Internet. The Library that in 1865 had not yet attained its 100,000th item had grown by 2003 to an enormous scholarly resource of over 19 million books, more than 5 million music items, over 57 million manuscripts, nearly 5 million maps, over 900,000 motion pictures, and more than 14 million visual materials items.

Fellows, Advisors, and Specialized Centers

In 1875, Librarian Spofford asked Congress to pay a "competent historical scholar" to care for the manuscript collection. His request was not granted until the Library moved into the Jefferson Building in 1897, when Herbert Friedenwald of Johns Hopkins University took charge. Spofford did, however, succeed in attracting several scholars to his small staff. Theodore Gill, for example, came to Washington from Columbia University to join the Smithsonian Institution's scientific staff but moved to the Library in 1867. Philip Lee Phillips, who Spofford hired in 1876, became a leading authority on maps and mapping, and Cyrus Adler was a language instructor at The Johns Hopkins University before he joined the Library staff in 1892. Hungarian-born Louis C. Solyom, whom Spofford hired as a cataloger, had an amazing talent for languages: he spoke more than a dozen and could read 30 different European and East European languages. This early inclusion of experts on the Library staff inaugurated the tradition of directly involving scholars and specialists with building the collections and assisting researchers.

Like Spofford, Herbert Putnam was keenly aware of the need to have scholars develop the collections. For the salaries he could offer, however, it was a difficult ambition to realize. The Library was fortunate to secure the services of several men who would shape their fields, such as Oscar Sonneck in American music and James B. Childs in government document bibliography. They exemplify the influence the Library has had in nourishing and shaping growing fields of scholarship: Sonneck was the first important scholar of American music in the United States, and he constantly promoted the study and performance of American music as a scholarly pursuit at a time when most critics did not consider it worthy of serious study. Childs was a pioneer discoverer and bibliographer of government publications, a field that he helped to shape through his writings and through patient collecting of documents worldwide, making the Library's collection the most valuable source of official material from many countries.

Putnam reached scholars and intellectuals in another way as well: he established a private, informal dining room on the northwest corner of the Jefferson Building's third floor, where he entertained guests at luncheon. The luncheons became a well-known Washington tradition including authors, scholars, scientists, government officials and other contemporaries important in a wide variety of endeavors. "I found at last a little group of men who could talk," wrote H. G. Wells after he lunched at the Round Table in 1906. "It was like a small raft upon a limitless empty sea."

After the Trust Fund Board was established, Putnam was able to attract a group of consultants to build the collections and to answer inquiries from scholars and researchers. As mentioned above, endowed chairs for experts in music, geography, the fine arts, aeronautics, and American history, and also consultants in poetry and Hispanic literature appeared by the late 1930s. Most often such experts came from the ranks of university professors or from research positions. They were the first of a long and distinguished procession of scholars in residence who have enriched both the Library's collections and its programs.

By selecting Archibald MacLeish as Putnam's successor, President Franklin D. Roosevelt added a new intellectual dimension to the post of Librarian of Congress. And MacLeish arrived determined to make the Library a great cultural resource center. With financing from the Carnegie Corporation, he established one-year fellowships to bring in young faculty members from colleges and universities to survey holdings in specific fields and to recommend purchases. MacLeish hoped these fellows would provide as well "the increasing liaison between the Library of Congress and American scholarship that the Library so pointedly needs." The program later expanded to include members of the Library staff and other government agencies, and in 1943 MacLeish recruited area specialists from the Office of Strategic Services to prepare lists of essential contemporary materials from war-related countries. The fellowship program survived into the 1950s, although with the cessation of Carnegie funding in 1944 its impact decreased.

MacLeish also brought poets, artists, and writers to the Library, beginning with a series of poetry readings in the spring of 1941. When the Librarian hired Allen Tate as poetry consultant and editor of his newly established *The Library of Congress Quarterly Journal of Current Acquisitions,* Tate organized a group known as the fellows in American letters, including such prominent writers as Carl Sandburg, Katherine Anne Porter and Mark Van Doren. The group inaugurated a recording program in which novelists and poets read selections from their works. Added to the concert series established by the Coolidge Foundation in the mid-1920s, the literary programs greatly enhanced the Library's cultural offerings.

Archibald MacLeish and Luther Evans both employed members of the scholarly and creative communities as advisors. MacLeish launched a Librarian's Council of scholars, book collectors, and librarians in April 1942 to make suggestions "for the conduct of our services, the development of our collections, and the initiation and control of bibliographic studies." Evans formed a Library of Congress Planning Committee including representatives of the same communities to examine the Library's mission during the late 1940s, a committee that recommended that the Library create a National Library Advisory Council and develop a national acquisitions program that would bring to the United States all currently published material of interest to researchers in every field. While its report failed to make any immediate impression on Congress, the Planning Committee's advice provided a blueprint that affected subsequent collection development and some of its suggestions were later accepted; for example, the national acquisitions program reappeared in the 1960s with the PL-480 program and the National Program for Acquisitions and Cataloging.

Between 1939 and 1944, Librarian of Congress Archibald MacLeish was determined to make the Library a great center of cultural resources. To that end, he brought in young faculty members from outside the Library to develop the collections. He also brought poets, writers, and artists to the Library. In 1943, Allen Tate (above) became poetry consultant and the first editor of The Library of Congress Quarterly Journal of New Acquisitions. *Tate helped MacLeish form the Fellows of the Library of Congress, a group of writers that inaugurated a recording program in which novelists and poets read selections from their works.*
Photograph: Gerald Holly.
The Nashville Tennessean, 1969.

L. Quincy Mumford created liaison committees of scholars in the humanities, the social sciences and the sciences in 1962 to provide advice on the Library's role and services, and also an advisory committee on the Public Law 480 program that included representatives of the major scholarly societies and library associations. The Librarian named a number of outstanding scholars as consultants and continued the cultural programming initiated during the 1940s, including concerts in the Coolidge Auditorium, poetry readings, dramatic performances, lectures, and motion picture showings. Between 1968 and 1980, the Library became a partner in a joint doctoral program with George Washington University, with two goals: to enrich graduate study through introducing use of the Library's collections and to promote the education of scholars who would be able to administer special collections in research libraries.

In 1965, the Carnegie Corporation funded a symposium on American literature that took place at the Library of Congress, and the Library assumed direction of an American Revolution Bicentennial Office, recruiting a staff of professional historians and an advisory group of scholars of the Revolutionary era. A grant from the Morris and Gwendolyn Cafritz Foundation supported a series of five symposia on the Revolution between 1972 and 1976, with a number of distinguished scholars and writers participating, and the Library published the proceedings as well as a number of bibliographic works and documentary sources; for example, the *Letters of the Delegates to Congress, 1784–1789,* which received support from the Ford Foundation.

Mumford's successor Daniel Boorstin, a well-known scholar of American history and culture, took a more active role in incorporating scholarship into the Library's programs. His ambitions were aided by congressional passage of a 1976 bill that established the American Folklife Center in the Library, guided by a board of trustees that included scholars of folk culture. The new Center supplemented and broadened the work of the Archive of American Folk-Song, which had been part of the Library since the late 1920s, drawing on the work of musicians and specialists in folk culture. Its charge was to provide assistance and "coordinated leadership" to the field and to

In 1986, Librarian Boorstin named Robert Penn Warren (above) to be the Library's first Poet Laureate Consultant in Poetry. During his 12 years (1975–1987) as Librarian, Boorstin strengthened the Library's scholarly and outreach programs. To mark the the U.S. Bicentennial in 1976, the Library hosted five symposia on aspects of the American Revolution that highlighted outstanding scholars and the Library's exceptionally strong collections for the period. Boorstin also presided over the establishment of the American Folklife Center (1976), initiated the creation of the Center for the Book (1977), and organized a Council of Scholars (1980). LC/Poetry Office.

engage in model projects; its activities included documentation projects, performances, publications, consultancies, and assistance to scholarly research. Scholars of folk culture and ethnomusicology were most immediately involved with the Center, but its interests in other fields, such as linguistics and in non-music materials, grew steadily.

Boorstin established two other centers: the Children's Literature Center (1978) and the Center for the Book (1977). A Children's Literature Section had existed since 1963, but primarily as a reference and bibliographical office. The new Center, in contrast, initiated programs and projects, using private gifts to bring authors and illustrators to the Library as well as scholars of children's literature. The Center for the Book almost immediately gathered a wide audience of librarians, publishers, authors, editors, writers, and scholars. Its program of symposia, lectures, and projects examining the historical role of books, reading, and libraries, helped to encourage the new and growing field of book and publishing history. But the Center's activities also extended to media other than print—for example, television—and consequently attracted even wider attention. The establishment of state center affiliates proceeded apace until all states were covered by 2003. The three centers have helped to bring scholarly work to the attention of an interested public through numerous public events, and their activities have been reinforced and extended through the establishment of the annual National Book Festival in 2001, which features authors, illustrators, and scholars reading from their works and discussing their careers.

Boorstin also founded the Council of Scholars, a privately funded group, to provide advice about the Library's relations to the scholarly world, to explore the extent to which the collections supported scholarship, to prepare "an inventory of knowledge in the world today," and to sponsor programs to examine intellectual issues. The first symposium, on creativity, took place in 1980 and the Library published the participants' papers in 1982. Other symposia followed, on topics such as "Work," "Modern Scholarship," and "Time." Private gifts supported such new programming as, for example, the Mary Pickford Foundation's donation for the Mary Pickford Theater in the Library's Madison Building, built to further the awareness of the history and development of motion pictures. Film historians participated in the inaugural symposium, "Mary Pickford, Her Times, the Films." While *The Quarterly Journal*, the Library's first and only scholarly journal, was discontinued in 1983, the creative arts received new recognition with the appointment in 1986 of the first Poet Laureate/Consultant in Poetry, Robert Penn Warren. James Billington, the scholar of Russian history and culture who succeeded Boorstin in 1987, announced his intention to provide "an atmosphere hospitable to world-class scholars," and to give the Library a catalytic role in the nation's intellectual growth and leadership. As the former director of the Woodrow Wilson Center for Scholars, Billington came to his post thoroughly grounded in the world of learning. In January 1990, he established an Office of Scholarly Programs and formed the James Madison National Council to enhance the Library's programs and services at all levels, including its resources for scholars. The Office of Scholarly Programs was intended to foster relationships between the Library and the academic and cultural communities by presenting lectures, colloquia and other forums for cultural and scholarly expression and by attracting eminent scholars, writers, musicians, and creative artists to the Library to pursue research and provide advice on improving the collections. Thus, scholarly conferences at the Library proliferated: for example, 1987 saw the first Wheatland Conference, a joint endeavor with the Wheatland Foundation that brought together dozens of American and foreign writers for a three-day discussion of modern literature. The celebration of the bicentennial of the U.S. Congress included two major conferences: "Understanding Congress" and "Knowledge, Power, and the Congress," both including scholars, legislators, representatives of the media, and other experts. There were also the 1990s "Decade of the Brain" lecture series, which led to the publication of a series of published volumes and, for the Library's bicentennial, several conferences beginning with "The Frontiers of the Mind in the Twenty-First Century" in 1999 and including "Democracy and the Rule of Law in a Changing World Order," and "John Bull & Uncle Sam: Four Centuries of British-American Relations" in 2000. A series of Bradley lectures, culminating in 2001, focused on "Classic Texts That Have Mattered to Western Citizenship, Statecraft, and Public Policy." Major exhibitions, too, have provided occasions for public lectures, scholarly conferences, concerts, and publications that bring expert knowledge and opinion to bear on important subjects. Such events are often jointly sponsored by the Office of Scholarly Programs, the custodial divisions, the American Folklife Center and the Center for the Book. Cooperative projects with other agencies and organizations interested in the advancement of scholarship have been fostered as well, notably participation with the U.S. Information Agency's International Visitor Program and its Fulbright program.

In October 2000, Librarian Billington announced a $60 million gift from Madison Council chair John Kluge to establish a center for scholars in the Library and the John W. Kluge Prize in the Human Sciences. Opened in 2002, the Kluge Center is housed in the Jefferson Building, and it hosts scholars pursuing research in the Library's collections. A number of privately funded fellowships are awarded yearly to scholars, both senior and junior, from around the world and to Library of Congress staff who are working on their own research projects. The Kluge Center aims to bring scholarship together with the public policy milieu of the nation's capital, and its fellows participate in an active program of presentations, forums, conferences, and similar events. With a center for scholars in place at the Library, its alliance with experts and specialists has become institutionalized to an extent never before possible.

Pictured above is Kluge Fellow Gregg Brazinsky from George Washington University, working in his office in the Library's new John W. Kluge Center. As Librarian of Congress since 1987, James H. Billington, a scholar of Russian history and culture, has moved the Library forward in many directions. He created the Madison Council (1990), a private sector group that has supported scholarly activities such as the "Decade of the Brain" program and major books developed in connection with important exhibitions. The Madison Council also supported the development of the National Digital Library, which was launched in 1994 to make the Library's collections more widely available via the Internet. In late 2000, Madison Council chairman John W. Kluge gave the Library a $60 million gift to establish a new center for scholars and the Kluge Prize in Human Sciences.
Photograph: LC/Levon Avdoydan.

Services to Scholars

Researchers were admitted to the Library's stacks by written permission from the late nineteenth century to 1992, when the stacks were closed for security reasons. However, the Library staff also set aside 52 study rooms in the Jefferson Building for scholars' use and with the completion of the Adams Building in the late 1930s, an additional 174 private rooms for "serious investigators" became available as well. Since that time, perpetual crowding and collection and staff space needs have limited private study space. The assignment of shelves where books may be held for repeated use in the reading rooms has been the chief substitute. The special format divisions of music, maps, manuscripts, prints and photographs, and motion pictures, broadcasting and recorded sound have similarly made arrangements for keeping materials available to researchers working on long-term projects. Since many collections are now stored off-site and at some distance from Capitol Hill, researchers should ascertain before arriving at the Library whether the materials they want to use are available; if not, an advance request must be filed to bring the material from storage.

In 1901, Congress authorized the Library to loan books outside the District of Columbia, thus enabling Herbert Putnam to begin the interlibrary loan service long desired by American librarians. It was a radical step at the time, but it signaled as did no other action the transition in the role of the Library as a storehouse to a laboratory—an active partner for every researcher who needed assistance with obtaining materials. "They must be required for serious research," Putnam specified, "that is to say, for an investigation calculated to advance the boundaries of knowledge. They are not lent for the purpose of private study or self-cultivation. . . There is a risk, to the charge of which I know of but one answer: that a book used is, after all, fulfilling a higher mission than a book which is merely being preserved for future use." The Library of Congress still provides interlibrary loans of books not commonly available in other research libraries.

Another service to scholars appeared in 1938 with the establishment of the Photoduplication Service. Since that time it has provided scholars—locally and by long distance—with copies of materials from the Library's collections for their research, for book illustrations, for lectures and conferences. Materials in the Library's collections that have already been copied to protect the originals, or material microfilmed or copied from other library or archival collections for the Library of Congress may also be duplicated for purchase. The Service also cares for the card-operated photocopy machines as a convenience for researchers needing quick copies on a self-serve basis.

Beginning with World War I, the amount of research performed in the Library increased dramatically, but exactly who was using the collections and for what purposes remained buried in enormous numbers of call slips. A rare picture of the research population appeared in 1937, when it was reported that the 1,150 researchers who had been assigned to study rooms or tables were calling for 240,000 volumes annually. These researchers came from the United States and 21 foreign countries, representing 136 American and 14 foreign universities. Among them were 140 who were doing research for the federal government, 171 faculty members, 339 graduate students, and 74 holders of fellowships or grants. About 50 books published during that year were recognized as incorporating research in the Library's collections.

In 1939, Chief Assistant Librarian Martin Roberts produced a pamphlet titled "The Library of Congress in Relation to Research," which encompassed not only general descriptions of the collections, but also the organizational methods, the services, and the interpretive assistance. It was the first attempt by the Library to address its scholarly constituency directly. Roberts's enumeration of collections was necessarily "exemplary rather than exhaustive," but he described more thoroughly "the apparatus through which the materials are made available" which, he noted, "is of almost equal importance with the materials themselves." Under that heading he discussed the methods of organizing, cataloging and classifying the materials and described the printed catalogs, guides, lists, and bibliographies prepared by the several divisions, and also the Union Catalog. He called attention to the edited documentary collections issued by the Library: the *Journals of the Continental Congress*, *The Records of the Virginia Company of London*, and *The Harkness Collection* of early Peruvian material; and to the publications on the origins and contents of important documents such as the Declaration of Independence and the Constitution.

While the Library itself could not undertake or finance extensive research outside its own functions and operations, Roberts stated, it continued to supervise projects funded externally and to provide space and materials. The extensive list of such projects that he appended included, for example, the 1904 publication of the American Library Association's *A.L.A. Catalog,* the Archive of American Folk-Song began in 1928, and the *Guide to the Diplomatic History of the United States*, published in 1935. By 1943, the Library had published the first volume of *Eminent Chinese of the Ch'ing Period, 1644–1912*, edited by Arthur W. Hummel, chief of the Asian Division. This work was prepared between 1934 and 1942 by a group of over 50 scholars and sponsored jointly by the Library and the American Council of Learned Societies. The responsibility for preparation of the *Handbook of Latin American Studies*, a joint project of the National Research Council, the American Council of Learned Societies, and the Social Science Research Council, was assumed by the Library's Hispanic Foundation in 1945. A 1948 grant from the Rockefeller Foundation supported the preparation of the Library of Congress Series in American Civilization, a series planned to deal with American achievements in such fields as art, business, education, religion, and scholarship. Eminent scholars were recruited as authors for these volumes, which concentrated primarily on the twentieth century.

During the late 1950s, Librarian Mumford formed an internal Committee on the Control and Organization of the Collections to develop statements of the Library's objectives. This Committee affirmed that the Library would make available its collections and facilities for public use but "within the limitations imposed by the Library's primary obligation to provide services to the Congress and to agencies of the Federal Government." The Library would provide free reference service on the premises; reference service by correspondence or referral of the request to a local, state, or regional library agency; interlibrary loan; photoduplication at cost; preparation and publication of specialized catalogs and bibliographies; and cooperation with other institutions in developing and improving library resources and services. These services offered by the Library to the public had not changed substantially since the early twentieth century. During the past four decades they have been enhanced through the addition of an online catalog and database searching services and the availability of collection materials via the Internet.

Scholars and the Organization of the Collections

At the turn of the twentieth century, scholars in the United States urgently needed more and better library collections and better means to gain access to those resources. Many universities across the country had adopted the graduate study model of European institutions, but lacked the imposing library resources of foreign universities. Researchers working at one library had no means of knowing what books were available in other libraries, and even if they did, libraries did not generally lend material by mail. Almost no bibliographies existed for current book and periodical literature, let alone government documents, manuscripts, maps, music, prints, photographs, or other specialized material.

Librarian Herbert Putnam developed new services that would revolutionize the recording and use of research materials nationwide. Late in 1901, the Librarian announced that the Library of Congress would sell its printed catalog cards to any library wishing to purchase them and that it would collect printed cards from other libraries to form a Union Catalog of titles available nationwide. The Library's Card Section would also send free complete sets of the Library's cards to selected libraries nationwide, which would allow users to consult the Library of Congress's catalog at remote locations.

Since the Library staff cooperated with the American Library Association to establish a standard set of cataloging rules for libraries by 1907, it soon became possible for researchers to expect to see the familiar format of a Library of Congress catalog card in every library. Gradually, too, many other libraries and particularly research libraries, adopted the Library of Congress classification, one of the two systems (the other is the Dewey Decimal System) most used in American libraries even today. The Library of Congress's system of cataloging became a lingua franca of library research in the United States, drawing American scholars and librarians together through the use of a standard system. But knowledge about the Library's collections was not limited to catalog cards. Other descriptions of its resources began to be published as early as 1901 when Philip Lee Phillips' *List of Maps of America in the Library of Congress* appeared, and over the years numerous other lists and specialized bibliographies have been published. Scholars can also send their own reference inquiries to the staff and be sure of obtaining assistance.

From the late 1920s, new efforts were made to make the Library's collections accessible and to extend that accessibility to library holdings nationwide. A grant from John D. Rockefeller supported the expansion of the Union Catalog to encompass the holdings of hundreds of American libraries and the compilation of descriptions of thousands of special collections. Knowledge of these holdings depended upon mailed inquiries, however. During the 1940s, several publication projects were initiated to issue the Library's catalog in book format, and then, in the mid-1950s, to turn it into the *National Union Catalog* (NUC), which included the Library of Congress's own cataloging plus the holdings of all American libraries that reported them to the Library of Congress. Virtually every large library subscribed to the NUC before 1960, as they did to several other union lists that the Library began publishing.

In December 1958, the Library obtained foundation support to begin the *National Union Catalog of Manuscript Collections* (NUCMC). Comprising thousands—sometimes tens of thousands—of items, manuscript collections had long posed a problem for researchers because of the impossibility of knowing where they resided and what might be found in each collection. It was this bibliographic problem that NUCMC aimed at solving, and as more and more collections were added, its value increased. With the appearance of the NUC and NUCMC, interlibrary loans skyrocketed and scholars were able to plan research trips to include all repositories owning material relevant to their inquiries. The key remaining resource not yet in print format was the old National Union Catalog, and in 1959 the ALA began cooperating with the Library to publish the full catalog in a 754-volume set, completed in 1981.

Book catalog development, however, was overshadowed by the use of computers to store catalog and bibliographic information. The Library's MAchine-Readable Cataloging (MARC) format appeared in the late 1960s; today, huge databases containing Library of Congress cataloging data plus that of thousands of other libraries are readily available to users through the World Wide Web. The rapid development of online resources, made possible because of the accumulation of standard, authoritative cataloging information over decades, has become the Library's greatest service to all researchers, extending instant access to its collections worldwide. The development of useful methods of access for large collections and the cooperation with other libraries to make universal coverage possible was the most important service the Library provided to users during the twentieth century. The partnerships developed within the federal government, with private foundations, with private citizen donors, and with other libraries brought together all the important parties to support research resources through continuing contributions to database size and quality.

In addition to providing catalog and bibliographic information electronically, the late twentieth century saw the formation of a National Digital Library, privately funded, to bring the Library's resources, and those of other libraries, to the World Wide Web. Important historical collections, the bulk of them materials from the Library of Congress's collections, are accessible through the Library's Web site. Scholars will not find all the Library's collections available on the Web, since both economics and copyright restrictions make complete coverage impossible. However, researchers can take advantage of Web access to some of the finest specialized materials in the Library's collections. They can also use the Web site to obtain information about the Library itself since the materials range from the daily schedule of open hours to such technical issues as matters of cataloging policy.

American scholars and scholarship depend heavily on the major research libraries, all of them built slowly and painstakingly over centuries of collecting. No library is altogether comprehensive; each depends on others for unique or specialized materials. However, the bibliographic apparatus, also erected slowly and painstakingly first by the Library of Congress and then through cooperation by many institutions, may be, in the early twenty-first century, as close to comprehensive as can be achieved, and it is readily available online. With the addition of electronic capabilities to its traditional services, the Library is able to serve scholars, researchers, and specialists worldwide.

Cole, John Y. "The Library of Congress and American Scholarship, 1865–1939," pp. 45–61 in Phyllis Dain and John Y. Cole, eds., *Libraries and Scholarly Communication in the United States: The Historical Dimension*. New York: Greenwood Press, 1990.

Gabriel, Ralph H. "The Library of Congress and American Scholarship," *ALA Bulletin* 44 (October 1950): 349–351.

THE LIBRARY OF CONGRESS AND AMERICAN LIBRARIANSHIP

by Jane Aikin

When the American Library Association (ALA) was founded in 1876, the Library of Congress was the largest library in the United States. Librarian

Librarian Spofford in his office. The Library rooms in the U.S. Capitol are surrounded by books and copyright deposits. Although made a vice-president of the American Library Association at its founding in 1876, he confined his participation in the new organization to primarily bibliographic projects. His idea of the Library accorded with the model of the great independent European national libraries, and therefore he did not take an active role in the new association.

LC/Prints and Photographs Division. LC-USZ62-44185.

Ainsworth Rand Spofford attended the ALA's organizational meeting, and he served a term as one of the vice presidents. Nevertheless, Spofford confined his profession-related activities mostly to cooperation with bibliographic projects. Since his conception of the role of the Library of Congress accorded with the tradition of independent European national libraries, he never considered taking an active role in the growing library community. Some librarians, notably Melvil Dewey, thought that the Library of Congress—not only as the nation's largest library but also as the official copyright depository—should assist other libraries. Dewey proposed, for example, that catalog records be created at the same time that the Library staff recorded copyright books, so that other libraries could use them for their own cataloging. But neither he nor the ALA was able to persuade Spofford. While the Association did pass resolutions of support for the Librarian's appropriations requests, for most librarians, the Library of Congress was not a source of assistance during the nineteenth century.

In 1896, before the Library moved from the Capitol to the new building, a prominent publisher and ALA member, Richard R. Bowker, proposed to New York Congressman Lemuel Quigg that the pro-

Richard Rogers Bowker about 1890

Because of the Library's imminent move into the new Jefferson Building, publisher R.R. Bowker successfully advocated that librarians be involved in the 1896 congressional hearings about the Library's future. The American Library Association sent six library experts to the hearings. They proposed a new leadership role for the Library among American libraries, along wih a larger staff and expanded national activities.

LC/Prints and Photographs Division. LC-USZ62-59870.

fessional library community be asked for advice on the Library's future administration and functions. As a result, the ALA was invited to send witnesses to the Joint Committee on the Library's hearings on the Library's organization and role. The six librarians informed the congressmen that their Library required much more than a new organizational structure; it should assume a leadership role in the library community. While none criticized Spofford, they spoke of the urgent needs for better administration, a larger staff, and expanded activities. What many librarians wanted was to have the Library of Congress designated as the national library, which would make it possible to broaden its role to include assistance to libraries nationwide. However, the resulting organization plan significantly strengthened the authority of the Librarian by making him responsible for hiring the staff and administering Library operations. It also provided for a departmental organization, but did not include a change in the Library's name or its activities.

President McKinley exercised his prerogative of appointing a new Librarian in 1897, giving the post to his old friend, journalist John Russell Young. While Young was not a librarian, he did select several experienced staff members, and he authorized J.C.M. Hanson and Charles Martel to adopt new cataloging rules that drew on existing practices in the library community. Hanson also established the Library's first card catalog, and the two men began constructing a new classification system. But Young's tenure was short. When he died early in 1899, President McKinley did something that no president had done before: he asked ALA leaders' advice and nominated

When President McKinley came to appoint a new Librarian of Congress in 1899, he took the advice of the ALA and named Herbert Putnam, director of the Boston Public Library, an experienced librarian and expert and innovative manager. Under Putnam, the Library and the ALA began a long partnership. LC/Center for the Book.

Herbert Putnam, director of the Boston Public Library and one of the librarians testifying at the 1896 hearings, to be Librarian of Congress.

With the appointment of Putnam, an experienced library administrator who was well known as an expert manager and innovator, the ALA and the Library of Congress began a long partnership. Putnam thought that a national library should be more than a massive collection of books, and in July 1901 he stated at the ALA convention that the Library should "reach out" to other libraries. While specifying that the Library had as its first duty service to the Congress and the federal government and as its second, assistance to researchers in Washington, D.C., "There should also be possible a service to the country at large: a service to be extended through the libraries which are the local centers of research involving the use of books."

Putnam obtained support for his ideas from President Theodore Roosevelt, telling him that a national library for the United States "should mean in some respects much more than a national library in any other country hitherto meant." Librarians in the United States, he informed the president, were interested in employing uniform methods and promoting efficiencies in their services; and they looked to the Library of Congress for leadership. The Library, consequently, "is now in a position to 'standardize' library methods, to promote cooperation, to aid in the elimination of wasteful duplication [and] to promote the interchange of bibliographic service."

Within three years, Putnam obtained a large increase in the Library's appropriation, revised the organizational structure, instituted an interlibrary loan service, established a Bibliography Division to compile and distribute bibliographies, and organized a card service to disseminate the Library's cataloging. Catalog Division Chief J.C.M. Hanson became chair

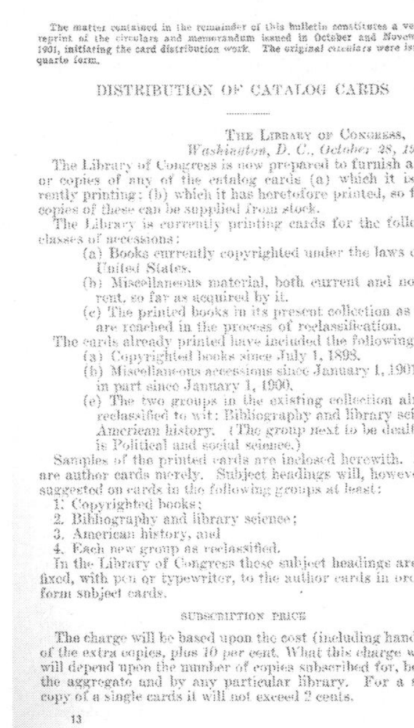

The matter contained in the remainder of this bulletin constitutes a verbatim reprint of the circulars and memorandum issued in October and November of 1901, initiating the card distribution work. The original circulars were issued in quarto form.

DISTRIBUTION OF CATALOG CARDS

THE LIBRARY OF CONGRESS,
Washington, D. C., October 28, 1901.

The Library of Congress is now prepared to furnish a copy or copies of any of the catalog cards (a) which it is currently printing; (b) which it has heretofore printed, so far as copies of these can be supplied from stock.

The Library is currently printing cards for the following classes of accessions:

(a) Books currently copyrighted under the laws of the United States.
(b) Miscellaneous material, both current and noncurrent, so far as acquired by it.
(c) The printed books in its present collection as these are reached in the process of reclassification.

The cards already printed have included the following:

(a) Copyrighted books since July 1, 1898.
(b) Miscellaneous accessions since January 1, 1901, and in part since January 1, 1900.
(c) The two groups in the existing collection already reclassified to wit: Bibliography and library science; American history. (The group next to be dealt with is Political and social science.)

Samples of the printed cards are inclosed herewith. They are author cards merely. Subject headings will, however, be suggested on cards in the following groups at least:

1. Copyrighted books;
2. Bibliography and library science;
3. American history, and
4. Each new group as reclassified.

In the Library of Congress these subject headings are prefixed, with pen or typewriter, to the author cards in order to form subject cards.

SUBSCRIPTION PRICE

The charge will be based upon the cost (including handling) of the extra copies, plus 10 per cent. What this charge will be will depend upon the number of copies subscribed for, both in the aggregate and by any particular library. For a single copy of a single cards it will not exceed 2 cents.

13

In a 1901 bulletin, Distribution of Catalog Cards, *Librarian Putnam announces the sale and distribution of the Library's printed catalog cards. Finding that the Library of Congress could no longer ignore "the opportunity and appeal" of the idea of centralized cataloging, in the announcement he explained: "American instinct and habit revolt against multiplication of brain effort and outlay where a multiplication of results can be achieved by machinery. This appears to be a case where it may."* LC Archives, Library of Congress Card Section Bulletin, No. 7, June 15, 1904.

of the ALA's Catalog Rules Committee in 1901, and the rules eventually adopted by that committee accorded with those of the Library of Congress. Henceforth the Library would not only make its cataloging available; for at least four decades it was the main professional authority on how cataloging should be performed.

Although he frequently had to remind librarians that the Library's first duty was to Congress, Putnam approved many mutually beneficial projects. He proposed cooperation with state libraries to obtain local documents and in 1910 began publishing the *Monthly Checklist of State Publications* as a comprehensive record of state and municipal publications. By having the card service provide free depository cards to selected libraries, he disseminated knowledge of Library of Congress holdings, and he also had the service begin collecting printed cards from other libraries to form a Union Catalog of library holdings nationwide. For the ALA, the Librarian had the *A.L.A. Catalog* (1904)—a standard list of books recommended for library collections—printed by the Government Printing Office. The *Catalog* included Library of Congress catalog card numbers to facilitate card orders, and Putnam also had the *A.L.A. Portrait Index* (1906) printed at federal expense. At the St. Louis Exposition in 1904 the ALA, at Putnam's invitation, shared the Library's exhibit space.

Putnam largely achieved his ambition of turning the Library of Congress into a model institution that other libraries would emulate during his first few years as Librarian, and he described its new organization, methods, and services at length in his 1901 *Annual Report*. His office became an important source of information and advice about library operations in general, responding to requests from librarians, library trustees, local officials, and the general public. Putnam hired only professional librarians for the most technical work, and he encouraged them to "reach out" by being active in the profession. By 1903, for example, 47 Library of Congress staff members were ALA members, and 26 of them attended the ALA's annual conference; the Library staff also accounted for nearly half the members of the District of Columbia Library Association. Putnam himself served as president of the ALA in 1903–1904; he was constantly a member of its Executive Board or its Council, and he chaired the Association's International Relations Committee for many years.

The tradition that the Library's staff attends ALA and other library association conferences has endured; they have been constantly present as speakers, as resources, and as representatives of the Library to the profession. For more than 50 years the Library has had its own booth in the ALA exhibits area at the midwinter and summer conferences. And when the Association holds conventions in Washington, D.C., the Library staff mounts a full schedule of tours and demonstrations for visiting librarians. Library staff members also have been active in more specialized organizations; for example, the Special Libraries Association, the Music Library Association, and the American Association of Law Libraries. And while the Library of Congress's influence on the broad library community has been exercised most through its cataloging and classification products and services, its special format divisions (maps, prints and photographs, music, manuscripts, microforms, motion pictures, rare books), the National Library for the Blind and Physically Handicapped, the Law Library, the Copyright Office, and the African and Middle Eastern, Hispanic, European, and Asian divisions and their specialized staffs have been continually interested in a broad array of professional endeavors.

Most librarians in public, college, and university libraries have accepted and used Library of Congress cataloging and cards since early in the twentieth century. Many also adopted the Library of Congress classification, although the peak years for reclassification did not occur until the 1960s. And most librarians have also used the *List of Subject Headings* that Hanson began to publish in 1909. Under Charles Hastings's leadership, the card service began cooperating with publishers to provide card numbers for each entry in publications such as the *Cumulative Book Index*, *Book Review Digest*, the *United States Catalog*, and the *Catalogue of United States Public Documents*—all standard ordering sources for librarians. As the card service steadily issued catalog cards for most of the output of American publishers, the Library became an authoritative source of bibliographic information.

The Library did not assume leadership in some areas. For example, Putnam did not develop a national legislative reference service until 1914, long after such services appeared in state capitals. Similarly, the Library of Congress deferred to the Surgeon General's Library and the Department of Agriculture Library in the fields of medicine and agriculture; as the National Library of Medicine and the National Agricultural Library, those libraries became the national leaders in their respective fields. But nevertheless, the Library of Congress's leadership among public and academic libraries, in particular, was well-established to the extent that criticism from Putnam or his staff could block unwanted initiatives. And while there was always dissent, especially where the Library's practices did not fit librarians' special needs, criticisms during Putnam's tenure were generally muted.

The Library of Congress's services to other libraries were quickly and relatively easily established, but they were not readily expanded. After the first years of the twentieth century, the Library's budget increased very little until well into the 1920s. Yet librarians in research libraries wanted more and faster cataloging of foreign books, while public librarians asked for simpler cataloging and cards that included Dewey Decimal numbers. All wanted cards for articles in periodicals and cataloging for scholarly society publications. But Putnam refused the ALA's request that the Library undertake a project to compile a union catalog of periodicals, and he also rejected the National Association of State Libraries' request for a catalog of state laws.

When the United States entered World War I, however, Putnam strongly supported the library community. He interceded with federal authorities to allow continuing importation of library materials, and he convinced them to designate the ALA to provide library services to American troops. Housed at the

After the United States entered World War I, Herbert Putnam interceded with federal authorities to designate the ALA to provide library services to the troops through the Library War Program. It was headquartered in the Jefferson Building. Here Librarian Putnam is seen standing in front of a card catalog surrounded by ALA volunteers.

LC/Prints and Photographs Division. LC-USZ62-90451.

Library of Congress and headed by Putnam the ALA's War Service drew on volunteers from the library community, but it also relied heavily on the Library's resources, including significant volunteer time from the staff. Within a few months, the War Service staff collected books and periodicals and established a privately funded system of libraries for soldiers in training camps, on overseas transports and, eventually, in Europe. The War Service was aptly termed "an organizational triumph," and it accrued the library community both national gratitude and prestige.

Cooperative Services for Librarians

The post-war period provided new opportunities to expand the role of the Library of Congress. Its potential as an exhibition center and as a symbol of American democracy emerged when in 1921 the Declaration of Independence and the Constitution were transferred from the State Department. Three years later, in connection with a gift to the Music Division, Putnam agreed to sponsor three privately funded chamber music concerts, which led to another gift for the construction of the Coolidge Auditorium, a permanent concert series, and an endowment for the Music Division. Private funding would enable the Library to collect comprehensively, to improve services, to enhance its role as a cultural center, and to support other activities that appropriations could not cover; and Putnam actively sought additional endowments. But he also promised to continue "in whatever ways might be practicable, to render at least the by-products of our operations serviceable to other libraries [of whatever type] in effecting economies in their own administration."

This description of library-related services as "by-products" and named last in a list of the Library's interests might have been discouraging had there not also been important advances. In 1927, John D. Rockefeller provided $250,000 for improving the Union Catalog and other bibliographical tools important to the profession. When Rockefeller funding ceased, Putnam requested and obtained an appropriation to continue to build the Catalog. And this passage of events recurred in the 1930s: with gifts that provided project funding, the Library staff began new services benefiting libraries, which Congress later sustained with appropriated funds.

The war years and the early 1920s had not been encouraging for librarians who depended on Library of Congress cataloging, since the Library's appropriation was insufficient to sustain a high level of production. At the ALA's 50th anniversary conference in 1926, the Association honored the 25th anniversary of the card service. "No event in American library history, no work done by American librarians, has more significance than the beginning and continuing progress of this unique plan of cooperation in the most laborious and exacting part of the internal work of our libraries," the citation read. Even as they commended the Card Division, however, ALA members were seeking to remedy the budget reductions and staff losses that resulted in cataloging and card printing arrears.

Two initiatives developed from the ALA's discussions. First, the Catalog Section sought to achieve a long-standing goal by proposing to Putnam that the ALA pay catalogers to supply Dewey Decimal numbers for Library of Congress cards. Putnam agreed, and several years later he obtained an appropriation to continue the Dewey work. The second initiative aimed at the production of more cards representing foreign titles, out-of-print books, specialized materials, and series. Rising cataloging costs were causing concern in libraries nationwide, and librarians were eager to cooperate to solve the problems, but they wanted the product to be Library of Congress catalog cards. The ALA therefore proposed an office at the Library to solicit catalog information produced by other libraries. When the General Education Board granted the Association $45,000 for a three-year experiment, 32 libraries joined the effort. The establishment of the Cooperative Cataloging and Classification Service as part of the Library on July 1, 1935, ensured continuation of both the Dewey work and cooperative cataloging.

Cooperative cataloging, however, was handicapped from the outset because the cataloging rules had not been revised since 1907, because contributed entries in foreign languages raised difficult cataloging problems, and because the Card Division experienced serious printing delays during the 1930s. Rule revision had begun in 1931, but progressed slowly. Lacking updated rules, the contributing libraries sent cataloging that disagreed with current Library of Congress practice, and the catalogers insisted on revising it. A period of mutual exasperation resulted, and by 1937, with as much as 39 percent of card orders delayed because cards were out of stock or the books were not cataloged, the ALA Catalog Section appointed a committee to investigate. Their efforts captured Putnam's attention, and the printing situation slowly improved with the assistance of deficit appropriations.

Another initiative came from the Association of Research Libraries (ARL), which proposed that the Union Catalog staff circulate titles of requested books that were not in the Catalog. The resulting *Weekly List of Unlocated Research Books* eventually found 65 percent of all titles requested and those not located went on the *Select List of Unlocated Research Books*, which research libraries used as an acquisitions tool. But when the ARL requested improvements in the bibliography of doctoral dissertations that the Library had published since 1912, Putnam declined. And when the ARL leaders asked the Librarian to cooperate in the publication of a printed book catalog of Library of Congress holdings, he again refused.

During the late 1930s, ALA Executive Secretary Carl Milam tried to persuade the Librarian to take an interest in the proposal that a federal library bureau become part of the Library's operations, but Putnam would not consider the idea. Milam, however, also took an interest in Putnam's recurring differences with Congress and the Roosevelt administration. Under strong pressure to retire, Putnam discussed the situation with the ALA leader but never requested formal Association support. Ultimately, in 1938 he asked President Franklin D. Roosevelt to select a new librarian, and Roosevelt named Archibald MacLeish.

World War II, Post-war Planning, and Interdependence

The nomination disappointed many ALA members, especially those who hoped that Milam would be named Librarian. Roosevelt had ignored the library community in his search, and after having all offers of advice spurned, the Association reacted strongly. Accustomed to having a librarian in the post, the ALA leaders protested that MacLeish could neither understand technical matters nor successfully administer a large organization. While others both inside and outside the profession thought that MacLeish would make an excellent Librarian, the Association testified against the appointment during Senate hearings. Nevertheless, the nomination was confirmed.

It soon became clear that MacLeish's opponents had greatly underestimated him. The new Librarian signaled respect for the library profession by obtaining support from the Carnegie Corporation to appoint a Librarian's Committee of senior librarians to analyze Library of Congress operations and recommend changes, and he took the Committee's advice in reorganizing the Library. In his 1940 *Annual Report*, the most important since Herbert Putnam described his organization in 1901, MacLeish addressed the reorganization and also the issue of making Library of Congress resources available to other libraries, writing that "The reference staff and facilities of the Library of Congress are available to members of the public, universities, learned societies and other libraries requiring services which the Library staff is equipped to give and which can be given without interference to services to the Congress and other agencies of the Federal Government." The new Librarian also invited several senior members of the profession to join scholars and collectors on his Librarian's Council, formed to provide advice on the Library's future directions. As the United States entered World War II, MacLeish also became a leading advocate for the war effort and for the spread of democracy. The ALA greeted his appearance at the 1942 convention with a thunderous ovation.

The Librarian enlisted L. Quincy Mumford of the New York Public Library to restructure the Library's processing operations, because the Librarian's Committee had criticized cataloging methods. The long-awaited revision of the catalog rules finally appeared in 1941, but it drew severe criticism:

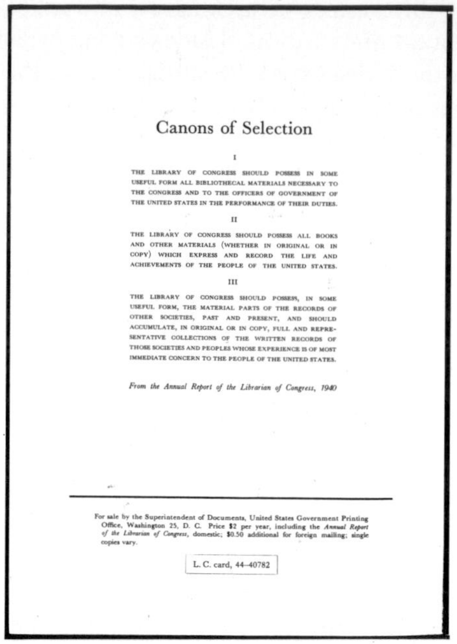

Canons of Selection

I

THE LIBRARY OF CONGRESS SHOULD POSSESS IN SOME USEFUL FORM ALL BIBLIOTHECAL MATERIALS NECESSARY TO THE CONGRESS AND TO THE OFFICERS OF GOVERNMENT OF THE UNITED STATES IN THE PERFORMANCE OF THEIR DUTIES.

II

THE LIBRARY OF CONGRESS SHOULD POSSESS ALL BOOKS AND OTHER MATERIALS (WHETHER IN ORIGINAL OR IN COPY) WHICH EXPRESS AND RECORD THE LIFE AND ACHIEVEMENTS OF THE PEOPLE OF THE UNITED STATES.

III

THE LIBRARY OF CONGRESS SHOULD POSSESS, IN SOME USEFUL FORM, THE MATERIAL PARTS OF THE RECORDS OF OTHER SOCIETIES, PAST AND PRESENT, AND SHOULD ACCUMULATE, IN ORIGINAL OR IN COPY, FULL AND REPRESENTATIVE COLLECTIONS OF THE WRITTEN RECORDS OF THOSE SOCIETIES AND PEOPLES WHOSE EXPERIENCE IS OF MOST IMMEDIATE CONCERN TO THE PEOPLE OF THE UNITED STATES.

From the Annual Report of the Librarian of Congress, 1940

For sale by the Superintendent of Documents, United States Government Printing Office, Washington 25, D. C. Price $2 per year, including the *Annual Report of the Librarian of Congress*, domestic; $0.50 additional for foreign mailing; single copies vary.

L. C. card, 44–40782

Although opposed by the ALA at his Senate hearings, Archibald MacLeish became Librarian in 1939. MacLeish set up a Librarian's Committee of senior librarians to analyze the Library's operations and suggest changes and took their advice in restructuring the Library's administration. In his Canons of Selection of 1940, MacLeish enumerated his collections philosophy for the Library: ...all bibliographical materials necessary to the Congress and to the officers of Government...all books and... materials...which express and record the life and achievement of the people of the United States... and possess in some useful form, the material parts of the records of other societies, past and present...full and representative collections of the...records of those ...peoples whose experience is of most immediate concern to the people of the United States. LC Archives.

librarians complained that the Library of Congress perpetuated detail-oriented, over-elaborate cataloging that most libraries could not afford. Therefore the Processing Department addressed revising the rules for descriptive cataloging and began a new publication, *Cataloging Service Bulletin*, in the mid-1940s to report new Library practices quickly so that other librarians could consider adopting them.

The long cataloging controversy significantly influenced the relationship between the Library and the ALA. Late in the 1940s, after the Association accepted the revised rules, the Library of Congress agreed that in future changes would not be made without consulting the profession. Since that time, rule-making has been a cooperative venture requiring extensive consultation, and every new edition or extension of cataloging rules has been the product of lengthy discussions among all interested parties.

During MacLeish's tenure, the Library also began to cooperate more closely with other research libraries and with the ARL. In 1942, the Library, the ARL, and Edwards Brothers of Ann Arbor, Michigan agreed to publish *A Catalog of Books represented by Library of Congress Printed Cards, 1898–1942*, the project that Putnam had vetoed. The Library also joined with other research libraries to develop the Farmington Plan, a cooperative acquisitions program intended to ensure broad coverage of European materials for American libraries. But the Plan could not begin operations until the war ended, and MacLeish therefore used his considerable influence with the Roosevelt administration to encourage the establishment of an Interdepartmental Committee on the Acquisition of Foreign Publications to obtain as many wartime publications as possible. At the war's end this effort was converted into the Cooperative Acquisitions Project for European Wartime Publications (1945–1948), in which the Library acquired publications of the war years for American research libraries. The Library also housed a Documents Expediting Project, established in 1946 and developed by library leaders and others to acquire certain normally unavailable federal publications and distribute them to libraries that paid a subscription fee. At the same time, the Library's Photoduplication Service began microfilming large collections of research material, such as domestic and foreign newspapers, official gazettes, archival material, manuscripts, and unique collections. Librarians could purchase their own positive copies of these films, which assisted specialized collection building. And book catalogs of Library of Congress holdings began to appear during the late 1940s, providing subscribers with facsimiles of the new cataloging records the Library created.

MacLeish's successor, Luther Evans, a political scientist who acquired Library of Congress experience before he became Librarian, also enjoyed good relations with the library profession. Evans viewed the American library system as "an integrated national resource," and he thought that Library of Congress acquisitions efforts should be "directed toward enriching the total national holdings." The Librarian aggressively sought additional appropriations to build the Library's collections and services, emphasizing its national role in the post-war world. But Congress refused to provide the increased funding, citing the need to determine "what the policy of the Library of Congress is going to be in the way of expansion and service to the public and to the Congress."

In the wake of the congressional rebuff, Evans formed a Planning Committee chaired by Keyes D. Metcalf of the Harvard University Library. The

Librarian Luther H. Evans in the Library's Great Hall examining the front page of an engrossed and signed Constitution of the United States with Librarian Emeritus Putnam (left), Chief Justice Fred Vinson, Library Committee Chairman Senator Theodore F. Green, and President Harry S Truman. The occasion was Constitution Day, 1951. Named Librarian of Congress by President Truman in 1945, Evans served until 1953. He promoted the Library of Congress as a leader and partner among the nation's libraries, but was not able to obtain sufficient funds from Congress to expand the Library's national role.
LC/Prints and Photographs Division. LC-USZ62-314464.

Committee reported that the Library's resources were inadequate to carry out its responsibilities as the national library and recommended that its national status be officially recognized. The group also recommended organizing a Federal Library Council to promote cooperation among federal libraries and a National Advisory Council to aid the Librarian in addressing research library problems. Congress never officially recognized the Planning Committee's report, but other advisors in succeeding years repeated its recommendations.

The Association of Research Libraries established a Committee on National Needs in 1950, which discussed with the Library's senior staff the inadequacies of the collections and services of American research libraries in the light of post-war demands and began to develop plans to remedy the deficiencies. They addressed a variety of issues: obtaining acquisitions from remote and war-torn areas; stimulating the production of catalogs and bibliographies for Asian and Middle Eastern materials; improving the representation of current foreign newspapers in American collections; developing accessions lists for Asia, Africa, the Middle East, and Eastern Europe; improving guides for area studies; cataloging arrearages of foreign publications, developing special area union catalogs, standardizing subject headings, developing a union list of current scientific serials; investigating the possibility of federal subsidy for research libraries, acquiring rare Chinese and Malayan publications through cooperative microfilming projects, and surveying libraries' holdings of and services for Asian and Middle Eastern publications. The establishment of this group and its close relationship with the Library, Evans observed, indicated that the research library community had decided to undertake an ongoing role in determining national information requirements and to organize cooperative activities to meet those needs. Other library groups shared this resolve as well; for example, the Council of National Library Associations (CNLA) began formulating a national plan for acquiring important domestic and foreign research materials on microfilm, and Library representatives on the ALA's Board on Resources of American Libraries' Subcommittee on Cooperative Microfilm Projects, took part in a project to gather information on deteriorating files of American newspapers that needed to be filmed. And at the request of the Association of College and Research Libraries, the CNLA established a Joint Committee on the Safeguarding of Library Materials, which included representatives from a number of national associations of librarians and scholars and met at the Library of Congress.

Much of the support that the Library continued to provide to other libraries during the 1950s and early 1960s was little noticed. Catalogers mounted long-term projects in cooperation with colleagues outside the library and with the major professional and scholarly associations to create romanization schemes so that books in nonroman languages could be represented by printed cards and to develop cataloging rules for nonbook formats—maps, music, manuscripts, prints and photographs—so that these too might be represented in catalogs. In cooperation with law librarians, classifiers worked to complete the final segment of the Library of Congress Classification: Class K: Law. The Library also took over the editing of the Dewey Decimal Classification, thus greatly expanding its Dewey activities.

Two publications, *New Serial Titles* (NST) and the *National Union Catalog* (NUC), represented new cooperative efforts. While the Library had previously collected information on other libraries' holdings in the Union Catalog, it had not published that information. Urged by the ALA and the library community, the Library expanded its own printed book catalogs and serials list by 1956 to enable librarians everywhere to consult bibliographic tools that included the holdings of every contributing library. These tools made it possible for librarians and researchers nationwide to locate the nearest copy of a needed book or journal and to make acquisitions decisions with neighboring libraries' holdings in mind. Librarians used these tools in printed format until online catalogs matured, but only new catalog records were included until the ALA sponsored a pilot retrospective NUC for the years 1952–1955. The Library began editorial work in 1967, with the assistance of the ALA's Subcommittee on the National Union Catalog and Mansell Publishing, Ltd, on the complete National Union Catalog in book format, completed in 1981 and including all pre-1956 imprints.

By the mid-twentieth century, the Library of Congress's collections, services, and participation in cooperative projects increasingly affected the operations of other libraries while librarians nationwide also contributed to its work. Libraries large and small depended on its cards, book catalogs, classification schedules and subject headings for their own cataloging operations. Scholars, institutions, professional organizations, government agencies and other libraries helped, through their requests for assistance and sometimes their financial support, to determine the Library's agenda for producing information through bibliographic and other publications. Librarians strengthened national library services by submitting catalog copy for cards, by assuming collecting responsibilities in assigned fields through the Farmington Plan and other cooperative acquisitions programs, and by providing advice on Library initiatives. In the postwar years, the emphasis was distinctly on furthering the library community's interdependence, although many still considered the Library of Congress the primary source of support.

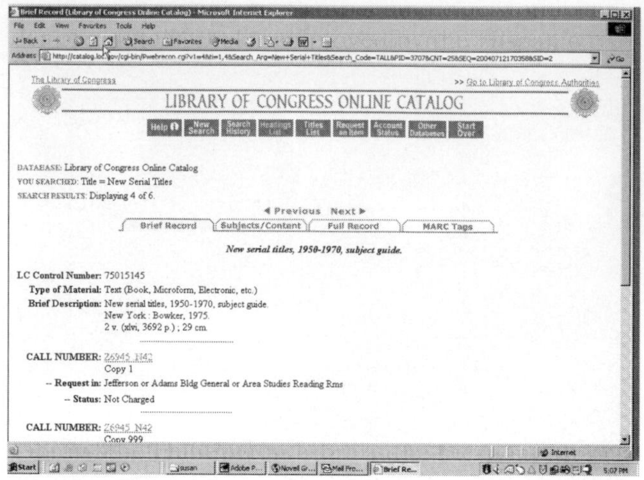

In 1954, President Dwight D. Eisenhower nominated L. Quincy Mumford, the director of the Cleveland Public Library and the president of the American Library Association, to be the 11th Librarian of Congress. Between 1954 and his retirement in 1974, Mumford expanded the Library's technical processing, acquisitions, and cataloging services for other libraries. Romanization schemes were developed so that books in non-roman language could be represented by printed cards, and cataloging rules were created for non-book formats such as maps, manuscripts, music, and prints and photographs. Under Mumford's leadership, in the mid-1960s automation was successfully introduced into the Library's cataloging procedures. The Library's publication New Serials Titles, *greatly expanded in the 1950s, is depicted above as an entry in the Library's online catalog. Librarian Mumford also began planning for the Library's third major building, expanded the overseas acquisitions and cataloging programs, and initiated the publication of the Library's pre-1956 National Union Catalog, "the largest single bibliographical undertaking in the Library's 167-year history."*

New Federal Programs and the Library's National Role

When Librarian Evans resigned to become Director General of UNESCO in 1953, President Eisenhower nominated L. Quincy Mumford, director of the Cleveland Public Library and the current president of the ALA. The library community applauded Mumford's appointment, and the ALA gave the nomination full support. As the new Librarian worked to obtain more support for the Library in Congress, he formed an in-house Committee on the Control and Organization of the Collections (1958) to examine current operations and consider alternatives. While recognizing the interdependence of libraries and the need for cooperative projects, it was clear to Mumford that external demands for Library resources and services would probably always exceed the ability to fulfill those demands. The Librarian also recognized that the crowded condition of the Library's two buildings would limit new activities. "Sheer lack of physical space, not lack of concern for solving technical library problems, has forced the Library of Congress to seem unresponsive to suggestions for a number of cooperative or experimental projects of interest to the library world," he commented, adding that Congress had addressed the Library's needs, including providing services to other libraries—since 1954 increased appropriations had helped to strengthen Library programs. Nevertheless, space continually had to be converted from public use to book storage or staff work areas, and the new building Congress had authorized was only in the planning stages.

The library community, however, found ways of obtaining Library of Congress support. In 1956, Verner W. Clapp, a senior Library staff member, had become president of a new funding agency sponsored by the Ford Foundation to address library problems: the Council on Library Resources, Inc. (CLR). Under his leadership, the Council provided funding for a number of activities that would benefit librarians but appropriated funds could not support; for example, compilation of the *National Union Catalog of Manuscript Collections*, beginning in 1958. The

Council also supported an experiment in which Library staff cataloged books before publication (1959) so that catalog information could be printed in newly published books. Librarians were quite disappointed when Mumford declared the experiment unsuccessful, and a service that had seemed to many to hold great promise had to wait another 15 years before its development as Cataloging in Publication (1974). CLR funds also assisted the Library by financing a study of stack use and a survey on the feasibility of automation.

Professionals in research libraries, in particular, deplored Librarian Mumford's instinct to keep the Library in the background; and they began to advocate library needs on Capitol Hill. Eventually Douglas Bryant of Harvard was asked in 1962 by Senator Claiborne Pell, a member of the Joint Committee on the Library, to provide a statement on the current and potential future role of the Library of Congress and in general on the role of the federal government in research library activities. Bryant proposed that the Library of Congress become the national library and expand its activities commensurately, but he suggested moving it into the executive branch and establishing an advisory board. He also advocated federal aid for a variety of research library needs and activities, among them, acquiring, cataloging, and preserving material; and the adaptation of modern technology for library purposes.

Almost simultaneously, the federal library establishment was the subject of a survey undertaken by former Librarian Luther Evans for the Brookings Institution. After considering the Library of Congress's potential leadership role among federal libraries, Evans too recommended removing the Library (excluding the Legislative Reference Service) to the executive branch. His purpose was to bring the Library administratively nearer other federal libraries and to allow it to better address their problems.

In response to the Bryant Memorandum, Mumford sent a rejoinder to Congress. Asserting that the Library of Congress was the *de facto* national library and that its role as such was amply recognized and supported, he contended that neither "history, logic or expediency" dictated a transfer to the executive branch. He also observed, however, that Bryant's memorandum was useful in calling attention to the problems of research libraries, and he proposed that a national commission be appointed to address library problems in general. To improve the Library's communications with the library community and the scholarly world, Mumford established three new advisory committees, one of which consisted of representatives from the ALA, the Special Libraries Association, the ARL and the CLR. He addressed Evans's recommendations by cooperating with the Bureau of the Budget in 1965 to establish a Federal Library Committee, housed at the Library of Congress.

Writing in the *ALA Bulletin* in 1963, Frederick H. Wagman, president-elect of the ALA and a former Library of Congress staff member, tried to put the Library's role into perspective. To increase its already large contributions to American libraries, he wrote, the Library needed support: "Most of us take the Library of Congress for granted. We rarely reflect on the extent of its service to us or on how a great many of our libraries would have to operate if LC did not give us the service it does. We often think how helpful it would be if LC could do more, but we rarely try to help it do more." Reminding readers that as part of the legislative branch the Library could not marshal its own support, Wagman asked his colleagues to inform their congressmen of the importance of the Library's services, and he noted that more was needed than support for the card service; increases in book funds and staff were crucial to allow the Library to handle the additional acquisitions and cataloging that helped other libraries save money.

Probably the most intractable problems research librarians faced in the early 1960s were still foreign acquisitions and timely cataloging. The Cold War, the Korean War, and the first earth satellite, the USSR's Sputnik, brought new demands, not only from Congress and federal agencies, but also from scholars and researchers nationwide for the most recent and authoritative information on little-known places. Congress addressed these needs through two programs: Public Law 480 (passed in 1958 but not implemented until the early 1960s) and the National Program for Acquisitions and Cataloging (NPAC; 1965), the latter a program suggested by the ALA and the ARL and supported by the Library. Under these programs, Congress charged the Library with obtaining foreign publications required for research nationwide and providing cataloging information for them. While the programs depended on annual appropriations and on the supply of foreign currency available for materials from PL-480 countries, funding was sufficient to permit the Library to mount its own acquisitions operations abroad. Increased appropriations also allowed the Library to increase cataloging production by 103 percent between 1965 and 1970, fulfilling an unprecedented 70 percent of the cataloging needs of U.S. research libraries. While later appropriations did not suffice to maintain the programs as originally envisioned, acquisitions for many areas have been continued on a subscription basis so that participating libraries could continue to add to their collections.

With a grant of $100,000 from the Council on Library Resources, a study of automation for research libraries and specifically the Library of Congress was conducted between 1961 and 1963. The survey team's report, *Automation and the Library of Congress* (1964), concluded that automation was technologically feasible, that it would augment and accelerate library services and that it would help libraries adapt to changes in research and facilitate the development of a national system of research libraries. It would be possible, the investigators concluded, to create this national system by tying individual libraries into a central computer through standard communication lines. "Such a system," the Librarian's annual report for 1963 noted, "could bring growing collections in research libraries under more effective bibliographical control, save time and space in the use and maintenance of now-unwieldy catalogs in card form, and relieve arrearages in cataloging and processing that result from the ever-increasing volume of publication, particularly in the field of serial publication." The Library would develop automated solutions to library problems in part as a means of addressing the common needs of large research libraries.

By 1966, librarians and computer experts at the Library had developed the MAchine-Readable Cataloging Format (MARC) that during the 1970s was adopted as the national (and later international) standard for exchanging bibliographic records among computer systems. MARC-formatted electronic catalog records were not the first computer bibliographic operation in libraries—the National Library of Medicine had begun developing its MEDLARS network in 1961. However, the advent of MARC as a general-purpose cataloging system quickly became the most important innovation for libraries generally. During the following decades, the development of MARC formats for all forms of material and for all languages occupied a significant number of the Library's systems, cataloging, and serials staff.

With MARC well under way, Librarian Mumford announced at a meeting of the newly established National Advisory Commission on Libraries (May 22, 1967) the intention of the Library of Congress to play a major role in the planning and operation of the emerging national library and information network. Invited to provide a statement of "the Library's view of itself as the National Library," Mumford commented that to achieve his objectives there would have to be support for a national service; formal legislative recognition of the Library of Congress as the national library; and adequate appropriations. But he assured the Commission of the Library's commitment to a central role in the development of a national library and information network.

Other participants, however, noted that the Library had not vigorously sought appropriations for national library functions, even though Mumford had accepted responsibility for a national preservation program. One participant declared that the Library "responds rather than initiates," that it remained isolated from other libraries and "an empire unto itself." Others voiced doubts that the Library could exert national leadership, given its own administrative needs.

The Commission's report, submitted to President Lyndon B. Johnson on October 3, 1968, contained only two recommendations relating to the Library of Congress: that it be designated as the national library and that a board of advisors be established. President Richard M. Nixon did not act on either recommendation, but he did create a permanent National Commission on Libraries and Information Science (NCLIS) in 1970. An NCLIS report issued in July 1975 declared that the Library of Congress should be designated as the national library and its national responsibilities recognized.

Late Twentieth-Century Initiatives: Preservation, Networking, and Digitization

Taken together, the Library's achievements during the post-war period had been of considerable assistance to the library community, and librarians acknowledged the importance of its contributions—publishing union catalogs, developing MARC, organizing and administering the PL-480 and NPAC programs, and completing a number of research projects related to library technical processes. A bevy of ALA awards from the early to mid-1970s went to individual Library of Congress administrators for their conduct of these and other activities which had, one citation declared, "immediate and wide-ranging impact" for other libraries. No doubt the complaints from librarians, particularly those of the 1960s from the research library community, had had an effect, but the community had also supported the Library's initiatives, and while continually urging quicker action, found the results beneficial. Another strong advocate of further Library of Congress involvement with other libraries was the Council on Library Resources, whose President, Verner Clapp, had detailed knowledge of the Library's complicated administrative structure and its staff and of the difficulties it encountered in mounting projects that librarians wanted and needed. The later years of the century would feature new initiatives in networking library bibliographic processes, a shift of some library activities from local computer systems and bibliographic utilities to national interconnectivity and the Internet, and interest in an old but increasingly pressing problem: preservation.

Librarians had long been concerned about the deteriorating condition of items printed on wood pulp paper and the proper measures to take when library materials suffered damage due to natural and man-made disasters. By the mid-1960s, the ARL and others in the profession were calling for a national program of preservation at a major research library; namely, the Library of Congress. Librarian Mumford created a Preservation Office in the Library in 1967 and acknowledged a national responsibility to disseminate information about techniques, methods and developments in restoration and preservation. Staff lectures, workshops, advisory services, and presentations, together with the publication of pamphlets on preservation problems helped to fulfill this responsibility. By 1970, Mumford had also established a Preservation Research Laboratory to assess the problems of deacidifying brittle books, restoring records on nitrate film, and salvaging materials damaged during floods, fires, and other disasters.

The ALA became briefly involved in a controversy involving the Library in 1971, when a Library staff member complained of job discrimination. The ALA Council passed a resolution authorizing an inquiry into the Library's practices. However, when Mumford reported the matter to Congress, the Joint Committee on the Library refused to allow him to appear before the ALA inquiry team, stating that the Association was "infringing on and usurping the oversight responsibilities of Congress." By launching an Affirmative Action Plan, establishing a Human Relations Council and developing a training, appraisal, and promotion program, Mumford made progress that satisfied the ALA. Meanwhile, the Library staff members who had complaints turned to the courts for assistance.

When Mumford retired on December 31, 1974, President Gerald Ford selected historian and author Daniel Boorstin as Librarian of Congress. The ALA formally opposed the nomination, largely for the same reasons it had opposed MacLeish in 1939. But with a strong bipartisan coalition of congressmen approving Boorstin, ALA opposition again had no effect.

Boorstin established an internal Task Force on Goals, Organization, and Planning to review the Library's organization and activities. Private funding supported eight advisory groups representing the Library's constituencies; among them, librarians. The Task Force recommended establishing a Board of Advisors for the Library and an office to coordinate the services of the Library to other libraries. Neither was approved, although the Task Force's insistence that the Library must "become a more *useful* part of the national life" seemed to echo the criticisms made at the National Advisory Commission meeting nearly nine years earlier. Boorstin characterized the reorganization as designed to address the Library's statutory missions, but his statement was couched in more active terms than Mumford had employed: "To support the nation's libraries and help them, for example, secure bibliographic control over the world's publishing."

The Task Force report also reflected the growing recognition by the library community that "there is no hope for one institution to go the whole way alone" in establishing a national bibliographic system. Some libraries obtained MARC records by subscribing to the Library's tape service and mounting the tapes on their own institutions' computer systems. But increasingly institutions joined one of the so-called "bibliographic utilities" that subscribed to the tapes for member libraries— the Ohio College Library Center (OCLC), the Washington Library Network (WLN) or the Research Libraries Group's

New technologies proliferated during the tenure of Librarian of Congress Daniel J. Boorstin (1975–1987). By the early 1980s, selected libraries were authorized to enter records online. The Library of Congress adopted the Cooperative Database Building System to expand its MARC database rapidly, and for the same reason, used the Research Libraries Information Network's Chinese-Japanese-Korean terminals to input vernacular bibliographic records in the RLIN database. Here, members of the Library's Executive Session observe a demonstration in the Shared Cataloging Division of the new CJK (Chinese-Japanese-Korean) terminals, which were to be used to create machine-readable records for the minigraphic holdings in those languages. LC Archives.

Research Libraries Information Network (RLIN). Through cathode ray tube terminals, local library staff members could gain access to utility records, match the records to the books they wanted to catalog, and order their catalog cards from the utility. When a library recorded acquisition of a book in the utility's database, the catalog record included a symbol for that library, creating a union catalog that librarians and users could search at terminals installed in library reading rooms.

In partnership with the National Library of Medicine and the National Agricultural Library, the Library of Congress in the early 1970s was engaged in a National Serials Pilot Project, intending to convert the three libraries' serial holdings to machine readable format in conformity with national and international standards to provide a file of cataloging data that other libraries could eventually use. Supported by the National Science Foundation and the National Endowment for the Humanities, the pilot program was an important development, but progress was too slow for librarians who were already cataloging by computer and ready to convert all their serial records to electronic format. Since all wanted standardized cataloging, they asked whether the Library might join a comprehensive database building effort, combining records from several different sources. The Council on Library Resources provided funding and technical support, and the Ohio College Library Center agreed to mount a large database, to be assembled via tape loads from member libraries. Named CONSER (Conversion of Serials; later called the Cooperative Online Serials Program), the project began with the Library of Congress, National Agricultural Library, National Library of Medicine, National Library of Canada, and other libraries as members. Data input began in 1976, and funding agencies provided assistance for several projects that added large numbers of records from specialized fields. Member libraries were responsible for contributing their cataloging, but each catalog record received quality review by Library staff or other CONSER participants. Financial restrictions kept the Library from eventually assuming management of CONSER as first planned, but it retained an important role in CONSER activities.

The Library established an Office of Network Development in 1978 and formed a Network Advisory Committee and Bibliographic Advisory Committee to provide advice on its evolving role in the national library and information network. NCLIS had funded a study to assist the Library in this area as well, and the final report of the consultants noted continued support from the library community for a strong leadership role by the Library of Congress. Otherwise, many feared that the library community might adopt their own programs "from which shifts to better, more comprehensive services may take years." The Council on Library Resources, also aware of the potential for duplication of effort, used funding from the NEH and private foundations to establish a Bibliographic Service Development Program in November 1978, to coordinate a nationwide effort and with the intention of linking different institutional computer systems so that bibliographic and other records could be shared among all participants. The Linked Systems Project was the result: a cooperative effort involving CLR, the Washington Library Network, the Ohio College Library Center, the Research Libraries Group, and the Library of Congress.

Grants from funding agencies also provided the resources for cooperation with other libraries to contribute catalog records to the MARC files. A COMARC pilot project funded by the CLR operated 1974–1978 to obtain contributions to the database. The NEH assisted a 1978 project with Northwestern University to contribute cataloging records for Africana collections. Under the BSDP, the CLR supported the Library's project to convert its name authority file to electronic format and to involve other libraries that were willing to contribute their own authority records. The Name Authority Cooperative formed in 1978 gathered records containing the proper forms of names used in cataloging, thus centralizing access to information needed to ensure standardization of catalog entries. By the mid-1980s, the partners in this effort were using the BSDP's computer-to-computer links to transmit information, and between 1988 and 1990 the CLR funded a two-year pilot project to expand the use of the computer links to full catalog records. As other libraries' cataloging began to enter the MARC distribution channels, initially the Library established the bibliographic and input conventions to be followed and trained librarians from selected libraries to submit records, but by the early 1980s began authorizing some libraries to enter records online.

New products also began to enter the library community as the Library's Cataloging Distribution Service began issuing cataloging and other technical publications in microform during the 1980s. The Service also began performing retrieval from the MARC database, allowing librarians to obtain records by card number, by classification, language, and geographic coverage; for those librarians engaged in converting their own catalogs to machine readable format, the Service provided abbreviated records to assist matching. By the late 1980s, products were being issued on CD-ROM as well, including bibliographic records, name authorities, subject headings, MARC manuals, cataloging rule interpretations, and proceedings of Network Advisory Committee meetings.

Meanwhile, the preservation of library materials posed more difficult tasks than the Library or the library community had expected in 1970. In the hope of finding a solution to the brittle book problem, Library staff pursued research on methods of deacidifying books. Eventually deciding in favor of the dimethyl zinc process, senior staff planned to construct a plant to handle Library material and to serve as a model. However, a test facility experienced two fires, and in the early 1990s the Library adopted the Bookkeeper mass deacidification technology instead. As this effort proceeded, the Preservation staff continued its efforts on behalf of other libraries by issuing a monthly newsletter and by joining the ALA in sponsoring conferences on the best preservation practices and the organization of preservation programs in institutions. By the mid-1990s, they had established a series of Preservation Awareness Workshops on making preparations for recovery after disasters and forming plans for emergency responses to library needs. By the early 1990s, preservation had advanced significantly both at the Library of Congress and in other libraries. The establishment of a Commission on Preservation and Access (1986) and an Office of Preservation at the National Endowment for the Humanities signaled widespread recognition by foundations, librarians, and institutional officials that a broad-based attack on the brittle books problem was essential as well as coordination to assure that a virtual national collection would survive. A national invitational conference at the Library explored the development of cooperative preservation programs in the states and assembled experts from a wide range of institutions to provide advice on the future of the Library's program. With the Association of Research Libraries, the Library developed an information packet on permanent, durable book paper, and the staff participated in the committee work of the American National Standards Institute and the International Standards Organization, as well as the International Federation of Library Associations. Cooperative preservation microfilming efforts continued, while in 1992, the National Film Preservation Act provided for a film preservation program.

Librarian James Billington, who took office in 1987, established a Management Analysis and Planning Committee to evaluate all aspects of the Library's operations. Library of Congress services to external constituencies received extended consideration, and Billington attended regional forums, visited libraries, and gathered hundreds of suggestions. His National Advisory Committee of external experts, including members of the library community, recommended more collaboration with other libraries, and discussed "the need to refocus the Library's leadership role."

Billington's response to the Library community and to Library users came with a series of electronic initiatives and the conversion of existing technology to World Wide Web-based products and services. The Library made its bibliographic databases available on the Internet in 1993, and following a successful pilot effort known as American Memory, began a National Digital Library Program to provide online access to selected materials from the collections. A 16-member National Digital Library

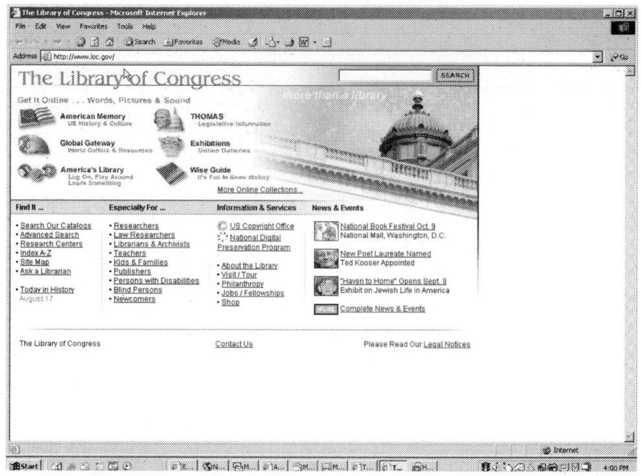

With Librarian James H. Billington's leadership, the Library of Congress Web site was officially launched in June 1994, one year after the Library's bibliographic data was made available online. Determined to expand the Library's electronic resources as a means of sharing the Library's collections and the knowledge of its specialists, Librarian Billington is taking full advantage of new funding and cooperative arrangements with libraries worldwide.

Federation was formed to promote cooperation in digitizing materials, and a year later the Ameritech Corporation provided $2 million to fund a three-year grant competition, in which 33 libraries received support to digitize their own unique collections of Americana, using systems and standards compatible with the Library's system and making the collections available on the Library's American Memory Web site. As these projects proceeded, further development of the Library's Web site made home pages available for all of the reading rooms and for the service units most important to other libraries; for example, the Cataloging Distribution Service and the Cataloging Directorate.

As the digital environment began to affect other areas of library service as well, in 1998, the Library cooperated with Library Solutions, Inc., of Berkeley, California, to sponsor an institute on "Reference Service in a Digital Age," which dealt with issues of staffing and training for reference service in the new environment. Four years later, the Library collaborated with the Online Computer Library Center to produce QuestionPoint, a collaborative virtual reference service available worldwide at all hours, as a cooperative venture among libraries. Interlibrary loan requests began to be accepted and answered through OCLC, RLIN, or email, with some requests answered with digitized products. A congressionally approved National Digital Information Infrastructure and Preservation Program (2000) charged the Library to cooperate with the public and private sectors in the long-term preservation of digital materials, and following a bicentennial conference titled "Bibliographic Control for the New Millennium, the Cataloging Directorate developed plans for the bibliographic control of World Wide Web resources and began to identify partners in the library and vendor communities.

Two other new initiatives benefiting the library community appeared in the form of new cataloging and acquisitions programs. In 1995, the staff created a new Program for Cooperative Cataloging, which by 1997 united the several programs under which electronic contributions of records to the cataloging databases were received. Several years later the program had enrolled more than 300 institutions. With the members sharing responsibility for policy-making while the Library provides the secretariat, this program enables fuller cooperation and interchange than any other cooperative cataloging program the Library has undertaken. And continuing the decades-old programs for acquiring materials from foreign sources to benefit research libraries, the Library sought congressional approval for a Cooperative Acquisitions Revolving Fund to allow continuation of these efforts. In the fiscal 1998 appropriations bill, provision was made to allow recovery of direct and indirect costs associated with the acquisitions program from participating libraries and capitalize the fund with these collected proceeds as the first congressionally mandated revolving fund in the Library.

The digital age has removed the library community's focus from centralized services at the Library of Congress to massive databases and collections available to all via the World Wide Web. Yet librarians remain extremely interested in the Library of Congress and tend to regard its achievements in some measure as the entire profession's contribution to the nation. In the year 2004, the Library of Congress is much less the acknowledged leader of the American library community than it was a century ago, but it remains perhaps its most important icon.

Cole, John Y. "LC and ALA, 1876–1901," *Library Journal* 86 (Oct. 15, 1973): 2965–2970.

Evans, Luther H. "The Strength by Which We Live," *ALA Bulletin* 44 (October 1950): 339–345.

Rosenberg, Jane Aikin. The Nation's Great Library: *Herbert Putnam and the Library of Congress*, 1899–1939. Urbana, IL: University of Illinois Press, 1993.

Wagman, Fred. "Toward Understanding of the Library of Congress," *ALA Bulletin* 57 (April 1963): 322–323.

Young, Arthur P. *Books for Sammies: The American Library Association and World War I.* Pittsburgh: Beta Phi Mu, 1981.

THE LIBRARY OF CONGRESS AND THE SMITHSONIAN INSTITUTION: A LEGISLATED RELATIONSHIP

by Nancy E. Gwinn

Although situated administratively in the legislative branch of government, the Library of Congress is at the heart of the nation's federal libraries. Over the years, the Library has developed many relationships with those libraries, most especially with the other national libraries, the National Library of Medicine and the National Agricultural Library. But none of these interactions have been as close and entangled as the Library of Congress's relationship with the Smithsonian Institution, which, as a trust instrumentality of the United States, stands outside the three branches of government. The circumstances surrounding the establishment and early years of the Smithsonian in the mid-nineteenth century resulted in the legislating of a relationship between these two great institutions that has remained active and productive, though occasionally controversial, to this day.

The Founding of the Smithsonian Institution

In 1835, U.S. Secretary of State John Forsythe informed President Andrew Jackson that James Smithson, a well-regarded British scientist and member of the Royal Society of London, had left a bequest to the United States of America. Valued at well over $500,000, the bequest provided an opportunity to establish America's first truly national establishment of learning. Whether to accept the gift was a matter of intense debate for those in Congress who either did not wish to be beholden to any Englishman or who felt the United States government did not have the appropriate authority to receive such a gift. Having successfully surmounted this obstacle, the House of Representatives and the Senate nevertheless debated another 10 years about the characteristics of the new Washington institution. After all, Philadelphia, New York, and Boston were the existing centers of the nation's cultural and scientific infrastructure. The fledgling city that had become the national capitol was far from assuming any sense of grandeur. Yet the broad outlines of architect Pierre L'Enfant's city design could be seen, anchored with the U.S. Capitol Building, the partially built Washington Monument, the White House and the U.S. Patent Office. The landscape was wide open to provide a setting for a national institution of learning.

The Mall in Washington, D.C., ca. 1865, with the Smithsonian Institution in the foreground and the Capitol, looking almost as it does today, in the distance.
Photograph: Mathew Brady, Smithsonian Institution Archives.

Suggestions from many quarters fell on a continuum between those whose ideal was pure scholarship to those who felt the nation's want of practical, technical skills. Avid proponents argued for a national university, an agricultural school and experimental farm, a museum of natural history, a teacher's training school, and lectureships. John Quincy Adams thought the nation was embarrassed by the lack of an astronomical observatory. Others wished to emulate learned institutions like the Royal Society of London. The idea that eventually gained the most ground was for construction of a great national library.

On August 10, 1846, President James K. Polk signed into law the act that created the Smithsonian Institution. It was clear that the United States Congress could not make up its mind about the nature of the institution, for the act called for a building that would contain a museum with geological and mineralogical cabinets, a chemical laboratory, a library, a gallery of art, and the necessary lecture rooms. The act also established a Board of Regents to create and oversee the institution. Although views differed, some thought the legislation seemed to favor national library advocates, since it called for "the gradual formation of a library" by spending not more than an average of $25,000 a year for book purchases. To help this process along, in 1846 the Congress also gave copyright deposit status to the Smithsonian, as well as to the Library of Congress.

The Board of Regents hired the distinguished American physicist Joseph Henry as the first Secretary of the Smithsonian; he was an acknowledged leader with his own strong ideas. Based on the model of a learned society, Henry wanted the

Prominent American physicist and the first secretary of the Smithsonian Institution (1846–1878), Joseph Henry opposed locating a national library at the Smithsonian. Instead he envisioned the Smithsonian as a place for scientific research and the Library of Congress as a more appropriate national library.
LC/Prints and Photographs Division. LC-USZ62-14760.

Smithsonian to stimulate original scientific research and experimentation and to publish the results in documents that could be exchanged for proceedings of scientific societies all over the world. Rather than a huge, comprehensive national library, he preferred a working collection of scientific materials that could be loaned to scientists and naturalists in direct support of their research programs. He tried to deflect the push for a comprehensive library and posed a more limited view: in addition to forming a complete collection of the transactions and proceedings of all the learned societies in the world and the most important current scientific periodicals, the library could become a bibliographical center containing catalogs of all the different libraries in the United States. But some of the Regents still held strong pro-library views and persuaded Henry to hire Charles Coffin Jewett, the respected librarian of Brown University, as his first assistant secretary, to help carry them out.

With the 1855 completion of the interior of the Smithsonian Building (its turreted towers inevitably meant it would be dubbed the "Castle"), to an outsider it appeared that the institution was well on its way to becoming a national library. Thanks to the vigorous international exchange system inaugurated with the distribution in 1848 of the first volume of the *Smithsonian Contributions to Knowledge*—combined with the heavy, if sporadic, receipts of copyright deposits—the Smithsonian's library collection approached 25,000 volumes and attracted around 16,000 visitors annually. With Henry's encouragement, Assistant Secretary Jewett compiled and published a global listing of publications of learned societies as a basis for the exchange, and also made the first attempt to survey the library resources of the country.

Even though Henry and Jewett clashed with such force that Henry eventually fired Jewett in 1854, the library continued to grow apace. But Henry had never wanted more than a scientific library, writing grumpily to Harvard botanist Asa Gray in 1856 that "exclusive of those [books] read by persons connected with the institution, not more than one person in the course of a month visits it [the library] for the purpose of research." Copyright deposit, he commented later, had chiefly brought in "sheets of music, labels of patent medicines, novels, and elementary works of instruction," and he persuaded Congress to repeal the deposit provision in 1859 from both the Smithsonian and the Library of Congress. Still, by the 1860s, an average of 4,000–5,000 books a year were arriving through the exchange system to fill the increasingly crowded shelves.

The Library of Congress at Mid-Century

The Library of Congress of the 1850s offered no alternative to the Smithsonian as the national library. Housed in the U.S. Capitol Building, which had yet to acquire its grand wings and majestic dome, by 1850 the collection contained only about 55,000 volumes. The small annual appropriation allowed by Congress inhibited growth. Successive Librarians of Congress, hired as political appointees, exercised little influence over the collections. Vermont

Senator George Perkins Marsh of Vermont, like his colleague, Senator Rufus Choate of Massachusetts, favored a national library at the Smithsonian because they considered the Library of Congress ill-equipped to assume the role because of its small appropriations. Marsh said of the Library "...there is no one branch of liberal study... in which it is not deficient."
Smithsonian Institution Archives.

Representative George Marsh, one of the most vocal advocates for a national library, confirmed this during the Smithsonian debate, when he commented that although the Library of Congress collection had "been almost wholly purchased and selected from the best European sales catalogs," there was not "one branch of liberal study. . . in which it is not miserably deficient." This was not surprising given that the Joint Committee on the Library, and usually its conservative Chairman Senator James Alfred Pearce, selected all the books. To compound this picture, disaster struck the Library of Congress on Christmas Eve, 1851, when a raging fire in the stacks destroyed two-thirds of the books.

Disaster often breeds opportunity, however, and the fire proved a wake-up call to the Congress. In 1852, members voted to build a new fireproof room of stone and iron in the Capitol Building for the Library and moved vigorously to replace all of the lost books. In 10 years, the Library's collection rose to nearly 80,000 volumes, the fourth largest in the United States. But all was not well, as reported by the young new assistant librarian Ainsworth Rand Spofford in the 1861 annual report. "All the books in the outer rooms and the larger portion of those in the main Library were found covered with accumulated dust and in many cases hidden amid rubbish and in dark and out-of-the-way corners, inaccessible save to the most persevering explorer . . . . Several valuable and costly works were found perishing from carelessness and abuse and in one case, an entire set of books were found ruined by wet and consequent mold." Remarking on the Library's many deficiencies, Spofford decried the lack of nearly all publications of the U.S. government in the collection, including, for example, the vastly important accounts of coastal, railroad, and geological surveys. Most important, in light of what was to come, Spofford exhorted the congressional members: "This Library, it is to be remembered, is the only one commonly visited by travelers and by the American people. It is in some sense the Library of the Government. . . ."

Spofford's inaugural statement presaged the beginning of an influential career for the young librarian, as well as a new era for the Library of Congress. On the last day of 1864, President Lincoln appointed Spofford as Librarian of Congress; he was the first person truly qualified for the job. Afterwards the persistent bookman continued to pressure members of Congress to take their Library seriously. His first success came on March 2, 1865, when Congress voted a $160,000 appropriation to expand the Library's reading room in the Capitol with fireproof wings on each end and required once again the deposit of copyrighted materials to enhance the collection. Spofford shared the vision and desire of the intellectual politicians of the 1840s to create for the American people a great national library.

The Smithsonian Deposit

In the 10 years following the institution's 1846 founding, Secretary Henry worked hard to achieve a compromise with the Board of Regents between his desire to create the premier scientific institution and the Board's—and Congress's—desires for a more broadly based icon of national culture. Henry feared that the Smithson endowment, barely sufficient for his scientific purposes, could not support the broader vision. He acceded to the congressional desire for a prominent building, accepting the notion that the Smithsonian would have to take in government-owned collections returned to Washington from various exploring expeditions and therefore create a museum. But his concern about the direction of the library and the rising costs of its care and maintenance resulted in "a condition of apparently irreconcilable warfare" between Henry and librarian Jewett. Through his friends, Jewett mounted a vicious attack on Henry's policies in the newspapers. After Henry solidified his position with the Regents, he fired his insubordinate assistant in 1854. The controversy and resulting congressional investigation further convinced him that something had to be done about the Smithsonian's library.

Charles Coffin Jewett, the Smithsonian librarian whose dream of building the nation's preeminent library at the Smithsonian ended abruptly in 1854 when secretary Henry fired him. In 1866, Henry transferred the Smithsonian's library to the Library of Congress.
LC/Prints and Photographs Division. LC-USZ62-13081.

Henry's adopted sphere of operation was the international world of science; his goal was nothing less than to promote the scientific progress of the human race. But he did not think the Smithsonian could, or should, do it all. The secretary was never happier than when another institution agreed to assume a Smithsonian-instigated program if it had better resources, for this would remove a drain on the institution's funds, which could then be devoted to his preferred areas of original research and publication. When in 1846 Henry first articulated a plan for the Smithsonian to his friend Alexander Dallas Bache, he wrote that "... but few cases can occur in which a person will travel from a distance to consult a book in Washington, and when such a case does occur the book ought to be found in the library of Congress." Following the fire in the Library, he used his annual reports to Congress to advocate earnestly in public, writing in 1851: "The libraries of the country must be supplied by the country itself; by the General Government; by the State governments; by cities, towns, and villages, and by wealthy and liberal individuals. It is to be hoped that in the restoration of the library of Congress, a foundation will be laid for a collection of books worthy of a government whose perpetuity principally depends on the intelligence of the people."

If the Smithsonian's library could have been restricted to science from the beginning, the scenario that emerged in the 1860s might have been quite different. On January 24, 1865, the Smithsonian Castle suffered a disastrous fire. Although the main library escaped the blaze, it consumed all of the institution's early records and nearly all of the stock on hand of duplicate annual reports and other public documents, as well as books intended for distribution to libraries. The supposedly fireproof building clearly was not. After another small fire broke out in his office a year later, and with strong support from the Regents, Henry took immediate action. In February 1866, Henry and Librarian of Congress Spofford presented a plan to both the Joint Committee on the Library and the Board of Regents to deposit the Smithsonian's library in the new and empty fireproof wings of the Library of Congress. On April 5, 1866, President Andrew Johnson signed the act that legalized the deposit, acceded to conditions imposed by the Board of Regents, and defined the relationship that exists to this day.

The act specified that following the removal of the library to the Library of Congress, the Smithsonian would continue to have the use of it, as would the public, and that the Smithsonian, through its secretary, would have the use of the Library of Congress "subject to the same regulations as Senators and Representatives." The act charged the Library of Congress to care for and preserve the Smithsonian Library "in like manner" as its own collections and allowed the Smithsonian to reclaim the library only if it reimbursed the Treasury for the expenses incurred in binding and taking care of the collection, or if there were other mutually agreeable conditions. Finally, the legislation authorized the Librarian of Congress to hire two additional assistants to manage the Smithsonian collection. By December 1867, Librarian Spofford was able to report that the approximately 40,000 volumes had been received and all the books cataloged and shelved. Only the scientific transactions, proceedings, and journals were kept separate, however, as Spofford immediately integrated other publications with the rest of the Library's collection.

What the Smithsonian did not surrender was ownership of the library, which became known officially as the Smithsonian Deposit. Indeed, the institution referred to the Deposit in its publications as its main library and for decades continued to build it through the international exchange program. Smithsonian staff carefully accessioned all library materials received before forwarding them to the Deposit, and the institution's annual reports listed and described some of the more important additions.

The two institutions also began the custom of mutually supporting the Deposit through salary subvention. As one of the two new assistants, Dr. Theodore Gill, a Smithsonian zoologist, moved with the Deposit to the Library of Congress payroll to be in charge of the collection; the other, Jane Turner, stayed at the Smithsonian to accession exchange items as they were received and forwarded. This practice continued, with the Library sometimes paying a whole salary and sometimes splitting an employee's salary costs with the institution, until the 1950s.

The Library, the Smithsonian, and International Exchange

Joseph Henry understood that for a learned institution to become an accepted participant in the global exchange of scientific information required barter goods in the form of regular scientific publications. He launched the Smithsonian *Contributions to Knowledge* and persuaded shipping companies to carry the publications at no cost on a space-available basis to Europe and Latin America and to bring back foreign publications on the same basis. Soon he had a network of exchange agents and consular offices to handle and forward shipments at key locations abroad. Having established a capacity much larger than could be filled by the Smithsonian alone, Henry offered use of his system to any American government agency, scientific and learned society or educational institution for only the cost of transporting preaddressed packages to Washington. Tremendously successful, by 1881 the Smithsonian was shipping over 100,000 pounds of publications and had been designated by the U. S. State Department as the official U.S. international exchange agent, a status confirmed by the first international convention for the exchange of official documents and scientific and literary publications, signed in Brussels in 1886.

From the start of his tenure, Librarian of Congress Spofford eagerly sought congressional approval for printing extra copies of official federal publications for exchange with other countries as a way of enhancing the utility of the library's collections. The Smithsonian's exchange service provided the obvious means, particularly as, by the end of the Civil War, the service had already handled 20,000 publications of the U.S. Department of Agriculture, the U.S. Patent Office, the National Observatory, the Postmaster General, the Census Office, the Surgeon General, and other federal agencies. Congress authorized the scheme in 1867, and Henry immediately sent a circular through the Department of State to foreign ministers in the United States and to U.S. ministers stationed abroad to determine how many and which governments would be interested. Eighteen countries responded favorably and several sent immediate shipments of their publications to the United States. Unfortunately, a series of technical and political problems plagued the project on the American side; not until 1874 was Librarian Spofford able to order the first documents to be shipped to Canada, Japan, and Germany. Two years later, once Henry and Spofford were able to establish a routine schedule, they agreed that the official documents could be sent to universities and societies, as well as to their official national counterparts. Once again the Library of Congress and the Smithsonian were intertwined in a program that would help to consolidate the Library's position as the de facto national library.

Cooperative programs among institutions, always beneficial in concept, are not without cost or trouble in execution. The growing relationship between the Smithsonian and the Library of Congress required constant maintenance, but with a legislated basis, the stimulus to resolve problems was ever present. The Library of Congress still depended on the Smithsonian to feed its science collections through the exchange program. The Smithsonian was a working, scientific institution with a growing collection of natural history specimens, to which other objects and artifacts were added daily. The work of identifying, classifying, and displaying the flora and fauna of the United States, not to mention the emerging and broadly based museum displays, required the daily use of books, journals, and other documents.

Initially, Smithsonian staff found it relatively easy to retrieve the Smithsonian Deposit books and journals required in their work. But with Spofford's acquisitive energies, which in addition to the Deposit and exchange publications had resulted in the purchase of several large collections and the reinstatement of copyright deposit status, the Library of Congress quickly filled to overflowing all available space. Although Congress authorized construction of a new building in the 1870s, the space shortage in the U.S. Capitol Building became so acute that Library staff were unable even to open the boxes of journals and books sent by the Smithsonian, much less sort or retrieve what the institution's increasing staff of scientists and curators required. In frustration, Joseph Henry's second assistant secretary, Spencer Fullerton Baird, and other staff acquired large personal book collections in order to have the documents needed at hand. In 1878, Joseph Henry died and Baird was appointed second secretary. He donated his extensive personal library to the Smithsonian to found the new U.S. National Museum Library and to constitute "working collections" near staff offices. He authorized staff to secure two copies of exchange publications, one to keep in the working collections and one to forward to the Library. Now the Smithsonian annual reports combined the number of volumes in the institution's Main Library Collection, the Smithsonian Deposit, with its local working collections to compose an aggregated figure to describe the institution's total library holdings. Never again did the Smithsonian relinquish its local library.

Still, the Smithsonian Deposit volumes remained a critical resource for the institution's research staff. As the opening of the Library's splendid new Renaissance palace on Capitol Hill neared, the Board of Regents and Secretary Samuel P. Langley, who had succeeded Secretary Baird, reaffirmed its ownership of, and need for access to, the Deposit and expressed concern about how the Smithsonian collection would be housed. Librarian Spofford reassured the officials, stating that the collection would be arranged in a separate stack of the new building with a special reading room adjacent. In 1900, the Library created a Smithsonian Division with Francis Henry Parsons in charge, and the next year, to the scientists' delight, implemented twice-daily delivery of books to the institution. Still, Langley wrote, it was plain that "no scientific establishment can exist and perform its functions without at least a considerable working library," and he continued to build the local collection.

The Smithsonian Library was to continue in this bifurcated state until the middle of the twentieth century. In its 1919 *Annual Report*, the Smithsonian asserted that according to the records, 888,129 publications had been deposited at the Library of Congress, with another 156,275 publications populating the U.S. National Museum Library and its 38 sectional libraries; another 35,000 volumes were housed at the National Zoological Park, with the Bureau of American Ethnology, at the Smithsonian Astrophysical Observatory, and in other areas of the institution. Whenever the leadership changed at either the Library of Congress or the Smithsonian Institution, the basis for the agreements concerning the Deposit were reviewed, usually because of concerns on one side or the other: the problems connected with trying to manage a separate collection on the Library's side; the continuing problem of access, loan, and record-keeping on the Smithsonian side. The Library sometimes complained that the institution was sending inappropriate items, such as reprints or circulars, along with routine exchange items, when the Library's Smithsonian Division primarily held the scientific journals and society transactions and proceedings. The institution had given permission at the time of the legislation for the Library to integrate nonscientific or duplicate materials with its other collections, with the result that duplicate runs were held in different places, usually with neither one complete, and a third growing at the Smithsonian. The institution nevertheless continued to send important collections to the Library. In 1930, Samuel Langley's aeronautical library, containing 1,736 volumes and 923 pamphlets, joined the collections of the Library's new Division of Aeronautics, which thus acquired nearly complete sets of early aeronautical magazines worldwide. A year later, the institution forwarded 876 maps and seven atlases, many with considerable historic interest. Meanwhile, the Smithsonian retained important collections closely tied to its research interests, such as the William H. Dall collection on mollusks and the extensive holdings of the Bureau of American Ethnology.

A Mid-Twentieth-Century Turning Point

After the United States entered the Second World War in 1941, the country's burgeoning need for scientific and other data highlighted the problems and inconsistencies that had advanced over the early decades of the twentieth century. The United States suddenly had a strategic need for information about the flora and fauna of East and South Asia and the tropics and for maps of lands half a globe away. Both the Library of Congress and the Smithsonian Institution were called on for research data and information. While the valuable holdings of each were moved out of Washington in 1941–1942 to safer storage locations at Washington and Lee University in

After the attack on Pearl Harbor in 1941, both the Smithsonian and the Library of Congress moved their most valuable collections outside of Washington, D.C. to safer locations at the University of Virginia, Washington and Lee University, the Virginia Military Institute, and Denison University in Ohio. This photo shows the Library's collections at the University of Virginia.
LC Archives.

Lexington, Virginia, and other sites, the scientific journals gathered from all over the world had critical importance. A September 1940 survey on the Library's scientific holdings had reported on deficiencies. While "not numerous compared with similar collections," there was a gap in holdings from Latin American countries. "Probably the greatest need in our scientific collections," the survey concluded, "are the works of the scholars of the past, particularly collected sets and rarities of the sixteenth to eighteenth centuries. The Library is really in desperate need of works in the sciences, whether monographic treatises or encyclopedias, that cover these centuries." The Smithsonian Deposit volumes, the survey noted, were practically all that the Library possessed of scientific literature. By the early summer of 1942, the Library reported that submarine blockades had severely crippled the exchange system with the result that accessions of learned society volumes had dropped by 50 percent.

But past collecting activities proved their worth. More than 35 war agencies made inquiries, borrowed books, or sent research workers to use the Smithsonian's collections, and the Library of Congress experienced the same surge of use. "Never before in the history of the world have books played so significant a part in the successful waging of war," wrote the Smithsonian's librarian in 1944. "It seems a far cry from the broomsticks of a scientific library to the battlefields of Africa or the South Pacific, but this is a scientific war, and many lives have been saved by the exactly right bit of information about an insect, a plant, an animal, the shoreline of a far-away island, or other natural features of strange lands found in little-known journals and documents on library shelves." Information and scientific expertise were not the only commodities offered. The Smithsonian and the Library of Congress cooperated with the American Library Association's program to help libraries in war-torn areas and contributed tens of thousands of duplicate periodicals and other materials to the effort.

Both the Library of Congress and the Smithsonian were called on for research and information during World War II. The war also highlighted deficiencies in the Library's overall science collections, which still depended largely on materials in the Smithsonian deposit. Map collections were an exception. Pictured here are war conflict maps from the Library's collections on display in the U.S. Capitol.
LC Archives.

In 1942, Leila F. Clark became custodian of the Smithsonian Deposit and librarian of the Smithsonian Institution with the Library and the Smithsonian each paying half her salary. Clark was the first person with an academic degree in librarianship to be appointed to this dual role and the last to hold it. Over the next decade, the Library's difficulties in managing the Smithsonian Deposit grew. Although Librarian of Congress Archibald MacLeish assured Smithsonian Secretary Charles Abbott in 1942 that he saw "no cause to disturb our mutual relations as regards the Smithsonian Deposit," the problems of housing, identifying, and record-keeping predicated change. In 1944, MacLeish announced a major re-organization of the Library; the Smithsonian Division was discontinued, its custodial functions transferred to the Stack and Reader Division and its reference functions absorbed by the General Reference and Bibliography Division.

Once again, a change in leadership raised the matter of the two institutions' relationship to a high level. Luther Evans stepped into the post of Librarian of Congress in 1945 and in 1953, the Smithsonian's Board of Regents appointed psychologist and former president of Tufts College Leonard Carmichael as the seventh secretary. Library of Congress staff saw the opportunity to reconsider the policies and arrangements that had grown over the years. A 1952 memo from Raymund L. Zwemmer, chief of the Library's Science Division, pointed out to Librarian Evans that the Smithsonian Deposit was no longer maintained as a separate entity, since material from other sources had been added to complete some sets. He recommended combining all of the volumes in the Library of Congress classification system for science (Q), "irrespective of source." Nevertheless, recognizing the Smithsonian's historical claim and research needs, Zwemmer later suggested that scientific journal sets be combined at one place or another depending on the availability of duplicate sets, the relative importance of the subject matter to the collections and activities of either place, and the availability of funds for binding and servicing.

In the same period, Smithsonian Librarian Clark advised Secretary Carmichael that it was time to recognize that the Deposit was no longer the main library of the Smithsonian. Rather, the 500,000 volumes housed in over 40 locations in the Smithsonian should be considered as the institution's library, and steps taken to improve staffing and management of the collection. Pointing to the rich collections in systematic zoology, botany, paleontology, and in certain subfields of anthropology, especially in physical anthropology and in the study of the Indians of North and South America, she proposed that the Smithsonian assume "the responsibility for building up and maintaining the national library of the literature of these subjects." Cracks were becoming apparent in the legislative glue of the Deposit that bound the two institutions.

Over lunch in May 1953, the Smithsonian Secretary and the Librarian of Congress reached toward a new foundation for the acknowledged historical relationship of their institutions. Secretary Carmichael agreed that the Library's management of its scientific collections would be more effective if the Library were allowed to integrate all volumes without regard to whether or not they were part of the Smithsonian Deposit. But he did not surrender the marks of ownership, requesting that book plating of the volumes, which had ceased in 1942, be re-established. Evans and Carmichael agreed that the Smithsonian could continue to keep the scientific journals it needed, with missing volumes filled in as necessary by the Library, through a "semi-permanent loan" arrangement. But Carmichael requested that objects from the Langley Aeronautical collection, deposited at the Library in 1930, be returned to the institution, along with any duplicate items still existing.

In July 1953, just two months later, Librarian Evans resigned to become Secretary-General of UNESCO. It took nearly a year to fill the post. Two years later, new Librarian L. Quincy Mumford took up the conversation again. Although much of the original process of handling the Smithsonian Deposit had "fallen into innocuous desuetude," staff of both institutions were chafing under the burdensome record-keeping still required. Much of the Deposit had already been integrated with the Library's collections, and both institutions were plagued with incomplete sets of scientific journals. Further, the Library was no longer dependent on the Smithsonian for international exchange of publications, having built up its own independent exchange operation after the Second World War. With her retirement looming in 1957, Librarian Clark also felt it was time to end the dual funding of her position and for the Smithsonian to assume total support of the position.

Finally, in response to proposals from Librarian Mumford, on January 22, 1958, Secretary Carmichael cut most of the Deposit string, writing the Librarian that "you have my assurance that the Smithsonian Deposit will not be withdrawn from the Library of Congress." He agreed that the Smithsonian Library would continue to send its thousands of publications to the Library of Congress, but would discontinue placing the Deposit stamp on any of it, thus removing any means of identification. (Beginning in 1959, the Library would no longer count and report annually the number of items received for the Deposit.) Further, the Smithsonian would assume full responsibility for the salary of its librarian. There were still issues to be worked out concerning sets of scientific journals. But he made sure one legislative strand remained firmly in place. There would be "no curtailment of the privileges of the institution" that had been recorded in the 1866 Act, which were to have the use of the Library of Congress on the same basis as members of Congress.

In fact, the entire 1866 Act was still in place with regard to items identified as Smithsonian Deposit. Secretary Carmichael did not surrender rights of ownership, as the Smithsonian's legal staff reaffirmed in 1962 in response to questions from a curator. The institution " has by statute the right to the same use of the material in the Deposit as it had when the Deposit was housed in the Smithsonian Institution, it is entitled to the use for indefinite periods of any material in the deposit, whether duplicated by other Library of Congress collections or not, but to permanently recall any of this material would require the assent of Congress." Although the removal of the entire Deposit from the Library was never an issue, Smithsonian curators were becoming increasingly apprehensive of the Library's attempts to reconcile the Smithsonian privilege to retrieve Deposit material with its own policies for access and interlibrary loan.

Once again, a change in leadership brought the matter into the open. Shortly after S. Dillon Ripley took the oath as Smithsonian secretary on February 1, 1964, the Smithsonian formed an ad hoc Smithsonian Deposit-Library of Congress committee "to ensure that Smithsonian Deposit books are readily available for Smithsonian research and to ensure that Smithsonian investigators have maximum use of non-SD Library of Congress material." Headed by scientist George Watson, the committee offered Secretary Ripley a series of recommendations, urging him to reiterate firmly the Smithsonian's legal title to the Deposit and its legislated right to "unlimited use of its own library," which included unlimited loan periods and possible transfer of certain specific items. He also asked the secretary to remind Librarian Mumford that the 1866 statute allowed Smithsonian curators to borrow Library of Congress books, but he admitted that staff had been extensively delinquent in returning books that were not part of the deposit, a "black-eye for the SI." The desirability of a special reading room for Smithsonian staff, so they could conveniently use the Library's books that couldn't be loaned, and the need to appoint a Smithsonian Deposit liaison were also raised. Secretary Ripley started his negotiations with Librarian Mumford on October 20, 1964, at a luncheon meeting.

In his opening remarks Mumford expressed worry that the Smithsonian would withdraw a mass of volumes. Secretary Ripley responded with a discussion of the research-scholar emphasis in the Smithsonian and the need for cooperation between the institution and the Library in library matters, particularly concerning the availability of books for research. From this point to the present day, the leaders of each agency continued to express the essence of these points of view each time concern over acquiring collections erupted: the Library's desire for comprehensive collections of publications and manuscripts and the institution's desire to serve efficiently the needs of its scholars for research materials.

At the 1964 luncheon, the two negotiators reached a satisfactory agreement. Librarian Mumford agreed to reinforce the right of Smithsonian staff to have both Smithsonian Deposit and Library of Congress books available for indefinite loan periods, to make study desks and reserved book spaces available to Smithsonian scholars, and to welcome the appointment of a liaison librarian. He agreed to have staff work on a list of Deposit books to be transferred to the Smithsonian. On his part, Secretary Ripley conceded that the volumes sent to the Library since 1958, which had not been identified or stamped in any way, could not now feasibly be located, nor could the Library entertain the workload of establishing separate processing routines for these materials. For the moment, the issues were resolved.

Meanwhile, Secretary Ripley had a more serious problem on his hands, the status of the Smithsonian Library. The collections were scattered and disorganized and the central card catalog and shelf lists "in almost total confusion." According to a consultant,

> "over the years, filing has been done by a great number of different persons following a variety of rules, and in many cases, no rules at all. The catalog entries are, in many instances, incorrectly or carelessly done. The classification represents a composite picture of all approaches to a systematic arrangement of book material, but only rarely does it follow the standards of today. To use these catalogs is not only frustrating but takes an exorbitant amount of time."

An internationally acclaimed ornithologist and lover of books himself, Ripley understood the scientist's need to have easy access to books and documents. Having set upon a path to revitalize the Smithsonian's programs in research and education, he was frustrated by the "state of chaos" he found in the library. He vowed to bring it into the modern age by appointing a Director of Libraries to undertake a complete reorganization, one who had "the qualifications and ability to establish a library which will rank with other great research libraries in the government and the country."

> Ripley reported his visionary plans to Congress in his 1968 *Annual Report.*
> "In connection with our plans for mobilizing information in the Smithsonian, our library must occupy a paramount place. To a library-minded curator like myself, no single part of the institution can yield primacy of place to our library and to our library-like resources which in essence are the collections... The library program aims to create an innovative and totally responsive integrated system of Libraries and services capable of serving the goals of the institution directly through research, education, and service programs of its own, as well as secondarily through its support of the work of the institution's professional staff."

In appointing Russell Shank as the first director of the new Smithsonian Institution Libraries, Ripley was certain he had found the right person for the job.

From Collection to Collecting—Controversy Emerges

S. Dillon Ripley's tenure as secretary marked a period of phenomenal growth in the Smithsonian. The opening of what is now the National Museum of American History just before he took office was only the first of several museums launched as the institution began to mushroom into the world's largest museum complex. Ripley complemented the new edifices with new outreach programs as diverse as the *Smithsonian Magazine*, the Smithsonian National and Resident Associates, and a carousel on the Washington Mall, and expanded research programs in environmental studies, ecology and conservation. As the program activities grew, so did the Smithsonian Institution Libraries, which slowly resolved its internal issues and began to enhance and refine its collections. No longer as dependent on the Library of Congress, the Smithsonian's needs for documentation of, and historical context for, its object and specimen collections began occasionally to impinge on what the Library considered its realm.

Librarian Mumford outlined the essence of the argument in 1971 when he wrote to Secretary Ripley shortly after astronaut Michael Collins was appointed as the first director of the new National Air and Space Museum, whose capacious building opened in July 1976. "For years there has been an understanding of the general roles of these two organizations," he reported.

> "The Smithsonian Institution would principally collect artifacts, the Library of Congress would principally collect published materials and manuscripts. I recognize that there can be no absolute delimitation of interests; in some fields—photographs and prints, for example—we both collect actively. The collecting of personal papers, however, has been traditional with the Library of Congress and, until the establishment of the Air and Space Museum, appeared to be accepted by the staff of the Smithsonian."

He and succeeding Librarians used essentially the same argument over the years, whenever the Smithsonian acquired archival or rare material that the Library felt was better housed on Capitol Hill than on the Mall. "We feel strongly," he wrote, "that scholars working with written material—published or unpublished—can be served best by the concentration of such materials and that the best interests of scholars and researchers should govern our policies and practices."

Ripley responded in the same way his successors were to meet this pronouncement, agreeing that the Smithsonian's main interest was artifacts and the Library of Congress focus was published material and manuscripts. In this case, of course, the museum's assembling of needed reference documentation for aerospace artifacts was standard procedure and might include appropriate biographical material. "... There should be no conflict of interest here," he offered, "and any such material can easily be shared"—an argument used by the Library as well.

Over the next three decades, these points of view between the Library of Congress and Smithsonian leaders have been politely reiterated with great courtesy on both sides, but never completely resolved. In 1974, industrialist and bibliophile Bern Dibner, who had created the Burndy Library, a great library of the history of science and technology located on the grounds of the Burndy Corporation, donated approximately 10,000 rare books and manuscripts to the Smithsonian Institution in honor of the nation's bicentennial. As he was surrendering his office to historian Daniel J. Boorstin, Librarian Mumford once again objected. He pointed to the strength of the Library's collection of rare scientific materials and suggested that further dispersion of new collections among "competing government agencies" was not in the best interest of scholars and the nation. Mumford recommended a more coordinated acquisition policy. Ripley's response to Mumford was firm. He did not consider the Smithsonian's library activity to be in competition with the Library of Congress. He wrote:

> "Our goal, nevertheless, is to have at the institution the kinds of library collections that directly support the advanced research, exhibits, and educational programs of many hundreds of professional curators and research scholars on our staff. I consider library collections to be essential to their endeavors .... The Dibner gift with its dual character, goes right to the heart of our major research and exhibition programs, almost as if it had been assembled specifically for us."

Coming from Yale and "shaken" to discover the meager support for the Smithsonian's own library, Ripley wrote later, he had worked since 1964 to develop a rare book facility to support scholarly work in the fields of science and history of science. The Burndy gift stayed, becoming the nucleus of a growing collection of rare materials in the Dibner Library of the History of Science and Technology, developed according to Ripley's principles.

The leadership changed again, but the arguments did not. Robert McCormick Adams became the ninth Smithsonian Secretary in mid-1984, and James H. Billington succeeded Dr. Boorstin in September 1987. As the 1990s approached, it became clear that the next point of contention would be in the area of music, specifically over archival and manuscript material of a great personage.

In 1986, Congress had appropriated $1,000,000 to the Smithsonian for the purchase and conservation of a collection of Duke Ellington items relating to his musical career, which belonged to Ellington's son Mercer. Given the Library of Congress's own extensive music collections, Librarian Billington was understandably perturbed. Once again the Librarian of Congress engaged the Smithsonian Secretary in a discussion of the collecting priorities of both institutions, asking to negotiate a memorandum of agreement that would once and for all clarify the role of the Library as the principal repository for published and manuscript material, and the Smithsonian as the same for artifacts. And again Secretary Adams pointed out that there could never be such a simple solution, that "sharply defined jurisdictional boundaries" could never be established. After all, the Library of Congress was collecting artifacts, witness its wonderful musical instruments used by the Julliard Quartet. "Scholarship and public service both grow up around our two organizations," Adams posited, "taking different forms, reaching different audiences, differentiating themselves creatively rather than competing with one another."

The GAO Investigation

This time, however, the interest of Congress heightened the tension. Earlier, several senators had asked both organizations and the National Archives and Records Administration (NARA) for information that would address senatorial concern over the expense of the major national cultural institutions. Specifically they wanted to know whether the Smithsonian and NARA were going to continue to build library and archival resources that might be seen to be duplicative with the Library of Congress, and what the future needs of these institutions might be. When Duke Ellington's sister began to negotiate with both institutions over the purchase of her own collection of her brother's work, the question of competition, which would result in a bidding war that would raise the price to taxpayers, added to congressional concerns. Tension heightened when other collections came on the market, including a private collection of rare recordings of Ellington's work, a manuscript collection of jazz musician Charles Mingus, and a collection of architectural drawings that contained James Renwick's original designs for the Smithsonian's "Castle" building, the Corcoran Gallery, and other Washington, D.C., sites. Controversies over these collections finally spurred Senator Ted Stevens of Alaska to request that the General Accounting Office (GAO) undertake an investigation of whether the Library of Congress, the Smithsonian Institution, the National Park Service and the National Archives and Records Administration "bid competitively against one another to acquire historic artifacts." Should the review find this to be the case, Senator Stevens further asked GAO if the agencies did anything to guard against it and if mechanisms were needed to prevent it.

In its 1992 report, GAO determined that neither the National Park Service nor the National Archives had a problem. The issue was between the Library of Congress and the Smithsonian, which had competed in at least four instances involving jazz music and architectural drawings with one or the other agency winning; in three cases, one agency paid more than the amount being negotiated by the other. Senator Stevens accepted the report and asked the Librarian and the Secretary to respond to its recommendations to:

- Clarify their institutions' collecting roles to prevent duplicated effort,
- Formulate acquisition policies to discourage competition against other agencies,
- Reach agreement and establish more specific guidelines as to which agency will take the lead in acquiring artifacts for areas of overlap, and
- Instruct their staffs to inform agency counterparts when potentially overlapping collections become available.

Senator Ted Stevens requested the General Accounting Office to investigate competition for collections among several major national cultural institutions. The 1992 GAO report found that indeed such competition existed in certain collecting areas between the Library of Congress and the Smithsonian Institution. The heads of both institutions complied with the report's recommendations and agreed to seek mutually acceptable solutions when potential for competitive bidding arose. They also agreed to periodic meetings and to continue their historically collegial relationships.
Courtesy: Office of Ted Stevens.

Both leaders complied, to the satisfaction of Senator Stevens. Secretary Adams issued a new policy to his staff, "Smithsonian Institution Collecting Coordination Within the Federal Establishment," which stated that "the Smithsonian will avoid competitive bidding with other federal organizations for collections of common interest, and will seek mutually acceptable agreements whenever the potential for competitive bidding with such organizations becomes apparent." Staffs of both agencies began to meet and apprise one another whenever either developed an interest in a music collection. That the two staffs were also relieved was clear when the Smithsonian's chief music curator reported that the Musical History Division's relationship with the Library's music staff had been long and harmonious and that meetings would be held periodically to ensure the collegiality would continue and strengthen.

This comment underscores an important point about the relationship between America's two largest national cultural organizations: whatever the strains and stresses that naturally occurred as the two agencies grew and expanded their programs and activities, their leaders and staffs remained cordial, willing to negotiate differences, and determined to act in the best interests of the American people, the ultimate owners of their immense collections. There have been many mutually satisfying activities and collaborations over the years; the staffs have interacted successfully on numerous levels. The two organizations borrowed artifacts from each other for exhibitions, engaged colleagues on professional committees and joint projects and spoke at each other's symposia and seminars. The Library of Congress has occasionally transferred to the Smithsonian artifacts, such as coins, paper currency, and the personal belongings of noted Washington collector Joseph Meredith Toner, which came in with printed or manuscript materials. Both agencies have strong programs in folklife that have spurred joint efforts, such as the conservation of wax cylinder field recordings of Native American songs and stories. In 2001, the Library's American Folklife Center and the Smithsonian's Center for Folklife and Cultural Heritage signed an Interagency Agreement for the "Save Our Sounds" program to preserve recordings of America's vast musical heritage.

In 1987, Library of Congress and the Smithsonian Libraries staff resolved the last remaining confusion about the ownership of the Smithsonian Deposit. The Smithsonian Institution Libraries would keep those Deposit volumes that were still at the institution and still needed, while making available to the Library a number of volumes of older natural history journals required to complete gaps in the Library's collections. Smithsonian staff continue to transfer unneeded books and other publications to the Library of Congress, as they have since 1866. The two staffs also continue periodically to negotiate borrowing privileges and access rights. Although the Smithsonian Institution Libraries has grown to a collection of 1.5 million volumes, including 40,000 rare books and manuscripts, the Smithsonian remains the Library of Congress's largest borrower of materials for the use of its scholars and researchers. Still an active statute, the 1866 Act that governed the transfer of the Smithsonian Deposit to the Library of Congress laid the groundwork for a legislated relationship that, despite the occasional controversies, has proven to be productive and meaningful for over 135 years.

Cole, John Y. and Nancy E. Gwinn. "Debating National Culture in Nineteenth Century Washington: The Library of Congress and the Smithsonian Institution," in William E. Brown Jr. and Laura Stalker, eds., *Getting Ready for the Nineteenth Century: Strategies and Solutions for Rare Books and Special Collections Librarians*. Chicago: American Library Association, 2000.

Gwinn, Nancy E. "The Origins and Development of International Publication Exchange in Nineteenth Century America." Ph.D. dissertation, The George Washington University, 1996.

Smithsonian Institution. Office of the Secretary. Record Unit 613 (1972–1980).

THE LIBRARY OF CONGRESS AND THE NATIONAL ARCHIVES

by John Y. Cole

The National Archives Building in Washington, D.C., was constructed under the supervision of architect John Russell Pope and opened in 1935. The recently renovated rotunda is the home of the Declaration of Independence and the U.S. Constitution, which were housed at the Library of Congress from 1921 until 1952. Today the billions of government records in the collections of the National Archives are also housed in a major facility in College Park, Maryland, in 20 regional centers, and in 13 presidential libraries across the country.
LC/Prints and Photographs Division. LC-H814-A04-030.

Known officially as the National Archives and Records Administration (NARA), the National Archives was established in 1934 to identify and ensure the preservation of the records of the U.S. government that have continuing historical value. Because of the relative lateness of its creation as a national institution, it began under the shadow—but nevertheless with the support—of the Library of Congress. Herbert Putnam, Librarian of Congress from 1899 to 1939, encouraged the creation of what became the National Archives, telling President Theodore Roosevelt as early as 1907 that there was a clear distinction between the personal papers gathered by the Library of Congress and the governmental records that such a national "hall of records" would accumulate.

The gestation period for the National Archives, which is part of the executive branch of government, was lengthy and convoluted. Once established, agreement on how to divide the collecting and custodial responsibilities between the Library of Congress and the new National Archives for "government records and documents" did not come easily—primarily because by 1934 the Library had established traditions and policies that, in the end, it was reluctant to give up. Today the governmental, public records function of the National Archives remains paramount, but its role as a resource for historians also is of great importance. Moreover, the combined resources of the two institutions have satisfied the lifetime research needs of many historians and genealogists, who continue to travel between their respective reading rooms, despite the attractions of the Internet.

Early History

The federal government was slow to recognize the importance of its own records. In the nineteenth century, governmental records of individual departments often were poorly kept and usually inaccessible. Key documents of recognized national importance, for example the journals of the Continental Congress and the priceless originals of the Declaration of Independence, the Articles of Confederation, and the Constitution, were retained in the Department of State.

The first serious discussions about centralizing federal records in a single institution were prompted by the flood of Civil War records. In 1878, the Secretary of War endorsed the idea of an inexpensive, fireproof hall of records, but no general solution was attempted prior to the passage of the first Records Disposal Act of 1889. This legislation provided for disposal of unneeded material, but a separate building was essential for storage. Preliminary plans were drawn up in the 1890s, and in 1903 a bill was finally enacted that authorized the purchase of a site and the construction of a separate building to house the nation's archives. President Theodore Roosevelt showed interest in the project, but there was a controversy over the proposed site that alienated some members of Congress. However a private citizen, Lathrop Withington of Newburyport, Mass., prevailed upon Massachusetts Senator Henry Cabot Lodge to introduce a bill modeled after the organic act of the British Public Records Office that would have converted the still-proposed modest hall of records into an independent national archives, complete with a professional staff. The bill was referred to the Joint Committee on the Library, chaired by Senator George P. Wetmore of Rhode Island, who consulted with his friend Chief Assistant Librarian of Congress Ainsworth Rand Spofford, who had built the Library of Congress into a national institution when he served as Librarian from 1864 to 1897. Then in his early 80s and a respected figure with many powerful friends in Congress, Spofford opposed the bill. Wetmore deferred to Spofford, and the bill died in committee.

Spofford had always felt that all government-related research, archival, and scholarly activities should be centralized at the Library of Congress. While Librarian of Congress, he had succeeded in centralizing U.S. copyright activities at the Library, an achievement that forced the construction of the Library's first separate building in 1897. One of the few government officials to recognize the value of manuscripts and archives, as Librarian in the 1870s he had started acquiring manuscripts and was forced to stop only because the Library ran out of space in the Capitol Building.

Spofford died in 1908, the same year that historian J. Franklin Jameson, who more than any other single individual would become the moving force in the creation of the National Archives, began to work seriously to create a "movement" on behalf of the project. Jameson, who held the first doctorate awarded in history from the Johns Hopkins University, taught at Brown University and the University of Chicago before becoming the first academically trained historian to be elected president of the American Historical Association (AHA). In 1895, he had served on an AHA Historical Manuscripts Commission that established guidelines for the development of the manuscript collection of the Library of Congress once it occupied its new building, so he was familiar with the Library and its policies. In 1905, he left academia to become the first director of the Department of Historical Research at the Carnegie Institution in Washington, D.C. Here he was well-positioned to pursue his interest in promoting a national records repository. In December 1907, Jameson was pleased to learn that Librarian of Congress Herbert Putnam did not share Spofford's views regarding a hall of records; and that Putnam saw no conflict between collecting historical manuscripts at the Library of Congress and providing "a better storehouse" for the masses of records produced by the federal government.

Ironically, the movement toward a national archives for government records had been delayed somewhat by the rapid development of the Library of Congress's Manuscript Division since its establishment in 1897. The 1895 AHA Commission, concerned about the scattering of manuscript collections among many institutions, had encouraged the growth of collections in established agencies such as the Library. Putnam took full advantage of the recommendation, arguing that manuscripts of truly national interest should in fact be gathered at the Library. In March 1903, the Librarian persuaded President Theodore Roosevelt to issue an executive order to transfer from the Department of State to the Library of Congress, not only a remarkable assemblage of the personal papers of most of the Founding Fathers—Washington, Jefferson, Madison, Hamilton, Monroe, and Franklin—but also the records and papers of the Continental Congress. At the Library, Putnam explained in his 1903 *Annual Report*, these papers and records would be preserved and rendered accessible for historical and "other legitimate uses."

President Theodore Roosevelt was persuaded by Librarian Putnam in 1903 to issue an executive order that transferred the personal papers of most of the Founding Fathers, as well as the records and papers of the Continental Congress, from the Department of State to the Library of Congress. Roosevelt also was the first president to give his papers directly to the Library of Congress. The first installment arrived in 1917.
LC/Prints and Photographs Division.
LC-USZ62-13026.

Viewing the records of the Continental Congress primarily as a manuscript collection, not as government records, Putnam consistently supported Jameson's national archives initiative. He hosted luncheons at his "Round Table" (a private dining room within the Library) at which Jameson could forward his idea. He also arranged for the Library's Superintendent of Building and Grounds, Bernard Green to provide advice about the construction of a National Archives Building. The Library supplied favorable testimony at congressional hearings in 1911 and 1912, and in 1916 Putnam himself provided "good suggestions, " according to Jameson, on the latest plan. World War I intervened, however, and there were further delays in the early 1920s.

Between 1910 and 1928, there were intermittent congressional proposals that the archives be placed under the administrative supervision of the Librarian of Congress. There is no evidence that Putnam initiated any of the proposals; moreover, since the Library of Congress was running out of space, its Manuscript Division had stopped accepting all "archival collections." Jameson and Putnam remained on such excellent terms that Putnam hired Jameson as chief of the Library's Manuscript Division in 1928.

Nevertheless, the seeds of a future complication in the relationship between the Library of Congress and the National Archives were planted in the early 1920s. In 1920, a committee of scholars, concerned about the preservation of the Declaration of Independence and the Constitution in the Department of State, made recommendations concerning the care of the two "sacred documents" and their possible public exhibition. On September 29, 1921, President Warren G. Harding acting on the recommendation of Secretary of State Charles Evans Hughes, issued an executive order transferring the two documents from the Department of State to the Library of Congress. In his 1921 *Annual Report*, Putnam stated that the order was issued "at the instance of Gaillard Hunt, formerly Chief of the Division of Manuscripts, now Editor for the Department of State and in charge of its Library and Archives."

On September 30, the day after Harding signed the order, Putnam went to the State Department in the Library's Model T Ford truck, signed a receipt, and returned to the Library with the documents which he placed in his office safe. Congress soon appropriated funds to build "a sort of shrine" in which the documents could be displayed for public viewing in the Library's Great Hall. The exhibition opened on Feb. 18, 1924, in the presence of President Calvin Coolidge, and the ceremony took place "without a single utterance, save the singing of two stanzas of "*America*." The newspapers reported that the Declaration of Independence and the U. S. Constitution had finally found a permanent home.

In the presence of Librarian Putnam (left) and President and Mrs. Coolidge (center), the U.S. Constitution and Declaration of Independence were put on public display in the Library's Jefferson Building in 1924. In 1952 they were permanently transferred to the National Archives for care and display.
LC/Prints and Photographs Division.
LC-USZ62-57285.

Two years later, in 1926, Congress appropriated funds for a national archives building in downtown Washington, D.C., and construction began in 1931. At the laying of the cornerstone on February 20, 1933, to the dismay of Library of Congress officials, President Herbert Hoover announced that "the most sacred documents of our history—the originals of the Declaration of Independence and the Constitution of the United States" would be displayed in the new archives building once it was completed. Moreover, later that year architect John Russell Pope commissioned artist Barry Faulkner to create two large murals about the documents for the rotunda of the new building's Exhibition Hall. The murals depict Thomas Jefferson presenting the Declaration of Independence to John Hancock, and James Madison presenting the final draft of the Constitution to George Washington.

On June 19, 1934, President Franklin Roosevelt approved the creation of the National Archives of the United States. The act stipulated that "all archives or records belonging to the Government of the United States (legislative, judicial, and other) shall be under the charge and superintendence of the Archivist." A National Archives Council was created to advise the Archivist on the categories of material to be transferred to the new institution, and included the Librarian of Congress was a member. The same act established a National Historical Publications Commission, chaired by the Archivist. The chief of the Manuscript Division of Library of Congress became one of the commission members.

Librarian of Congress Putnam disliked all suggestions that the documents would be moved to the National Archives, citing the executive order of President Roosevelt and the congressional appropriation for the Great Hall "Shrine" as the Library's authority for their possession. President Roosevelt and R.D.W. Conner, the president's selection as the first Archivist of the United States decided not to insist until after Putnam, who already had served as Librarian of Congress for 35 years, decided to retire. This did not happen until 1939, when poet and writer Archibald MacLeish became Librarian of Congress.

Next, however, World War II intervened. In December 1941, MacLeish sent the Declaration and Constitution to Fort Knox, Kentucky for safekeeping. On October 1, 1944, with the approval of the War Department and the Joint Chiefs of Staff, they went back on display at the Library. The new Archivist of the United States, Solon Buck, did not press for their return. In 1950, President Harry Truman approved the Federal Records Act, which placed virtually all national archival and records management authority in the Office of Administrator of General Services, which administered the National Archives. Nevertheless, on September 17, 1951, the Library of Congress hosted a reopening of its "permanent" encasement for the Declaration and Constitution, newly sealed in helium by the Bureau of Standards. But once again the cast of characters had changed and a new Archivist of the United States, Wayne Grover, found that in spite of the ceremony at the Library, a new Librarian of Congress, Luther H. Evans, agreed that the documents must to go to the National Archives. A political scientist who had served as the head of the WPA's Historical Records Survey, which was headquartered at the National Archives, before coming to the Library of Congress in 1939, Evans felt that the Federal Records Act had settled the matter. The problem was how to execute the transfer smoothly in the face of certain strong opposition from Evans's fellow senior managers at the Library.

In the end, Grover and Evans worked together secretly to obtain approval from President Truman and congressional leaders, particularly Senator Theodore Green of Rhode Island, the chairman of the Joint Committee on the Library. Next Evans asked the Joint Committee, at its meeting on April 30, 1952, to order him to transfer the documents, which it did unanimously. Only then did he inform his senior staff about the change. The National Archives began remodeling its Exhibition Hall to receive the documents.

In a ceremony at the Library of Congress on Saturday, December 13, 1952, Librarian Evans turned the Declaration and the Constitution over to the commanding general of the Air Force Headquarters Command. Twelve members of the Armed Forces Special Police carried the carefully-encased documents down the Library's steps where they were placed on mattresses in a Marine Corps armored personnel carrier. With a full military escort and to the accompaniment of two military bands, they paraded down Constitution Avenue to the National Archives Building and placed the documents in the custody of Archivist Grover. The formal enshrining ceremony at the National Archives on Monday, December 15, at which the Chief Justice of the United States presided, was equally impressive. A highlight was a "roll call of the states" in the order in which they ratified the Constitution or were admitted to the Union. In his remarks, President Truman noted that the Declaration and Constitution were now to be exhibited for the first time with the Bill of Rights, which had been transferred from the Department of State and put on display at the National Archives in 1938. Senator Green traced the history of the three documents and Librarian of Congress Evans and Archivist of the United States Grover unveiled the shrine. Finally, the Marine Corps Band played the *Star-Spangled Banner*, and President Truman was escorted from the hall, followed by the bearers of the flags from the 48 states.

On July 5, 2001, the Declaration, the Constitution, and the Bill of Rights, by now known collectively as the Charters of Freedom, were removed for conservation treatment while the National Archives Building was being renovated. On Constitution Day, September 17, 2003, the leaders of all three branches of the federal government gathered to rededicate the renovated National Archives Rotunda and unveil the newly re-encased Charters of Freedom.

The custody of presidential papers has been another area of "shared responsibility" between the Library of Congress and the National Archives, but it never engendered the emotions or controversy of the dispute over the founding documents. Since the administration of Herbert Hoover, presidents have been memorialized by library-museums that have preserved their papers and commemorated their achievements. These presidential libraries have been administered by the National Archives since 1940. However the Library of Congress is the nation's oldest and most comprehensive presidential library. While the recently built presidential libraries each hold the papers of a single chief executive, the Manuscript Division of the Library of Congress has in its custody the papers of 23 presidents.

The collection began shortly after the Thomas Jefferson Building opened in 1897 with the gift, from the descendants of Francis P. Blair, of the papers of Andrew Jackson. Soon thereafter, Librarian Putnam persuaded President Theodore Roosevelt to issue an executive order transferring to the Library the State Department's historical archive, which included the papers of George Washington, Thomas Jefferson, James Madison, and James Monroe. In later years, the Library assiduously acquired other presidential papers, obtaining some by purchase—the papers of James K. Polk and Andrew Johnson for example—and many more by gift, including those of William McKinley, Woodrow Wilson, and Calvin Coolidge, for example. For nearly 20 years, Librarian Putnam patiently solicited the donation of Abraham Lincoln's papers from Lincoln's son Robert Todd Lincoln. The collection was donated in 1919.

The pattern was broken by President Franklin D. Roosevelt. In December 1938, he announced that he planned to donate his papers, books, art objects, and mementos to the people of the United States and to preserve them in a library and museum to be built on his family estate at Hyde Park, N.Y. His papers would not go to the Library of Congress, but to the first special presidential library. National Archivist R.D.W. Conner knew about Roosevelt's plans; it appears that the Library of Congress did not. However, with Librarian Putnam on the verge of retirement, in June 1939 President Roosevelt nominated his successor, Archibald MacLeish, who took the oath of office in July 1940 and throughout his four years as Librarian remained a close Roosevelt advisor and occasional speech writer.

On August 16, 1957, President Eisenhower signed a bill that authorized the Presidential Papers Program at the Library. The new law enabled the Library to arrange, index, and microfilm the papers of the presidents in its collection to preserve them and to make them "more readily available for study and research."

Because of its focus on the records of the federal government, the National Archives is a more specialized institution than the Library of Congress. With the dispute over the custody of the founding documents well behind them and the system of modern presidential libraries clearly an executive and therefore a National Archives responsibility, the roles and relationship of the two organizations is well defined. Today the Library and the National Archives cooperate on specific projects where collection overlap or mutual interests have brought them together. For example, both were involved in the WPA Arts projects, which were initiated in the mid-1930s just as the National Archives was being created and did not end until the early 1940s. The bulk of the administrative records from government agencies most directly involved, such as the Agricultural Adjustment Agency (AAA), the Works Progress Administration (WPA), the Civilian Conservation Corps (CCC), the National Recovery Administration (NRA), and the National Youth Administration (NRA) are in the National Archives, many of them transferred from the Library of Congress. However both agencies have strong holdings of WPA arts project "products," such as photographs, folklore and social-ethnic studies, motion pictures, architectural drawings and surveys, posters, prints, paintings, maps, theatrical costume and set designs, music manuscripts, imprint inventories, unpublished manuscripts, transcripts, and research materials; historical records and archival surveys; and books and pamphlets. As interest in the WPA arts projects has increased in recent years, both agencies have cooperated—with other federal agencies—in making research collections and projects more readily available.

"See America, Visit Montana," a travel poster produced by the WPA Art Project in New York City for the U.S. Travel Bureau. Both the Library and the National Archives have strong holdings of WPA arts project products and cooperate with each other when the collections overlap, making research collections and projects more readily available.
LC/Prints and Photographs Division.
LC-USZC4-4241.

The Modern Archives Institute is another area of cooperation. Providing hands-on experience in basic archival principles and practices, the institute was started in 1945 as a joint project of The American

University, the National Archives, and the Maryland Hall of Records. The Library's Manuscript Division became a sponsoring organization in 1949. In 1977, the National Archives began administering the two-week institute; the Manuscript Division of the Library of Congress continues to be a principal program partner.

Cole, John Y. "The Nation's Reading Rooms," in *Washington, D.C.: The Smithsonian Book of the Nation's Capitol.* Washington, D.C.: Smithsonian Books, 1992. pp. 180–189.

Gustafson, Milton O. "The Empty Shrine: The Transfer of the Declaration of Independence and the Constitution to the National Archives," *The American Archivist* 39 (July 1976): 271–285.

AMERICAN LITERATURE AND THE LIBRARY OF CONGRESS: A PERSONAL PERSPECTIVE

by John C. Broderick

The story of the Library of Congress and American literature is one of collections, people, and programs, sometimes in creative collaboration, sometimes going their separate ways. (For this essay, "American literature" comprises original publications, literary manuscripts, correspondence, notebooks, etc. of the principal American poets, novelists, dramatists, and essayists, and background material necessary to full understanding of the writers' milieu.)

In some respects, the Library for decades neglected American literature as thoroughly as it was being neglected in the disdainful groves of academe. Until the 1940s, some important materials for study of American literature came into the Library, it is true, but almost surreptitiously, resulting in valuable holdings but without an overall plan for responsible growth. Nevertheless, one early survey of the nearly 6,000 titles of American fiction, 1774–1900, credits the Library with about half the known titles, including some 200 unique to the Library. These figures continue to increase.

In common with other subject fields, American literary books and pamphlets subject to copyright deposit requirements were regularly available for selection from 1870 onwards. For decades, however, books and pamphlets added to the general collections were subject to ordinary wear and tear. In recent times staff members and visiting scholars alike have found valuable and otherwise interesting publications in the general stacks, the worse for wear. To counteract an officially acknowledged weakness in American literature, Librarian of Congress Archibald MacLeish in 1943 directed the Rare Book Division to maintain a list of 27 living American authors (whom he named), whose deposited first editions should be automatically transferred to that division for maximum care. (The list subsequently grew to more than 500 names, no longer limited to American writers.) As with any program dependent on the accuracy of foresight, some dodos have been listed and some worthies overlooked. Nevertheless, the MacLeish initiative was a prerequisite to progress.

Private collectors who augment public collections (rather than disperse their treasures) frequently do so with books that are cared for to the utmost. Lessing J. Rosenwald's insistence that he wanted only books and manuscripts in a high state of excellence is singular only in his consistency in meeting his own standard. Subject collections, even if not of "Rosenwald quality," are often welcome complements to routinely acquired holdings.

The Library of Congress has hardly been lacking in such rare collections, acquired through gift or purchase. The Peter Force Collection of Americana, the G.V. Yudin Collection of Russian literature, and the Vollbehr Collection of incunabula, to name just three, all made the Library prominent—and, in some cases, preeminent—in their particular subject fields. But there were no comparable special collections of American literature in the early history of the Library of Congress—no Owen Aldis Collection, the seedbed of the Yale Collection of American Literature, no brothers Berg, whose literary collection is one of the treasures of the New York Public Library, no C. Waller Barrett Collection (University of Virginia), all the more impressive because formed so recently. The only major American writers represented by special collections in the Library before World War II were Benjamin Franklin, Walt Whitman, and Henry James. Omitted from consideration are such statesman-authors as Thomas Jefferson, Abraham Lincoln, Ulysses S. Grant, Theodore Roosevelt, and Woodrow Wilson, all represented by rich resources in the Library, because their public writings, however admirable a contribution to our cultural history, are not belles-lettres.

A signed and dated photograph from 1890 of Walt Whitman, who was, according to John C. Broderick, one of the few major American writers represented in the Library before World War II.

LC/Prints and Photographs Division. LC-USZ62-115977.

The Franklin collection, including publications and manuscripts, originating in an 1882 purchase from Henry Stevens, was greatly augmented by the transfer of Franklin papers from the Department of State authorized in 1903. The 200 titles in the Stevens purchase had grown to some 800 in the Rare Book Division. Walt Whitman's manuscripts—drafts, notebooks, and correspondence—were the gift of Thomas Harned in 1918. These were supplemented by a comprehensive collection of Whitman publications formed by Carolyn Wells Houghton and bequeathed to the Library in 1922. The Henry James collection of his publications came as the bequest of Mrs. Clarence Jones also in 1922.

The Benjamin Franklin Collection, including papers and manuscripts, originated in an 1882 purchase from Henry Stevens, and was greatly augmented in 1903 by the transfer of the Franklin papers from the Department of State.
LC/Prints and Photographs Division. LC-USZ62-90398.

Until the acquisition of the Feinberg Whitman collection in 1969, therefore, the Library seemed largely constrained to constructing, brick by brick, its edifice of research materials for the study of American literature. The MacLeish initiative in behalf of the rare book collection was a start. As for manuscripts, the build-up in American literature followed David C. Mearns's assumption of the position of chief of the Manuscript Division in 1951. A practicing historian, Mearns recognized the need to broaden the Library's manuscript holdings beyond the traditional strengths of American political, military, and diplomatic history. There was soon, therefore, renewed emphasis on American cultural history, especially literary history and criticism, as well as the history of science and the arts. In the mid-1950s, letters of solicitation were systematically sent to more than 300 achievers in all fields of American life, including literary figures. This shotgun approach yielded some significant personal archives, though usually after an interval of years or even decades.

Purely historical collections continued to be the bread and butter of the Library's Manuscript Division, but a few writers (Owen Wister, Kenneth and Elizabeth Madox Roberts, MacKinlay Kantor, James A. Michener) were beginning to make their presence known. All of those named, of course, were rather historically-minded novelists. In the latter stages of the manuscript acquisition "push" of the 1950s, the Library benefited from the advice and counsel on literary matters offered by Randall Jarrell, its Consultant in Poetry, 1956–1958.

The Consultant in Poetry and the Whittall Series

The Consultantship in Poetry (originally called the Chair of Poetry in English) had been created in 1936 through an endowment fund donated by Archer M. Huntington. After an initial shakeout period, when the first incumbent, Joseph Auslander, held the position (1937–1941), the Consultanship became a one- or two-year appointment, except that Robert Pinsky agreed to serve a third term to take part in commemoration of the Library's bicentennial in the year 2000. Since Auslander, with the exception of Randall Jarrell, few Consultants have interested themselves in routine improvement of the Library's American literature holdings. With the financial backing of Mrs. Gertrude Clark Whittall, Auslander succeeded in adding to the Library's collections literary books and manuscripts, mostly British, but including manuscripts of Mrs. Whittall's favorite poet, Edwin

In the latter stages of the manuscript acquisition "push" of the 1950s, the Library benefited from the advice and counsel offered by its Consultant in Poetry, Randall Jarrell (right), here in the poetry office with Delmore Schwartz in 1958.
LC/Prints and Photographs Division. LC-USP6-3359-C.

Arlington Robinson. Before Auslander left the Library in 1943, he had the title of "Gift Officer." Consultants undertook some special assignments when asked, of course. Howard Nemerov, for example, during his year as Consultant, helped finalize a general purpose brochure (1964) designed to acquaint writers with the benefits of placing literary manuscripts and personal papers in the Library. (Nemerov also served as Poet Laureate, 1988–1989, only the second former Consultant to do so, the other being Robert Penn Warren.)

One acquisition initiative, however, interested the Consultant. Beginning in the 1940s, spearheaded by Allen Tate (1943–1944), most Consultant have been assiduous in building the collection of recordings of poets reading their own work within the confines of the Library's Recording Laboratory. The Archive of Recorded Poetry and Literature, housed in the Music Division, also includes recordings of programs of readings, lectures, and dramatic performances presented at the Library, a series which began in earnest in 1951 when Mrs. Whittall established a series of three funds (subsequently merged) to support a series of literary programs, as she had also done for the music program.

The Whittall series was to become a principal focus among official activities of the Consultant in Poetry, but its beginnings were stormy indeed. The Consultant at the time the programs began was Conrad Aiken (1950–1952). Aiken's contempt for Mrs. Whittall's taste in poetry was exceeded only by that for Library officials responsible for administrative oversight for the Poetry Office and the Consultant. Mrs. Whittall (then 84), he referred to as a "millionaire nonagenarian female." Of the "top brass of the bureaucracy" he wrote a friend: "None of them knows *anything* about literature, none of them have the least notion of a sensitive regard for it or pride in it." What was needed, obviously, was an administrator whom the poets could respect but one who could deal with the preferences of a most generous but opinionated donor.

That need was met by the appointment of Roy P. Basler in 1952. Basler was to take on increasingly important administrative responsibilities in the Library, especially when director of the Reference Department, 1958–1968, but for American literature his major contribution was his 22-year direction of the literary programs. (Basler reflected on his experiences in *The Muse and the Librarian*, 1974.) Best known as editor of the writings of Abraham Lincoln, Basler held the doctorate in English, had taught and written widely on literature, and was a writer of poetry himself.

The ever-expanding Whittall series has brought almost all contemporary American writers of note to the Library for readings or lectures, from Robert Bly in robe, chains, and stocking feet to Allen Ginsberg in a three-piece suit! Some writers (Denise Levertov) declined invitations on principle during the war in Vietnam, but most eventually joined the distinguished roster of readers. Early programs in the series, reflecting Mrs. Whittall's preferences, disproportionately featured silver-tongued actors and actresses reading poetry of the past. Gradually authors reading their own work displaced the likes of Claude Rains, Charles Laughton, Vincent Price, and—for 20 consecutive years—Arnold Moss. Burgess Meredith, who read at the Library five times himself, when told of Moss's string, pondered a moment, then said, "I wouldn't cast Arnold Moss for a single role." When I succeeded Basler's stewardship of the programs, 1974–1988, I retired Moss and included local poets (contrary to Basler's practice), but otherwise continued the series along familiar lines. The character of the series from year to year depended on particular recommendations by the incumbent Consultants as well.

The three-day National Poetry Festival, October 22–24, 1962, planned by Basler and Consultant Louis Untermeyer and funded by the Bollingen Foundation was the Library's first great literary extravaganza, occasioned by the 50th anniversary of *Poetry* magazine. The gathering, though shadowed by the Cuban missile crisis, went on as planned and featured readings by 29 American poets, including 13 who had been or were to become Consultants in Poetry. One entire evening was devoted to Robert Frost, then 88 and with barely three months left in his long life. Frost read 18 of his own poems and three by

Robert Frost, one of the many poets participating in the three-day National Poetry Festival in 1962, occasioned by the 50th anniversary of Poetry *magazine. One entire evening was devoted to Frost, who was 88. He read 18 of his own poems and a few by others. The readings were interspersed with his extensive autobiographical and self-critical commentary.*

LC/Prints and Photographs Division.

other writers, the readings interspersed with his extensive autobiographical and self-critical commentary. Frost's first Coolidge Auditorium program was in 1941; he served as Consultant in Poetry from 1958–1959), and this was to be his 10th and last appearance. Of 11 lectures during the Festival, Jarrell's "Fifty Years of American Poetry" was the tour de force.

Two comparable gatherings took place after Basler's retirement in 1974. They were the two Consultants' Reunions (1978, 1987), which attracted overflow audiences for the poetry readings. The 1987 gathering was also a three-day affair, March 29–31, the first evening arranged jointly with the National Endowment for the Arts and celebrating the appointment of Robert Penn Warren as the first Poet Laureate Consultant in Poetry. The next two evenings featured readings by the Consultants themselves, to great acclaim.

The Poet Laureate

Despite the 1987 "celebration" of the first Poet Laureate, it was common knowledge that the Library for years had opposed the creation of the laureateship as originally proposed: a presidential appointment without regard to the existence of the Library's Consultantship. However, by 1985 the principal advocate, the late Senator Spark Matsunaga of Hawaii, was willing to accept: 1) appointment by the Librarian of Congress, and 2) unifying the laureateship with the consultantship. Even so, Librarian of Congress Daniel J. Boorstin went down swinging, in vain voicing the Library's objections to the very end. As foreseen, the laureateship has overshadowed the traditional position of Consultant in Poetry. Senator Matsunaga's vision, however, has been thoroughly validated. And the laureates themselves have even warmed to the idea.

The Collections (Manuscripts)

One might expect the Library's close involvement with so many American writers over the past half-century to have led to the acquisition of literary manuscripts and personal papers of a goodly number, but the facts are otherwise. Consultants, laureates and Whittall readers usually have had established institutional loyalties or commitments elsewhere before their association with the Library. Hence major manuscript collections of contemporary poets are few in number: those of Archibald MacLeish, Muriel Rukeyser, Edna St. Vincent Millay, Merrill Moore, Louis Simpson, and a few others. Louis Untermeyer's gift of his correspondence with Frost, along with some Library-related manuscripts, deserves mention. Some Whittall series theatrical performers have also placed their papers in the Library, led by Hume Cronyn and Jessica Tandy, Margaret Webster, and Lillian Gish.

Through the years, many consultants in poetry had established institutional loyalties or commitments elsewhere before their association with the Library. As a result, the Library's post-World War II manuscript collections of contemporary poets are few in number. Edna St. Vincent Millay, seen here in a 1940 photograph, is one of the exceptions. LC/Prints and Photographs Division. New York World-Telegram and the Sun Newspaper Collection. LC-USZ62-116346.

Several American novelists have also appeared in the Whittall series, but invariably after, not before they had donated their literary manuscripts to the Library. Yet few institutions rival the Library of Congress in holdings of manuscripts of important writers of fiction since World War II. Many of these gifts came in a five-year period in the 1960s, ending in 1969, when changes in the tax laws made such gifts monetarily almost worthless as charitable tax deductions. Since I represented the Library in personal negotiations for most of these gifts (and deposits), the mere recital of the familiar names is a source of nostalgic pleasure for me: John Barth, Truman Capote,

Another serious drawback for acquisitions was a change in the tax law in 1969, making gifts of papers monetarily almost worthless. Several major collections, however were acquired, among them, those of John Barth, Truman Capote, Marcia Davenport, and Ralph Ellison (shown here in 1966). Ellison was first approached in 1964, and ultimately, the materials were received posthumously. LC/Prints and Photographs Division. New York World-Telegram and the Sun Newspaper Collection. LC-USZ62-12629.

Marcia Davenport, Ralph Ellison (approached first in 1964, material received posthumously), Bernard Malamud, Vladimir Nabokov (an earlier acquisition), Philip Roth, William Styron, and John Updike. Some (but not all) of these writers discontinued their gifts to the Library after 1969.

Then there are "the ones that got away," a staple of every fishing story. The biggest names and the closest to being landed are Ernest Hemingway and Katherine Ann Porter. Miss Porter, in particular, was in the net when she jumped out, to great dismay and disappointment within the Library. The Hemingway decision was also hard to take. David Mearns wrote Mrs. Hemingway: "We have buried our hopes with muffled drums."

Unique to the Library is the collection of Unpublished Dramas, deposited for copyright, usually in typescript form, and given the dynamic way in which plays are revised before performance, of great interest when the work is that of a major playwright. They might even be called the equivalent of Shakespearean quartos. The Manuscript Division initially sought the transfer of particular titles to add to existing collections, such as that of Maxwell Anderson or Clare Boothe Luce. In the late 1980s, however, a systematic program of wholesale transfer of the dramas began. Although the bulk of the collection cannot be regarded as "literature," however broadly construed, there are gems imbedded in the dross, and the dross itself, taken as a whole, is a unique measure of the American mind.

Despite the Library's successes in gathering important materials for the study of twentieth-century American literature, its manuscript holdings for the classic American writers of the nineteenth century were scattered and incidental: an Emerson journal here, a Thoreau commonplace book there, a few poems of Emily Dickinson. The main repositories for such writers as these being already determined, no realistic prospects were in view for a large cache of materials of this kind. The determined researcher could find some letters and other manuscripts for just about every prominent American writer of the past, but no preeminent collection—except for Whitman.

For these reasons, acquisition of the Charles E. Feinberg-Walt Whitman Collection assumed an importance hard to overestimate, because of the volume and quality of the collection and the nature of its subject, America's greatest poet. (When the Chilean poet Pablo Neruda, Nobel laureate to be, visited the Library in 1966, his only mission was to see hand-written manuscripts of Whitman. Once he had seen two or three, he quickly departed.) As it turned out, acquisition of the Feinberg Collection, like the Battle of Waterloo, was "a near-run thing." Some balked at the price tag: one million dollars, payable over a 10-year period. David Mearns remembered when the collection could have been had for about one-third that price. The Congressional Joint Committee on the Library, asked to support the Library's purchase, expressed a "profound hope" that "this worthy object" be attained, but said nothing about special funds to achieve "the worthy object." The Library was able to meet the first few installments largely though the generosity of Arthur Houghton and Mrs. Charles Engelhard. By the fourth installment, matters were critical. That installment was met partially by emptying some small gift funds appropriate for the purpose, including (ironically) a small Mearns fund. After one allowed deferral, acquisition funds were finally earmarked for the purchase, completed in 1979. Henceforth no serious scholar can complete research on Whitman without recourse to the Library of Congress collection.

When the Chilean poet Pablo Neruda visited the Library in 1966, the future Nobel laureate's only mission was to see handwritten manuscripts of Whitman. The acquisition of the Feinberg Collection cost one million dollars and finally was completed after some difficulties in 1979. The multiple copies of Whitman publications in the Feinberg and the Carolyn Wells Houghton collections, give the Library the kind of bibliographic riches for a major writer dear to the heart of bibliophiles and textural scholars.
LC/Prints and Photographs Division. LC-USZ62-48982.

The Collections (Rare Books)

Soon after his appointment as curator of rare books in 1940, Arthur Houghton expressed the desirability of building up in the Library of Congress the "greatest" collection of American literature and American history. Soon thereafter, an internal report acknowledged that the American literature collection was "weak in relation to the collections of American historical material."

The past half-century has seen numerous steps toward righting that balance, beginning with MacLeish's 1943 directive effecting automatic transfers of selected copyright deposits by certain authors. Multiple copies of publications by Whitman in the Feinberg collection, added to those in the Carolyn

Wells Houghton collection, give the Library for a major writer the kind of bibliographic redundancy dear to the hearts of bibliophiles and textual scholars. The Library has been able to fill some gaps in the holdings of earlier twentieth century American writers (Faulkner, Hemingway, Fitzgerald, etc.) through the gifts of Herman Finkelsein and others and the occasional receipt of a special run of publications by a single author, such as those of the Kentucky regionalist Jesse Stuart, the gift of the late Register of Copyrights, David Ladd. An archival set of the Armed Services Editions, published for the American servicemen and women, 1943–1947, though not limited to American writers or to literature, provides a record of a major cultural initiative affecting American reading habits. More than 122 million books were distributed to the armed forces through this program. Another archival set of similar interest is the Dell paperback series, the twentieth-century counterpart to the division's Dime Novel collection for the nineteenth.

Two nineteenth-century writers for whom special strengths have been developed are Washington Irving and Mark Twain, Irving through gifts by Leonard Keebler, and Twain through collections of Roy J. Friedman and Frances R. Friedman. The Rare Book and Special Collections Division also holds records and publications of the Mark Twain Society. Even the Rosenwald Collection contains a surprising segment, the first and/or early editions of Stephen Crane, one of Mr. Rosenwald's earliest collecting interests.

Some other holdings useful to studying aspects of American literature are the fine printing collection in the Rare Book and Special Collections Division and, in the Manuscript Division, the papers/records of publishers (B. W. Huebsch, Kenneth McCormick), literary agents (Luc Kroll), and writers' retreats (MacDowell Colony).

Space limitations prevent more than a passing reference to a major additional asset: the Library's comprehensive general collections of books, pamphlets, newspapers, and periodicals, which form an essential supplement to the more specialized materials discussed earlier.

Entering the twenty-first century, the Library holdings not only in general materials, but an impressive body of literary manuscripts and original publications of some of the principal voices of the twentieth century and earlier, are more than adequate to advanced study of American literature. That study, once an academic stepchild, is now one of the leading disciplines in the humanities—and not only in the United States. Materials gathered by the Library of Congress and other research libraries are essential components supporting continued academic research, which in turn validates the Library's efforts.

The nineteenth-century writer Mark Twain, for whose work special strengths have been developed through the acquisition of the collections of Roy J. Friedman and Frances R. Friedman. The Rare Book and Special Collections Division also holds the records and publications of the Mark Twain Society.
LC/Prints and Photographs Division. LC-USZ62-112728.

Perhaps the Library of Congress has not yet achieved for American literature the status sought by Arthur Houghton in 1940 (the "greatest "collection), but through its procedures, its people, and its programs, it is working on it.

Broderick, John C. "The Greatest Whitman Collector and the Greatest Whitman Collection," *The Quarterly Journal of the Library of Congress* 27 (April 1970): 109–128, 170–176.

________. "The Poet Laureate of the United States," *Dictionary of Literary Biography Yearbook*: 196 (Gale, 1987): 30–35.

Basler, Roy P. *The Muse and the Librarian*. Westport, Conn.: Greenwood Press, 1974.

THE LIBRARY OF CONGRESS IN FICTION AND FILM

by Abby L. Yochelson

"Life in a library is supposed to be quiet, reflective, helpful—not bloody or kinky." (Margaret Truman, *Murder at the Library of Congress*, 1999). Although most people would view libraries in such a fashion, the Library of Congress as depicted in the creative world of fiction and film often is a dangerous place to work or visit, with corpses falling left and right, bombs exploding, journalists assaulted, spies and drug runners passing information, and even a Bengal tiger prowling in the ruins in a distant future.

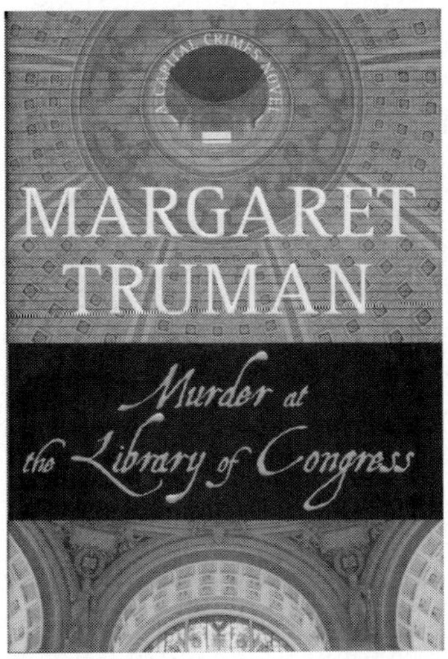

"Murder at the Library of Congress" (1999), is one of Margaret Truman's murder mysteries set in and around Washington, D.C.'s governmental and cultural institutions. The victim is the Library's most prominent Hispanic scholar, and as the plot unfolds the reader learns a great deal about the Library and quite a bit about its own folkways and legends
Photograph: Rob Sokol. LC/General Collections.

On a more positive note, the Library of Congress also is a place, causing several fictional characters to aspire to work at the Library or to improve their minds. With its grandiose and gorgeous architecture, it is a Mecca for tourists and a fine venue for hosting receptions and parties. The Library is part of official Washington, standing alongside the United States Capitol and symbolizing all that the capital and the federal government represents. The Library of Congress is even a place to undertake research—perhaps the one place to get the essential answer to solve a mystery, find treasure, learn of humankind's past, or stave off alien invasion.

Most of the books featuring the Library are of the mystery or thriller genre with science fiction providing a significant body of work. Although the Library of Congress figures in the story line of only a few movies, Hollywood has more often used the Library, especially the Jefferson Building, when "the official Washington shot" is required.

"The official Washington shot" is usually a long eastward look up the Mall, displaying the Capitol Building with the Library behind it; or an overhead shot of Washington monuments and government buildings. Such footage appears in *Night of the Living Dead* (Image Ten, 1968), *Live Wire* (New Line Cinema, 1992), *The Pelican Brief* (Warner Brothers, 1993), *In the Line of Fire* (Columbia Pictures, 1993), and *GI Jane* (Buena Vista Pictures, 1997). *In the Line of Fire* is the most vivid of these, showing views of the Library in the course of an extended chase and fight across neighboring roofs by a Secret Serviceman (Clint Eastwood) and a presidential stalker. Occasionally the Library has been disguised as another building, as in *The Seduction of Joe Tynan* (Universal Pictures, 1979), in which Senator Joe Tynan (Alan Alda) is shown striding down a hallway supposedly in the U.S. Capitol but which in reality is one of the ornate corridors in the Jefferson Building.

The Neptune Fountain gracing the First Street side of the Jefferson Building appears in two films. *Filial Love* (American Éclair, Universal Films Manufacturing Company, 1912), an early silent film shows a young boy disembarking at Union Station and stopping at the fountain to freshen up before he asks for President Taft at the Capitol and is directed to the White House. In the first version of *Born Yesterday* (Columbia Pictures, 1951), Billie Dawn (Judy Holliday) and Paul Verrall (William Holden) purchase ice cream bars from a vendor in front of the fountain and enjoy them on Neptune Plaza after visiting the Library.

As a working institution, the Library of Congress appears in *Washington Merry-Go-Round* (Columbia Pictures, 1932) both versions of *Born Yesterday* (1951 and Hollywood Pictures/Buena Vista, 1993), *The Thief* (United Artists, 1952), *All the President's Men* (Warner Brothers, 1976), *Wag the Dog* (New Line Cinema, 1997), and *Battlefield Earth: A Saga of the Year 3000* (Morgan Creek Films/Warner Brothers, 2000). Perhaps the most famous scene occurs in *All the President's Men*, when *Washington*

Post reporters Bob Woodward and Carl Bernstein follow up a tip that Howard Hunt requested material on Senator Ted Kennedy at the White House Library and the Library of Congress. Stonewalled at the White House, they request call slips for White House requests at the Library but are refused because such requests are confidential. Ultimately they sit down in the Main Reading Room, where an attendant dumps all the call slips for a year in massive stacks on their desks. As they plow through them, the camera recedes, showing the expanse of the circular Reading Room, ultimately from the top of the dome, where the people become distant specks. The 1951 version of *Born Yesterday* has Billie Dawn reading the Gettysburg Address in the Great Hall, then viewing the Constitution, Declaration of Independence, and Bill of Rights. In the 1993 remake, with Melanie Griffith and Don Johnson, the Main Reading Room is shown instead, as Billie dons glasses for the first time to read de Tocqueville's *Democracy in America*; becomes confused by the vocabulary and is directed to an unabridged dictionary. Her first apartment, she exclaims, was smaller than that book.

Judy Holliday and William Holden on the steps of the Thomas Jefferson Building while shooting the 1950 film "Born Yesterday." Interior scenes included the display of the U.S. Constitution and Declaration of Independence, which were at that time still on view in the Great Hall.
Photograph: Columbia Picture Corporation. LC Archives.

The Library's catalog lists only one book under the subject "Library of Congress—fiction." It is Margaret Truman's *Murder at the Library of Congress*, one in her series of murder mysteries set in and around Washington, D.C.'s governmental and cultural institutions. The novel describes much of the Library, from the Librarian's Office to Public Affairs, to the Hispanic and Manuscript Divisions, the Rare Book Reading Room, the Main Reading Room, and the stacks, in pursuit of rumored diaries relating to Christopher Columbus's voyage and clues to the murder of a noted scholar employed by the Hispanic Division.

Charles Goodrum, a longtime employee of the Library of Congress, wrote four mysteries: *Dewey Decimated* (1977), *Carnage of the Realm* (1979), *Best Cellar* (1987), and *A Slip of the Tong* (1992). The books are set in the fictional Werner Bok Library located on the Mall between the National Gallery of Art and the National Museum of Natural History. Although most readers have assumed that the site is really the Library of Congress, Goodrum himself has described the Werner Bok as bits and pieces of many libraries including the Folger Library, Boston Public Library, the Huntington Library, the Pierpont Morgan Library and the Library of Congress. Much of the description, nevertheless, is of architectural elements in the Library of Congress. Some items mentioned as belonging to the Werner Bok collections are unique to the Library of Congress, as are references to such Library colloquialisms as "Mahogany Row," the site of early executive offices. In all of Goodrum's books, characters from the Werner Bok climb Capitol Hill to conduct research at the Library or consult with colleagues. Of the four, *Best Cellar* relates most directly to the Library: its plot revolves around the notion that the books in the original Library of Congress were not destroyed when the Capitol was burned by the British in 1814 but were taken to a safe place. The intention was to hide the books away so that Thomas Jefferson, then financially embarrassed, could sell his library to Congress—a plot quite foreign to the generally accepted view of Jefferson as the Library's patron saint. Readers looking for more details about the Library itself will find in *A Slip of the Tong* material about inventorying and processing the Asian collections and about Houdini's magic tricks, as taught by experts in the Rare Book and Special Collections Division.

Clearly the Library's labyrinthine passages and stacks have stimulated novelists' imaginations. For example, in R. B. Dominic's Murder, *Sunny Side Up* (1968) one character notes that there are "Hundreds of ways to get from one place to another. All sorts of bays to lurk in." Another at one point declares that "That Mr. Rivers in the Semantics Division said once there were corners in this pile where a body could lie undisturbed for months." Moreover, the Library offers unusual weapons and hiding places. The nozzle on a fire hose in the stacks is used for the first murder in Francis Bonnamy's *Dead Reckoning* (1943). In *Murder at the Library of Congress* the victim is hit on the head with weights typically used by conservation and preservation experts to hold down curled pages or maps; the weight is Linotype lead melted into bricks and covered with cloth. At the Werner Bok Library, a murdered employee's head is wedged against a thin steel beam from the elevator shaft in the stacks, intended to appear as an accident. A gun is used for the Main Reading Room murder in *Murder, Sunny Side Up*, and the murderer makes use of one of the many doorways into the stacks to escape and stash his weapon. Even lacking murder, authors have imagined the Library as a dangerous place. In Charles McCarry's *Shelley's Heart* (1995), a journalist is assaulted in the men's room so that his press credentials can be used by an assassin at a press conference on inauguration day. The Library also becomes a place for passing on information rather than gathering it. In *The Thief* (1952), an atomic physicist films top secret Atomic Energy Commission documents and uses the Library to pass the films to his contact. In three different scenes he enters the Jefferson Building through the First Street entrance, walks through the Great Hall, and enters the Main Reading Room. After pausing at the Central Desk and looking for the contact, star Ray Milland walks to an alcove, browses the shelves, pulls a book from the American history section and places the film container behind it. The contact immediately pulls the book and finds the film. For the second drop, Milland uses the card catalog in the Main Reading Room, opens a drawer and places the film in the front. As he walks away, another researcher nearly opens the same drawer before the contact is able to retrieve the film. In the last scene, Milland enters the Great Hall, desperate to make contact because the network has been discovered. Watching from the balcony above and then the Visitors' Gallery, the contact sees that Milland is being followed and refuses to communicate.

In the Ellery Queen short story "Mystery at the Library of Congress," a drug ring uses the Main Reading Room to pass information about contacts. Desk attendant Norma Shuffing brings preselected books to reader Balcolm. From their titles—all including the word "burning"—, he guesses the identity of the contact—a redheaded reader seated nearby who will meet him the next day. Ellery Queen subsequently solves the riddle of the clue. In David Morrell's *Assumed Identity* (1993), an individual tying a shoe on the steps of the Jefferson Building drops a small envelope. This is retrieved by a character named Buchanan, who enters the building and reads the instructions in a stall in the men's room. He then uses a directory in the Library's reference collection to locate the place of his next contact.

The beauty of the Jefferson Building has inspired novelists for many years. In Francis Parkinson Keyes's *Queen Anne's Lace* (1930), the admiration comes from a honeymooning couple visiting Washington in the late nineteenth century. In *Pop Goes the Weasel* (1999), James Patterson's Detective Alex Cross stops during his investigation of serial killings (including the murder of a Congressional Research Service employee) to look at the newly renovated Main Reading Room with its "amazing dome," while J. R. Salamanca's *A Sea Change* (1969) features references to the wall inscriptions and quotations, the sculpture, and even the odor. Martha Cooley, in *The Archivist* (1998) pays tribute to "vaulted ceilings and marble floors, its magnificent circular reading room fitted with mahogany benches, rows of soft reading lamps, and heavy brass-trimmed doors that kept out all noise." In Barbara Michael's *Smoke and Mirrors* (1989), two senate election campaign staff members arrive to consult old newspapers. One points out to the other the "squatty green cupola" and "impressive" décor of the Jefferson Building, and contrasts the Madison Building's "stark cube of pale-gray marble, polished till it glistened." But in *Dead Reckoning*, one character simply finds the Library depressing, criticizing the architecture as "a cross between the Baths of Diocletian and the Old Union Station."

In both fiction and reality, the Library is a sumptuous social venue. Simultaneous receptions in the Madison and Jefferson Buildings for a G7 summit meeting provide an opportunity for a diversionary bomb and the theft of the Gutenberg Bible in Michael Bowen's *Corruptly Procured* (1994). Lawyer Janet Pete in Tony Hillerman's *The Fallen Man* (1996) attends a dinner and concert featuring fifteenth-century music played on the Library's period instruments. In James McCourt's *Delancey's Way* (2000), the Great Hall is the setting for a Venetian masked ball complete with life-size cardboard effigies of all the presidents and First Ladies, and guests view fireworks from the Congressional Page School in the Jefferson Building Attic.

Characters whose line of work is bookish often express ambitions to work at the Library. In Robert Hellenga's *The Sixteen Pleasures* (1994), Newberry Library book conservator Margot imagines a ghostly double who went to Harvard, apprenticed in London, was profiled in a Dewar's whiskey ad and went on to become the first woman head of the conservation department at the Library. In Cooley's *The Archivist*, a young man aspires to become an archivist following a college graduation trip to Washington, where he visits the Library. Later, however, he abandons the idea, preferring the literary archives of "an elite academic setting." Dr. Michael Pritchard in A Sea Change, however, realizes his ambition to work at the Library when he becomes a stack assistant in the Manuscript Division. Attending George Washington University's evening classes, he obtains a doctorate in classics and is eventually promoted to a high-graded position. *Murder at the Library of Congress* features an enthusiastic intern, Sue Gomera, who works in the Main Reading Room and catalogs Cuban newspapers in the Hispanic Division while studying to become a librarian. A lucrative position is not her objective; instead, like many aspiring librarians, she finds "something special about bringing people and books together," and hopes some day to become Librarian of Congress.

Described as "the aristocrats of their profession," in *Murder, Sunny Side Up*, librarians on the Library's staff are generally favorably depicted. Other staff members, particularly those who assist with retrieving materials, are often portrayed as knowledgeable and helpful, although Dominic's gently humorous narrative reveals that youthful deck attendants occasionally play poker in the stacks. He also deftly describes the ambition of librarians who dream of greatness—"of confounding the world with an improved decimal system" and the passion for order among staff behind the scenes who muse that "if the Library did not have to cope with tourists and people who want to use books, it would be the perfect place to work." Other novelists have presented less favorable views. In Amanda Cross's *The James Joyce Murder* (1967), the staff besiege the discoverer of a James Joyce manuscript, becoming perhaps a trifle overeager to acquire the treasure. Frank Odenkirk, the murdered Congressional Research Service employee in *Pop Goes the Weasel* is described as haughty, and murder victim Michele Paul in *Murder at the Library of Congress*, disliked for his arrogance and rudeness, is discovered to be selling material to a private collector and aiding a scheme to falsify valuations of items donated to the Library. The head of the Manuscript Division is a stalker who makes obscene phone calls to a library intern, while the upper administration of the Library is rather too obliging to an important donor. There are also some stereotypical characters. The head of the Rare Book Division in Oliver Bleeck's *No Questions Asked* (1976), encountered in the course of investigating the theft of Pliny's *Historia Naturalis*, is described as extremely polite and helpful, but he "spoke a kind of mandarin English touched up with plenty of commas and semicolons," and "parted his hair in the middle and wore a bow tie." Miss Fly, a map librarian in *Dead Reckoning*, is spinsterish, and so inefficient, gossiping, and flirtatious that the author apologizes for her fictional presence, stating that the Map Division is "efficient and distinguished" and "with nothing misfiled."

Both *Murder at the Library of Congress* and *Murder, Sunny Side Up* provide lengthy statistical descriptions of the institution and its collections, and numerous individual items and collections appear in other books. *No Questions Asked* mentions the Library's pornography collection: a taxi driver comments that the Library has "the world's biggest collection of dirty books" but will allow only "Congressmen or government big shots" to borrow them. In James Grady's thriller *Six Days of the Condor* (1974), filmed as *Three Days of the Condor* (Paramount, 1975), the Central Intelligence Agency uses a front called the American Literary Historical Society. Its task is to keep track of all espionage and related acts recorded in literature; its staff reads spy thrillers and murder mysteries and for that reason is relocated "conveniently close to the Library of Congress." *Dead Reckoning* includes research in the Library's map collection for clues to buried pirate treasure. Japanese antiques specialist Rei Shimura, a character in Sujata Massey's *The Bride's Kimono* (2001) locates in the Asian Division a diary written in nineteenth-century Japan, while archaeologists and amateur detectives Elsie Mae Hunt and Tim Mulligan in Aaron Marc Stein's *Death Takes a Paying Guest* (1947) examine manuscripts on Ecuadorean pre-Columbian sites in the Library. In Richard Timothy Conroy's *India Exhibition: A Mystery at the Smithsonian* (1992) a State Department employee is assigned to the Smithsonian to work on an exhibition about an Indian independence leader. He consults the Library of Congress for material but fearing that he would find so much, he abandons the quest. Later forced to take it up again, he discovers, as many researchers have, the necessity for broadening or narrowing the search depending upon his objective.

The Library's vast music collections have appeared in at least one book and one film. A serviceman in Claudia Crawford's *Bliss* (1994) discovers on returning home from the South Pacific that his mother has given away his record collection, including discs by Burl Ives, Pete Seeger, and Woody Guthrie. Years later, the family discovers that the Library has reissued the old 78 rpm recordings in a four-volume album. *Wag the Dog* features the creation of a mythical war in Albania in order to divert attention from a presidential scandal two weeks before an election. Dustin Hoffman, as a Hollywood producer, has a folk song written by Willy Nelson, "Good Old Shoe" recorded on a fake album that he plans to plant and unearth from the Library's collections for the publicity campaign.

The congressional connection appears in several books and films. R. B. Dominic's *Murder, Sunny Side Up* (1968) revolves around a congressman's involvement in hearings for Ova-Cote, a new egg preservation technique. When the chair of the congressional committee is murdered during a hearing, the witnesses and staff undertake additional research in the Library, and a tour is arranged for a group of constituents. Dominic is therefore able to describe the elegant and generally empty Members Reading Room and the work of the Congressional Research Service: "great experts on housing, on treasury practice, on foreign trade, on Russian rocketry" and all other subjects of interest to Congress. In this telling, staff members have "raised the practice of aiding and comforting congressmen to a fine art." In *Murder at the Library of Congress*, Senator Richard Menendez, a strong Library supporter, is asked to raise support for a special purchase and becomes furious when he is not immediately informed of a brewing scandal at the Library. In the film *Washington Merry-Go-Round*, a newly elected member is asked to support a bill, but after researching it at the Library, he discovers it is fraudulent—intended to honor a man who stole land from Native Americans. Jeffrey Archer's *Shall We Tell the President* (1977) tells the story of the research of Special FBI Agent Marc Andrews, who searches senators' schedules to discover which of them plans to assassinate the newly elected president, and Michael Bowen's *Washington Deceased* (1990) sends a senator's daughter to the Library to do essential research to clear her father, who has been jailed for bribery.

Several works of science fiction feature a future Library of Congress. Often in a world destroyed by overpopulation, environmental devastation, totalitarian control, or alien invaders, a ruined Library provides desperately needed information or the Library remains intact as the only source of knowledge. The devastated Library appears in the film *Battlefield Earth: Saga of the Year 3000* (Morgan Creed Films/Warner Brothers, 2000), where the one remaining literate human being, Johnny, rallies others to fly to Washington, D.C., to search successfully in the abandoned collections for the secret of radioactivity and its power to destroy the ruling Psychlos—ultimately saving the earth and humanity. In David H. Keller's short story "Biological Experiment" (1928), the world of 3928 has sterilized humans; most are illiterate, and thus the Library exists only as a closed repository of books. When a night watchman steals 10 books from the Library, he precipitates a furor, which ends only with the discovery that the Librarian has engineered the plot in an effort to save the human race. *The Puppet Masters* (1951), by Robert Heinlein, finds the America of 2007 under attack from another planet, but the Library's comprehensive historical collections provide the key to defense. The Library of this period, in Heinlein's imagination, is open 24 hours, contains private study rooms, and provides all materials on film.

William F. Nolan and George Clayton Johnson's *Logan's Run* (1967) is set in 2072, an "ideal" world in which everyone's needs are fully met but no one is permitted to live past 30. A hunter of people who hide from their mandated deaths, Logan, comes to Washington, D.C. to find his leader, Ballard, and locates him at the ruined and abandoned Library of Congress. The screen version of *Logan's Run* (Metro-Goldwyn-Mayer, 1976), however, showed this scene as occurring in the Capitol Building rather than the Library. Another film on the theme of overpopulation, *Soylent Green* (Metro-Goldwyn-Mayer, 1973) is set in 2022. Edward G. Robinson plays a New York researcher who refers to the Library of Congress only briefly; a New York librarian provides the clue to the mystery.

The future does not even solve the free versus fee debate over information. Two vastly different versions of the Library of Congress glimpsed in Neal Stephenson's *Snow Crash* (1992) and Bruce Sterling's *Heavy Weather* (1994) approach the totally computerized future from opposite viewpoints. In 2031, in Heavy Weather, all the Library's contents have been digitized and are available to everyone since it all is in the public domain. In *Snow Crash*, the term "LC" is a measurement of data meaning information equivalent to all pages of materials deposited in the Library of Congress. At some past point, the Library of Congress merged with the Central Intelligence Agency just as the federal government fell apart. With all information commercialized, digitized, and sent to the Central Intelligency Corporation in Langley, Virginia, the words "library" and "Congress" have ceased to have meaning. All information from the CIC is for sale and "stringers" ceaselessly upload data into the database.

The science fiction novels and films provide radically different views of the future Library of Congress: a ruined heap, an essentially dead depository providing useful clues to the past, a working library providing 24 hour service, or the ultimate electronic repository of information, either all freely available or all available at great cost.

Within the fictional descriptions of the Library of Congress are embedded a history of the Library itself. Writers' and filmmakers' products recall a time when readers were permitted to enter the stacks, when the Constitution and the Declaration of Independence were displayed in the Library, when the Great Hall and the Main Reading Room and the corridors of the Jefferson Building had grown dark with the accumulated dirt of a century and more before their 1990s renovation. Enough of the future is now visible to reveal that computers, not microfilm, will display the wealth of the Library's information. The ultimate destiny of the Library remains open to the imagination.

ACQUISITIONS

The Library of Congress receives some 22,000 items each working day and adds approximately 10,000 items to its collections daily. In fiscal year 2003, more than 1,800,000 items (books and print materials, audio materials, talking books, manuscripts, maps, microforms, music, visual materials, and machine-readable materials) were added to the Library's collections, bringing the total number of items to nearly 128 million. The majority of the collections are received through the copyright registration process, but materials are also acquired through purchase, government transfer (state, local, and federal), Cataloging in Publication (a pre-publication arrangement with publishers), exchange with libraries and other organizations abroad, and gifts from individuals and organizations.

With an initial appropriation of $5,000 in 1800, Congress signaled its intention to enlarge the 243-volume collection that it had already accumulated, mostly works of history, classics, politics, law, economics, and geography, with relatively few titles in literature, but it was not until 1806 that an annual appropriation was authorized. When the British burned the Capitol during the War of 1812, destroying most of the books, Congress decided to purchase Thomas Jefferson's private collection of over 6,000 volumes. The former president's library was probably the most carefully selected and most comprehensive library in the United States at that time, and it included materials that up to that time might not have been considered appropriate to the Library of Congress, including books in the fine arts, the sciences, belles lettres, and books in foreign languages.

Despite the introduction of new subjects to the Library, subsequent purchases did not develop the collection along those lines, except for an increase in attention to scientific and technical books. During the early nineteenth century, Congress's Joint Committee on the Library took responsibility for approving acquisitions, frequently authorized Committee members to select and purchase materials, and employed British agents to purchase and ship needed items from abroad. Congress also supported between 1840 and 1852 the initiative of a French citizen, Alexandre Vattemare, to arrange an international exchange system for cultural materials; passed a copyright deposit law in 1846 (only to repeal it in 1859); and paid attention to the recreational needs of congressmen and their families by approving the acquisition of fiction and other light reading material. After a catastrophic fire in 1851, the Joint Committee replaced most of the collection. But while continuing to acquire materials within the subject areas of traditional congressional concern, the Joint Committee's selection procedures continued to be at best haphazard and sporadic until Ainsworth Rand Spofford became Librarian in 1864. Spofford persuaded Congress to pass legislation that redefined the Library's mission and hence its acquisitions operations: the Copyright Law of 1870; the act of April 5, 1866, providing for the deposit of the Smithsonian's collection; the act of March 2, 1867, providing that 50 copies of every public document should be made available to the Library for international exchange; and the appropriation at the same time of $100,000 for the purchase of the Peter Force collection, which set a precedent for special appropriations for the purchase of important material.

As Librarian of Congress from 1864 to 1897, Ainsworth Rand Spofford developed the Library of Congress into a national institution. The centralization of copyright deposit activities at the Library of Congress in 1870 was his greatest achievement, for it enabled the Library to acquire without cost all books, maps, music, prints, photographs, and other items being registered for copyright in the United States. LC/Prints and Photographs Division. LC-USZ62-23839.

During the next several decades, more exchanges were negotiated and copyright deposits rapidly enlarged the collections. But classes of material other than these—privately printed works, state and municipal documents, retrospective items, and foreign works other than public documents and scientific societies' publications—still had to be individually purchased on an appropriation that did not exceed $11,000 until 1898. Thus Spofford, an indefatigable bibliographer, scanned "with unwearying assiduity"

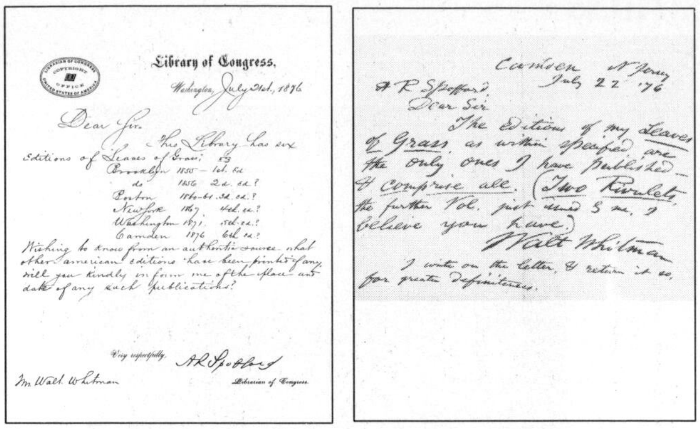
Library of Congress,
Washington, July 21st., 1876
Dear Sir.
The Library has six editions of Leaves of Grass; viz
Brooklyn 1855 – 1st. Ed
do 1856 2d. ed.?
Boston 1860-61 3d. ed.?
New York 1867 4th. ed.?
Washington 1871 5th. ed.?
Camden 1876 6th ed.?
Wishing to know from an authentic source what other american editions have been printed if any, will you kindly inform me of the place and date of any such publications?
Very respectfully, A R Spofford
Librarian of Congress.
Mr. Walt. Whitman

Camden N Jersey
July 22 '76
A R Spofford
Dear Sir
The Editions of my Leaves of Grass as within specified are the only ones I have published – & comprise all. (Two Rivulets, the further Vol. just issued by me, I believe you have.)
Walt Whitman
I write on the letter, & return it so, for greater definiteness.

In 1876, Librarian Spofford wrote to poet Walt Whitman, wanting to know "from an authentic source" if the Library of Congress had acquired all the published editions of Leaves of Grass. *"For greater definiteness" Whitman promptly and affirmatively responded on the back of Spofford's letter.* LC/Manuscript Division.

and continual vigilance dealers' catalogs and auction brochures for material that would fill gaps in the collections as well as for newly published items. Overwhelmed with copyright deposits, however, he fell far behind in acquiring and cataloging material. When Librarian John Russell Young established an Order Department in 1898 and Herbert Putnam continued it as the Order Division (1900), the collections were in such disarray that it was difficult to determine whether the Library already owned an item or needed to order it. Under the leadership of William Parker Cutter, the division's 13-member staff established new routines for obtaining recommendations for purchases; determining where orders should be placed; recording purchased gift and exchange material; and preparing invoices for payment by the Chief Clerk. Acquisitions work became increasingly important with the establishment of the Card Service in 1901, since other librarians informed the Library through their card orders of titles they were buying. Scholars visiting the Library often recommended purchases as well, and the specialists Putnam hired as chiefs of the divisions of maps, documents, manuscripts, music, and prints reviewed those collections, striving to fill gaps and expand coverage. Each recommended item had to be individually approved by Librarian Putnam before an order could be placed. Putnam was eager to expand the collections rapidly and continually requested a $100,000 appropriation for acquisitions. In fiscal 1908 through 1910, Congress did provide that sum but economy-minded congressmen decreased it to $98,000 the following year.

Beginning in 1900, Putnam frequently traveled abroad to purchase material, but on his first journey he found that the Library had bought so little in foreign countries that the dealers were unacquainted with it. The Librarian selected dealers and placed "blanket orders" to acquire every item in particular subject areas. On occasion, he approved bidding on desirable items at auctions, competing with dealers and collectors for rare or unusual items. After World War I, when a large number of collections were entering the book market, William A. Slade reported that he had obtained about two-thirds of the items on which the Library had placed bids.

Nevertheless, Putnam always insisted that "The bulk of our acquisitions is the 'ordinary run' of material current and noncurrent." In 1900–1901, for example, the Library acquired 76,481 items, of which 34 percent were purchased; 17 percent acquired from the Smithsonian Deposit or other federal departments; 13 percent were gifts; 10 percent were copyright items; 9 percent were added to the Smithsonian Deposit; 8 percent came as international exchanges; and 8 percent through the exchange of duplicates. Exchanges included primarily official publications received as the result of intergovernmental agreements; however, publications from learned institutions, organizations, libraries, and book dealers also might be received; and in return, the Library provided material from its large duplicates collection.

Library of Congress acquisitions have been deliberately limited for non-budgetary reasons. An important policy dating to the late nineteenth century is that in clinical medicine and agriculture the Library has not attempted to collect comprehensively because the Army Medical Library (now the National Library of Medicine) and the Department of Agriculture Library (now the National Agricultural Library) had long been collecting in those fields. Another limitation was imposed because of the very high volume of copyright deposits: beginning with Putnam's administration, Library staff systematically evaluated the copyright receipts and decided which items the Library should retain. In addition, there have always been certain classes of material that the Library does not collect, or acquires only selectively.

Usually unable to purchase rare or valuable material but seeking to build comprehensive collections despite the Library of Congress's relatively late entry into the foreign book trade, Putnam seized every opportunity to expand the collections. For example, he asked Congress in 1903 to allow other federal libraries to transfer material to the Library of Congress, and the same year a presidential executive order provided for the transfer of the records of the Continental Congress and the papers of Washington, Madison, Jefferson, Hamilton, Monroe, and Franklin from the State Department to the Library. The only deterrent came to be lack of space; by 1922 the Librarian had to decline further transfers from government agencies.

Putnam also entered a joint venture with the American Historical Association and the Carnegie Institution's Bureau of Historical Research to copy manuscripts abroad to build the collections in American history. In 1905, he contracted with a professional copying firm in London and employed Professor Charles Andrews to select from the material related to American history at the British Museum and the Bodleian Library, Oxford University. This launched a long-term copying effort: French and Spanish archives, for example, were added in 1914, and Mexican material in 1919. Gifts from James B. Wilbur (1925) and John D. Rockefeller Jr. (1927) funded larger copying projects for the replacement of transcripts with photostats. Reproductions of rare books, maps, manuscripts, pamphlets, and missing numbers of periodicals as well as entire newspaper files were added year by year in a major retrospective collecting effort. During World War II, the American Council of Learned Societies and the Library sponsored extensive microfilming in Great Britain, which was intended to preserve important historical materials against the ravages of war as well as to make them more widely available.

Block acquisitions, or the acquisition of entire collections, occurred occasionally during the Library's first one and one-half centuries, but it became more frequent after 1925. For example, Putnam acquired the G. V. Yudin collection of Russian material for a very small sum in 1906–1907, the East Asiatic literature collection of the John Crerar Library in 1928 through priced exchange, and the Vollbehr Collection of incunabula by appropriation in 1930. Private collectors like John Boyd Thacher sometimes donated their collections to the Library or placed material there on deposit and later bequeathed title. After Elizabeth Sprague Coolidge in 1925 donated funds to build an auditorium for the performance of chamber music and established an endowment for the Library's music collections and activities, Putnam was able to persuade Congress to approve the formation of the Library of Congress Trust Fund Board to receive, hold, and administer gift and bequests. The establishment of the Board provided to be catalytic; from that time forward the Library's collections have been significantly enriched by gifts of material in all formats and money.

Librarian Archibald MacLeish produced the "Canons of Selection" that formed the Library's first written acquisitions policy. They stated that the Library would acquire material needed by Congress and the federal government; that it would obtain material about the "life and achievements" of the

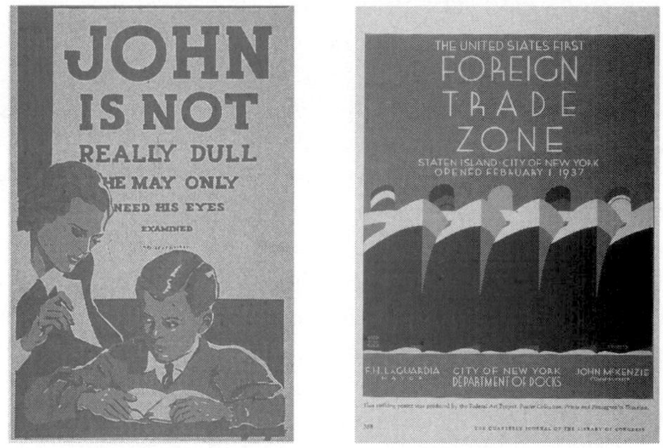

Transfer of materials from other government agencies (local, state, federal) has been an important way for the Library to acquire research materials and specialized collections. These two posters, for example, were produced by the Federal Art Project in the 1930s and acquired through the Library of Congress Project of the District of Columbia Works Projects Administration (1939–1941).
LC/Prints and Photographs Division.

American people, and that it would collect material about other societies, particularly those peoples "whose experience is of most immediate concern to the people of the United States." He also initiated a more active acquisitions strategy, stating that "The Library of Congress no longer waits for dealers to offer books, or for collectors to give them, or for publishers to deposit them for copyright. The Library of Congress now takes active and affirmative steps of its own and on its own account to find out what it lacks and to secure what it needs." He assigned significant responsibility for book selection to the Reference Department, and initially placed the old Accessions Division within the Processing Department. Changes in the division's work included establishing a central serial record, appointing a selection officer and a gifts officer, allocating acquisitions funds by subject field, and designating specialists to review the collections and make recommendations in each field. However, in 1943 a separate Acquisitions Department was established that included three divisions: Exchange and Gift; Order; and Serial Record. While specialists throughout the Library continued to provide recommendations for individual purchases and outside specialists served as consultants who surveyed the collections in their fields and also provided recommendations, an interdepartmental Acquisitions Committee (later known as the Acquisitions Seminar) was also established to advise on the allocation of funds and to consider policy issues. For the first time, all unsolicited materials received were systematically evaluated under the direction of a selecting officer, and in 1946 the division became responsible for selecting and purchasing current material from national bibliographies and trade lists. The importance that MacLeish attached to acquisitions and collection building became even more apparent with the launching in 1943 of a new journal titled *The Library of Congress Quarterly Journal of Current Acquisitions*.

World War II revealed serious deficiencies in the Library's collections. The Library was receiving only about half the material that Librarian Luther Evans thought should be collected: "we must possess," he wrote, "a far more comprehensive and a more genuinely universal resource than the narrow concept of 'representation' held in other days, permitted." Especially in demand were current materials relating to the war-torn countries in which the Allies would fight: maps of foreign cities, plans, information relating to industries, armaments, trade, and much more. With the outbreak of war, such publications became nearly unobtainable, and a federal Interdepartmental Committee on the Acquisition of Foreign Publications was formed to try to obtain them. Assistance also came from the State Department's diplomatic and consular offices abroad, from the Alien Property Custodian, and the Office of War Information, all of which channeled publications to the Library of Congress.

At the end of the war, the Interdepartmental Committee's work in obtaining European material also ended, but, with assistance of the State and War Departments, the Library began a Cooperative Acquisitions Project for European Wartime Publications (1945–1948). During that period, the Library re-established relationships with dealers abroad and mounted a special Library of Congress Mission to Germany to secure as many publications as possible for American libraries and to obtain the release from storage in Germany of shipments kept abroad for U.S. libraries for the duration. When the newly purchased materials were received, Library staff redistributed the publications to 113 participating U.S. libraries, each of which paid $1 for each volume or set of periodical issues shipped.

In the post-war period, the Library depended on the State Department's newly established publication procurement program for the acquisition of materials in countries where that program was operating. State has continually assisted the Library by helping to establish purchasing arrangements, forwarding information on new publications, stimulating exchanges with foreign institutions, and acquiring publications for the Library in places where other means of procurement were virtually nonexistent. For other foreign materials, as in the past, Library representatives were sent to purchase materials and negotiate exchanges. The "blanket" order system in use during the war, in which foreign agents or Library representatives selected materials for the Library, however, was in part replaced with an "open" order system in which current book trade bibliographies, as they reappeared country by country, were received by mail, checked, and orders sent by return air mail. The Library also was able to make reciprocal agreements with some overseas institutions whereby each would select and purchase materials from the current national book trade.

In August 1947, Evans merged the Acquisitions Department into the Processing Department, aligning acquisitions with the other processing operations and allowing the elimination of redundant positions. Nearly simultaneously, a flurry of new acquisitions activities commenced, including the development of a federal Documents Expediting Project formed through the cooperation of the American Library Association and the Association of Research Libraries to provide libraries with publications not available through the Superintendent of Documents, the inauguration of the Farmington Plan, and the organization of the United States Book Exchange, a corporation intended to facilitate the exchange of duplicates among libraries. All three involved the Library in new forms of cooperative acquisitions activities aimed at the development of library collections throughout the country.

As early as 1942, the Library had joined with the leaders of other U.S. research libraries in designing the Farmington Plan (planned at a meeting in Farmington, Connecticut) to obtain new foreign books on a cooperative basis. Operations had to await post-war re-establishment of the foreign book trade, but in 1948 the Plan began with the publications of France, Sweden, and Switzerland. Thirty-one research libraries accepted responsibility for specific subjects, with the Library of Congress undertaking to collect in 26 fields otherwise not covered. Each member library received current foreign publications in its fields of interest, ensuring that at least one copy of each book of interest to scholars or researchers in the United States would be made available in this country. The Plan did not cover books in non-Roman languages or publications outside the commercial book trade. Between 1950 and mid-1957, the Library consequently served as fiscal and distribution agent for an acquisitions project aimed at current USSR publications sponsored by the American Council of Learned Societies (ACLS) and the Social Science Research Council (SSRC) and funded by the ACLS and the Ford and Rockefeller foundations. Seven major U.S. research libraries received the publications, which were procured through the Department of State.

The development of collecting policies after the war took place chiefly through a staff Acquisitions Seminar (later the Acquisitions Committee), which considered the issues relating to various types of publications and presented draft policies to the Librarian. The Seminar began a systematic survey of acquisitions policies in 1949, recognizing that World War II and the continuing global engagement of the United States had greatly enlarged the range of materials needed by Congress and other branches of the federal government. The Library's senior staff decided that it would be necessary to limit the acquisition of older materials so that resources could be concentrated on securing all books and periodicals currently published worldwide "which embody the product of scholarship and research (save in medicine and agriculture), or which usefully represent the condition, the state of mind, or embody the laws of any people, or which constitute work of significant literary or esthetic merit."

Adhering to the principle that research collections grow best from the comprehensive acquisition of current materials, the Seminar recommended that the Library complement rather than duplicate collecting activities of other U.S. research centers and collect comprehensively only in areas of existing collection strength (such as Chinese material), in areas of unique opportunity, such as American copyrighted works, and in areas of official need (such as law). Recognizing the historic and continuing need to microfilm material abroad, especially collections related to American history, they faced another imperative as well: the need to not only safeguard materials through copying but also make them accessible to American scholars. Thus, the Library pursued extensive filming operations in, for example, Great Britain, France, Germany, Italy, Japan, and Mexico and it took advantage of the Fulbright Scholars program by asking program fellows to film important materials abroad, in partnership with the American Historical Association and the Ford Foundation.

Putting the Seminar's policy into operation required several steps. The Copyright Office took steps to tighten its procedures for obtaining U.S. copyrighted works and waived the fee for foreign works deposited for U.S. copyright in favor of the deposit of two copies plus a completed catalog entry. The procurement of non-copyright U.S. items, a constant problem, received more attention, and open orders were placed with dealers in 55 countries, including the zones of Germany. Where possible, selections were made from national bibliographies, but these still covered only the principal publishing centers of the world. Eastern Europe, much of Asia, the Middle East, and Africa lacked an organized book trade and negotiations were fraught with linguistic and legal difficulties. Exchange agreements effectively secured the publications of the more developed countries. But since the scope of the Smithsonian Exchange was largely scientific and excluded many institutions and organizations, the Library sought to further develop its own exchanges. For this purpose, the extensive collection of duplicate materials proved extremely valuable.

By its sesquicentennial year of 1950, the Library of Congress was receiving material from every area of the globe in which significant publication was ongoing. Agents abroad procured and forwarded publications as they were published, thus enabling the Library to keep control of current materials. In the process, however, a large backlog of foreign material accumulated because it could not be cataloged immediately. To help with access to such material, a series of publications describing acquisitions from specific countries began in April 1948 with the first issue of the *Monthly List of Russian Accessions*, initially funded by the ACLS and the Rockefeller Foundation and from 1951 through 1969 with appropriations. In December 1951, the Library began publishing the *East European Accessions List*, a cooperative venture to which over 125 libraries contributed by 1958. It was funded by Rockefeller and the National Committee for a Free Europe and later by contributions from federal agencies. With the addition of coverage of periodicals by 1958, the titles of these two publications changed to the *Monthly Index of Russian Accessions* and the *East European Accessions List.* When funding ceased, the East European index was discontinued, but the scope of the Russian accessions list broadened in January 1962. Publication of *Southern Asia: Publications in Western Languages* began in January 1952 in cooperation with the SSRC, the ACLS, and the Wenner-Gren Foundation. The Library also began publishing *New Serial Titles* in 1951 to provide other libraries with information on its new current subscriptions.

When the outbreak of the Korean War multiplied the demands from federal agencies for strategic information, funds were diverted from other purchasing to obtain collections of Korean, Manchurian, Formosan, and Mongolian publications. The Acquisitions Committee received a formal charge (October 1952) that broadened its scope of activities: it was to recommend policies, review the canons of selection, advise on plans for developing the collections, recommend allotments for subject fields, designate areas of special emphasis, and examine proposals for the purchase of entire collections and expensive items. The Committee continued to survey the collections in subject fields and by type of publication.

Acquisitions policies received even closer scrutiny after L. Quincy Mumford became Librarian in 1954. The Acquisitions Committee embarked on a project to complete a Selection Manual, while codifying policies and making them more rigorous. Mumford changed the membership and functions of the Committee in 1959, placing it under the chairmanship of the Chief Assistant Librarian and stipulating that it report to the Librarian. Over the next decades, the group continued to review and revise acquisitions policies for various types of material. By the late 1950s, for example, the Library ceased to acquire foreign doctoral dissertations because the Midwest Inter-Library Center (later the Center for Research Libraries) collected them; had relinquished the collection of government documents in medicine and agriculture to the National Library of Medicine and the National Agricultural Library; and strictly limited the collection of textbooks, paperback reprints, minor works of fiction, juvenile literature, personally subsidized biographies and belles-lettres, publications of secondary schools, and house organs. By 1958, less than one-quarter of the items that entered the Library were retained for the permanent collections. Older materials that remained uncataloged were re-evaluated and many items used for exchange or discarded.

The USSR's launch of Sputnik, the first earth satellite, in 1957 promoted renewed American attention to science and technology and heightened the demand for foreign books and journals. Under legislation regulating the Wheat Loan Fund for India, Public Law 82-48, the Library received authorization to purchase government of India documents for placement in several research libraries in the United States and to send American publications to Indian research institutions. Then Congress passed amendments to the Agricultural Trade Development and Assistance Act of 1954 (Public Laws 83-480 and 85-931) authorizing the Library to use U.S.-owned foreign currency to acquire foreign materials that would provide information of technical, scientific, cultural, or educational significance. The act additionally provided for funds for processing such materials and for acquiring materials that might be deposited in other U.S. libraries. When Congress voted an appropriation in 1962, the Library established centers in India, Pakistan, and Egypt to acquire publications. Gradually, coverage was extended to Indonesia, Ceylon, Nepal, Brazil, Israel, Poland, Sri Lanka, and Yugoslavia. The overseas centers issued acquisitions lists that became the *de facto* national bibliographies for countries that lacked them, and the New Delhi office began microfilming newspapers, official gazettes, and selected periodicals from South and Southeast Asian countries. The Library also was a member of the Latin American Cooperative Acquisitions Project, which sent traveling agents to contact local booksellers and publishers directly (1960–1973).

The health of the PL-480 program, however, depended on the supply of foreign currency, and in 1968 an amendment to the law required countries to pay in U.S. dollars rather than in their own currencies. As the supplies of national currencies dwindled, some offices had to be closed. However, the Library received congressional authorization beginning in 1975 to use non-PL-480 foreign currencies in a Special Foreign Currency Program. For some countries, such as Indonesia and Sri Lanka, the library was able to substitute cooperative acquisitions programs in which research libraries paid a fee to have the Library of Congress obtain publications for them. In recognition of these arrangements, in August 1974 the title of the *PL-480 Newsletter* changed to *Foreign Acquisitions Program Newsletter*.

Under the Higher Education Act of 1965, the Library received additional responsibility for acquiring foreign material. Librarian Mumford cooperated with the ALA and the ARL in developing the centralized acquisitions and cataloging program that constituted Title II-C of the act: "Strengthening College and Research Library Resources." It provided a mandate for the Library of Congress to assist other libraries by acquiring all currently published library materials worldwide that might be of value to scholarship and providing cataloging and bibliographic information for them. Named the National Program for Acquisitions and Cataloging (NPAC), it allowed the Library to establish additional overseas offices to facilitate acquisitions and cataloging, to expand blanket orders, to hire additional catalogers, and to train them. At the close of the first year, nine overseas offices were acquiring the publications of 21 countries, subscriptions for the bibliographical services of 17 foreign institutions had been placed, and 29 cooperating American libraries were receiving sets of catalog cards for about 150,000 publications. The acquisitions and cataloging operations for the program were combined in a new Shared Cataloging Division (1966) and the Library made special arrangements with the U.S. Bureau of Customs for rapid clearance of books and cataloging data.

New publications spread the NPAC story: accessions lists from the overseas offices and the *NPAC Progress Report* (1966–1977), which was later united with the *Foreign Acquisition Program Newsletter* (1974–1977), in *LC Acquisitions Trends* (1977–1982). The Library staff also continually provided information about the programs and about other overseas acquisitions efforts to member libraries and librarians and to academe through semiannual reports at the ALA conferences and meetings of the Seminar on the Acquisition of Latin American Library Materials, the Association for Asian Studies, the Middle East Library Association, and other professional meetings. Library staff also convened occasional meetings of participants in NPAC and held special events, such as a Workshop on Acquisitions from the Third World (1977).

The automation of acquisitions processes began during the late 1960s, but it was not until February 1971 that the first computer-produced purchase orders were mailed to vendors, completing the first phase of a three-part program for the creation of LOIS, the Library Order Information System. The automated system included the collection and printing of data for regular and subscription orders, production of an in-process list, scheduled follow-ups on outstanding orders and production of all fiscal records and forms. The final phase was initiated in 1977, and LOIS records were integrated into the MARC Search Service beginning in August 1978.

In addition to the PL-480 and NPAC programs, in the mid-1960s Congress provided for a Special Reserve Fund to purchase unusual materials, generally rare published works or single manuscripts to supplement existing collections. The Library staff made good use of these funds to fill gaps in the collections. The selection staff also, when time allowed, undertook to identify items no longer needed in the collections (e.g., duplicate copies, superseded editions, and duplicate sets of serials). These efforts helped gain space to shelve new materials and also saved money on duplicate subscriptions and binding expenses. An effort to review foreign-language material held in cataloging and other arrears in the mid-1980s resulted in a large number of unneeded items, which were used for exchanges.

Librarian Daniel Boorstin reorganized the Acquisitions Committee to include representatives of all Library departments, and he established a Collections Development Office within the Office of the Deputy Librarian in 1978. Intended to bring together various collection-related functions, the new office included units from both Processing Services and Research Services. While its concerns were always larger than the acquisitions function, the Collections Development Office director chaired the Acquisitions Committee and oversaw the development of acquisitions policies, and also the Preservation Policy Committee. The Acquisitions Committee's duties remained much the same as they had been in the past: to insure that the acquisitions and selection policies met the Library's research and reference needs, to review acquisitions policy statements, to advise on plans for the development of the collections, and to allocate book funds.

The Collections Development Office centralized selection, weeding, preservation and allocations operations at a time when Congress began to reduce funding for government operations. In the mid-1970s, funding for the overseas programs declined, and as overseas centers closed, greater selectivity became necessary. In 1978, a Hispanic Acquisitions Project tested the possibility that purchasing material, receiving gifts, and negotiating exchanges might proceed from a single point. Focusing all available expertise by geographic area made the acquisitions process more efficient. While the project was later absorbed into the Exchange and Gift Division (1981), the staff retained responsibility for purchases as well as exchanges. A new African and Middle Eastern Acquisitions Section later replicated the Hispanic project's focused approach, and the geographic focus reappeared in the 1997 reorganization of the division.

In spite of the changes in the overseas programs, acquisitions thrived during the early 1980s. Primarily, this was due to the continuing strength of the U.S. dollar abroad, minimal increases in the costs of foreign publications, a general decline in the volume of foreign scholarly publications, and the increased efficiency of the Library's computer operations. In fiscal 1983, for example, quantities of all forms of material purchased for the collections increased while costs were up only slightly over those of the previous years. The Collections Development Office began in December 1983 a systematic series of seminars on foreign acquisitions needs and problems, and developed a selection policy for machine-readable materials, while also instituting a multi-year project of reviewing cataloging arrearages and discarding or transferring unneeded material. The Acquisitions Policy Statements and the *Selection Manual* that had been prepared over more than a 30-year period continued to be revised and new statements written. A contractor prepared a three-volume study of acquisitions practices in Processing Services, the Copyright Office, and the Congressional Research Service that also paid some attention to the roles of staff in Research Services and the Collections Development Office. One result of the study was the development of functional requirements for automated acquisitions operations throughout the Library. Preservation copying programs underwent review in 1985, including the microfilming of brittle books, newspapers, serials, and special collection materials and the copying of deteriorating photographs and sound recordings. The Indian Special Foreign Currency Program, a unique chapter in the Library's acquisitions history that had begun with PL-480 funding in 1962, ended in 1985, when the supply of currency was exhausted and a modified dollar-funded program was put in place to continue activities.

In 1986, the acquisitions picture changed. Congress reduced the Library's appropriation at the same time that the purchasing power of the dollar declined. Faced with a budget reduction of 13.3 percent (about half of which was later restored), the Order Division reduced purchases of noncurrent materials and nonbook material such as microforms, prints, and photographic materials and maps while blanket orders were trimmed by 15 percent. More than 2,000 serial subscriptions were canceled, because the prices of serials over the last decades of the twentieth century constantly increased. As the later 1980s continued to see a sharp decline in the value of the dollar, prices increased. All of the Special Foreign Currency programs were appropriations-funded by 1988, and of the 23 field offices, only six remained. While Acquisition Policy Statements continued to be developed and revised, the staff also began preparing Acquisition Impact Statements, to identify potential problems in the custody, organization, or preservation of large collections being considered for acquisition.

Planning proceeded during the late 1980s to replace LOIS with a new, comprehensive acquisitions system, dubbed ACQUIRE, which was installed by the mid-1990s. Designed as a shared system for staff working in the Order, Exchange and Gift, and Copyright Acquisitions Divisions, ACQUIRE united all records for subscriptions, orders, and incoming material to eliminate duplicate orders, facilitate claiming missing serial issues, and provide financial and statistical information.

The general Library reorganization of 1988–1990 placed acquisitions functions in Collections Services, while the functions of a Collections Policy Office became a shared responsibility with Constituent Services. Copyright acquisitions was transferred to Collections Services, though a further reorganization in 1995 returned it to the Copyright Office under joint supervision of that office and the director of Acquisitions and Support Services. At the same time, all processing functions became part of a new Library Services directorate that encompassed acquisitions, cataloging, public service, and preservation.

The mid-1990s saw a number of new acquisitions and collections-oriented initiatives. The Office of Scholarly Programs coordinated the work of six teams and 22 consultants examining the collections of African American materials, international business materials, materials on twentieth-century Chinese social science, environmental studies, Islamic materials, and Latin American and Hispanic American materials. The decision to join The Johns Hopkins University Press's Project Muse in 1996 marked the Library's first purchase of full-text electronic publications. In addition to the rise of fee-based materials, other new trends that tended to decrease acquisitions were the declining level of government publishing in print format, increased reliance on the Internet for dissemination of material, and growing privatization of government printing and publishing. By 2004, the acquisition and processing of electronic resources had become an important Acquisitions Directorate activity.

In the mid-1990s, the staff examined the idea of restructuring acquisitions activities to focus on areas of the world rather than sources of materials, and in 1997 the Acquisitions and Support Services directorate was reorganized to combine the operations performed in the Exchange and Gift, Order, and Overseas Operations divisions and to realign acquisitions activities along geographic lines. Three new divisions were formed: the African/Asian Acquisitions and Overseas Operations Division, the Anglo-American Acquisitions Division, and the European and Latin American Acquisitions Division. Each division acquires all types and formats of material—serials, monographs, microforms, maps, moving images, music, photographs, sound recordings, and electronic publications—by whatever means is appropriate, including purchase, exchange, gift, or transfer. The reorganization enabled staff members to focus their individual area and cultural expertise to their best advantage, and the arrival of the Voyager integrated library system in 1999 provided for the online integration of files, enabling the acquisitions staff to create the first records for every item the Library orders or receives as well as search all files to guard against unnecessary duplication.

Mary R. Bucknum of the Motion Picture, Broadcasting, and Recorded Sound Division checks a newly arrived shipment of current music and spoken word CDs that have been sent on a standing order from a company in California for approval and possible inclusion in the collections.
Photograph: LC/Jim Higgins, Photographic Section.

Meanwhile, in 1994 the Library's Madison Council formed an Acquisitions Committee to help the Library acquire special items and collections, with subcommittees focused on Americana, the visual arts, rare books, and the performing arts. Notable purchases supported by the Madison Council in recent years include 260 manuscripts in Persian, Arabic, and Urdu; additions in the Jefferson Library project to reconstruct the collection in the original catalog of Thomas Jefferson's library; funds toward the purchase of the

Mark Dimunation of the Rare Book and Special Collections Division and Cindy Hileman of the United States Acquisitions Section review possible replacement editions for books originally in Thomas Jefferson's personal library, which was purchased by the Library of Congress in 1815. With Madison Council support, in 1999 the Library launched a project to replace books from Jefferson's library that were lost in a fire in 1851, when the Library was still in the U.S. Capitol.
Photograph: LC/Jim Higgins, Photographic Section.

1507 map by Martin Waldseemüller, which was purchased in 2003; more than 100 digital photographic prints documenting the September 11, 2001, attack on the World Trade Center and the Pentagon; and a complete set of *Curtis's Botanical Magazine*, a landmark of botanical literature and natural history illustration.

Efforts to scrutinize the Library's collections and collecting patterns continued. Collections policy statements continued to be formulated and revised, and in 1995 the Collections Policy Office published the complete set of *Library of Congress Collections Policy Statements* for distribution by the Cataloging Distribution Service and the federal documents depository library program. A "Characteristics of the Collection" project revealed in 1995 that half of the Library's classified book collections were in English and one-third of the titles were published in the United States. More than half the classified materials were published after 1970, and the percentage of titles in the humanities, social sciences, and sciences had remained much the same since the mid-1950s. Among the various efforts to reappraise collections policy during the 1990s were the continual efforts to identify serials that were received in multiple copies and to cancel titles that were no longer needed, in accordance with collections policy statements. A jointly sponsored conference with the Association of Research Libraries in 1998 considered the future needs of area studies collections and how the overseas offices might contribute better to fulfilling national collecting needs. (JA)

Downs, Robert. "Wartime Cooperative Acquisitions," *Library Quarterly* 19 (July 1949): 157–165.

Library of Congress Information Bulletin 50 (July 29, 1991): 293–296; 56 (September 1997): 292–295.

Rosenberg, Jane Aikin. *The Nation's Great Library: Herbert Putnam and the Library of Congress, 1899–1939*. Urbana, Ill.: University of Illinois Press, 1993.

ADAMS BUILDING

Called the Annex Building when it opened to the public in 1939, the Library's handsome second building was named for President John Adams in 1980; concurrently the Library's Main Building was named for Thomas Jefferson. Today it serves as the Library's major book stack and computer center and as its center for research in science, technology, and business. Approximately 10 million books are stored

The John Adams Building, which opened in 1939, was originally known as the Library's "Annex." The second of the three Library buildings on Capitol Hill, in 1980 it was named for the second president. Photograph: LC/Jim Higgins.

in its stacks. Two major reading rooms are located on the fifth floor of the Adams Building: the Science Reading Room on the north side and the Thomas Jefferson Reading Room on the south.

In 1928, at the urging of Librarian of Congress Herbert Putnam, Congress authorized the purchase of land directly east of the Library's Main Building for the construction of an Annex Building. On June 13, 1930, $6,500,000 was appropriated for its construction, for a tunnel connecting it to the Main Building, and for changes in the east front of the Main Building, including the construction of the Rare Book Room. An additional appropriation approved June 6, 1935, brought the total authorization to $8,226,457.

The simple classical structure was intended, essentially, as a functional and efficient bookstack "encircled with work spaces." It was designed by the Washington architectural firm of Pierson & Wilson with Alexander Buel Trowbridge as a consulting architect. The contract stipulated completion by June 24, 1938, but the building was not ready for occupancy until December 2, 1938. The move of the Card Division started on December 12, and the building opened to the public on January 3, 1939.

The dignified exterior of the Adams Building is faced with white Georgia marble and pink granite from North Carolina. The building is five stories in height above ground, with the fifth story set back 35 feet. It contains 180 miles of shelving (compared with 104 miles in the Jefferson Building) and can hold 10 million volumes. There are 12 tiers of stacks, extending from the cellar to the fourth floor. The south entrance on Independence Avenue has never been used.

The pair of bronze doors at the south or Independence Avenue side of the Adams Building. The male figure beneath the seal of the United States represents manual or physical labor, and the female figure beneath the book symbol represents intellectual labor. These figures and the lanterns on either side of the doors contain elements of the Art Deco style. LC Archives.

The building's decorative style contains elements of the "Art Deco" inspired by the Exposition des Arts Décoratifs held in Paris in 1925, and today it is recognized as one of the few distinguished Art Deco buildings in Washington, D.C. The history of the written word is depicted in sculptured figures by Lee Lawrie on the bronze doors at the west (Second Street) and east (Third Street) entrances. Decorative features in the first floor lobbies and corridors and in the fifth floor lobbies and reading rooms are worth special note.

On the fifth floor, the North Reading Room is decorated by the murals of artist Ezra Winter that illustrate the characters in Geoffrey Chaucer's

Canterbury Tales. Winter, who had earlier painted an acclaimed Art Deco mural for Radio City Music Hall in New York City, also contributed the murals that decorate the South Reading Room. The themes are drawn from quotations from Thomas Jefferson's writings, which are inscribed in the murals and reflect Jefferson's thoughts on freedom, labor, the living generation, education, and democratic government. The characters and costumes depicted are those of Jefferson's time. A portrait of Jefferson with his residence, Monticello, in the background is in a lunette over the reference desk at the north end of the room.

The north and south reading rooms on the fifth floor of the Adams Building are enlivened by four 72-foot-long murals by artist Ezra Winter. Chaucer's pilgrims ride toward Canterbury above the north room. The South Reading Room is dedicated to Thomas Jefferson. Here Winter brings to life five passages from Jefferson's writings, depicting the value of freedom, the virtues of labor, the rights of the living generation, the importance of education (shown), and the role of people in democratic government.
LC Archives. LC-USP6-128-A.

On April 13, 1976, in a ceremony at the Jefferson Memorial marking the birthday of Thomas Jefferson, President Gerald Ford signed into law the act to change the name of the Annex Building to the Thomas Jefferson Building. This change, initiated by Librarian of Congress Daniel J. Boorstin, lasted four years. In 1980, the structure acquired its present name, which honors John Adams, the man of letters and president of the United States who in 1800 approved the law establishing the Library of Congress.

In 1977, Librarian Boorstin proposed to the Architect of the Capitol a major restoration and renovation of the Library's Thomas Jefferson and John Adams Buildings. In 1984, Congress appropriated \$81.5 million for the project. The architectural firm of Arthur Cotton Moore & Associates was selected to design the work, which was completed in two phases between 1986 and 1994. (JYC)

Roberts, Martin A. "The Annex of the Library of Congress," in *Report of the Librarian of Congress for the Fiscal Year Ending June 30, 1937.* Washington, D.C.: Government Printing Office, 1937, pp. 354–359.

AFRICAN AND MIDDLE EASTERN DIVISION AND COLLECTIONS

African and Middle Eastern Division

The African and Middle Eastern Division Reading Room on the second floor of the Jefferson Building. The division includes materials in vernacular scripts, like Amharic, Arabic, Armenian, Georgian, Hebrew, Persian, Turkish, and Yiddish. The division's three sections—African, Hebraic, and Near East—offer in-depth reference assistance to the rich and varied collections of related materials. Photograph: Carol Highsmith.

The African and Middle Eastern Division (AMED) was created in 1978 as part of a general Library of Congress reorganization. AMED combined three disparate sections—African, Hebraic, and Near East, which cover some 78 countries and regions from Southern Africa to the Maghreb and from the Middle East to Central Asia. The division, led by chiefs Julian Witherell (1978–1991) and Beverly Gray (1994–), coordinates and directs the component sections. Each section plays a vital role in the Library's acquisitions program; offers expert reference and bibliographic services to the Congress and researchers in this country and abroad; develops projects, special events, and publications; and cooperates and participates with other institutions and scholarly and professional associations in the United States and abroad.

Although proposed earlier, it was not until 1960, with increased national academic and government interest in sub-Saharan Africa, that the African Section was established. It was administered initially by the General Reference and Bibliography Division. The section focused on virtually all topics relating to sub-Saharan Africa. The Hebraic Section began operation in 1914 as part of the Division of Semitic and Oriental Literature, and concentrates on Jewish culture, Israel, the Hebrew language, Biblical studies, and the ancient Near East. Its founding may be traced to Jacob H. Schiff's gift in 1912 of about 10,000 Hebraica books and pamphlets. In 1945, the Near East Section was created as part of the Orientalia Division to serve as a focal point of the Library's programs for this pivotal area. It covers North Africa, the Arab world, Turkey, Iran, Afghanistan, the Caucasus, Central Asia, and Islam.

Volumes about Africa and the Middle East were in one of the first major purchases by the Library of Congress, the 1815 acquisition of the Thomas Jefferson library. Although sporadic receipts of publications from and about the region were reported in annual reports of the Librarian of Congress, there was limited systematic acquisition effort for this part of the world prior to World War II. Today, AMED is recognized as a major world resource center for Africa, the Middle East, the Caucasus, and Central Asia.

The Hebraic and Near East sections have custody of material in the non-Roman alphabet languages of the region. Included in these collections are books, periodicals, newspapers, microforms, and rarities including cuneiform tablets, manuscripts, incunabula (works printed before 1501), and other early African and Middle Eastern publications; in 2003, together they numbered about 600,000 volumes. The Hebraic Section collections contain more than 160,000 volumes in Hebrew and related languages, including Yiddish, Ladino, Syriac, and the languages of Ethiopia. Materials in more than 35 languages are held by the Near East Section, the major holdings of which are Arabic (the largest, with more than 150,000 volumes), Persian, Turkish, Central Asian, Armenian, and Georgian. While the African Section has no formal custodial responsibilities, it maintains a pamphlet collection of about 22,000 items.

To enhance further holdings already strong in the fields of history, literature, economics, linguistics, art, religion, and philosophical studies, division curators participate in acquiring materials of research value. Noteworthy grants and gifts have also served to strengthen these collections. For example, in 1960, a grant from the Carnegie Corporation provided initial support for the African Section, including staff travel to many African countries to obtain publications for the collections. A gift of two Deinard collections, the last received in 1921, and which total nearly 20,000 volumes, substantially increased the Hebraica collections. Generous gifts from Mr. and Mrs. Arthur Dadian in the 1990s created an endowment of now $783,000 to develop and maintain the Library's Armenian holdings.

In the spring of 1997, the division moved from the John Adams Building to its present location on the second floor of the Thomas Jefferson Building. The new AMED Reading Room houses a 10,000-volume reference collection and a rotating display of current events journals, arranged and maintained by each of the three sections. Researchers may consult specialists who provide extensive reference assistance in identifying materials in their custodial collection as well as related sources about Africa, the Middle East, the Caucasus, and Central Asia in Roman script and in other formats or specializations found in the Library of Congress general collections and in other units such as the Geography and Map Division, the Manuscript Division, the Rare Book and Special Collections Division, and the Law Library.

In several display cases in the reading room, the division mounts small exhibits. Staff have, for example, curated an exhibit: "Oil and Petroleum in Africa and the Middle East," for members of the Domestic Petroleum Council, whose annual dinner was co-sponsored by the African and Middle Eastern Division. Major exhibits featuring AMED collections have been mounted in the Library's galleries. "From the Ends of the Earth: Judaica Treasures of the Library of Congress" was prepared to mark the 75th anniversary of the Hebraic Section, and a version of this exhibit later traveled to several North American cities.

Special events and outreach activities have long been part of the division's agenda. Working through the three sections, it sponsors many library, cultural, and scholarly programs. The Africana Librarians Council of the African Studies Association has held several of its semiannual meetings at the Library. Officials of the International Summer Seminar in Jewish Genealogy accepted an invitation from the Hebraic Section to serve as host for the 1995 meeting and make readily available to participants its outstanding genealogy-related resources. As part of its 50th anniversary celebration, the Near East Section held a conference on "Arab-American Cultural Relations," and more recently, it co-sponsored with the Embassy of Tunisia a panel of international experts who spoke on "Tunisia: Past, Present, and Future." Lectures, including a research seminar series, are another important and ongoing part of the division's outreach program. Well-known speakers such as MacArthur Fellow and human rights lawyer Gay McDougall, Nobel Laureate Elie Wiesel, and Egyptian philosopher Zaki Naguib Mahmoud have participated.

Another role of the division is to enhance access to the collections. For example, the African Section has been in the forefront in adapting Library automation technology to its needs. Its serial publication, *U.S. Imprints on Sub-Saharan Africa: A Guide to Publications Cataloged at the Library of Congress*, was based on a complex retrieval of records from the Library's online catalog. The two custodial collections maintain retrospective national union catalogs for the non-Roman alphabet material in their respective charge. In 1978, part of the Near East National Union Catalog was automated, and volume one of the print edition was issued.

The publications issued under the division auspices form a widely acclaimed body of material. The African Section has compiled more than 40 publications ranging from official publications of African nations to short subject guides on contemporary issues such as *Abuja: The New Federal Capital of Nigeria*. Titles prepared in the Near East Section include *The Holy Koran at the Library of Congress* and *American Doctoral Dissertations on the Arab World*. The catalog of the successful exhibit initiated by the Hebraic Section, "Scrolls from the Dead Sea: The Ancient Library of Qumran and Modern Scholarship," published jointly by the Library and the Israel Antiquities Authority, received several awards for its design.

The African and Middle Eastern Division continues to exert a vital influence in the development of area studies librarianship. Its specialists represent the Library at key cooperative area studies programs in which it is an institutional member, such as the Cooperative Africana Project, the Council of Archives and Research Libraries in Jewish Studies, and the Middle East Microform Project. Division staff members are recognized for their scholarly publications; they serve as officers in area studies organizations; and they participate in national and international meetings on their areas of expertise. Additionally, AMED offers a contribution to the field by training young scholars and future librarians through briefings, presentations, internships and volunteer positions, and mentoring promising candidates, thus helping to guarantee future study of these vital areas in world culture. (BG, MG)

Africana Collections

Among the best in the world, the Library's collections of Africana—material from or relating to Africa—concern the countries of sub-Saharan Africa, an area which includes the Indian Ocean Islands and excludes the North African countries of Algeria, Egypt, Libya, Morocco, and Tunisia. The African Section is the focal point of the Library's collection development, reference, and bibliographic activities for sub-Saharan Africa. Although most Africa-related material is dispersed in the general book and periodical collections, impressive works of Africana may also be found in the collections of manuscripts, maps,

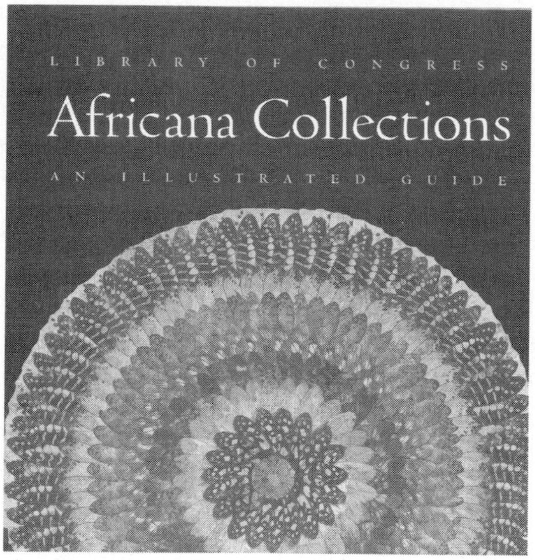

The cover of Africana Collections: An Illustrated Guide *features a popular West and Central African art form—creating pictures from butterfly wings in intricate patterns, as can be seen in this geocentric example purchased in Bangui, Central African Republic.* LC/African and Middle Eastern Division.

microforms, music, newspapers, prints, photographs, and films in the various custodial divisions of the Library. Every major field of study, except technical agriculture and clinical medicine, is represented. Holdings in economics, history, linguistics, and literature are especially strong.

Beginning with the Thomas Jefferson Collection, which included several books on Africa, the Library has a longstanding role in acquiring and providing access to material about Africa. This goal has been accomplished by pursuing and acquiring materials by copyright, by purchase, by the exchange of publications, and by encouraging collectors or creators of Africana to donate their treasures to an institution pledged to preserve them for future generations. The growth of the collections over the years has been phenomenal. In 1901, the Library's collection of materials about the entire continent of Africa included about 1,830 volumes and 78 pamphlets. Measuring the largest single block of material in the general collections (that is, surveys, yearbooks, histories, and general descriptive works under the DT classification), as an example, the Library owned about 50,000 books and periodicals in 1997 in this category alone. Currently numbering more than 22,000 items, the African Section's Pamphlet Collection includes brochures, speeches, conference papers, and other ephemeral materials.

The Library's field office in Nairobi, Kenya, which obtains materials from Eastern, Central, and Southern Africa and the Indian Ocean Islands, and in Cairo, Egypt, whose acquisition responsibilities include Mauritania and Sudan, manage networks of bibliographic representatives resident in each of 28 countries in Central, Eastern and Southern Africa whose assignment is to contact any organization likely to issue publications. Because of small press runs, on-the-spot collecting of African publications has been critical.

The Library has sought to obtain materials reflecting the political, economic, social, and technological developments in contemporary sub-Saharan Africa. Its collection of materials published in Africa during the last 30 years offers scholars of contemporary African states unparalleled resources for investigation. Publishers include government ministries, government printing offices, research institutes, banks, non-governmental organizations (NGOs), commercial publishers, courts, university departments, and libraries. Researchers are offered a wealth of national, provincial, and municipal documents ranging from presidential speeches, tourist brochures, annual reports of government agencies, ministries or research organizations, statistical abstracts, project reports and budgets, to multi-volume, long-range development plans. The Law Library has extensive collections of laws and regulations, gazettes, constitutions, international agreements, and unofficial legal materials such as compilations of laws, digests, dictionaries, and legal encyclopedias of African countries. In the Newspaper and Current Periodical Reading Room, the Library receives newspapers from all the African capitals and from many major cities, too. It is estimated that approximately 6,000 Africana periodicals arrive regularly, providing scholars with timely information.

The Library of Congress's Africana historical collections are rich with primary documents and secondary sources in a variety of languages and formats. Texts, maps, visual images, artifacts, and recordings document the observations of non-Africans as they traveled to parts of the continent, of Africans who encountered them willingly or under coercion, and of the resistance and adaptation of Africans to the cultural and political onslaught of the non-Africans. In the Library's Manuscript Division, Rare Book and Special Collections Division, and general collections, resources are available to study the development of commercial and diplomatic relations; the creation and dissolution of colonial governments; and the reestablishment of sovereign nations. For example, among the writings of Africans captured in slavery are the first and subsequent editions of Ghanaian Ottobah Cugoano's (ca. 1745–ca. 1790) *Thoughts and Sentiments on the Evil and Wicked Traffic of the*

Slavery and Commerce of the Human Species ... (1787) and Nigerian Olaudah Equiano's (ca. 1745–ca. 1802) autobiographical *Interesting Narrative* (1789). Of special note is the American Colonization Society (ACS) Collection, a key resource for scholars of Liberian history and related topics, which numbers more than 190,000 pieces in the Manuscript Division.

The collections of the Library of Congress are particularly strong in the humanities including information about the art, handicrafts, music, dance, film, oral and written literatures that enrich life in African communities and have influenced societies wherever peoples of African descent have settled. Of the 400 to 1,000 languages spoken in Africa, the Library of Congress tries to collect materials in as many African languages as there are materials published or recorded and it is known for its outstanding collection of dictionaries, grammars, and similar linguistic studies. The Library is proud to count in its collections Maxamed Daahir Afrax's *Maana-Faay: qiso (novel)* (published between 1981–1991), reportedly the first novel written in Romanized Somali script and Nazi Boni's *Crépuscule des temps anciens* (1962) the first novel published in Burkina Faso (then Upper Volta).

Researchers have the opportunity to listen to the sounds of Africa in the Performing Arts Reading Room or in the Folklife Reading Room, which houses the Archive of Folk Culture. A wide spectrum of music and sound recordings are represented including contemporary music; traditional music including that associated with specific ceremonies or events such as weddings or funerals; songs and ballads written for political parties and protest movements; and national anthems.

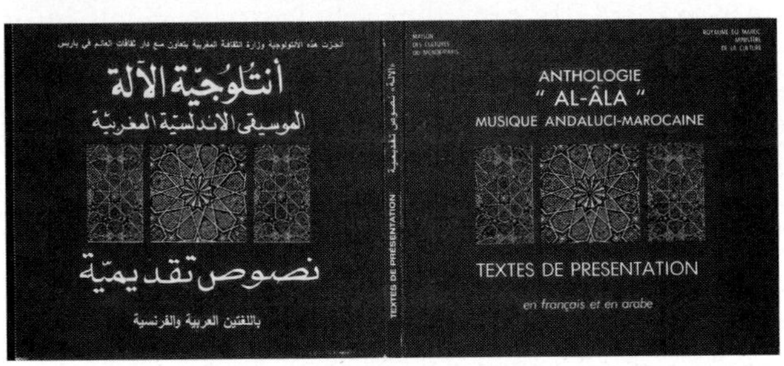

One of the 72 compact discs that form the anthology of nawbas *titled* Anthologie al-Ala: musique andaluci-marocaine. LC/Music Division.

From ancient hand-drawn charts to the latest satellite surveys, the Geography and Map Division houses more than 150,000 maps and atlases on Africa, offering diverse types of information such as political and geographic divisions, environmental conditions, or ethnological data. For example, the collection includes the 1477 Bologna edition of Claudius Ptolemy's *Geography*, which was based on Ptolemy's writings (ca. 150 A.D.) and on what was known in Europe about Africa from Arab and European writers up to that time.

A dazzling array of graphic resources are available, which portray how Africans were viewed by others and how Africans saw themselves and other peoples. These materials include drawings reproduced as etchings and lithographs in rare books, newspapers, or periodicals, or as individual images such as photographs and daguerreotypes, or as films and videotapes. These resources may be found in such diverse locations as the general collections, the Microform Reading Room, the Rare Book and Special Collections Division, the Prints and Photographs Division, and the Motion Picture, Broadcasting and Recorded Sound Division. In the later division, for example, a researcher may compare the coronation of the last emperor of Ethiopia, Haile Selassie I as recorded on five reels of 35 mm film in 1930, to the coronation of one of the traditional rulers of Uganda, the Kabaka of Buganda, Ronald Mutebi (Mutebi II) in 1993 on videocassette.

All in all, the vast, multimedia, multilingual Africana collections of the Library of Congress offer researchers unequaled opportunities to study sub-Saharan Africa. (JZ)

Library of Congress Africana Collections: An Illustrated Guide. Washington, D.C.: Library of Congress, 2001.

Hebraic Collections

The Library of Congress has collected Hebraic from its earliest days. Among the volumes acquired from Thomas Jefferson in 1815 was a Mishnah (with Latin translation) and a Hebrew grammar. But the systematic acquisition of Hebraic dates back only to 1912, when New York financier and philanthropist Jacob H. Schiff purchased for the national library a collection of Hebraic from the well-known bookseller and bibliographer Ephraim Deinard. In 1914, Schiff purchased a second Deinard collection. A third Deinard collection was added in 1916 and a fourth and final Deinard collection was acquired in 1921. The approximately 20,000 volumes in Deinard collections form the nucleus of the national library's Hebraic collections.

Today, the Library's Hebraic collections number more than 160,000 volumes of Hebrew, Yiddish, and related languages. The collection includes materials in Hebrew, Yiddish, Ladino (Judeo-Spanish), Judeo-Persian, Judeo-Arabic, Aramaic, Syriac, Coptic, Ge'ez, Amharic, and Tygrina, as well as materials in the languages of the Near East prior to the rise of

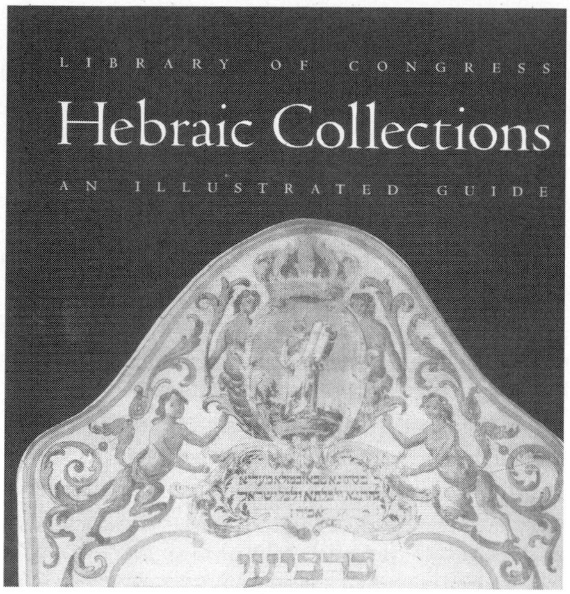

The cover of Hebraic Collections: An Illustrated Guide *shows a ketubah dating from 1805 in Ancona, Italy. The ketubah is both a lavishly illustrated marriage document and a work of art. It features a cartouche adorned with a decorative crown and a depiction of Moses holding the tablets of the Ten Commandments. Beams of light emanate from Moses's forehead as he gazes down the mountain.* LC/ Hebraic Collections.

The Washington Haggadah *from Central Europe, and created in 1478, is known as The Washington Haggadah because of its presence in the Library of Congress. This illumination illustrates the passage "This Bread of Affliction" from the Passover Seder recitation.* LC/Hebraic Collections.

Islam in the seventh century. Strengths of the collection include Bible, rabbinics, liturgy, Hebrew language and literature, responsa, Jewish history, and Israel related materials.

Housed in the rare book collection of the Hebraic Section is a collection of 37 clay tablets that were acquired in the 1920s and 1930s from Kirkor Minassian, a New York art dealer and expert on the Near East. These tablets, some dating back to almost 2000 B.C.E., represent the earliest examples of writing in the collections of the Library of Congress. Among the Library's more than 200 Hebrew manuscripts are an eighteenth century Hebrew translation of the *Koran* from Cochin (India); a fifteenth-century monumental *Scroll of Esther* from Central Europe; a selection of nineteenth century-decorated *Ketuboth* (Jewish marriage documents) from Italy, Corfu, Turkey, and Iran; a decorated eighteenth century *Scroll of Esther* from Italy; an early Ethiopian Psalter in Ge'ez from Ethiopia; and the Library's most noteworthy Hebraic manuscript treasure: *The Washington Haggadah*, a Hebrew-illuminated manuscript completed by Joel ben Simeon in 1478.

Some 140 Hebrew titles are thought to have been printed before 1501. Of these, the Library holds 38 (nine are second copies). Included among this trove is the first book of the Bible printed in Hebrew, a Psalter with the commentary of David Kimhi, which was published in Italy in 1477; a copy on vellum of the first complete Hebrew Pentateuch, which appeared in Bologna in 1482; and the first book printed in Lisbon, Portugal, a Hebrew commentary on the Pentateuch by Nahmanides, which was issued in 1489. Especially noteworthy is the Library's copy of Moses of Coucy's *Sefer Mitzvot Gadol*, published in 1488, which includes the only known autograph of Gershom Soncino—the premier printer of early Hebrew books—on a deed of sale pasted-in on the last leaf of the volume.

The Library's collections also are rich in printed rarities from the sixteenth century. Among these is the first book printed in any language on the African continent, *Sefer Abudarham*, which was published in Fez Morroco by Samuel Nedivot, who learned the craft of printing in Portugal and took it up again in Morocco where he and his family found haven after their expulsion from Portugal. The first Rabbinic Bible (1516–1517) published in Venice by Daniel Bomberg, whose press was the most important Hebrew press in sixteenth century Europe, is held in the Hebraic collections, as are individual tractates from Bomberg's folio edition of the *Talmud* (1519–1523)—the first complete edition of the *Talmud* to appear in print. It was this edition that set the layout and the pagination for virtually all subsequent editions of the Babylonian *Talmud* that have appeared to this day. The Library also owns the first edition of the *Zohar* (*The Book of Splendor*), a classic of Jewish mysticism, which appeared in Mantua, Italy in 1558. The second volume of the Library's three-volume set is printed on blue paper, indicating that it was a deluxe edition prepared for a wealthy sponsor or patron.

The 25,000-volume Yiddish Collection includes monographs, pamphlets, serials, and newspapers. The collection is especially strong in late-nineteenth century imprints, including religious, labor, literary, Zionist, and socialist tracts. Well represented are the fruits of the classics by Yiddish luminaries such as Mendele Mokher Seform, I.L. Peretz, and Sholem Aleichem. Modern Yiddish literature is represented by a wide range of twentieth century European, Israeli, and American Yiddish poets and writers. Yiddish works on social science, history, and linguistics are also available. Among the collection's Yiddish printed rarities are works especially intended for women: an early edition of the *Tsena U-re'ena*—a Yiddish paraphrase of the Bible; a worn volume of *Tehinot*—special supplicatory prayers for women; and the first American Yiddish cookbook, Hinde Amchanitzky's *Lehr-Bukh Vi Azoy Tsu Kokhen un Baken* (New York, 1901). Also available for consultation is a rich microfilm collection of Hebrew and Yiddish monographs, newspapers and serials, as well as microfilms of Hebrew manuscripts held in the Russian State Library (Moscow), Russian Academy of Sciences (St. Petersburg), Preussiche Staatsbibliotek (Berlin), and the Hungarian Academy of Sciences (Budapest).

Unique to the Library of Congress are more than 1,000 original Yiddish plays in manuscript and typescript written between the end of the nineteenth and middle of the twentieth centuries that were submitted for copyright registration to the Library of Congress. Intended for the American Yiddish stage, they document the hopes, the fears, and the aspirations of several generations of immigrants to America. And of particular interest to historians and genealogists is the Library's comprehensive collection of more than 500 *yizker-bikher* (memorial books) documenting Jewish life in Eastern Europe before the Second World War.

With the enactment of U.S. Public Law 480 (PL-480) in 1958, the Library of Congress greatly enhanced its ability to collect Israeli publications comprehensively. PL-480 mandated that 25 American research libraries, including the Library of Congress, be supplied with a copy of virtually every book of research value published in Israel. The program lasted from 1964 to 1973 and provided the participating institutions with an average of 65,000 items. Since 1973, substantial efforts and resources have been expended to maintain this high level of acquisitions. The collection includes an extensive array of monographs; a broad selection of Hebrew periodicals, current and retrospective, popular as well as scholarly; and a wide range of Hebrew and Yiddish newspapers reflecting every shade of opinion, from the religious to the secular and from the far right to the extreme left. In addition, an extensive collection of government documents has been assembled. In recent years, the Library has enriched its collection with examples of modern Hebrew fine printing, including a selection of Israeli and American artists' books in Hebrew. (MG)

Karp, Abraham J. *From the Ends of the Earth: Judaic Collections of the Library of Congress*. Washington, D.C.: Library of Congress, 1991.

Library of Congress Hebraic Collections: An Illustrated Guide. Washington, D.C.: Library of Congress, 2001.

Near East Collections

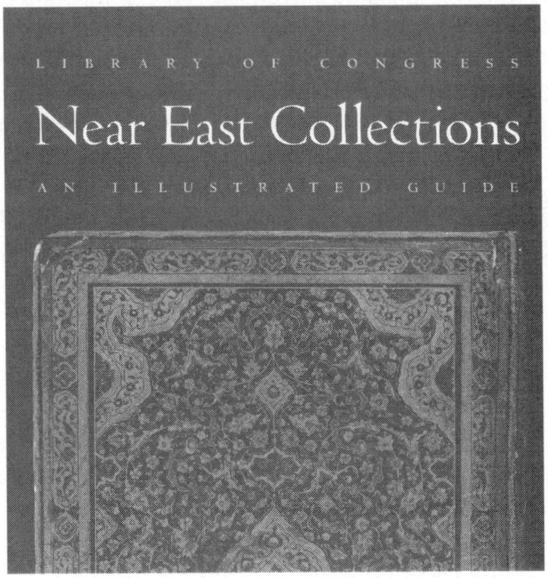

The cover of Near East Collections: An Illustrated Guide *features an example of particularly rich bookbinding from the Minassian collection of Islamic book bindings. It is enameled with an intricate golden vine and highlighted with petite burgundy and blue flowers.* LC/Near East Section, housed in Rare Book and Special Collections Division.

Originally part of the Orientalia Division, the Near East Section (NES) was created in 1945 following the allied victory in World War II and America's growing interest in the lands and peoples of the Near East. The NES became the custodian of materials in more than 35 vernacular languages of the lands from the Atlantic coast of North Africa to the steppes of Central Asia, and from the Caucasus mountain range in the North to the tropical Gulf States in the South. The section shares responsibility for the African countries of Mauritania, Sudan, Somalia, and Djibouti, which are part of the League of Arab States, with the African Section, and for the history and languages of the Ancient Near East, with the Hebraic Section. Combined with the large number of works in the general collection and the many other divisions of the Library, the Arabic, Armenian, Central Asian, Georgian, Persian, and Turkish language materials form the core of the NES collection.

The Arabic language monograph collection is the largest. It consists of approximately 125,000 titles and 150,000 volumes, and increases at an estimated rate of 5,000 volumes a year. The Arabic language collection also includes newspapers, manuscripts, and microfilms that cover topics ranging from religion to history and science. Together, those materials represent the intellectual heritage of all the Arab countries of the Near East and North Africa and to a lesser extent that of other, primarily Muslim, countries that have published in Arabic.

In 1945, the Arabic manuscript collection was vastly expanded when the Library purchased 1,300 manuscripts from Shaykh Mahmud al-Imam al-Mansuri, professor of religion at Al-Azhar University in Cairo. These supplemented the manuscripts and other rare items that had been acquired in the 1920s and 1930s from the New York dealer Kirkor Minassian, whose collection was especially rich in Islamic materials. Today, the manuscript collection includes approximately 1,700 items, most of which have been divided into three categories. The first consists of about 100 items, bought in the 1930s from Minassian, for which a bibliography was prepared in 1961 by Professor Salah al-Din al-Munajid. Some of the most valuable pieces include a fifteenth century copy of a manuscript on medicine by Najib al-Din al-Samarqandi, and a sixteenth century manuscript by Muhammad bin 'Ali al-Hanafi al-Hashimi on weaponry.

The second and largest category is that of Shaykh al-Mansuri's estimated 1,300 manuscripts that focus primarily on religious matters. Among the important works in that collection are a fifteenth century copy of a commentary on the Qur'an by Ibn 'Abdallah al-Taftazani, and an eleventh century copy of a manuscript on the *hadith*, the Prophet Muhammad's traditions, by Abi Bakr al-Suyuti. Other manuscripts in the Mansuri collection, written between the twelfth and the eighteenth centuries, include works on the four schools of Islamic jurisprudence, the Arabic language and literature, history, medicine, mathematics, logic, and philosophy. Finally, the third set of manuscripts, numbering 244, was given to the Library in 1983 by Jacob Baker. They include manuscripts in Arabic, Persian, and Turkish dealing primarily with religious topics such as a thirteenth century copy of a commentary on the Qur'an by Nasr ibn Muhammad al-Samarqandi, and a fourteenth century study of the *hadith* by Ibn Musa al-Shahrazuri. A few dealt with more secular subjects such as language and literature.

The Near East Section recently purchased the entire collection of Islamic manuscripts on microfiche from the British Library. It included 15,000 manuscripts on 45,000 microfiche.

The Arabic periodical collection contains over 5,000 titles, both current and non-current, and includes government serial publications as well. Those publications come from all over the Arab world as well as from countries with large Arab communities in Europe and the Americas. In 1968, a program was initiated to preserve representative newspapers on microfilm. Over 200 titles are included in this program, among the most outstanding are *Al-Ahram* (Cairo, 1876–); *Filastin* (Jerusalem, 1911–1961); *Al-Nahar* (Beirut, 1934–); and *Al-Huda* (New York, 1898–).

Although the NES was established in 1945, it was only in 1959 that a specialist in Turkic languages was named to assist in the development of the Turkish collection. Within the past 40 years, the collection has grown to over 30,000 titles and 35,000 volumes in Romanized script and another 10,000 volumes in Ottoman Turkish in Arabic script. This constitutes the single largest collection of Turkic publications in the United States. There are, in addition, major holdings related to the Turkic world in other divisions of the Library.

Although the collection is very strong in materials published in the post-1923 period, when Turkey decided to Romanize its alphabet, the Turkish area specialists made a systematic effort to acquire important books and serials dating from earlier eras such as those published in the nineteenth century by the Bulaq Press in Egypt. Older publications such as *Vankulu Lugati* (*Vankulu's Dictionary*), published in Istanbul in 1729, and Katib Çelebi's *Cihannuma* (*Universal Geography*), published in Istanbul in 1732, were also purchased over the years.

A unique part of this collection is the 284 volumes given to the Library by Sultan Abdul Hamid II in 1884. Those books (in Turkish and Arabic) provide a representative view of Turkish intellectual life at the end of the nineteenth century, and are available to researchers on microfilm. Many of the more fragile volumes are preserved in the NES rare materials collection. In 1893, another gift was made to the Library by Sultan Abdul Hamid consisting of a 51-volume

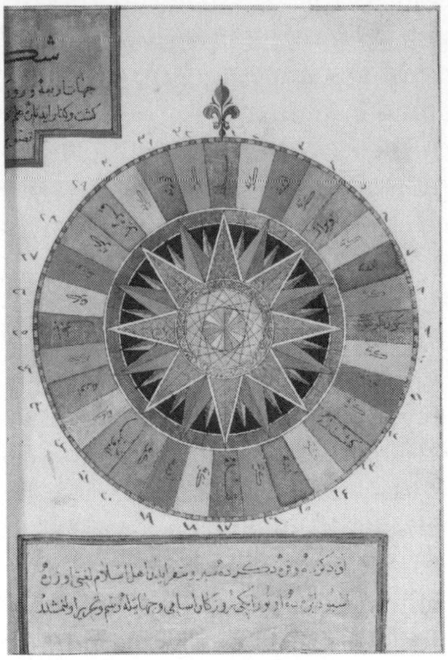

The military arts and sciences were important to the Ottoman state. This highly ornamented device is a chart of the points of a compass from Katip Çelebi's Tuheftü'l-Kibar fi Esfar'il-Bihar *(The naval wars of the Turks) Istanbul, 1792.*
LC/Near East Section.

photographic survey of the Ottoman Empire's military, educational, and health institutions, as well as its historic monuments.

The NES has also acquired over 125 manuscripts in Ottoman Turkish that focus primarily on religious subjects. Among these are a 1526 copy of *Farid Attar's Tezkiret'l-Evliya* (*History of the Saints*) by Muhammad Haravi, one of only three copies known to exist as well as Yazioglu Mehmed's *Muhammediye* (*Poem in Praise of the Prophet Muhammad*), and a Turkish translation of Zakariyah Qazwini's *Acâibü&l-Mahlukât* (*Wonders of Creation*), both written at the end of the sixteenth century.

The Turkish serial collection includes approximately 630 titles in the Arabic and Romanized scripts. Among the major holdings in newspapers are *Aksam* (1942–1964), *Baris* (1971–), *Cumhuriyet* (1924–), *Hürriyet* (1948–1949, 1973–), and *Milliyet* (1962–1965, 1970–). The government serial publications are extensive including a complete set of *Turkish Republic Statistics* dating back to 1923. Complete or near complete runs of serials by the Turkic peoples of the Soviet Union since 1955 are also part of the Turkish serial holdings and include all the journals of the various writers' unions.

Materials from Tajikistan, Azerbaijan, Kazakhstan, Kirgistan, Tashkent, Turkmenistan, and Uzbekistan are an intrinsic part of the NES collection. There are more than 17,000 volumes in this collection and 1,100 items in the Arabic script, dating from the pre-1939 period. Later materials are in Cyrillic script. Linguistically, more than 35 languages are included in the NES's vernacular materials from the area. Among the useful works are encyclopedias in Tajik, Uzbek, Tatar, and other languages.

Persian monographs were first donated to the Library of Congress in 1872–1873 by American missionaries who had lived in Persia. After diplomatic relations were established between the United States and Persia in 1883, the collection was expanded by private donations from Persian citizens and others. It was only after 1945, and the establishment of NES, that a more systematic form of acquisition of Persian, Afghan, Pushto, Kurdish, and other Iranian language research materials began in earnest. Today, the collection consists of approximately 45,000 catalogued volumes, and almost as many titles that are not catalogued or exist only on microfiche. The vast majority are in Farsi, but some are also in Pushto, Dari, and Kurdish. These cover a wide range of subjects from religion to politics, history, art and architecture, language, and philosophy. The collection of Persian classical materials includes the *Shahnameh* (*Book of Kings*) by Firdawsi (935–1025), and the poetry of 'Umar Khayyam (d. 1123). Others include catalogues of rare books in Iran's Royal Library and the shrine of Astanah-i Quds in Meshdad, a collection of the *Ariyana Almanac* from the 1920s, and the *Safarnameh* of the Qajar Shah Nasir al-Din (1848–1896).

The Persian collection has a large section on modern Iranian politics, including works on the rule of Shah Muhammad Reza Pahlavi; the opposition movements at the time of the Shah; the collected works of the leaders of the 1978 Iranian Revolution; dissident literature published by opposition groups in exile since 1978; and an extensive collection of works on U.S.-Iranian relations. The periodical collection holds approximately 500 titles (including dissident literature), some of which date back to the early part of this century such as *Salnameh-i Ariyan* (the *Aryan Directory*) and *Salnameh -i Pars* (the *Pars Directory*). Moreover, 326 newspapers in Farsi published between 1871 and 1978 have been microfilmed, and for these a published bibliography exists. That bibliography also cites the titles of 23 Afghan newspapers published in the same period. Despite the difficulty in getting materials from Iran in recent years, the newspaper and periodical collection has continued to grow rapidly over the past two decades. Also, there are an estimated 200 manuscripts among the Persian holdings, collected over the years. Many are exquisitely illuminated with Persian miniatures, such as copies of Firdawsi's *Shahnameh*.

Western books about Armenia and Georgia entered the Library's general collections in the nineteenth and twentieth centuries. Yet in 1945, at the time of the creation of NES, the Library had scarcely

200 Armenian language books and even fewer Georgian language works. In the late 1940s, an Armenian-American, Arthur Dadian, created, with the approval of Luther Evans, the Librarian of Congress, the Committee for the Armenian Collection of the Library of Congress. The goal of the committee was to help the Library acquire Armenian language materials, and its remarkable success eventually led the Library to hire a specialist in the field of Armenian studies. Today, the Library holds more than 14,000 Armenian and Georgian language books, and 200 serial and periodical titles. The collection, as a whole, is made up of over 25,000 items that include manuscripts, rare books, and microfiche and microfilm collections of newspapers and periodicals, including virtually every commercially produced microfilm and microfiche set on Armenia and Georgia. In 1991, Marjorie Dadian created an endowment from the estate of her husband to continue the expansion and maintenance of the Armenian collection, and in 1997, that endowment was augmented by an additional bequest from her own estate.

The section's earliest Armenian published works date to the 1600s and were printed in Istanbul, seat of the Ottoman Armenian Patriarchate, and Ejmiatsin, home of the Katholikos, the head of the Armenian Church. A great number of these early works, however, came from the Armenian diaspora in Europe, India, Russia, Iran, and the Arab world. Today, the Armenian and the Georgian collections also have been enriched by Soviet era academic monographs and serials. The several medieval and early modern Armenian manuscripts include a fourteenth century tetraevangile, two seventeenth century missals, and several seventeenth century illuminated calligraphy sheets, and embroidered and inscribed ecclesiastical fabric. The 14-volume diary, handwritten by Armenian American David Atamian, provides an important narration of the 1915 Armenian Massacre.

Following the independence of Armenia and Georgia in 1991, NES acquired numerous monographs, newspapers, pamphlets, and other materials to help researchers document the transformations taking place in that region. *Hayastani Hanrapetut'yun*, the state newspaper from Yerevan, Armenia, and *Sakatvelos Respublika*, its analogue from Tblisi, Georgia, are among the most important titles added to the collection. (LA)

Library of Congress Information Bulletin 54 (July 10, 1995): 311–315.

Library of Congress Near East Collections: An Illustrated Guide. Washington, D.C.: Library of Congress, 2001.

AMERICAN FOLKLIFE CENTER AND COLLECTIONS

The American Folklife Preservation Act

The American Folklife Center was created when the American Folklife Preservation Act, Public Law 94-201, passed both houses of Congress at the end of 1975 and was signed into law by President Ford on January 2, 1976. The legislation defines the term "American folklife" as "the traditional expressive culture shared within the various groups in the United States: familial, ethnic, occupational, religious, regional." It states that "the diversity inherent in American folklife has contributed greatly to the cultural richness of the Nation and has fostered a sense of individuality and identity among the American people."

Scholar and fiddler Alan Jabbour (left), was the first director of the American Folklife Center, serving from 1976 until 1999.
LC/American Folklife Center.

The American Folklife Preservation Act was nearly 10 years in the making. The intrepid advocacy of folklorist Archie Green kept the bill alive through years of backroom debate. The argument that the bill would provide cultural balance to the more elite National Endowment for the Arts and the Humanities (founded in 1965) proved effective, both in advancing the legislation and in simultaneously pressing the endowment to acknowledge the importance of folk cultural traditions. Also, the bill coincided with plans for the celebration of the bicentennial of the American Revolution, which took a grassroots turn, emphasizing local, ethnic, and other cultural traditions.

The legislation originally conceived a foundation within the Smithsonian Institution, but for a variety of reasons the host agency became the Library of Congress, where an archive of folk music and folklore (currently known as the Archive of Folk Culture) had been created in 1928. The Library supported the legislation, but final passage of the bill caught the institution in transition between retiring Librarian of Congress L. Quincy Mumford and a new Librarian, Daniel J. Boorstin. The Center's board of trustees was appointed by the Speaker of the House and the president pro tempore of the Senate; and Boorstin convened the board for its inaugural meeting, during which it elected distinguished folklorist Wayland D. Hand as its first chairman. In September 1976, the Librarian appointed Alan Jabbour as the Center's first director. Jabbour had served as head of the Library's Archive of Folk Song (1969–1974) and had been director of the Folk Arts Program at the National Endowment for the Arts from 1974 through 1976. In October 1998, after 23 years, the American Folklife Center achieved permanent authorization from Congress with the passage of Public Law 105-275, the Legislative Branch Appropriations Act of 1999. In 1999, Alan Jabbour was succeeded as director by Peggy A. Bulger, who came to Washington from the Southern Arts Federation, based in Atlanta, Georgia. In the early years of the twenty-first century, Bulger has presided over a flurry of activity and a major expansion in Center staff, collections, and projects

The Center is under the direction of a board of trustees and the supervision of the Librarian of Congress. In addition to four members each appointed by the Speaker of the House and the president pro tempore of the Senate, the board consists of four members appointed by the president of the United States from federal departments and agencies concerned with some aspect of American folklife traditions and arts, and a number of ex officio members: the Librarian of Congress; the secretary of the Smithsonian Institution; the chairman of the National Endowment for the Arts; the chairman of the National Endowment for the Humanities; and the director of the Center. In 1998, the law was amended to add four additional appointments by the Librarian of Congress and two additional ex officio members: the presidents of the American Folklore Society and the Society for Ethnomusicology.

Early Initiatives

One of the first initiatives of the Center was a noontime concert on the plaza in front of the main entrance of the Library's Thomas Jefferson Building on September 23, 1976, featuring Washington bluesmen Big Chief Ellis, John Cephas, Phil Wiggins, and James Bellman. The successful event led to a 20-year series of programs on what was dubbed "Neptune Plaza," in honor of the fountain featuring Neptune between the plaza and First Street. In 2002, the series was reincarnated under the rubric "Homegrown: The Music of America," and it is now conducted in cooperation with state folklorists from around the country.

Spanish dancers and musicians on Neptune Plaza in front of the Jefferson Building at one of the American Folklife Center's public noontime concerts. The dome of the U.S. Capitol is in the background. The concerts began in 1976, the year the Center was established by Congress.
LC/American Folklife Center.

The Center's next initiative was one of many designed to underline and celebrate the nation's ethnic and cultural diversity. On January 24–26, 1977, the Center sponsored its first conference, "Ethnic Recordings in America: A Neglected Heritage," in order to highlight the importance of the vast corpus of ethnic recordings produced by American commercial recording companies in the first half of the twentieth century. Subsequent conferences have included "The Archive of Folk Song: A 50th Anniversary Symposium" (1978); "The Washington Conference on American Folk Custom" (1980); "Folklife and the Elderly" (1981); "The Washington Conference on Folk Art" (1983); "The Kalevala and Finnish Identity in Finland and America" (1985); "Cultural Conservation: Reconfiguring the Cultural Mission" (1990); "Folk Heritage Collections in Crisis" (2001); and "Living Lore: Celebrating the Legacy of Benjamin A. Botkin" (2001).

In 1979, the American Folklife Center began a project based on an existing archive collection that proved to be one of its most rewarding: the Federal Cylinder Project. Over the decades, the archive had received many wax cylinder recordings of ethnographic material collected in the field from 1890 through the 1930s, primarily of Native American music and spoken word. The Library's Recording Laboratory, in fact, had developed a special expertise to meet the engineering challenge of copying them for preservation and access. Some had been copied onto disc in the 1930s and 1940s, and more were copied to magnetic tape, beginning in the 1960s. But many of the 10,000 cylinder recordings housed in the archive had never been preserved.

The Center devised a plan for preserving, cataloging, and disseminating copies of the recordings, for which it received private funding support, at first from the Bureau of Indian Affairs and the L.J. and Mary C. Skaggs Foundation, and then from the Ford Foundation. All the wax cylinders were preserved by duplicating them onto tape; about three-fourths were cataloged in detail; and copies of perhaps two-thirds of them have thus far been returned to the tribal communities of origin.

Documentary Field Projects

During 1977, the Center launched two field documentary projects: the Chicago Ethnic Arts Project and the South-Central Georgia Folklife Project. These projects established a pattern that characterized the Center's fieldwork for the next two decades. Though one was urban and one rural, both emphasized the importance of documenting artistic traditions professionally, using sound recordings and still photography, and both resulted in substantial additions to the folk archive and public products created from the documentary materials gathered.

Major field documentation projects restored an activity that had characterized the Folk Archive in the 1930s. The Center's innovation was in expanding that fieldwork to include not only music but also verbal arts, material culture, occupational traditions, and other aspects of culture not documented by the archive in an earlier generation. Similarly, the basic tools of documentation expanded to include not only sound recordings but also photography. And, finally, the process of fieldwork expanded from the classic one or two fieldworkers to teams of professionals—fieldworkers, photographers, and local historians—assembled by the Center for their knowledge of and familiarity with the particular area or subject under investigation.

The ideal of fieldwork—making a permanent record for the archive through documentation in the field—characterizes the whole history of folklore and folklife activities at the Library of Congress, from the archive's inception in 1928 through the Center's work in the present day. Field projects provided a major infusion of documentary material and caused a substantive transformation of the Archive of Folk Culture, adding over a half million items in various media to the collections.

Center field documentation projects and cultural surveys have included the following: Chicago Ethnic Arts Project (1977); South-Central Georgia

Folklife Project (1977); Ethnic Broadcasting in America (1977–1978); Blue Ridge Parkway Folklife Project (1978); Paradise Valley Folklife Project (1978–1982); Rhode Island Folklife Survey (1979); Montana Folklife Survey (1979); Ethnic Heritage and Language Schools Project (1982); Pinelands Folklife Project (1983); Grouse Creek [Utah] Cultural Survey (1985); Lowell [Massachusetts] Folklife Project (1987–1988); Italian-Americans in the West Project (1989–1991); Maine Acadian Cultural Survey (1991–1992); New River Gorge [West Virginia] Folklife Project; Working in Paterson [New Jersey] (1994); and Coal River [West Virginia] Folklife Project (1994).

The American Folklife Center's David Taylor interviews Anne Murphy during the American Folklife Center's 1994 project to document the occupational heritage of Paterson, New Jersey. Mrs. Murphy is showing Taylor a photo of workers (including herself) at Newberger's Towel Factory, ca. 1918, and describing her work. LC/American Folklife Center.

Field Documentation Training Schools

Drawing upon experience gleaned from its many field documentation projects and responding to a need for practical training in fieldwork, the American Folklife Center launched a series of field documentation training schools. The schools have been conducted during the summer months at several locations around the United States, in partnership with local colleges and universities, and with support from other organizations and agencies. The first was held in Washington, D.C., in 1992, in partnership with the National Park Service and the Smithsonian Institution, designed specifically for participants from the Native American community. Others have been held in Colorado Springs, Colorado, in cooperation with Colorado College and the University of New Mexico's Center for Regional Studies (1994 and 1995); Gambier, Ohio, in cooperation with Kenyon College's Rural Life Center; Bloomington, Indiana, in cooperation with Indiana University's Folklore Institute and the Evergreen Institute (2000 and 2001); Salisbury and Crisfield, Maryland, in cooperation with Salisbury University and the Ward Museum of Wildfowl Art (2003); and Provo, Utah, in cooperation with Brigham Young University (2004).

The Archive of Folk Culture

Founded in 1928 within the Music Division, the Archive of American Folk Song made important contributions to ethnography, folklore and folk music research, public programming, and cultural documentation and preservation in every decade of its history. The heads of the Archive have been Robert W. Gordon (1928–1932); John A. Lomax (1933–1942), whose son Alan who worked with his father from 1937 to 1942, was given the title Assistant in Charge; Benjamin A. Botkin (1942–1945); Duncan Emrich

Urban folklorist, author, and editor Benjamin A. Botkin broadened the public's understanding of folklore. Head of the Archive of American Folk Song from 1942 to 1945, here he reads into a microphone in the Library's Recording Laboratory. LC Archives.

(1945–1955); Rae Korson (1956–1969); Alan Jabbour (1969–1974); and Joseph C. Hickerson (1974–1989). After several years without an official "head," due in part to budget restrictions, Michael Taft was appointed to that position in 2002. Though the archive was originally established to collect American folksong, it began documenting folk music beyond the borders of the United States as early as 1935, when Alan Lomax recorded in the Bahamas, and by 1940 it had expanded its documentary scope well beyond folk music into folklore, verbal arts, and oral history. From the 1950s through the 1970s, it was called simply the Archive of Folk Song.

The archive became part of the American Folklife Center in 1978, and its name was changed again to the Archive of Folk Culture in 1981. It ceased to function as an administrative unit at that time but continued as an umbrella designation for the collections of the Center. The archive has grown exponentially since 1976, in part because of acquisition of major collections, both national and international, but also because of the field documentation initiatives undertaken by the Center itself. A striking aspect of the growth is the increase in visual documentation from a negligible supplementary role to a place of honor alongside the manuscripts and sound recordings. This shift is primarily a consequence of the use of still photography and, to a limited extent, film and video in field documentation. In addition, during the early years of the twenty-first century, the Center entered into cooperative agreements with private organizations that have brought in large collections featuring storytelling, oral narrative, and other forms of spoken word.

Today, the Archive of Folk Culture contains more than 3 million items and is truly the national folk archive. It is, in fact, not just an archive of music or individual items, but an archive of ethnographic collections, which are multiformat, unpublished, created works that document aspects of human culture in field situations. In addition to the documentary materials from the Center's own field projects, its holdings include the classic recordings of African American and British American folk music made by John and Alan Lomax for the Library of Congress in the 1930s and early 1940s; unique recordings of ex-slaves narrating their pre-emancipation experiences; documentary recordings of American music, culture, and life made during the New Deal period; vast collections of American Indian music, narrative, and ritual encompassing many tribal groups and regions of the country, including 3,500 recordings assembled between 1895 and 1940 by the Smithsonian Institution's Bureau of American Ethnology and several hundred recordings made in the 1940s and early 1950s by the Bureau of Indian Affairs of the U.S. Department of the Interior; wide-ranging collections documenting the folklife of the many immigrant groups that came to the United States in the nineteenth and twentieth centuries; and materials concerning the American folksong revival from the 1930s through the present.

In addition, the archive holds national institutional collections from the American Dialect Society, the American Folklore Society, the National Folk Festival, the Folk Arts Program of the National Endowment for the Arts, and the International Storytelling Foundation. In October 2000 (Public Law 106-380), Congress created the Veterans History Project, a nationwide effort that has resulted in an immense collection of oral history materials; and in 2003, the Center agreed to accept the "born digital" oral history materials from a similar nationwide project, StoryCorps, conceived to gather the stories of friends and families.

In 2004, the American Folklife Center acquired the Alan Lomax Collection, which comprises the ethnographic documentation collected by the legendary folklorist over a period of 50 years, from the time he left his position as head of the Archive of American Folk Song at the Library of Congress in 1942 through the end of his long and productive career as folklorist, author, radio broadcaster, filmmaker, concert and record producer, and television host. The Alan Lomax Collection had been housed at Hunter College in New York City, and managed by the Association for Cultural Equity, which Lomax founded in 1985 to preserve, research, and disseminate world folk performance traditions. The collection comprises sound recordings, motion picture film, videotapes, scholarly books and journals, photographic prints and negatives, and manuscript materials.

Folklorist Alan Lomax in 1942. From 1933 to 1942 his father, John A. Lomax, was "honorary consultant and curator of the Archive of American Folk Song." Son Alan worked with his father and was given the title Assistant in Charge of the Archive from 1937 to 1942. In 2004, the American Folklife Center acquired the Alan Lomax Collection, an unparalleled ethnographic collection documenting traditional music, dance, tales, and other forms of creativity.
LC/American Folklife Center.

Included in the collection are original sound recordings of traditional singers, instrumentalists, and storytellers made by Lomax during numerous field trips to the American South, the Caribbean, Britain,

Scotland, Ireland, Spain, and Italy as well as original video footage, shot in the South and Southwest, Washington, D.C., and New York City, which was used as the basis of Lomax's *American Patchwork* television series. In addition, the collection includes audio, video, and film from around the world made by other collectors and assembled by Lomax for his cantometric and choreometric studies of song and dance.

In fact, the archive is rich in the documentation of music and folklife traditions from many regions and nations, such as Africa, including collections from Ethiopia, Morocco, Nigeria, and South Africa elsewhere in the Americas, including the Bahamas, Brazil, Canada, Chile, Haiti, Mexico, Panama, Trinidad, and Venezuela; Asia, including materials from Cambodia, China, India, Japan, Korea, Nepal, Sri Lanka, Thailand, and Tibet; Europe, including extensive material from Bulgaria, France, Great Britain, Greece, Hungary, Ireland, Portugal, Romania, Spain, and the former Yugoslavia; the Mediterranean and the Middle East, including Afghanistan, Iran, Iraq, Israel, and Turkey; and the Pacific Islands, including a major collection made during 1940 and 1941 in Bali, Fiji, Java, the Kangean Islands, Madura, the Marquesas, New Caledonia, Samoa, and the Society Islands.

International and Domestic Outreach Programs

The international collections in the Archive of Folk Culture are reflected in the international programs and activities of the American Folklife Center. In 2002, the United States began to include folklorists from the Center on its official delegation to the meetings of the Intergovernmental Committee on Intellectual Property and Genetic Resources, Traditional Knowledge and Folklore of the World Intellectual Property Organization (WIPO), an agency of the United Nations that meets biannually in Geneva, Switzerland. The Center has been instrumental in supplying case-study examples on the use and misuse of traditions, and has also suggested wording for U.S. positions. It has advised the secretariat of WIPO on professional ethics among folklorists, explained archival policies for collections of traditional materials, and supplied bibliographic references on folklore and intellectual property issues. The Center has served on delegations for the Organization of American States (OAS) and UNESCO, contributing to their discussions on cultural diversity. The Center also regularly hosts librarians, archivists, and cultural specialists from such places as Great Britain, Europe, the Middle East, Russia, Central Asia, Africa, and South America, as well as others who seek information on organizational development and administration, cultural programming, and collection management and preservation for organizations, agencies, and programs in their respective countries.

Each year, in fact, the Center serves several thousand in-person visitors and responds to thousands more telephone requests and correspondence (by letter and by e-mail), from both persons who wish to use the collections in the archive and those with general inquiries about folklife. The Center's Folklife Reading Room is used by members of Congress and their staffs; teachers and students at all levels; researchers, including folklorists, anthropologists, linguists, ethnomusicologists, and historians; community, ethnic, and tribal officials; record and book publishers and editors; the public media; government workers, librarians, and archivists; senior citizens and other public groups; and interns who gain experience in folklife and archiving techniques while assisting in the work of managing the archive.

Collections Preservation

The turn of the twentieth century witnessed a growing awareness that the audio documentation of the previous 100 years, which began with the invention of the Edison cylinder recording machine in 1877 (commercially available in 1889), was in great danger of deterioration and loss. In December 2000, the American Folklife Center hosted a symposium entitled "Folk Heritage Collections in Crisis," at which librarians, archivists, audio engineers, computer scientists, preservation specialists, folklorists, ethnomusicologists, lawyers, and recording company executives shared their ideas and experiences and made proposals on how to respond to the problems of collection preservation, access, and property rights. Earlier in the year, the Center had been awarded a grant from the National Park Service and the National Trust for Historic Preservation (through the White House Millennium Council's preservation program "Save America's Treasures"). The grant provided funds to the American Folklife Center and the Smithsonian Institution's Center for Folklife and Cultural Heritage for preserving the unparalleled collections of recorded sound at the two institutions. Under the rubric "Save Our Sounds," the two Centers identified collections in most need of attention, raised private funds to match the grant, publicized the cause of audio preservation, and helped to establish best practices for collection management and preservation as it occurs at folklore archives throughout the United States.

Ethnographic Thesaurus Project

Another collaborative project that addressed the concerns of archivists, this one between the Center and the American Folklore Society, was the Ethnographic Thesaurus Project, launched in 2001 with an initial grant from the National Endowment for the Humanities and eventually funded with a grant from the Andrew W. Mellon Foundation. The thesaurus will establish consistent terminology to describe traditional materials located in a wide variety of archival settings.

"To Preserve and Present American Folklife"

The American Folklife Preservation Act includes the mandate that the American Folklife Center "preserve and present American folklife," and activities fulfilling the second half of that mandate have been many; in addition to the concert series mentioned earlier, the Center has sponsored lectures, workshops, consultancies, and other educational activities. Major exhibitions, usually the outcome of field documentation projects, have included "Folk Art and Folklife" (1978), in two parts: a photographic exhibition (with sound stations)—"Sketches of South Georgia Folklife," drawn from the South-Central Georgia Folklife Project—and "Missing Pieces," an exhibition of Georgia folk art; "Buckaroos in Paradise: Cowboy Life in Northern Nevada" (1980), at the Smithsonian Institution's Museum of History and Technology, with material gathered during the Paradise Valley Folklife Project; "The American Cowboy" (1983), made possible by major support from United Technologies, in three sections: the late nineteenth-century reality of cowboys and open-range cattle in the West; the rise and diffusion of myth-making about cowboys; and the contemporary reality of cowboys and cattle management in the Western states; "Old Ties, New Attachments: Italian-American Folklife in the West," with material from a five-state documentary project of the same name that was conducted in conjunction with the Library's observance of the Quincentenary of Columbus's voyage to the New World.

Like exhibitions, publications have been a central function of the Center from the start. A canvass of folklife activities in federal agencies, undertaken by Linda Coe, resulted in the Center's first publication, *Folklife and the Federal Government* (1977). Since then, nearly every conference or field project has generated an accompanying publication. In January 1978, the Center inaugurated a quarterly news magazine, *Folklife Center News* (edited by Alan Jabbour, 1978–1980; Brett Topping, 1980–1986; and James Hardin, 1988–2004) to address its constituency and share its activities more broadly. Other notable publications were *Folklife and Fieldwork: A Layman's Introduction to Field Techniques* (1979; revised 1990, 2002), by Peter Bartis; *One Space, Many Places: Folklife and Land Use in New Jersey's Pinelands National Reserve* (1986), by Mary Hufford, on the relation between culture and natural landscape; *American Folk Music and Folklore Recordings: A Selected List* (1984–1992), edited by Jennifer Cutting, et al., an annual selection of the best folk recordings issued by commercial recording companies; *Folklife Annual* (1985–1990), edited by James Hardin and Alan Jabbour, a series of essays on folklife; and bibliographies and finding and reference aids for using the collections of the Folk Archive and the Library of Congress.

The most famous publications drawn from materials in the archive are doubtless the documentary folk music recordings issued in the 1940s under the series title *Folk Music of the United States*. By 1976, when the Center was created, the archive had produced 67 recordings in long-playing record (LP) form. In addition, a special 15-album bicentennial series, *Folk Music in America*, edited by Richard K. Spottswood, was released over a period of several years overlapping with the early years of the Center.

The Center continued this practice by issuing in 1978 an LP album *Folk-Songs of America* (AFS L68), featuring the field recordings created in the 1920s and 1930s by Robert W. Gordon, the first head of the archive. A year later, the Blue Ridge Parkway Folklife Project yielded a double-LP set, *Children of the Heav'nly King* (L69-70). And a few years later, *Omaha Indian Music* (L71) appeared. By the late 1980s, the Center's production of recorded publications ceased. It was a period of transition between the old LP format and the new digital compact disc. In addition, the Center was refocusing its publications strategy on working with private-sector partners rather than publishing and distributing directly.

The first fruits of the partnership strategy came out of the Endangered Music Project. It was proposed by Mickey Hart, a percussionist for the Grateful Dead and a longtime documentarian and advocate for grassroots music, American and worldwide. He proposed a series featuring the collections in the archive representing music of the world's cultures, in collaboration with the record company Rykodisc. The first in the series presented musical traditions from rainforest cultures of the tropical Americas. Entitled *The Spirit Cries*, it was released in early 1993. The second in the series, *Music for the Gods* (1994), presents music from Bali and nearby islands in Indonesia, drawn from the Fahnestock South Sea Collection, which was donated to the Center in 1986. Other releases have featured music from West Africa and the African American traditions of Brazil and the Caribbean.

The Center has also entered into a private-public partnership with Rounder Records for reissue in compact disc format of 20 records from the LP series for which the archive is famous, *Folk Music of the United States*. The initiative is in cooperation with the Library's Motion Picture, Broadcasting, and Recorded Sound Division, which includes the Recording Laboratory that originally issued the LP recordings. Thus, the legendary field recordings of the 1930s and the 1940s continue to live for a new generation in the latest technological format.

"American Memory" and the National Digital Library

From the cylinder recording machine, invented by Thomas Edison in 1877, to the compact disc as a medium for reproducing and distributing field recordings, the Folk Archive in its day and the American Folklife Center today have taken advantage of the latest technological innovations to carry out their missions in preserving and presenting American folksong and folklife. Likewise, Librarian of Congress James H. Billington has made it a hallmark of his administration to find new technologies for sharing the Library's collections with all people. In 1990, he launched the American Memory Project to digitize and make available over the Internet collections that illuminate facets of American history and culture. One of the first collections identified for online presentation was the Center's Sidney Robertson Cowell WPA Northern California Folk Music Project Collection, and the Center has made a major commitment to what has become the Library's National Digital Library Program. It has put online, in addition to the Cowell Collection, materials from the Paradise Valley Folklife Project; the Charles L. Todd and Robert Sonkin Migrant Worker Collection; the Juan B. Rael Collection of Hispanic music from the Southwest; Omaha Indian Music; and many more. These collections, free Center publications, and other information on the Center's programs and activities can be reached through the Center's Web site.

Through its Web site, the Center also makes available information about many collections donated by states and congressional districts under "Local Legacies," a project that encouraged individuals and organizations to document their own local traditions and activities as "gifts to the nation" during the Library's bicentennial celebration in 2000. The Veterans History Project, created by Congress in late 2000, partners with many individuals and organizations to collect and preserve oral histories and documentary materials from veterans (and those who supported them) of World War I, World War II, and the Korean, Vietnam, and Persian Gulf wars. These stories will be registered on a searchable database, and many will be available on the Veterans History Project Web site. A 2003 partnership with StoryCorps, a private organization created to help people interview their own friends and family, brings to the Center digital copies of these interviews, its first "born-digital" collection. (The participants receive a compact disc copy.) Thus does the American Folklife Center find itself, at the beginning of a new century, in the words of Folk Archive founder Robert W. Gordon, "a national project with many workers," newly engaged in its mission "to preserve and present American folklife." (JH, AJ)

Volunteers conduct an interview during the World War II Reunion in Washington, D.C. in May 2004. The Veterans History Project, administered by the American Folklife Center, urges grassroots participation in its efforts to record the stories of wartime veterans. Photograph: LC/Michaela McNichol.

Jabbour, Alan. "The American Folklife Center: A Twenty-Year Retrospective," in James Hardin, ed., *Folklife Center News*. Part 1, vol. xviii, nos. 1 and 2 (Winter-Spring 1996): 3–19; Part 2, vol. xviii, nos. 3 and 4 (Summer-Fall 1996): 3–23.

Library of Congress American Folklife Center: An Illustrated Guide. Foreword by Peggy A. Bulger. Preface by James Hardin. Washington, D.C.: Library of Congress, 2004.

AMERICANA

The Library's collections relating to American history and culture are its single most important collection strength. They are multimedia, multiformat, and so pervasive that they can be found not only throughout the general book collections but also, in varying degrees, in most of the institution's specialized research collections. Americana, for example, is the major subject in the collections of the Manuscript Division, which holds what is perhaps the most extensive and comprehensive collection of personal papers and organizational records relating to American history and culture ever assembled. Americana also dominates the collections of the Rare Book and Special Collections Division and the American Folklife Center. It is a principal strength of the collections in the following divisions: Geography and Map; Motion Picture, Broadcasting, and Recorded Sound; Music, and Prints and Photographs.

This poster by James Montgomery Flagg was originally published on the cover of "Leslie's Weekly" on July 6, 1916. More than four million copies were printed between 1917 and 1918 as the United States entered World War I. Because of its overwhelming popularity, the poster was also adapted for use in World War II and given its unforgettable title. LC/Prints and Photographs Division. Poster Collection. LC-USZC4-3859.

The Peter Force Collection purchased by the Library in 1867, is generally acknowledged as the foundation of the Library's Americana collections. The copyright amendment of 1865 and especially the centralization of all U.S. copyright registration and deposit activities at the Library in 1870 brought the Library unsurpassed "national collections" of Americana. Between 1865 and 1897, copyright deposit added to the Library holdings approximately 350,000 books and pamphlets; 47,000 maps and charts; 250,000 musical compositions; 12,000 engravings, lithographs, and chromolithographs; 33,000 photographs; 3,000 etchings; and 6,000 dramatic compositions.

In the twentieth century, specialists and curators in the Library's various divisions have obtained retrospective and unusual items, piece by piece, and numerous collections of personal papers and significant individual items have been acquired from American presidents, members of Congress, American politicians, Supreme Court justices, diplomats, scientists, artists, musicians, and other public figures. Organizations such as the National Association for the Advancement of Colored People (NAACP) have similarly placed their archives at the Library. Many other notable collections have been acquired through the years, and they are too numerous to list. But, as an example, the huge and invaluable Marian S. Carson Collection of Americana, acquired in 1993–1996, is a comparable landmark to the Peter Force Collection, encompassing more than 10,000 manuscripts, photographs, prints, drawings, books, and broadsides from the Colonial era through the 1876 Centennial celebration.

The strength of these special collections is supplemented by the Library's enormous holdings in American history and culture throughout the general book collections. In the early 1950s, the Library's reference staff began to discuss the feasibility of gathering together in one publication "a series of bibliographical studies of civilization in the United States." Planners felt that such a project would enable the Library to accomplish two objectives simultaneously: contribute to a wider diffusion of knowledge about the United States throughout the world, and prevent "wasteful duplication of work resulting from repeated attempts to give individual answers to questions that might be more satisfactorily answered within the compass of one carefully prepared reference work."

In 1960, the Library published *A Guide to the Study of the United States of America: Representative Books Reflecting the Development of American Life and Thought*, a one-volume, 1,193-page work that was prepared under the direction of Roy P. Basler, by Donald H. Mugridge and Blanche P. McCrum. The 6,487 entries, most of them annotated, were followed by an appendix, "Selected Readings in American Studies," a list of 190 titles. A supplement to the *Guide*, covering books published in the years 1956–1965 and listing nearly 3,000 titles, was published in 1976. It was prepared under the direction of Basler by Oliver H. Orr Jr. and the staff of the Library's

Bibliography and Reference Correspondence Section.

Many of the contributors to *A Guide to the Study of the United States of America* took part in a Library of Congress program that offered a course for academic credit: an orientation seminar on "Americana in the Library of Congress" that was presented by the Library's specialists from 1968 to 1980 as part of a new joint doctoral program in American Thought and Culture with George Washington University.

The multimedia strengths of the Library's Americana collections have come to the fore in the digital age. The American Memory program of the Library's National Digital Library is based on the richness of these collections. Beginning in 1995, American Memory began to use the Internet to disseminate digital versions of the Library's historical collections of American history and culture. At the end of fiscal year 2003, 123 multimedia historical collections containing more than 8.5 million items from the collections of the Library and other institutions were available on the American Memory Web site. The collections document the breadth of U.S. history—from the nation's founding, the wars it fought, the invention of baseball and motion pictures, the beginnings of the conservation movement, the Great Depression, the New Deal, photography, the civil rights movement—to modern music and dance. Moreover, as in the case of the thousands of New Deal arts documents that are part of American Memory, the collections cut across different formats (for example, typewritten oral history manuscripts and field notes, audio recordings, music recordings, photographs, motion pictures, theater scripts, set designs and production notebooks; posters, architectural drawings) to illuminate a particular period of American history. (JYC)

American Treasures in the Library of Congress. Introduction by Garry Wills. N.Y.: Harry N. Abrams, 1997.

"First Seminar in New LC-GWU Doctoral Program," *Library of Congress Information Bulletin* 27 (September 26, 1968): 579–581.

Gathering History: The Marian S. Carson Collection of Americana. Washington, D.C.: Library of Congress, 1999.

Virga, Vincent and the Curators of the Library of Congress. *Eyes of the Nation: A Visual History of the United States*. N.Y.: Alfred A. Knopf, 1997.

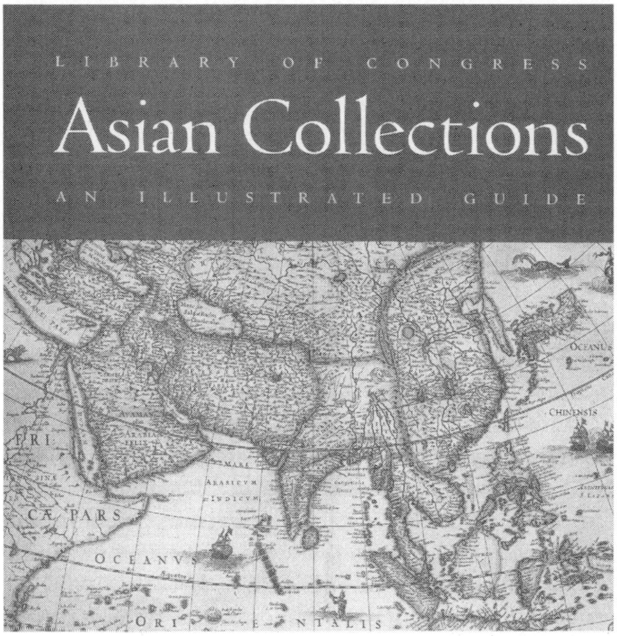

Administrative History and Historical Development

Although the Library of Congress first received Chinese publications in 1869, the Division of Chinese Literature was not officially established until July 1, 1928, more than 75 years ago. Its founding chief, Asian scholar Arthur W. Hummel, headed the division until 1954, seeing it through several reorganizations and name changes. In 1932, the Division of Chinese Literature became the Division of Orientalia. The Chinese and Japanese Sections were established within the division in 1938. The Orientalia Division became the Asiatic Division in 1942, and in the same year the Indic Section was formed. When the Library's Reference Department was reorganized in 1944, the name was changed back to the Orientalia Division. Finally, in 1978, the Asian Division in its current form was created to include the Chinese and Korean Section, the Japanese Section, and the Southern Asia Section, which includes South and Southeast Asia. The Korean Section was established as a separate section in 1990. The Asian Division was reorganized in 2004 into the following area collection teams: Chinese and Mongolian; Japan; Korea; Southeast Asia; and South Asia.

In his 1928 Annual Report, *Librarian of Congress Herbert Putnam proudly announced the appointment of Arthur W. Hummel (above), "an American sinologist very appropriate in temperament, learning, and experience" as the new Chief of the Division of Chinese Literature, which Putnam feels "is certain to be the center on this hemisphere for the pursuit of oriental studies."* LC Archives.

After Arthur W. Hummel (1928–1954), the chiefs of the Asian Division were Horace I. Poleman (1955–1965); Warren Tsuneishi (1966–1978, 1988–1992); J. Thomas Rimer (1982–1986); Mya Thanda Poe (1994–2001); and Hwa-Wei Lee (2003–present).

The Asian Division encompasses several different projects that have developed at the Library of Congress through the years. For example, Project F for the Development of Indic Studies was established on November 16, 1938, with a three-year grant from the Carnegie Foundation, and with assistance from the American Council of Learned Societies (ACLS). "Indic" applied not only to India but to all countries influenced by Indic culture. This project was to include all subject fields. The Library mounted a comprehensive exhibit: "Indic Manuscripts and Paintings" representing the main phases of Indic literature. Horace I. Poleman who was director of this project, went to South Asia for a year in 1939. Project F continued until June 30, 1942, and on July 1, 1942, the project was made a permanent part of the Library of Congress as the Indic Section of the Orientalia Division with Poleman as the Head. On his return from the region, he gave lectures at universities under the auspices of the Association of American Colleges. A comment in the ACLS Indic Committee's memorandum says: "In studying India, we concern ourselves not only with a survey of an important past, but we forecast a not less important future with which America of the second half of the twentieth century will have to live in increasingly close understanding and cooperation" would apply to Asia and the rest of the world. The ACLS project purchased microfilm apparatus for use in India.

Other major programs which developed the South and Southeast Asia collections were the PL-480 and the NPAC programs in the 1960s and 1970s. In 1961, under the amendment to Public Law 480 in the 83rd Congress, millions of dollars in local currencies owed as repayment for agricultural commodities, which by agreement with the foreign governments were made available for education and other purposes. With the strong support of the Committee on South Asia and the Far Eastern Association, the Library of Congress established the American Book Procurement Center in New Delhi. In 1963, the Jakarta office was established to acquire Indonesia materials under the PL-480 program. A separate office was set up in Karachi in 1965 to acquire materials from Pakistan. These programs developed into cooperative acquisitions programs, and continue to thrive despite the end of the PL-480 funding in all these countries at the end of the 1990s. The Library of Congress and American universities have built up comprehensive in-depth Asian collections from the region, which they could not have done with their own resources and funds. The Overseas Offices also have extensive preservation programs to microfilm and microfiche materials from Asia and other parts of the world, which are thus made available to the scholarly community.

In East Asia in the late 1960s, the Library of Congress jointly developed the Foreign Language Acquisitions Project with the Association for Research Libraries. In the early 1970s, Warren Tsuneishi and Donald Jay went on a survey trip to Bangkok, Hong Kong, and Tokyo. The Library decided to establish a field office in Tokyo in 1972. A large number of Asian publications were acquired from Japan until the office closed in 1985.

The Asian Division mounted three exhibitions in the mid-1980s that showcased the Asian collections. One commemorated United States-Thailand relations, "Amity and Commerce: 150 Years of the United States and Thailand Accord," which focused on a copy of the first treaty between an Asian country and the United States. The exhibit also displayed important old materials and a remarkable collection of musical instruments given by the reigning monarch, King Bhumibol Adulyej.

Another exhibit was on Japanese calligraphy, which depicted the artistic shape and form of this ancient style of communication. This exhibition, entitled "Words in Motion: Modern Japanese Calligraphy," included more than 130 examples of calligraphic art, historic documents, and an audiovisual presentation featuring revolutionary computer software that could be used to catalog in Chinese, Japanese, and Korean. During the exhibition, the Library's Center for the Book and the Asian Division cosponsored a symposium, "Calligraphy and the Japanese Word."

In June 1985, as part of the nation-wide Festival of India, the Asian Division coordinated the mounting of the 150-item exhibit, "Discovering India." Included in the exhibit were delicate paper fragments in Indian scripts; copyright deposits that reflect the influence of the designs, games, and music of India on the mainstream of American culture; historic eighteenth century maps; Landsat satellite images; and illustrations from Rudyard Kipling's *The Jungle Book*.

Exhibits were mounted on two occasions for the visits of the 14th Dalai Lama in 1979 and in 1984 depicting Tibetan culture with rare Tibetan books, maps, and rare books in Western languages. In 1986, a joint exhibition entitled "Riders on Earth Together: Expression of Faith in the Middle East and Asia" was mounted by the African and Middle Eastern Division and the Asian Division. The exhibition displayed from the collection of the two divisions a selection of beautiful and historically important documents and objects that illustrated the power of various faiths, past and present.

In the early 1990s, with funding of one million dollars on the occasion of the 200th anniversary of the U.S. Congress from the International Cultural Society of Korea, later known as the Korea Foundation, the Korean Section was formally established. The grant was used to strengthen the acquisition of scholarly publications, and to promote a variety of scholarly and cultural programs for the Korean collection in the Library. The Korean Trust Fund provided support for study trips by analysts in the Congressional Research Service (CRS). In 1998, funding was provided to CRS to invite Asian participants to the CRS Seminar on the Asian Economic Crisis and Pacific Rim Science and Technology: Implications for U.S. Policy held in the Library of Congress. In addition, the Fund assisted the Law Library to visit Korea, which led to the establishment of the first Asian site of the Law Library's Global Information Network (GLIN). Travel of Law Library staff and personnel from Korean organizations participating in GLIN continued to be funded. The compilation of the *Korean Catalog of Korean Rare Books* and the *Bibliography of English Books on Korea in the Library of Congress Available On-line* was completed with the use of these funds.

In 1992, the Japan Foundation Center for Global Partnership (CGP) and the Library of Congress agreed to establish the Japan Documentation Center (JDC) at the Library and the Tokyo Acquisitions Facility in Tokyo. Their main mission was to collect and disseminate current information on a wide range of Japanese policy issues, serve the reference needs of congressional and other researchers on policy information pertaining to Japan, and inform and educate the American public on Japanese information through newsletters in printed and electronic forms, seminars, and other activities. The JDC sponsored symposia in 1994, 1995, and 1996. In 1997, JDC co-sponsored with the Asia Pacific Technology Program at the U.S. Department of Commerce the Fifth International Conference on Japanese Information in Science, Technology and Commerce at the Library of Congress.

On May 30, 1997, the Asian Division, with the support of the Hong Kong Economic and Trade Office in Washington, D.C., held a symposium on Hong Kong: From Fishing Village to Financial Center, with panelists from Hong Kong and the United States. An exhibition on the same theme was mounted with the Interpretive Program Office, which explored Hong Kong's history showcasing 43 documents, books, manuscripts, maps, and photographs from the Library's collections, which highlighted the city's development into an international finance center.

The Asian Division acquired in the early twentieth century approximately 4,800 titles on about 15,000 fascicles of rare Japanese printed books and manuscripts of the pre-Meiji (pre-1867) period. In 1996, Shojo Honda compiled a bibliography, *Pre-Meiji Works in the Library of Congress: Japanese Literature, Performing Arts, and Reference Works*, which was published by the Library. From 1997 to 2002, Professor Kenji Watanabe of Rikkyo University led a team of faculty and students to survey on several visits the division's Japanese rare books. Their work resulted in the publication in 2003 of the *Catalog of Japanese Rare Books in the Library of Congress* by Yagi Shoten in Tokyo. This latest *Catalog* included also the listing of 628 works in Honda's bibliography. The Library's cataloging staff has been cataloging these materials for online bibliographic records since the project started.

The Henry Luce Foundation made a three-year grant to the division in 2000 for the purpose of expanding the acquisition of recent publications from China and encouraging scholarly use of the Library's collections of materials from East and Southeast Asia by fellowships. Through the Luce-funded Chinese Acquisition Project, the staffs of the African/Asian Acquisitions and the Overseas Operations Division and the Asian Division designed a new model of working with selected Chinese scholars and librarians in six regions of China to select, in a timely manner, new publications of particular interest to the Library of Congress. Six awards were made for the Luce Foundation-sponsored International Studies Fellowship; the competition was conducted by the American Council of Learned Societies. (HWL, MTP)

Hummel, Arthur W., "The Growth of the Orientalia Collections," *The Library of Congress Quarterly Journal of Current Acquisitions* 11 (February 1954): 69–87.

Library of Congress Asian Collections: An Illustrated Guide. Washington, D.C.: Library of Congress, 2000.

The Chinese Collections

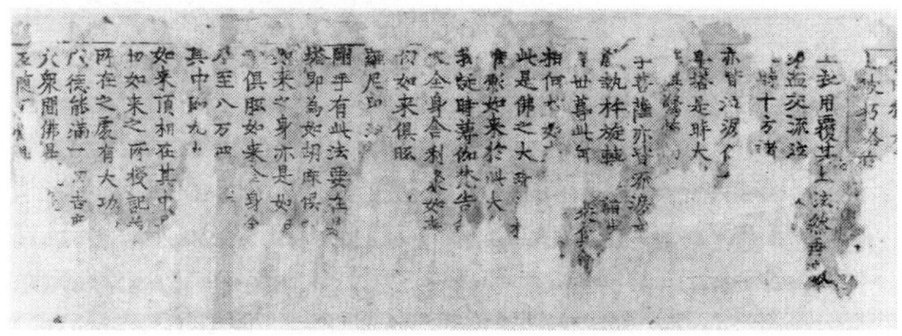

Buddhist Sutras from the Thunder Peak Pagoda (975 A.D.) The earliest example of Chinese printing in the Library of Congress. LC/Chinese Section, Asian Division.

The Chinese collection of the Library of Congress dates back to 1869, when it received 10 works, consisting of some 934 volumes from the Chinese government as the result of an international exchange system authorized by Congress two years earlier. The books included the Confucian classics and works on medicine, botany, language, philosophy, and mathematics, each with a notation "Presented to the Government of the U.S.A. by His Majesty the Emperor of China, June 1869."

Ten years later, in 1879, the Library acquired the Caleb Cushing collection of 237 titles in 2,547 volumes including history, medicine, classics, poetry, rituals, ethics, astronomy, essays, and dictionaries. Cushing, the first United States Ambassador to China, had acquired his collection during his six-month stay in Macau in 1844 when he negotiated the first U.S. treaty with China. In addition, Cushing's personal papers can be found in the Manuscript Division of the Library.

The 1869 exchange volumes and the Cushing collection were to remain the extent of the Chinese collection until the beginning of the twentieth century when William Woodville Rockhill, an American scholar and diplomat who served as Minister to China from 1905 to 1909, sent to the Library the first of what eventually were to be three donations of Chinese, Manchu, Mongolian, and Tibetan books.

The Chinese government presented 198 works from its exhibit at the Louisiana Purchase Exposition of 1904. China followed this in 1908 with another presentation to the Library in acknowledgment of America's return of its unused portion of the

Boxer Indemnity Fund. This gift was a complete set of the Chinese encyclopedia, the *Ku chin t'u shu chi ch'eng*, originally printed in 1728, and with 5,040 volumes considered to be the world's largest printed encyclopedia.

Three men played key roles in developing this foundation into a broad, systematic Chinese collection during the first half of the twentieth century. Herbert Putnam used his 40 years as Librarian of Congress (1899–1939) to expand the Library from a "national" to a "universal" library. To strengthen the Asian collections, Putnam turned to Walter Tennyson Swingle for help. A botanist with the U.S. Department of Agriculture who dedicated a long career to searching out Asian plants that could be useful in the United States, Swingle also collected tens of thousands of Chinese and Japanese books for the Library between 1913 and 1937. After 1928, Swingle's collecting was reinforced and guided by Arthur W. Hummel, a former missionary teacher in China and the first chief of the Library's Orientalia Division. Hummel, who served until 1954, presided over the growth of the Library's Asian collections to world-class status. Three areas of special strength may be singled out. The Library's collection of Chinese gazetteers or local histories (*fang chih*) is especially good. Containing information on each province's history, geography, economy, folklore, culture, and literary developments, gazetteers serve as good records of change over time since they were frequently revised. The second area is the *ts'ung shu* (*collectanea*) volumes of reprints that brought together manuscripts, monographs, and reprints of rare works no longer available. Rare books constitute the third area. Swingle, with the support of Hummel, made a major effort to acquire rare Chinese material, especially books from the Ming Dynasty (1368–1644). These were still widely available at reasonable prices from the 1920s through the war years. A large number of rare items were added to the collection in 1929 with the acquisition of the library of Wang Shu-an, a well-known professor at China's Tsinghua University. The Wang collection included 94 rare palace editions, 276 titles printed during the Ming Dynasty, and a Sung book printed between 1131 and 1162. The broad scope of the Wang acquisition enhanced the growing Chinese collection, filling gaps especially in the area of Chinese literature.

Hui-chiang chih (Gazetteer of the Muslim Regions), 1772.
LC/Chinese Section, Asian Division.

The Library's access to Chinese rare books was also expanded during World War II when the Director of China's National Library, T. L. Yuan, temporarily transferred rare books from Peking to the Library to save them from possible destruction. The Library microfilmed the books and made the films available to interested libraries. Wang Ch'ung-min, a specialist in rare Chinese works, compiled a catalog that was revised and supplemented by Yuan and published by the Library in 1957. The catalog lists 1,777 rare books in the Chinese collection.

The Chinese collection holds other unique materials. This includes a collection of state examination papers used to select the mandarins who governed traditional China. These were donated by Kiang Kang-hu, a scholar and politician who played an active role in Chinese history during the first half of the twentieth century. Also part of the Chinese collections are 10 books published by the Taiping Kingdom that offer insight into the early years of this internal rebellion that shook China from 1851 to 1864. They include volumes of Taiping edicts, an almanac, a book on Taiping rituals, religious hymns, a primer for children, a book of children's rhymes, and a bibliography of Taiping publications.

Another unique collection of nineteenth-century Chinese material came from the family of William Gamble (1830–1886), an American who went to China in 1858 as a missionary printer. The Gamble collection consists of some 277 Chinese publications and 120 items in English and other languages, dating mainly from the first half of the nineteenth century. The collection includes Christian missionary publications in Chinese and translations of western works on subjects such as geography, astronomy, and mathematics.

Within the Library's Chinese collections are valuable examples of traditional Chinese cartography. Before China adopted a mathematical system of mapping in the wake of the 1894–1895 Sino-Japanese War, Chinese maps were primarily concerned with aesthetics or local administrative priorities, frequently depicting internal waterways or coastal regions and walled cities. Many examples of traditional Chinese cartography can be found in the Geography and Map

Division. The Arthur W. Hummel Collection consists of some 85 scrolls, wall maps, and atlases dating from the Ming dynasty (1368–1644) through the nineteenth century. The Langdon Warner Collection has 30 items, including manuscript maps, atlases, and fan maps of China and Korea.

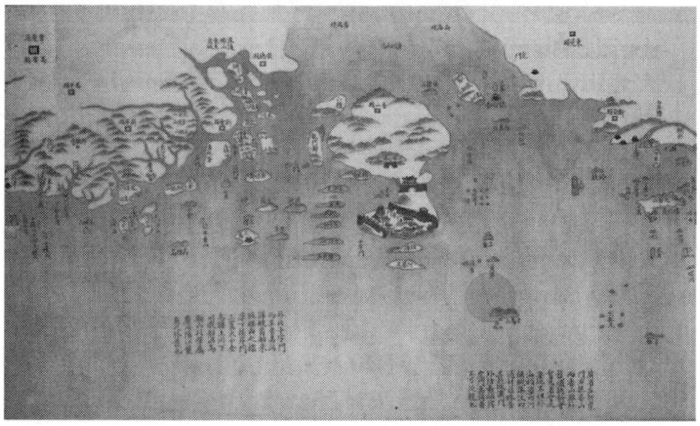

Eighteenth-Century Chinese Scroll Map.
LC/Chinese Section, Asian Division.

The revolution and wars that engulfed China during the first half of the twentieth century have also influenced the Library's Chinese holdings. The Library was able to obtain the only copies of some 4,000 unique and valuable publications issued by both the Nationalist and the Communist sides during the war years from 1939 to 1945. These publications cover subjects ranging from the social sciences and government to military strategy and wartime propaganda. The material also includes valuable Chinese Communist Party publications concerning party policies in the areas of northwest China under its control during World War II. Literary works are another particularly rich part of this collection, especially a number of modern Chinese plays written in the wartime capital of Chungking. These include works by the well-known writers Lao She (author of *Rickshaw Boy*) and Tsao Yu (*Sunrise* and *Thunderstorm*).

During the 1950s and 1960s, the Library acquired probably the best holdings on the People's Republic of China available in the West. Of special interest from that period are some 600 to 700 provincial newspapers. Following the 1972 visit to China of President Richard Nixon, the Library re-opened contact with the National Library of Peking. A formal exchange agreement was signed in 1979. From 1980 until 1987, the Library received a massive influx of Chinese publications, averaging some 24,000 titles each year.

Of the collection's nearly one million books, manuscripts, and other publications, the Library has more than 12,000 Chinese periodical titles and regularly receives about 45 Chinese-language newspapers and has more than 15,000 reels of microfilm. With a grant from the Chiang Ching-kuo Foundation for International Scholarly Exchange, the *Research Guide to Chinese Microforms* was prepared and is available online.

The Naxi Collection

Speaking a language belonging of the Tibeto-Burman family, the Naxi, previously called "Moso," live between Tibetan and Chinese cultural influences in the rugged northwestern Yunnan province. Their traditional religion drew heavily on Bon, the pre-Buddhist religion of Tibet. The Naxi use three different forms of writing. The contemporary form is essentially a mix of Chinese and Naxi. An older system, found in manuscripts as far back as the fourteenth century, was a syllabic or phonetic script called "Ggo-Baw" that was used only for transcribing mantras and *dharani* (magic formulas). Ggo-Baw used simple characters resembling those used by the nearby Lolo and Nosu tribes as well as Chinese characters. Perhaps most interesting is the third system, a unique form of pictographs dating back to at least the thirteenth century and recorded in manuscripts used in religious ceremonies.

The Library holds a unique collection of 3,342 Naxi pictographic manuscripts, about two-thirds of which came from the colorful explorer, adventurer, and scientist, Joseph Rock. The remainder came to the Library in 1945 as a gift from Quentin Roosevelt, a grandson of President Theodore Roosevelt. The Library holds two rare Naxi funeral scrolls, one painted on cloth and the other on paper. The cloth scroll is about 40 feet long and contains a series of individual paintings depicting devils, humans, and gods that represent the three realms through which the spirit must travel after death. The pictographic language is still used today in a simplified form by Naxi priests for a rural population of 295,000 farmers and traders. For two years, beginning in 1998, Professor Zhu Bao-Tian from the Yunnan Provincial Museum prepared a descriptive record of each manuscript at the Library. His work was funded by the Chiang Ching-kuo Foundation for International Scholarly Exchange.

The Manchu and Mongolian Collections

Two important dynasties stand somewhat apart in China's history. The Yüan Dynasty (1280–1368) was Mongolian and the Ch'ing Dynasty (1644–1912) was Manchu. Both Mongols and Manchus have their own written languages, taken from the Syrian Estrangelo alphabet introduced by Nestorian Christian missionaries in the seventh or eighth century. Many of the Library's approximately 80 Mongolian manuscripts and xylographs are Buddhist religious texts. Of the non-religious texts, the *Great Yuan Gazetteer* (*Ta Yüan i t'ung chih*) is especially important. Kublai Khan ordered the first draft of this book in 1285 and his grandson Timur (Ch'eng tsung), who ruled from 1284 to 1307, had the work revised. The Library's fourteenth-century manuscript consists of six books bound in 10 volumes, each volume with a large seal showing it had been seen by the Yüan Emperor in 1303. Another valuable Mongol work is *The Epic Poem of King Gesar*, printed in 1716, and one of the classics of Mongolian literature. In 1992, the Library's New Delhi Field Office began acquiring and cataloging modern publications from Mongolia, which now total nearly 2,500 volumes of monographs, 160 serial titles, and more than 2,000 microfiche.

The Manchu collection consists of about 400 titles covering philosophy, religion, language, literature, politics, and Chinese classics. Of particular interest are *The Book of Old Manchu Speech to Keep Up Good Manners; History of the Manchu Tribes*, printed in 1744; and *Ritual of the Manchus*, printed in 1776. The Edward Barrett collection of 114 titles, some wholly in Manchu and others in Manchu and Chinese, provide valuable insight into the economic affairs of the Ch'ing Dynasty. It contains reports to the throne on the condition of the Treasury, on the types and quality of valuables received and stored in the palace, on rental income from imperial lands, and on the distribution of payments to Manchu and Mongol bannermen (soldiers).

Hu, Shu Chao. *The Development of the Chinese Collection in the Library of Congress*. Boulder, Colorado: Westview Press, 1979.

The Japanese Collection

One of the Library's earliest visitors from East Asia was a Japanese diplomatic delegation that came to Washington in 1860. During a call on the House of Representatives, two members of the delegation were escorted to the Library of Congress, then located inside the Capitol. According to newspaper reports of the time, the Japanese were surprised to find a Japanese grammar text, translated from a Portuguese Jesuit book printed in Nagasaki in 1604.

Despite this early visit and a limited exchange of government publications, the Library's first important effort at building its Japanese collections came later, in 1907 and 1908 with the purchase of some 9,000 volumes (over 3,000 titles) of important works on Japanese history, literature, Buddhism, Shinto, geography, music, and arts. This fine collection came to the Library through the efforts of Asakawa Kanichi, a Yale University historian, who was commissioned by the Library of Congress and Yale to acquire books during his 18-month stay in Japan in 1906 and 1907.

Japanese Poets. A drawing of part of a group known as The Thirty-Six Poetic Geniuses, a list of outstanding Japanese poets from the time of the poetry anthology Manyoshu (759) to the end of the 10th century.
LC/Japanese Section, Asian Division.

An important gift of Japanese art to the Library was received in 1905 from Crosby Stuart Noyes, journalist and editor of the *Washington Evening Star*. His gift to the Library included watercolors, drawings, woodblock engravings, lithographs, and illustrated books, all of which were produced between the mid-eighteenth century and the late nineteenth century and a fascinating series of over 100 colored woodblock prints, essentially political cartoons, on the Sino-Japanese War of 1894–1895 and the Russo-Japanese War of 1904–1905.

By 1930, American academic interest in Japan was increasing and the Library hired its first Japanese specialist, Sakanishi Shio. It was Sakanishi who pioneered the development of the Library into a first-rate resource for scholars of Japan, while also actively promoting Japanese studies in the United States.

The Library's Japanese collections include both traditional and modern material, reflecting the periods before and after Japan's decisive break with its past in the mid-nineteenth century. The Meiji

Restoration of 1868 put Japan on a new footing as the nation began a period of rapid modernization and took on an increasing role in East Asian affairs.

Nature painting on silk from Album of Twelve Original Watercolor, artist unknown, 1890. LC/Japanese Section, Asian Division.

Today's Pre-Meiji Printed Books and Manuscripts Collection consists of some 5,200 titles, with most dating from the early seventeenth century to 1867. Among its items is a rare edition of the Japanese literary masterpiece, *Genji Monogatari* (*The Tale of the Genji*), published in Kyoto in 1654 and written in the first decade of the eleventh century by Lady Murasaki Shikibu. *Genji Monogatari* is considered to be the world's earliest novel. The collection also holds a rare volume of *Heike Monogatari*, written during the Kamakura period (1185–1333) and representing a new type of *monogatari*, the war tale. The Library's volume is especially valuable because it indicates how the text should be chanted during a performance. Another rare book in the Pre-Meiji Collection is the *Yoshitsune Azuma Kudari Monogatari*, printed with moveable type between 1624 and 1643. Bronze moveable type was brought to Japan from Korea at the end of the sixteenth century. In Japan, it was often combined with wooden moveable type to print books for a short period between 1600 and 1650. This form of printing gave way to woodblock printing until the end of the Edo period when wooden moveable type came into use again. The *Yoshitsune Azuma Kudari Monogatari* tells part of the story of Japan's eleventh-century tragic hero, Minamoto Yoshitsune. The Library's copy is one of only two known to exist. The other is in Japan.

In the West, perhaps the best known Japanese poetic form is the "haiku." The haiku reached its peak during the Tokugawa period (1615–1868) with the poetry of Matsuo Basho. The collection holds many haiku anthologies by common people such as merchants, shopkeepers, women, and artisans.

Another rare manuscript is *Kabuki Sugatami*, written by the kabuki actor Nakamura Nakazo in 1776, a valuable source for the study of kabuki and its history.

The Japanese collection also contains the world's second oldest example of printing that is still in existence and that has a date of printing recorded in contemporary historical documents. It consists of three printed strips of Buddhist sutras used as prayer charms, printed between 764 and 770 A.D. The prayers were placed in one million wooden pagodas that were distributed equally to 10 temples throughout Japan to mark the end of an eight-year civil war. The project involved the work of 157 people over a six-year period, making it one of the earliest examples of mass production.

Eighth-Century Buddhist Ddarani Prayer Charms. These printed prayers are considered to be the world's second oldest examples of printing. LC/Japanese Rare Book Collection, Asian Division.

Despite the importance of the Pre-Meiji Collection, the modern holdings are also significant. With the end of World War II, the Library's holdings of Japanese material increased rapidly and are today the most extensive collection outside Japan. Valuable Japanese government records that throw light on Japanese decision-making before the war were transferred to the Library from the Washington Documentation Center. Among them are records from the former Japanese Imperial Army and Navy, the South Manchuria Railway Company, and the East Asian Research Institute (Toa Kenkyujo). The Library also has a microfilm copy of the archives of the Japanese Foreign Ministry from 1868 to 1945. Japanese scholars have also used the Library's pre-1945 records of the Police Bureau of Japan's Ministry of Home Affairs.

With Japan's increasing exposure to the West following Commodore Perry's missions in the 1850s, print makers began to portray the strange foreigners coming to their shores and the exotic nations they represented. This fascination with foreigners is well illustrated by the Chadbourne Collection of Japanese prints in the Prints and Photographs Division. A gift to the Library from Mrs. E. Crane Chadbourne in 1930, the collection consists of 187 late eighteenth and nineteenth century prints, the majority showing American and European visitors in Japan and imagined scenes of foreign cities.

The Geography and Map Division holds many early Japanese maps. These include the Shannon McCune Collection of scrolls, atlases, wood blocks, and fan maps of Japan and Korea from the fifteenth to the nineteenth centuries. More modern maps provide insight into the early period of Japanese expansion in northeast Asia. These include a collection of Japanese Army manuscript route maps of Korea and China prepared from 1878 to the 1880s and manuscript maps concerning the Russo-Japanese War (1904–1905) from Theodore Roosevelt's papers. Japanese material in other divisions of the Library includes pre-1946 newsreels and movies in the Motion Picture, Broadcasting and Recorded Sound Division; posters, ukiyo-e, other prints, and photographs in the Prints and Photographs Division; and recorded music and scores in the Music Division.

The Asian Division's Japanese collection has more than 1.1 million books and serials. Its holdings include major Japanese newspapers such as *Asahi shinbun*, *Yomiuri shinbun,* and *Nikkei weekly*. Technical reports in English are held in the Science, Technology and Business Division.

The Korean Collection

The Library's Korean collection has made up for a relatively late start and is probably the largest and most comprehensive outside Korea. The collection is primarily contemporary, although it contains a number of valuable pre-nineteenth-century publications in traditional format. Korea absorbed early cultural influences from China, including language, and many of its early classics were written in Chinese. Old Korean books appear quite different from their counterparts in China and Japan. They tend to be larger and are often printed on tough, durable paper. Because of the quality of the paper, Korean versions of Chinese classics sometimes survived the original printings in China. For example, the only existing version of an important fourteenth-century Chinese map, *Sheng-chiao Kuang-pei t'u* (*Map of the Vast Reach of China's Moral Teaching*), is a fifteenth-century Korean work containing a copy of the original.

Korea made a special contribution to the technology of printing by developing moveable cast metal type, beginning in 1403. Although China first used moveable type made of clay, it was in Korea that printing with moveable metal type reached a high point in the fifteenth century. Korean printing technology spread to China and Japan, but moveable type was not a commercial success and by the nineteenth century had been almost completely displaced by the older woodblock printing. This in turn soon gave way to European typography. The Asian Division holds some fine examples of Korean printing from metal moveable type. These include the collected writings of the renowned sixteenth-century Confucian scholar and statesman Yi I, printed in 1744, and the 1834 reprint of the works of the "father of Korean literature," Ch'oe Ch'i-won (857–915). Examples of rare woodblock-printed books include a history of the Koryo Dynasty (*Koryo Sa*), printed in 1590, and the law code of the Yi Dynasty (*Kyongguk Taijon*), printed in 1630.

The Library has some 422 titles in 2,900 volumes of rare Korean books, printed on mulberry paper in Chinese characters, many of which were acquired in the 1920s. While the majority of the Korean rare books are in the Asian Division, 13 titles are in the Law Library. There are also rare Korean maps in the Geography and Map Division, including those provided to the Library by the American geographer Shannon McCune. Unique Korean photographs also may be found in the Prints and Photographs Division.

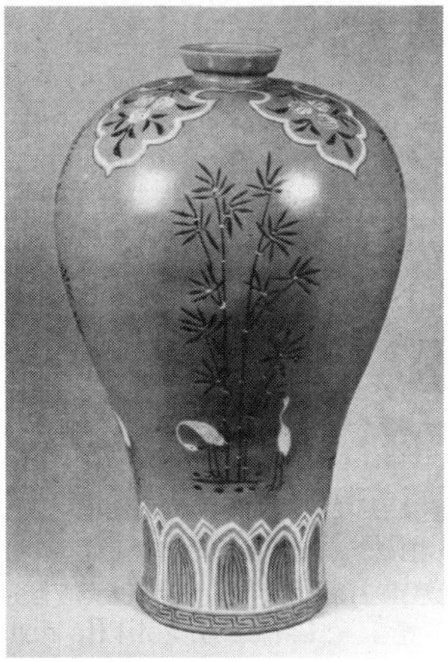

Korean vase from the Koryo period (918–1392). From Choson Yujok Yumul Togam (Illustrated Book of Ruins and Relics of Korea), a 17-volume set published in Pyongyang in 1994.
LC/Korean Collection, Asian Division.

The most important contributor to the Library's classical Korean book collection was Dr. James S. Gale, a Canadian missionary who arrived in Korea in 1888 and spent the next 40 years there. A prodigious scholar, Gale translated many of Korea's literary classics into English and wrote numerous books on Korean history, literature, and culture. Gale also helped the Library procure a number of Korean classics, including rare books from the estate of the Korean scholar Kim To-hui. In 1927, the Library received the major portion of Gale's own library, more than doubling its Korean holdings.

The Library began systematic acquisition of Korean-language publications in 1950 and the collection now includes books, periodicals, and some 250 newspapers that go back to the 1920s. Through a 1966 exchange agreement between the United States and the Republic of Korea, the Library has built up an especially strong collection of Korean government publications. Another strength of the contemporary collection is Korean trade publications, systematically built up since 1955.

The Asian Division has 10,000 items from North Korea that are vital to scholars and government officials trying to understand developments in the north. The Library receives the two major North Korean newspapers, one a government paper and the other the Party paper, as well as several dozen North Korean periodicals. Two newspaper titles have been microfilmed. In 1998, the acquisition of North Korean published material was regularized through a book vendor.

As noted earlier, the rapid development of the Korean collection during the 1990s is in large part due to the generous support of the International Cultural Society of Korea, which presented the Library with a gift of one million dollars in December 1989, on the 200th anniversary of the U.S. Congress.

The Southern Asian Collection

The title of a slim nineteenth-century volume in the Library's collection of Indian books almost shouts out to be noticed—*Was the Ramayana Copied from Homer?* by Kashinath Trimbak Telang, Senior Fellow at Elphinstone College and Advocate at H.M.'s High Court in Bombay. The yellowing pages contain Telang's indignant but scholarly rebuttal to the German Indologist, Albrecht Weber, who he accused of suggesting that the Indian epic, the *Ramayana*, "is nothing more than a Buddhist saga dovetailed to the Homeric story of the Trojan War." The book, inscribed "To Professor Weber, with the author's compliments," is part of Weber's Indological library, the first major purchase of books about the Indian subcontinent by the Library of Congress in 1904. Weber's terse, handwritten comments in the margins, not always complimentary, are perhaps as interesting as the text itself.

The possibility of classical Greek influences on Indian culture was one of the great issues that captivated nineteenth-century European scholars of India. Western interest in India's past started with the work of the Jesuits and was carried forward by Europeans working for the East India Company in the eighteenth century. The founding of the Asiatic Society of Bengal in 1784 marked the beginning of a sustained scholarly effort to understand India's complex civilization and languages. The first president of the Asiatic Society of Bengal, Sir William Jones, or "Oriental Jones" as he was sometimes called, spurred European interest in India when he found that Sanskrit was related to Latin and Greek. Today, the chief languages of Europe, including English, and the languages of the northern part of the Indian subcontinent are all classified as part of the Indo-European family of languages. Translations of classical Indian works by French and German scholars in the nineteenth century influenced the founding of the German Romantic Movement in the nineteenth century as well as the Transcendentalist movement in the United States.

The purchase of the Weber collection of over 4,000 books and pamphlets in 1904 laid the foundation for the Library's extensive holdings on South Asia. The Weber collection includes texts in Sanskrit of India's sacred Hindu works, the Vedas, Brahmanas, and Upanishads as well as the stories of the Puranas and the great epics in the Mahabharata and the Ramayana. The Weber collection also contains material in other Indian languages, Indian works on music, science, history, geography, and grammar and most of the writings on India by nineteenth-century European scholars. In addition, there are a number of Weber's notebooks with his handwritten transcriptions of rare Indian texts for his pioneering critical editions.

It was not until 1938, however, that the Library began to develop the southern Asian collection systematically, thanks to a grant from the Carnegie Corporation. A Sanskritist with a doctorate from the University of Pennsylvania, Horace I. Poleman, was brought into the Library to head "Project F—Development of Indic Studies," which in 1942 became a permanent section of what is today's Asian Division. During a field trip to India and Southeast Asia in 1939, Poleman reinforced and expanded the Library's relationships with universities, museums, and government publishers and obtained microfilms of rare manuscripts, as well as pamphlets, recordings of Indian music, and movies of traditional ceremonies of the Malabar coast. The music and movies can be found in the Library's Music Division and Motion Picture, Broadcasting, and Recorded Sound Division.

Distinguished Islamic scholar Hadji Agua Salim (left) visited the Library on February 5, 1953. With Librarian of Congress Luther Evans (center) and Horace I. Poleman, Chief of the South Asia Section, he examines a 200-year old manuscript written on palm leaves in the old Javanese language. LC Archives.

Besides being the home of Hinduism, South Asia is also the birthplace of Buddhism. The Southern Asian collection holds some unique remnants of Buddhism's journey along remote settlements on the southern fringe of Sinkiang's Taklamakan desert. The "Crosby Khotan Fragments" contain parts of Buddhist texts as well as illustrations of the Buddha and bodhisattvas. During a 1903 journey to Central Asia, Oscar Terry Crosby, an American who later became an Assistant Secretary of the Treasury, purchased this bundle of manuscripts in the oasis town of Khotan, famous for its jade and carpets. Following in the footsteps of the explorers Sven Hedin and Sir Aurel Stein, Crosby found local Khotan businessmen well aware of the demand for Silk Road antiquities in the West and not beyond manufacturing them to satisfy the demand. One of the Library's Khotan fragments is, in fact, a fake done in a script invented by a local entrepreneur.

A number of magnificent early books reflecting the West's fascination with India can be found in the Library's Rare Book and Special Collections Division. These include such beautiful works as the Daniell brothers' massive volumes of aquatints of Indian views and the earliest work on Indian flora, Hendrik van Reede tot Drakestein's *Horti Malabarici* of 1686. The William M. Carpenter Collection in the Prints and Photographs Division also holds valuable early twentieth-century photos of India.

Before World War II, there was virtually no interest in the United States in the modern languages of South Asia. Scholars were then fixated on the classical languages of Sanskrit, Pali, Prakrit, Arabic, and Persian. In 1945, however, this began to change. Disrupted by the war, the Library's acquisition program was then resumed and orders were placed with five Indian dealers for a broad array of publications. Horace I. Poleman, the Asian Division's Indologist, made another trip to India in 1947, buying publications in modern languages, recordings of Indian music, and legal texts. During the 1950s, the collection grew rapidly. By 1953, the Library was receiving 86 contemporary newspapers and periodicals in the languages of India, Pakistan, and Ceylon. The collection's growth was spurred even more in 1962 when the Public Law PL-480 program began, enabling the Library to use rupees from Indian purchases of U.S. agricultural products to buy Indian books. The Library's Field Office in New Delhi was opened the same year to implement the program, marking the beginning of the thorough and systematic acquisition of publications in the modern languages of South Asia. A field office was opened in Karachi in 1965 to oversee the acquisition of modern Pakistani publications.

Today, the Southern Asian collection holds material in over 50 modern languages of India, Pakistan, Bangladesh, Sri Lanka, Nepal, and the Maldives. The majority of these publications are in the fields of literature, religion, philosophy, history, and politics, but all subjects are included.

Nepalese Manuscript. This manuscript from Nepal, in Newari and Sanskrit, dates from around 1900.
LC/Southern Asian Collection, Asian Division.

Among the Library's unique holdings are World War II records in English and Hindi from the Indian National Army, that operated against British forces from Burma with Japanese support. In addition, the Motion Picture, Broadcasting, and Recorded

Sound Division has an excellent collection of audiovisual material from India, including a large collection of 78 r.p.m. recordings of Indian music made by British and American companies working in India in the first half of the twentieth century. More music from India, Sri Lanka, Nepal, and Pakistan can be found in the Library's Archive of Folk Culture. The Archive also holds recordings of Nestorian Christian services at several churches in the Indian state of Kerala, made by Prince Peter of Greece and Denmark in 1949.

The Southeast Asian Collection

A region of great diversity, modern Southeast Asia consists of Brunei, Myanmar (Burma), Cambodia, Indonesia, Laos, Malaysia, the Philippines, Singapore, Thailand, East Timor, and Vietnam. The Library started systematic acquisition of Southeast Asian publications following the end of World War II and as American interest in the region grew with the development of the Cold War. Today, the Library's Jakarta Field Office ensures that the Library's contemporary holdings in the languages of Southeast Asia reflect the full range of publications available in the region. The Library's holdings also include material from the island states of the Pacific. Despite its focus on contemporary publications, the Southeast Asian collections also contain earlier, rare material.

Indonesian/Malay

The Library's Southeast Asian collections got an early start when, in 1866, the Smithsonian Institution transferred a collection of books to the Library. These included unique books and manuscripts in the Malay and Bugis languages that were collected in Singapore in 1842 by the United States Naval Exploring Expedition, commanded by the colorful Lieutenant Charles Wilkes, who later served as a model for Captain Ahab in Herman Melville's classic *Moby Dick*.

Among these books are two editions of an important Malay history, the *Sejarah Melayu*, or "Malay Annals" written in Jawi, a local adaptation of Arabic script. The Wilkes Expedition also brought back several works in the script used by the Bugis people from South Sulawesi who ran an extensive seaborne trading network, of which Singapore became a central part. The Manuscript Division holds the papers and journals of a number of participants in the Wilkes Expedition, including Wilkes himself; his second in command, William Leverreth Hudson; and one of the Expedition's sailors, Joseph G. Clark.

Of particular interest to scholars of Indonesia are some of the early manuscript maps of the Indonesian archipelago in the Geography and Map Division. One set of 14 maps was previously owned by Gilbert Elliot, the First Earl of Minto, who served as Governor General of India from 1807 to 1814 and who led Britain's 1811 expedition to expel the Dutch from the island of Java. Another set consists of eighteenth century Spanish manuscript maps showing coastal areas, primarily of Sumatra.

The Philippines

When the Spanish arrived in the Philippine Islands in the sixteenth century, they found a system of writing based on Indic script in use. However, no literature or official records written before 1521 were found. Thus, early accounts of the Philippines are virtually all in Spanish. After 1898, when the Philippines fell under U.S. administration, English became the primary language of government and education. The Library's holdings on the Philippines before it achieved full independence in 1946 are therefore largely in these two languages.

Early Spanish accounts such as Diego de Aduarte's 1640 *Historia de la Provincia del Sancto Rosario* and the first book printed in Manila, *Doctrina Christiana*, as well as a copy of the treaty between General Bates representing the United States and the Sultan of Jolo in Arabic script and in English, can be found in the Rare Book and Special Collections Division. The Manuscript Division has material from the Spanish period such as records of the Catholic Church in the Philippines from 1707 to 1799, a 1654 history of the Jesuits in Mexico, Guatemala and the Philippines, and a microfilm copy of the Urbanite collection from the Vatican Library.

Doctrina Christiana *(1593). The first book printed in the Philippines.* LC/Rosenwald Collection, Rare Book and Special Collections Division.

The Manuscript Division also holds valuable material on the Philippine campaign of the Spanish–American War, notably the papers of General John J. Pershing. Of special interest to students of the beginning of American involvement in the Philippines is the Wildman brothers' unique collection of documents and photographs covering the period 1897 through the 1900s. Rounsevelle Wildman was American Consul in Hong Kong during the Spanish–American War and the ensuing Philippine–American War from 1899 to 1901. He maintained close contact with pro-independence Filipinos in Hong Kong. His brother, Edwin, covered the Philippine–American War as a correspondent and his journals and photos are also part of the Wildman Collection. Other material on the Philippine independence movement against Spain and the war against the United States includes Filipino General Emilio Aguinaldo's papers and the Philippine–American War collection of some 300 documents.

The American colonial period and World War II are well covered by material in the Manuscript Division. Of special value to scholars are the papers of William Howard Taft, who before becoming president of the United States chaired the Second Philippine Commission (1900–1901) and served as Governor of the Philippines from 1901 to 1904. A large collection of documents from General Leonard Wood, an army officer who served as Governor General of the Philippines from 1921 to 1927, covers an especially difficult period in American-Filipino relations. The papers of Andres Soriano, who served on General Douglas MacArthur's staff during World War II, are also in the Manuscript Division. A number of rare photographs from the late 1890s to World War II are held in the Prints and Photographs Division.

Myanmar (Burmese), Cambodian, Lao, and Thai

Although Myanmar (Burma), Cambodia, Laos, and Thailand are each unique states with their own histories, they share important traditions. Their writing systems use alphabets derived from the early Indian script known as Brahmi and their predominant religion has been Theravada Buddhism since the gradual decline of other Indian-derived religions by the thirteenth century.

The Library holds many palm leaf manuscript texts of the *Tipitaka*, Theravada Buddhism's basic text, and the extensive commentaries written on it. In 1905, King Chulalongkorn (Rama V), the well-known Thai reformer, presented the Library with a modern Thai version of the *Tipitaka*. A Burmese *Tipitaka*, written in Pali using Burmese script, was presented to the Library in 1949 as part of a large Burmese donation. The Library holds an especially fine collection of 124 early Burmese Theravada palm leaf manuscripts in Pali.

The Library has a good selection of traditional Thai historical texts primarily on microfiche. An important Burmese history, the *Hmannan Mahayazawindawgyi* (*The Glass Palace Chronicle*), written by a group of scholars appointed by King Bagyidaw in 1829, was part of a 1949 Burmese donation that included a number of other important works of Burmese language and literature.

The Library has several rare accounts of early European contacts with Thailand. Among the earliest is the French diplomat Marquis Alexandre de Chaumont's record of his 1685 mission. Accompanied by a large delegation of Jesuits, Chaumont aimed to convert King Narai to Christianity, a mission doomed to failure. The Rare Book and Special Collections Division has a copy of Chaumont's book, *Relation de l'ambassade de Mr le chevalier de Chaumont a la cour du roy de Siam*, published in Paris in 1686. It also has several editions of *Yoyage de Siam, des peres jesuites, envoyez par le roy aux Indies & a la Chine*, by Guy Tachard, one of the Jesuits in the Mission.

Among the Library's collections is unique American material that provides a glimpse of nineteenth-century Thailand. The first treaty between the United States and an Asian state was negotiated by Edmund Roberts with the Thai government in 1833. Roberts's journal and personal papers are in the Manuscript Division as are the papers of John Barrett, United States Minister to Thailand from 1894 to 1898. Barrett's large collection of photos of Thailand from the 1890s are held separately in the Prints and Photographs Division. Of special interest to historians of nineteenth-century Thailand are two serial titles, the English-language newspaper *Bangkok Recorder*, which was started by the American Dan Beach "Mo"

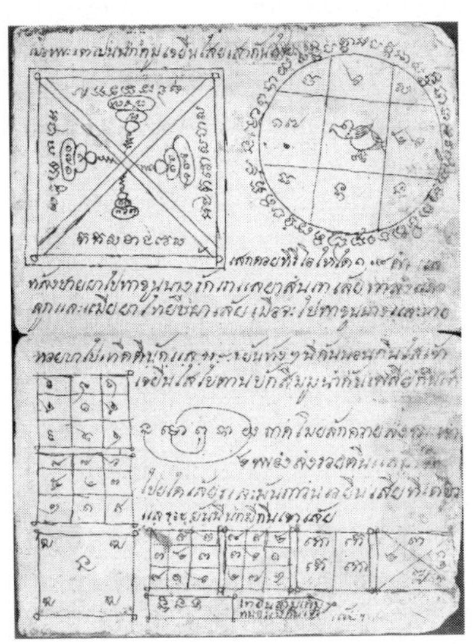

"Nong Rak Chaophi Oei." A manuscript from Thailand, probably nineteenth century.
LC/Southeast Asian Collection.

Bradley in 1865, and a major Buddhist periodical, *Thammachaksu* (*The Eye of the Law*).

During World War II, the United States supported the anti-Japanese resistance in Thailand, the Free Thai Movement. The American largely responsible for bringing about this relationship was Kenneth Landon, a former missionary in Thailand and later Washington's leading expert on Thailand, serving with both the Office of Strategic Services, and the Department of State. Dr. Landon donated hundreds of pages of transcripts of Free Thai radio broadcasts to the Library, along with a small but important collection of post-World War II Thai books on politics as well as Thai political fiction.

Vietnamese

Vietnam has traditionally stood apart from the rest of Southeast Asia, separated by its close historical and cultural ties to China. Although fiercely proud of its independence from China after 939 A.D., Vietnam continued to follow many Chinese traditions, including the use of Chinese as the official language of the court and elite. In the seventeenth century, Alexandre de Rhodes, a French Jesuit, and his fellow missionaries devised a romanized alphabet for written Vietnamese that eventually replaced Chinese characters and is currently in use.

Vietnam has a strong tradition of written dynastic history. Although many of the Library's early Vietnamese histories are reprints in modern Vietnamese, the Asian Division has a small collection of important Vietnamese books in traditional format. In 1918, the Director of the Ecole Francaise d'Extreme Orient in Hanoi gave the Library several valuable works published in Chinese. Two of these books were printed for the Library from the original wooden blocks at the imperial palace in Hue. One of these, *Kham Dinh Viet Su Thong Giam Cuong Muc,* is a nineteenth century history of Vietnam. The other, *Dai Nam Nhat Thong Chi*, is an early Vietnamese gazetteer. Besides these two large works, the French gift included two copies of the best-known work in Vietnamese literature, *Kim Van Kieu*, written by Nguyen Du in 1813. One copy is in Chinese characters used phonetically, a form of writing called "Chu Nom;" the other is in standard romanization, "Quoc Ngu."

In 1920, the Library received another important Vietnamese history printed on the palace library blocks in Hue, the *Dai Viet Su Ky Toan Tho* (*Complete Annals of the Great Viet*). Rounding out the Library's collection is an 1884 Shanghai reprint of the *An-Nam Chi Luoc*, written toward the end of the thirteenth century and probably the oldest Vietnamese historical work that has been preserved.

More modern holdings reflect America's intense military and political involvement in Indochina from the 1950s to 1975. Acquisition of French-language publications from Indochina was stepped up in the late 1940s. By the early 1950s, the Library was receiving Vietnamese-language newspapers and signs of growing interest in Vietnamese internal politics were in evidence, such as the Library's acquisition of an intriguing book on Vietnam's Cao Dai religion, published in 1950 under the auspices of the Commander in Chief of the Cao Dai army and Saigon's Minister of Armed Forces, General Tran Quang Vinh. The Library also holds copies of reports on government and administrative reform in South Vietnam from Michigan State University's "Vietnam Advisory Group."

An extensive record of the television coverage of the Vietnam War can be found in the Library's Motion Picture, Broadcasting, and Recorded Sound Division. Included are special reports that appeared on ABC, CBS, and NBC; historic footage from Nippon News covering the Japanese occupation during World War II; travelogues on French Indochina produced in the late 1940s; and a French film collection on the colonial period with perspectives from the Viet Minh and Ho Chi Minh and some scenes from 1901.

Another interesting source of material on the war is found in the Manuscript Division, which holds the notes and records of Neil Sheehan, author of *A Bright Shining Lie: John Paul Vann and America in Vietnam* (1988).

With the end of the war and the arrival of hundreds of thousands of refugees from Indochina, the Library began to see a large increase in demand for publications in the languages of the region. Today, the Asian Division's holdings in Vietnamese include some 75 newspapers, about half published in Vietnam and the rest published by the overseas Vietnamese community. The Division also receives 247 Vietnamese periodicals, over half published in Vietnam, and a broad selection of fiction and non-fiction published in Vietnam. Many of these books come through an exchange program between the National Library in Hanoi and the Library of Congress, initiated before the end of the war in 1973.

The other languages of Indochina are represented by small but growing collections in Khmer, Lao, and Hmong (an upland minority group in Laos, Thailand, Burma, and China). The Motion Picture, Broadcasting and Recorded Sound Division holds materials on several Lao minority groups such as the Khammu and Hmong as part of the Indochina Archives Project of the Social Science Research Council. The diaries of Souvanna Phouma, former

Prime Minister of Laos, can be found in the Manuscript Division.

Pacific Collections

The Library holds a fascinating collection of South Pacific material that predates World War II. In 1934, the Fahnestock brothers, Bruce and Sheridan, began a three-year voyage to study the cultures of the Pacific. During a second sailing expedition in 1940,

The Fahnestock brothers Sheridan and Bruce at the Presto disc-cutter in 1940. Their Pacific Islands research and collecting formed the basis for much pre-World War II scholarship about southeast Asia. LC/Asian Division.

the Fahnestocks made extensive recordings of music from American Samoa, Fiji, French Polynesia, New Caledonia, and Australia before their ship hit a reef near Australia and sank.

A third voyage in 1941, as war loomed in the Pacific, resulted in rare recordings of music on the islands of Indonesia including Bali, Madura, and the Kangean islands. With the outbreak of war, the Fahnestocks joined the United States Army's Small Ships Section in New Guinea, the unit that inspired the 1960s television series "The Wackiest Ship in the Army." In 1986, Margaret Fahnestock Lewis, the widow of Sheridan Fahnestock, gave the Library much of the material the brothers had collected on their three expeditions. The Library's Archive of Folk Culture is the home for the Fahnestock South Sea Collection, including recorded music of the South Pacific and Indonesia, recordings of Fijian legends, manuscripts, logs, correspondence, and photographs.

Balinese dancers photographed by the Fahnestocks in 1941. LC/American Folklife Center.

The Archive of Folk Culture also holds other rare Asian material, including the Benjamin Ives Gilman Collection of wax cylinder recordings made at the 1893 World's Columbian Exposition in Chicago and including Javanese and South Pacific music. The Hornbostel Demonstration Collection of 120 pressed cylinder copies from wax field recordings includes Chinese, Japanese, Southeast Asian, and Indian music recorded in the early years of the twentieth century. In addition, the Archive of Folk Culture holds many more recent recordings of music from Asia and the Pacific.

The Tibetan Collection

During the 1904 British invasion of Tibet, the 13th Dalai Lama fled Lhasa, seeking refuge first in Mongolia, then at the lamasery of Kumbum near Koko Nor. In early 1908, he arrived at Wu T'ai Shan, a large temple complex located on one of China's four sacred Buddhist mountains.

On June 17, 1908, another distinguished visitor arrived at Wu T'ai Shan, having walked much of the distance from Peking to call on the Dalai Lama. Standing 6'4" tall, William Woodville Rockhill, the United States Minister to China, still had the stiff bearing of the French military officer he had once been and was not given to strong expressions of emotion. But after two meetings with the Dalai Lama, Rockhill could barely conceal his excitement in a 12-page letter describing the meetings to President Theodore Roosevelt. The letter is among Roosevelt's papers in the Library's Manuscript Division. The Dalai Lama presented Rockhill with a number of gifts, one of which was a beautiful Buddhist text called the *Sutra of the Perfection of Wisdom*, now in the Asian Division's rare book collection, a gift from Mrs. Rockhill in 1942.

Rockhill played an important role in the development of the Library's Asian collections, especially in making the Library one of the world's leading centers for Tibetan books. During his youth in France, Rockhill developed a strong interest in Tibet that remained with him during his years as an officer in the French Foreign Legion, a stint as a rancher in New Mexico, and a long career as a diplomat and China specialist, best known as the framer of America's "Open Door" policy towards China at the turn of the century. However, Rockhill remained first and foremost a scholar. A book Rockhill published in 1891, *The Land of the Lamas*, grew out of his 1888–1889 journey into eastern Tibet and Mongolia. The

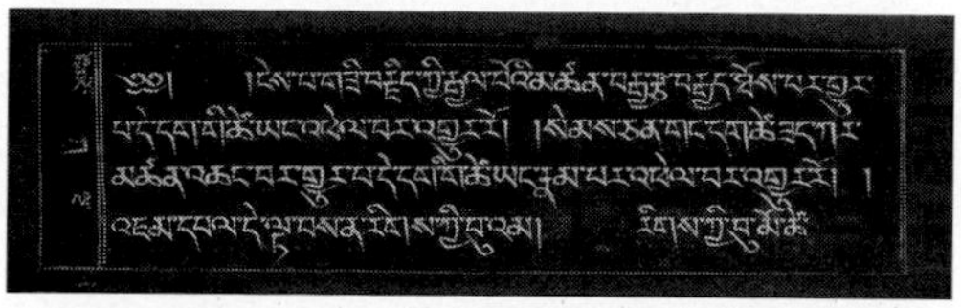

Tibetan Amitayus Sutra. This unusual manuscript is written in silver ink on dark blue paper. LC/Rockhill Tibetan Collection, Asian Division.

Smithsonian Institution sponsored Rockhill's second trip to Tibet and Mongolia in 1891–1892 and published his detailed travel diary. Throughout his long career, Rockhill published a number of other scholarly works on Tibet and China and his personal library became the heart of the Library of Congress's extensive holdings on Tibet.

Religion occupies a central role in traditional Tibetan society and the Library's holdings of Tibetan Buddhist scriptures are especially strong. The Tibetan Buddhist canon is contained in the *Kanjur*, in over 100 volumes of sutras, and the *Tanjur*, in over 200 volumes of commentaries. Of special value to scholars, the Tibetan canonical texts are accurate translations of the original Buddhist texts, written in Sanskrit between 500 B.C. and 900 A.D. Although many of the originals were lost, they may be reconstructed using the Tibetan translations. The Library of Congress has several rare woodblock printings of the *Kanjur* and *Tanjur*, as well as a complete set of the *Bonpo* canon, the scriptures of Tibet's pre-Buddhist religious tradition.

Rockhill's donation included an edition of the *Kanjur* he acquired from the monastery of Derge in eastern Tibet. The Library of Congress also has a *Tanjur* printed at the Narthang monastery in central Tibet. This rare work was originally obtained by another leading Tibetologist, Berthold Laufer, who collected Tibetan texts for two libraries in Chicago, the Newberry and the John Crerar. In 1928, the Crerar Library transferred an important group of Laufer's Tibetan books, including the *Narthang Tanjur*, to the Library of Congress.

During one of his expeditions in western China, the colorful explorer Joseph Rock obtained another valuable addition to the Library's holdings of Tibetan sacred texts. On behalf of the Library of Congress, Rock purchased a complete set of the *Kanjur* and *Tanjur* in 1926 from the famous Tibetan monastery of Choni in China's Kansu province. The fine quality of Choni's wooden blocks and its excellent Tibetan paper, strengthened by the lamination of eight sheets together to make an individual page, make the *Kanjur* and *Tanjur* purchased by Rock of the highest caliber. They are also very rare, since the monastery at Choni, including the printing blocks for the *Kanjur* and *Tanjur*, was completely destroyed by fire in 1929 during a period of armed conflict between Buddhists and Muslims in Kansu. The only other complete copy of the Choni *Kanjur* and *Tanjur* is said to be in China, although a partial set is in Japan.

The contributions of Rockhill, Rock, Laufer, and others have made the Library's Tibetan-language collection one of the largest in the West. Besides the Buddhist and *Bonpo* scriptures, the collection contains a wide range of history, biography, traditional medicine, astrology, iconography, musical notations, grammars, social science, and secular literature. Aside from covering their own history, Tibetan historical materials are of special interest to scholars because they are sometimes able to fill in blank spaces in the history of India and Inner Asia.

In recent times, the Library's New Delhi Overseas Office was well-positioned to take advantage of the upsurge in Tibetan publishing in India, Nepal, and Bhutan following the flight of the Dalai Lama to India in 1959 and the influx of refugees. As a result, the majority of the Library's books in the Tibetan language are reprint editions purchased by the New Delhi Office since 1962. Of the Library's approximately 10,800 Tibetan volumes, about 6,500 were purchased by the New Delhi Field Office.

With normalization of relations between the United States and China that began in 1972 and the end of China's Cultural Revolution in 1976, Tibetan-language publications from the People's Republic of China became increasingly available to the Library. Exchange agreements with scholarly institutions in China and three procurement missions to Tibet by Library staff in the 1990s have helped the Library obtain current Tibetan publications, including new printings of old woodblock texts as well as modern Tibetan literature. About 2,000 of the Library's Tibetan volumes are modern publications from the People's Republic of China. In 1990, the Library acquired 340 volumes of woodblock texts, recently printed in monasteries in Tibet, and in 1999 more than 300 volumes of xylographs from the famous Derge Printing House were acquired. In addition, the Library has about 40 serial titles, 430 reels of microfilm, and 7,200 microfiche of Tibetan material.

Extensive Western-language holdings related to Tibet are also found outside the Asian Division. Tibet has long fascinated Westerners and early accounts of travelers found eager readers over the centuries. The first European to travel from India over the Himalayan mountain range to enter Tibet was the Portuguese Jesuit Antonio de Andrade. Driven by stories of a Christian community supposedly living in Tibet, Andrade disguised himself as a Hindu and left Agra in March 1624 with a group of Indian pilgrims. After numerous adventures, he reached Tsaparang in western Tibet five months later. A copy of Andrade's account of the journey, *Nvevo descvbrimiento del gran Cathayo, o reynos de Tibet*, published in Lisbon in 1626, may be found in the Rare Book and Special Collections Division. Another rare, early work on Tibet found in the Rare Book and Special Collections Division is a language text, *Alphabetum Tibetanum Missionum Apostolicarum Commodo Editum,* by Antonio Agostino Giorgi, published in Rome in 1762.

The Library's Archive of Folk Culture has an interesting set of wire recordings made in 1950 by the anthropologist Prince Peter of Greece and Denmark in Kalimpong, northeastern India's "gateway" to Tibet. The recordings include recitations of traditional Tibetan stories, such as "The Story of the Rabbit" and part of the epic "History of King Gesar" as well as esoteric "lamaist" ceremonies. When Prince Peter was making his recordings, Kalimpong was a major center for Tibetan political activity, intensified by the People's Liberation Army's ongoing occupation of Tibet. Prince Peter made an especially timely recording of a November 15, 1950, luncheon conversation between senior Tibetan officials, Chinese scholars, Indian and Chinese diplomats, and the sister of the Dalai Lama.

Besides the 2,000 photographs taken by Joseph Rock in western China, many of which are of Tibetan lamas and monasteries, the Prints and Photographs Division has a collection of "Scenes of Tibet" from the 1930 to 1933 German expedition led by Ernst Schaefer. The Motion Picture, Broadcasting, and Recorded Sound Division holds a large collection of recorded Tibetan music and many films and videos of Tibet. Among the latter is the exhaustive film record of the German-Tibetan expedition of 1938–1939 that began in Darjeeling, India, and continued on to Lhasa. The film footage contains some interesting scenes of a Tibetan New Year's Festival in Lhasa and shots of various Tibetan officials. (All collection descriptions prepared by HEM and the staff of the Asian Division.)

AUTOMATION

During an examination of the Library's financial procedures in 1940, representatives of the General Accounting Office noted several operations that could be performed with greater efficiency with equipment used elsewhere for similar purposes. Two years later, tabulating machines entered the Library, and on July 15, 1942, the Tabulating Office appeared as a unit within the Administrative Department. Its operations included payroll and other personnel records and also billing for the Card Division.

By the mid-1950s, the tabulating machines were being used for Library tasks as well as business operations. Billing the purchasers of printed cards continued to be an important application, as well as maintaining purchasers' accounts and preparing sales analyses; for other offices, the machines proved useful for equipment inventories and budget calculations. The Tabulating Office also worked with book charges, records for the assignment of study facilities and, until 1961, the publication of *New Serial Titles*. The staff and equipment, which included the interpreter, the card-printing punch, sorters, and collator, were housed in the southwest corner of the ground floor of the Jefferson Building. With a reorganization of the Administrative Department in 1958, the unit became the Tabulating Section, but because of increasing interest in applying electronic data processing in libraries, it began to seem likely that the equipment would be obsolete within a few years.

Librarian L. Quincy Mumford established an interdepartmental Committee on Mechanized Information Retrieval in January 1958 as a step toward automation, and in early 1961 created the position of Information Systems Specialist (ISO) in the Librarian's Office to guide both the plans for data processing and its integration into the Library organization. Meanwhile, the Tabulating Section moved in 1960 from the ground floor to the cellar of the Jefferson Building where more space and better power sources were available. After a computer feasibility study was completed, the Section became the Data Processing Office in 1963, and on January 15, 1964, the Library installed the first computer, an IBM 1401. The 1401 was a transistor-based mainframe requiring the peripheral devices of a card read punch, printer, and magnetic tape unit. During the early days of data processing, the office consisted of about 20 staff members, half operating keypunch equipment and the rest operating computer equipment. Since the operating system for the 1401 was contained on a deck of punch cards, signs reading "Do Not Drop" adorned the walls, and operators carefully guarded their duplicate decks. In 1966, the Office moved to newly designed quarters, including a computer room, on the ground floor, southwest corner of the Adams Building, with space also directly above on the first floor. The ISO occupied space on the fourth floor.

While fiscal processing still dominated the Data Processing Office's work, the Library moved further toward bibliographic applications in the early 1960s. This occurred by necessity: because of its sheer size, its many and varied collections, and unique needs, traditional manual processing systems were increasingly inadequate to deal with the recording and maintenance of collections. To assess the feasibility of computerized operations, the Library received a grant from the Council on Library Resources, Inc. in April 1961, which resulted in *Automation and the Library of Congress*, the January 1964 report of a survey team headed by Gilbert W. King.

The King report concluded that automation was feasible, both technically and financially, in three areas: bibliographic processing, cataloging, and document retrieval. The major recommendation was that the Library produce "system specifications" for its internal operations and also for the services provided to other libraries. The specifications would guide the design of a Central Bibliographic System. By the end of 1965, the Information Systems Office had a staff of seven, including librarians, computer programmers, and technicians; and it had begun to develop specifications for automating bibliographic operations and to design a format for machine-readable catalog records. Henriette Avram was assigned to the second task, and her study, "A Proposed Format for a Standardized

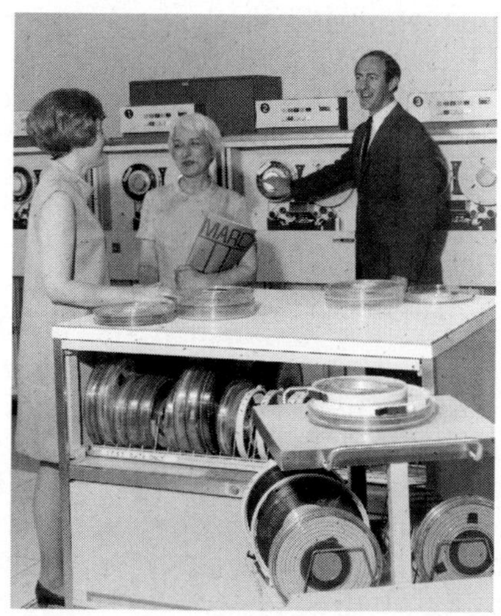

Henriette Avram (center), director of the Machine Readable Cataloging (MARC) Pilot Project, on May 14, 1968, with two colleagues in the "computer room" of the Information Systems Office. By the mid-1970s, she would be widely recognized as the most influential person in library automation worldwide. LC Archives.

MAchine-Readable Catalog Record" (June 1965) led to the development of MAchine-Readable Cataloging (MARC). The Information Systems Office, the Data Processing Office, and the Processing Department combined efforts on the MARC experiment, mounting a year-long pilot project in November 1966 to test the format. Meanwhile, automation of other processes and services moved forward in many areas of the Library, project by project.

The Library awarded a contract to the United Aircraft Corporate Systems Center in June 1966 to develop the first three phases of the planned seven-phase Central Bibliographic System: survey of the manual system, analysis of system requirements, and functional description. While in this phase of development the Library was treated as a single entity, the staff recognized that the entire institution could not depend on a single system for the many and varied tasks that automation could facilitate. During the 1970s and 1980s, systems staff developed several automated systems, of which the most widely used were Multiple Use MARC System (MUMS) and SCORPIO: Subject Content Oriented Retriever for Processing Information On-line.

MUMS replaced the batch processing system for MARC records. The system had produced the weekly tapes of new MARC cataloging for the Library and for other libraries that subscribed to the service, but tapes had to be mounted and they required serial searching while disk storage would allow records to be processed online. The disk-based MUMS became available in 1974. As MUMS development proceeded, the staff adapted another batch retrieval system, STAIRS, from the House of Representatives' Information Systems group to produce SCORPIO in 1974 for the Congressional Research Service. While MUMS was an input and updating system for cataloging and associated records, SCORPIO was a text retrieval system. Over the years, many new features and databases were added to SCORPIO, and it was used throughout the Library and in congressional offices.

In 1970, a reorganization of central automation took place. The Information Systems Office moved from the Librarian's Office to merge with the Data Processing Office under the Administrative Department, and a MARC Development Office was established in the Processing Department. The ISO included a Computer Applications Office, a Computer Service Center (the direct descendant of the Tabulating Section), and a Systems Development and Standards Office. Its responsibility was to develop and augment systems for the full range of Library applications. Located on the first floor of the Adams Building, the chief responsibility of the MARC Development Office was to develop bibliographic control in the Processing Department, plan the conversion of cataloging and associated data to machine-readable format, and issue the automated bibliographic records on MARC tapes, as book catalogs, as special lists, and other printed products.

Another reorganization of the Library's automation establishment occurred in 1976, when an Automation Planning Committee was established in the Librarian's Office. The desire to "move toward a more united Library of Congress automation program," resulted in the establishment of a Bibliographic Systems Office in the Administrative Department, including the MARC Development Office (from the Processing Department), the Copyright Systems Applications Office (from the Copyright Office), and the Library Systems Applications Office (from the Information Systems Office). The new office had responsibility for implementing, coordinating, and integrating the Library's plans for automated systems related to bibliographic services and automated services to legislative offices and executive agencies. Its offices were in the Jefferson Building and in the Copyright Office in Crystal City, Virginia. A Network Development Office (NDO) established in the Librarian's Office became responsible for the development, in collaboration with other organizations, of a national library networking system. The NDO moved in 1978 to the office of the Associate Librarian for National Programs, while an Automation Planning and Liaison Office (APLO) appeared in Processing Services to work with the ISO and the NDO in developing or refining processing systems. With this reorganization, the three elements of the Library of Congress's late twentieth-century automation program were internal systems development and support in the ISO, MARC and other cataloging activities support in ISO and APLO, and relations with networks and with national and international organizations, including worldwide standardization activities, in NDO.

By the late 1970s, with the development and implementation of MARC, MUMS, and SCORPIO, more user support became a priority. The Bibliographic Systems Office established a MARC support office to handle training, hardware problems, and programming and systems issues. The Information Systems Office continued to have responsibility for the installation and maintenance of computer equipment for users through its Computer Service Center. SCORPIO training and user support devolved to the Congressional Research Service, assisting primarily CRS staff and congressional offices but also Library staff and users in the Main Reading Room, where terminals had been installed in 1975 for public use. The consolidation of software systems and user support began to be considered by a design team in September 1977, but due to fiscal constraints such consolidation had to be accomplished through the gradual modification of existing systems rather than new system design.

The Information Systems Office and the Bibliographic Systems Office merged in 1978 to form the Automated Systems Office (ASO) under the Associate Librarian for Management, with branches for systems engineering and operations and systems development. Still spread among several buildings, the staff was eventually united on the ground floor of the Madison Building in 1980–1981. Processing Services also moved to the Madison Building, and established a Director for Processing Systems, Networks, and Automation Planning, whose office included the Automation Planning and Liaison Office, the Network Development Office, the Catalog Management and Publication Division, the Cataloging Distribution Service, and the Serial Record Division. The new directorate responded to the continuing need to increase coordination across units within Processing Services. Responsibility for the MARC communications formats also moved at that time from ASO to the Automation Planning and Liaison Office, thus locating in Processing Services the direction of the Library's standards activities and other technical matters associated with machine-readable cataloging. In 1984, the directorate was renamed Bibliographic Products and Services, and the Network Development and MARC Standards Office became a separate unit.

A milestone in networking and interlibrary communication appeared in 1985 with the initial implementation of the Linked Systems Project, which linked the Library of Congress's computer system to the computer system of the Research Libraries Group for the purpose of building and maintaining shared databases of cataloging information. Funded by the Council on Library Resources and participating institutions, the computer-to-computer telecommunication link or Standard Network Interconnection, allowed designated partners to add information to the Library's databases and provided for the online distribution of cataloging and associated records. Its use soon expanded to the Online Computer Library Center, Inc., and the Western Library Network. MUMS and SCORPIO were tied together in the mid-1980s, producing the Library of Congress Information System (LOCIS). Under LOCIS, users could employ both SCORPIO and MUMS command language, thus providing a single-user interface to both systems. With computer use multiplying among both users and staff, the goal quickly became to make even casual users largely self-sufficient. With the last cards filed in the card catalog at the end of 1980, the Computer Catalog Center established in 1977 near the Main Reading Room had to be enlarged and staff made readily available to help solve technical problems. Computer use again surged when microcomputers began to be employed in office applications in 1983, and a few years later a Committee on Automation Planning convened to determine the character and volume of the Library's future automation needs. In 1987, the Committee issued a five-year Strategic Information System Plan, which included redesign of the systems supporting online retrieval, data input, and file maintenance.

In June 1989, the Automated Systems Office became the directorate for Information Technology Services (ITS) within the Office of the Librarian while the following year the Network Development and MARC Standards Office and the Automation Planning and Liaison Office became part of Collections Services, with APLO assuming responsibility for working across all Collections Services directorates. Both units moved into a new Acquisitions and Support Services directorate in 1994, and in 1995 into Library Services. Meanwhile, a pilot project tested the feasibility of remote access to LOCIS via dialup and Telnet services; by 1991 this service had become known as LC Direct, but work also began on use of the Internet, which carried the potential to support cooperative cataloging, interlibrary loan, and document transfer. In the Computer Catalog Center, a new interface named ACCESS introduced in 1991 assisted users to do searches without training and with little staff assistance, employing terminals incorporating an attractive graphical user interface and touch screens.

The growing popularity of the Internet soon overtook these services. User evaluation of the American Memory pilot project (which began in 1990) indicated that secondary schools were making the most frequent and effective use of the American Memory materials being distributed through CD-ROMs, and discussion began about possible future distribution over the Internet. In 1992, the Library presented its first online exhibition "Revelations from the Russian Archives." With Congressional approval, worldwide online access via the Internet to Library of Congress computerized databases became a reality in April 1993; the Library of Congress Information System (LOCIS) included access to the Library's catalogs and other records. In July, the Library enhanced Internet access by implementing Machine-Assisted Realization of the Virtual Electronic Library (LC MARVEL), a software system that made it simpler to conduct Internet searches and provided access to full texts of information circulars published by the Copyright Office and basic information about the Library's services. In 1993, Internet users gained access to texts and images from four major Library of Congress exhibitions, including

"Rome Reborn: The Vatican Library and Renaissance Culture" and "1492: An Ongoing Voyage." The same year, the Library began testing the Law Library's Global Legal Information Network (GLIN). The Library's World Wide Web site server was launched in June 1994 at the American Library Association's

A 1997 version of the Library's home page on the World Wide Web. LC Archives.

annual conference in Miami, Florida. It soon included a growing number of home pages that linked various Library departments and projects to outside libraries, publishers, and other organizations—as well as to individual users. Specially configured personal computers, called bibliographic workstations, and including Web access and technical software packages, appeared in staff work areas.

The American Memory pilot project, which disseminated primary source materials from the Library's Americana collections to schools and libraries through CD-ROMs, came to a close in 1994. However, its success had led to a proposal to Congress for a more comprehensive, five-year National Digital Library (NDL) program. In October 1994, the Library announced it had received $13 million from the private sector to establish the NDL program, which would make parts of the Library's Americana collections available through digital conversion and electronic distribution. The American Memory Office staff was absorbed into the NDL program. A working group including NDL staff, special collections and computer staff, designed an NDL Web site; the computer staff continually enhanced the technology infrastructure and provided support. Congress agreed to provide $15 million for the NDL program and asked the Library to raise an additional $45 million, a goal the Library exceeded.

However, the Library still had not, by the mid-1990s, achieved the systems integration sought since the 1970s. With appropriations funding, however, in May 1998 the Library contracted with Endeavor Information Systems of Des Plaines, Illinois to build an integrated library system (ILS) to replace the Library's older or "legacy" systems and unite all functions: acquisitions, cataloging, inventory, serials control, circulation, and the online catalog. An Integrated Library System Program Office reporting to the Deputy Librarian and to the Associate Librarian for Library Services handled the transition to the new system, which involved the work of more than 80 teams of staff members pursuing individual tasks. The initial system implementation in 1999 involved installing new software on nearly 3,000 work stations, training over 3,000 staff members, and loading approximately 12 million bibliographic records and five million authority records. Capabilities continued to be added to the system; for example, data import and export to and from the Research Libraries Group and the Online Computer Library Center Inc., while ITS and APLO worked for over two years to complete planning for "Y2K," to ensure the availability and integrity of the computer systems and data after December 31, 1999. In the wake of the September 11, 2001 terrorist attack, automated systems staff revised existing plans for preserving backup system tapes and developed specifications for a new remote computing facility.

The Automation Planning and Liaison Office and the Network Development and MARC Standards Office were among the units in Library Services moved into a new Operations Directorate in March 1999. Both were heavily involved in ILS planning and implementation and continued to support the Library's Web development, MARC, computer-to-computer linkages, interchange of digital material, and multiple National Information Standards Organization and International Organization for Standardization activities, including enhancement of the international information retrieval protocol, Z39.50 and a developing initiative to catalog digital resources. In 2002, the ILS program office was dissolved and its staff also became part of Operations Directorate, with the recognition that their work would continue to support ILS users throughout the Library.

A Digital Futures Task Group, established in 1998 and co-chaired by the associate librarian for library services and the director of the National Digital Library Program, created a Library-wide five-year plan to collect and create significant publications in electronic formats, to build collaborations with national and international institutions, to make the Library's collections and resources more widely accessible and more widely used, and to inspire technical and strategic innovation. Concurrently,

Librarian Billington commissioned a study from the National Research Council. Released in July 2000, *LC21: A Digital Strategy for the Library of Congress* encouraged the Library to pursue an aggressive strategy of creating, acquiring, describing, and preserving electronic resources. In October, the Library established the position of Associate Librarian for Strategic Initiatives to address the Library's technology infrastructure and policies and to collaborate with the public and private sectors. In December, Congress appropriated $99.8 million for a National Digital Information Infrastructure and Preservation Program (NDIIPP). An advisory board for this effort convened in May 2001, and initial planning culminated in "Preserving Our Digital Heritage: Plan for the National Digital Information Infrastructure and Preservation Program" in October 2002. The plan outlined the steps that the Library would take to develop a network of partners and the technical architecture to support long-term digital collection, storage, and preservation. Congress approved the plan in December, releasing $35 million for the program's next phase. An August 2003 announcement solicited applications for projects to advance the nationwide program; awards totaling $15 million to eight institutions and their partners were announced in September 2004.

The National Digital Library and Information Technology Services became the two principal component parts of the Office of Strategic Initiatives. ITS's post-2001 activities included construction and deployment of the Collaborative Digital Reference Service in alliance with OCLC and the initiation of digital archiving projects with the Internet Archive and the American Physical Society Information Technology Services remains the Library's central computing facility and chief source of technical support, working closely with the Automation Planning and Liaison Office and with the Network Development and MARC Standards Office. ITS's responsibility is to provide reliable, secure, and effective telecommunications and automated systems and services to the Library, and to plan, design, and implement systems that embody the future digital library and information infrastructure. Library systems, applications, and facilities supported by the ITS staff are located in every division to provide support for current systems while developing new applications to meet current and future needs. ITS employs computer programmers, systems analysts, systems programmers, telecommunications specialists, telephone and computer operators, data technicians, data analysts, and administrative support staff. More information is available on the ITS home page at the Library's Web site.

Just 40 years after the installation of the first computer, the Library has transferred most operations from manual to electronic, moving through several generations of technology along the way. The cumulative record of digitization shows 8.5 million American historical items, more than 125 multimedia historical collections, and more than 50 exhibitions available on the Library's Web site in late 2004. More than 2.6 billion transactions were recorded on the Library's computer systems, and the online public access catalog had an average of more than 30 million transactions per month in fiscal 2003, an increase of seven million over 2002. Use of the American Memory collections increased from 38.8 million per month in 2002 to nearly 47 million in 2003. The Library's Web site, American Memory, and the National Digital Library extend the contents of Library of Congress collections to the many who cannot use them in Washington, D.C. (JA, JYC)

Goodrum, Charles and Helen Dalrymple. "Computerization at the Library of Congress: The First Twenty Years," *Wilson Library Bulletin* 57 (October 1982): 115–121.

Library of Congress Information Bulletin 52 (September 6, 1993): 319–321; 53 (September 5, 1994): 323–324; 53 (October 31, 1994): 407–413, 416.

Rohrbach, Peter T. FIND: *Automation at the Library of Congress: The First Twenty-Five Years and Beyond.* Washington, D.C.: Library of Congress, 1985.

BECKLEY, JOHN JAMES (1757–1807)

John Beckley was the first Librarian of Congress, albeit a part-time one. When the position of Librarian was established on January 26, 1802, President Thomas Jefferson asked his friend and political ally John Beckley—who also was serving as the clerk of the House of Representatives—to fill the post. Beckley served concurrently in both positions until his death in 1807. (The next Clerk of the House, Patrick Magruder, also held both jobs).

Beckley was born in England on August 4, 1757, and came to Virginia at age 11 as a scribe for John Clayton, clerk of court for Gloucester County and a well-known botanist. Following Clayton's death in 1774, Beckley served in several increasingly important political positions, including clerk of the Virginia House of Delegates. After the seat of Virginia government was moved from Williamsburg to Richmond, he became one of Richmond's first city councilmen and then its second mayor.

When the federal government was established in New York in 1789, Beckley was elected the first clerk of the House of Representatives. He was an ardent "Democratic-Republican," and closely associated with Thomas Jefferson. In 1791, just before Congress moved from New York to Philadelphia, he married Maria Prince, and they moved to Philadelphia, where Beckley was active in city, state, and national politics. Sadly, he and Maria also lost several children. Only Alfred, who was born in 1802, the year after the Beckleys moved to Washington, survived.

In Philadelphia, John Beckley campaigned vigorously for Jefferson and other Republican candidates, attacking the Federalists (and particularly Alexander Hamilton) in the press and through writings published under pseudonyms such as "Americanus." The Federalists removed him from office when they were elected in 1787, but with the election of Jefferson as president in 1801, he was re-elected clerk of the House of Representatives. Beckley and Maria moved to the new capital city of Washington, where he became involved in local as well as national politics.

On the day that John Beckley was reappointed clerk of the House of Representatives, December 7, 1801, Congress also formed a committee, headed by John Randolph of Virginia, to decide what to do with its library. The result would be the law of January 26, 1802, that defined the role and functions of the new institution and established the post of Librarian of Congress. Beckley decided that as clerk of the House of Representatives he also could perform the duties of Librarian. He had some experience in this type of work, having been responsible for books and documents when he was clerk of the Virginia Senate. He applied to Secretary of State James Madison and obtained the appointment from President Jefferson on January 29, 1802.

The major decisions in the Library were made by the Joint Committee on the Library, not by the Librarian. Beckley and his assistants, however, carried out the wishes of the Joint Committee and particularly of President Jefferson, who took a keen interest in the Library and frequently provided advice regarding purchases. Jefferson also became involved in the ordering and shipping of the books themselves, on at least one occasion having to straighten out confusion resulting from the mixing of his personal book orders from Europe with those of the Library.

Beckley prepared the Library's first printed catalog, which was printed by William Duane in April 1802. The *Catalogue of Books, Maps, and Charts, Belonging to the Library of the Two Houses of Congress* lists the collection of 964 volumes according to their size and appends a list of nine maps and charts.

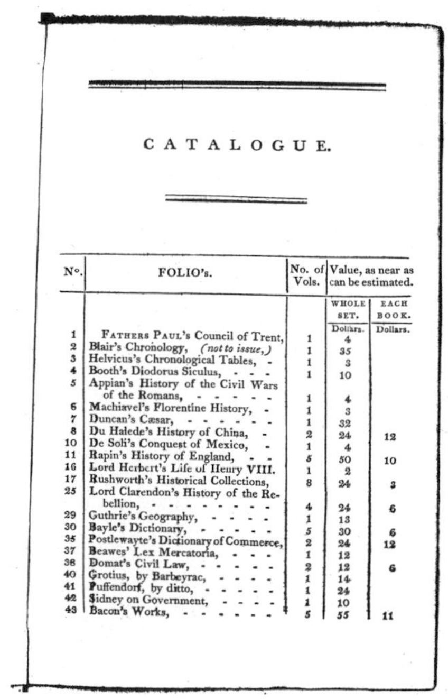

CATALOGUE.

N°.	FOLIO's.	No. of Vols.	Value, as near as can be estimated.	
			WHOLE SET.	EACH BOOK.
			Dollars.	Dollars.
1	FATHERS PAUL's Council of Trent,	1	4	
2	Blair's Chronology, *(not to issue,)*	1	35	
3	Helvicus's Chronological Tables, -	1	3	
4	Booth's Diodorus Siculus, - - -	1	10	
5	Appian's History of the Civil Wars of the Romans, - - - - - -	1	4	
6	Machiavel's Florentine History, -	1	3	
7	Duncan's Cæsar, - - - - - - -	1	32	
8	Du Halede's History of China, -	2	24	12
10	De Soli's Conquest of Mexico, -	1	4	
11	Rapin's History of England, - -	5	50	10
16	Lord Herbert's Life of Henry VIII.	1	2	
17	Rushworth's Historical Collections,	8	24	3
25	Lord Clarendon's History of the Rebellion, - - - - - - - - - -	4	24	6
29	Guthrie's Geography, - - - - -	1	13	
30	Bayle's Dictionary, - - - - - -	5	30	6
35	Postlewayte's Dictionary of Commerce,	2	24	12
37	Beawes' Lex Mercatoria, - - -	1	12	
38	Domat's Civil Law, - - - - - -	2	12	6
40	Grotius, by Barbeyrac, - - - -	1	14	
41	Puffendorf, by ditto, - - - - -	1	24	
42	Sidney on Government, - - - -	1	10	
43	Bacon's Works, - - - - - - - -	5	55	11

John Beckley, the first Librarian of Congress, was also the Clerk of the House of Representatives. One of his tasks was the preparation of the Library's first catalog (above). The books were listed by size.
LC/Prints and Photographs Division. LC-USZ62-61724.

With his many duties, it is remarkable that Beckley found much time to deal with Library matters as he did, using help from clerks assigned to him in his House of Representatives position. Significantly, he also began soliciting donations to the Library from personal friends, including Benjamin Rush. Another friend, Samuel H. Smith, editor of the *National Intelligencer*, took note of this trend and encouraged it in his newspaper in articles on February 13, 1803, and again on April 11, 1806: "Gentlemen desirous of having the publications exhibited in this public and conspicuous place may forward them, to Mr. Beckley the librarian, who will thankfully receive, and carefully preserve them, for the use of the Representative Bodies of the American nation."

Beckley also personally escorted distinguished visitors through the Capitol and showed off the Library's quarters. In June 1804, Charles Willson Peale, who was accompanying the famous German naturalist Baron Alexander von Humboldt, recorded in his diary: "We went first to the Library where Mr. Beckley received us with politeness. . . The Library is a spacious and handsome Room, and although lately organized, already contained a number of valuable books in the best taste of binding."

The Library lost this impressive room in December 1805 when the House of Representatives took it back and assigned the Library to a former committee room. In the same month, Beckley fired one of his clerks, Josias Wilson King, a Federalist who three years earlier had sought the job of Librarian for himself. King quickly prepared a memorial to the House that accused Beckley of failing to live up to an earlier promise to share the Librarian's salary with him or to provide additional compensation in accordance with an 1804 authorization by the House of Representatives. Beckley was exonerated, but King's accusations—preserved in the Library's early record books—have become part of Beckley's story as Librarian.

During the last years of Beckley's involvement with the Library, the dominant force was Senator Samuel Latham Mitchill, who proposed and obtained the first annual appropriation for the purchase of books and personally ordered many of them.

John Beckley died on April 8, 1807. His son Alfred inherited a large tract of unsettled land in what today is West Virginia and built the first house in a village that became the city of Beckley, named so by Alfred to honor his father.

John Beckley's biographers Edmund and Dorothy Smith Berkeley stress that despite his many other activities, Beckley took his duties as Librarian of Congress seriously. They also emphasize that by assisting Congress in the development of its library and by helping the institution obtain public approval, the first Librarian of Congress created a firm foundation on which others have been able to build. (JYC)

Berkeley, Edmund and Dorothy Smith Berkeley. "John Beckley: The First Librarian of Congress," *The Quarterly Journal of the Library of Congress* 32 (April 1975): 83–117.

Berkeley, Edmund and Dorothy Smith Berkeley. *John Beckley: Zealous Partisan in a Nation Divided.* Philadelphia: The American Philosophical Society, 1973.

BIBLIOGRAPHY DIVISION (1900–1940)

Ainsworth Rand Spofford was the first Librarian of Congress to compile specialized bibliographies from the Library's collections. Even though his pressing responsibilities left him little time for such work, Spofford managed to produce a bibliography on libraries for the Bureau of Education's 1876 special report on libraries, and in 1892, at the request of Treasury Secretary Charles Foster, he produced a listing of books, pamphlets, and periodicals on banking and finance.

Spofford's successor, John Russell Young, had a larger staff that produced lists of books for Congress on important topics of the day: Cuba, the Philippines, Hawaii, Alaska, and interoceanic canal and railway routes. But it was not until 1900 that Librarian Herbert Putnam established a Division of Bibliography. One of Putnam's ambitions was to make the Library of Congress the center of U.S. bibliographic work, and as a first step, he intended to broaden the assistance provided in response to inquiries from the public. "The service of the Library of Congress is little to be estimated by the number of inquirers who frequent it in person," he said. "It may render services in value immeasurably exceeding its cost without issuing a single volume to a reader within its walls."

Funded by the appropriations act of April 7, 1900, the new division was organized immediately. As chief, Putnam named Appleton Prentiss Clark Griffin, a noted bibliographer who had worked at the Boston Athenaeum and the Boston Public Library before coming to the Library of Congress in 1897. When Chief Assistant Librarian Spofford died in 1908, Putnam named Griffin to replace him and transferred Henry Herman Bernard Meyer from the Order Division to head the Division of Bibliography.

In particular, Putnam wanted the six-person division staff to compile full bibliographies on topics of interest to Congress. One long bibliography, four shorter bibliographies, and 23 typed lists appeared during 1901, with subjects ranging from mercantile marine subsidies to the theory of colonization and the Trans-Siberian Railway. The Government Printing Office printed the more important bibliographies, and the Library distributed the typed or mimeographed lists free.

The division staff also provided citations to books, collections, or other authorities in response to inquiries, and they recommended items to be purchased for the Library's collections. In the early years, they also constructed their own reference aids. For example, because there were no comprehensive indexes to periodicals in 1901, the staff began a card index. They had carefully inscribed more than 18,000 references covering 126 subjects by 1903.

The Bibliography Division at work on the east side of the first floor of the Jefferson Building soon after its creation. It was established by Librarian Putnam primarily to compile bibliographies on topics of interest to Congress.
LC Archives.

Since the staff consistently produced more bibliographies than the Library's printing budget could accommodate, Meyer published bibliographies in other government publications whenever the opportunity appeared, and he searched for other outlets. For example, to help reduce the duplication of work by state librarians and legislative reference librarians that occurred when legislatures in different states took up the same subjects, in 1910 Meyer entered an agreement with the professional journal, *Special Libraries*, to publish one short bibliography each month. Three years later, he began sending the division's typed lists to the legislative reference librarians' new Public Affairs Information Service for duplication and distribution.

The Division of Bibliography handled congressional requests even after Putnam established the Legislative Reference Service in 1914, for the Service's small staff could do only part of the work. By that date, the division staff was producing over 200 bibliographies annually. With the coming of World War I, they undertook several major projects: *The United States At War: Organizations and Literature*, and a comprehensive guide, *European War Literature*, that included books, periodicals, broadsides, prints, photographs, and music. They began a comprehensive bibliography on the origins and causes of the war, and assisted the American Library Association's Library

War Service in its work of assembling reading material for soldiers in training camps.

As new tasks abounded, "We have become a machine for grinding out information almost to the exclusion of everything else," Meyer reported to Putnam in 1920. Continually flooded with requests, his seven-member staff had to spend most of their time on congressional work. Bibliographies on important topics such as agricultural credit, cooperative marketing, trusts, railroads, tariffs, taxation, cost of living, foreign debts, League of Nations, World Court, Muscle Shoals, hours of labor, and immigration appeared as typewritten and mimeographed lists. A bibliography on standardization appeared annually in the *Standards Yearbook*, and one on the Permanent Court of International Justice came out in the Court's annual report. A list of federal commissions, boards, and committees appeared as a Senate Document. And mail from the general public continued to pour in: from just under 1,500 queries in 1909, the volume rose to over 3,000 in 1921–1922.

Meyer assumed the extra responsibility of overseeing the Legislative Reference Service in 1921, and William Adams Slade succeeded him as chief of the division in 1923. When Slade resigned in 1930, Florence Hellman became Acting Chief Bibliographer, supervising an all-female staff. She had been assistant chief of the division since 1914, but because women were not given high administrative posts during Herbert Putnam's tenure, Miss Hellman became the Library's first woman division chief only after Putnam retired.

During the Depression, the division turned its attention to the numerous "alphabet" agencies of the New Deal, compiling lists of books to satisfy the demand for information on such subjects as the National Recovery Administration and the Agricultural Adjustment Administration. The Library was still unable to print all the bibliographies, but in 1937 division bibliographies began to be cited routinely in the *Monthly Catalog of United States Government Publications* and in two commercial publications: *Bibliographic Index* and *The Vertical File Catalog.*

When Archibald MacLeish reorganized the Library in 1940, the Bibliography Division became the Bibliography and Reference Correspondence Section of the General Reference and Bibliography Division. MacLeish also organized an interdepartmental advisory committee to guide bibliographic work. The members decided that their first project would be to standardize bibliographic practices, and in 1944, *Bibliographical Procedures and Style: A Manual for Bibliographers in the Library of Congress* appeared. It proved to be an essential tool, since more and more bibliographies were produced in succeeding years, in response to congressional and outside requests, and to inform readers about the Library's collections. Abandoning the idea of having a single unit handle all the Library's bibliographic work served to encourage bibliographic output by all the divisions and to greatly expand the coverage beyond legislative topics to a wide variety of subjects. (JA)

BILLINGTON, JAMES H. (1929–)

James Hadley Billington was sworn in as the 13th Librarian of Congress on September 14, 1987. He was born on June 1, 1929, in Bryn Mawr, Pennsylvania, to Nelson and Jane (Coolbaugh) Billington. His father, who did not go to college, nevertheless transmitted to his son his love of reading. Billington's early schooling was in public schools in the Philadelphia suburbs. His interest in the former Soviet Union began to develop when in high school he became interested in reading *War and Peace* in Russian, a project at which he succeeded over a number of years with the help of a tutor, a Russian émigré. He was class valedictorian at Lower Merion High School.

A noted Russian scholar and the author of several books on Russian history, James H. Billington became the thirteenth Librarian of Congress in 1987. In his speech at the swearing-in ceremony, Billington defined his task as moving the Library "out more broadly and in more deeply" by making its resources more widely available in order to share its unparalleled collections, and to "turn information into knowledge" and eventually, "distilling it into wisdom." Here Billington is pictured in the Jefferson Congressional Reading Room. Photograph: Roger Foley.

Billington received his undergraduate degree from Princeton University, graduating as valedictorian of the class of 1950. In 1953, he earned his doctorate from Oxford University, he was a Rhodes Scholar at Balliol College. He served in the U.S. Army from 1953 to 1956, attaining the rank of first lieutenant. In 1957, he became a history instructor at Harvard University, where the following year he was promoted to assistant professor and also became a fellow at the Russian Research Center.

In June 1957, he married Marjorie Anne Brennan. They have four children.

In 1958, he published a pioneering work, *Mikhailovsky and Russian Populism*, the first major biography of an influential nineteenth century Russian liberal journalist and social critic. While on the Harvard faculty, he was a Fulbright professor at the University of Helsinki in 1960–1961 and a guest professor at the University of Leningrad in 1961.

Moving to Princeton University in 1962, he taught history as an associate professor for two years and then as professor from 1964 to 1974. During this period, he returned to the Soviet Union as a research professor at the University of Moscow in 1964 and then as visiting research professor at the Institute of History of the Soviet Academy of Sciences in Moscow in 1966–1967. In 1966, Billington published the encyclopedic and widely praised book, *The Icon and the Axe: An Interpretive History of Russian Culture*. From 1971 to 1973, he served as chairman of the Board of Foreign Scholarships, which directs international academic exchanges under the Fulbright-Hays Act.

From 1973 to 1987, Billington was the director of the Woodrow Wilson International Center for Scholars, the national memorial in Washington, D.C., to America's 28th president. Under his directorship, eight new programs were established at the center, beginning with the Kennan Institute for Advanced Russian Studies, named after his friend, the Sovietologist George F. Kennan.

Under his direction, in 1976 the Wilson Center launched *The Wilson Quarterly*, "the news magazine of the world of ideas" in Billington's phrase. He also initiated a series of scholars' guides to educational and research resources in Washington, D.C., a series that includes many detailed descriptions of the collections of the Library of Congress. In 1980, he published a major work, *Fire in the Minds of Men: Origins of the Revolutionary Faith*, the story "not of revolut*ions*, but of revolution*aries*: the innovative creators of a new tradition."

When Daniel J. Boorstin announced his intention to step down as Librarian of Congress, Billington's name was immediately mentioned as a potential candidate. He was nominated for the post by President Ronald Reagan on April 17, 1987. The U.S. Senate held hearings on the nomination on July 14 and he was confirmed 10 days later. He took the oath of office in a ceremony in the Library's Great Hall on September 14, 1987. Participants in the ceremony included the congressional leadership, President Reagan, and Chief Justice William H. Rehnquist, who administered the oath on the Library's 1782 Aitken Bible, the first complete Bible printed in the independent United States.

In his speech at the swearing-in ceremony and in a press conference on that occasion, Billington proposed two directions in which the Library of Congress should move. The first was "out more broadly," to be accomplished by making its resources more widely available, especially by using new technologies "to share the substantive content" of its unparalleled collections. The second direction, "in more deeply," referred to strengthening the Library's role as a catalyst and leader in turning "information into knowledge" and eventually "distilling it into wisdom."

"Frontiers of the Mind in the Twenty-First Century" was the theme of a symposium that brought together 50 scholars to discuss achievements of the past century and developments in the next. Experts in fields from cosmology to the behavioral sciences gathered at the Library on June 15–17, 1999. Here, Mary Douglas, a scholar in cultural analysis, talks with James Billington and her husband, James Douglas (left).
LC/Public Affairs Office.

Billington immediately took personal charge of the Library, instituting his own one-year review through a Management and Planning (MAP) Committee, a process that included regional forums in nine cities. The result was a major administrative reorganization based on goals and institutional values identified through the MAP study.

To help the Library share its resources more widely, he instituted several projects to test new technologies that might extend direct access by libraries and schools to the Library's databases and collections. The American Memory Project, for example, began providing electronic copies of selected American history and culture collections. In 1993, Billington obtained congressional approval to make available on the Internet an online computer version of its bibliographic data. The Library of Congress World Wide Web site opened in mid-1994. In late 1994, the Librarian announced a pilot National Digital Library Program, supported primarily by private funds that would create several million digital items from the Library's Americana collections and make them accessible to everyone over the World Wide Web.

Billington also envisioned a new educational role for the Library, one that would bring the institution greater public visibility without drawing extensively on public funds. In 1988, he sought and obtained congressional approval for the Library's first development office and the establishment of a private sector support group. The creation in 1990 of the James Madison Council, a private sector support body consisting mostly of business executives and prominent cultural figures, opened a new chapter in the Library's history. The Madison Council quickly became a major supporter of the National Digital Library, and the Kellogg Foundation contributed $3 million for educational services associated with the digital collections. The Council also supported exhibitions, publications, films, and cultural programming that advertised the Library and its mission throughout the nation and the world.

Billington always has been ambitious for the Library of Congress and eager to serve as its spokesman, not only with members of Congress but also among librarians, scholars, and the general public. In 1997, he took full advantage of the completion of the renovation and restoration of the Jefferson and Adams Buildings to extend the institution's reach nationally and internationally. Increased use of the Library's Web site, expanded media coverage, and a strengthened visitor services and docent tour program helped keep the Library and its programs strong and in the public eye. Under Billington's guidance, the Library used its bicentennial in 2000 to move the institution on several fronts. For example, Congress authorized 84 positions for the National Digital Library Program, giving it permanent government support, and Madison Council Chairman John W. Kluge gave the Library a gift of $60 million to create within the Library a center for scholars and a Nobel-level prize for lifetime achievement in the humanities

Librarian and Mrs. Billington and President George W. Bush and First Lady Laura Bush celebrated the First National Book Festival on September 7, 2001 with a dinner at the Jefferson Building with a group of Festival sponsors, authors and guests. During an extremely full weekend, James H. Billington and Laura Bush presided over the hugely successful inaugural festival.
Photograph: LC/Marita Clance.

or social sciences. It was the largest monetary donation in the Library's history. On September 8, 2001, Billington and the First Lady Laura Bush presided over the first National Book Festival; it was held on the U.S. Capitol grounds and at the Library.

Librarian Billington's specialized knowledge of Russia has served the Library of Congress well. In June 1988, he accompanied President and Mrs. Reagan to the Soviet summit in Moscow. He was representing the Library in Moscow during the decisive days of 1991 when the Soviet Union fell apart. He recorded his impressions in a book, *Russia Transformed: Breakthough to Hope* (1992). In April 1993, he accompanied a bipartisan delegation of U.S. House of Representatives leadership to Ukraine and Russia, and in August 1995, he was part of a bipartisan U.S. Senate delegation to Siberia and Mongolia.

In 1999, he provided the leadership for a congressionally funded Russian Leadership Program, one of the largest and most inclusive one-time foreign visitation programs ever developed by the United States. Its name was changed in 2000 to the Open World

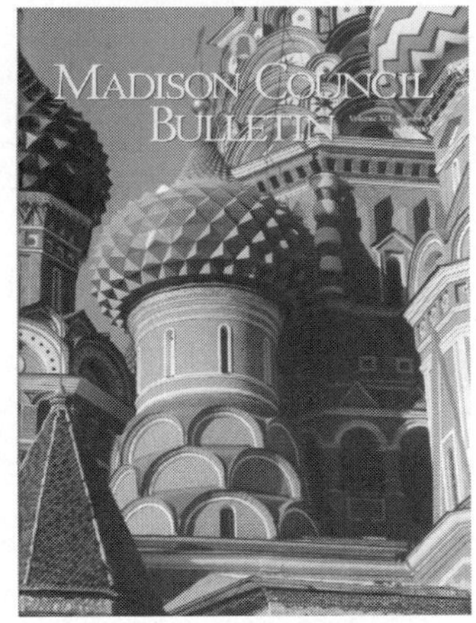

Librarian Billington envisioned a new educational role for the Library. In 1988, he sought and received congressional approval for the Library's first development office and private sector support group which led to the creation in 1990 of the James Madison Council. The council consists of public spirited citizens who help the nation receive the benefits of the Library's incomparable resources. The Madison Council quickly became a major supporter of the National Digital Library and many other outreach programs, as well as acquisitions for the collections.
Madison Council Bulletin, XII, Number 1, Spring 2001.

Program and it became an independent entity housed at the Library of Congress with Billington as Chairman of its Board of Trustees. Total funding appropriated by Congress for the Open World Program from 1999 through fiscal year 2004 was $64.5 million and by mid-2004 the program had hosted more than 7,500 of Russia's new and future political and cultural leaders. In 2004, Billington published *Russia In Search of Itself*, an examination of Russia's efforts to find a post-Soviet identity. (JYC)

Nomination of James H. Billington to be Librarian of Congress. Hearing before the Committee on Rules and Administration, U.S. Senate. July 14, 1987. Washington, D.C.: Government Printing Office, 1988.

BOORSTIN, DANIEL J. (1914–2004)

Daniel J. Boorstin, the 12th Librarian of Congress, was born in Atlanta, Georgia on October 1, 1914. He was one of two sons of Samuel Aaron Boorstin, a lawyer, and of Dora (Olsan) Boorstin. His grandparents on both sides of his family were

Daniel J. Boorstin, Librarian of Congress 1975–1987, was nominated by President Gerald R. Ford. Boorstin was a Pulitzer prize-winning historian, and a former Director of the National Museum of American History, and distinguished professor of history at the University of Chicago. Boorstin brought with him, as President Ford put it, "a love of learning and a scholar's appreciation of the importance of libraries and of the unique contribution of the Library of Congress to American Life." LC/Public Affairs Office.

Russian-Jewish immigrants. He grew up and attended public schools in Tulsa, Oklahoma. After graduating from Tulsa Central High School in 1930, he entered Harvard College, which awarded him the bachelor's degree summa cum laude in 1934. As a Rhodes Scholar from Oklahoma, in 1934, he entered Balliol College, Oxford, from which he received his B.A. in Jurisprudence (first class honors) in 1936 and his Bachelor of Civil Laws (first class honors) in 1937. Simultaneously, he was enrolled as a student at the Inner Temple, London, and passed the English bar examinations. He became a Barrister-at-Law in 1937.

Boorstin returned to the United States in 1937 as a Sterling Fellow at Yale University Law School, where he worked toward a doctor of judicial science degree, which was awarded in 1940. From 1938 to 1942, he was an instructor on the faculty of Harvard University, where he taught English and American history and literature, and also legal history at the Harvard Law School. His first book, *The Mysterious Science of the Law*, was published by Harvard University Press in 1941. He was admitted to the Massachusetts bar in 1942.

While teaching at the Harvard Law School, he met his future wife, Ruth Frankel, the sister of a legal assistant who worked for him. They were married in 1941 and she became his most trusted editor and the mother of their three sons.

After a brief tour as a lawyer with the Lend-Lease Administration, Boorstin joined the faculty of Swarthmore College. In 1944, he left Swarthmore for the University of Chicago, working as one of a group of teachers under President Robert M. Hutchins to establish an interdisciplinary program in the social sciences. He rose rapidly through the ranks of the history department, becoming a full professor in 1956. In 1966, he was appointed to an endowed chair, the Preston and Sterling Morton Distinguished Service Professor of History.

In 1969, after a productive and prestigious 25-year academic career and many honors in the United States and abroad, Boorstin left the University of Chicago to become director of the Smithsonian Institution's National Museum of History and Technology (today known as the National Museum of American History). Focusing on the Smithsonian's participation in the forthcoming U.S. bicentennial in 1976, he brought new intellectual energy to the institution, along with exhibitions such as "A Nation of Nations" that provided a new, broad social context for a new generation of Smithsonian exhibitions. He stepped down as director in 1973 to become Senior Historian.

On June 30, 1975, President Gerald R. Ford nominated Boorstin to be Librarian of Congress. The Senate hearings on the nomination lasted three days. Opposition from the American Library Association echoed the association's opposition to the nomination of Archibald MacLeish to be Librarian of Congress in 1939: Boorstin's background, "however distinguished it may be, does not include demonstrated leadership and administrative qualities which constitute basic and essential characteristics necessary in the Librarian of Congress." The nomination was strongly supported, however, by a bipartisan group of congressmen including Senators Mark O. Hatfield, Adlai E. Stevenson, and Charles H. Percy; and Representatives Carl Albert, Speaker of the House of Representatives, and John J. Rhodes, Minority Leader of the House of

Representatives. Thus in 1975, as in 1939, the Congress readily accepted the nomination of an author and in this case a historian, to head the Library. Confirmation occurred, without debate, on September 26, 1975, and on November 12, 1975, Daniel J. Boorstin took the oath of office as the 12th Librarian of Congress.

For the first time in the Library's history, the new Librarian took the oath of office at a formal ceremony in the Library. Held in the Jefferson Building's Great Hall, the occasion symbolized what was to be a hallmark of the Boorstin administration: public emphasis on the institution's dual role as both a legislative and a national institution. The ceremony's participants included national leaders from both the legislative and the executive branches of government, including President Gerald Ford, Vice-President Nelson Rockefeller, and Speaker of the House Carl Albert, who administered the oath of office. Representative Lucien N. Nedzi, chairman of the Joint Committee on the Library, presided. In introducing President Ford, Nedzi commented on the Library's dual role: "As its name reveals, the Library is the

As President Gerald R. Ford looked on, Daniel Boorstin placed his hand on the Thomson Bible from the Library's Jefferson collection, held by Speaker of the House of Representatives Carl Albert, and took the oath of office, making him the 12th Librarian of Congress. At the ceremony, held in the Library's Great Hall on November 12, 1975, Boorstin pledged himself "to try to keep alive and flourishing the tradition of the book." LC/Prints and Photographs Division. LC-USZ62-133568.

Library of Congress—a fact in which the Congress of the United States takes great pride—and, of equal importance, if not more so, it is a national library that serves all of the people of the United States."

One of Boorstin's first official acts was to create, on January 16, 1976, a staff Task Force on Goals, Organization, and Planning, which was charged with the responsibility of carrying out "a full-scale review of the Library and its activities." The Task Force effort was supplemented by advice from eight outside advisory groups, each representing one of the Library's principal outside constituencies.

Boorstin established greater public visibility for the Library, more systematic interaction between the Library and the world of scholarship and learning, and he developed programs and administrative structures that formalized these relationships. The year-long study of the Library by the staff Task Force on Goals, Organization, and Planning and its outside advisory groups helped create and sustain new relationships, and the Task Force reports were the basis for an administrative reorganization of the Library in 1978.

Among his early personal initiatives, Boorstin obtained congressional approval in 1976 of the American Folklife Center and the following year for the Center for the Book, which was established "to keep the book flourishing" by stimulating public interest in books, reading, and the printed word. The next year, the Library opened the Performing Arts Library at the Kennedy Center, a joint project of the two organizations. In 1980, Boorstin established a Council of Scholars, a link between the Library and the world of scholarship. Both the Center for the Book and the Council of Scholars were supported primarily by private donations.

A highlight of the Boorstin administration was the occupancy of the new James Madison Memorial Building in 1980; when it opened, it was the largest library building in the world. In collaboration

The opening of the James Madison Memorial Building in 1980 was a highlight of Boorstin's librarianship. At the time it was the largest library building in the world, containing 2,100,000 square feet with 1,500,000 square feet of assignable space. It also was the third largest public building in the Washington, D.C. area, exceeded only by the Pentagon and the F.B.I. building.

with Architect of the Capitol George M. White, Boorstin also initiated legislation, approved in 1984 that eventually led to the renovation and restoration of the Library's two older structures, the Jefferson and Adams Buildings. The Mary Pickford Theatre in the Madison Building, opened in 1983, greatly enhanced public access to the Library's unparalleled motion picture collections.

As Librarian of Congress, Boorstin fought hard and publicly for the Library's appropriation, even curtailing evening and Sunday opening hours in response to budget cuts. During his administration, the Library's annual appropriation increased from $116 million to $250 million. As Librarian of Congress, he took special interest in library preservation problems and in the development of the collections, which he dubbed "a multi-media encyclopedia."

Librarian Boorstin presents Mrs. Lessing J. Rosenwald with a copy of The Early Illustrated Book: Essays in Honor of Lessing J. Rosenwald. *Published by the Library, the book is based on papers presented at a Library symposium in May 1980, a year after Mr. Rosenwald's death. The Rosenwald collection of illustrated books, donated to the Library from 1943 to 1979, is the premier collection of its kind in the United States.* LC Archives.

Boorstin saw one of his principal roles as Librarian "to be a catalyst, an avenue between the world of ideas and what goes on at the Library." His success in this role was widely acknowledged. On December 10, 1986, he announced that he would leave his position as Librarian of Congress on June 15, 1987, "in order to devote more time to writing and lecturing." *The New York Times* noted that he had made the position of Librarian of Congress "perhaps the leading public intellectual position in the nation."

On April 17, 1987, President Ronald Reagan announced his intention to nominate James H. Billington as Boorstin's successor. On July 21, just three days before Billington's confirmation, the House of Representatives approved a bill designating Boorstin as Librarian of Congress Emeritus. The Senate concurred to the House amendment on July 22 and it was signed into law (Public Law 100-83) by President Reagan on August 4, 1987. Boorstin's only predecessor as Librarian of Congress Emeritus was Herbert Putnam, Librarian of Congress from 1899–1939, who served as Librarian Emeritus from 1939 until his death in 1955.

Throughout his career, Boorstin was a prolific author. He continued his work as an historian while Librarian of Congress, carefully pointing out that his research and writing took place in the morning at home–and not at the Library. His books include the trilogy: *The Americans: The Colonial Experience* (1958), which won the Bancroft Prize; *The Americans: The National Experience (1965),* which won the Parkman Prize; and *The Americans: The Democratic Experience* (1973), which won the Pulitzer Prize; *The Genius of American Politics* (1953); *The Image* (1962); and his world history trilogy: *The Discoverers* (1983), *The Creators* (1992), and *The Seekers* (1998).

Daniel Boorstin died on February 28, 2004; he was 89 years old. At a public memorial service at the Library, his successor as Librarian of Congress, James H. Billington, eulogized him as "a great American," a key figure "in the coming of age of our Nation's Capital," and "a matchless chronicler of the uniqueness, the innovative spirit and the everyday practicality of our shared American experience." (JYC)

Cole, John Y., ed. *The Republic of Letters: Librarian of Congress Daniel J. Boorstin on Books, Reading, and Libraries, 1975–1987.* Washington, D.C.: Library of Congress, 1989.

Leonard, Angela Michele, ed. *Daniel J. Boorstin: A Comprehensive and Selectively Annotated Bibliography*. Westport, Conn.: Greenwood Press, 2001.

Nomination of Daniel J. Boorstin of the District of Columbia to be Librarian of Congress. Hearings before the Committee on Rules and Administration, U.S. Senate. July 21 and 30 and September 10, 1975. Washington, D.C.: Government Printing Office, 1975.

CATALOGING DISTRIBUTION SERVICE

The mission of the Cataloging Distribution Service (CDS) is "To serve the information needs of the Library of Congress and its national and international constituencies by developing and marketing products and services which provide access to Library of Congress resources." For over a century, the distribution of Library of Congress cataloging has been perhaps the Library's most important contribution to improving library services nationwide. "LC cards" were a standard of American library practice for most of the twentieth century, and they have also been constantly used in libraries worldwide.

In 1870, the Library of Congress became the official copyright agency of the United States, receiving copies of every item published and submitted for copyright protection. Since the Library cataloged many copyrighted items for its collection, in 1876 Melvil Dewey suggested that the Library begin cataloging "for the whole country." Other librarians echoed Dewey's plea, but Librarian Ainsworth Rand Spofford did not consider the task appropriate to the Library's mission.

After Herbert Putnam became Librarian in April 1899, librarians renewed Dewey's request. Although no library had ever developed a national cataloging service, they knew that Putnam planned a broader role for the Library of Congress. Moreover, J. C. M. Hanson, the chief of the Library's Catalog Division, had begun a card catalog, and he designed the Library's printed cards with other libraries' needs in mind. In 1900, at Putnam's request, a printing and binding branch of the Government Printing Office moved into the Library's basement, and the Librarian began conferring with librarians on developing a card service. Next, he consulted the Public Printer about legislation to provide "such copies of the card indexes and other publications of the Library as may not be required for the ordinary transactions of the Library, and charge for the same a price which will cover their cost." The Public Printer added the words "and ten percentum added," and in that form the bill passed in 1902. It is the legislation under which the CDS's sales are still carried out.

Putnam announced the sale and distribution of the Library's printed cards at the August 1901 American Library Association (ALA) Conference and in a circular sent to more than 400 libraries on October 28, 1901. He and Hanson created a Card Section within the Library's Catalog Division and appointed Charles Harris Hastings as chief. After the initial period of organization, his six-person staff filled all orders for Library of Congress catalog cards within 24 hours, and at the end of the first year, Hastings reported receipts of $3,785.19 and 212 subscribers. After two years, the service was self-supporting, and Putnam declared the experiment a success.

The Card Section within the Catalog Division in the early 1900s, soon after it was established. LC/Prints and Photographs Division. Levin C. Handy. LC-USZ62-88888.

From the outset, the card service staff did more than fill card orders. They sent proof slip copies of cards to subscribers and depository cards to selected libraries nationwide, worked with publishers to record card numbers in national bibliographies and other publications, sent free samples to library schools, dispatched specially selected sets to libraries, and loaned card sets on request. They also filled standing orders for particular series, languages, and subjects. As the card service's emissary to the library community, Hastings constantly received ideas for additions and changes to the cards, and he managed to incorporate many of the librarians' suggestions. One of the most-wanted additions was Dewey Decimal Classification numbers, which through the united efforts of Hastings, Dewey, and the ALA, finally commenced in 1930.

Originally housed in the Catalog Division on the second floor, southeast curtain of the Jefferson Building, the Card Section soon required expansion as the stock of cards increased. The catalogers moved to the first floor in 1910, making way for more tiers of stacks. By 1914, when the Section became the Card Division, the stacks held 43,500,000 cards and there were 1,986 subscribers. Forty-one staff members climbed up and down steel stairs to fill orders, working under bare light bulbs. The inventory, subscribers, staff, and orders increased steadily until 1932–1934, when the Depression decreased receipts. But even then, the number of subscribers did not diminish; they simply sent smaller orders. When Hastings retired in

By 1913, the growing stock of catalog cards overflowed three tiers of storage space. Card Section staff continually climbed up and down to fulfill orders for catalog cards from across the nation—and increasingly from around the world. In 1914, Librarian Putnam expanded the Card Section into the Card Division, headed by Charles H. Hastings, who had been in charge of the card service since it began in 1901. LC/Prints and Photographs Division. LC-USZ62-60729.

1938, the service had 6,311 subscribers and sold nearly 14 million cards annually.

The Depression also brought shortages in printing capacity and staffing. Delays in fulfillment mounted, and subscribers' complaints increased. In 1938, the problems were aggravated when the division moved to temporary quarters in the southwest courtyard to await completion of new offices on the third floor of the Adams Building. Early in 1940, the move was finally accomplished, and in the reorganization of the library effected by Archibald MacLeish, the Card Division relinquished some book selection and cataloging duties in order to concentrate on filling orders more promptly. In the immediate post-war years, increased appropriation and management improvements enabled the staff to fill orders within three working days.

Hastings's successor was the division's assistant chief, John Cronin, who supervised the introduction of a second great innovation in American library cataloging: the modern book catalog. At the request of the Association of Research Libraries, the Library of Congress made its card catalog available to Edwards Brothers of Ann Arbor, Michigan, and Edwards used the new photo-offset process to create *A Catalog of Books Represented by Library of Congress Printed Cards Through 1942* with a supplementary set covering 1942–1946. With these sets in progress, in 1947 Cronin further undertook to publish ongoing book catalogs of the Library's holdings through the Government Printing Office. The book catalogs were intended to substitute for the depository catalogs and proof sheets that many librarians had been filing for nearly 50 years. Nevertheless, librarians wanted more, and in 1956, in response to their requests, the Library's book catalogs were expanded to include the holdings of other libraries and renamed the *National Union Catalog*.

The Card Division continued to sell cards as well as book catalogs during the 1950s, 1960s, and 1970s as librarians used the *National Union Catalog* and trade publications to locate card numbers and order cards. Cards began to be printed for nonbook materials in the early 1950s: maps, motion pictures, films, filmstrips, talking books, and books in raised characters. Cards also began to be produced for books in nonroman languages such as Arabic, Chinese, Japanese, and Korean. Publishers were invited to send advance copies of their books to the Library for rush cataloging and to obtain pre-assigned card numbers before publication, thus allowing card numbers to be printed in new books. The availability of card numbers in new books had a significant impact, since 80 percent of Card Division sales were for current American imprints, and in 1956, card sales for the first time topped $1 million. By the early 1960s, the Library had begun assisting distributors and publishers to make complete card sets available with new books at the time of sale in the so-called "Cards-with-Books" program. It was a period of enormous growth in library holdings nationwide: whereas in 1950 the division sold around 20 million cards, at peak in 1968 the total reached nearly 79 million while the number of subscribers jumped from 8,500 to 25,000.

In the mid-1960s, the Card Division, with almost 600 staff members, was the Library's largest administrative unit. It operated in two shifts and sometimes seven days per week, handling 60,000 orders daily. Again in need of space, in 1964 the division moved to the Navy Yard, a mile away on the Anacostia River. With an office occupying space larger than a football field, the staff navigated the aisles on custom-made stools with oversize casters that had to be cleaned and oiled once a month. To help improve service, the division began to mechanize in 1968. In the first phase of the Card Automated, Reproduction and Distribution System (CARDS), optical character recognition equipment began handling card orders, accounting, billing, and inventory control. In a second phase, bibliographic information was stored electronically so that seldom-ordered cards could be printed on demand rather than supplied from inventory. By the end of fiscal 1972, more than 265,000 records were stored on disc and tape and over eight million cards had been printed since the first production run in September 1971.

With the development of the MARC format, catalog records began to be distributed on computer tape and, as increasing numbers of librarians began cataloging by computer in the 1970s, card orders decreased dramatically. Also not-for-profit organizations such as the Ohio College Library Center and the Research Libraries Group began using MARC tapes to produce ready-to-file line-printer catalog cards for their member libraries. This meant that the Card Division was no longer the principal source of printed cards. Beginning in 1974, the sales of book catalogs, technical publications, and MARC tapes exceeded 50 percent of the division's net sales. The decline in card sales prompted cutbacks in staff and reorganization,

Malhotra, Nirmal.
Source material on education of scheduled castes and scheduled tribes / Nirmal Malhotra, Najma Rizvi. — Delhi : Anamika Publishers & Distributors, 1997.
455 p. ; 23 cm. I-E-97-901435; 68-92; 93-13
Includes bibliographical references and indexes.
ISBN 8186565140

1. Socially handicapped—Education—India—Sources—Bibliography. 2. India—Scheduled tribes—Education—Sources—Bibliography. I. Rizvi, Najma. II. Title.

Z5814.S72M35 1997 97-901435
[LC4097] AACR 2 MARC

Library of Congress

The Card Division became the Cataloging Distribution Service in 1975. This 1997 Library of Congress catalog card presents the basic bibliographical elements available online and freely to all libraries, including author, title, publication and ISBN information, subject headings, and Library of Congress classification number.
LC Archives.

and on February 1, 1975, the Card Division became the Cataloging Distribution Service (CDS) Division. The last word was dropped a year later. The new name reflected more accurately the Service's role as distributor of Library of Congress cataloging on MARC tapes, microform publications, proofsheets, book catalogs, and technical publications for catalogers. Despite the new name, however, Library of Congress cards did not disappear; and the Library remained committed to providing printed cards as long as demand existed, although the free depository card sets were discontinued in 1982, just after the CDS moved from the Navy Yard back to Capitol Hill.

By the early 1980s, the Library had stored 5.5 million card images, all of which had to be available for speedy distribution. In the summer of 1978, a Card Automated Reproduction DEMAND System had been installed to produce MARC cards, and the Library contracted with Xerox Electro-Optical Systems to develop the DEMAND optical disk system to provide for on-demand printing of the Library's non-MARC cataloging records. Delivered in August 1982, it stored card images electronically at the rate of 200,000 images on one side of an optical disk and printed 12 copies per second on high-resolution laser printers. Just before it was implemented, the Government Printing Office branch that had been located in the Library since 1900 closed.

The electronic MARC records provided new opportunities for disseminating catalog information. The Alert Current Awareness Service introduced in 1981 allowed subscribers to select among subject categories tied to the Library's classification system and receive automatic weekly shipments of cards for new books on those subjects. MARC Reselect, introduced in 1983, provided for fulfillment of orders for subsets of the MARC database—by format of material, language, country of publication, and other keys. The Select MARC: Retrospective Conversion Service begun in 1985 offered retrieval and transfer to computer tape of the catalog records needed by librarians who were converting their entire card catalogs into online catalogs.

The Service began issuing some of its products on microfiche in 1983, and a pilot project for distributing information on compact disc began in 1986 with a contract to Online Computer Systems, Inc. for development of software and documentation. Representing a new generation of mass-storage devices, the compact disc allowed the Service to provide bibliographic files and technical publications to small libraries that had personal computers but no access to minicomputers or mainframes. The first product, *CDMARC Subjects* included the Library's complete subject headings database, retrieval software, and indexing; *CDMARC Names* provided name authorities; and *CDMARC Bibliographic* contained the Library's machine-readable bibliographic files. By the late 1980s, the MARC Distribution Service was also providing records on tape for a variety of materials: Hebrew books, the *National Union Catalog of Manuscript Collections*, Chinese/Japanese/Korean records, materials cataloged by other national libraries, and computer files. These were joined over the next several years by records for microform masters, an index of Hispanic legislation, an inventory of nitrate film holdings, and *CDMARC Serials*. Librarians could profit from the Library's own training program on the fundamentals of descriptive cataloging by purchasing *Cataloging Concepts* on CD, and they could evaluate through the *MARC Diagnostic*

Service how well their cataloging data conformed to the USMARC standards.

In 1990, only about 40 percent of CDS sales were still in book format, but the best-selling titles were still books: the 13th edition of the *Library of Congress Subject Headings* and the companion volume *Free-Floating Subdivisions: An Alphabetic Guide*, a manual for librarians constructing their own subject headings. The Service assumed responsibility that year for the newly acquired National Translations Center, and distributed MARC tapes of its records until it was closed in 1993. Electronic products steadily became more popular. At mid-decade, the CDS introduced two new Windows-based compact disc products: *Classification Plus* (1996) and *Cataloger's Desktop* (1994), just as Internet file transfer protocol began to be used to speed the distribution of MARC records. These products offered access to the Library's technical apparatus for cataloging, including the classification schedules, the subject headings, documentation for all the MARC formats, and cataloging rules and interpretations. A CDS home page including the *CDS Catalog of Bibliographic Products and Services* went up on the Library's Web site.

During reorganization of the Library's administrative structure, in 1990 the CDS moved from the Processing Department to Constituent Services, and in 1995 to National Services. For many years self-supporting, the Service posted receipt shortfalls in 1996 to 1998. To offset these shortfalls, the CDS reduced staff, and eliminated products for which there was least demand. Among them was printed catalog cards, and that service was accordingly discontinued effective March 1, 1997.

The Service celebrated the 100th anniversary of the card service in the autumn of 2001 with a forum to consider current cataloging issues and ideas for reshaping the Service to meet future needs. A high priority was to offer customers electronic alternatives to the publications they had used in print, microform, and other formats. Thus in 2002, the Service introduced its first Web-based subscription service, *Classification Web*, which provides access to the Library's classification schedules and subject headings in a way previously available only within the Library. Development proceeded concurrently for the introduction of the *Cataloger's Desktop on the Web* in 2004. During the early years of the new century, the Service ceased distributing microfiche products and stopped supplying MARC records on tape reel and tape cartridge, and its card-based Alert Service was scheduled to phase out in 2004.

At the end of 2003, the CDS was providing products and services to approximately 7,900 libraries and information concerns with receipts of over $4.5 million. Its sales included print publications, 34 percent; MARC Distribution Services, 28 percent; *Classification Web*, 19 percent; CD-ROM, 14 percent; Alert Service, 5 percent; and microfiche catalogs, less than 1 percent. Throughout the history of the CDS, the constant goal has been to reduce the amount of time it takes to provide catalog information and cataloging-related services to the librarians who need them and to help librarians save money on processing services. For nearly three-quarters of a century, the Service was a manual operation that supplied mostly cards and operated by mail. Only in the last few decades have rapid improvements in computer and communications technology made possible the ideal: the instant transmission of catalog information to all who want it worldwide. (JA)

Edlund, Paul. "A Monster and a Miracle: The Cataloging Distribution Service of the Library of Congress, 1901–1976," *The Quarterly Journal of the Library of Congress* 33 (October 1976): 383–421.

CATALOGING IN PUBLICATION (CIP)

As long ago as the late nineteenth century, librarians wished that they could obtain cataloging information for books before publication. When the Library of Congress began its printed card service early in the twentieth century, current cataloging became readily available but librarians still had to order the cards. No other solution appeared until the 1940s, when the Library entered an agreement with Rutgers University Press to publish a review journal, *The United States Quarterly Book Review*. Publishers sent copies of their new books to the *Review* in advance of publication, and the Card Division borrowed them for cataloging. But the *Review* covered only about one-fourth of all titles published.

In 1953, the American Book Publishers Council and the Library began the "All the Books" program, intended to achieve complete coverage of publishers' output. The Council urged publishers to participate, and the Library pre-assigned card numbers so that the numbers could be printed in the books themselves, in advertising, and in announcements. This enabled librarians to order cards by card number and at a discount of four cents off each 10-cent card. However, it was soon discovered that, even when the Library received the very first bound copy of a book, there was not enough lead time for cataloging and card printing.

With a $55,000 grant from the Council on Library Resources, Inc. (CLR), the Library of Congress and the Department of Agriculture Library experimented from July 1958 through February 1959 with asking publishers to send page proofs of new books to be cataloged. The 157 publishers who cooperated received facsimiles of Library of Congress cards for reproduction in their books. On a "rush" schedule, catalogers were able to complete work on a total of 1,203 works in an amazing 7 hours and 10 minutes. The project staff then surveyed 200 libraries to assess the results.

Librarian L. Quincy Mumford ultimately decided that the project, called "Cataloging in source" could not be continued because of high costs, the disruption of publishers' schedules, the pressure on the Library staff, and a high error rate. Many of the errors, however, were inevitable because the cataloging was based on books that were not yet in final form. Mumford's decision greatly disappointed librarians, many of whom thought the experiment successful enough to continue. Instead, the Library made an agreement with the R. R. Bowker Company to catalog all the books received for review in Bowker periodicals. Catalog information was then made available through the Bowker publications *Publishers Weekly* and the *American Book Publishing Record*.

At a meeting preceding the June 1969 conference of the American Library Association (ALA), a joint committee of the ALA's Resources and Technical Services Division and the American Book Publishers' Council decided to take a new look at pre-publication cataloging. While Verner Clapp, president of CLR, investigated the willingness of publishers to participate and surveyed libraries to determine the potential impact on their processing operations, the committee studied the results of the 1958–1959 experiment and joined with Library staff to find solutions to the problems. All agreed that the cataloging information should be printed on the reverse of the title page so that every purchaser of a book would have it; but that to avoid errors, data that was apt to change in the publication process should be omitted. To decrease time pressures, galley proofs would be used, and the turn-around period would be 10 days from receipt to completion. This plan seemed likely to achieve current bibliographic control of U.S. publications.

Fully 97 percent of the librarians surveyed favored a new program, while publishers also affirmed their intent to cooperate. Thus in July 1971, the Library began the Cataloging in Publication Program (CIP), covering monographs published in the United States Matching grants from CLR and the National Endowment for the Humanities supported the first two years' work. By June 30, 1973, almost all of the larger publishing houses and university presses and many smaller firms were participating—a total of about 500 publishers. When foundation support ended, Congress approved funding for CIP as part of the Library's permanent operation. Federal government agencies were invited to send their publications to the program beginning in September 1973.

The basic objectives of the CIP program were to distribute LC cataloging data at an early stage in the manufacture of a book, and in machine-readable format; to make catalog cards available before publication; and to include cataloging data in each CIP book. Librarians had several options for using the information. They could pre-order cards and match them up with the books when books were received; they could order printed cards and use the CIP data for temporary control; or they could convert the CIP data printed in the books to their own catalog card reproduction masters. When CIP records began to be distributed via the MARC distribution service in October 1971, librarians were able to use the records in their own online catalogs.

As publishers learned about the program, it grew rapidly: by 1974, 610 publishers were participating and cataloging was being provided for about 65 percent of all monographs published in the United States. As librarians in other countries monitored the success of the program, they too began planning to capture the output of domestic publishers, and interest spread so quickly that the Library held an international conference on CIP in 1976. Processing of biomedical titles submitted for cataloging in publication was transferred to the National Library of Medicine in 1984 to eliminate any possibility of duplication of that library's cataloging. A CIP advisory group composed of representatives of library and publishing associations and book jobbers met regularly, and the division offered workshops to inform publishers about the program during the 1980s and 1990s, as well as soliciting librarians' suggestions about the program at American Library Association and other library meetings. A *CIP Publishers Manual* appeared in 1985.

Studies of CIP effectiveness were conducted after the program's 10th and 20th anniversaries. The first survey showed that about 80 percent of U.S. libraries used CIP data and more than 2,000 publishers had joined the program. About 30,000 titles were cataloged annually, accounting for the entire output of the American trade publishing industry. In a study completed in 1992, SKP Associates estimated the overall savings to libraries at over $122 million annually as CIP took the place of local cataloging and computers eased the tasks of recording information, correcting errors, and speeding communications.

As early as 1996, publishers began transmitting their texts via the Internet, and librarians began sending the catalog information back electronically. When the published book is received, the Library staff corrects and updates the catalog information so that individual libraries need not. In addition to providing the information to publishers, the Library also distributes the records in machine-readable format to libraries, bibliographic services and book dealers worldwide. Many of them use the catalog records in their products and services to alert libraries to new publications and to assist book orders. The CIP home page on the Library's Web site provides information for publishers on eligibility for the program and on the submission of material needed to obtain CIP data.

Late in 1999, the program recorded its millionth record and in June 2001 celebrated its 30th anniversary. In 2003, the CIP program provided cataloging for more than 50,000 titles annually, and included virtually all U.S. trade book publishers. Its *New Books* project, an effort to link electronically auxiliary information such as author biographies, images of book jackets, and summaries or additional subject terms to catalog records was planned to be integrated with the Electronic Cataloging in Publication program after an ongoing development phase. (JA)

The Cataloging in Publication Program: A Brief History, 1971–2001. Washington, D.C.: Library of Congress, 2001.

CATALOGING OF COLLECTIONS

Between 1802, when the first catalog of the Library of Congress's collections appeared, and 1879, when the publication of book catalogs ended, the Library produced at least 57 different catalogs and supplements. In the catalogs of 1802, 1804, and 1808, the books were listed according to size: folios, quartos, octavos, and duodecimos. For each size, the descriptions began with the earliest acquisition and proceeded chronologically to the most recent. Separate sections for maps, state laws, gazettes, and U.S. government publications appeared in several catalogs. A listing by subject first appeared in 1812.

When Congress purchased Thomas Jefferson's library in 1815, Jefferson also provided his catalog, arranged by subject and under subject, alphabetically by author. As the collection grew, Librarians Watterston and Meehan published supplements to Jefferson's catalog, and they added an alphabetical author index and indexes to newspapers and society transactions. By the time Ainsworth Rand Spofford became Librarian in 1864, the Library's holdings exceeded 80,000 volumes and the 10-page catalog of 1802 had grown to 1,398 pages.

Spofford's first published catalog (1864) was arranged alphabetically by author, but the Librarian also compiled a two-volume subject catalog that was published in 1869. He planned to completely recatalog the library, expanding all catalog descriptions. Volume one of his new catalog appeared in 1878, but the set never went beyond "C" because the ever-growing burden of copyright registration absorbed all the staff's time. The catalogers simply filed their handwritten 5" x 8" author slips to await the printing of another volume.

When Librarian John Russell Young organized the Library, he established a Catalog Department and hired James Christian Meinich Hanson as its chief in 1897. Hanson developed the Library's first card catalog, a dictionary-style arrangement of authors, titles, and subjects on 3" x 5" cards. In the hope that Library of Congress cataloging might become useful to other libraries, he revised the Library's cataloging rules to accord with current library practices as codified by Charles Ammi Cutter, Melvil Dewey, and Klas Linderfelt, and he used the American Library Association's (ALA) *List of Subject Headings for Use in a Dictionary Catalog* as a base for expanding subject cataloging. With the assistance of classifier Charles Martel, Hanson developed an outline for a new classification system, and he planned for subject entries based on ALA practice. His transformation of the Library of Congress's catalog so impressed his colleagues that in 1900 he was named chairman of the ALA's Catalog Rules Committee. Under his leadership, the committee eventually produced the *Catalog Rules: Author and Title Entries* (1908), the first set of cataloging practices to be adopted by both British and U.S. libraries. *Subject Headings Used in the Dictionary Catalogues of the Library of Congress* followed, first appearing between 1909 and 1914. The cataloging staff has been compiling new editions and supplements ever since.

In 1897 Librarian Young hired experienced cataloger J.C.M. (James Christian Meinich) Hanson as the first chief of the Library's new Catalog Department. Hanson developed the Library's first catalog, revised its cataloging rules to comply with widely approved practices, and with his colleague Charles Martel, shaped the Library's new classification system. When Librarian Putnam decided to print catalog cards for sale in 1901, Hanson planned the content and format of the cards. He left the Library in 1910 to become associate director of the University of Chicago Library.
LC/Prints and Photographs Division. LC-USZ62-6059-A.

Librarian Herbert Putnam separated the ordering and binding functions from cataloging and renamed the Catalog Department the Catalog Division. He also established within it a Card Section to sell Library of Congress catalog cards to other libraries. Begun as an experiment, the card service was immediately successful, and it significantly changed cataloging routines because the most pressing need became to acquire and catalog new books quickly in order to provide cards to libraries nationwide. Due to card sales, the Library's cataloging methods increasingly influenced the practices of other libraries. Library of Congress cataloging was—and is—highly detailed, enabling users to find books by author, title, subject, added entries, and other keys. Its adoption demonstrated that in American libraries services to readers would be a top priority.

Since the original plan for the Jefferson Building did not includc a public catalog, one-fourth of the desks had to be removed from the Reading Room to make room for the card cases. Like other libraries, the Library of Congress also kept an "official" card catalog and a shelflist in the Catalog Division to expedite catalogers' work. The official catalog included "authority" cards for names and subjects, because these references to work already completed serve to remind catalogers of established practices as they catalog new books. The shelflist, kept in order by classification number, helped the staff determine how to number new books so that they would fit with those already entered.

The public and official catalogs, however, were not the only catalogs in the Library. There were separate catalogs for the Law Library, for maps, for music, and for copyright items, plus a host of other files. Staff in the manuscripts, prints and photographs, and serials areas had their own methods of recording these specialized items, and units that acquired materials in non-Roman languages also developed their own listings. These special catalogs were located in the reading rooms or offices of the units handling the material, and they were kept up to date by those units. In addition, each deck in the stacks included its own catalog of entries for the books on that deck. Thus, the Library's cataloging involved far more staff than those in the Catalog Division.

For more than two decades, the Catalog Division revised the 1908 cataloging rules as needed, often without advice from other librarians. But because Library of Congress cataloging was used in so many libraries, the card service printed the rule changes for free distribution. To expand the stock of cards available for purchase, the service printed cards for publications acquired by other federal libraries, and in 1910 began accepting catalog copy from selected research libraries that acquired many items that the Library of Congress did not own. While the Library could not catalog every book published, the card service provided a product that American librarians increasingly found indispensable.

When Charles Martel became chief of the Catalog Division in 1913, the staff had cataloged more books than the Library acquired each year in order to convert the collection to the new classification system. Thereafter, however, it was only during 1916 through 1918 that cataloging output exceeded acquisitions—because of wartime decreases in publishing. There were no appropriations for additional staff, and because salaries remained low, expert catalogers who left could not be replaced with equally qualified professionals. It took several years to train a new cataloger sufficiently to work independently, and the senior catalogers were fully occupied in handling the most highly specialized work. Every catalog record completed was revised by the senior staff before being printed.

By the early 1920s, the continued staff losses and card service budget cuts seriously eroded cataloging output. Finding that the card service could not supply cards for many books, especially foreign books and scholarly monographs, the ALA concluded that a cooperative effort might solve the problem. In 1932, the Association obtained a grant from the General Education Board to solicit catalog information from research libraries and print cards for those titles, and they secured Librarian Putnam's permission to house the project at the Library. In 1935, it became part of a new Cooperative Cataloging and Classification Service established by the Librarian, and when the grant expired in 1940, the Library took over the cooperative cataloging program. Another part of that Service, a project to print Dewey Decimal Classification numbers on Library of Congress cards also began at the ALA's behest in 1930 but was soon integrated into the Library's work.

In the Catalog Division in the late 1920s, staff members worked at desks hemmed in by official card files, reference books, and numerous book trucks containing volumes that awaited attention.
LC/Prints and Photographs Division. LC-USZ62-75117.

Instituting the two ALA projects, assembling a card catalog for the Adams Building (opened in 1938) and cooperation with the ALA on a new edition of the 1908 catalog rules, plus the regular work, kept the Catalog Division staff hard-pressed. Highly detailed original cataloging continued to be the norm, and because the Library was the central American cataloging authority, the catalogers continued to check all catalog records contributed by other libraries. As a result, the cataloging arrears grew alarmingly, and

Putnam told Congress in 1936 that with 750,000 books uncataloged, more staff was essential.

When Archibald MacLeish became Librarian in 1939, he ordered a comprehensive review of processing operations by a Librarian's Committee that included Carleton B. Joeckel (University of Chicago), Keyes D. Metcalf (New York Public Library), L. Quincy Mumford (New York Public Library), Paul North Rice (New York Public Library), Andrew Osborn (Harvard College Library), and Francis R. St. John (Enoch Pratt Free Library). Finding that of the Library's 5.8 million volumes about 1.5 million were not fully processed and that the arrears were growing at the rate of 300,000 volumes annually, the committee recommended reorganization, the use of simplified cataloging and more cooperative cataloging, changes in personnel policies, and new methods of cost analysis.

On July 1, 1940, MacLeish united the Accessions Division, Catalog Division, and Card Division in a new Processing Department temporarily directed by Mumford (September 1, 1940–January 25, 1942). The new department assumed responsibility for obtaining printed books and pamphlets and integrating these into the Library's collections. Catalogers were organized into two divisions: the Descriptive Cataloging Division, which physically described the books; and the Subject Cataloging Division, which assigned subject headings and classification numbers. A new Central Processing File tracked books while they were being processed. Additional units handled the physical preparation of the books for the shelves and card filing. A Processing Committee was created on July 8, 1943, as an interdepartmental advisory group to ensure coordination of cataloging and processing policies with the needs of the Acquisitions and Reference Departments and the Law Library. The cataloging of material received via copyright deposit, initially the responsibility of the Processing Department, was shifted to the Copyright Office in 1945 when a Copyright Cataloging Division was established in that office.

Meanwhile, the 400-page preliminary edition of the revised *A.L.A. Catalog Rules, Author and Title Entries*, begun by the ALA and the Library in 1930, finally appeared in 1941. It drew criticism from the profession: many librarians thought it was too Library of Congress-oriented and that the Library's practices were not cost-effective for other libraries. After reviewing the recommendations of the Librarian's Committee, Herman Henkle, director of the Processing Department (1942–1947) and Lucile Morsch, chief of descriptive cataloging (1940–1950; 1962–1965) and other staff members developed a statement of principles, examples, and a questionnaire that were sent to selected librarians nationwide. Their responses and comments appeared in a report titled *Studies in Descriptive Cataloging* (1946). Librarian Luther Evans then appointed an Advisory Committee on Descriptive Cataloging to help ensure that the rules would both meet the Library's needs and express the balanced judgment of the profession.

Drawing on the recommendations, Morsch completed *Rules for Descriptive Cataloging in the Library of Congress*, which the ALA approved at its 1949 conference. The Association endorsed the *Rules* as a new approach to description: the many specific rules were replaced by more general principles, which left more decisions to the individual cataloger. Throughout the long revision process, the library accepted changes recommended by the ALA's Division of Cataloging and Classification and loaned staff to the ALA to assist the revision of its *A.L.A. Cataloging Rules for Author and Title Entries* (1949). Ever since, the Library has continually consulted all professional groups that have a stake in its cataloging.

To simplify cataloging procedures and at the same time manage the cataloging arrearage more efficiently, the Processing Committee established a system of four priorities for cataloging: catalogers had to process books marked "rush" in a day, and for "hasten" books they had a week. "Regular" items, however, might wait up to 12 months, and material designated "Priority 4" received only a brief listing. The staff also instituted limited, or brief cataloging and collective listings for some classes of material and began limiting the amount of authority research performed and the number of added entries.

The demand for Library of Congress cataloging continued to increase. In 1947, the Library began to issue printed cards in book format on a monthly basis, with different series for author entries, subject entries, motion pictures and filmstrips, maps and atlases, and music and phonorecords. Librarians who purchased the book catalogs could copy entries for their own card catalogs and thereby save on both cataloging and card ordering, and they could follow the Library's cataloging rule interpretations and obtain subject heading guidance through the *Cataloging Service Bulletin* begun in 1945. In 1956, the book catalogs became the *National Union Catalog* (NUC), including not only Library of Congress cataloging but also catalog records contributed by other libraries. One result was to reduce the amount of cataloging other libraries sent to the Library of Congress under the cooperative cataloging program, which was phased out.

The Department still concentrated primarily on print publications, and materials in special formats and in non-Roman languages continued for the most part to be cataloged in the custodial divisions. During the late 1940s and through the following decade, staff committees began working to develop transliteration systems for material in Asian, Slavic, Middle Eastern, and other languages and to develop explicit cataloging rules for all formats of material: prints and photographs, music, recordings, manuscripts, motion pictures and microfilms—so that cards could be issued for them. A Law Processing Committee reviewed policies and special problems pertaining to legal material, and an Orientalia Processing Committee studied and revised the cataloging rules for Chinese, Japanese, and Korean materials. The Processing Committee decided in 1958 that printed cards should be filed into the general card catalog regardless of language. Therefore, as the new rules were approved by the Library, by the ALA, and by other relevant professional organizations, the catalog came to contain material in every language.

Nevertheless, cataloging rules still troubled both the Library and librarians generally. The Library's efforts to expedite cataloging in some cases conflicted with the elaborate procedures embedded in the cataloging code, and at the request of the ALA, the Library in 1951 assigned Seymour Lubetzky to consider alternatives. Lubetzky's *Cataloging Rules and Principles* (1953) set forth a new set of principles of author and title entry and led to another full-scale code revision beginning in 1956. This revision, pursued in collaboration with the British and Canadian library associations, was also the subject of an International Conference on Cataloging Principles, held in Paris in 1961.

Cataloging for a growing international publishing output was a major concern for all American research libraries by the late 1950s. The federal government and many educational institutions were developing programs in foreign area studies, which implied significant expansion of American library collections. But librarians found it difficult to acquire foreign publications, particularly those from less-developed countries. Moreover, trained catalogers with knowledge of Asian, African, and Middle Eastern languages were hard to find. Several library associations, principally the ALA and the Association of Research Libraries (ARL), worked to make Congress more aware of these needs, citing the fact that the Library of Congress provided cataloging for only about half the foreign books being acquired nationwide.

In 1958, Congress amended the Agricultural Trade Development and Assistance Act of 1954 (Public Law 480) to authorize the Library of Congress to purchase publications abroad with U.S.-owned foreign currencies and to catalog them to benefit research libraries throughout the country. Begun in January 1962 in India, Pakistan, and Egypt, by 1969 the program covered eight South Asian, Middle

Cataloging expert Lucile M. Morsch served as Deputy Chief Assistant Librarian of Congress from 1953 to 1962 and president of the American Library Association in 1957–1958. Here she poses in front of the Library's exhibit at the 1957 annual ALA conference in Kansas City, Missouri. Chief of the Descriptive Cataloging Division (1940–1950, 1962–1965), she was deeply involved in the development of standardized cataloging rules and catalog code revision, nationally and internationally.
LC Archives.

Eastern, and European countries. The staff in the local centers were trained to assist in establishing catalog entries, and research libraries participating in the program also provided cataloging assistance for some of the new materials and cash contributions to support cataloging at the Library. In the Descriptive Cataloging Division, the PL-480 work resulted in the establishment of new units for Indic, Arabic, and South Asian languages. Expecting to add to the staff to cover this work, the division abandoned the limited cataloging policy it had followed between 1951 and 1963 and returned to providing full descriptions for each item.

Three years later, Congress added the National Program for Acquisitions and Cataloging (NPAC). Authorized by the Higher Education Act of 1965 (Title II, Part C), the act directed the Library to acquire all material published worldwide that might be valuable for scholarship and to publish catalog information promptly. NPAC funding enabled the Processing Department to again increase staff, to organize a Shared Cataloging Division to handle NPAC materials (1967) and to establish centers abroad to acquire publications and cataloging information. At a January 1966 conference in London of national libraries and the producers of the national bibliographies of England, France, West Germany, Norway, and Austria, it was agreed that the Library would use for cataloging purposes the descriptions listed in the national bibliography of each country of publication and that the publishers would supply the Library with copy in advance of publication. By 1968, the Department's 1,200 staff could catalog in 60 languages and the Library provided over 70 percent of the current cataloging needed by American research libraries—a more than 20 percent increase over the pre-NPAC period. NPAC continued to expand rapidly in the early 1970s, covering 40 countries by 1974, and the number of languages in which cataloging was performed rose to 144.

Under the stimulus of the PL-480 and NPAC programs, the 1960s became a period of explosive growth as the Processing Department constantly recruited new staff. A Cataloging Instruction Office was established in 1964 to help language specialists learn to catalog and to provide other training programs. At the same time, the organization of a separate section for children's literature gave catalogers the new duty of preparing annotated catalog cards for children's books (1966). The Library's role as the central U.S. cataloging facility was further reinforced by the appearance of the new, comprehensive *Anglo-American Cataloging Rules* (1967), in part the result of the Paris conference of 1961, which adopted much of Lubetzky's work. The new code was edited by C. Sumner Spalding the chief of the Descriptive Cataloging Division, with the assistance of Lucile M. Morsch, the Library's representative on the ALA Catalog Code Revision Committee, and supported by a grant from the Council on Library Resources, Inc. Use of the new rules in the Library's catalogs began March 20, 1967, just two months after publication, and news of the Library's applications of particular rules was announced in the *Cataloging Service Bulletin*.

In 1968, the Processing Department was reorganized into three units: acquisitions and overseas operations; cataloging; and catalog maintenance, production, and publication. Recognizing that the most-demanded materials were not being cataloged quickly enough, Director William Welsh instituted a seven-class system that gave top priority to American trade books and U.S. and state government publications. Simultaneously, the Descriptive Cataloging Division continued to expand coverage to a number of African languages while pursuing additional romanization schemes for obscure languages. The essential tasks over the next decades were to absorb a high volume of international acquisitions and to keep the Library's manual systems running smoothly while computer systems were developed. To that end, when in 1970 the Main Reading Room card catalog had grown to about 15.5 million cards in 12,849 trays, the staff expanded it into 21,257 trays to provide for the 30 million cards that they expected to file during the next 10 to 20 years. But financial pressures forced the staff to cease filing cards in the Adams Building catalog in 1969; in 1973 it was removed to storage, replaced by a complete set of the *National Union Catalog*.

Just as during the late nineteenth century Hanson viewed the changes in the Library's cataloging as a development that would affect all libraries, the Library made services to other libraries an essential part of the Library of Congress's automation program. The Department sponsored conferences on machine-readable cataloging during 1965–1967 to obtain librarians' advice on its MARC pilot project and established a Technical Processes Research Office in 1967 to conduct research on issues related to bibliographic control. A cooperative project with the Government Printing Office to test the use of electronic photocomposition resulted in publication of the seventh edition of the Library's subject headings the same year. The Library joined the National Library of Medicine and the National Agricultural Library in a U.S. National Libraries Task Force on Automation and Other Cooperative Services. The three libraries agreed to coordinate their automation programs through the adoption of standard practices and to establish joint databases for machine-readable cataloging at the Library of Congress.

Within a decade, the Library launched MARC and expanded its scope to serials, motion pictures and filmstrips, manuscripts, maps, sound recordings, and to all Roman alphabet languages, with catalog records distributed on tape to subscribing libraries via the Cataloging Distribution Service's MARC Distribution Service. They also began work on the conversion of the Library's retrospective catalog records to machine-readable format, a project completed in the early 1980s with the assistance of an outside contractor, Carrollton Press. With automation, catalogers' annual production increased from around 60,000 to over 180,000 catalog records by the late 1970s, and in 1977 the Library announced the decision to close the card catalog and rely on computers henceforth. The staff established a Computer Catalog Center near the Main Reading Room to make the Library's online files available to users. Four years later, its size had to be tripled to keep pace with staff and readers' increasing reliance on the online catalog.

Code revision began again in the mid-1970s, when the Processing Department cooperated with the ALA, the British Library, the Canadian Committee on Cataloging, and the Library Association of Great Britain to bring the North American and British texts of the *Anglo-American Cataloging Rules* into conformity and to incorporate the new International

Standard Bibliographic Description, an international standard for descriptive information. Edited by Paul Winkler of the Library staff and Michael Gorman of the British Library, the new code, dubbed AACR2, appeared in 1978. The Library's *Subject Cataloging Manual: Subject Headings*, which appeared in 1984, provided simultaneous recognition of the growing complexity of formulating subject headings for use in online catalogs. A new Office for Descriptive Cataloging Policy, created in March 1979, coordinated the development of all catalog descriptions, cataloging rules, and romanization schemes, and the Cataloging Instruction Office developed training courses to ensure that the staff would be well-versed in AACR2 rule changes. The cataloging staff also entered a joint effort with the ALA to train the nation's catalogers. Holding more than a dozen regional institutes around the country between 1979 and 1981, they discussed AACR2 with over 2,000 professionals each year. These institutes were followed by a series of ALA/Library of Congress name authority institutes and subject headings institutes in 1982–1983. To supplement AACR2, the Library began publishing a series called *Library of Congress Rule Interpretations* in 1981, circulating each draft to the library community for comment before publication. And during the late 1970s, a concerted attack was mounted by the Descriptive and Shared Cataloging Divisions on the cataloging arrearage, with good progress on Japanese, German, Thai, Yudin Collection, Indonesian, Korean, Latin, and Persian titles and also non-music sound recordings. Following up on that effort, it was decided to resume minimal-level cataloging of selected material, in machine-readable format, and to store this low-priority material compactly at a remote location.

The name of the Processing Department changed in 1978, amid a general Library reorganization, to Processing Services, and the following year saw a review of cataloging priorities, which resulted in placing primary emphasis on the content and need for a particular item rather than its source. Two years later, the staff shifted functions from the Library's Automated Systems Office to establish an office of processing systems, networks, and automation planning as computer and telecommunications technology development continued to dominate library cataloging. In 1973, the Library entered for the first time into a cooperative cataloging project that it did not host—a cooperative called Conversion of Serials (CONSER), formed to enter serials cataloging into the Ohio College Library Center's (OCLC) database. The definition of the role of a participant in an evolving national network was a project that preoccupied many librarians as computer capabilities matured, and after a series of meeting with the major cataloging database producers, the so-called "bibliographic utilities": the Ohio College Library Center, the Research Libraries Group (RLG), and the Washington Library Network (WLN), foundations and other interested parties, the Library developed a position paper titled "Toward a National Library and Information Service Network: The Library Bibliographic Component." A Network Advisory Committee was organized to provide advice on the Library's role in the evolving national library and information network.

At the same time, the Library made agreements with the National Library of Canada and several European national libraries to exchange machine-readable cataloging, and when the Government Printing Office agreed to make its name authority records compatible with those of the Library (as a step toward coordinating the two agencies' cataloging practices), a Name Authority Cooperative (NACO) was formed. During 1980–1981, 15 large libraries, including three state libraries, one historical society and 11 university libraries began contributing their name authority records to the database as well, and the National Library of Medicine contributed headings for its biomedical serials. In a further move toward relying on cooperative efforts, the Library delegated to the Government Printing Office all cataloging for federal documents. Several years later, libraries began contributing not only name but also series authorities and complete bibliographic records. All these contributions were made available in the same way the MARC records were made available, through the Library's Cataloging Distribution Service. A *NACO Participants' Manual* first appeared in 1994, and numerous technical publications for participating libraries followed.

By 1980, the growing interest of libraries and bibliographic utilities in the pursuit of increasingly complex automation activities had made the need for better cooperation across automated operations evident in the Library, and a new position, director of processing systems, networks, and automation planning was established with Henriette D. Avram as the first incumbent. This office cooperated with the Network Advisory Committee in identifying and addressing needs in facilitating access to bibliographic information, and it worked with such outside groups as the Council on Library Resources on the Council's Linked Systems Project, a plan to develop linkages among computer systems; on the further development of the name authority service; and on mechanisms for nationwide network governance. The office was also concerned with extension of the MARC formats, the guidance of changes to MARC and with integrating these with national and international standards, in cooperation with the ALA's Representation in Machine-Readable Form of Bibliographic Information (MARBI) Committee, the American National

Standards Institute, the International Organization for Standardization, the International Federation of Library Associations, and UNESCO.

In 1981, Processing Services moved to the James Madison Building and officially adopted AACR2 and the new 19th edition of the Dewey Classification. But an even more important milestone preceded these changes: on December 31, 1980, the last cards were filed in the card catalog. The public catalog was removed from the Main Reading Room to nearby stacks, but conversion of all the records in the catalog to machine-readable format soon followed, and the catalog itself was eventually reproduced on microfiche (1989). When it became the official catalog of the Library of Congress, the online catalog included fully cataloged books in all languages other than Chinese, Japanese, Korean, Arabic, Persian, and the Hebraic alphabet. It did not yet include audiovisual material, music and sound recordings. Thus considerable work remained to be done to provide machine-readable records of all materials in the collection. The gradual expansion of the MARC formats and the Library's continuing work to maintain them was recognized in 1984 when the Network Development Office became the Network Development and MARC Standards Office.

Other important developments of the early 1980s included the implementation of a new system of cataloging priorities that emphasized the research value of publications and the current need for them, while retaining the emphasis on English language material and providing for material that would never be cataloged in full to be given low priority. In recognition of the increasing importance of audiovisual materials, manuscripts, music, and rare books in the Library's collections, the staff responsible for cataloging those items were consolidated in a Special Materials Cataloging Division in 1981. The first compact disc sound recording was cataloged in 1983, and the first software packages in 1987.

Even before the two millionth MARC record entered the system in 1985, catalogers had begun using the growing online bibliographic and authority files as principal aids to cataloging books in most languages, serials, and maps. TOSCA (Total Online Searching for Cataloging Activities), as the new procedure was called, promoted productivity increases, and the Library installed the Research Libraries Group's Chinese-Japanese-Korean terminals for catalogers working in these languages. With the development phase supported by private funding and the Council on Library Resources, the so-called JACKPHY/MARC program produced the first romanized Japanese, Arabic, Chinese, Korean, Persian, and Yiddish MARC catalog records in 1983. Cataloging for music and sound recordings and for films and graphic materials went online in the mid-1980s, while the 10th edition of the *Library of Congress Subject Headings* (1986) was converted to machine-readable format.

Cooperative cataloging activities continued to increase as the Library began accepting other libraries' cataloging online through a project involving the University of Chicago, Harvard University, and later the University of Illinois at Champaign-Urbana. As NACO had become the coordinating mechanism for the receipt of bibliographic records and series authority records as well as name authority records, the cooperative program was named National Coordinated Cataloging Program (1988), and the Linked Systems Project provided the computer-to-computer links that allowed the online exchange of cataloging records. In the National Coordinated Cataloging Program three-year pilot project funded by the Council on Library Resources (1988–1991), cataloging responsibilities were assigned among eight participating research libraries that agreed to contribute full bibliographic records and authority work online, with the Library of Congress providing the terminals to access its computer and also the documentation and training materials.

As part of a Library reorganization, Processing Services became part of Collections Services in 1990, and in 1996 it became part of a new Library Services department that encompassed acquisitions, cataloging, public service, and preservation. An Office for Subject Cataloging Policy, created in 1989, became responsible for the continuing publication of the Library's classification and subject headings and for determining policies relating to them. Also that year, a Cataloging Forum, an independent grass roots organization for staff interested in issues of bibliographic control, began presenting monthly programs featuring experts on such topics as the information highway and online classification.

In 1989, Processing Services launched the Whole Book Cataloging Project, designed to test whether catalogers could effectively handle both the physical description of items and the creation of subject access. The administrative division between the two dated from the 1940s, but staff interest in making cataloging a more stimulating activity as well as the desire to integrate functions and shorten the cataloging cycle inspired the experiment. When the project proved successful, cataloging was reorganized, with an Enhanced Cataloging Division created in 1991 to handle copy cataloging (the adaptation of cataloging records other libraries had contributed to the bibliographic utilities) and minimal level cataloging, while in 1992 five new subject-based divisions appeared in the Cataloging Directorate: Arts and Sciences, History and Literature, Regional and

Cooperative, Social Sciences, with additional units for Cataloging in Publication, Cataloging Policy and Support, Decimal Classification, and Special Materials. Descriptive and subject catalogers and preliminary cataloging and shelflisting technicians began working together in teams. A "Whole Serials Cataloging" program followed up the successful effort, and a new four-priority cataloging system reduced emphasis on English-language items, although new American books needing prepublication cataloging remained the highest priority while minimal level cataloging was lowest. Simultaneously, the staff expanded use of collection-level cataloging for special materials, which meant that a single catalog record might describe hundreds of similar or related objects. Collection-level cataloging has been used for items kept in the Prints and Photographs Division, which developed the *Thesaurus for Graphic Materials* (1995) to handle topics relating to image collections. Similar manuals such as the Motion Picture, Broadcasting and Recorded Sound Division's *Archival Moving Images Materials* (2000), and the Geography and Map Division's *Map Cataloging Manual* (1991) were developed as special aids to describing nonbook materials.

Part of the cataloging reorganization was due to the Library's efforts to reduce arrearages. In 1989, Librarian James Billington had formed a Special Project Team to undertake a comprehensive census of unprocessed material. Defining "arrearage" as materials that were in process longer than a reasonable amount of time or that would not be processed in the foreseeable future, the team counted 38 million items, with arrears growing at the rate of 1.8 million items annually—more than one-third of the Library's holdings. A report went to Congress in December 1990, and in response to the congressional request that the Library make arrearage reduction its highest priority, Billington made the problem a focus of his 1991 budget request. The resulting appropriation included over 160 new staff positions, and staff throughout the Library lent time to the work. Testing different procedures and approaches, they achieved a 2.4 percent decrease the first year, and by the end of 2000, total arrearage had been reduced by more than 50 percent.

An obvious avenue to arrearage reduction was to obtain cooperative cataloging. In response to a directive from the House Appropriations Committee, Billington established a Special Project Team to review all cooperative cataloging programs in which the Library participated and to develop a new formal plan for this activity. Late in 1992, representatives from the National Coordinated Cataloging Program, the Conversion of Serials Policy Committee, and Library staff met to discuss the future of cooperative cataloging programs, and in April 1993 the Library formed a Cooperative Cataloging Council and planned an ambitious program, which included international partners with the input of authority data from the British Library and the National Library of Canada. With numerous contributions from libraries being received under agreements made at different times and for different types of materials, in 1997, the Program for Cooperative Cataloging became the umbrella organization for the all efforts to provide contributions to the Library's databases: The Cooperative On-line Serials Program, the Name Authorities Cooperative, the Subject Authorities Cooperative, and the Bibliographic Cooperative. Around 340 institutions had joined the program by 1999. The Library serves as the secretariat for the program, but members formulate the policies. For example, participants approved new standards for this program, the so-called "core bibliographic record," which included the use of authority records, a classification number, and at least one subject entry. As the program reached its 10th anniversary, member libraries nationwide and abroad had contributed more than 350,000 bibliographic records and over 1.2 million name and series authorities to the pool of shared cataloging created according to mutually agreed-on standards. More than 74,000 subject headings were incorporated into the *Library of Congress Subject Headings* and more than 8,000 numbers into the Library of Congress Classification. The program provides the Library with communication channels with the library community and promotes discussion about evolving cataloging policies and practices and about ways in which the Library might respond to other libraries' needs. Member libraries benefit by having access to high-quality cataloging, from staff training conducted by program trainers, and from the documentation distributed to program participants free of charge.

By the mid-1990s, the combination of funding for centralized cataloging, cooperation with libraries worldwide, and the efficiencies of online systems enabled the Library to set new cataloging records, and by 2003 it was creating approximately 270,000 new records annually, of which about 69 percent received original cataloging. An electronic newsletter, *LC Cataloging Newsline*, began publication in January 1993, and on April 30, 1993, the Library's bibliographic records became available worldwide to users of the Internet, providing instant access to the record of Library of Congress holdings. To capitalize on the opportunities presented by access to the World Wide Web, a Bibliographic Enrichment Activities Team was formed in the Cataloging Directorate to employ electronic capabilities to enrich bibliographic data. Its activities have included providing table of contents within bibliographic records; linking bibliographic records to publishers' online descriptions of their new books; linking records to *H-Net Reviews*, which provides online reviews of books in the humanities and social sciences; and linking records with electronic texts provided by the *Making of America* project of the University of Michigan and Cornell University and Indiana University's *Wright American Fiction, 1851–1875*.

A notable occurrence was the beginning of an effort in partnership with OCLC and RLG, to convert from the Wade-Giles system of romanization for Chinese-language records to the pinyin system, a development encouraged by the National Library of Australia's success in achieving automatic conversion of its Wade-Giles records. After three years' work, on October 1, 2000, the conversion to pinyin went into effect with OCLC, RLG, and the Library converting existing romanized Library of Congress bibliographic and authority records; making them available in the Library's online catalog and through its Web site, and distributing them through the MARC distribution service.

With the implementation of the Voyager integrated library system in 1999, the Library staff became able for the first time to perform cataloging, circulation, inventory control, binding, serials check-in, reference, and acquisitions operations online in a unified bibliographic database, significantly easing many tasks and coordinating operations that could previously be related only manually. This milestone was shortly followed by another: the Library of Congress Bicentennial Conference on Bibliographic Control for the New Millennium held in November 2000 resulted in a set of 29 agenda items for the further development and enhancement of bibliographic records in relation to the wealth of digital resources available on the World Wide Web. Many of these would require long efforts, and they were represented in the directorate's first strategic plan, covering 2003–2008. The plan included six strategic goals: to provide national and international leadership in the development and promotion of cataloging policy, practice, standards, and programs; to provide appropriate, high-quality bibliographic and inventory control data for onsite and remote resources; to attain cataloging currency and meet arrearage reduction targets; to provide leadership in the application of bibliographic control/access to digital content; to ensure a secure environment for Cataloging Directorate staff, collections, and data; and to develop staff resources and provide effective personnel management. Thirty initiatives were to be undertaken during the first two years. One of these addressed electronic resources, aiming at improving approaches to resources available on the World Wide Web in collaboration with other institutions and organizations. An initial project, the Virtual International Authority File, involved cooperation with Die Deutsche Bibliothek to provide open access on the World Wide Web to the two libraries' authority files.

Today, the Library catalogs all types of materials including books, journals, government documents, microforms, computer files, sound and video recordings, prints, drawings, photographs, films, manuscripts, Braille books and music, and other formats. The Library catalogs at several levels of detail: full, core-level, minimal-level, and collection-level. Cataloging is still performed in many areas of the Library, although most of the books, music, sound recordings, microforms, and computer files are handled in the Cataloging Directorate. Other types of materials are cataloged in special units and in the custodial divisions; for example, serials are cataloged in the Serial Record Division and maps and cartographic materials in the Geography and Map Division. The Cataloging Policy and Support Office coordinates cataloging policy for all areas in the Library except for copyright cataloging. Cataloging rules and other publications used by Library of Congress catalogers are listed on the Cataloging Directorate's Web site. Among these are a number of publications that serve as standards for the library community, including subject headings, the classification, its rule interpretations, and specialized manuals for cataloging particular kinds of material such as maps and serials. The Library also maintains and further develops the MARC formats and code lists, the Z39.50 American National Standards Institute/National Information Standards Organization standard for information retrieval among computer systems, and the metadata standards for describing the contents of electronic files and databases.

Through the extensive use of cooperative cataloging and the less full "core record" that still contains the most essential catalog information, the Library has been able to significantly decrease the costs of this complicated, time-consuming, highly skilled work as well as decrease the cataloging arrears of over a century. Today other libraries rely most heavily on the Library of Congress for three kinds of cataloging data: full original cataloging, Cataloging in Publication, which provides pre-publication cataloging to keep abreast of new materials, and Dewey classification numbers. The interdependence of the cataloging community has grown steadily over the twentieth century, making contributions by each library increasingly important. The Library of Congress increasingly relies on other libraries, both nationwide and abroad, for assistance in covering publications worldwide. Its cataloging objective remains the same as it was a century ago: in serving the Library and the Congress, to serve other libraries as well. (JA)

Lacy, Dan. "The Library of Congress: A Sesquicentenary Review II: The Organization of the Collections," *Library Quarterly* 20 (October 1950): 235–252.

Milner, Sigrid P. "Library Observes 50 Years of Cataloging for the Nation," *Library of Congress Information Bulletin* 49 (December 17, 1990): 444–447.

CENTER FOR THE BOOK

In "A Design for an Anytime, Do-It-Yourself Energy-Free Communications Device," published in a 1974 article in *Harper's Magazine*, historian Daniel J. Boorstin praised the "wonderful, the uncanny, the mystic simplicity" of the book. The next year President Gerald R. Ford nominated Boorstin as the 12th Librarian of Congress, and two years later Boorstin proposed legislation to establish a Center for the Book in the Library of Congress. With enactment of Public Law 95-129, approved on Oct. 13, 1977, Congress endorsed a program to "stimulate public interest and research in the role of the book in the diffusion of knowledge." President Jimmy Carter approved the legislation to indicate his "commitment to scholarly research and to the development of public interest in books and reading."

Tara Holland, Miss America 1997, and official spokesperson for the Center's "Building a Nation of Readers" national reading promotion campaign, speaks at the Library in March 1997. On the left is Librarian of Congress Emeritus Daniel J. Boorstin, who founded the Center in 1977. Center for the Book Director John Y. Cole is next to Ms. Holland, and Carolyn Staley of the National Institute for Literacy is at the far right. LC/Center for the Book.

The Boorstin initiative for a Center for the Book was endorsed by the Publishers Advisory Group, one of eight outside advisory bodies established in 1976 as part of a year-long Task Force on Goals, Organization, and Planning. Dan Lacy of McGraw-Hill headed the Publishers Advisory Group, which urged the Library to create "a new body to fill and greatly enlarge the role of the former National Book Committee," which had promoted books, reading, and libraries from 1954 to 1974 with support from the publishing community. In late 1977, Librarian Boorstin named former Task Force chairman John Y. Cole to head the new Center.

Dan Lacy was Deputy Chief Librarian when this photograph was taken in 1951; from 1947 to 1949 he served as Assistant Director of the Processing Department. In 1976, the new Librarian of Congress, Daniel J. Boorstin, asked Lacy to chair a Publishers Advisory Group for the Library. In this capacity Lacy was instrumental in the creation of the Center for the Book in October 1977. LC Archives.

The legislation creating the Center authorized the Librarian of Congress to raise private funds to support the Center's activities; indeed, there was an understanding with Congress that the Center's program would be privately funded. The first contribution, $20,000 from McGraw-Hill, Inc. was used in 1977 and 1978 to convene four planning meetings to discuss the new Center and its potential activities. Other major contributors in 1978 were Time-Life Books and Mrs. Charles W. Engelhard Jr.

Today the Library of Congress funds the Center's four full-time staff positions, but its entire program and all of its individual projects must be supported by private contributions from individuals, corporations, or foundations or transfers of funds from other government agencies.

The Center for the Book's 25-year history, summarized below, reflects the gradual emergence of reading promotion and literacy as central concerns of the U.S. book, library, and educational communities; and the gradual "decentralization" of the Center for the Book idea and projects to the 50 states and the District of Columbia.

Books, Reading & Technology 1978–

Television was the dominant communications technology of the mid-1970s and one of Librarian Boorstin's immediate goals was for the Center for the

Book "to do something more to integrate television and the printed word within the educational process." In 1978, the belief that television was a promising vehicle for promoting books and reading was controversial; today it is taken for granted. The Center for the Book soon became pioneer in using new media to remind people of the "wonderful world of books."

Following its first symposium, "Television, the Book, and the Classroom," held at the Library on April 27–28, 1978, the Center developed a joint reading promotion project with CBS Television: 30-second "Read More About It!" messages following major CBS programs. Similar projects with cable, public television, and other commercial television networks soon

The Center has emphasized using new technologies—from television to the computer—to promote books and reading. For its pioneering "Read More About It" project on CBS Television (1979–1999) the Center compiled approximately 400 prime-time messages that sent viewers to their local libraries and bookstores for recommended books. Here in 1981, Mickey Mouse and Fess Parker film a "Read More About It" message for the CBS Television special "Walt Disney: One Man's Dream."
LC/Center for the Book.

followed. The Center prepared approximately 400 "Read More About It!" messages for CBS Television before the project ended in 1999.

In 1983, Congress authorized a major Center for the Book study about "the changing role of the book in the future." A major conclusion focused on the threat, not of technology, but of "the twin menaces of illiteracy and aliteracy—the inability to read and lack of the will to read," two menaces that had to be defeated "if our citizens are to remain free and qualified to govern themselves." New technologies were to be enlisted "with cautious enthusiasm in a national commitment to keep the Culture of the Book alive."

Today the Center continues its interest in technology and print culture though different projects and programs, often with state centers. "Read More About It" continues on the Library's Web site via American Memory's Learning Page, where users interested in learning more about digitized Library of Congress collections can find reading lists from the Center for the Book that send them to their local libraries and bookstores to "Read More About It!"

The Study of Books, Printing, and Libraries, 1978–

From the outset it was expected that the Center for the Book would encourage the traditional, scholarly study of books and of the role of books in society. Approximately one-third of the Center for the Book's more than 100 publications since 1978 have been on historical topics. Today the Center is a key organization in the new scholarly field of "book history."

Fifteen librarians, scholars, publishers, collectors, and editors from throughout the United States met at the Library on April 13–14, 1978, to discuss contributions the new Center might make to the history of books, printing, and libraries—and to what was the beginning to be called "print culture studies." Lectures, conferences, and publications began almost immediately. In 1979, book historian Elizabeth Eisenstein became the Center's first resident scholar. *The Early Illustrated Book*, the Center's first major scholarly conference (1980), honored the important Library of Congress donor, collector Lessing J. Rosenwald. In 1994, the Center won an award for its contribution from the American Printing History Association, and it hosted the second annual conference of the Society for the History of Authorship, Reading and Publishing (SHARP). Four years later it hosted a program marking the 50th anniversary of the American Library Association's Library History Round Table.

The International Role, 1978–

The Center for the Book's international program had two "founding impulses:" 1) the Library of Congress is a "world library," acquiring materials in most formats and most languages from most countries; and 2) when the Center was founded, "the international flow of books" was an important topic of concern to publishers and librarians alike. On February 23, 1978, in cooperation with the Association of American Publishers (AAP), the Center sponsored a meeting to explore issues related to the international flow of books and to consider how it might become a useful catalyst in U.S. government international book and library programs.

With support from the U.S. International Communications Agency (USICA), a 1979 conference at the East-West Center in Hawaii on "The International Flow of Information: A Trans-Pacific Perspective" culminated in a two-week tour to the

United States for the 17 participants from 12 East Asian and Pacific Rim countries. In 1983, the Center sponsored and published *U.S. Books Abroad: Neglected Ambassadors,* a study by publisher Curtis G. Benjamin. From 1987 to 1994, in cooperation with the U.S. Information Agency, the Center helped organize and staff a U.S. government exhibit booth at the Frankfurt Book Fair. From 1987 to the present, the Center has helped inspire comparable book and reading centers in libraries and educational institutions in England, South Africa, Scotland, Australia, and Russia.

Honoring Books and Book People, 1979–

Shortly after its creation, the Center began organizing and hosting events that honored "the book," important individuals in the book world, and notable series of books. In 1979, the Center and the Authors League of America sponsored "The Book," a lecture by historian Barbara Tuchman, a member of the Center for the Book's first National Advisory Board. Other programs have included: "Books in Action: The Armed Services Editions," a 1983 celebration of the 40th anniversary of the paperbacks distributed to American servicemen and servicewomen during World War II; "Amassing American Stuff," a 1995 symposium and oral history project featuring the publications and participants in the New Deal Arts projects of the 1930s and early 1940s, with a special emphasis on the Federal Writers Project (1935–1943) and its publications; and "Rivers of America," a 1997 symposium and oral history project marking the 60th anniversary of the 65-volume series of illustrated books about American rivers published between 1937 and 1974.

Historian Barbara W. Tuchman's The Book *(1979) was the first presentation in the Center's continuing series of "Viewpoint" talks by well-known book people.* LC/Publishing Office.

The Community of the Book, 1981–

As its program grew in the early 1980s, the Center began to gather and publish information about its organizational partners. Its first directory was *U.S. International Book Programs 1981*, a 61-page booklet that described 32 organizations and their programs. Between 1986 and 1993, it published three editions of *The Community of the Book: A Directory of Organizations and Programs.* The third edition (1993), a 150-page book, provided detailed descriptions of the programs of 109 organizations, by then all "reading promotion partners" of the Center for the Book. The introduction, "Is There a Community of the Book?" asserts that indeed there is such a community; it stretches from the people who create books, the authors, through book designers, publishers, printers, booksellers, distributors, librarians, scholars, educators, and students, to the general public and especially to the reader. The Center for the Book attempts to harness the energies and organizational skills of book professionals and the entire "community of the book" to bring authors and readers closer together.

Directory information about the Center for the Book's organizational partners, state centers, and many other national and international organizations concerned with books, reading, literacy, and libraries is now available on the Center's Web site. It includes links to other Web sites whenever possible. More than 250 organizations are included.

Promoting Reading, 1981–

The concept of "reading promotion," while not well known when the Center for the Book was established, nevertheless was an "implied" national mission for the new organization. In 1981, the Center developed "Books Make a Difference," the first in a series of reading promotion projects that also incorporated themes that other organizations were encouraged to use, for example "Read More About It!" and "A Nation of Readers."

In 1987, the Center launched its first national reading promotion campaign, "The Year of the Reader." From 1989 to 1992, First Lady Barbara Bush was honorary chair of three other national campaigns: "Year of the Young Reader," "Year of the Lifetime Reader," and "Explore New Worlds—READ!" First Lady Laura Bush became the honorary chair of "Telling America's Stories," the campaign for 2001–2004.

Also in 1987 the Center initiated its national reading promotion partners' program. Today more than 90 national organizations—private and governmental—concerned with promoting reading and literacy are Center for the Book partners. Each is encouraged to share program information and to use Center for the Book promotional themes and organizational networks to benefit their own projects.

State Centers, 1984–

State centers were not part of the original plan for the Center for the Book. While the idea was discussed as early as 1979 at a national Center for the Book program in California, the first formal proposal for an affiliated state center was submitted in 1984 by Broward County Library in Fort Lauderdale. Florida's argument that the national Center for the Book's mission needed grassroots advocates at the state level was persuasive, and the Florida Center for the Book was established the same year. Basic guidelines for state centers were created: each must be statewide in its book, reading, and literacy promotion activities and must raise its own funds; and each must use its affiliation with the Library of Congress judiciously as both incentive and leverage in obtaining statewide involvement and support. Most state centers have an institutional home: a state library, a large public library system, a university, or a state humanities council. State centers must apply to renew their affiliation every three years, outlining in their applications past accomplishments as well as future programming and funding plans.

In 1987, when James H. Billington became Librarian of Congress, there were 10 affiliated state centers. With the approval of the New Hampshire Center for the Book in December 2002, the total number of affiliates reached 50—in addition to the D.C. Center for the Book, which is hosted by the District of Columbia Public Library. Today the most popular state programs are state book festivals; state book awards; the creation of state literary maps and state author databases; state literary landmark projects, the "Letters About Literature" project, which promotes student essay contests about how books and authors helped shape or change a student's life; and "One Book" projects in which an entire community reads and discusses a single book.

Promoting Libraries, 1985–

In the mid-1980s, the American Library Association (ALA) and other library groups began a renewed public relations effort on behalf of libraries. Because the Center for the Book's state affiliate program was underway, the Center was a natural and willing partner. In 1985, the ALA chose "A Nation of Readers," a Center for the Book reading promotion theme, as its theme for National Library Week and for a traveling photography exhibition cosponsored with the Center. The next year the Center hosted its first annual Library of Congress reception to celebrate National Library Week and became a supporter of the ALA's Banned Books Week.

From 1987 to the present, the Center has hosted programs and sponsored publication on many library-related topics, including the role of the public library; libraries and scholarly communication; libraries and learning opportunities for children; libraries and Head Start programs; "USIA Libraries Abroad" (1993); the history of libraries in Washington, D.C.; libraries and literacy; and the history of national libraries. In 1996, the University of New Mexico Press published, in association with the Center, *Library: The Drama Within*, a book featuring photographs of 48 libraries around the world by Diane Asseo Griliches. In the spring of 2003, the Center hosted a joint ALA-Library of Congress traveling photography exhibit, "Beyond Words: Celebrating America's Libraries."

Promoting Literacy, 1989–

When the Center for the Book was established, "literacy" was not yet a popular concept or phrase. In 1980, the Center sponsored its first program that specifically mentioned the topic: "Literacy in Historical Perspective," a conference that emphasized how historical research about literacy could help contemporary policymakers. The Center's literacy promotion efforts began with its 1989 "Year of the Young Reader" campaign. Aided by a presidential proclamation and the efforts of honorary chair First Lady Barbara Bush, the campaign enlisted several dozen literacy and reading promotion organizations as Center for the Book partners.

In 1992, the Center launched a five-year Library-Head Start program to demonstrate how libraries that serve young children can work with Head Start teachers in children's literacy and language development projects. In 1996, it supported and published a major report that urged the strengthening of adult literacy programs in public libraries. From 1998 to 2004, the Center's major literacy effort was the administration of the Viburnum Foundation Family Literacy project, which provided for the planning and promotion of family literacy programs among rural public libraries and their community partners. More than 175 small public libraries participated in the project. In 2004, with additional funding from the Viburnum Foundation, the project was reorganized and named the Reading Powers the Mind family literacy project.

The National Book Festival, 2001–

Since the first Festival in 2001, the Center for the Book has played a key role in the National Book Festival, which is held in Washington, D.C. The Festival is organized and sponsored by the Library of Congress and hosted by First Lady Laura Bush.

The Center for the Book coordinates the Festival's author and reading promotion programs. At the 2003 Festival, there were seven pavilions for author and storytelling performances and two "reading promotion" pavilions: the "Let's Read America" pavilion at which 60 of the Center for the Book's organizational partners distributed information about their programs and the Pavilion of the States, highlighting information about library, literacy, and reading promotion projects in all 50 states, the District of Columbia, and four U.S. territories. Most of the state tables were staffed by people from the state: state librarians, center for the book coordinators, and state humanities council representatives.

Since 1977, approximately 150 individual authors have discussed and autographed their new books at the Library of Congress under the Center's auspices. In January 2000, Juan Williams signed his biography of Thurgood Marshall for a fan. Mr. Williams also was featured in the "History & Biography" pavilion in the 2003 and 2004 National Book Festivals.
LC/Center for the Book.

The National Book Festival is strengthening the Center for the Book by reinforcing its current programs and by expanding its reach to include new audiences and organizational partners. It is helping the Center come closer to fulfilling their ambitious vision of Librarian of Congress Daniel J. Boorstin, at the planning meeting held at the Library of Congress on October 20, 1977, one week after the Center was founded: "You may wonder why the Library of Congress, which, of all places on earth, is a center for the book should now become a place for the establishing of the Center for the Book. It is to organize, focus, and dramatize our nation's interest and attention on the book, to marshal the nation's support—spiritual, physical, and fiscal—for the book." (JYC)

Library of Congress Information Bulletin 62 (January 2003): 3–13.

CHILDREN'S LITERATURE CENTER

The Children's Literature Center was created in 1963 as the Children's Book Section in the Reference Department to provide reference and bibliographic services to government officials, children's book specialists, publishers, writers, illustrators, and the general public, but not to serve children directly. In the Library's reorganization of 1978, it was renamed the Children's Literature Center and became a part of the newly established Office of the Assistant Librarian for National Programs. In subsequent years, it joined Public Service Collections in the Library Services Directorate.

In his *Annual Report* for 1898, under the heading "the juvenile library," Librarian of Congress John Russell Young described his plan for a separate reading room for children, noting that the Library's rule of not admitting those under 16 years of age was a "hardship" that deprived children "at the outset of their lives of what may be a precious opportunity in the bending of the mind toward knowledge." He hoped to transfer "some 10,000 to 12,000 volumes suitable for children" to the new reading room's shelves. Young, however, died not long after the report was issued, and his successor, Herbert Putnam, saw no need to pursue Young's plan, deferring to newly announced plans to establish a District of Columbia Public Library that would provide a full range of library services to children.

In the years that followed, there were several unsuccessful attempts to create a children's department in the Library of Congress. In 1944, the American Association of University Women (AAUW) and the Association for Childhood Education International (ACEI), concerned about difficulty of access to the wealth of materials for children within the Library, proposed a children's book consultant. Librarian of Congress Luther Evans agreed that the institution "owed an obligation in this field as in any other to aid persons making serious and scholarly inquiries in a subject" and included funding for a consultant in children's literature in his 1947 and 1948 budget requests. Congress, however, denied funding.

In December 1951, Evans accepted funds from the AAUW and the ACEI for a study of the potential uses of the Library's children's book collections and Frances Clarke Sayers, coordinator of children's services at the New York Public Library, became the principal investigator. Sayers recommended the creation of a center to provide reference and bibliographical services that would enable a researcher to identify and locate children's material throughout the Library's collections. The AAUW and the ACEI obtained endorsement of Sayers' recommendation from the American Library Association's Division of Libraries for Children and Young People. However, Congress did not approve the establishment of such a unit until 1962. The Children's Book Section opened in March 1963.

Because the cost of bringing all children's books together was deemed prohibitive, the books remained dispersed throughout the general and special collections. Thus, the Children's Literature Section, a unit of the General Reference and Bibliography Division, was not established as a custodial unit but as a reference and referral unit.

The first head of the Children's Book Section was Virginia Haviland, a noted children's book authority who came to the Library with a one year's leave of absence from the Boston Public Library, where she had been Reader's Advisor for Children. She coined the Center's motto "Serving Those Who Serve Children: A National Reference Library of Children's Books" and immediately set to work assembling a specialized reference collection. With her newly hired children's book specialist Margaret N. Coughlan, she began compiling bibliographies and catalogs that would call attention to the Library's extensive children's collections.

Nationally known Boston Public Library children's literature specialist Virginia Haviland came to the Library of Congress in 1963 to become the first head of the new Children's Book Section. Under her leadership, the section was renamed the Children's Literature Center in 1978. LC Archives.

Particularly notable among these publications are *Children's Literature: A Guide to Reference Sources* (1966) and its two supplements: *Fables: From Incunabula to Modern Picture Books* (1966) and *Folklore of the North American Indian* (1969); *Yankee*

Doodle's Literary Sampler of Prose, Poetry & Pictures (1947); and *Samuel Langhorne Clemens: A Centennial for Tom Sawyer* (1977).

Most popular among the numerous subject bibliographies was *Books for Children*, an annual selection of the year's most noteworthy children's books.

In addition to her numerous publications, Haviland initiated annual National Children's Book Week programs that brought distinguished authors and illustrators to the Library.

Through her prolific writing and active involvement in library organizations, including the American Library Association, the International Board on Books for Young People, and the International Federation of Library Associations and Institutions, she established the Children's Literature Center nationally and internationally as a force in the children's book and library community.

Sybille A. Jagusch succeeded Haviland in 1983. Building on the foundations laid by her predecessor, the new chief's initiatives included the creation of the Children's Literature Center Fund. Gifts from individuals, corporations, and foundations now made possible numerous lectures, symposia, celebrations, exhibitions, and publications.

Programs included "Independent Spirits: Picture Book Makers for Children" (1990); "Holding on to Dreams: the Books of Childhood" (1991); "For the Heart of the Child: The Enduring Picture Book: A Symposium and Exhibition"(1996); "From Sea to Shining Sea—An American Sampler: Children's Books from the Library of Congress" (1998).

A number of programs were held in cooperation with other organizations including, in 1991, the prestigious annual May Hill Arbuthnot Honor Lecture, which was presented by noted British folklorist Iona Opie. Another notable program made possible by interagency cooperation was the Center's co-sponsorship with the John F. Kennedy Center for the Performing Arts, in 1992, of the play Dragonwings by Chinese-American writer/playwright Laurence Yep. Publications followed many of the programs, including *Stepping Away From Tradition: Children's Books of the Twenties and Thirties* (1988); *Stick to Reality and a Dream: Celebrating America's Young Readers*, by Katherine Paterson (1990); *Window on Japan: Japanese Children's Literature and Television Today* (1990); *Antonio Frasconi at the Library of Congress* (1993), and *Leo Lionni at the Library of Congress* (1993).

Stepping Away From Tradition: Children's Books of the Twenties and Thirties *(Washington, D.C.: Library of Congress, 1988), papers from a symposium at the Library on November 15, 1984 sponsored by the Children's Literature Center and the Center for the Book.* LC/Publishing Office.

A summary of the Center's activities was created in the 1998 film *Serving Those Who Serve Children: The Children's Literature Center in the Library of Congress*. (SJ, MC)

CLASSIFICATION OF COLLECTIONS

The first books purchased for the Library of Congress arrived in 1801, and in its 12-page catalog (1802), the entries are arranged by size and format: folios, quartos, octavos, duodecimos, and maps and charts. In 1808, Librarian Patrick Magruder issued another book catalog, also arranged by size but with special types of material, such as statutes and other federal documents, listed separately. The first subject arrangement appeared in the 1812 book catalog. The 18 subject classes came from the Library Company of Philadelphia, which had adapted a scheme developed from the English philosopher and statesman Francis Bacon's division of knowledge into memory, reason, and imagination. To these the Library of Congress added two format divisions: gazettes, and maps and charts. Within each subject class, however, arrangement was still by size.

When the British set fire to the Capitol Building in 1814, destroying the Library, Congress replaced the books by purchasing the private library of Thomas Jefferson. Jefferson had his own classification of 44 "chapters," also based on Baconian principles. He devoted 15 chapters to history (ancient, modern, and natural); 14 to philosophy, including jurisprudence, ethics, government, mathematics, physics and

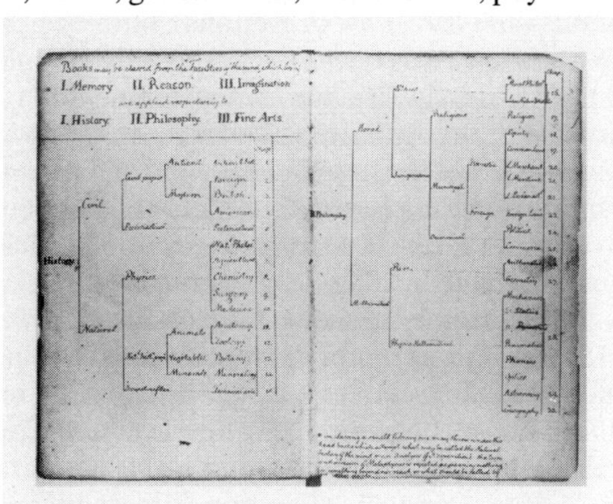

When Jefferson's personal library arrived at the Library in 1815, it came with Jefferson's personal classification system. His scheme, in turn, was derived from Francis Bacon's division of knowledge into three categories: Memory (History); Reason (Philosophy); and Imagination (Fine Arts). LC/Prints and Photographs Division. LC-USP6-628.

geography; and another 14 to Fine Arts (architecture, art, gardening, music, poetry, oratory, and criticism). The last chapter was for general or multidisciplinary works. But members of the Congressional Joint Committee on the Library disliked classification schemes, and they wanted to dispense with Jefferson's arrangement altogether. Librarian Watterston did not agree, but he also modified Jefferson's arrangement. While not especially pleased with Watterston's changes, Jefferson graciously commented that the new arrangement might be easier for readers to use.

Librarians John Silva Meehan and Ainsworth Rand Spofford further modified Jefferson's scheme. Of the two, Spofford made the most extensive changes, but the paucity of space in the Library's Capitol Building quarters defeated attempts to keep the books in strict order. As Spofford revised it to accommodate the rapidly growing collection, the classification still included 44 classes, but it had little resemblance to the original.

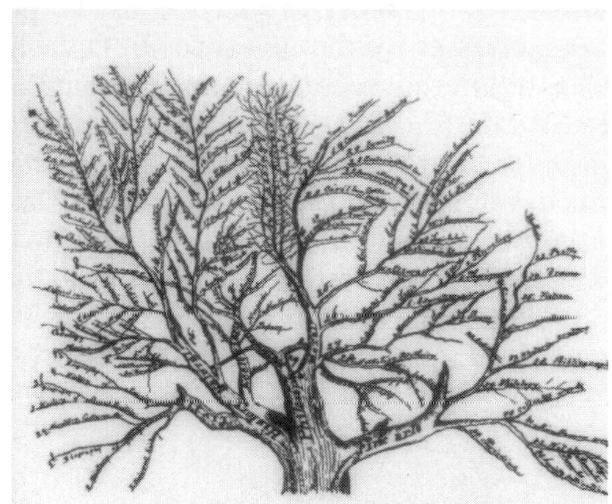

This "tree of classification," anonymously penned in the 1890s, attaches fields of knowledge and their subdivisions to branches and twigs, illustrating the gradual expansion and modification of the Library's Jefferson-based classification system. LC/Prints and Photographs Division. LC-USZ62-6015.

In 1897, Librarian John Russell Young hired James Christian Meinich Hanson, an expert on cataloging and classification, to head the new Catalog Department that Young was establishing. Hanson decided that the old classification system was inadequate, and he persuaded Young to hire an expert classifier, Charles Martel, to build a modern classification scheme. They considered adopting the Dewey Decimal Classification, Charles Ammi Cutter's Expansive Classification, and others, but ultimately decided to devise their own system.

Developed over several years, the outline of the new scheme came partly from Cutter. Martel used Cutter's Book Arts class to develop Class Z: Bibliography and Library Science, which he had completed by the time Herbert Putnam became Librarian in April 1899. Putnam wanted to reconsider the classification issue because he hoped to employ an existing system that would transfer readily to other libraries, and he thought the Dewey system would be adaptable for that purpose. Melvil Dewey, however, refused to allow the Library to make any changes in Decimal Classification, which destroyed any hope of adopting it. Thus Putnam agreed that Martel should proceed. By 1903, the outline of the classification was complete, consisting of 21 classes and including three mnemonic classes: Music (M), Geography (G), and Technology (T).

The Library's needs dictated classification priorities. Class Z had to be developed first because those books had to be organized first: the bibliographical material provided essential assistance in working on other classes. Similarly, Americana required early attention because of its importance in the Library's collections, and Martel therefore began work on classes E and F (American History) next. Thereafter he moved to D, World History, in which he used double letters for subclasses for the first time. In D, each country has a different second letter; for example, DA for Great Britain.

Under Martel's supervision, Library subject specialists developed the detailed schedules. Class M, Music, appeared in 1904 and Class Q, Science, in 1905, but no more schedules were published until 1910

Charles Martel was the chief architect of the modern Library of Congress classification system. In the 1890s, he worked at the Newberry Library in Chicago with J. C. M. Hanson who, soon after he became chief of the Library's Catalog Division, brought his friend and former colleague to the Library of Congress. Given the title of Chief Classifier in 1903, in 1912 he was named chief of the Catalog Division. He became a consultant in 1929, but did not formally retire until 1945.
LC Archives.

when Philosophy (B-BJ), Fine Arts (N), Geography (G), Political Science (J), the Social Sciences (H), Medicine (R), Technology (T), and Naval Science (V) all appeared. General Works (A), Agriculture (S), and Education (L) followed in 1911; Americana (E-F) in 1913; Auxiliary Sciences of History (C), and General Literature and British and American Literature (PN, PR, PS) in 1915; and Universal and Old World History (D) in 1916. After the schedules were printed, at intervals the Library has issued lists of additions and changes and, eventually, new editions.

After a long period when no schedules were issued, Religion (BL-BX) appeared in 1927; Classical Languages and Literature (P-PA) in 1928; the Modern European Languages and Literatures (PB-PH) in 1933, and the languages and literatures of Africa, Asia, Oceania, and America (PJ-PM) in 1935. In 1936 and 1937, Romance Languages and Literatures (PQ) completed the basic classification. Works of fiction were originally classed in PZ, but in response to requests from research libraries that wished to classify it with the appropriate literature classes, in 1968 the Library began providing those class numbers and by 1980 had decided to apply literature class numbers to all fiction in English. A project begun in the early 1940s to construct Class K, Law, encountered many delays, but with the assistance of grants from the Council on Library Resources, Inc., KF, American Law, finally appeared in 1969, with the other subclasses following. From time to time classifiers have thoroughly revised portions of the classification to reflect advances in knowledge, and they have further developed or established some subclasses, such as JZ (International Relations) and KZ (Law of Nations), both completed in 1997. Class K was declared "essentially complete" in 2002 after nearly 30 years of development in consultation with the American Association of Law Libraries and libraries around the world. The entire Library of Congress classification system was converted, over a 10-year period, to an online tool, which became available in 2003.

The Library of Congress classification was developed with the Library's future needs in mind. Initially it did not seem especially suited to the needs of other libraries. Nevertheless, librarians were very interested in the classification, and by 1906 several federal libraries and one state library were planning to adopt it. In 1920, the five largest U.S. academic libraries (Chicago, Columbia, Cornell, Harvard, and Yale) were using the classification for all or part of their collections, and other institutions slowly followed. By the 1970s, nine-tenths of the largest U.S. libraries and over half of all U.S. academic libraries employed the Library of Congress classification system for all or part of their collections. Now available on compact disk and on the World Wide Web, the classification scheme is readily accessible by computer in libraries large and small. On the Internet, when users search the online catalog, they may browse parts of the classification simply by typing in the class numbers that cover the relevant subject. (JA)

Immroth, John Philip. *A Guide to the Library of Congress Classification*. Littleton, Colo.: Libraries Unlimited, 1968.

Martel, Charles. "The Library of Congress Classification," in William Warner Bishop and Andrew Keogh, eds., *Essays Offered to Herbert Putnam by His Colleagues and Friends on His Thirtieth Anniversary as Librarian of Congress: 5 April 1929*. New Haven: Yale University Press, 1929.

Rosenberg, Jane Aikin. *The Nation's Great Library: Herbert Putnam and the Library of Congress, 1899–1939*. Urbana, Ill.: University of Illinois Press, 1993.

COLLECTIONS ACCESS, LOAN AND MANAGEMENT DIVISION

The Collections Access, Loan and Management Division, created in Library Services in 2002 as part of the merger of the Collections Management Division and the Loan Division, is responsible for providing access to the Library's general collections and other collections as assigned, both for on-site and off-site use, and for maintaining those collections. Steven J. Herman, then chief of the Collections Management Division, was named the first chief of the division. The Library's general collections comprise approximately 12 million book and bound serial volumes, shelved on more than 530 miles of shelves. Each working day, members of the division respond to more than 2,500 requests for items from the collections.

The division serves the on-site public directly by delivering items at book service desks in the Main Reading Room, the Local History & Genealogy Reading Room and the Science and Business Reading Room, and at special search desks in the Main Reading Room and the Science and Business Reading Room. In addition, it provides access to the collections, both the content and the artifact itself, to users off-site, through such programs as interlibrary loan, digital document delivery, and loan to special borrower categories, including members of Congress and their staff, embassies, the federal judiciary and other authorized groups. Simultaneously, the division's staff of approximately 240 employees is involved in extensive behind-the-scenes activities in support of collections management, from support of the Library's inventory management program (effective inventory control and tracking) to collections maintenance work, running the gamut from erecting shelving and cleaning collections to shelfreading and shifting collections from crowded areas.

History

The organizational lineage of the Collections Management Division stretches back to 1897, when the Library's collections and services were transferred from the Capitol Building to the new Library of Congress Building. The Main Reading Room Division was established, and one of its principal responsibilities was the service and care of the collections. From 1897 to 1939, the Main Reading Room served all readers who came to the Library for general research and reference assistance; special service for members of Congress was provided in the Congressional Reading Room, and authors and scholars were assisted at study tables and in study rooms. In 1939, with its name already changed to the Reading Rooms Division, the division expanded its public services to include the new Annex Building.

In the 1944 reorganization of Librarian of Congress Archibald MacLeish, the Reading Rooms Division became the Stack and Reader Division and began close cooperation with two new divisions—the Loan Division and the General Reference and Bibliography Division. The reorganization gave the Stack and Reader Division responsibility for the service and custodial care of the general collections, materials shelved in the Hispanic Foundation, the proceedings and transactions of learned societies and academies, the literature of geography, and aeronautical publications. The division began administering a Special Facilities for Research program to assign study tables, study rooms, reserve shelves, and stack passes to qualified researchers.

The Collections Management Division was established in the Library Services Directorate in 1978. It was created to provide access to the Library's general collections and to maintain those collections. Particular problems at the time were the relatively high (up to 30 percent) not-on-shelf rate in response to individual book requests, and the diffusion of responsibility for collection service and maintenance. The new division combined all functions necessary to serve and maintain the general collections into one administrative unit. It also initiated an inventory/improvement program to gain greater physical control over the collections, and a greatly expanded special search program to help individual readers find materials not readily retrievable. Steven J. Herman, then chief of the Stack and Reader Division, was named the first chief of the Collections Management Division.

As stated above, the MacLeish reorganization of 1944 gave birth to the Loan Division. Previously, circulation activities were decentralized. In establishing the Loan Division, MacLeish stated that: "The Loan Division, as its name implies, administers all outside loans...and, as a result of this centralization of responsibility, is enabled to exercise uniform controls, and establish uniform procedures governing the Library's lending operations. It passes upon applications for the borrowing privilege..., maintains records of loans, prescribes conditions of use, recalls overdue materials, administers the Library Station in the Capitol..." Elsie Rackstraw was appointed as the first permanent chief of the new division on July 10, 1944. Throughout its nearly 60-year history, it continued the activities as envisioned by Librarian MacLeish. Changes along the way included an expansion of the

the Treasury Henry Morgenthau to request space at the Bullion Depository at Fort Knox, Kentucky. Morgenthau immediately agreed, and on December 23, just after the Japanese attacked Pearl Harbor, the Library staff locked the Constitution, the Declaration of Independence, the Gutenberg Bible, the Stradivarius violins, and a copy of the Magna Carta belonging to the British, in bronze containers. When the Attorney General formally issued a ruling holding the Librarian responsible for the safety of these items, the containers were sealed, packed in metal-bound boxes, and loaded on an armed, escorted truck for the drive to Union Station.

The Baltimore and Ohio Railroad's Pullman sleeper "Eastlake" headed west at 6:30 p.m. the day after Christmas, with the boxes in Car A-1, compartment B. In adjoining compartments sat armed Secret Service agents and the escort-in-charge, Verner W. Clapp, the new Chief Assistant Librarian of Congress. At 10:30 the next morning, a delegation of more agents and troops met the train with an Army truck to convey the boxes to the Bullion Depository at Fort Knox.

Clapp occasionally returned to inspect the physical condition of all items deposited, and the Declaration was removed once, briefly, for the dedication of the Jefferson Memorial and the Jefferson bicentennial celebration in April 1943. On that occasion, the Library published a pamphlet entitled *The Declaration of Independence: The Evolution of a Text* (1943) by Julian Boyd, the newly appointed editor of Jefferson's papers. The pamphlet also included facsimile reproductions of the principal documents connected with the Declaration, and Librarian MacLeish stated that the publication "may prove to be one of the most important single events in the history of the Library."

The Declaration of Independence and the Constitution returned to the Library in the fall of 1944, several months after the Normandy invasion. On October 1, the exhibit reopened, an occasion that featured a military guard of honor and the rendition of the national anthem by the Marine Band.

Pursuing the Library's charge to preserve the Declaration, in May 1949 Librarian Luther Evans asked the National Bureau of Standards for assistance with preservation. After making a study of the causes of deterioration in parchment and ink, the Bureau requested the Libbey-Owens-Ford Glass Company to develop a method for preserving the documents. On the 175th anniversary of the Constitution, September 17, 1951, the documents were sealed in a bronze and glass container filled with helium, which the Bureau recommended as an inert gas that would not readily combine with other elements. To prevent cracking, relative humidity was kept between 24 percent and 35

This 1944 cartoon by Karl Kae Knecht, which appeared in The Evansville Indiana Courier, *was dedicated to Librarian of Congress Archibald MacLeish. It celebrates the return of the Declaration of Independence and the Constitution to public display at the Library in 1944 after the documents had been removed for safekeeping during World War II.* LC/Prints and Photographs Division. LC-USZ62-132001.

percent, and filters were added to screen out harmful ultraviolet light rays.

Meanwhile, in December 1950 Evans considered sending the documents to Fort Knox or somewhere else for protection for the duration of the Korean War, but he feared it would alarm the public. Nothing came of a substitute plan to exhibit them in state capitals. That same year, however, Congress passed the Federal Records Act, which specified that all federal agency records not in current use must be transferred to the National Archives. This act seemed to supersede the legislation placing the Declaration and Constitution at the Library of Congress, and Archivist Wayne C. Grover and Librarian Evans agreed to move them to the Archives building, which would provide a safer, temperature-controlled environment. Evans then consulted with congressional leaders and the president and turned the matter over to the Congressional Joint Committee on the Library, which on April 30, 1952 approved the transfer. "It is naturally an emotional wrench to surrender the custody of the principal documents of American liberty," wrote Evans. "Logic and law require it, however."

An armored Marine Corps personnel carrier equipped with mattresses transported the encased and crated documents on December 13, 1952, the 161st anniversary of the ratification of the Bill of Rights. Accompanied by tanks, a motorcycle escort, a color guard, two military bands, and four servicemen with submachine guns, the carrier slowly traversed Constitution and Pennsylvania Avenues to the Archives building.

While the Declaration of Independence and the Constitution are no longer at the Library of Congress, the Library's Manuscript Division still houses the papers of the Continental Congress and other early state papers, as well as the papers of many presidents. Jefferson's handwritten rough draft of the Declaration of Independence, received from the State Department with Jefferson's papers in 1903, is one of the Library's greatest treasures. A digital image of that document may be viewed on the Library's World Wide Web site. A new fragment of the draft discovered by Julian Boyd and exhibited for the first time on July 4, 1995, is included in the online exhibit. (JA)

The Constitution of the United States: An Account of Its Travels Since September 17, 1787, compiled by David C. Mearns and Verner W. Clapp. Washington, D.C.: The Library of Congress, 1942.

Gustafson, Milton O. "The Empty Shrine: The Transfer of the Declaration of Independence and the Constitution to the National Archives," *American Archivist* 39 (July 1976): 271–285.

Mearns, David C. "The Declaration of Independence: the Story of a Parchment," in the *Annual Report of the Librarian of Congress for the fiscal year ended June 30, 1949*, pp. 36–55.

DEWEY DECIMAL CLASSIFICATION

Melvil Dewey devised his Decimal Classification (DC) while he was a student at Amherst College, publishing the first edition in 1876. It became popular as a scheme for arranging public library collections, which at that time were being established rapidly and in great numbers. The Library of Congress almost adopted the Decimal Classification around the turn of the century. When Herbert Putnam became Librarian, he thought that because of its national role the Library should adopt an existing classification scheme, and he investigated the available systems. Dewey was enthusiastic about having the Library adopt his classification, but when it became evident that Putnam wanted the right to make changes in it he refused, citing the inconvenience to libraries already using the system. Putnam therefore approved developing a scheme uniquely suited to the Library of Congress.

Melvil Dewey devised his Decimal Classification System while he was a student at Amherst College, publishing the first edition in 1876. He later became director of the New York State Library and a leading figure in the American library movement. His system became popular with public libraries, but the Library of Congress created its own classification system in the early years of the twentieth century.
LC/Prints and Photographs Division. LC-USZ62-40188.

The issue came up again when Putnam established the Library's card service. Librarians were enthusiastic about the service, but many wanted Dewey numbers included on the cards. For many years that was not possible because the catalogers would have to classify each book both in the Library of Congress Classification and in the Decimal Classification, and Congress was unlikely to approve undertaking work not needed for the Library's own collections. By the 1920s, however, over 90 percent of all U.S. libraries used the Decimal Classification, and Dewey sought the support of the American Library Association (ALA) for having Dewey numbers added to Library of Congress catalog cards.

The ALA proposed to Putnam that the Association pay catalogers to work at the Library to assign the Dewey numbers. Putnam agreed, provided funding was available, and in April 1929 the ALA requested a three-year contribution from every library that subscribed to the Library of Congress's card service. With pledges of over $5,000 plus $500 from the ALA and a contribution of personnel time from the Library, the ALA Office for DC Numbers on L. C. Cards opened on April 1, 1930 with David J. Haykin in charge. As part of the arrangement, the DC Editorial Office, which was responsible for updating and printing the DC, had already moved into the Library in 1927. The Decimal Classification work became the first of many joint ALA-Library of Congress efforts to make the cataloging and card services more useful to other libraries.

Several years later, in the depths of economic depression, libraries' payments for the DC work fell short of the amount required, and Haykin and Charles Hastings, chief of the Card Division, convinced Putnam that the Library should take over the work. Putnam testified to the need at the Library's 1933 congressional appropriations hearings; Congress ultimately approved three new positions, and on July 1, 1934 the ALA Office became a section in the Card Division. One year later, Putnam united it with another ALA-sponsored cataloging project in a new Cooperative Cataloging and Classification Service headed by Haykin. Dewey catalogers classified between 20,000 and 40,000 books annually over the ensuing decades, and receipts from DC card sales were returned to the U.S. Treasury, making the office self-supporting.

When Archibald MacLeish reorganized the Library in 1940, the DC work became part of the Subject Cataloging Division of the Processing Department. The staff continued to work with the DC Editorial Office to revise the classification as needed, but the policy of classifying all books was altered to one of selectively classifying books likely to be purchased by "popular libraries." In 1953, at the request of the publisher, Forest Press, and the ALA, the Library agreed to undertake the editorial work for the 16th edition on a contract basis and established a Dewey Decimal Classification Editorial Office in the Processing Department. Work proceeded on the basis that policy would be set by the joint ALA-Forest Press Decimal Classification Editorial Policy Committee, with the advice of the ALA's Special Advisory Committee on the Decimal Classification. Forest Press contributed funds annually thereafter to support the editorial work. With the assumption of responsibility for the DC editorial work, the Library was maintaining the two classification schemes most used by libraries in the United States—the DC and the Library of Congress Classification. A Spanish edition of the DC appeared in 1956, produced by the Columbus Memorial Library of the Pan American Union with assistance from Library staff, and the classification was translated into many other languages in succeeding years. Benjamin Custer succeeded Haykin as Decimal Classification editor in September 1958, the 16th English edition of the *Dewey Decimal Classification* was published in October, and the Library's Decimal Classification section merged with the DC Editorial Office on November 24 to form the Decimal Classification Office. Produced in consultation with over 300 specialists, the 16th edition expanded many topics that had not been developed before, and all purchasers received a free update publication titled *Decimal Classification Additions, Notes and Decisions*. An eighth abridged edition intended for school libraries and smaller public and college libraries was published in June 1959.

Beginning in 1960, the English-language focus of the DC classification work broadened to include a substantial number of foreign language works and juvenile publications in English. Simultaneously, the R. R. Bowker Company began printing DC numbers in *Publishers Weekly*, and its monthly *American Book Publishing Record* arranged titles by Decimal class number. A guide to the use of the classification, which expanded on the basic rules provided in the introduction and also explained the practices of the Decimal Classification Office, appeared in 1962. As relations between the DC and its foreign counterpart, the Universal Decimal Classification (UDC) as well as assistance for foreign librarians using the DC became more important, the DC editor began participating in the work of the Subcommittee on UDC of the U. S. National Committee for the International Federation for Documentation. With the assistance of Forest Press and the ALA, in the early 1960s the Office undertook a field survey of the use of the UDC in selected countries with the objective of enhancing its usefulness abroad.

By 1965, when the 17th edition appeared, over 80 percent of the cards sold by the Library of Congress included DC numbers. At the same time, the number of books classified annually in DC increased from 40,000 to 50,000, and jumped to over 70,000 by the late 1960s. The Office assigned numbers to nearly all U.S. nonfiction titles cataloged by the Library of Congress, all current nonfiction published abroad and cataloged by the Library, and all current titles, other than belles-lettres, in French, German, Italian, Spanish, and Portuguese received through the Library's National Program for Acquisitions and Cataloging.

During the 1968 reorganization of the Processing Department, the Decimal Classification Office became the Decimal Classification Division, and with the inception of the MARC format for online cataloging, DC numbers were provided for all MARC records, with a further expansion of coverage to adult fiction in English as a service to academic libraries, many of which classified fiction. The additional work caused the staff to abandon foreign language classifying for a short period between 1969 and 1972, but by the mid-1970s nearly all English-language titles cataloged by the Library and a selection of those in other western languages were being covered. The *British National Bibliography* (BNB) began using Dewey numbers by the late 1960s, adopting the 18th edition when it appeared in January 1972. Consistency of classification and editorial policy among the national bibliographic agencies, always a concern, received close attention as the BNB and Forest Press provided grants during the early 1970s for personnel exchanges with the BNB and the *Australian National Bibliography* as well as with *Canadiana*, the Canadian national bibliography.

With an extension of the work to audiovisual materials, the Dewey staff classified more than 100,000 volumes by the mid-1970s. John Comaroni became head of the division in 1980, when the 19th edition and 11th abridged edition appeared and output advanced to more than 120,000 titles. *A Manual on the Use of the Dewey Decimal Classification* appeared in 1982, and the division staff designed workshops to instruct librarians on applying the DC as well as working with teams engaged in translating the classification into Italian and Arabic and expanding language coverage to Chinese and Russian.

Forest Press became a division of the Online Computer Library Center, Inc. in 1988, and the Electronic Dewey, a version of the classification for online use, became available from the Press in January 1993. Further electronic products include a CD-ROM version called *Dewey for Windows* (first issued in 1996), which features the 21st edition of the classification, and WebDewey and Abridged WebDewey, made available in 2002. Continuous revisions and updates to the classification appear on the Dewey home page on the Internet, on *Dewey for Windows*, and new print versions are issued approximately every seven years.

The division celebrated the 125th anniversary of the Decimal Classification in 2001, when work was underway on the 22nd full and 14th abridged editions, and the classification was being used in more than 130 countries and published in more than 30 languages. In fiscal 2003, the division classified nearly 97,000 books for Dewey users and the 22nd edition was loaded into the WebDewey database. Machine-readable catalog records including Dewey classification numbers are distributed through the Cataloging Distribution Service's MARC distribution service.

For most library users in the United States, the Decimal System has provided the first encounter with a library classification. The simplicity of the classification, with just 10 major classes, or areas of knowledge, has always made it attractive to small and medium-sized school, public, academic, and special libraries. While university and research libraries have generally adopted the Library of Congress Classification as better suited to their very large holdings, the Decimal Classification has maintained its popularity for more than a century. It is the most widely used classification worldwide, and the Library's Decimal Classification program continues to provide an important outreach service to national and international constituencies. (JA)

Rosenberg, Jane Aikin. *The Nation's Great Library: Herbert Putnam and the Library of Congress, 1899–1939.* Urbana, Ill.: University of Illinois Press, 1993.

EMPLOYEES AND EMPLOYMENT

The Library of Congress was located in the U.S. Capitol from 1801, when the first shipment of books arrived from England, until 1897, when the Library moved into the Thomas Jefferson Building. Until 1828, the staff consisted of only one person: the Librarian of Congress—and the incumbent had also served as the clerk of the House of Representatives from 1802 until 1815, when the job of Librarian became full-time. In 1828, Congress provided for an assistant librarian, and a third staff member, a messenger, was added in 1831. Two years later, Congress authorized a second assistant librarian, but that position was not made permanent until 1841. A laborer, whose major duty was to make fires, was added in 1844. A third assistant librarian was employed in 1855 and a second laborer in 1861—bringing the size of the Library's staff on the eve of the Civil War to seven.

Edward B. Stelle, the first Assistant Librarian. Stelle held the position twice, the first time from its creation on May 24, 1828 until May 1829, and secondly from 1830 until 1861. In 1828, he became the second Library employee; when he left in 1861, the Library had a staff of seven.
LC/Prints and Photographs Division. LC-USZ62-6008.

The president of the United States has appointed the Librarian of Congress since the Library's organizing act of 1802, and during the nineteenth century it was a political appointment. Friends and relatives of congressmen and senators often became employees; in fact, few could obtain positions without congressional support. In 1861, when President Abraham Lincoln named John G. Stephenson, a physician and political supporter from Indiana as Librarian of Congress, Stephenson replaced most of the staff with friends of the new administration. Ainsworth Rand Spofford, Librarian of Congress 1864–1897, was the first Librarian to begin selecting well-qualified staff members whenever possible. Nevertheless, between 1865 and 1897, only five staff members had previous library experience. The Library's first female employee, technically speaking, was Jane Wadden Turner, who managed the Smithsonian Institution's exchange service between 1857 and 1886, a service administered by the Library of Congress beginning in 1867. In 1893, Spofford hired Bessie A. Dwyer, the first woman employed directly by the Library of Congress. Spofford also hired the Library's first African American to be employed at a beginning professional level, Daniel A. P. Murray, who served as an assistant librarian from 1871 until he retired in 1922. Congress gradually

Daniel A.P. Murray, hired as an assistant librarian by Librarian of Congress Ainsworth Rand Spofford in 1871, was the Library's first African American to be hired at a beginning professional level. His most significant achievement was as a bibliographer of African American literature. In 1979, Library employees established the Daniel A.P. Murray Afro-American Culture Association to further awareness and appreciation of African American culture.
LC Archives.

increased the Library's staff, particularly after Spofford successfully centralized all U.S. copyright registration and deposit activities at the Library in 1870. By 1896, there were 42 staff members crammed into the Library's rooms in the Capitol, 18 of them assigned to copyright work and 24 to general library duties.

The Library's appropriations act for 1898, approved by Congress on February 19, 1897, and effective July 1, 1897, reorganized the institution with an eye to its future growth and organization. Spofford

those paid in college and university libraries. MacLeish commented that the staff needed "broader technical sophistication" since less than one-fourth of the professional staff had even the bachelor's degree in library science. But he also asked the Civil Service Commission to bring the classification of positions in the Library in line with federal practice and to correct inequities. The commission was not able to complete its work for several years, during which staff turnover multiplied, a problem further exacerbated by the passage of the Selective Service law. As in other federal offices, beginning April 18, 1942, all wartime appointments were limited to the duration of the war plus six months, so that returning ex-servicemen could retain their jobs. And all federal employees were working longer hours: between February 2 and December 22, 1942, the work week was extended to 44 hours without increased compensation and beginning February 11, 1943, a 48-hour week was imposed.

Ultimately, the Civil Service Commission's work resulted in 600 grade and salary increases. MacLeish established a Personnel Office and issued General Order #1014, which recognized employees' right to organize and provided new procedures for recruitment and for resolving grievances. He also began issuing a *Staff Information Bulletin* (1942) and organized an in-service training committee, and at the suggestion of union representatives, created a Staff Advisory Committee (1942) to make suggestions for improving operations. Eager for all staff to participate in problem-solving, in 1943–1944 the Librarian started a monthly Professional Forum, broadened in 1950 to the Staff Forum. Attendance was voluntary, but the forum had to be held in two sessions because the entire staff could not fit into the Coolidge Auditorium.

In 1942, the staff had formed the Library of Congress Recreation Association; by 1949, its name had expanded to the Library of Congress Welfare and Recreation Association. Among its activities were a baseball team, a bowling league, a writers' group, a drama club, a choral society, and an art cinema league. Some units, such as the Filing Unit and the Orientalia Division, were holding monthly staff luncheons in the 1940s, and a Political Science Group luncheon featured invited speakers. Foreign language "tables" or discussion groups seem to have first appeared in April 1951, when the association sent out a call for interested staff members to establish them; they have come and gone through the years and reappeared during the 1990s.

Luther Evans retained MacLeish's Staff Advisory Committee and the Professional Forum but also organized Staff Discussion Groups of 25 or fewer members each, which met every three months. During the first half of each meeting, the groups discussed matters the members suggested; in the second half, topics were selected by the Staff Advisory Committee. Attendance was compulsory, and Evans promised to listen to and answer all suggestions and recommendations. The Librarian also ordered department directors to hold meetings with their chiefs and supervisory personnel and also to have general staff meetings in between Staff Discussion Group meetings.

In the wake of highly publicized fears that the federal government employed Communists, President Truman established a loyalty program for executive branch employees (Executive Order 9835, March 19, 1947). Thus in May 1947, Librarian Evans created a three-member Library of Congress Loyalty Review Board. The Board was charged to conduct investigations of the loyalty of employees and to determine what action might be taken in cases in which disloyalty was found. By 1951, the Board had adjudicated 64 cases, of which three were returned to the Library for further consideration after review by the Loyalty Review Board. In 1953, the name of the program was changed to the Security Program, but thereafter, the hunt for disloyal government employees quietly died away.

In 1949, the Library started a "Special Recruitment Program" to attract outstanding library school graduates to regular positions at the Library, offering a four-month orientation program and then a full-time job to the 15 members of the first class. In 1970, the Library altered what was now called the "Intern Program" to include qualified staff members as well as candidates nominated from accredited library schools in the United States. In 1988, the program was lengthened to nine months to allow more time for work experiences throughout the Library. Due to budget constraints, the program was discontinued after the 1993–1994 class.

Discrimination and Equal Employment Opportunity

In January 1962, the Washington *Afro-American* raised allegations of racial discrimination in the Library of Congress. Librarian L. Quincy Mumford immediately affirmed the Library's policy of non-discrimination in employment, investigated the allegations, and named several part-time Fair Employment Practices Officers to hear complaints and try to resolve them. A study conducted in 1962 revealed that 24.9 percent of the staff were African Americans and that they constituted 36.6 percent of the employees in grades 1–4; 12.9 percent of the employees in grades 5–11; and .9 percent of those in grades 12–18. A second study (1971), showed that African Americans accounted for 38 percent of all Library employees, but they were 73.9 percent of those in grades 1–4; 48.3 percent in grades 5–8, 16.1 percent in grades 9–11; 5.5 percent of those in grades 12–13; 1.6 percent of those in grades 14–15; and 3.9 percent in grades 16–18. That same year, Howard R. L. Cook, a Congressional Research Service research assistant, and other black employees organized the Black Employees of the Library of Congress (BELC) to challenge the Library's hiring, promotion, and personnel practices. The Library did not officially recognize BELC until two years later, when it was said to include 96 percent of all black employees and one-fifth of the white employees.

From June 23–26, 1971, 20 to 30 deck attendants engaged in a four-day work stoppage and presented a memorandum of grievances on position classification, promotion policy, and working conditions. Those who refused to return to work were suspended, and 11 employees who did not return to work on Monday, June 28 as ordered were dismissed. Simultaneously, at the annual conference of the American Library Association in Dallas, the ALA Council was asked to make an inquiry into allegations by an ALA member that the Library "discriminates on racial grounds in recruitment, training, and promotion practices." But when the ALA proposed sending a fact-finding team, the Joint Committee on the Library forbade the Library to cooperate with the ALA because the inquiry was an infringement on congressional oversight responsibilities. The ALA team proceeded, and reported early in 1972 "a pattern of actions for which it could conceive no other motivation than racial discrimination."

Meanwhile, Mumford replaced the Library's Fair Employment Practices Program with a new Equal Opportunity Program (1971) and formed a Human Relations Council (1972) and ad hoc Human Relations Committees in each of the departments to aid communication between staff and management. For fiscal 1972, the Library developed a comprehensive affirmative action program under the Equal Employment Opportunity Act of 1972, which mandated annual plans for improvement. A report on the new programs was favorably received at the June 1972 ALA meeting, where Library officials promised to take further steps to achieve equal opportunity and advancement for all employees.

Two months later, Howard Cook was discharged and on November 25, 1975, he and another employee, David Andrews, filed a complaint with the Library's Equal Employment Opportunity Office on behalf of all black employees, female employees, and Spanish-speaking employees. Barbara Ringer, a former assistant register of copyrights, also filed a suit alleging that the Library's employment process discriminated on the grounds of both sex and race. On February 28, 1973, the District Court ruled for Ringer, who subsequently served as Register of Copyrights from 1973 to 1980. After another visit by ALA representatives in June 1973, a report detailing the Library's efforts to combat discrimination was accepted. In 1981, the EEO office concluded that the complainants had not proved discrimination, but in February 1982, Cook, Andrews, and BELC sued the Library in the U.S. District Court, alleging violations of Title VII of the 1964 Civil Rights Act and requesting that their case be considered a class action on behalf of African American employees. Others who joined the case were Joyce Thorpe, James Bradford, Carolyn Torsell, Tommy Shaw, and Oscar Scott. Class action was eventually granted by the U.S. Court of Appeals (1988), as applying to all African Americans qualified for professional and administrative positions since 1975. On August 14, 1992, the court ruled that the competitive selection process as applied by the Library discriminated against black employees and required changes in the Library's personnel system as well as compensation. Attorneys for both sides were charged with working out a settlement, a long process that culminated in approval on September 22, 1995. Judge Norma Holloway Johnson of the U.S. District Court reserved jurisdiction for a four-year period to ensure compliance and implementation, and after several appeals were dismissed, in 1997 the Library began the process of providing back-pay awards, promotions, and reassignments. On September 8, 2003, Judge Gladys Kessler of the U.S. District Court denied an appeal to modify the settlement approved in 1995.

A Quarter Century of Modernization

By the mid-1970s, the mechanisms for enhancing staff opportunities were falling into place. For example, the 1974 Affirmative Action Plan established a Librarian's Affirmative Action Advisory Committee that included representatives of all employee organizations. It also included provisions for improving the Upward Mobility Plan to include training opportunities and evaluation of employment tests and qualification requirements by an outside consulting firm. Tuition support, career counseling, and other training were provided for employees below the GS-7 level in the Training, Appraisal, and Promotion Program (TAP), designed to allow employees an opportunity to move into higher-graded positions for which they showed aptitude but lacked the necessary qualifications. Several years later, a flextime program that provided more latitude in work schedules was the subject of an experiment (1976) and eventual adoption (1977).

Library of Congress Regulation 2026 established a labor-management program on October 24, 1975, providing that union representation would for the first time include collective bargaining. In the

Librarian of Congress Billington talks to Clara Elgi LeGear at the Geography and Map Division's 1988 Christmas party, which featured a display of Mrs. LeGear's many publications through the years. In 1973, she completed 11 years of service as the Library's Honorary Consultant in Historical Cartography, a period of voluntary service preceded by 47 years of full-time employment. Her continuous association with the Library for 58 years is unequalled in the Library's history. Dana Pratt, the Library's Director of Publishing, is on the right. LC Archives.

ensuing elections, the American Federation of State, County, and Municipal Employees was selected to represent the Library's professional and nonprofessional employees, with the Congressional Research Employees Association selected to represent employees of CRS and the Law Library of Congress United Association of Employees selected by Law Library staff. Bargaining took place over a two-year period, and contracts were finally signed for Library employees on June 14, 1978, and for CRS staff in 1979.

The Library of Congress Professional Association (LCPA) was established in 1969. A voluntary staff organization, it was created "to foster communication and promote cooperation among the staff, to improve the knowledge and skills of Library employees, and to create an independent platform for discussing issues affecting staff." It welcomed all staff and retirees "regardless of job description," because "we advocate that all staff are professionals and therefore all have a role to play in helping LCPA and LC achieve their respective goals." Through the years, LCPA has developed a variety of staff activities, including a continuing education fund, an arts and crafts show, language tables, and specialized interest groups. Many of its programs are supported by proceeds from its popular annual book sale.

The Library began to pay special attention to women's and family needs by the mid-1970s, hiring the first full-time Women's Program coordinator in 1976. Early activities centered on addressing concerns about part-time employment and the need for a day-care center. Part-time employment increased slightly between 1975 and 1981, but the Little Scholars Child Development Center did not open until 1993. The first Hispanic employment program coordinator began work in 1984, along with a program for handicapped employees. Throughout the 1980s and 1990s, affirmative action plans continued programs of various types: fellowships, internships, career development, incentive awards, employment seminars, details, job fairs, and a career interest group.

Employee organizations continued to appear. In November 1979, the Daniel A.P. Murray Afro-American Culture Association was formed to further awareness and appreciation of African American culture through educational, scholarly, cultural, benevolent, civic, and nonprofit social activities. Another organizing effort in 1992 revived the old Library of Congress Welfare and Recreation Association as the Library of Congress Recreation Association (LCRA) including the Choral Society, the Philatelic Club, the Tennis Tournament, the Film Society, the Dance/Exercise Class, the Travel Club, the Bible Group and the Recorder Club. More than an umbrella organization for special interest groups, the LCRA soon began offering an array of products and services for employees, and beginning in 1999, canceled membership fees. A chapter of the national organization of Blacks in Government was organized at the Library in 1996. Another active, ongoing group is the Library of Congress Gay, Lesbian or Bisexual Employees (LC-GLOBE), an educational, recreational, and cultural forum.

In 1993, Librarian Billington announced a new initiative aimed at recruiting minorities and preparing them for mid-level managerial positions at the Library. The Leadership Development Program was made possible by a grant of $1 million from John Kluge, the chairman of the Library's Madison Council. The first class was in 1995. By 2004, more than 35 Library of Congress staff members had participated in the program, which had become a 12-month orientation that included practical work experience, professional mentoring and development opportunities, and specialized training sessions about leadership and new technology and information systems.

Another set of opportunities for Library employees appeared in 1997 when the Library of Congress Internal University (LCIU) was established to provide training and educational programming and services to Library management and staff members. Hundreds of courses are offered each year online and in classrooms throughout the Library. The LCIU also supports a Learning Support Center in the Library's Adams Building, a state-of-the-art computer center for staff training, particularly self-paced learning; supports training efforts by other offices, such as the Office of Security's emergency preparedness training program; and sponsors a mentoring program.

Employment Statistics in 2003

According to the Library's 2003 *Annual Report*, as of September 30, 2003, there were 4,151 "full-time" employees in permanent positions working at the Library of Congress. The attrition rate for permanent employees in fiscal year 2003 was 5 percent. The average years of service at the Library was 17, the average age was 48, and there were 1,879 males and 2,272 females on the staff. By racial origin, the breakdown was 2,182 White, 1,613 Black, 256 Asian, 82 Hispanic, and 18 American Indian. (JYC, JA).

Davis, Donald G. Jr., ed. *Second Supplement to the Dictionary of American Library Biography*. Westport, Conn.: Libraries Unlimited, 2003. Includes biographies of the following former Library of Congress staff members: Frances Neel Cheney, Robert B. Croneberger, Benjamin A. Custer, Virginia Haviland, Frazer G. Poole, and Vernon D. Tate.

Fairness and Equal Opportunity at the Library of Congress. Washington, D.C.: Library of Congress, November 1998.

Pierson, Harriet Wheeler. *Rosemary: Reminiscences of the Library of Congress*. Washington, D.C., 1943.

Rosenberg, Jane A. "Patronage and Professionals: The Transformation of the Library of Congress Staff, 1890–1907," *Libraries and Culture* 26 (Spring 1991): 251–268.

Wiegand, Wayne A., ed. *Supplement to the Dictionary of American Library Biography*. Englewood, Colo.: Libraries Unlimited, 1990. Includes biographies of the following former Library of Congress staff members: Luther H. Evans, Archibald MacLeish, Blanche P. McCrum, David C. Mearns, L. Quincy Mumford, Jesse H. Shera, and Harold Spivacke.

Wynar, Bohdan S., ed. *Dictionary of American Library Biography*. Littleton, Colo.: Libraries Unlimited, 1978. Includes biographies of the following former Library of Congress staff members: John James Beckley, Verner W. Clapp, Bernard R. Green, Appleton P. C. Griffin, J. C. M. Hanson, David J. Haykin, Patrick Magruder, Charles Martel, John S. Meehan, Herman H.B. Meyer, Lucile M. Morsch, Daniel A. P. Murray, Herbert Putnam, Thorvald Solberg, Oscar G. T. Sonneck, Ainsworth Rand Spofford, John G. Stephenson, Frederic Vinton, George Watterston, and John Russell Young.

EUROPEAN DIVISION AND COLLECTIONS

The European Division

Europe has been a major focus of the Library of Congress since the founding of the institution in 1800, yet the European Division dates from only 1978. Europe's historical and contemporary importance to the United States and the volume of library materials originating in Europe in part explain why responsibility for the continent has been the responsibility of a number of administrative units rather than one. In addition, the diversity of European languages and cultures and the post-World War II geopolitical division of the continent into Eastern and Western blocs worked against treating the area as a single administrative unit until the late 1970s.

Throughout most of the nineteenth century, Europe, especially western Europe, dominated the foreign focus of the Library. In 1800, when Congress ordered the first books for its library, it turned to London rather than to American booksellers with a list of classical and European authors, mostly in English translation. When considering the purchase of Thomas Jefferson's library (1814–1815), which included a significant number of books in French, Congress debated extending the language policy. Over the objections of some members, it ultimately decided to expand beyond the English language in order to include large quantities of materials published in classical and modern languages from continental Europe. Later, in the spirit of post-Civil War nationalism, the model of European national libraries—especially the British Museum Library—guided the development of the Library of Congress from a legislative library in the Capitol Building to a major cultural institution housed in its own magnificent building. When the new building opened in 1897, the mission and objectives of the institution expanded greatly. Librarian Herbert Putnam (1898–1939) focused on improving the European collections and making them available to both government and scholarly clienteles. In 1900, Putnam himself undertook a major trip to London, Paris, The Hague, Amsterdam, Brussels, Vienna, and Berlin to strengthen the Library's acquisitions from Europe and its contacts with European government officials and scholars. Putnam's reorganization of the Library kept European materials integrated with the general collections. Reader services involving European materials and subjects, including publishing bibliographies, were the responsibility of many different administrative divisions. In 1906, Putnam acquired 80,000 books and bound serials, 68,000 of which were in Russian, from Siberian merchant and bibliophile Genadii Yudin. In 1907, a Slavic Section was established within the Catalog Division to process this collection.

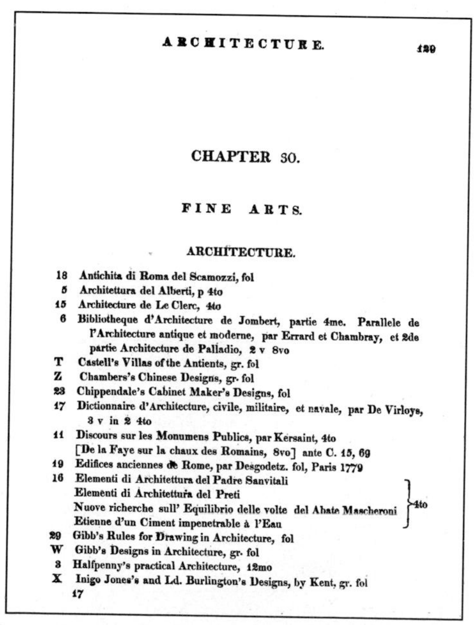

ARCHITECTURE. 129

CHAPTER 30.

FINE ARTS.

ARCHITECTURE.

18 Antichita di Roma del Scamozzi, fol
5 Architettura del Alberti, p 4to
15 Architecture de Le Clerc, 4to
6 Bibliotheque d'Architecture de Jombert, partie 4me. Parallele de l'Architecture antique et moderne, par Errard et Chambray, et 2de partie Architecture de Palladio, 2 v 8vo
T Castell's Villas of the Antients, gr. fol
Z Chambers's Chinese Designs, gr. fol
23 Chippendale's Cabinet Maker's Designs, fol
17 Dictionnaire d'Architecture, civile, militaire, et navale, par De Virloys, 3 v in 2 4to
11 Discours sur les Monumens Publics, par Kersaint, 4to
[De la Faye sur la chaux des Romains, 8vo] ante C. 15, 69
19 Edifices anciennes de Rome, par Desgodetz. fol, Paris 1779
16 Elementi di Architettura del Padre Sanvitali
Elementi di Architettura del Preti
Nuove richerche sull' Equilibrio delle volte del Abate Mascheroni
Etienne d'un Ciment impenetrable à l'Eau } 4to
29 Gibb's Rules for Drawing in Architecture, fol
W Gibb's Designs in Architecture, gr. fol
3 Halfpenny's practical Architecture, 12mo
X Inigo Jones's and Ld. Burlington's Designs, by Kent, gr. fol
17

A page from the 1815 catalog of Thomas Jefferson's library, which he sold to Congress after the burning of the Capitol by the British in 1814. The architecture titles on this page represent only a fraction of the large number of European books added to the Library's collection through the Jefferson purchase.
LC/Rare Book and Special Collections.

Although Putnam's 40-year administration demonstrated a strong interest in Europe, except for the Slavic Section, which became the Division of Slavic Literature (1929–1939), it did not establish any formal administrative units focused on the continent. Putnam developed European collections and reader services most notably through large special projects and a system of scholarly consultants, supported by substantial gift funds, grants, and endowments. Scholarly consultants specializing in European history and other humanities and social sciences subjects worked with the Division of Bibliography on both collection development and the publication of bibliographies. The collections continued to grow, as did the work in reader services. In 1938 the division moved to the John Adams Building, and a reference service area was established adjacent to the custodial and cataloging unit.

Librarian Archibald MacLeish (1939–1944) continued the scholarly development of the Library and many of Putnam's initiatives. Europe remained the focus of large, ongoing special projects, such as the

with different European countries throughout the first decades of the century. Immediately after World War II, however, the U.S. government signed treaties with most post-war European governments to secure the regular exchange of official documents, a system that remained intact until the end of the century.

In 1905, the Library initiated a Foreign Copying Program, a special project of copying archival material in foreign repositories that related to American history. Ninety-six percent of the thousands of volumes of transcripts, photostats, microfiche, and microfilm produced by the Foreign Copying Program is European. The staff coordinated the copying efforts with groups specializing in American history, including the American Historical Association, and has received substantial private grant support. The program has brought together extensive European documentation of European settlement history, of American colonies, of European participation in the American Revolution, and later, of diplomatic and cultural relations between Europe and the United States. For example, at the end of the century, the Library undertook projects to copy an extensive collection of papers of Lafayette still held by his descendants and to copy documents relating to American history in newly accessible Russian archives.

World War I and World War II both generated intense research and information needs for Congress, the U.S. government, scholars, and many segments of the American public; and both spawned increased acquisition efforts. Many materials acquired by agencies throughout the U.S. government were later transferred to the Library, creating extensive collections of European printed, pictorial, cartographic, and other documentation of the first half of the twentieth century. Following World War II the Library's special Mission to Europe (1945–1948), supported by the War Department and the Department of State, organized a cooperative overseas acquisition project to obtain multiple copies of European publications of the war period for distribution to American libraries and research institutions. It also located and forwarded stacks of books ordered before the war by American libraries but never shipped. Most of these materials had been accumulated for the libraries by book dealers in Germany located in what became the Russian zone.

The Library continued to meet its responsibilities to Congress and to American libraries by assuring and sustaining high research level collections related to Europe. The National Program for Acquisitions and Cataloging (NPAC), a part of the Higher Education Act of 1965, allowed the Library to establish 12 offices in Europe alone to collect comprehensively all materials of value to scholarship, and to produce and distribute bibliographic information about them. Materials acquired but not needed for the Library collections were to be used for exchange. By the early 1980s, when the Library had fully automated its cataloging the European offices were closed, and commercial European vendors were contracted to supply most current publications. In some cases for Eastern Europe the Library worked with national libraries and/or literary and scientific academies that served as vendors. The Library also contacted west European commercial vendors to supply materials not available directly from communist sources. In the 1990s, after the dissolution of the Soviet Union, the Library once again turned to commercial dealers to meet the fluctuating change in the east European publishing world.

The Size and Scope of the Collections. The Library's holdings of books and other materials from almost all European countries are larger than holdings anywhere else in the world except for the countries of origin. In the general collections alone, the particularly strong German collections encompass approximately 2.25 million volumes; the French collections number more than one million items. About 700,000 volumes are in Russian, with approximately an equal number of volumes in other languages of the former Soviet Union. Italian items number about 500,000. Smaller European countries are also well-represented: the Dutch and Flemish collections consist of about 180,000 items; the Hungarian collection amounts to about 130,000; the Czech and Slovak collections are estimated at more than 100,000 volumes. In general, all these collections are well-balanced in subject focus. The Library's special emphasis on materials related to American history makes it the world's largest repository of publications and documents related to American–European ties, including records of European exploration of the New World, genealogical records, and materials describing the experiences of American artists, literary figures, and diplomats in Europe. As the importance of materials published in European languages far exceeds the geographical limits of Europe, these collections also support international studies in all parts of the world.

The European collections are strongest in the humanities and social sciences, with special strengths in language, literature, history, geography, political science, law, the arts, and economics. Reference materials in all these areas, but particularly in the social sciences and humanities, are represented as comprehensively as possible. For most European countries the Library offers in-depth coverage of a wide variety of subjects throughout all periods, but is especially

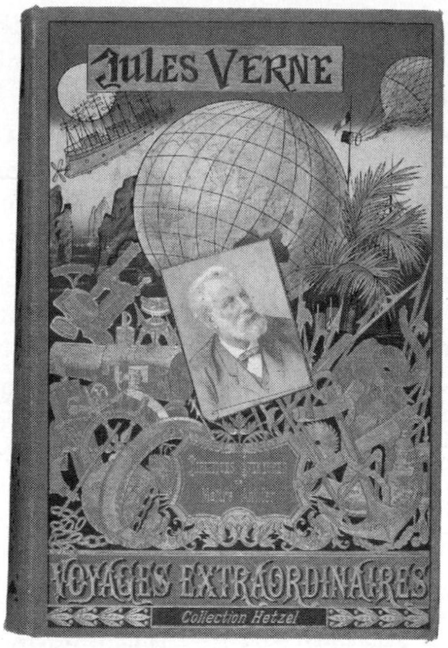

The many special collections related to European studies include items on individual countries, on distinct European eras, and on individual Europeans such as authors Jules Verne and Hans Christian Andersen. Jules Verne's Voyages Extraordinaires *is part of the Willis E. Hurd Collection.*
LC/Rare Book and Special Collections Division.

strong from the Renaissance to the present. A particular strength of the collections is literature that was once considered *libri prohibiti*. For many decades the Library collected books and periodicals that were not available to researchers in Central and Eastern Europe under the Communist régimes. These include *samizdat* publications, émigré literatures, and works of Western authors on Central and Eastern Europe.

The many special collections related to European studies include some on individual countries like Bulgaria, Portugal, and Russia. Other special collections exist on the Reformation, the French Revolution, the Russian Empire, the Third Reich, World War II propaganda, and World War II resistance material. Still others focus on individual fields of endeavor having a strong European tradition or presence, for example, aeronautics, anarchy, gastronomy, Reformation, or magic. Some focus on individuals, for example, Hans Christian Andersen, Sigmund Freud, Martin Luther, and Jules Verne. The Library also excels in European rarities or rarities related to Europe in a wide variety of fields and formats—books, manuscripts, letters, maps, drawings, musical scores, musical instruments, films, and photographs. In 1992, the Library acquired as its 100,000,001st item—the first printed account of the fifteenth-century Portuguese discoveries in the New World. (CA)

Yudin Collection. Gennadius Vasilievich Yudin (1840–1912), a Russian merchant in the liquor trade and a bibliophile, lived in Krasnoiarsk, Siberia. His home was a two-month journey from St. Petersburg, but he ordered books by telegraphing agents in Moscow and St. Petersburg and occasionally purchased material from scholars' private collections. In approximately 30 years, he managed to accumulate 80,000 volumes. Most of his books were in Russian, and he was especially interested in Russian history, literature, and bibliography, and in Siberian material. Shelved by size, the books were kept in a two-story log building twice as large as the Yudin family's nearby home. But remarkable as it was, for both size and quality, the collection was little-known, even in Russia. On the verge of retirement by 1903, Yudin hoped to follow the Russian custom of giving his library to a public institution.

Alexis V. Babine, a Russian émigré who became a librarian after entering the United States, was at that time a staff member at the Library of Congress. Librarian Herbert Putnam dispatched him to Siberia to view the collection in 1903 and, assured of its value, purchased Yudin's library but called it "primarily a gift" since "the sum paid scarcely exceeded a third of what the owner himself had expended in the accumulation of it over a period of thirty years." Yudin, for his part, was pleased to learn that Putnam hoped to establish a Russian section in the Library of Congress. While he would have liked to send his books as a gift "with the sole idea of establishing closer relations between the two nations," his financial

The Yudin Collection of more than 80,000 items, which came to the Library early in the twentieth century, is the nucleus of the Library's Russian and Siberian collections. Most of the books were in Russian, but among the manuscripts is documentation of Russian discovery and settlement in the Far East and in the United States. This nineteenth century Russian drawing shows the great Chinese "Hall of Supreme Harmony," the main hall in the Forbidden City, Beijina China.
LC/Prints and Photographs Division.

circumstances dictated a sale instead. Yet he remained happy that his library would be "accessible to everyone interested in Russian literature and progress."

The collection included the best editions of every important Russian writer, historian, and critic. In addition, it contained 60 sets of scholarly society publications and periodicals, such as the collections of the Imperial Russian Historical Society, the publications of the Imperial Russian geographical society, the Moscow Society of Russian History and Antiquities, and the *Historical Review (Istoricheskii vestnik)*. Large holdings of periodicals dated from the late eighteenth century and newspapers from the 1800s. Among the manuscripts were materials documenting Russian discovery and settlement in the Far East and America. The literature holdings began with the early stages of literary awakening, dating from the accession of the Romanovs and especially Peter the Great and his successors, with especially complete nineteenth-century holdings encompassing literature, literary history and criticism. Also rich in the fine arts, in local history, ethnography, genealogy, travel and description, political science, law, institutional history, and in the literatures of various groups and sects, the collection represented the largest Russian holdings outside Russia.

Transporting the books to the United States proved something of a problem. Five hundred packing cases had to be made to order to ship the books west through Russia and Germany to Hamburg. The transport took three months, expedited by Russian authorities who, in response to an appeal from the American Embassy, cleared the railway lines and directed that the shipment be given right of way. The Yudin collection formed the nucleus of the Library of Congress's holdings of Russian and Siberian material. Its acquisition at an early date in the Library's development meant that Russian history and culture would remain an important part of continuing acquisitions interests, and it made the Library of Congress preeminent among American collections of Russian material. (JA)

Babine, Alexis Vasilievic. *The Yudin Library, Krasnoiarsk (Eastern Siberia)*. Washington, D.C.: Press of Judd and Detwiler, 1905.

Library of Congress European Collections: An Illustrated Guide. Introduction by Michael H. Haltzel. Washington, D.C.: Library of Congress, 1995.

Yakobson, Sergius. "An Autobiography of Gennadii Vasil'evich Yudin," *The Library of Congress Quarterly Journal of Current Acquisitions* (February 1946), pp. 13–15.

EVANS, LUTHER H. (1902–1981)

Luther Harris Evans, the 10th Librarian of Congress (1945–1953) and the third director-general of the United Nations Educational, Scientific, and Cultural Organization (UNESCO), was born on his grandmother's farm near Sayerville, Bastrop County, Texas, the son of George Washington Evans, a railroad foreman, and Lillie Johnson. Evans worked on his family's farm until he graduated from high school, when as valedictorian he spoke on the League of Nations. Through teaching and work in cotton fields, Evans financed his education at the University of Texas, receiving his A.S. degree in 1923 and master's in political science in 1924. Following a summer in Europe, where he studied the League of Nations first-hand, Evans began teaching and graduate work at Stanford University, where he received a doctorate in political science in 1927. In 1925, he married Helen Murphy, a University of Texas classmate.

Luther H. Evans, the 10th Librarian of Congress (1945–1953), was brought to the Library in 1939 by Librarian of Congress Archibald MacLeish. He soon became MacLeish's principal lieutenant, holding several key positions and serving as Acting Librarian of Congress during Librarian MacLeish's absences.
Drawing by Lila Oliver Archer.
LC/Prints and Photographs Division. LC-USZ62-58936.

From 1927 to 1935, Evans taught at New York University, Dartmouth, and Princeton. On the recommendation of Raymond Moley, a member of President Franklin D. Roosevelt's "Brain Trust," in 1935 Evans went to Washington, D.C. to develop a national survey of historical records. Later in the year, when the project evolved into the Historical Records Survey (HRS) of the Works Progress Administration (WPA), he became its first director. Under his leadership, it became one of the most successful of the New Deal arts projects.

Evans also had political connections that, in the autumn of 1939, brought him to the attention of the newly appointed Librarian of Congress Archibald MacLeish. He offered Evans the job of director of the Library's Legislative Reference Service (LRS). Evans quickly became MacLeish's principal lieutenant, a position formalized less than a year later when he became chief assistant librarian as well as director of the LRS.

MacLeish was a wartime advisor to President Franklin D. Roosevelt, and Evans served as Acting Librarian of Congress during MacLeish's frequent absences. He played an influential role in shaping a major administrative reorganization. Once they adjusted to Evans's blunt style, the Library staff appreciated their chief assistant librarian, who believed in sharing decision-making. When MacLeish resigned to become assistant secretary of state, most of the Library's staff hoped Evans would be named to head the Library. Although Roosevelt had other plans, he died before filling the post, and President Harry S. Truman was willing to consider the advice of the American Library Association (ALA). Evans was included on its list of three "acceptable" nominees and Truman, who liked him immediately, sent his nomination to the Senate on June 18, 1945. Hearings were held on June 29 and confirmation took place without objection the same day. On June 30, Evans took the oath of office as the 10th Librarian of Congress.

MacLeish had insisted that the Library of Congress contribute actively to the cultural and scholarly life of the nation. Evans shared MacLeish's views, and in many ways Evans's eight-year administration was an extension of the MacLeish years. But Evans also plunged into technical library issues and promoted the Library of Congress as a leader and partner among American libraries. In the process, he established an international role for the Library. These were considerable accomplishments, because Evans ran into opposition in Congress and never was given what he considered an adequate appropriation.

As soon as he took office, Evans emphasized the national role of the Library of Congress, which had, he believed, "an inescapable responsibility" to serve the entire country. The challenges of the post-war years meant "no spot on the earth's surface is any longer alien to the interest of the American people." In such a world, the Library of Congress could be "a powerful instrument of peace and progress." Thus the new Librarian asked Congress to nearly double the Library's appropriation in fiscal 1947. But not only was his request rejected by an economy-minded Congress, his broad vision of the Library's future also

The Lincoln Cathedral copy of the Magna Carta was sent to the Library by the British for safekeeping at the beginning of World War II. After the Japanese attacked Pearl Harbor, the Library sent the Magna Carta, along with other Library of Congress treasures, to Fort Knox, Kentucky. On December 26, 1941, Evans (left) supervised the removal of the document from the Library. LC/Prints and Photographs Division. LC-USP6-359C.

was challenged when the Appropriations Committee questioned the Library's authority to serve "as a national and indeed an international library." With Evans on the defensive, the Library's appropriation grew only slowly, but his leadership ability pushed the institution forward in spite of fiscal constraints.

Most of the Library's accomplishments between 1945 and 1953 can be traced to Evans's initiatives or concerns. Important acquisitions and bibliographical achievements included the Library of Congress Mission to Europe to obtain multiple copies of European publications for the war period, microfilming projects for the Middle East, and leadership in developing the Farmington Plan, a cooperative acquisitions effort among research libraries. Evans's colleague, Assistant Librarian Verner W. Clapp, asserted that Evans invented the phrase "bibliographical control," and his open management style was a positive contribution. He consulted frequently with his department directors and mixed freely with the staff. He believed that in a democracy the free flow of information was a necessity, and he courageously applied his belief, speaking out against censorship at home and abroad. Evans was one of the few government officials to openly resist the intimidation of Senator Joseph R. McCarthy, even hiring an administrator in 1952 a month after she was dismissed from the State Department as a "security risk."

Such actions made Evans a controversial Librarian of Congress. Many members of Congress disliked his aggressive, opinionated style and criticized both his ambitious plans for the Library and the time he spent away from the institution, particularly in UNESCO activities. In a profile of Evans, Chief Assistant Librarian Verner Clapp speaks of his dogmatic manner, his "totally uninhibited laugh," and his "constitutional inability to praise a subordinate to his face." Yet the staff respected him.

Nominated as Librarian of Congress by President Truman, Evans (above) took the oath of office on June 30, 1945. He worked hard to promote the Library and its collections both nationally and internationally, declaring that in the postwar years "no spot on the earth's surface is any longer alien to the interest of the American people." LC Archives.

Evans's interest in international affairs remained strong throughout his librarianship. In late 1945, he was a member of the U.S. delegation to the London conference that established UNESCO, and the new organization benefited from his earlier interest in the League of Nations. He continued to work for UNESCO and involved the Library of Congress in its activities, particularly in the development of a Universal Copyright Convention. In 1953, Evans allowed his name to be considered for the vacant post of director-general. He was elected and resigned as Librarian of Congress, effective July 5, 1953.

Evans served from 1953 to 1958 as UNESCO's director-general. He received good marks as an administrator but, ironically, given his personal views, became entangled with the U.S. government's loyalty program as it applied to American citizens working for UNESCO. The organization grew rapidly during this period, however, and Evans effectively developed its technical assistance and educational programs.

Evans returned to Texas in 1958, but he soon became the director of a Brookings Institution survey, recommending ways to coordinate the planning and operation of federal libraries. A suggestion in his report showed that he still held strong and controversial views: he called for the transfer of the Library of Congress to the executive branch of government, where he felt it would obtain the support it deserved. In 1962, he became director of International and Legal Collections for Columbia University Libraries and helped develop a new library for the School of International Affairs. After retiring from this post in 1971, he became president of World Federalists U.S.A. and played an active role in groups such as the American Civil Liberties Union and the United Nations Association. He died in San Antonio, Texas, where he had made his home since 1977.

The principal contribution of Luther Evans's career was to the Library of Congress. In his budget proposal for fiscal 1947, he articulated for the first time a modern, post-war vision of the institution's national and international roles. For the next eight years, he expanded his ideas and advocated his views in more than 100 articles and 400 speeches. His vision, in large measure, has been fulfilled by subsequent Librarians of Congress. (JYC)

Sittig, William J. "Luther Evans: Man for a New Age," *The Quarterly Journal of the Library of Congress* 33 (July 1976): 251–267.

EXCHANGE AND GIFT

The exchange and gift functions have been essential to the Library since its earliest days. Gifts have come, for example, as single volumes or sets, as collections focusing on particular subjects, and as individuals' entire libraries or complete personal papers. Exchanges have taken place chiefly with foreign and domestic governments, universities and colleges, research centers, organizations, and businesses. Certain types of publications worldwide, both historically and currently, can readily be obtained through exchange—especially those of agencies and organizations that do not rely on commercial publishers to distribute their publications. Exchanges have been arranged by the State Department through executive agreements or informally by the Library staff on the basis that the Library would provide a full or partial set of U.S. government publications in return for the exchange partner's publications.

As early as 1828, the Library was authorized to dispose of duplicate copies of books, pamphlets, and other items to members of Congress and to state and college libraries, and in 1834 the Joint Committee on the Library was given the authority to provide U.S. government publications in return for gifts made to the Library of Congress, with an initial limit of 25 copies. The Library's first exchange agreement, with France, was approved by the Joint Committee in 1837, and a joint congressional resolution of July 20, 1840 authorized the Library staff to exchange documents as well as duplicate books. Through this resolution, Congress formally recognized the possibilities of a continuing exchange program for promoting international intellectual cooperation. Between 1840 and 1852, a French citizen, Alexandre Vattemare, received congressional support for his international exchange system, but the disappointing results of his efforts led to the repeal of the legislation that had supported it. And in January 1857, Congress approved a joint resolution transferring the responsibility for international exchange of books and periodicals from the Library of Congress to the State Department and the Bureau of the Interior.

During the nineteenth and early twentieth centuries, however, the federal government's chief exchange agency was the Smithsonian Institution's International Exchange Service, which was primarily oriented toward scholarly materials in the sciences. As a result of mutual agreement between the two agencies, Congress transferred the Smithsonian Library to the Library of Congress in 1866, and the following year approved the exchange of documents with foreign governments through the Smithsonian exchange service, providing 50 copies of government documents for exchange purposes. In 1900, Librarian Herbert Putnam organized the Smithsonian Division in the Library to care for the material received through exchange and housed the books and staff on the second floor of the Jefferson Building, east north curtain. Putnam also asked Congress to increase the number of exchange copies of government to 100. The Librarian listed nearly 50 foreign exchange partners in his 1901 *Annual Report*, but that number steadily increased, ultimately extending to thousands of institutions at home and abroad.

The Smithsonian material helped to lay the foundations of the Library's science collections, but other transfers from federal agencies have also greatly enriched the holdings. From the Department of State, for example, came the papers of George Washington, Thomas Jefferson, James Madison, James Monroe, and Alexander Hamilton, all purchased by the government in the early nineteenth century. And during the years following World War II, important collections of materials entered the Library when wartime agencies divested their large war-related files; among these were the Office of War Information's collection of photographs, confiscated Nazi Party archives and other German organizations' files, and from the Washington Document Center hundreds of thousands of Japanese items used for intelligence purposes. In the post-war years, materials from the federal agencies

Librarian of Congress Archibald MacLeish established The Library of Congress Quarterly Journal of Current Acquisitions *in 1943. This October 1945 issue was devoted to the first installment of what would become one of the most significant gifts in the Library's history: the Lessing J. Rosenwald Collection of Illustrated Books.* LC/Publishing Office.

far exceeded receipts from other sources.

During Putnam's administration, all gift and exchange material was routed first through the Order (later Accessions) Division for acknowledgment. Serials were recorded in the Division of Periodicals and documents in the Division of Documents. However, as the quantity of material increased and exchange arrangements became more numerous and complicated, the Exchange and Gift Division was established as a part of the Acquisitions Department on July 1, 1943, composed of units formerly part of the Accessions, Documents, and Catalog Divisions. Housed in the Adams Building, Exchange and Gift became the receiving unit for all library materials except those purchased by the Accessions Division. The new division had four sections for exchanges: American and British, European, Hispanic, and Orientalia. Other sections dealt with gifts, with receiving and routing Russian material, and the *Monthly Checklist of State Publications*, the latter representing an important category of material that the Library tried to collect comprehensively. The Documents Expediting Project established in 1946 to procure federal publications not available from the Government Printing Office or from issuing agencies for subscribing libraries also became part of the division, and the United States Book Exchange (USBE) was established in the Library in 1948 as an independent, nonprofit, self-supporting corporation that would receive surplus publications and distribute them. As a central clearinghouse for the international exchange of publications, it accepted member libraries' duplicates, credited their accounts, and sent them lists of items available, for which credits could be traded. After a decade, growing space problems forced the move of USBE to another location, but the Library continued to use USBE services in its exchange operations.

In the post-World War II period, exchanges were fostered by an increasing number of agreements negotiated by the State Department. With other national libraries and institutions abroad, the Library sometimes established "priced exchanges": current American publications were purchased as selected by foreign institutions and the Library received in exchange publications of equivalent value issued in the other country. Such agreements proved particularly useful in countries that lacked a well-organized commercial book trade. By the late 1950s, the Library had over 16,000 exchange agreements, including as many as 174 in the Soviet Union alone. These agreements included the usual institutional and governmental partners, but in the post-war period more attention began to be paid to such organizations as research

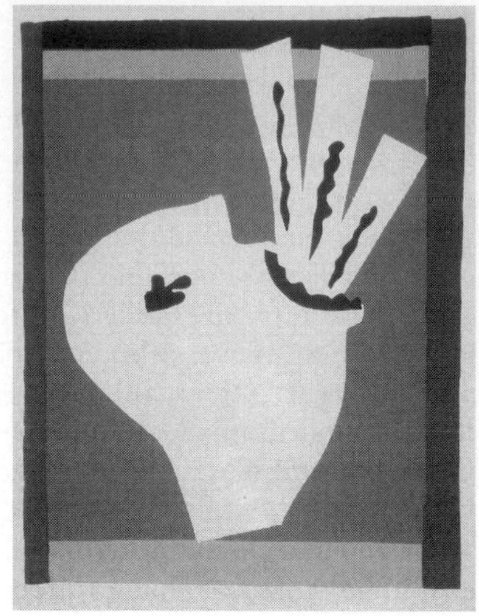

Duplicates from the Lessing J. Rosenwald Collection were exchanged in the mid-1980s for a copy of Henri Matisse's greatest illustrated book, Jazz *(above), until then the most important* livre d'artiste *or artist's book not in the Rosenwald Collection.*
LC/Rare Book and Special Collections Division.

centers, laboratories, observatories, and other scientific and technical institutions.

With the resumption of diplomatic relations with Mainland China during the early 1970s, exchange relations were re-established, assisted by a 1979 visit by a delegation of 12 American librarians led by William J. Welsh, the Deputy Librarian. As a result, 34 exchange agreements were negotiated with Chinese institutions by 1980, and receipts from the People's Republic of China grew dramatically. This new exchange capability meant that the Library had agreements in force worldwide, centering on official agencies, international organizations, semiofficial bodies, and educational and research institutions of all types. A shift of the responsibility for distributing exchange material abroad, from the Smithsonian Institution to the Superintendent of Documents, was begun on a contract basis in 1978.

Materials received through exchange and gift include books, pamphlets, serials, documents, manuscripts, maps, microforms, posters, prints, photographs, magnetic tapes, videotapes, and digitized information. All are examined by selection officers who designate which items are to be added to the Library's collections. Items not selected are added to the Library's large duplicates collection to be used for exchange, for transfer to other government libraries, for sale, as donations to educational institutions, or for disposal according to federal surplus property regulations. Members of Congress are able to make selections for libraries or public agencies in their districts; for example, schools. Executive agencies and local government representatives are also able to make selections from the duplicates collection. Materials also may be loaned to congressional offices.

Legislation has significantly affected gifts made to the Library. The Tax Reform Act of 1969 abolished individual donors' tax deductions for gifts of material such as their letters, papers, compositions, drawings, or literary works. Library officials subsequently found that the flow of gift material decreased since donors often preferred to deposit their papers rather than donating them, in the hope that the law would be changed. However, collectors and inheritors of intellectual property were not affected by the act, and they remained important sources of gift material. In 1986, the alternative minimum tax was imposed on charitable gifts of appreciated art, but it was rescinded in 1993. Gifts to the Library have provided some of the choicest, rarest, and most costly items and collections—the private library of Joseph M. Toner; the Stradivarius instrument collection from Gertrude Clarke Whittall; the rare illustrated books of Lessing J. Rosenwald; the Mary Pickford collection of motion pictures, Alfred Whital Stern's collection of Lincolniana—and also numerous personal and family papers collections from statesmen, authors, scientists, scholars, composers and musicians, and numerous others.

By the late 1970s, when the Library had over 13,000 active exchanges, the division moved from the Jefferson Building to the Navy Yard Annex pending the occupation of the Madison Building in the early 1980s. During the 1970s and 1980s, as the staff gained more experience with dealing with developing nations, it became evident that these countries often had greater interest in trade publications than in the government publications that had traditionally appealed to exchange partners. The division consequently began relying more on surplus and duplicate material for these exchanges, and the staff began working more closely with the Library's field offices abroad. More traditional international exchange partners, who still wished to receive U.S. government publications, began getting them mostly in microfiche format by the early 1980s, a generally acceptable alternative because it required less shelf space and posed fewer preservation problems. In the late 1970s, a special Hispanic Acquisitions Project was planned to include exchanges. The staff distributed lists of available books in more than 30 subject fields so that exchange partners might select needed items, a labor-intensive but effective method of making exchanges attractive. In 1981, the project was made a permanent part of the division, with responsibilities for both purchase and exchange. The division applied this strategy to African and Asian exchanges with similar success.

The 50th anniversary of the Exchange and Gift Division occurred in 1993, at which time exchanges were being maintained with more than 15,000 international organizations, educational institutions, and learned societies worldwide and the Library had amassed, primarily through gift and exchange, the most comprehensive collection of foreign official government documents found anywhere. However, from 1994 onward, materials obtained by exchange decreased each year, reflecting a general conversion of government publishing to electronic format and also a mail embargo following the discovery of contamination in government mailrooms in the wake of the September 11, 2001 terrorist attack. In 1997, the Library's acquisitions activities were reorganized along geographic lines, to replicate the earlier successful experiment. The Exchange and Gift Division disappeared; in its place the Acquisitions directorate has divisions for African/Asian Acquisitions and Overseas Operations, Anglo-American Acquisitions, European and Latin American Acquisitions, plus the Serial Record Division. An examination of exchange processes included sending a questionnaire regarding the exchange process to all the Library's general exchange partners in 2002, with the intention of centralizing the production and distribution of exchange lists and of offering partners a wider range of choices for their selection of materials. A regular schedule of mailings was established, which was planned to serve

Recent arrivals in the Central and Eastern European Acquisitions Section, European and Latin American Acquisitions Division, Library Services.
Photograph: LC/Jim Higgins, Photographic Section.

as a building block for a Web-based exchange program that would provide more efficient processing and better service to exchange partners. (JA)

Library of Congress Information Bulletin 49 (December 17, 1990): 429–432.

Ostrowski, Carl. *Books, Maps, and Politics: A Cultural History of the Library of Congress, 1783–1861*. Amherst and Boston: University of Massachusetts Press, 2004.

Stevens, Robert D. *The Role of the Library of Congress in the International Exchange of Official Publications: A Brief History*. Washington, D.C.: Library of Congress, 1953. p. 85.

EXHIBITIONS

The Library of Congress has presented exhibitions to the public since at least the 1830s, when it was located in the west front of the U.S. Capitol. The *National Intelligencer* of March 30, 1830, notes an exhibition in the Library of oriental manuscripts collected by William B. Hodgson, consul-general at Algiers and in 1832, the Library Committee authorized Librarian of Congress John Silva Meehan (1829–1861) to visit public libraries on the east coast to instruct himself "in modes of managing libraries for preservation, exhibition, use, etc." However, the public use of the Library attracted few notices in the press, or in the Library's records, during Meehan's long librarianship. An exception is an article in an 1835 issue of a local literary magazine in which the author complains about "chatting ladies" who were turning over pages of Audubon's *Birds of America* in the Library's room.

Ainsworth Rand Spofford, Librarian of Congress (1864–1897), took a different and more aggressive approach. Eager to develop the Library's national reputation, he wanted to begin an exhibitions program that would display the Library's treasures, particularly those acquired through copyright deposit. No space for such displays was available in the Capitol, but exhibitions were part of a preliminary plan for the new building that Spofford presented to Congress in 1895. He designated second-floor gallery space for "the arrangement and display" of the Library's graphic arts collections, pointing out that after being "so long buried from view," the collections would present "to art-students and to the general public. . .a most instructive illustration of the progress of the arts of design." Adjoining the art gallery would be rooms "well-adapted for an extensive and very instructive display of specimens of early-printed books, choice and illuminated manuscripts, rare Americana, interesting autographs, and illustrated works." Exhibited in glass cases, these items would "constitute a museum of the arts of typography, illustration, etc., of much interest and value."

In his revised plan for the new building that was submitted to Congress on January 18, 1897, Spofford was more specific regarding the special rooms and facilities needed in the new building. He announced his plan for several separate exhibit spaces, including extensive "halls" for the "gallery of art" and to display maps and charts. In addition, there were to be separate rooms to exhibit early-printed books, early Americana, early specimens of engraving and the progress of book design, and "specimens of book binding, ancient and modern." When he became Librarian of Congress on July 1, 1897, John Russell

In 1901, the new Jefferson Building was a popular tourist attraction. This photograph shows prints from the Library's collection on display in the second floor southwest gallery. LC/Prints and Photographs Division. LC-USZ62-37241.

Young accepted Spofford's recommendations in principle, and much of the new building's commodious second floor was soon devoted to the exhibit halls and rooms. By June 1900, the Library's Prints and Photographs Division had mounted five exhibitions of European prints and one of photographs and etchings by American artists.

Librarian Herbert Putnam (1899–1939) undertook another kind of project in 1904, when the Library presented a major exhibit as part of the U.S. government pavilion at the Louisiana Purchase Exposition in St. Louis. Emphasizing the "National Library. . . as a function of our Government," Putnam proudly pointed out that the exhibit marked "the first direct participation of the Library in any of the great international expositions." Another Putnam initiative was obtaining the transfer of the original copies of the Declaration of Independence and the Constitution of the United States from the Department of State to the Library in 1921. The documents, encased in a specially designed "Shrine," went on public display in the Library's Great Hall in 1924. They remained in the Library's custody until 1952, when they were transferred to the National Archives.

As Librarian of Congress from 1939 until 1944, Archibald MacLeish, like his predecessors, viewed exhibits as an important means of enlarging knowledge about the Library and its collections. He also envisioned a new public role for the institution and included exhibitions as an important part of his plan. On December 18–21, 1940, the Library celebrated the 75th anniversary of the proclamation of the

13th Amendment, which ended slavery in the United States, with a music festival and a series of exhibits "dealing with the struggle of the Negro race for freedom." Foreseeing the need for a more formal structure and focused programming, particularly with an important Jefferson anniversary occurring in 1943, on October 16, 1942, MacLeish established an Exhibits Office and a Committee on Exhibits.

The exhibition portion of the Library's celebration of the bicentennial of the birth of Thomas Jefferson opened at the Library on April 12, 1943. In the *Annual Report of the Librarian of Congress* for 1943, MacLeish called the Jefferson Bicentennial

Catalog of the Library's 1943 Jefferson Bicentennial exhibition, which Librarian of Congress Archibald MacLeish called "perhaps the most ambitious" in the Library's history. Jefferson items were displayed in the Great Hall and by many divisions throughout the Jefferson and Adams Buildings. LC Archives.

Exhibits program "perhaps the most ambitious exhibit ever mounted" at the Library. It consisted of nine groups of materials selected with reference to Jefferson's various interests and displayed throughout the Library's two buildings. The Librarian noted that much remained to be done regarding exhibitions, but that the Library would make every effort to pursue an exhibitions program "on a permanent basis." A month later, the Library opened its first national print exhibition. A juried show supported by the Library's Joseph Pennell Fund, the print exhibition became an annual event. The prize-winning prints were added to the Library's collections.

A 1943 photograph of the Jefferson Bicentennial exhibition in the Library's Great Hall. LC Archives.

When MacLeish's chief assistant, Luther H. Evans, became Librarian of Congress in 1945, he began a series of exhibitions to honor significant anniversaries in the histories of U.S. states and territories. The first, which marked the centennial of Florida's admission to the Union, was opened by Senator Claude Pepper of Florida on March 3, 1945.

In 1945, Librarian of Congress Luther H. Evans inaugurated a series of exhibitions to use the Library's collections to honor significant anniversaries of U.S. states and territories. Kansas and Nebraska: Centennial of the Territories, 1854–1954, *is an illustrated catalog that describes all 231 items in this 1954 exhibition. It includes the address presented at the opening by Kansas Senator Andrew F. Schoeppel.* LC/Publishing Office.

Accompanied by handsome catalogs, the Library's 26 state and territorial exhibitions between 1945 and 1972 amply fulfilled Evans's hope of illustrating how the Library's book, manuscript, and pictorial collections could, on a state-by-state basis, help Americans "come to know what is ours, and what we may become." Beginning with Senator Pepper, members of Congress were invited and frequently participated in the openings of the exhibits about their respective states. The catalogs of the state exhibitions were the focal point of an article describing the Library's exhibition program in the July 1954 issue of *American*

Archivist. The authors, Herbert J. Sanborn and Nelson R. Burr of the Library's Exhibits Office, also presented guidelines for issuing catalogs "that will be popular and at the same time, in keeping with the dignity of the institution, have appeal to the scholar and the specialist."

In his *Annual Report* for 1950, Evans enthusiastically stated that the Library's exhibitions were attracting "unprecedented public interest." The major reasons, he felt, were a growing "general recognition of the powers of visual presentation" and the Library's "eagerness," within certain limits, "to dedicate its resources to cooperation with institutions serving a common purpose." The Library actively loaned items for exhibitions and in return, hosted exhibitions from other institutions. Through the Department of State, Library of Congress exhibitions traveled abroad. The report lists 125 exhibitions in the fiscal year 1950. Particularly notable and, according to Evans, "the most widely noticed exhibit ever produced under the auspices of the Library of Congress" was the display, from October 23 to November 6, 1949, of three ancient Hebrew scrolls, part of the "Dead Sea Scrolls" recently discovered in Qumran, Israel.

Exhibitions were an important Library of Congress activity from 1950 through the administrations of Librarians Mumford (1954–1974) and Boorstin (1975–1987). Boorstin, in particular, pushed the Library to mount imaginative exhibitions that would appeal to a wide public. Two notable and successful examples were "Fifty Years of Animation: Building a Better Mouse" (1978) and "The American Cowboy" (1983). Librarian of Congress James H. Billington (1987–) implemented an even more ambitious new program of major exhibitions and exhibition-related publications and activities. To reflect the broad, educational focus of this new initiative, in 1989 the Library changed the name of the Exhibits Office to the Interpretive Programs Office.

In the 1970s and 1980s, Library of Congress exhibitions became more numerous and covered a range of topics that reflected the breadth of the Library's collections. This exhibition catalog accompanied an exhibit celebrating 50 years of Walt Disney's animated films. Fifty Years of Animation: Building a Better Mouse, *on display from November 1978 through January 1979, featured items from the Copyright Office and the Motion Picture, Broadcasting and Recorded Sound Division.*
LC/Interpretive Programs Office.

Public attention to Library of Congress exhibitions greatly increased in the mid-1990s as the renovation and restoration of the Thomas Jefferson Building neared completion. With support from the Madison Council and other private-sector donors, the Library launched "Great Libraries and Written Traditions," a series of cooperative exhibitions featuring treasures from other institutions. The first, "Rome Reborn: The Vatican Library & Renaissance Culture," held in early 1993, also reopened the renovated southwest second floor gallery in the Jefferson Building and its new cases, which were designed by architect Michael Graves. A permanent addition to the gallery, the cases were funded by a gift from Mrs. Charles William Engelhard Jr. The exhibition was accompanied by a 323-page book of essays and a catalog that described individual exhibition items. In 1995, a similar 480-page volume published by Yale University Press served the same purpose for "Creating French Culture: Treasures from the Bibliothèque Nationale de France," the second exhibition in the "Great Libraries" series. The opening of "American Treasures of the Library of Congress," a permanent installation featuring items rotated into the exhibition

President Ronald Reagan at the 1983 exhibition The American Cowboy, *with (left to right) Library of Congress exhibits officer William Miner, Librarian of Congress Daniel J. Boorstin, and First Lady Nancy Reagan. Drawing heavily on documentation gathered by the Library's American Folklife Center, the exhibition also presented images of cowboys from the movies and popular culture.*
LC/American Folklife Center.

"Creating French Culture: Treasures from the Bibliothèque Nationale de France" was a major Library of Congress exhibition in 1995, and part of the Library's series of exhibitions about major libraries and written traditions. Text and images from the exhibition were reproduced on the Library's Web site. This book from the exhibition, an artistic treasure as well as a valuable artifact, was a gift from Henri d'Albret, king of Navarre, to his bride, Marguerite d'Angouleme, in 1527.
Courtesy Bibliothèque Nationale de France.

from various Americana collections," took place on May 1, 1997. A book accompanied the exhibition. The Vatican Library, Bibliothèque Nationale, and American Treasures exhibitions brought the Library of Congress into an era of major exhibitions that relied primarily on private support but aimed at a wide audience and that produced significant books.

As part of the 1997 reopening of the Jefferson Building after its renovation, specialized exhibit galleries and a Visitors' Center for the general public were established near the building's entrance. Today, three exhibit galleries feature three different Library of Congress collections: the Caroline and Erwin Swann Memorial Exhibit Gallery for Caricature and Cartoon; the George and Ira Gershwin Room, highlighting the Gershwin Archives; and the Bob Hope Gallery of American Entertainment, which presents a sampling from the Library's Bob Hope Collection.

Exhibitions were a highlight of the Library's bicentennial celebration in 2000. Attractive brochures were produced for each of the three major exhibitions illustrating the bicentennial theme of "Libraries, Creativity, Liberty." They were "John Bull and Uncle Sam: Four Centuries of British-American Relations," a joint exhibition with the British Library (libraries); "The Work of Charles and Ray Eames: A Legacy of Invention" (creativity); and "Thomas Jefferson" (liberty). An exhibition of Jefferson's original library was developed as part of a bicentennial project to reconstruct that library.

In 2001, the Library opened a companion exhibit to its highly successful "American Treasures" installation: "World Treasures of the Library of Congress" in the Jefferson Building's second-floor northwest gallery. Establishing a permanent West Coast presence for the first time, in October 2003, the Library opened the new Library of Congress/Ira Gershwin Gallery in the Walt Disney Concert Hall in Los Angeles.

In 1992, the Library began making portions of major exhibitions available on the Internet. By 2004, the Internet had become a key element in the institution's exhibitions program. By late 2004, images and brochure or publication text from more than 50 Library of Congress exhibitions, including three traveling exhibitions, were available on the Library's Web site. Besides bringing images and information to those far away from the Nation's Capital, the widespread availability of the images and information was helping shape decisions about the topics and nature of future exhibits, printed exhibit catalogs, traveling exhibitions, and the exhibition talks presented weekly by Library of Congress subject specialists. (JYC)

Library of Congress Information Bulletin 55 (October 21, 1996): 376–377; 59 (June 2000): 134–135, 141; 60 (June 2001): 142–145.

Sanborn, Herbert J. and Nelson R. Burr. "Exhibition Catalogs," *The American Archivist* 17 (July 1954): 265–271.

FEDERAL LIBRARY AND INFORMATION CENTER COMMITTEE (FLICC)

During the last decade of the nineteenth century, federal agencies' libraries began to be recognized as important resources. In 1896, when the

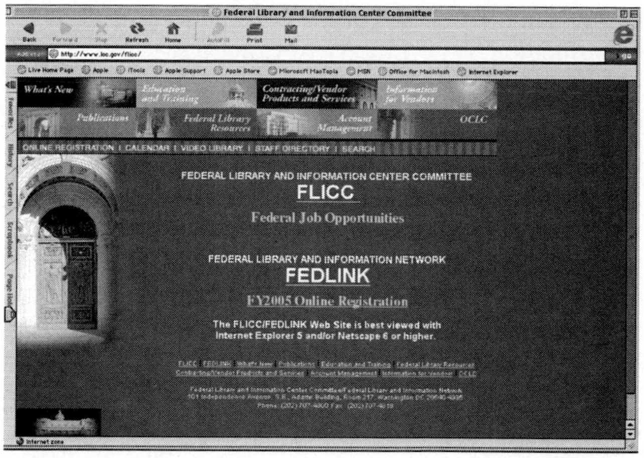

Congressional Joint Committee on the Library held hearings to assess "the condition of the Library of Congress," Melvil Dewey suggested that a board of eminent citizens oversee the federal libraries. But no formal ties existed until Librarian of Congress Herbert Putnam began efforts to foster interlibrary cooperation. His first act was to begin sending Library of Congress cataloging to other federal libraries so that they would have a record of new additions to the Library's collection.

The Library soon began providing printing services for other federal libraries' catalog cards, and the staff compiled a list of the serial publications in other federal library collections. The overlaps in coverage that they discovered caused Putnam to seek legislation allowing federal librarians to donate material to the Library of Congress. He did so in the hope that they would focus their own collections on specialized material suited to their own agencies' needs. But Putnam did not have the authority to consolidate federal libraries and could only try to facilitate their use of the Library of Congress's classification, catalog rules, and cards as a means of fostering cooperation.

In 1935, the American Library Association (ALA) recommended coordination of federal library activities, and two years later, the ALA's Special Committee on Federal Relations suggested forming a Federal Library Council to work with the Bureau of the Budget to coordinate library development with national planning. The ALA's proposals were not adopted, but as urged by the District of Columbia Library Association, librarians began meeting in August 1941 as an "Informal Federal Librarians' Council." Five years later, they recommended that the Library form a federal library council, and the Library of Congress's Planning Committee endorsed the idea in 1947.

For a long time, no action was taken to form the council, but Department of the Interior Librarian Paul Howard was instrumental in keeping the idea alive, and he convinced Librarian L. Quincy Mumford of the need for coordination. Additional support came from a study by former Librarian of Congress Luther Evans, sponsored by the Brookings Institution with funding from the Council on Library Resources, Inc. (CLR). Evans's report, *Federal Departmental Libraries* (1963), included the recommendation that the Bureau of the Budget form a Federal Library Council. A conference of experts convened by Brookings endorsed the idea, and the District of Columbia Library Association held a symposium on the subject early in 1965.

With three-year funding from CLR, the Library of Congress and the Bureau of the Budget established the Federal Library Committee on March 11, 1965, and Paul Howard became the first executive secretary. Librarian Mumford later requested that Congress provide an appropriation for the Committee, thus assuring its continuation.

In 1984, the Committee was renamed the Federal Library and Information Center Committee (FLICC). It provides leadership and assistance to the more than 2,500 libraries and information centers in the federal government. Working from an office at the Library of Congress, an executive director and staff work to improve federal library and information center resources and facilities through professional development, promotion of services, and coordination of resources. FLICC serves as a center for gathering data, planning, and identifying common problems and solutions. It coordinates cooperative services and activities among federal libraries, and makes recommendations on federal library and information center policies, programs, and procedures.

The Committee includes the Librarian of Congress (or a designate) as chair; the directors of the National Agricultural Library, the National Library of Medicine, and the National Library of Education; representatives from cabinet-level executive departments; and from legislative, judicial, and independent agencies. Quarterly meetings are held. However, most activities take place in working groups, where volunteers from federal libraries address topics such as information technology, education, preservation and binding, personnel issues, and cooperative projects.

In 1973, FLICC contracted with the Ohio College Library Center (now the Online Computer Library Center) to experiment with online cataloging in federal libraries. The Federal Library and Information Network (FEDLINK) that grew from that initial contract assists federal libraries' online cataloging, resource sharing, and other electronic activities. Member agencies subsidize a wide array of computer training programs for library personnel, and FEDLINK functions as a central contracting source, procuring commercial services for the federal library establishment as a whole. The Committee's current mission statement defines its task as: "To foster excellence in federal library and information services through interagency cooperation and to provide guidance and direction for the FEDLINK Program."

The Committee issues the *FLICC Newsletter* and sponsors an annual information policy forum and annual symposium on information professionals. Its Web site provides information on its many current activities. (JA)

Cole, John Y. *Capital Libraries and Librarians.* Washington, D.C.: Library of Congress, 1994.

FLICC Newsletter no. 154, Fall 1990.

Library of Congress Information Bulletin 43 (41) October 8, 1984, pp. 329–33; 55 (12) June 24–July 8, 1996, p. 261.

Mumford, L. Quincy. "The Establishment of the Federal Library Committee: A Symposium," *D.C. Libraries* 36 (3), Summer 1965.

FEDERAL RESEARCH DIVISION

The origins of the Federal Research Division (FRD) are found in the Aeronautics Division (1930–1953), which had major collections of aeronautical periodicals, technical reports, and captured German and Japanese aviation documents, and in the need of the United States to develop a defense posture during the Cold War. Recognizing that the exploitation and analysis of unique Library collections had significant national security value throughout the Cold War period, Librarian Luther H. Evans issued General Service Order No. 1358 on March 5, 1948, announcing that a new organization, the Air Research Unit, was being established in the Aeronautics Division to provide "certain research services to the United States Air Force in connection with the collections of the Library and with other materials available to the Library." The Library was to be reimbursed for these services by funds transferred from the Air Force. This unit, headed by John F. Sterns, was located on the third floor of the John Adams Building. On July 22, 1948, the unit was renamed the Air Research Division (ARD) with Sterns as chief. By this time, the division had a staff of 60 organized into the Urban Area Report, Special Report, Technical Analysis, and Research and Abstracting sections.

The first *Annual Report of the Air Studies Division* (FY49) noted several reasons for its establishment and early successes. These included "The Library's own philosophy of serving, on an ever-broadening front, all those who can use or profit by its collections and its skills"; "the support given that philosophy by the operating portions of the Library"; and the "cooperative development of a new program designed to improve the services available [from the Library] to Government." The report also noted the start of an enduring theme of service that has continued throughout the division's history: "Tailor the cloth to the customer's needs."

In addition to its service to the executive branch, the division also had a significant internal Library function—it assumed payroll responsibility for between eight and 13 subject and descriptive catalogers in turn for priority cataloging "in terms of Air Force interests." Another important ARD contribution was its work on the Slavic Union Catalog, which had been transferred from the Union Catalog Division. By October 1949, the staff had eliminated an arrearage of 50,000 cards and had begun to fill a gap of an estimated 10,000 entries in coverage.

The division was enlarged and renamed the Air Studies Division (ASD) on January 17, 1949. Annual expenditures for fiscal 1949 were $621,000, and the staff had increased to 98 by September 30, 1949. A further increase in staffing to more than 130 in the next year plus the separation of functions led on May 1, 1951 to a split into two divisions: the Air Research Division (ARD) and the Air Information Division (which in 1964 became the Aerospace Technology Division).

When Air Force research requirements and funding were reassigned to the Defense Intelligence Agency (DIA), the Air Research Division was renamed the Defense Research Division (DRD) on September 10, 1963. The mission of performing science and technology research continued, but the work broadened as the division began serving all three armed services on a nearly global basis. New work also included "quick response" work to assist DIA's "crisis demands."

Substantial staff growth and the decreasing amount of available space in the Library's Capitol Hill buildings led to the relocation of the DRD and several other divisions to 214 Massachusetts Avenue NE in September 1967. By the end of fiscal 1968, division staff numbered 229 with a $2,883,000 budget. Soon afterward, however, government-wide budget cuts caused a major reduction in force among the Library's reimbursable programs. Although the division survived, its companion division, the Aerospace Technology Division, was abolished. The Library decided to broaden the DRD's mandate, and on April 8, 1970, changed its name to the Federal Research Division (FRD) to reflect the new government-wide client base. During this time, the division staff decreased from 279 at the beginning of fiscal 1970 to 113.

The FRD established new research programs for the National Aeronautics and Space Administration, the National Institutes of Health, the Naval Scientific and Technological Information Center, and the Environmental Protection Agency. In August 1982, the division offices were relocated to the Washington Navy Yard, and new interagency agreements were developed with several Department of Defense organizations in the mid-1980s, among them the implementation of the *Area Handbook/Country Studies Series* for the Department of the Army. Nevertheless in the late 1980s, the Defense Intelligence Agency reduced the division's budget, with a staff reduced to 35, the division began a vigorous marketing effort, expanding its client base from two or three large defense sponsors to a mix of medium-sized and small accounts that included: the departments of Education, Energy, Health and Human

Services, Interior, Justice, Transportation, Treasury, and Veterans Affairs; and agencies such as the Social Security Administration, the Postal Service, the U.S. Institute of Peace, the Inter-American Foundation, the Army Corps of Engineers, the Defense Manpower Data Center, and the National Defense University. Projects were also completed for the U.S. Court of Veterans Appeals and the Administrative Office of the United States Courts. An initiative in fiscal 1991 was the establishment of a new computer-searchable database of formerly classified Department of Defense and Central Intelligence Agency documents concerning American Vietnam War soldiers missing in action. This analytical index was first made available through the Library's Main Reading Room and later on the Internet. Users could obtain texts of the documents through the Photoduplication Service, the Microfilm Reading Room, and the Loan Division.

In fiscal 1994, with funding from Information Technology Services (ITS), the division started digitizing the *Country Studies Series* for inclusion among the Library's Web site offerings. In addition, the Southeast Asia POW/MIA Database was supplemented by a companion effort—known as the U.S. Russia Joint Commission Archival Documents Database—that provided full-text documents from former Soviet archives concerning unaccounted American personnel from World War II onward. At the same time, the division moved briefly to a General Services Administration complex at 1900 Half Street SW, known as the Buzzard Point Annex; it returned to the Capitol Hill complex in December 1996 for the first time since 1967, relocating 45 staff members to the north study rooms on the fifth floor of the Adams Building. Soon after this move, however, revenue shortfalls in two successive years led to additional staff reductions to an all-time low of 14 permanent staff. At the beginning of fiscal 1999, the Cold Regions Bibliography Project, which was funded by the Army Corps of Engineers and the National Science Foundation, was reassigned from the Science, Technology, and Business Division to FRD. By the turn of the century, the division was serving between 30 and 40 federal agency clients and federal contractors annually, including agencies such as the Federal Emergency Management Agency, the Army Materiel Command, the International Trade Administration, the U.S. Census Bureau, the Department of Agriculture, various Library of Congress offices, and agencies involved in the war on terrorism.

On October 1, 2001, the Library of Congress Fiscal Operations Improvement Act of 2000 (Public Law 106–481) took effect. The Act gave FRD, and other Library fee-based activities, the authority to establish a revolving fund in the U.S. Treasury and to deposit federal agency funds without fiscal year limitation. This new authority allowed FRD to perform its research functions and to manage its finances on a more reliable basis. With the more stable funding base, the staff increased to 30 and was augmented, as needed, by expert/consultant contractors and other Library staff working for FRD on an overtime basis. (RW)

FORCE (PETER) COLLECTION

Newspaper editor and printer Peter Force assembled a book, pamphlet, and document collection that became the Library of Congress's first great collection of Americana and incunabula. Force devoted

Historian and archivist Peter Force, whose preeminent collection of Americana, purchased by the Library in 1867, became the foundation of the Library's Americana and incunabula collections. Smithsonian Institution Archives.

many years to the collection of materials from Colonial and Revolutionary America, and he used them for his *American Archives*, planned as a multi-volume set of the important original documents of American history from 1492 to 1789. He conceived the work in 1822 and in 1831 he combined forces with the Clerk of the House of Representatives, Matthew St. Clair Clarke, to present a memorial to Congress. Congress authorized the project on March 2, 1833, and Force completed nine volumes, covering 1774–1776. Because his lengthy project was expensive, in 1855 Secretary of State William L. Marcy abruptly ended it.

Force went heavily into debt to purchase material from dealers over a 45-year period, and the termination of his work was a severe financial as well as psychological blow. It was necessary for him to sell his books, but he wanted the collection kept intact. Even though Force had not sought rare editions or fine bindings, Librarian Ainsworth Rand Spofford unhesitatingly stated that the library was "the largest and best collection of the sources of American history yet brought together in this country." Directors of several libraries and historical societies made offers for the Force collection, but they were unsuccessful. In the meantime, Spofford decided that the Library of Congress should have it, and he began lobbying the Joint Committee on the Library for funds. He also produced an eight-page special report for the Committee on January 25, 1867 that described the collection in detail.

Force's library consisted of 22,529 books and around 37,000 pamphlets, ranging from early voyages, the Puritan divines, Benjamin Franklin's publications, and colonial assembly proceedings to 245 volumes of newspapers printed before 1800, 700 volumes of journals printed during the nineteenth century, 300 maps, and 161 incunabula selected to illustrate the evolution of the art of printing. There were also 48 volumes of historical autographs and 429 volumes of manuscripts, including two of George Washington's journals. "When it is remembered that the Congressional Library is for the use of our national legislature, and represents the nationality of the American people, it is plainly of the utmost consequence to render it complete in all that can illustrate our history and progress as a nation," Spofford concluded, and he prevailed. On March 2, 1867, an act of Congress authorized the $100,000 purchase. Many of the books but none of the collections of pamphlets, maps, or manuscripts were included in the *Catalogue of Books added to the Library of Congress from December 1, 1866 to*

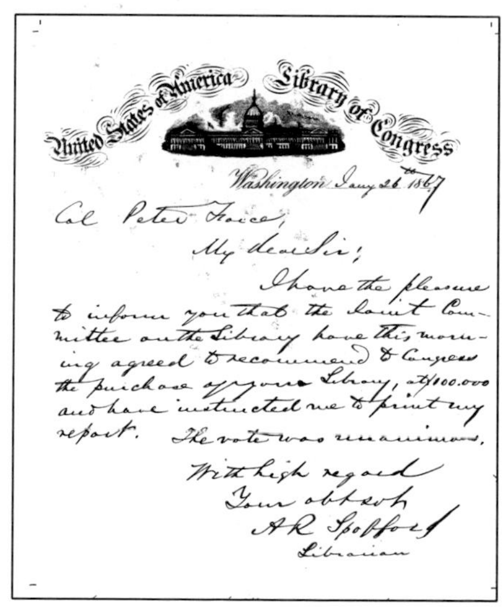

United States of America Library of Congress
Washington Jany 26th 1867
Col Peter Force,
My dear Sir;
I have the pleasure to inform you that the Joint Committee on the Library have this morning agreed to recommend to Congress the purchase of your Library, at $100.000 and have instructed me to print my report. The vote was unanimous.
With high regard
Your obt servt,
A R Spofford
Librarian

An early 1867 letter to Peter Force from Librarian of Congress Spofford, informing the archivist that the Joint Committee on the Library had agreed to recommend to Congress the purchase of his collection for $100,000.
LC/Prints and Photographs Division. USP6 666-0.

December 1, 1867. Although incomplete, this remains the only published catalog of the Force library. (JA)

Spofford, Ainsworth Rand. "The Life and Labors of Peter Force, Mayor of Washington," *Records of the Columbia Historical Society of Washington, D.C.* 2 (1899): 219–235.

Goff, Frederick R. "Peter Force," *Papers of the Bibliographical Society of America* 44 (1950): 1–16 U.S. Library of Congress.

Special Report of the Librarian of Congress to the Joint Committee on the Library Concerning the Historical Library of Peter Force, Esq. (Washington, D.C., January 25, 1867).

GEOGRAPHY AND MAP DIVISION AND COLLECTIONS

Administrative History

The Geography and Map Division began as a separate administrative unit within the Library with the establishment of a Hall of Maps and Charts in the newly constructed Library of Congress Building in 1897. Librarian of Congress John Russell Young appointed Philip Lee Phillips as the first chief. However, the official designation of a cartographic unit was not the beginning of map collecting in the Library, since the Hall of Maps and Charts was established for the express purpose of bringing together and organizing an estimated 27,000 maps and 1,200 atlases that had been stored haphazardly in odd corners of the Capitol Building.

The earliest known photograph of the Library's Hall of Maps and Charts, taken on October 18, 1898 in its original location on the second floor of the north side of the Jefferson Building.
LC/Geography and Map Division.

From 1800 onward, there is scattered evidence that the acquisition of maps periodically received special attention in the congressional library. In fact, the initial order for books from a London book dealer included three maps of the Americas and an atlas. Although this small cartographic collection was destroyed when the Capitol Building was burned by the invading British on August 24, 1814, maps continued to be added to the collection. For example, a major acquisition focus took shape in 1830 when the Joint Committee on the Library recommended the purchase of David H. Burr's 1829 county atlas of New York and the best maps of other states that were not already in the Library. Unfortunately, fire struck again on December 24, 1851, destroying 35,000 books and the extensive collection of maps.

Beginning in the 1850s, the need for a separate map collection within the Library was perceived by three different individuals, who raised the subject in public, but unofficial, forums. The first was Lt. Edward B. Hunt, U.S. Army, who was on detail to the U.S. Coast Survey, when he addressed the 1853 annual meeting of the American Association for the Advancement of Science, held in Cleveland, Ohio. The second proposal was presented two years later by Dr. Johann Georg Kohl at a Smithsonian Institution lecture. Kohl was an eminent German geographer, historian, librarian, Americanist, and world traveler, who had painstakingly hand copied the early maps of America he found in European libraries, museums, and archives. The third time the topic of a centralized map repository was addressed was when Prof. Daniel Coit Gilman of Yale University delivered a January 1871 lecture to the American Geographical Society in New York City.

Although these recommendations were not acted upon, the foundation for a separate map department was laid during the administration of Librarian of Congress Ainsworth Rand Spofford (1864–1897). In 1872, Spofford proposed a "map room of spacious dimensions" in the separate building he was advocating for the Library of Congress. In the meantime, during his tenure, a number of important acquisitions enriched the map collections. They included the Faden Map Collection, consisting of 101 manuscript and printed maps relating to the French and Indian War and the American Revolution; and the Peter Force Collection, which included over 1,200 manuscript and printed maps and plans documenting French involvement in the American Revolution. Spofford was also responsible for the Copyright Act of 1870, which centralized the mandatory deposit of all copyrighted material in the Library of Congress. Among the earliest maps to be submitted under this law were the detailed Sanborn and Parris fire insurance maps of American cities.

There have been nine administrative heads of the Library's map department since it was established as the Hall of Maps and Charts in 1897. The first and longest tenured chief was Philip Lee Phillips (1897–1924). He had the unenviable task of bringing order out of chaos when the Library's cartographic holdings were literally dumped on the second floor of the new building's north curtain. Assisted by a staff of two, he began to organize and describe these materials. The practices and procedures that he developed, especially those related to arrangement, cataloging, and acquisitions, provided the basis for policies that are still followed in the Geography and Map Division. He also established the division's strong publishing tradition. An untiring bibliographer and researcher,

Philip Lee Phillips, the "founding" head of the Library's map department, served from 1897–1924.
LC/Geography and Map Division.

Phillips published or edited 21 major cartobibliographies, guides, and checklists during his long career in the Library.

Phillips was succeeded as chief by Col. Lawrence Martin (1924–1944). With both academic training and professional experience in geography, Martin provided closer contacts with professional organizations such as the Association of American Geographers and the Geological Society of America. Reflecting an interest in boundary studies, his efforts focused on acquiring all editions and variants of three of the most significant maps for determining United States boundaries: John Mitchell's *Map of the British and French Dominions in North America* (1755); John Melish's large wall map, *Map of the United States* (1816); and John Disturnell's *Map of the United States of Mexico* (1846). A major contribution was strengthening the holdings of topographical maps series, both of the United States and foreign areas. During Martin's tenure, the collection increased from 500,000 items to nearly 1.5 million items, broadening the focus from antiquarian materials to current topographic and general materials that were to provide an important resource for the government during World War II.

Beginning in 1944, when Martin joined the Office of Strategic Services, the division underwent a transitional period, with two chiefs serving short tenures. Robert S. Platt, a geographer on leave from the University of Chicago, was appointed acting chief, serving until May 1946, when he returned to his teaching position. Burton W. Adkinson, who was appointed assistant chief in mid-1945, became chief in October 1947. However, he was reassigned to be Director of the Library's Reference Department in November 1949.

From the beginning of the 1950s to the end of the 1990s, there was greater administrative stability, with four individuals serving as chief, three of whom had also served long terms as assistant chief. These individuals were Arch C. Gerlach (chief, 1950–1967), Walter W. Ristow (assistant chief, 1946–1968; chief, 1968–1978), John A. Wolter (assistant chief, 1968–1978; chief, 1978–1991), and Ralph E. Ehrenberg (assistant chief, 1978–1991; chief 1991–1998). Prior to coming to the Library, Gerlach taught geography at the University of Wisconsin; Ristow served as map librarian at the New York Public Library; Wolter taught geography and served as map librarian at the University of Minnesota and the University of Wisconsin, River Falls; and Ehrenberg served as Chief of the Cartographic and Architectural Branch of the National Archives and Records Administration. In 1999, John R. Hébert, formerly a specialist in the Hispanic Division and a reference specialist in the Geography and Map Division, was named chief.

Since the mid-1950s, the cartographic collections has continued to grow steadily, resulting in three relocations, an increase and specialization of staff, and better organization and bibliographic control. In 1955, the division moved from the first floor of the north curtain of the Jefferson Building, where it had been located since 1900, to the ground floor of the Adams Building. In 1969, with the anticipated construction of a third building on Capitol Hill, the division was placed in temporary rental quarters in a warehouse on South Pickett Street in Alexandria, Virginia. It returned to Capitol Hill in 1980 as the first division to occupy the newly completed James Madison Building.

During the post-war years, the staff grew and became more specialized, initially to process the rapidly accumulating backlog of maps produced or captured by the U.S. armed forces during the war. Between 1947 and 2002, the staff grew from 16 serving a collection of approximately 2 million items, to over 50 full-time permanent employees serving a collection of approximately 4.8 million maps, 65,000 atlases, more than 500 globes and globe gores, and an ever increasing number of maps on CD. Until the late 1940s, the staff was not departmentalized, and the professional staff was expected to engage in a variety of functions including acquisitions, cataloging, and public service. With the increase in staff, administrative units were established within the division, focusing on such activities as acquisitions, cataloging, collections maintenance, and reference. In 1965, the division assumed its current name, Geography and Map Division, having been previously known as the Hall of Maps and Charts, the Division of Maps and Charts (1900–1929), and the Map Division (1929–1965).

With the expanding size of the collection, processing and bibliographic control became increasingly critical and sophisticated. While the first published efforts to classify the world's geographic areas into a numerical scheme, which were applied only to atlases, occurred in 1928, major revisions of the *Library of Congress Classification Class G* were published in 1954, with the addition of maps, and again in 1966, 1975, and 2001. A major innovation in the cataloging of cartographic materials began in 1968, when the Council on Library Resources provided a grant to the division for developing computer-assisted procedures. The completion of MARC Map revolutionized map and atlas cataloging, resulting in the comprehensive cataloging of the division's atlas and series holdings and the addition of approximately 10,000 records for cartographic materials each year. Major efforts were also devoted to codifying cataloging procedures and practices, resulting in the publication of the *Preparation Manual for the Conversion of Map Cataloging Records to Machine-Readable Form* (1971) and the *Map Cataloging Manual* (1991). Division staff also took a leading role in the Anglo-American Cataloging Committee for Cartographic Materials, an international endeavor to codify cataloging procedures, which resulted in the publication of *Cartographic Materials: A Manual of Interpretation for AACR2* (1982) and its revision published in 2003.

After a hiatus during Martin's tenure and the 1940s, the division resumed an active publication and exhibition program. Since Phillips published his first cartobibliography in 1896, the division has produced over 140 publications including cartobibliographies, exhibit catalogs and checklists, symposium proceedings, division guides, and cataloging manuals. Complementing the notable bibliographic publications initiated by Phillips, such as *A List of Maps of America in the Library of Congress* (1901), is an extensive list of cartobibliographies compiled during the last half of the twentieth century, focusing on such topics as American atlases, explorers' routes and trails, railroads, landownership maps, city panoramic maps, ward maps, Civil War maps, Revolutionary War era maps, and fire insurance maps. During the past 30 years, the division staff has also curated more than 25 formal exhibits focusing primarily on maps. While most of these exhibits consisted of 30 to 60 items displayed in the corridor gallery outside the current Geography and Map Division Reading Room, five were major Library exhibits consisting of 100 to 400 items. These included "Maps for an Emerging Nation: Commercial Cartography in Nineteenth-century America," displayed from August to October 1977, to coincide with the 7th International Conference on the History of Cartography, co-hosted by the division; "Images of the World: The Atlas Through History," displayed August to October 1984, in association with an international symposium sponsored by the division; "A World of Names," displayed September 1990 to April 1991, as part of the centennial celebration of the U.S. Board on Geographic Names, of which the Library is a member; "City of Magnificent Distances: The Nation's Capital," displayed October 1991 to March 1992, as part of the centennial celebration of the establishment of Washington, D.C.; and "Rivers, Edens, Empires: Lewis and Clark and the Revealing of America," displayed July–November 2003, as part of the bicentennial celebration of the Lewis and Clark expedition.

During the 1990s, the division undertook several initiatives to assist the transition to digital information and to obtain the support of commercial and private resources to enhance the division's programs. The first was to establish a corporate group, the Center for Geographic Information, and to assure the division's participation in the Library's national digitization program. These efforts have resulted in the establishment of a cartographic/geographic information systems (GIS) facility that produces maps for Congress and the development of a state-of-the-art large-format electronic scanning program that provides online access on the Internet to selected division maps and atlases. Starting with 26 digital map images in 1996 and adding approximately 1,000 images per year, by 2004 the online cartographic collection had grown to more than 7,000 images. These electronic images can be accessed through the Library's American Memory, Global Gateway, and Exhibitions online Web sites. The second initiative was the formation of a friends group, The Philip Lee Phillips Society, to further develop, enhance, and promote the division's acquisitions and outreach programs. Members of the society, which consists of approximately 200 map collectors, enthusiasts, and interested others, receive copies of the newly instituted division newsletter and an occasional papers series.
(REE, REG)

Collections

<u>Atlases</u>

The Geography and Map Division holds more than 65,000 atlases, ranging from general world atlases to those covering special subjects or themes. Additional atlases are found in the Rare Book and Special Collections Division. Geographical coverage of the atlas collection is heavily weighted toward the United States (47 percent), the world (19 percent), and Europe (16 percent). Some 20,000 atlases acquired before 1973 are described in Philip Lee Phillips and Clara Egli LeGear's *A List of Geographical Atlases in the Library of Congress, with Bibliographical Notes* (nine volumes, Washington,

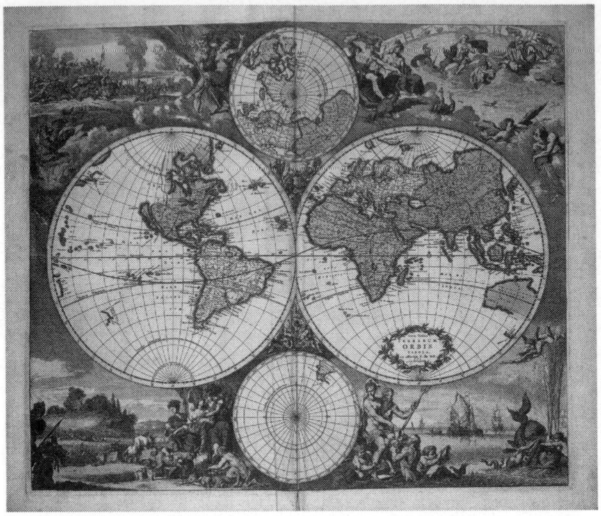

"Terrarum Orbis" (World Map) from La Feuille, Atlas, *early 1700s.* LC/Geography and Map Division.

D.C., 1909–1992) and LeGear's *United States Atlases* (two volumes, Washington, D.C., 1950–1953). These works represent a singular contribution to the fields of cartobibliography and the history of cartography by LeGear, who was associated with the division, first as a staff member and then as an honorary consultant and volunteer, for more than five decades.

The earliest atlases in the Library are general world atlases produced in Italy and southern Germany and based in large part on the work of Claudius Ptolemy, the great Alexandrian scholar who recorded and systematized classical Greek geographical knowledge during the second century. The Library holds 47 of the 56 known copies of Ptolemy's *Geographia*, dating from 1475 to 1883, as well as a bound collection of finely engraved maps assembled by Antonio Lafreri circa 1570, an important work in the emergence of the atlas.

With the publication of Abraham Ortelius's *Theatrum Orbis Terrarum* (*Theater of the World*) in 1570, the center of the European map trade shifted from Rome and Venice to Antwerp, the largest and most active port city in Renaissance Europe, inaugurating the Golden Age of Dutch cartography. The Library's holdings for this period are extensive, including 59 of the 82 known editions of Ortelius's *Theatrum*, published from 1570 to 1724; Gerard Mercator's *Atlas sive cosmographicæ meditationes de fabrica mundi et fabricati figura* (1595) as well as representative copies of subsequent editions published by Jodocus Hondius, who purchased the plates in 1606, by his son Henricus, and by Jan Janssonius; Gerard de Jode's *Speculum Orbis Terrarum* (*Mirror of the World,* Antwerp, 1578), one of 12 copies; Christopher Saxton's *An Atlas of England and Wales* (London, 1579), the first printed atlas of any country; Cornelius Wytfliet's *Descriptionis Ptolemaicae augumentum, siue Occidentis* (Louvain, 1597), the first atlas devoted exclusively to the New World; and Maurice Bouguereau's *Le Théâtre François* (Tours, 1594), one of nine known copies of the first national atlas of France.

Dutch cartography found its fullest expression during the seventeenth and eighteenth centuries with the production of multi-volume world atlases by Pieter van de Aa, Joan Blaeu, Johannes Cóvens and Cornelis Mortier, Abraham Goos, Johannes Janssonius, Reiner and Josua Ottens, Claes Janszoon Visscher, and Frederick de Wit. The division possesses excellent representative copies of all of these publishers, including Joan Blaeu's *Le Grand Atlas* (1667), a monumental 12-volume French edition. Also, the expansion of the European map trade to France, England, and Germany is well-represented, including such treasures as Nicolas Sanson's *Géographie universelle* (Paris, circa 1675), dedicated in manuscript to the Dauphin, son of Louis XIV; John Speed's *A Prospect of the Most Famous Parts of the World* (London, 1627); and Johann Baptist Homann's *Neuer Atlas* (Nuremberg, 1730), which revitalized German cartography.

Among the division's earliest works are those devoted to special subjects, most notably illuminated portolan atlases by Battista Agnese (Venice, 1544); Joan Martines (Messina, circa 1560); and Jean André Brémond (Marseilles, 1670). The Library's collection of printed sea atlases includes Benedetto Bordone's *Libro . . . de tutte l'isole del mondo* (Venice, 1528), the first book of island maps; Lucas Janszoon Waghenaer's *Spieghel der Zeevaerdt* (*Mariners Mirror*, Leyden, 1585), the first printed sea atlas; and a number of works associated with the privately owned Dutch East and West India Companies.

Notable French and British sea atlases include *The Neptune françois* (Amsterdam, Paris, 1693–1700), prepared under official French auspices; Jacques Nicolas Bellin's *Atlas maritime* (Paris, 1751); Sir Robert Dudley's *Dell'arcono del mare* (Florence, 1646–1647), the first maritime atlas to use the Mercator projection; and John Seller's rare *The English Pilot* (London, 1671), which initiated the printed chart trade in England. By the turn of the nineteenth century, most charts were produced as separates but the collection includes one American sea atlas by Edmund March Blunt, the leading American chart maker.

Complementing the sea atlases are atlases prepared to accompany the great voyages of discovery during the late eighteenth century. These include the works of Thomas Jefferys, Jean François de Galaup de La Pérouse, George Vancouver, Mikhail Teben'kov, and Charles Wilkes.

Plans of cities, towns, and private estates have been bound in atlas format since the sixteenth century. The division is fortunate to have copies of Antoine de Pinet's *Plantz, pouirtraitz, et descriptions de plusievrs villes et forteresses, tant del'Europe, Asie, Afrique, que des Indes, & terrees neuues* (Lyon, 1564), the earliest city atlas; George Braun and Franz Hogenberg's *Civitates orbis terrarum*, the first systematic city atlas (1572–1617); and Joan Blaeu's *Theatrvm civitatvm et admirandorvm Italiæ* (Amsterdam, 1663), considered among the finest topographical works ever published.

The Library's holdings of atlases from the nineteenth and twentieth centuries are voluminous (constituting over 90 percent of the atlas collection), reflecting the advent of lithography and the growing market for geographic and scientific information. The division's holdings are particularly strong in general and thematic atlases issued by American, British, and German publishers, including Alexander von Humboldt's *Atlas geographique et physique du Royaume de la Nouvelle-Espagne* (Paris, 1811), which records his observations during a 1799–1804 expedition to South and Central America; Heinrich Berghaus' three-volume *Physikalischer Atlas* (Gotha, 1845–1848), the first atlas to portray the physical geography of the world; Alexander Keith Johnston's *Physical Atlas* (Edinburgh, 1848), an English adaption of the Berghaus atlas; and Francis A. Walker's *Statistical Atlas Based on the Results of the Ninth Census 1870* (Washington, 1874), the first atlas published in the United States to focus exclusively on population.

The division also holds some 1,800 American county landownership atlases, dating from late nineteenth century to the early twentieth century that contain cadastral or landownership maps for the individual townships within a county. In addition, they often include county and township histories, personal and family biographies and portraits, and views of important buildings, residencies, farms, or prized livestock. (REG)

Special Collections

The Geography and Map Division maintains more than 100 individual collections that have been acquired through gifts, government transfers, and purchases or assembled by division specialists according to common themes. The geographic coverage of the division's special collections is worldwide but its primary focus is North and South America, with the strongest holdings in the general subjects of discovery and exploration, military campaigns, and settlement.

In 2003, the Library announced the successful completion of a multi-year campaign to purchase the only known copy of the 1507 world map by Martin Waldseemüller, the first map, printed or manuscript, to depict clearly a separate Western Hemisphere and to use the word "America." It was displayed for the first time in July 2003 in the Library's exhibition, "Rivers, Edens, Empires: Lewis and Clark and the Revealing of America."

Geography and Map Division Chief John R. Hébert closely examines the map of the world by Martin Waldseemüller, 1507. The map, the first to call the New World "America," was purchased in 2003. LC/Geography and Map Division.

Special collections relating to the Great Age of Discovery are described in two publications prepared in conjunction with the Library of Congress's Quincentenary Program: Louis DeVorsey Jr., *Keys to the Encounter: A Library of Congress Resource Guide for the Study of the Age of Discovery* (Washington, D.C., 1992) and John R. Hébert, *1492: An Ongoing Voyage* (Washington, D.C., 1992). Among the most noteworthy collections are 33 portolan charts dating from the mid-fourteenth century to 1770, described in Walter W. Ristow and R. A. Skelton, *Nautical Charts on Vellum in the Library of Congress* (Washington, D.C., 1977); six rare Renaissance maps of America donated by Lessing J. Rosenwald in 1949, described by Clara LeGear in Walter W. Ristow, *A la Carte: Selected Papers on Maps and Atlases* (Washington, D.C., 1972); the Henry Harrisse bequest, including the earliest cartographic depiction of Manhattan Island, described by Richard W. Stephenson in *Terrae Incognitae* (vol. 16, 1984); the Johann Georg Kohl Collection of 474 annotated manuscript facsimile maps relating to the discovery and exploration of the New World from 1500 to 1834, listed by Justin Winsor in *The Kohl Collection* (now in the Library of Congress) *of Maps Relating to America, with an index by Philip Lee Phillips* (Washington, D.C., 1904); and the *Lowery Collection: A Descriptive List of Maps of the Spanish Possessions Within the Present Limits of the United States, 1502–1820* (Washington, D.C., 1912).

For the student of nineteenth century exploration of the American West, the division has particularly rich holdings, highlighted by the Lewis and Clark Collection, transferred in 1925 from the files of the Office of Indian Affairs, U.S. Department of the Interior. The holdings are also particularly rich for military cartography. They include some 2,000 manuscript and printed maps in several collections associated with the French and Indian War and the American Revolution, described by John R. Sellers and Patricia Molen Van Ee in *Maps and Charts of North America and the West Indies, 1750–1789: A Guide to the Collections in the Library of Congress* (Washington, D.C., 1981); the Blair Collection of manuscript maps relating to Andrew Jackson's military campaigns during the War of 1812 and post-war activities with the Creek Indians, presented to the Library in 1903 by the descendants of Francis P. Blair, Jackson's adopted son; and perhaps the finest collection of extant Civil War maps, described in Richard W. Stephenson's *Civil War Maps: An Annotated List of Maps and Atlases in the Library of Congress* (Washington, D.C., 1989), including the collections of Confederate Major Jedediah Hotchkiss, chief topographer of the Army of Northern Virginia, and General Joshua Lawrence Chamberlain, a hero of the battle of Gettysburg.

Of the more than 2,200 Civil War maps in the Library's holdings, probably the most outstanding materials are found in the collection of maps compiled and collected by Jedediah Hotchkiss (1828–1899), a Confederate topographic engineer. Three representative items are illustrated here: two field notebooks and a finished manuscript map.
LC/Geography and Map Division.

Cartographic materials that document the development and growth of urban America are extensive and unequaled. These include the Sanborn Fire Insurance Map Company Collection of some 600,000 maps covering 12,000 American cities, from 1876 to the 1970s, and more than 1,800 panoramic views of

This panoramic map sketched by C.J. Dyer, presents a bird's eye view of Phoenix, Arizona, as it was in 1885.
LC/Geography and Map Division.

American cities and towns dating from 1837 to the 1920s. Each set depicts a wide variety of urban features such as streets, hotels, houses, mills and factories, court houses, schools and colleges, railway depots and round houses, fair grounds, cemeteries, canals, bridges, gas works, ferries, race courses, lumber yards, hospitals, banks, and churches, described in John R. Hébert and Patrick E. Dempsey, *Panoramic Maps of Cities in the United States and Canada* (Washington, D.C., 1984). The entire collection has been mounted on the Internet as part of the Library's American Memory National Digital Library program.

While the Geography and Map Division's special collections focus primarily on North America, coverage is worldwide. Maps and charts of Latin America are well represented by collections assembled by John Barrett, director of the Pan American Union (1894–1920); the Panama Canal Zone Library-Museum; the Portuguese-Spanish Boundary Commission, described in Lawrence Martin and Walter W. Ristow's "South American Historical Maps" in *A la Carte: Selected Papers on Maps and Atlases* (Washington, D.C., 1972); and Ephraim George Squier, an American journalist engaged in diplomatic and archaeological work in Central America and Peru from 1849 to 1865. The manuscript maps pertaining to Latin America are listed in the division's first online cartobibliography, which was prepared by John R. Hébert and Anthony P. Mullan: *The Luso-Hispanic World in Maps: A Selective Guide to Manuscript Maps to 1900 in the Collections of the Library of Congress* (Washington, D.C., 1999).

A prized addition to the division is the Hauslab-Liechtenstein Map Collection, which includes some 8,000 manuscript and printed maps primarily related to Europe with special emphasis on the Austro-Hungarian Empire and its separate provinces. Assembled by Franz Ritter von Hauslab, a member of the Austrian nobility and a distinguished military engineer who fought with Russian forces against Napoleon Bonaparte's armies, the collection reflects his lifelong interest in military affairs, the application of lithography to map printing, the portrayal of terrain on maps, and thematic mapping.

The only collection related specifically to Africa are maps acquired with the records of the American Colonization Society, an organization that assisted black Americans in settling in Liberia during the nineteenth century. For further information on this collection and other cartographic material relating to African Americans, see Debra Newman Ham, *The African-American Mosaic: A Library of Congress Resource Guide for the Study of Black History and Culture* (Washington, D.C., 1993).

The student of East Asia will find the division's collection of maps of China, Korea, and Japan one of the most extensive outside of Asia. The largest collection of rare Chinese maps were acquired through the efforts of Arthur W. Hummel, distinguished sinologist and head of the Library's Orientalia Division (1928–1954), and the generosity of Andrew W. Mellon. Among the cartographic treasures are an annotated wood-block folded atlas of China from the Ming Dynasty entitled "Looking At Distant Places as if They were on the Palm of Your Hand;" a seventeenth century silk scroll depicting in the form of landscape paintings four important frontier regions of the Manchu dynasty, including one illustrating a clash between Russian and Manchurian troops on the Heilungkian or Amur River; and a rare wall map of the world by the Jesuit missionary Ferdinand Verbiest, engraved on eight scrolls in Peking in 1674.

Korean cartography was directly influenced by Chinese cartographic traditions that reached the peninsula during the Koryo dynasty (918–1392). The bulk of the Library's collection of rare Korean maps and atlases were acquired by two eminent educators: the archaeologist Landgon Warner, leader of the first and second China expeditions of the Fogg Museum, Harvard University; and the geographer Shannon McCune, born in Korea of American missionary parents. These collections include both manuscript copies and wood-block impressions, which generally are rarer and more valuable than manuscript copies. The division's Korean atlases range in date from circa 1760 to 1896 and are representative of the traditional hand atlases produced since early in the Yi Dynasty (1392–1910).

While a number of very early rare manuscript and printed Japanese scroll maps date from the early seventeenth century, most of the division's rare maps by Japanese map makers date from the nineteenth century. These include a teaching collection of 11 maps assembled by McCune for a series of lectures on Japanese geography, and a large-scale manuscript map series of Japanese coast lines, major rivers, and roads, and terrain for the period 1800–1822, drawn by Ino Tadataka on 214 sheets, 207 sheets of which are in the division.

Maps of Southeast Asia are found in the Minto Collection, including manuscript maps of Java, Malaccas, and Sumatra drawn by British Army engineers about 1811, just prior to the British invasion and annexation of Java. This collection is described by John A. Wolter in the *The Napoleonic War in the Dutch East Indies: An Essay and Cartobibliography of the Minto Collection*, Phillips Society Occasional Paper Series, no. 2 (Washington, D.C., 1999). Additional maps of Southeast Asia are in the John Barrett Collection.

For the student of the map-making process, including compilation, construction, design, and printing, the division continues to add the archives of several noted cartographers, including William Morris Davis, who developed the block diagram for illustrating geomorphology and laid the foundation for this form of cartography; Richard Edes Harrison, whose innovative and distinctive perspective maps and land form maps provided a generation of World War II readers with a revolutionary image of the earth; Hal Shelton, a cartographic artist who represented three-dimensional relief in natural colors; Marie Tharp and Bruce Heezen, who undertook pioneering cartographic studies of the ocean floor; and John P. Snyder, a cartographic amateur who developed a complex map projection that provides the ability to continuously map the earth's surface using satellite data. The latter papers are described in John W. Hessler, *Projecting Time: John Parr Snyder and the Development of the Space Oblique Mercator Projection*, Phillips Society Occasional Paper Series, no. 5 (Washington, D.C., 2004). The division has also acquired selected cartographic materials from several professional organizations and commercial companies including the American Congress on Surveying and Mapping (ACSM) Map Design Competition and the Hammond World Atlas Corporation archives. (REG)

General Collections

The division maintains three general map collections: the MARC Map Collection; the Titled Map Collection; and the Series Map Collection. The MARC Map Collection consists of more than 170,000 titles (400,000 sheets) that have been acquired since 1967 and have been cataloged in the Geography and Map Division using the MARC Map format. Geographic coverage is worldwide. The collection is classified and filed according to the Library of Congress Classification Class "G" schedule. Online access to the bibliographic records is available.

The Titled Map Collection consists of some one million small-and medium-scale general and special purpose maps that were acquired by the Library prior to 1967. Coverage is worldwide and dates from the sixteenth century to the 1960s. With the exception of the states of Delaware, Maryland, Virginia, and the District of Columbia, the Titled Map Collection is unclassified and uncataloged. It is generally arranged geographically by regions, countries, provinces, and cities. Particularly noteworthy are thousands of photographic reproductions and facsimiles of manuscript maps from European archives and libraries relating to the Age of Discovery and the early settlement of America. Selected categories that have high reference use have been described in bibliographies published by the Geography and Map Division over the years. These include *Charts of Antarctica* (1959); *Aviation Cartography* (1960); *Civil War Maps* (1961, 1989); *Maps Showing Explorers Routes, Trails and Early Roads in the United States* (1962); *Land Ownership Maps* (1967); *Railroad Maps* (1984); *Marketing Maps of the United States* (1958); *Treasure Maps and Charts* (1973); and *Ward Maps of United States Cities* (1974).

The Series Map Collection consists of multiple sheets of maps published at a uniform size and utilizing standardized symbols. This collection includes approximately two million map sheets filed among 12,000 distinct series, and constitutes the largest and most comprehensive collection of medium- and large-scale map series ever assembled. Virtually every major national mapping organization is represented. This collection includes basic map series devoted to aerial navigation, census data, city planning, geology, hydrography, land use, and topography. The geographical coverage dates from the beginning of large-scale topographic mapping and nautical charting in the eighteenth century. Series produced prior to 1900 focus more heavily on Western Europe, reflecting the longer tradition of large-scale mapping in this region. However, series produced during the first half of the twentieth century provide good coverage for Europe, East Asia, and portions of Africa since these regions were heavily mapped by competing armies or colonial powers. And with the end of the Cold War, the division has once again begun acquiring current, large-scale topographic series of Eastern Europe and the former Soviet Union. (REG)

Globes and Terrain Models

Miniature representations of the earth in the form of globes and terrain models have a long history, and are well represented in the collections by approximately 400 terrestrial and celestial globes and armillary spheres, 150 globe gores (the paper segments used in the construction of globes), illustrations of globes, and treatises on globe construction and use. Globes come in a wide variety of sizes and formats, including pocket globes that were usually enclosed in fish skin cases, inflatable globes, dissected globes, and folded items such as R. Buckminister Fuller's "Dymaxion Globe." Among the most valuable globes found in the Division's holdings are Casper Vopell's globe, produced in 1543 by the Cologne mathematician and geographer; a pair of large, rare terrestrial and celestial globes constructed in 1688 and 1693, respectively by the famed Venetian cosmographer and globemaker, Vincenzo Coronelli, each measuring 110 centimeters in diameter and standing nearly two meters high on heavy mahogany stands; and examples by America's first commercial globe maker, James Wilson (1763–1855), who was largely self-taught in geography and the techniques of engraving and globe construction. Ronald Grim provides an enumeration of the division's globe holdings in *News of the International Coronelli Society for the Study of Globes* (2003).

The first American globes. These three globes were produced by James Wilson, America's first commercial globe maker. The larger 13-inch globe is dated 1811; the two smaller 3-inch globes probably were created in the 1820s.
LC/Geography and Map Division.

Another cartographic device used to represent or model the earth is the three-dimensional relief map, which was generally constructed for military or educational purposes from plaster, papier-mâché, sponge rubber or vinyl plastic. The core of the division's terrain model map collection consists of some 2,000 molded plastic relief quadrangle maps produced by the U.S. Army Map Service (AMS) at a horizontal scale of 1:250,000. Although more than two million plastic relief reproductions were produced from the 2,000 master molds from 1951 to the 1970s, the division's collection is the only known complete collection available for study in a public facility.

Terrain models were used extensively by military forces during World War II. Although thousands were produced in portable workshops behind front lines, aboard warships, and in permanent establishments in Pearl Harbor, London, and Washington, D.C., few have survived. The division has several examples, including models of Bangkok, Hong Kong, and two Pacific islands prepared by Navy terrain model units in Pearl Harbor and Washington, D.C., 1944–1945. Constructed with the aid of aerial photographs and reconnaissance reports, these models were cast in rubber for use in amphibious operations.

In addition, the division holds a study collection of 300 commercial terrain models produced in the United States and Europe from the 1890s to the present. Many were constructed for use in school classrooms, for business and industry boardrooms, and for wall decorations in private homes. Models are still an important cartographic format, as demonstrated by a solid plastic tactile relief model in three-sections of Capitol Hill and the Mall in Washington, D.C., made for the use of the blind and sponsored by Congress in 1988. (REG)

Cloth Maps

Despite the large number of cloth maps printed by British, American, and German service units during the war, very few examples of World War II cloth maps are preserved in American libraries. The largest collection of cloth maps was acquired in 1983 from the British Ministry of Defense's Mapping and Charting Establishment through the assistance of Ian Mumford, the British Liaison Officer assigned to the U.S. Defense Mapping Agency. It consists of some 60 escape and evasion maps and air-sea rescue charts produced during World War II under the direction of the British War Office's Secret Intelligence Service, M19 for both the European and Far Eastern theaters. The Service was established on December 23, 1939 to aid in the escape and safe return to the United Kingdom of prisoners of war and men lost at sea. These maps are described by Barbara Bond in *The Map Collector* (no. 22, March 1983). A set of almost 50 U.S. Army Air Force "Bailout" or "Survival Maps," issued by the Army Map Service, primarily for the Far East, are also on file. A third example of World War II cloth maps is a set of bombing target maps of cities and ports in England issued by the German General Staff, June–October, 1941. (REG)

Fire Insurance Maps

Cartographic materials that document the development and growth of urban America are extensive and unique. Through copyright deposits, government transfers, and exchanges, the Geography and Map Division has acquired the nation's foremost collection of city maps issued by fire insurance companies and underwriters. Developed in London in the 1790s and first published in the United States by the Jefferson Insurance Company of New York City in the 1850s, fire insurance maps are large-scale maps designed to provide insurance underwriters with detailed information concerning fire risks for individual residential and commercial properties. The maps depict street patterns, water systems, lot lines, individual buildings, and construction material, and their historical value for researchers is enhanced by updates.

By far, the largest number of fire insurance maps is found in the Sanborn Map Company Collection. The bulk of these maps were deposited for copyright by the company but about one-third were transferred in 1967 from the Commerce Department's Bureau of the Census, which originally purchased the maps. The Census Bureau maps contain paste-on correction sheets to reflect changes such as the construction or demolition of individual buildings. The entire collection is available on 35 mm black-and-white microfilm from Chadwyck-Healy, Inc. and is described in *Fire Insurance Maps in the Library of Congress: Plans of North American Cities and Towns Produced by the Sanborn Map Company* (Washington, D.C., 1981). Other fire insurance holdings include the work of H. Bennett, the Charles E. Goad Company, Ernest Hexamer, the Minnesota and Dakota Fire Underwriters Company, Charles Rascher, and Alphonso Whipple. All of these companies were eventually absorbed by Sanborn, Inc. (REG)

L'Enfant's Plan of Washington, D.C.

Pierre Charles L'Enfant's original plan for the capital of the United States was compiled under the direction of George Washington and extensively annotated by Thomas Jefferson. Submitted to President Washington on August 26, 1791, this event was commemorated by the Library two centuries later, on August 26, 1992, with the publication of a full-color facsimile reproduction and a newly created computer-generated, digitized version of the plan. Entitled *Plan of the City Intended for the Permanent Seat of the Government of the United States*, L'Enfant's plan forms the cornerstone of the Library's unrivaled collection of maps and atlases of the city of Washington, D.C. A study of the plan by Richard W. Stephenson is available under the title *"A Plan Who[l]y New": Pierre Charles L'Enfant's Plan of the City of Washington* (Washington, D.C., 1993). (REE)

Spatial Data and Geographic Information Systems

During the past decade, there has been a revolution in cartography. Beginning with efforts to automate the production of standard map products through various computer technologies, a new industry evolved known as geographic information systems (GIS) that encompasses such processes as automated cartography, remote sensing from earth-orbiting satellites, and sophisticated analysis of geographic information. Now, the emphasis is on varied uses of geographic information in digital formats.

The division acquires digital cartographic products, including such federally sponsored projects as the *Topological Integrated Geographic Encoding Reference (TIGER)/Line Census File*, developed by the Bureau of the Census and maintains a comprehensive collection of raster and vector data supplied regularly by the National Geospatial-Intelligence Agency (NGA). The division uses and supports GIS software developed by Environmental Systems Research Institute, Inc. (ESRI), Redlands, California, which enable users to browse, query, and display thematic spatial data for the United States and the world at county, state, and country levels. ESRI's latest GSI technology enables an enterprise architecture approach that allows multiple users to view and query central data through Internet and intranet access.

Because the development of GIS at an early stage was dominated by American firms, the division seeks to document its evolution. One of the pioneering firms, ERSI has donated the materials exhibited at its Annual Users' Conference starting with materials displayed in 1982. This is probably the single best collection of material to reveal the ways in which GIS has been applied to solving practical needs. Collaboration with the GIS community should speed the Geography and Map Division along the path to the electronic era and also interest producers of GIS products and software in the potential value of the division's historic materials to users of geographic information systems. (REE)

Library of Congress Geography and Maps: An Illustrated Guide. Introduction by Ralph E. Ehrenberg. Washington, D.C.: Library of Congress, 1996.

GIANT BIBLE OF MAINZ

The Giant Bible of Mainz, one of the Library's greatest treasures, is located in an exhibit case opposite the Gutenberg Bible in the Great Hall of the Jefferson Building. Produced between April 4, 1452 and July 9, 1453, it is an illuminated, handmade book of the greatest distinction and the Library's single most important acquisition after the purchase of the Gutenberg Bible in 1930. Moreover, at the same time that a scribe who signed himself *Calamus fidelis*, the "faithful Pen" laboriously produced the Giant Bible's formal Gothic script on vellum, somewhere in the same city Johann Gutenberg was struggling to reproduce that script with a new printing process. Neither knew that the Giant Bible of Mainz would be the last great hand-illuminated Bible.

The Biblia latina *(Giant Bible of Mainz, 1452–1453) was written and illuminated in Mainz, Germany, about the time that Gutenberg began printing his Bible. The Giant Bible, donated to the Library in 1952 on the 500th anniversary of its creation by philanthropist and rare book collector Lessing J. Rosenwald, is on display in the Great Hall of the Library's Jefferson Building.* LC/Rare Book and Special Collections Division.

As its name implies, the Bible is of unusually large size: nearly two feet tall and over 30 inches wide when opened. It is also in excellent condition for its circa 550 years; the pages are unsoiled, although the white pigskin binding bears some scars. Kept in the chapter library of Mainz Cathedral until 1631, the Bible passed into the hands of Gustavus Adolphus of Sweden, who presented the volumes to Duke Bernhard of Saxe-Weimar. Later the Bible appeared in the library of the Dukes of Gotha in eastern Germany, where it stayed until the mid-twentieth century when H.P. Kraus brought the Bible to America and the collector Lessing J. Rosenwald purchased it. The Bible is decorated with magnificent initial letters, and the margins of a few pages include birds, flowers, animals, and human figures. The most notable of these are at the beginnings of the texts of Genesis, Exodus, and Leviticus. The illumination was never finished. Little is known of the illustrations' origins, but scholars believe that three different artists designed them. Only because the calligrapher carefully dated each individual book as he completed it are the exact beginning and ending dates of his work known.

As one of the finest examples of early Renaissance manuscripts, the Bible is especially significant because it represents the cumulated knowledge of the making of manuscript books. Lessing J. Rosenwald gave the Bible to the Library of Congress in 1952, on the 500th anniversary of its creation, as part of the Rosenwald Collection. It is located in an exhibit case opposite the Gutenberg Bible in the Great Hall of the Jefferson Building, to represent the brief coexistence of handmade and printed books. (JA)

Goff, Frederick R. "The Great Bible of Mainz," *The Library of Congress Quarterly Journal of Current Acquisitions* 9 (August 1952), pp. 169–171.

Miner, Dorothy E. *The Giant Bible of Mainz, 500th Anniversary.* Washington, D.C.: Library of Congress, 1952.

Goodrum, Charles A. *Treasures of the Library of Congress.* New York: Harry N. Abrams, Inc., 1991.

GUTENBERG BIBLE

In a replica of a Renaissance bookcase in the Great Hall of the Jefferson Building is a copy of Johann Gutenberg's Bible. Most likely printed in 1455, it was the first book printed on his presses in Mainz, Germany, and the first printed book in the Western world. Gutenberg established his press about 1450 and printed approximately 180 copies of the Bible in 1454–1455, of which 35 are on vellum (fine parchment made from calf skin) and the rest on paper imported from northern Italy. Of these, 49 survived, but only 20 of the 49 are complete copies. The Library of Congress's Gutenberg Bible is probably the finest in existence. It is one of the three perfect copies on vellum—a tough, smooth, soft, white material that ages well. Bound in white pigskin over wooden boards with engraved brass clasps, the three volumes also have the earliest binding of any Gutenberg Bible, dating to the early sixteenth century. The other two perfect copies are in the British Library, London and the Bibliothèque Nationale, Paris.

The Gutenberg Bible has been considered the first product of the invention of moveable type printing in Europe. As the historians of print culture have explained it, Gutenberg made a type mold to

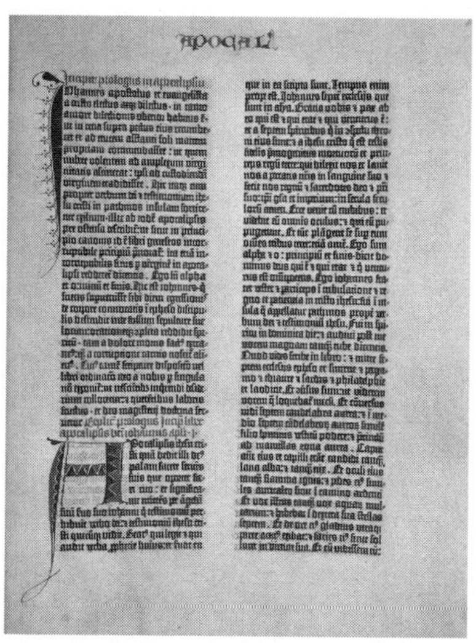

The Gutenberg Bible, the first book published in the Western world, is on display in the Great Hall of the Library's Jefferson Building. The Library's copy is one of three perfect vellum copies.
Photograph: Reid Baker. LC/Rare Book and Special Collections Division.

manufacture individual characters so that compositors could set type line by line by placing the metal characters in composing sticks. The sticks were locked into a form, inked with leather inking balls, and placed on the press. Blank sheets of paper or vellum were placed over the inked type and the printer lowered the platen to produce an inked impression on the page. Gutenberg kept two presses working simultaneously, and he later increased the number to six, but five years' labor was required to complete the approximately 180 Bibles of 643 leaves each.

Very recently, however, Gutenberg's printing method has been questioned. Employing mathematical models to compare the letters in two Bibles and a papal bull printed by Gutenberg, scholars have found that the individual letters differed so much in shape that they could not have come from the same mold. They hypothesized that Gutenberg instead employed a cruder printing method, sand casting. If molds were made of packed sand, they could not be reused and a printer would have to make molds over and over again, thus accounting for the differences in letters. Gutenberg remains the first European to print from separate moveable type, but the suspected use of sand molds makes the early history of printing more complex and more evolutionary than scholars had thought.

Seymour DeRicci, a scholar of early printing, refers to the Bible as "one of the most beautiful books ever printed; the quiet dignity of these 1,200 and odd pages of dark stately type, the deep black ink, the broadness of the margins, the fine texture of the paper, may have been equaled, but they never have been surpassed; and in its very cradle, the printer's art, thanks to the Gutenberg Bible, shines forth indeed as an art much more than a craft." The double-column text features "rubrications," capital letters, headings, and first lines printed in red and blue, all added by hand after printing. Since each column has 42 lines, the Bible is sometimes referred to as "the forty-two line Bible."

Gutenberg's financial backer, Johann Fust, took three copies of the Bible to Paris in 1458, selling one to the king of France, one to the archbishop of Paris, and one to the Benedictine monks of St. Blasius in the Black Forest in Germany. The monks' copper-engraved book plate is still in the Bible. Displaced by the French Revolution and the Napoleonic Wars, the monks resettled several times, finally moving around 1809 to the Monastery of Saint Paul in the valley of the Lavant River in the eastern part of Carinthia, Austria, near Klagenfurth.

A German chemical engineer, Dr. Otto H. F. Vollbehr, made a down payment for the Bible to the hard-pressed monks in 1926. When Congress purchased the Vollbehr collection for the Library of Congress in 1930, Librarian Herbert Putnam completed the negotiations, and Vollbehr finally handed the

Bible to the American minister in Vienna on August 16. At a total price of $370,000 (including interest and export duty), the Gutenberg Bible became the most expensive book ever purchased. Couriers carried it to Cherbourg, where Putnam waited on the *Leviathan* to carry it to the United States. On its arrival in Washington, D.C., the Bible went on permanent display at the Library in October 1930. To ensure that the volumes age similarly, the volume on display is rotated every three to four months and the pages are changed regularly. When not in use, volumes are kept in a vault at a temperature of around 50 degrees Fahrenheit. Opposite the Gutenberg Bible is a case containing the Giant Bible of Mainz, produced in the same city at the same time, but in manuscript rather than print.

Librarian of Congress Putnam examines one of the three volumes of the Gutenberg Bible. It came to the Library as part of the Vollbehr collection of incunabula, which was purchased for the Library by Congress in 1930 for $1.5 million.
LC/Prints and Photographs Division.

With the exception of a brief period of removal to Fort Knox for safekeeping during World War II, the Gutenberg Bible has been at the Library ever since 1930. On its 500th anniversary in 1954, an exhibition of significant Bibles was mounted. The Gutenberg Bible is now considered priceless. The Library's copy has been digitized by the electronic publishing firm Octavo on two compact discs. (JA)

Goodrum, Charles A. *Treasures of the Library of Congress*. New York: Harry N. Abrams, Inc., 1991.

U.S. Library of Congress. *Loan Exhibition of Incunabula from the Vollbehr Collection, Books Printed Before 1501 A.D., and Manuscripts of the Fifteenth Century Selected From the Private Library of Dr. Otto H. F. Vollbehr, Berlin, Germany; Spring, 1928.* Washington, D.C.: Government Printing Office, 1928.

"Has History Been too Generous to Gutenberg?" *New York Times*, January 27, 2001.

"The Hand of Technology Brings Gutenberg Bible to the Masses," *Washington Post*, July 12, 2003.

HISPANIC DIVISION AND COLLECTIONS

Administrative History

The Hispanic Division played a preeminent role in the emergence and development of the field of Luso-Hispanic studies in the United States, and its prominence continues today. The division began in 1936 when philanthropist Archer M. Huntington gave the Library of Congress funds "to equip and maintain" a reading room to be known as the Hispanic Society Room of Spanish and Portuguese Arts and Letters. On July 1, 1939, the Library established the Hispanic Foundation (now the Hispanic Division) as a "center for the pursuit of studies in Spanish, Portuguese, and Hispanic American culture," and charged it with creating "an unsurpassed collection of published material pertaining to Spain, Portugal, and the countries of Latin America." The Rockefeller Foundation also provided various grants to support the Hispanic Foundation, which first welcomed the public on Columbus Day, October 12, 1939. Dedicated by newly appointed Librarian of Congress Archibald MacLeish, it was the Library's first separate area studies reading room. It is located on the second floor of the Thomas Jefferson Building and the only location ever occupied by the division.

For the new Hispanic Society Room, architect Paul Philippe Cret redesigned space in the Thomas Jefferson Building in the style of the Spanish Renaissance. In 1940, a mural depicting the coat of arms of Christopher Columbus was added to the room's south wall. The first example of a mural on steel in any building, it was funded by executives from the Allegheny Ludlum Steel Corp., who also commissioned the artist for the project, Buell Mullen of Chicago.

In 1940, Librarian of Congress Archibald MacLeish, with funds given by the Brazilian government and by Nelson Rockefeller, Coordinator of Inter-American Affairs, commissioned the distinguished Brazilian painter Cândido Portinari to execute murals on the four walls of the vestibule to the Hispanic room. The scenes, completed in 1941, depict Iberian pioneers in Latin America and the conquest of the continent.

Lewis U. Hanke served as director of the Hispanic Foundation from 1939 to 1951, but in 1944 he was also named Chair of Latin American Studies, and Acting Assistant Director for Public Reference in the Reference Department. He brought to the Library the *Handbook of Latin American Studies*, a pioneering scholarly, annotated bibliography he had started at Harvard University in 1935 (at the time published by Harvard University Press), and made the *Handbook* the reference and bibliographic center of

"Teaching of the Indians" is one of four murals by Candido Portinari that decorate the Hispanic Division's reading room in the Jefferson Building. LC/Publishing Office.

the Hispanic reading room. As an integral part of the Hispanic Foundation, the *Handbook* has been sponsored by the Joint Committee on Latin American Studies of the National Research Council, the American Council of Learned Societies, and the Social Science Research Council. Each annual volume contains more than 5,000 annotated entries for selected monographs and scholarly articles in the humanities and social sciences, representing the active collaboration of 130 scholars and specialists worldwide. The *Handbook* was automated in 1988. In 1995, with an initial grant from the Andrew W. Mellon Foundation and the in-kind assistance of the Fundación MAPFRE América in Spain, the first 50 volumes (1935–1994) of the *Handbook* were digitized and published in a CD-ROM. Three years later, Hanke's heirs provided the funds to mount the *Handbook* CD-ROM on the World Wide Web, where it can be accessed in English, Spanish, and Portuguese.

In 1942, the Library named Chilean poet and critic Francisco Aguilera the first full-time Specialist in Hispanic Culture. In 1943, Aguilera created the Archive of Hispanic Literature on Tape, a repository of recorded literature. The next year, the Hispanic Foundation became part of the Public Reference Service in the Library's reorganized Reference Department.

Howard F. Cline served as director of the Hispanic Foundation from 1952 to 1971. Like Hanke, Cline was an innovative scholar. He increased social science coverage in the *Handbook*. Cline also initiated closer ties with professional associations in the rapidly growing fields of Luso-Hispanic studies. With a group of scholars, he founded within the Hispanic

Lewis U. Hanke, Director of the Hispanic Foundation from 1939 to 1951, photographed in 1951 in the Hispanic Society Room—the Library's first separate area studies reading room.
LC/Prints and Photographs Division. LC-USP6-1878-C.

Foundation the now thriving Latin American Studies Association (LASA), which today has more than 5,000 members. Cline was instrumental in reorganizing the moribund Conference on Latin American History (CLAH), affiliating it with the American Historical Association. He was also one of the founders of the Spanish and Portuguese Historical Studies Association (SSPHS). In 1955, Cline and Aguilera were founding members of the Seminar on the Acquisition of Latin American Library Materials (SALALM), a pioneering organization of librarians and area specialists and a vital network for acquiring area studies material. During Cline's tenure, the Hispanic Foundation published numerous works cooperatively with professional associations and university presses, such as the multi-volume *Handbook of Middle American Indians* (with the University of Texas Press, 1964–1986). Cline assisted in establishing the Library's Field Office in Rio de Janeiro and Assistant Chief Earl J. Pariseau became its first Field Director (1966–1968). The Rio Office strengthened immensely the Library's Brazilian collection, which today is the most complete in the world.

Librarian of Congress L. Quincy Mumford changed the name of the Hispanic Foundation to Latin American, Portuguese, and Spanish Division in 1972. The next year Mary Ellis Kahler, a historian of Brazil and Portugal, as well as a librarian, became chief. Kahler greatly improved the division's ties to the various library communities and was an active member of SALALM. Under her leadership, the division published major guides to Hispanic manuscript collections, such as the Mexican Harkness and Kraus collections, to the Portuguese manuscripts, and on materials relating to Bartolomé de las Casas. She strengthened the division's interest in Brazil and Portugal and became field director of the Rio Office (1978–1983). Until 1988, Kahler was the Hispanic Division's first Luso-Brazilian.

Director of Latin American Studies at the University of Florida William E. Carter was named chief in 1978 and served until his death in 1983. He brought an anthropologist's insight and perspective to the division, especially by improving the collections dealing with the indigenous peoples and cultures of Latin America and the Caribbean. He also was instrumental in changing the division's name back to Hispanic Division, as intended by the original founder Archer M. Huntington, and reinvigorated the division's ties with the Luso-Hispanic and Caribbean embassies and with international organizations—especially non-governmental organizations. Keenly interested in more efficient acquisitions procedures, Carter was the principal promoter of the establishment of the Hispanic Acquisitions Section in the former Exchange and Gift Division.

Assistant Chief John R. Hébert served as acting chief from mid-1983 to mid-1984, when literary critic Sara Castro Klarén was named chief. She served until the end of 1986, and during her tenure the division mounted a major exhibit on Miguel de Cervantes. Hébert again became acting chief until August 1988, when political scientist Cole Blasier came to be chief from the University of Pittsburgh, where he had been director of the Center for Latin American Studies. One of the founding fathers and a former president of LASA and an expert on Soviet-Latin American relations and foreign policy, Blasier brought to the division a new focus on global studies, and he developed the division's links to the MAPFRE Foundation in Madrid, which carried out the retrospective digitization of the first 55 volumes of the *Handbook*. Blasier maintained the position of Luso-Brazilian Specialist and created the position of Mexican Specialist. From 1989 to 1993, John Hébert coordinated the Library's Quincentenary Program, which included the exhibit "An Ongoing Voyage" and several publications; one was the first volume in the Library's new series of resource guides, *Keys to the Encounter: A Library of Congress Resource Guide for the Study of the Age of Discovery*, by Louis De Vorsey Jr. (1992).

After Blasier retired in January 1993, historian Georgette M. Dorn, who had been the division's Head of Reference and Specialist in Hispanic Culture, became chief in 1994. Dorn expanded the division's academic intern program, secured grants for bringing Iberia and Latin American library interns to the division, and raised funds for endowed fellowships for recent college graduates and graduate students. The division published *Hispanic Americans in Congress, 1822–1995* (1995), which is available on the division's Web site. In 1996, the division created English and Spanish Web pages for both the reading room and the

Handbook, and helped create pioneering Web sites about Puerto Rico, "The Portuguese in the United States," and "Spain in the United States" for the Library's American Memory project. In 1998, the division mounted on its Web page "The World of 1898: The Spanish-American War." In 2001, the division began working on a collaborative digitization project with the National Library of Spain entitled "The United States, Spain, and the American Frontier: Historias Paraleleas," which illustrated the history of the Anglo-American frontier from 1500 to the 1820s. In 2004, the division and Area Studies inaugurated the first phase of "The United States and Brazil: Expanding Frontiers, Comparing Cultures," a collaborative digitization project with the National Library of Brazil, which compares from the late eighteenth to the early nineteenth centuries.

The Hispanic Division's staff provides electronic and traditional reference service, prepares exhibits, such as the 1997 show of maps and photographs of the "Portuguese Communities in the United States," and organizes public programs such as symposia, lectures, and literary readings.

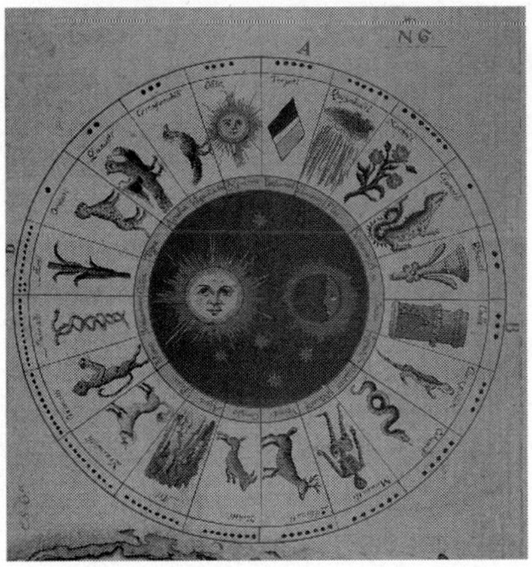

Calendar wheel, no. 6. Drawing, watercolor, and ink from Mariano Fernandez Echeverria y Veytia. Historia del origen de las gentes que poblaron la America septentrional. Early nineteenth century facsimile. Mexico. The sacred calendar ruled the life of each Mexica (Aztec). LC/Rare Book and Special Collections Division.

The Luso-Hispanic and Caribbean Collections

While addressing the annual meeting of the American Political Association in 1907, Hiram Bingham singled out the Library of Congress as one of the most important Latin American collections because the Library's interest in the Luso-Hispanic and Caribbean world dates to the beginning of the institution in 1800. Aided by congressional appropriations, exchange arrangements, and private donations, these have become the most extensive collections of the kind worldwide. The term "Hispanic" is used here as an all-inclusive term, from the broader Latin meaning of "Hispanic," encompassing the entire Iberian Peninsula and areas once under Spanish or Portuguese jurisdiction.

The Hispanic and Caribbean collections cover comprehensively the history, society, and cultures of the Iberian Peninsula, the countries of Latin America, and the Caribbean, their indigenous cultures, and other areas where Spanish and Portuguese influence have been significant, such as the southwestern and western United States, the Philippines and Guam until 1898, Macao, and parts of Africa. The collections consist of 2.5 million books and periodicals and approximately 11.5 million items such as maps, manuscripts, voice recordings, prints, photographs, motion pictures, and sheet music. Hispanic materials in various formats can be found in both the general and special collections of the Library.

Although there were a few books and maps about the Caribbean in the first congressional Library housed in the Capitol in the early 1800s, the fascinating history of the growth and development of the Hispanic and Caribbean collections really began with Thomas Jefferson, who recognized a need for a special relationship among the American republics and with the trans-Atlantic world. His private collection, purchased by the Library in 1815, included many items from and about the Hispanic and Caribbean areas. He owned, for example, most of the relevant works concerning the Iberian discovery and conquest of the Americas such as Francisco López de Gómara's *Historia de México* (Anvers, 1554), Bartolomé de las Casas' *Tratado comprobatorio del Imperio soberano universal que los Reyes de Castilla tienen sobre las Indias* (Seville, 1553), Agustín Zárate's *Histoire de la découverte et de la conquête de Pêrou* (Seville, 1781), and Fernando de Pizarro y Orellana's *Varones ilustres del Nuevo Mundo* (Madrid, 1639). Also, he had a facsimile copy of Cruz Cano y Olmedilla's famous 1775 map of South America and Spanish and other dictionaries and literary works such as an edition of *Don Quijote* by the Spanish Royal Academy of the Language. Other books by Miguel de Cervantes that came to the Library with the Jefferson collection include *Los seis libros de Galatea* (1784), *Novelas ejemplares* (1783), and *Los trabajos de Persiles y Segismunda* (1781).

After the Mexican-American War (1846–1848), when the United States began its rapid continental expansion, there was a practical need to acquire more information about Latin America, especially cartographic materials and commercial gazetteers of Mexico and Central America. In the wake of the war, General Winfield Scott transferred to the Library valuable manuscripts of colonial

Mexico. Other military leaders and explorers sent to the Library many maps, legal materials, land records, and other documents related to both the war and the territorial expansion. Unfortunately, all Jefferson's books about the Hispanic world were destroyed in the fire in the Library of Congress in the Capitol Building on December 24, 1851.

In 1866, the Smithsonian Institution transferred to the Library of Congress its collection of books and periodicals, greatly expanding the Hispanic collections. Among the books was Domingo Fausto de Sarmiento's *Recuerdos de provincia* (1855) and his *Civilización y barbarie* (1853). That same year, Mary Mann gave the Library *Life in the Argentina Republic in the Days of the Tyrants* (1858), her translation of a seminal work on Argentina. With the Smithsonian collection too, came materials on the flora, fauna, and natural history of Latin America, as well as reports from academies of sciences and humanities from the Hispanic world.

The Spanish-American War of 1898 further attracted the Library's attention to Hispanic culture at the same time that the opening of the Jefferson Building made expansion of the foreign collections possible. Thus, at the turn of century the Library received important transfers, among these the papers of General Leonard Wood and other personalities who participated in the war and the subsequent U.S. expansion into Cuba, Puerto Rico, the Philippines, and Guam.

Knowledge of the Library's growing collections began to attract important gifts, such as the papers of pioneer American anthropologist Ephraim George Squier, which related to the ancient history of the Americas, mainly Peru and Mexico. The Henry Harisse bequest of 1915 added a valuable collection centering on Columbus. A major manuscript collection given to the Library by Edward Stephen Harkness in 1928 and 1929 encompassed the first 200 years of Spanish rule in Mexico and Peru. Included in it are many items related to the careers of Cortés, Pizarro, and their contemporaries, from decrees conferring honors, signed by Charles V, to documents concerning states in Mexico and Spain and tailor's bills for Cortés. The Harkness Collection features the *Huexotzinco Codex*, formerly known as the *Codex Monteleone*, an original Mexican codex produced 10 years after the Spanish conquest.

To organize the growing Hispanic collection, the Library hired Cecil K. Jones in 1915 as Hispanic bibliographer. He entered into many exchange agreements with foreign governments and institutions, and once testified before Congress about the importance of collecting official publications, gazettes, and legal materials, as well as "works on history and literature in order to understand better the Luso-Hispanic nations." Librarian of Congress Herbert Putnam agreed that the Library "is in its position a library of record for the Hispanic American republic." At that time, the Library began collecting major Hispanic journals such as *Bimestre cubano*, *Cojo ilustrado*, *Revista de occidente*, *Revista de dos mundos*, *Caras y caretas*, and major newspapers such as *La Nación and La Prensa* (Argentina), *Diario de la Marina* (Cuba), and *El Mercurio* (Chile). Also, beginning in the late 1920s, the Library began copying manuscripts in the General Archive of the Indies in Seville.

In 1927, Archer M. Huntington, Hispanic poet, and president of the Hispanic Society of America, established the Huntington Endowment Fund of $100,000 as the first of several important donations intended to build the most comprehensive Hispanic and Caribbean collections. To continue supporting both acquisitions and services, Mr. Huntington provided a second endowment of $50,000 for an ongoing consultantship in Spanish and Portuguese literature (which in 1942 became the position of Specialist in Hispanic Culture). Augustinian friar David Rubio served as consultant of Hispanic culture from 1930 until 1942, and he and Jones developed basic collection development policies, later refined by Lewis Hanke and Howard F. Cline, that are followed to this day. During his tenure, Rubio acquired more than 100,000 volumes, making special efforts to develop the non-book collections, such as maps, manuscripts, and recordings. An example of these efforts was the work of John Lomax, who enriched the Archive of American Folk Song with folk recordings from the American Southwest, the Caribbean, and other areas. The archive also housed early recordings of indigenous people in the Helen H. Roberts Collection of ethnomusicological field recordings, and Helen Yurchenco's songs and stories by Sephardic Jews, and the Brazilian Literatura de Cordel collection.

The principal role of the Hispanic Division continues to be the development of the Hispanic collections, the facilitation of their use by Congress, other federal agencies, and scholars, and the interpretation of these collections. Editors of the *Handbook of Latin American Studies* have helped the Library acquire a broad array of materials. Thus, the general collection of books and periodicals dealing with the various Hispanic and Caribbean areas is now the most extensive in the world. Important journals such as *Sur, Revista Centroamericana*, *Martín Fierro*, and many others can be consulted in connection with the original works of writers, scholars, and intellectuals. The general collection not only houses materials published in the respective countries, dependent territories, or earlier colonies, but also works published about the Hispanic and Caribbean countries in other countries and in other languages. The Hispanic Division also

Reseacher Pablo Gonzalez looking for information in the Hispanic Division's reference collection.
Photograph: Carol Highsmith.

endeavors to acquire publications of Hispanic and Latin American centers from around the world.

The Spanish Civil War brought many Spanish intellectuals to the U.S. academic world. The Library has an important collection of books, periodicals, some manuscripts, and a significant number of posters relating to the Spanish Civil War. It was a prelude to World War II, when collecting materials worldwide became a recognized priority. Most Latin American countries were staunch allies of the United States during World War II, and receipts of books and periodicals from Latin America, especially those dealing with politics, became more urgent. During the Cold War, however, in various Latin American and Caribbean countries the influence of democracy encountered the appeal of Communism. When Fidel Castro firmly placed Cuba within the Soviet Union's sphere of influence, collecting all relevant materials for the use of the Congress and the federal government as well as for the scholarly community became even more urgent, and it is a matter of some pride to the division that exchanges with Cuba were never interrupted.

The establishment of the Library's Field Office in Rio de Janeiro, at the suggestion of Howard F. Cline, made the Brazilian collections the most extensive and complete worldwide. The collection of Hispanic and Caribbean newspapers published in the nineteenth and twentieth centuries is also significant, although for many early titles the sets are not complete. Early imprints include *El Monitor Araucano* and *Aurora* (1813–1814), published during the dawn of Chilean independence; *Gaceta de la Habana*, and the *Gazeta de México*. Eight current newspapers are received from Spain and six Portuguese newspapers represent Iberia. Currently, the Library subscribes to two or more newspapers from each of the Hispanic and Caribbean countries, and efforts are made to collect important regional newspapers from the larger countries. For example, from Brazil the Library receives newspapers from Belo Horizonte, Brasília, Curitiba, Porto Alegre, Recife, Rio de Janeiro, and Sao Paulo. To access a wider collection of periodical and government documents, the Hispanic Division is actively cooperating with the Latin Americanist Research Resources Project, a distributed network under the Association of Research Libraries, which was begun in 1994.

The Hispanic holdings contain unique resources in the fields of law and government because the Library has long pursued a policy of collecting legal codes, laws, statutes, official gazettes, ministry reports, parliamentary debates, and all other significant official publications of national agencies as well as selected provincial or state imprints from most of the Hispanic and Caribbean countries. Legal materials can be found in the Law Library, which also houses printed editions of treaties. The Library's collection of laws and official documents from the Hispanic and Caribbean countries is the strongest in the world. To enhance use of Hispanic government publications, the Hispanic Division, with the assistance of the Association of Research Libraries, has been working on the Latin American Microfilming Program (LAMP) for more than 20 years, microfilming nineteenth and twentieth-century Latin American memorias or ministerial reports and documents.

The Library's special collections contain a wealth of materials relating to the Hispanic and Caribbean areas. In the Rare Book and Special Collections Division, there are editions in many languages of *OS Lusiadas* by the Portuguese epic poet Luiz de Camoes. The Library has over 1,000 editions of works by Miguel de Cervantes, listed in *Works by Miguel de Cervantes y Saavedra in the Library of Congress*, compiled by Reynaldo Aguirre and edited by Georgette M. Dorn (1994). Also there is a compilation of documents known as Christopher Columbus's "Book of Privileges" (1492–1494), his *Nova Typis Transacta Navigatio* (1621) and the *Trevisan Codex*, a rare manuscript from the John Boyd Thacher collection and a report by a Venetian agent in Spain on Spanish explorations in America and the arrival of Portugal in Brazil and India. Also included are the *Papal Bull Inter cetera of May 1493*, defining the line of demarcation of future Spanish and Portuguese explorations, a devotional book entitled *Adoration of the Magi. Juan de Torquemada Meditationes seu Contemplationes devotissimae* (1479), an early depiction of Brazil in *Come ce peuple couppe et porte le Brésil* (1571). The Rare Book Room also houses one of the earliest books known to have been printed in Mexico City, a Christian Doctrine for the first bishop of Mexico, Fray Juan de Zumárraga, printed in 1544.

More contemporary treasures among rare books include *Picasso, con pinturas inéditas de la cueva de Nerja. Vicente Aleixandre* (1961) in which Spanish writer and Nobel laureate Vicente Aleixandre and Pablo Picasso collaborated to provide reflections on the paleolithic period cave drawings found near Málaga in Spain; Pablo Neruda's *España en el corazón* (1938) published on the Spanish Civil War battlefront and his *Bestiario* (1965) illustrated by woodcuts by Antonio Fransconi; Jorge Luis Borges' illustrated *Siete poemas sajones* (1974); and Spanish painter and sculptor Joao Miró's *Les essencies de la tierra* (1968).

Holdings in the Prints and Photographs collection include the Archive of Hispanic Culture assembled with a grant from the Rockefeller Foundation (1944) by noted Portuguese art historian Robert C. Smith, then assistant director of the Hispanic Foundation (1941–1944). The Archive is a photographic reference collection encompassing Latin American architecture, sculpture, painting, textiles, ceramics, and jewelry. Prints and Photographs also includes posters, prints, and the Historic American Buildings Survey collection, which contains a wealth of materials on Puerto Rico and Hispanic areas of the western and southwestern United States.

Notable Hispanic holdings in the Manuscript Division are the Edward Stephen Harkness Collections of manuscripts of Peru and Mexico, the Hans P. Kraus Collection of Spanish manuscripts, the Henry Monday collection of Mexican colonial materials, and a collection of Portuguese manuscripts. Important Cuban manuscripts are in the Delmonte Collection, the José Ignacio Rodriguez Collection, and Papeles de Cuba.

The Music Division has most of the important books on music from the major Hispanic countries. The Hispanic Division's close cooperation with the Library's Music Division and the Music Department of the Organization of American States has assured an impressive Latin American collection. The Music Division houses a significant recent acquisition of Uruguayan music and the Ayestarán Collection on materials of contemporary composers, which includes valuable holographs. In addition to published music from Cuba, the Music Division has letters from several Cuban composers and musicians, and contains extensive collections of musical recordings from Spain, Portugal, Latin America, and the Caribbean.

The Archive of Hispanic Literature on Tape

The Hispanic Division began to collect audio recordings of Hispanic writers in 1942 when Librarian of Congress Archibald MacLeish asked Uruguayan poet Emilio Oribe to record his poems. The Archive of Hispanic Literature on Tape was established in 1943 with assistance from the Rockefeller Foundation. Criteria for inclusion included recognition of a writer by critics, academics, award committees, and the public. Specialist in Hispanic Culture and Archive Curator Francisco Aguilera recorded noted poets such as Juan Ramón Jiménez, Gabriela Mistral, and Vicente Aleixandre (all became Nobel laureates), as well as Pedro Salinas, Jorge Guillén, and Pablo and Winett de Rokha during the Archive's first decade. Portuguese, Brazilian, Catalan, and Haitian French poets were added after 1951 and in 1958 Aguilera decided to also record prose writers, devising a well-integrated collection of noteworthy Luso-Hispanic oral literature. Today, this multi-lingual resource features 640 writers and noted intellectuals (among them, Daniel Cosío Villegas and Fernando Belaune Terry).

The collection was enriched with recordings by 140 writers as Aguilera made three trips to Latin America and Iberia during 1958–1961 under the auspices of the Rockefeller Foundation, Aguilera arranging tape recordings at radio stations or at U.S. Embassy or consular facilities in cities he visited. He recorded noted authors such as Jorge Luis Borges, Nicolás Guillén, Andrés Alencastre (who read poems in Quechua), Agustín Yáñez, Juan Rulfo, and Miguel Angel Asturias, who later won a Nobel Prize in Literature. And, at the Library, Aguilera and Georgette Dorn recorded Octavio Paz, Camilo José Cela, Pablo Neruda, and Gabriel García Márquez—all four of who later became Nobel laureates.

Aguilera and Georgette Dorn published *The Archive of Hispanic Literature on Tape: A Descriptive Guide* in 1974. Dorn had arranged with the Library of Congress Office in Rio de Janeiro and the United States Information Agency (USIA) to record prominent Brazilian writers for the Archive. More than 70 of the 82 Brazilian writers in the archive were recorded in Rio, among them the world famous novelists Jorge Amado and Nélida Piñon (the latter recorded on videotape). USIA offices in Barcelona, Madrid, Lisbon, Mexico City, Buenos Aires, Montevideo, and Port-au-Prince also recorded writers for the archive. At the Library, Dorn continued recording readings or interviews with most of the major writers of the "Boom in Latin American Literature" such as José Donoso, Carlos Fuentes, and Mario Vargas Llosa, who were fellows of the Woodrow Wilson Center for Scholars, as well as Julio Cortázar, Guillermo Cabrera Infante, Homero Aridjis, Luis Rafael Sánchez, Rosario Ferré, Pablo Antonio Cuadra, Juan Gustavo Cobo Borda, Antonio Benítez Rojo, Heberto Padilla, Angel Cuadra, and Leon Damas. Dorn also recorded writers in Ottawa, Puerto Rico, Barcelona, and Paris. U.S. Latino writers and some authors from the French

Caribbean were added in the late 1970s. Sabine Ulibarrí, Rudolfo Anaya, Denise Chávez, Luis Leal, and Carlos Morton became the first Latino writers added to the archive. Recent recordings include Ana Castillo, Isabel Allende, Katherine Vaz, Carlos Monsivais, José María Merino, and Bernardo Atxaga (the latter in Basque and Spanish). (GMD)

Library of Congress Hispanic and Portuguese Collections: An Illustrated Guide. Introduction by John R. Hébert. Washington, D.C.: Library of Congress, 1996.

Library of Congress Information Bulletin 58 (October 1999): 235–237, 239.

The Library of Congress looks to Thomas Jefferson, a lover of books and a man of wide intellectual interests, as one of its principal founders. As president of the United States from 1801 to 1809, Jefferson took a keen interest in the Library. On January 26, 1802, he approved the first law defining the role and functions of the new institution. Throughout his presidency, he personally recommended books for its collections. He also appointed the first two Librarians of Congress: John J. Beckley (1802) and Patrick Magruder (1807).

Thomas Jefferson, from the portrait by Rembrant Peale. The Jeffersonian concept of universality is the rationale for the comprehensive collecting policies of today's Library of Congress. His belief in the power of knowledge and the direct link between knowledge and democracy has helped shape the Library's philosophy of sharing its collections and services as widely as possible.
LC/Prints and Photographs Division. LC-USZ62-30743.

On August 24, 1814, the British army invaded the city of Washington and burned the Capitol, including the 3,000-volume Library of Congress. By then retired to Monticello, on September 21, in a letter to the Joint Library Committee, Jefferson offered to sell to Congress his personal library, the largest and finest private library in the country, to "recommence" its library. His key argument is one still used by the Library to justify the wide scope of its collections: "I do not know that (my collection) contains any branch of science which Congress would wish to exclude from their collection; there is, in fact, no subject to which a member of Congress may not have occasion to refer." The purchase of Jefferson's 6,487 volumes for $23,950 was approved in March 1815. On June 10, 1815, shortly after the wagons containing his books had departed for Washington, Jefferson wrote John Adams that "I cannot live without books" and he began purchasing books for a new personal library.

The library that Jefferson sold to Congress not only included more than twice the number of volumes that had been in the Library of Congress in the Capitol, it expanded the scope of that collection enormously and permanently. Jefferson was a man of encyclopedic interests who believed that the American national legislature needed ideas and information on all subjects and in many languages in order to govern. His library provided such a core, and was recognized at the time as "an admirable substratum for a national library."

The acquisition by Congress of Jefferson's library was the base for the expansion of the Library's functions. The Jeffersonian concept of universality is the rationale for the Library's comprehensive collecting policies. His belief that self-government depended on the free, unhampered pursuit of truth by an

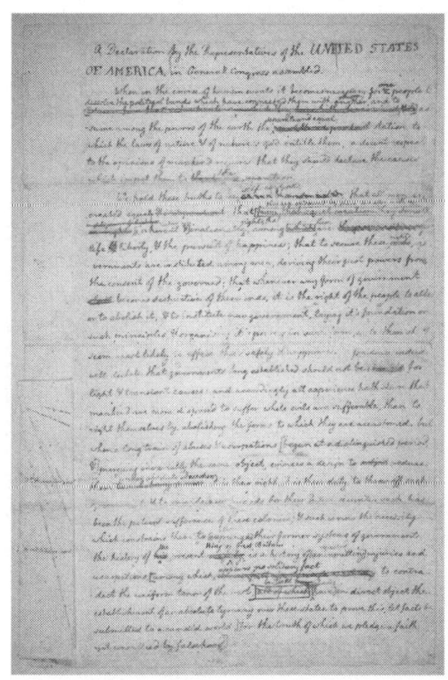
A Declaration by the Representatives of the UNITED STATES OF AMERICA, in General Congress assembled.

A principal Jefferson legacy to the Library is his personal library of 6,487 volumes, which was acquired by Congress in 1815 to "recommence" its library after its destruction when the British burned the Capitol in 1814. His personal papers in the Library's Manuscript Division are another legacy; they include Jefferson's rough draft of the Declaration of Independence (above). LC/Manuscript Division.

informed and involved citizenry has shaped the Library's philosophy of sharing its collections as widely as possible.

Between 1864 and 1897, Librarian of Congress Ainsworth Rand Spofford invoked Jefferson's legacy in transforming the Library into a national institution, even paraphrasing the third president, "there is almost no work, within the vast range of literature and science, which may not at some time prove useful to the legislature of a great nation." In 1943, the Library commemorated the bicentennial of Jefferson's birth with a large exhibition. Librarian of Congress Archibald MacLeish also commissioned two murals honoring Jefferson in the reading rooms in the Library's new Annex Building. In 1980, Librarian of Congress Daniel J. Boorstin named the Library's 1897 building for Jefferson. The renovation and restoration of the Jefferson Building, initiated by Boorstin in 1984, was completed in time for the celebration of the building's centennial in 1997.

In Jefferson's honor, in 1994 the database for legislation on the Library's Internet site on the World Wide Web was named THOMAS. The digitization of both the Thomas Jefferson and the George Washington Papers in the Library's Manuscript Division was supported in 1997 through a $2 million gift from a private donor.

On Jefferson's birthday in 2000, the Library's bicentennial year, the Library opened a major exhibition titled Thomas Jefferson: Genius of Liberty. *The book of the same title was an opportunity for prominent scholars to look again at Jefferson and his beliefs in the light of new scholarship.* LC/Publishing Office.

Jefferson and his Library of Congress legacy were major themes of the Library's bicentennial celebration in 2000. On Jefferson's birthday in 2000, the Library's bicentennial year, the Library opened a major bicentennial exhibition titled "Thomas Jefferson: Genius of Liberty." An accompanying publication contained essays by prominent scholars on the same topic.

In his preface to *Jefferson's Legacy: A Brief History of the Library of Congress*, published by the Library in 1993, Librarian of Congress James H. Billington asserted that "today's Library of Congress epitomizes Jefferson's faith in learning and his practical determination to make democracy work." Jefferson provided the Library with another form of inspiration: "It is only in the life of the mind and spirit that the horizons of freedom can remain truly infinite. We must rediscover what we should have known all along, that the pursuit of truth is the noblest part of Jefferson's legacy." (JYC)

Cole, John Y. *Jefferson's Legacy: A Brief History of the Library of Congress*. Washington, D.C.: Library of Congress, 1993.

JEFFERSON BUILDING

The Library of Congress was established in 1800 when the American government moved from Philadelphia to the new capital of Washington on the Potomac River. For 97 years, the Library was housed in various locations within the Capitol Building. The first separate Library of Congress Building, known today as the Thomas Jefferson Building, was suggested by Librarian of Congress Ainsworth Rand Spofford in 1871, authorized in 1886, and finally completed in 1897.

This bust of Thomas Jefferson by sculptor Jean-Antoine Houdon is in a niche in the Great Hall of the Thomas Jefferson Building.
Photograph: LC/Reid Baker.

When its doors were opened to the public on November 1, 1897, the new Library building was an unparalleled national achievement; its 23-carat gold-plated dome capped the "largest, costliest, and safest" library building in the world. Its elaborately decorated facade and interior, for which more than 40 American painters and sculptors produced commissioned works of art, were designed to show that the United States could surpass European libraries in grandeur and devotion to classical culture and to inspire optimism about America's future. A contemporary guidebook boasted: "America is justly proud of this gorgeous and palatial monument to its National sympathy and appreciation of Literature, Science, and Art. It has been designed and executed solely by American art and American labor (and is) a fitting tribute for the great thoughts of generations past, present, and to be." This new national "Temple of the Arts" immediately met with overwhelming approval from the American public.

Known as the Library of Congress (or Main) Building until June 13, 1980, when it was named for Thomas Jefferson, the Library's principal founder, the structure was built specifically to serve as the American national library, and its architecture and decoration express and enhance that grand purpose. The elaborate entrance pavilion and Great Hall lead to the central reading room where, properly prepared, the user can take full advantage of the Library's vast resources of knowledge and information. A national library for the United States was the dream and goal of Librarian Spofford; the new building was a crucial step in his achievement. It was a functional, state-of-the-art structure as well as a monument to American cultural nationalism, for it used and celebrated the latest technology to demonstrate the emerging role of the library as an efficient workshop.

"Just think! Every book that's ever been published in the United States is right here in the Library of Congress."
"Even 'The Poky Little Puppy'?"

The early years of planning and construction were filled with controversy and delay. After two design competitions and a decade of debate about design and location, in 1886 Congress finally chose a plan in the Italian Renaissance style submitted by Washington architects John L. Smithmeyer and Paul J.

Pelz. Structurally the architects followed the basic idea proposed by Librarian Spofford: a circular, domed reading room at the center of the building, surrounded by ample space for the Library's various departments. In the final Smithmeyer & Pelz plan, the reading room was enclosed by rectangular exterior walls, which divided the open space into four courtyards. The corner pavilions were devoted to the departments and to exhibit space.

Disputes continued after the building was authorized in 1886. Responsibility for clearing the site was debated (several buildings had to be razed) and the Capitol landscape architect, Frederick Law Olmsted, protested the building's location because it shut out "the whole view of the Capitol building from Pennsylvania Avenue—the main approach from Capitol Hill." Another controversy, this one about the selection of the proper cement for the foundation, proved to be architect Smithmeyer's undoing, and he was dismissed in 1888. Building construction was placed under the direction of Brigadier Gen. Thomas Lincoln Casey, Chief of the U.S. Army Corps of Engineers. Casey and his Superintendent of Construction, civil engineer Bernard R. Green, had successfully completed the construction of the Washington Monument and the State, War, and Navy (now Old Executive Office) Building and Congress trusted their work. The cornerstone was laid on August 28, 1890. Paul J. Pelz, who replaced Smithmeyer as architect in 1888, was himself dismissed in 1892 and replaced by architect Edward Pearce Casey, General Casey's son, who supervised most of the interior decoration.

The building's elaborate decoration, which combines sculpture, mural painting, mosaics, and architecture on a scale unsurpassed in any American public building, was possible only because General Casey and Bernard Green lived up to their reputations as efficient construction engineers, completing the building for a sum substantially less than that appropriated by Congress. When it became apparent in 1892 that funds for "artistic enrichment" would be available out of the original appropriation, Casey and Green seized the opportunity and turned an already remarkable building into a cultural monument.

The two engineers' nationalism complemented Spofford's national library aspirations. The 1893 World's Columbian Exposition in Chicago provided General Casey, his architect son Edward, and Bernard Green with an example of a cooperative artistic endeavor that combined architecture, sculpture, and painting; there are many similarities and parallels between the Chicago Exposition and the Library building. Both were artistic ventures on a massive scale and, for the most part, in the same Beaux-Arts design tradition. Many of the artists who contributed works to the Library building either helped design the imperial facades of the Chicago Exposition or exhibited their works within its pavilions; moreover, many of them repeated the idealistic themes and togaed likenesses they produced in Chicago.

In 1888 Congress placed Brigadier General Thomas Lincoln Casey (left), Chief of the U.S. Army Corps of Engineers, in charge of the building's construction. With his assistant Bernard Green, a civil engineer, Casey had recently completed major Washington, D.C. construction projects such as the Washington Monument and the State, War and Navy Building (today the Executive Office Building). LC Archives.

General Casey and Bernard Green were anxious to give American artists an opportunity to display their talents, and ultimately they commissioned no less than 42 American sculptors and painters "to fully and consistently carry out the monumental design and purpose of the building." The two men exercised final approval over the words and images seen throughout the building, even though the names, inscriptions, and quotations were chosen by many different people. The works of art were expected to address various areas of human achievement without entering into controversial areas such as politics and religion. The sculptors were assigned general themes, but the muralists, with guidance from the two engineers and Edward Pearce Casey, chose their own themes and, it appears, most of the inscriptions and quotations within their assigned areas. Librarian Spofford chose the authors (his favorites) who are portrayed in the nine busts in the portico above the front entrance, and the quotations in the Pavilion of Seals (the Northeast Pavilion). He also chose the figures portrayed in the 16 portrait statues on the balustrade of the Main Reading Room and the quotations in the four corridors on the second floor of the Great Hall. Charles W. Eliot, president of Harvard University, chose the inscriptions above the eight symbolic statues in the

Main Reading Room, and provided the Caseys and Green with advice about other inscriptions and decorative features.

In a report to Congress in 1896, Green stated that the total cost of the mural and decorative painting, the sculpture, and the three massive bronze doors at the main entrance was $364,000. Even with the additional costs of gilding the building's dome, including the Torch of Learning at its apex, and the construction of the Neptune Fountain in front of the building on First Street, the building was completed for $200,000 less than the total congressional authorization of approximately $6,500,000. In 1897, Green joined the Library's staff as Superintendent of the Building and grounds.

Patrons admire the Great Hall a few years after the Library of Congress opened to the public in 1897. Forty-two American painters and sculptors had been commissioned to create artworks to "fully and completely carry out the monumental design and purpose of the building."
LC/Prints and Photographs Division. LC-USZ62-59056.

Weather and the chemical effects of the nineteenth century method of tinning the copper beneath the gold leaf dome combined to produce perforations in the copper in the twentieth century, and the leaking gilded copper was replaced in October 1931. It was thought that gold leaf would conflict with the appearance of the building's aging granite exterior, and the new copper was left to acquire its current patina. In August 1993, however, the flame of the Torch of Learning at the apex of the dome was regilded, this time with 23 1/2 carat gold leaf.

Since 1897, three of the four interior courtyards of the Jefferson Building have been filled. The east courtyards have become bookstacks; the southeast bookstack was completed in 1910, the northeast in 1927. The northwest courtyard is occupied by two special structures: the Coolidge Auditorium, built in 1925 for chamber music recitals and a gift of Elizabeth Sprague Coolidge, and the Whittall Pavilion, given to the Library in 1938 by Gertrude Clarke Whittall to house five Stradivarius instruments she donated to the Library. A plaque commemorating Mrs. Coolidge and her gift is outside the entrance to the Coolidge Auditorium, on the ground floor. The names of four great composers—Mozart, Beethoven, Schubert, Brahms—are inscribed on the outside wall of the Whittall Pavilion, above the windows and the stairs leading down to the interior courtyard. The east side of the Jefferson Building was extended between 1929 and 1933, providing space for a Rare Book Room, a Union Catalog Room, and additional study rooms.

In 1924, a marble and bronze exhibit case known as the Shrine, designed by architect Francis Bacon, was installed on the west side of the second floor gallery in the Great Hall. There the Declaration of Independence and the Constitution of the United States were displayed until 1952 when the documents were transferred to the National Archives. As part of the general building restoration that began in 1986, the empty Shrine was removed from the Great Hall and placed into storage. The Main Reading Room closed for renovation and the installation of air conditioning on May 4, 1964, reopening on August 16, 1965. In 1984, Congress appropriated $81.5 million for the renovation and restoration of the Jefferson and Adams Buildings, which included the cleaning and conservation of murals in the Jefferson Building. Work started in 1986 and was completed in 1995, revealing once again to tourists and staff alike the bright colors and impressive iconography and works of art that brought the Jefferson Building unanimous praise when it opened its doors in 1897.

The renovation and restoration of the Jefferson Building began in 1986 and took eight years to complete. Here in the Pavilion of the Elements, two conservators work to bring "Water," one of artist Robert Leftwich Dodge's murals, back to its original vibrant colors.
LC Archives.

The Jefferson Building is a heroic setting for a national institution. Today it is recognized as a unique blending of art and architecture, a structure that celebrates learning, nationalism, and American turn-of-the-century confidence and optimism. The Jefferson Building also reflects its own time and prejudices. It emphasizes the achievements of western civilization, and most of the names and images on its walls evoke a society dominated by western thought. Thus, for many different reasons, the elaborate embellishment of the Jefferson Building is worth careful attention. The building is celebratory, inspirational, and educational. Few structures represent human aspiration in such dramatic fashion. (JYC)

Cole, John Y. *On These Walls: Inscriptions and Quotations in the Buildings of the Library of Congress.* Washington, D.C.: Library of Congress, 1995.

Cole, John Y. and Henry Hope Reed, eds. *The Library of Congress: The Art and Architecture of the Thomas Jefferson Building.* N.Y.: W.W. Norton and Co., 1997.

JOINT COMMITTEE ON THE LIBRARY

The U.S. Congress is the Library of Congress's most important client, and the Joint Committee on the Library is a key link between the Congress and its Library. Created in 1800 and established by statute in 1802, the Joint Committee has no legislative jurisdiction, that is, bills are not referred to the committee. However much of the legislative jurisdiction relating to the Library is assigned to the House Committee on House Administration and the Senate Committee on Rules and Regulations, from which the Joint Committee members are drawn. Because of this overlap and because of the substantial influence and strong personalities of many of the committee chairs through the years, the Joint Committee on the Library has been an important force in shaping the Library and its activities.

The Role and Responsibilities of the Joint Committee

The oldest continuing Joint Committee of the U.S. Congress, the Joint Committee on the Library was created on April 24, 1800, when President John Adams signed the bill establishing the federal government in Washington and creating the Library of Congress. The act appropriated $5,000 for "the purchase of such books as may be necessary for the use of Congress" after it moved to the new capital city of Washington. The books were to be housed in "a suitable apartment" in the Capitol, and a Joint Committee of Congress would oversee the purchase of the books, furnish a catalog, and "devise and establish" the Library's regulations.

More specifics were provided in an act of January 26, 1802, approved by President Thomas Jefferson, which stated that the expenditure of funds for the Library would be supervised by a joint congressional committee consisting of three members of the Senate and three members of the House of Representatives. The Library's appropriation for fiscal year 1811 officially made the Joint Library Committee a standing committee, which would be "appointed every session of Congress."

In his *History of the Library of Congress, 1800–1864*, William Dawson Johnston states that in 1802 the chairman of the newly named Library Committee "seems to have been" Senator Abraham Baldwin of Georgia. Documentation of the committee's membership and its chairmanship during its first few years is sparse and uncertain. However it is clear that from 1805 until the second session of the Sixty-Fourth Congress in 1916, the Joint Library Committee consisted of two separate Library committees—one for the U.S. Senate and the other for the U.S. House of Representatives, each with its own chairman. In practice, beginning in 1835 with the chairmanship of Senator William C. Preston of South Carolina, the ranking U.S. Senator served as the chairman of the committee; however this practice apparently was not formalized until 1916, when it was described in the second edition of the *Congressional Directory* for the Sixty-Fourth Congress, first session.

The size of the Joint Committee and its relationship to other legislative committees was redefined by the Legislative Reorganization Act of 1946. Prior to the act, the Joint Committee, comprising the separate House and Senate Committees on the Library, had consisted of five Senators and five Representatives. As a result of the 1946 act, the committee was composed of the chairman and four members of the House of Representative's Committee on House Administration, and the chairman and four members of the Senate Committee on Rules and Administration. In 1955, beginning with the Eighty-Fourth Congress, first session, the committee began designating a vice chairman and alternated the chairmanship and vice chairmanship each session between the chair of the House Committee on House Administration and the Senate Committee on Rules and Administration. This system changed in 1977 with the Ninety-Fifth Congress, first session, when the chairmanship and vice chairmanship began alternating between the House and Senate members every Congress, rather than every session. (The Committee on House Administration was named the House Oversight Committee between 1995 and 1999.)

Throughout the nineteenth century, the Joint Committee's responsibilities gradually extended beyond its supervisory responsibilities for the Library of Congress to include publication of the results of government-related exploration projects, the acquisition of art works for the Capitol, and the activities of the U.S. Botanic Garden, which was located at the foot of Capitol Hill.

Beginning in the 1830s and 1840s, books and libraries increasingly represented "culture" in the United States. Thus within the U.S. Congress it was appropriate for publishing projects, the acquisition of art for the Capitol, and, in the 1870s, the supervision of the Botanic Garden, to be assigned to the congressional committee that dealt primarily with books—and the Congress's library.

Before the librarianship of Ainsworth Rand Spofford (1864–1897), the Joint Library Committee managed the Library of Congress and its chairman was responsible for selecting most of its books. Spofford, however, expanded the Library from approximately 82,000 volumes in 1864 to nearly

800,000 in 1897, and increased the size of the staff from seven to 42. He also added new functions and made ambitious plans for the Library once it occupied its new building in 1897. Early that year Congress debated the Library's mission and oversight. As a result, in the reorganization and expansion of the Library that was approved on February 18, 1897 as part of the Library's appropriation, the Joint Library Committee's management responsibilities for the Library were transferred to the office of the Librarian of Congress, which was directed to "make rules and regulations for the government of the Library." The Joint Committee on the Library's formal role abruptly changed from management to providing oversight, advice, and guidance.

In 1925, by law the chairman of the Joint Committee was made a member of the Library of Congress Trust Fund Board. The 1970 Legislative Reorganization Act provided that the Librarian of Congress appoint the director of the Congressional Research Service (CRS) after consultation with the Joint Committee on the Library. The director, in turn, was required to submit an annual report to the Joint Committee.

Today the Joint Committee on the Library and its individual members, and especially its chairman, provides informal but frequent oversight and advice to the Librarian of Congress, particularly with regard to the approval and implementation of new Library of Congress programs.

The Library Committee in the Life of the Library: A Brief History

In the nineteenth century, many of the most bookish and intellectually inclined members of Congress were also members of the Joint Committee on the Library—and served as chairman of either the House or Senate Library Committee. Many of these individuals were cultural nationalists who by and large promoted U.S. government involvement in books, education, culture and science.

Senator Samuel Latham Mitchill was a significant early (1805–1808) chairman and Library of Congress supporter. Previously a professor of natural history, chemistry, agriculture, and botany at Columbia College, he was characterized by his contemporaries as a "living encyclopedia" and "a chaos of knowledge." On January 20, 1806, Mitchell urged the expansion of the Library: "Every week of the session causes additional regret that the volumes of literature and science within the reach of the national legislature are not more rich and ample." The next month Congress approved and President Jefferson signed an act that "continued" the earlier appropriation "made to purchase books for the use of Congress," and provided $1,000 a year for a period of five years for the purpose.

Scholar, editor, and orator Edward Everett of Massachusetts was chairman of the House of Representatives Library Committee the entire time (1825–1835) he served in Congress. Everett tried, without success, to build the Library's collections in new directions. In 1827, lamenting that "the most important sources of our early history are deposited in the archives of foreign governments," he reported a resolution that would "procure from the public offices in England copies of documents illustrative of the history of America." The resolution failed, as did a 1829 proposal that would provide for "standing orders" of state laws for the collections of the Library. He did succeed, however, in obtaining approval for a resolution providing for the distribution of duplicate public documents in the Library to members of Congress, state legislative libraries, universities, colleges, "incorporated Atheneums" and to the U.S. Military Academy at West Point.

In 1840, Senator Benjamin Tappan of Ohio, an amateur seashell collector and chairman of the Senate Library Committee in 1839–1840, learned about the U.S. Exploring Expedition, which had departed in 1838 on what would be a four-year around the world expedition to chart new waters and gather scientific specimens. Tappan became a strong supporter of the Exploring Expedition and legislation, which in 1842, authorized under the direction of the Joint Library Committee the publication of "an account of the discoveries made by the Exploring Expedition under the command of Lieutenant Wilkes." The committee also was placed in charge of the "objects of natural history" gathered by the Expedition.

The history of the publications of the Exploring Expedition is complicated, lasting from 1844 to 1874. Tappan retired from the Senate in 1845. Senator James A. Pearce from Maryland, chairman of the Joint Committee from 1846 until his death in 1862, tried to bring the expensive publishing project to a close, but failed. Moreover, the Joint Committee stayed in the publishing business even as the Expedition project was drawing to a close. In 1873, Congress authorized the publication of French documents relating to the discoveries and explorations made in the United States by the French government from 1614 to 1752. The volumes were to be edited by Pierre Margry but published under the direction of the Joint Committee on the Library–and the supervision of Librarian of Congress Ainsworth Rand Spofford.

The Library as a whole languished markedly from 1846 to 1862 when James A. Pearce was Library Committee chairman. An active, even domineering chairman, Pearce viewed the Library of Congress as little more than a gentleman's club. Nor did he believe it should extend its privileges or services much beyond those it provided to Congress. A southern sympathizer, he refused to order a subscription to the newly established *Atlantic Monthly* magazine for fear of engendering "sectional differences" between the North and the South. Pearce's death in 1862 gave Assistant Librarian of Congress Spofford his first real opportunity to begin transforming the Library of Congress into an institution of national significance. As Librarian of Congress, Spofford gradually took charge of the institution, assuming responsibility for choosing the books and establishing the rules for the Library's governance. Most important, he gained congressional approval for the expansion of the Library's collection and its national role, including the construction of its first building separate from the Capitol.

The support of the Joint Committee on the Library was crucial to Spofford, and he successfully persuaded congressmen friendly to him and to his national library cause to become committee members. In the mid-1860s, the list included three congressional friends from his adopted state of Ohio: Rutherford B. Hayes, James A. Garfield, and John Sherman. In the 1880s, his strongest support in the fight for a separate Library of Congress Building came from the two dominant members of Congress, both personal friends: Senator Daniel W. Voorhees (Indiana), who served as chairman of the Joint Committee 1879–1881, and Senator Justin S. Morrill (Vermont), chairman of the powerful Senate Committee on Buildings and Grounds.

In late 1896, on the eve of the Library's move into its new Capitol Hill Building, the Joint Committee held several days of hearings about the Library in order to develop a plan for its organization and management in the new structure. As mentioned earlier, it was the Appropriations Committee, not the Joint Library Committee that shaped the Library's expansion and organization. The 1898 appropriations act, approved by President Grover Cleveland on February 19, 1897 (to be effective July 1, 1897), gave the Librarian of Congress sole authority and responsibility for making the "rules and regulations" for governing the Library, including the selection of the staff, institutionalizing the authority Spofford had assumed during the past several decades. Another provision, however, added a new kind of oversight: for the first time, a president's nomination of a Librarian of Congress had to be approved by the U.S. Senate.

Since 1897, the Joint Committee on the Library has functioned both as a general oversight committee and as an informal advisory board. Librarian of Congress Herbert Putnam (1899–1939), in particular looked to the Library Committee for support. With advice and help from his Harvard friend Robert Luce of Massachusetts, chairman of the House Library Committee from 1924 to 1931, Putnam established precedents and gained approval for important Library activities such as the establishment of the Library of Congress Trust Fund Board (1925) and the purchase of the Vollbehr collection (1930). The Trust Fund Board was of special significance because it gave the Librarian new authority to accept gifts and trusts in the name of the United States. The Joint Committee on the Library still had to approve the gifts, however, and the committee chairman was made an ex officio trust fund board member. Senator Simeon D. Fess of Ohio, Senate Library Committee chairman (1925–1933), and House Library Committee member Ross Collins of Mississippi were also strong Putnam and Library of Congress supporters.

In 1950, Congress passed the Federal Records Act, which in effect, authorized the transfer of the Declaration of Independence and the Constitution to the National Archives from the Library of Congress, where they had resided since 1921. Librarian of Congress Luther Evans agreed with the decision, but the senior officers of the Library of Congress did not. Librarian Evans and Archivist of the United States Wayne Grover worked together secretly to obtain approval for the transfer from President Truman and congressional leaders, particularly Senator Theodore Green of Rhode Island, the chairman of the Joint Library Committee. As worked out ahead of time with Senator Green, in 1952 Evans asked the Joint Committee to order him to transfer the documents, which they did on April 30, 1952. Only then did Evans inform his senior staff about the change. The transfer took place on December 13, 1952.

Other committee chairmen and members helped the Library ease its continuing space shortage problem. For example, in the mid-1960s, Chairman Everett Jordan, a Senator from North Carolina, provided crucial support to Librarian of Congress L. Quincy Mumford (1954–1974) in Mumford's successful effort to obtain a third major Library of Congress Building. After the James Madison Memorial Building opened in 1980, committee members Claiborne Pell (chairman, 1979–1981) and Mark Hatfield (chairman, 1995–1997), helped the Library obtain the appropriations necessary for a major renovation and restoration (1984–1997) of the Library's Jefferson and Adams Buildings. Since then committee members, particularly Senator Theodore F. Stevens (Alaska), have supported several initiatives of Librarian of Congress James H. Billington, including efforts to increase Library funding from private sources; extending accessibility to the Library's collections through the National Digital Library; the celebration of the Library's bicentennial in 2000; the development of off-site storage facilities at Fort Meade, Maryland and plans for the Library's future National Audio Visual Conservation Center in Culpeper, Virginia; the inaugural National Book Festival in 2001; and the creation of the Library's John W. Kluge Center in 2002. (JYC)

Johnston, William Dawson. *History of the Library of Congress, 1800–1864*. Washington, D.C.: Government Printing Office, 1904.

Ostrowski, Carl. *Books, Maps, and Politics: A Cultural History of the Library of Congress, 1783–1861*. Amherst, MA: University of Massachusetts Press, 2004.

KLUGE (JOHN W.) CENTER

In October 2000, the Library's bicentennial year, Metromedia president and philanthropist John W. Kluge, head of the Library's James Madison Council, gave $60 million to the Library of Congress. Kluge provided the funding to establish the John W. Kluge Center within the Library and the John W. Kluge Prize in the Human Sciences. Located in the Thomas Jefferson Building, the Kluge Center officially opened in May 2003. The Kluge Center supports scholarly research in the humanities and social sciences, bringing the intellectual resources of academe to the public policy arena of Capitol Hill. Through individual research in the Library's collections, group discussions, lectures, and contacts with members of Congress and their staffs as well as the broader public policy community, the Center aims to both foster knowledge and bring new perspectives to the federal government.

In 2000 John W. Kluge, chairman of the Madison Council, made a gift of $60 million to establish the John W. Kluge Center at the Library of Congress and the John W. Kluge Prize in the Human Sciences. It was the largest monetary gift in the Library's 200-year history. Here, on May 7, 2003, Mr. Kluge (left) and Librarian of Congress James Billington officially open the Center in its newly renovated Jefferson Building quarters. LC Archives.

Scholar and author Leszek Kolakowski, the first recipient of the Kluge Prize, presents his acceptance speech on November 5, 2003. Photograph: © John Harrington, 2003.

The Kluge Prize in the Human Sciences is intended for scholars in such fields as history, philosophy, politics, anthropology, sociology, religion, linguistics, and criticism in the arts and humanities. As such, it includes a broad range of disciplines not covered by the Nobel Prizes. The award of one million dollars recognizes an individual's lifetime of intellectual achievement, similar to the John F. Kennedy Center's acknowledgment of individual accomplishment in the performing arts. The recipient of a Kluge Prize demonstrates unusual distinction within a given area of inquiry that also affects perspectives in other areas of study and in other walks of life. The Library solicits nominations for the prize, which are reviewed by a selection committee and by the Council of Scholars. The Librarian of Congress makes the final decision. The first Kluge Prize winner, announced in November 2003, was Leszek Kolakowski, whose principal scholarship has been in the fields of history of philosophy and philosophy of religion. Born in Poland but ejected from his position at Warsaw University and his Communist Party membership in the 1960s because of his increasingly unorthodox beliefs, Kolakowski has written on Marxism, Spinoza, Kant, modernism, authority and free will, and the relevance of philosophy in everyday life. Writing from exile, his works influenced the growing Polish opposition movement of the 1970s and 1980s. Additional writings have ranged from the examination of European Christianity of the sixteenth and seventeenth centuries to satirical plays and fables.

The Center also hosts scholars occupying three distinguished chairs: the Henry A. Kissinger

The Kluge Center also hosts scholars occupying distinguished chairs; one of them is the Henry A. Kissinger Chair in Foreign Policy and International Relations. Mr. Kissinger, whose papers are in the Library's Manuscript Division, is pictured above. Photograph: © Vivian Ronay, 2001.

Chair in Foreign Policy and International Relations, the Harissios Papamarkou Chair in Education, and the Cary and Ann Maguire Chair in American History and Ethics. Five other senior-level chairs were established with Kluge funding: American Law and Governance; Countries and Cultures of the North; Countries and Cultures of the South; Technology and Society; and Modern Culture.

To advise the Librarian regarding the selection of the senior fellows and the award of the Kluge Prize, an internationally chosen 21-member Scholars' Council had its first meeting in October 2001. All distinguished for achievement in their particular disciplines, Council members are asked to suggest ways to enrich Library of Congress resources, to nominate scholars for fellowships and chairs, and to advise the Librarian on trends and developments in their own fields. The term of service is five years with reappointment possible; however, the first appointments were made in groups: one group to serve one year, a second group for three years, and a third group for five years. New members are appointed every other year.

The several senior scholars share the Kluge Center's studies with up to a dozen post-doctoral scholars known as Kluge Fellows, with Library of Congress staff fellows, with other visiting scholars, and, on occasion, members of the Council of Scholars. The chairs, scholars, and fellows are in residence for varying periods of time. Kluge Fellowships are intended specifically for junior scholars worldwide who received their degrees up to seven years preceding the application. These fellows are selected through a review process administered by the National Endowment for the Humanities, with the final decisions made by the Librarian. Other fellowships offered through the Library are the J. Franklin Jameson Fellowship, jointly administered by the American Historical Association and the Manuscript Division; the Swann Fellowship in Caricature and Cartoon, administered by the Prints and Photographs Division; the Library of Congress Coca-Cola Fellowship for the Study of Advertising and World Cultures, administered by the Motion Picture, Broadcasting and Recorded Sound Division; the Library of Congress Rockefeller Fellowships in Islamic Studies; the Library of Congress International Studies Fellowships, administered by the American Council of Learned Societies and supported by the Andrew W. Mellon Foundation and the Association of American Universities; the International Fellowship program, administered by the American Council of Learned Societies and supported by the Henry Luce Foundation; and the David B. Larson Fellowship in Health and Spirituality, supported by a gift from the International Center for the Integration of Health and Spirituality.

While the Library of Congress has welcomed scholars and distinguished consultants throughout the course of its history, it has not had an established long-term program of fellowships. The gift of John W. Kluge provides the funding to allow the Library to support scholarship as a continuing presence within the institution and to bring the resources of intellectual and academic endeavor to the nation's capital. (JA)

Kluge scholars at work: Sergei Zhuk (left), whose topic of inquiry is "Peasant, Millennialism, and Radical Sects in Southern Russia and Ukraine, 1880–1970." Clarissa Burt's subject is "Felicity's Parting: Imitation, Trope, and Gender in Classical Arabic Poetry."

Photographs: LC/Levon Avdoyan.

LIBRARIAN, OFFICE OF

The central administrative office of the Library of Congress—the Office of the Librarian of Congress—grew relatively slowly until the Library itself began to expand significantly in the 1960s. The Office of the Librarian began, for all practical purposes, with what Librarian of Congress Herbert Putnam (1899–1939) called his" General Administration." In his 1901 *Annual Report*, Putnam noted that the entire Library consisted of 372 persons and that the "General Administration" included himself, the Chief Assistant Librarian, the Librarian's Secretary, the Chief Clerk, "and subordinate assistants."

At the end of fiscal year 2003 (September 30), the Library of Congress's staff of permanent, full-time employees numbered 4,151, and 510 of them were part of the Office of the Librarian. The Office of the Librarian and Deputy Librarian includes the offices of Communications; Congressional Relations; Development; General Counsel; Planning, Management, and Evaluation; Training and Development; and Workforce Diversity, as well as Human Resources Services, Integrated Support Services, the Office of the Chief Financial Officer, and the Office of Security and Emergency Preparedness. (JYC)

LIBRARY OF CONGRESS BICENTENNIAL

The Library of Congress celebrated its bicentennial on April 24, 2000. With the theme of "Libraries-Creativity-Liberty," the yearlong program of events presented the Library with a special opportunity to feature its collections, its role in American life, and the importance of libraries in a democratic society as providers of free and open access to knowledge and information.

"Libraries-Creativity-Liberty" was the theme of the yearlong Library of Congress bicentennial celebration in 2000.

Planning for the bicentennial began in December 1989, when Librarian of Congress Billington convened a staff group to discuss approaches to the celebration. He emphasized that the bicentennial must "demonstrate why the history of the Library of Congress is relevant to the institution's future and to the intellectual and cultural life of this country and of the world." Through a Bicentennial Steering Committee formally established in 1996, a program was developed and eventually carried out in partnership with the Library's staff, Congress, federal agencies, the American Library Association, national and international libraries, and Americans throughout the nation.

The Bicentennial Steering Committee consisted of Lindy Boggs, retired U.S. Representative, U.S. Ambassador to the Vatican, and Mark Hatfield, retired U.S. Senator (Honorary Co-chairs); John Y. Cole, Director, Center for the Book, and Jo Ann Jenkins, Library of Congress Chief of Staff (Co-chairs); Norma Baker, Director, Development Office; Jill Brett, Public Affairs Officer; Laura Campbell, Director, National Digital Library Program; Robert Dizard Jr., Acting Director, Congressional Relations Office; Geraldine Otremba, Director, Congressional Relations Office; Roberta Stevens, Bicentennial Program Manager; and Winston Tabb, Associate Librarian for Library Services.

Major bicentennial activities during 2000 included:

- A yearlong bicentennial "Gifts to the Nation" program that allowed the Library to acquire many significant items identified by the Library's curators and specialists. Through the generosity of the James Madison Council and contributions from other donors, the Library received gifts of Americana, maps, atlases, globes, rare books, foreign rarities, and performing and visual arts collections, as well as support for a number of Library programs. The Gifts to the Nation program resulted in 384 gifts totaling $109.8 million.
- A project was launched to reconstruct Thomas Jefferson's personal library, which was the original nucleus of the Library's collections and which he sold to Congress after the British burned the U.S. Capitol (the former home of the Library of Congress) in 1814. Although two-thirds of Jefferson's library was tragically lost in a second fire in 1851, the handwritten catalog survived. A generous contribution of $1 million from Madison Council members Jerral and Gene Jones provided the support for a global search, acquisition, and preservation of the missing titles and editions of this landmark collection.
- On the Library's official bicentennial date, April 24, 2000, bimetallic (gold and platinum) and silver commemorative coins were issued at a ceremony in the Great Hall of the Thomas Jefferson Building; the U.S. Postal Service issued the Library's bicentennial commemorative stamp at the same event.

On April 24, 2000, the date of the Library's 200th birthday, the U.S. Postal Service honored the Library by issuing a 33-cent commemorative stamp and the U.S. Mint issued two commemorative coins, a $1 silver coin and a $10 bimetallic (gold and platinum coin).

The Library's 200th birthday party on April 24 featured a program and concert on the U.S. Capitol's east lawn honoring 84 bicentennial "Living Legends," including top American singers and entertainers. Colin Powell (front and center, seated) was both a "Living Legend" and a program speaker.
LC Archives.

Librarian of Congress James H. Billington reading aloud to youngsters at the party.
Photograph: Susan Davis International.

Big Bird was there too. Photograph: Paul Hogroian.

Tito Puente entertaining the large crowd on the east Capitol grounds, with the Library's Jefferson Building in the background.
Photograph: LC/Christina Tyler Wenks.

- At a National Birthday celebration and concert on April 24 on the east lawn of the U.S. Capitol, the Library honored 84 "Living Legends," individuals selected by the Library for their significant creative contributions to American life.
- "Local Legacies" was a grassroots bicentennial initiative. Working through their congressional representatives and with local organizations and groups, people from all walks of life documented America's cultural heritage at the turn of the millennium. Seventy-seven percent of Congress (414 of the 535 members) registered nearly 1,300 projects from every state, trust, territory, and the District of Columbia. All told, more than 4,000 Americans participated by providing photographs, written reports, sound and video recordings, newspaper clippings, posters, and other materials as part of their projects, which are being preserved in the Library's American Folklife Center.

Other bicentennial projects and programs included poetry, exhibitions, symposia, publications, concerts, and the launching on April 24, 2000, of "America's Library," a new Web site for children and families. Library of Congress staff projects included publishing a series of articles in *The Gazette* highlighting staff achievements through the years; a "Bicentennial Background" series of articles in the

America's Library: The Story of the Library of Congress 1800–2000 *by James Conaway, was published in 2000 by the Yale University Press to mark the Library's bicentennial.* LC/Publishing Office.

Library's *Information Bulletin*; and creating bicentennial gardens around the Jefferson Building, planting a bicentennial tree, and collecting objects for a bicentennial time capsule, which was sealed at a Jefferson Building ceremony and program on December 20, 2000. Containing 85 objects documenting the daily life of the Library and its staff in 2000, the stainless steel capsule is to be opened on the Library's tricentennial on April 24, 2100. (JYC)

Annual Report of the Librarian of Congress for the Fiscal Year Ending September 30, 2000. Washington, D.C.: Library of Congress, 2001, pp. 6–42, 167–231.

Library of Congress Information Bulletin 60 (January 2001): 8–11.

LIBRARY OF CONGRESS IN THE CAPITOL BUILDING

The law creating the Library of Congress, approved on April 24, 1800, called for its books to be housed in "a suitable apartment" in the Capitol. In 1800 only the north wing of the Capitol was finished. The books brought by Congress from Philadelphia and the new books acquired for the Library were placed in the office of the Clerk of the Senate. During 1801, a temporary structure was built for the use of the House of Representatives, and the act of January 26, 1802, which established the rules and procedures "concerning the Library for the use of both Houses of Congress," provided for the move of the Library into the room in the north wing formerly occupied by the House. Here the Library remained until December 1805.

The Library of Congress occupied various spaces in the Capitol Building between 1806 and August 24, 1814, when the British burned the Capitol and the Library. On January 30, 1815, Thomas Jefferson's library was purchased by Congress to "recommence" its library, and a law approved on March 3, 1815, authorized the preparation of "a proper apartment" for the books. Blodget's Hotel at 7th and E Streets was serving as the temporary Capitol, and a room on the third floor became the new loca-

Blodget's Hotel at 7th and E Streets was the temporary home of the U.S. Capitol from 1815 to 1818 following the fire that destroyed the Capitol and the building that housed the Library of Congress during the same period.
LC/Prints and Photographs Division. LC-USZ62-55629.

tion of the Library of Congress. Here Jefferson's books were received and organized by Librarian of Congress George Watterston. In 1817, Library Committee Chairman Eligius Fromention, a senator from Louisiana, introduced a resolution advocating a separate building for the Library, but it failed. In late 1818, however, funds were appropriated to move the Library back into the Capitol.

The new quarters in the attic story of the Capitol's north wing proved inadequate. In 1818, Charles Bulfinch became Architect of the Capitol, and he soon developed plans for a spacious library room in the center of the west front of the Capitol. The new room, which measured 90 feet long and 30 feet wide, was occupied on August 17, 1824. On December 22, 1825, a fire started by a candle left burning in the gallery was controlled before it could cause serious damage. Investigations into fireproofing the room concluded that the expense would be too great. In 1832, a separate "apartment" was established for the law collection within the Capitol, and the Law Library began its close relationship with the Supreme Court. In 1842, the law collection was moved to a room in close proximity to the court.

On Christmas Eve, 1851, the Library of Congress suffered a disastrous fire. Approximately 35,000 of its 55,000 volumes were destroyed in the flames, caused by a faulty chimney flue. Architect of

Fire struck the Library again in 1851, and approximately 35,000 of its 55,000 books were destroyed. Architect of the Capitol Thomas U. Walter prepared a new plan to enlarge the Library's room, using fireproof materials in its construction. The elegantly restored room was opened in 1853 and was described by the press as the "largest room made of iron in the world."
LC/Prints and Photographs Division. LC-USZ62-1818.

the Capitol Thomas U. Walter presented a plan, which was approved by Congress, to repair and enlarge the Library room using fireproof materials throughout. The elegantly restored Library room was opened on August 23, 1853. Called by the press the "largest room made of iron in the world," it was encircled by galleries and filled the west central front of the Capitol. A month before the opening, President Franklin Pierce inspected the new Library in the company of British scientist Sir Charles Lyell, who pronounced it "the most beautiful room in the world."

In 1865, Librarian of Congress Ainsworth Rand Spofford obtained approval for expanding the Library by adding two new fireproof wings, each 95 feet long and 35 feet wide. They were completed in

1866. The Copyright Law of 1870 brought two copies of all copyright items to the Library, however, it immediately became apparent to Librarian Spofford that the Library would soon run out of space. He suggested a separate building and, in 1872 presented a plan to Congress for such a structure. In 1875, he reported to Congress that the Library had exhausted all shelf space and that "books are now, from sheer force of necessity, being piled on the floor in all directions." Unless Congress took quick action on the question of a separate building, he noted, its Librarian would soon be placed "in the unhappy predicament of presiding over the greatest chaos in America."

The new building, today called the Jefferson Building, was not authorized until 1886, nor opened until 1897. In the meantime, Library operations slowly ground to a halt as Spofford dealt as best he could with the unceasing flow of materials into the cramped

The Library in the Capitol Building filled up rapidly after the Copyright Law of 1870 began bringing copyright deposits into its rooms. All shelf space was gone by 1875. In this drawing from Harper's Weekly *on February 27, 1897, Librarian Spofford (right) emerges from the crowded stacks with a book for a reader. The new building finally opened on November 1, 1897.*
LC/Prints and Photographs Division. LC-USZC4-5714.

Library rooms in the Capitol. In the summer and fall of 1897, the Library's collections were moved to the new building from their many storage locations throughout the Capitol, including 13 rooms in the basement. The spaces in the west front of the Capitol, occupied for so many years by the general Library, were quickly dismantled and remodeled for other uses. Because of its close relationship with the Supreme Court, which ended only in 1935 when the court moved from the Capitol into its own building, the law library continued to keep a reference collection in the Capitol and moved into the Jefferson Building gradually. The Library retained a small "Capitol Station" in the Capitol to provide delivery of books and other Library materials; the books were sent from the Jefferson Building through an electronically operated book carrier in a narrow tunnel connected to the Capitol. Capitol Station did not formally close until December 31, 2002. While the timing of the closing was precipitated by the construction of the Capitol Visitor Center, begun in 2002, the center already was being phased out due to the growth of reference services via the Internet and the continuation of loan and reference services to Congress through Congressional Research Service (CRS) research centers in the House and Senate Office Buildings as well as the CRS Web site for Congress. (JYC)

Johnston, William Dawson. *History of the Library of Congress, 1800–1864.* Washington, D.C.: Government Printing Office, 1904.

The Original Library of Congress: The History (1800–1814) of the Library of Congress in the United States Capitol. Committee Print prepared for the Committee on Rules and Administration. U.S. Senate. 97th Cong., 1st Sess. Washington, D.C.: Government Printing Office, 1981.

LIBRARY OF CONGRESS, ADMINISTRATIVE REVIEWS AND REORGANIZATIONS

Created in 1800 as a collection of books for Congress, the Library of Congress is part of the legislative branch of the U.S. government. It has no formal charter or constitution. The Library's operations are authorized and supported by annual appropriations from Congress, and through the years Congress has approved its growth, changes in organization, and the gradual expansion of the scope of its activities, nationally and internationally. Several important reviews of the Library's overall structure and functions, some initiated from outside the institution and some from within, have also shaped the Library's administrative organization. The most recent general review, *LC21: A Digital Strategy for the Library of Congress*, a National Academy of Sciences Committee report, was commissioned by Librarian of Congress James H. Billington in 1998 and released in July 2000. The report called for the Library to develop a new strategic and collaborative strategy for acquiring and preserving electronic journals and books, Web sites and links, databases, and other digital creations. In response, on October 2, 2000, Librarian Billington established a new high-level Office of Strategic Initiatives to develop such strategies and administer the Library's principal digital and information technology offices.

Historically the major periods of administrative review and reorganization, outlined below, have been 1895–1897, 1939–1944, 1946–1947, 1962–1966, 1976–1978, and 1987–1990.

1895–1897

In 1895, the Library's book collection numbered approximately 850,000 and there were 42 staff members. With the first separate Library of Congress building nearing completion and occupancy, in 1896 Congress asked Librarian Spofford to report on "a complete reorganization of the Library of Congress." Basing his estimates on the work of other large libraries, the Librarian proposed dividing the materials among the departments of printed books, periodicals, manuscripts, maps and charts, and works of art; and the functions among departments of cataloging, binding, copyright, and building superintendence, with the separate law collection remaining in the Capitol. Spofford also requested 97 new positions of which 58 were for the Library and the rest for the copyright department.

When the Joint Committee on the Library decided to hold hearings about the Library and its organization in late 1896, it invited six prominent library directors, all members of the American Library Association, to provide advice. The librarians told the committee that the Library needed modern methods, more staff, more extensive services—particularly to other libraries—and a strong executive at the top. Spofford's plan, along with the recommendations made by these six librarians, influenced the reorganization of the Library contained in the legislative appropriations act for fiscal year 1898, which became effective on July 1, 1897.

The act increased the Library's staff from 42 to 108 and created separate administrative units for copyright, law, cataloging, periodicals, maps, manuscripts, music, and prints. It also provided for reading room attendants, a congressional reference library in the Capitol, and private House and Senate Reading Rooms in the new Library building. The office of Superintendent of Building and Grounds was created, with a staff of 79. During his 32 years in office, Spofford had gradually assumed full responsibility for directing the Library, and the 1897 law gave the Librarian the authority to make rules and regulations and to appoint staff on the basis of "special aptitude," which meant the staff remained outside the civil service system. Finally, the law required that the Senate approve presidential nominees for the office of Librarian of Congress.

1939–1944

In 1939, when President Franklin D. Roosevelt named Archibald MacLeish as Librarian of Congress, the Library's collection numbered approximately six million volumes and there were about 1,100 full-time employees. During Herbert Putnam's 40 years (1899–1939) as Librarian of Congress, the number of employees had increased from 134 to 1,100 and the number of administrative units reporting to the Librarian of Congress from 16 in 1901 to 35 in 1939. Aware of the Library's many needs, including reorganization, but lacking experience in library technical matters, on April 10, 1940, MacLeish appointed a special Librarian's Committee to study the situation and recommend changes.

The committee consisted of Professor Carleton B. Joeckel, University of Chicago Library School (chairman); Paul North Rice, chief of the Reference Department, New York Public Library; and Andrew D. Osborn, chief of the Serial Division, Harvard College Library. The work of the committee was supported by a grant from the Carnegie Corporation. The Librarian's Committee began its work on April 16, 1940, assisted by the Library's own staff and three individuals from other institutions:

Keyes D. Metcalf, director of the Harvard University Library; Francis R. St. John, assistant librarian, Enoch Pratt Free Library; and L. Quincy Mumford, assistant in charge of the preparation unit, New York Public Library. The committee's detailed 300-page report was submitted to Librarian MacLeish on June 15, 1940. The major purpose of the committee's effort was to analyze the Library's processing operations and to recommend structural and procedural changes in the existing system. Its final recommendations were in fact much more comprehensive.

In its report, the committee recommended organizing the Library's administrative units into three departments: Administration, Acquisition and Preparation, and Reference. They also recommended preparing a written statement of the Library's objectives, compiling procedure manuals for each unit, and reclassifying the staff, since salaries had fallen behind those in other federal agencies. Urging the adoption of processing methods that met Library needs while maintaining standards satisfactory for libraries nationwide, the committee advised MacLeish that, in order to eliminate the severe cataloging backlog, the cataloging staff should abandon the quest for technical perfection and strive instead for higher productivity.

On June 28, MacLeish announced the reorganization of the Library into three departments: Administrative, Processing, and Reference. But the reorganization took years to complete as the staff worked to integrate the functions of units that had operated autonomously for many years. The Administrative Department, for example, was created on July 1, 1940, and dissolved on June 30, 1943, when the Assistant Librarian became the Library's administrative officer. However, it was re-established on February 7, 1946, as the Department of Administrative Services, and the Assistant Librarian became the principal planning and public relations officer. Reorganized in March 1944, the Reference Department absorbed the Division of Bibliography. The Documents and Periodicals divisions were divided between Reference and Processing, while a separate Acquisitions Department established on June 30, 1943, became part of the Processing Department in 1947. The Smithsonian Division's functions were transferred to other units, and a Serials Division was formed. The organization finally evolved to six departments: Administrative, Processing, Reference, the Legislative Reference Service, the Law Library, and the Copyright Office.

1946–1947

In 1947, the Library 's book collection numbered approximately seven million volumes and there were about 1,200 employees. In April 1946, Librarian of Congress Luther H. Evans requested an increase in the 1947 appropriation from $5.1 million in 1946 to $9.8 million in 1947, but an increase of only $965,000 was approved. Several members of Congress felt that in recent years the Library had gone too far beyond its basic role of serving the national legislature and wanted a review of the Library's role and functions before approving additional funding.

In response, Evans immediately formed a Library of Congress Planning Committee, a distinguished group of scholars, librarians, businessmen, and federal executives who asked to consider the Library's future role. The chairman was Keyes D. Metcalf, director of the Harvard University Library. In its March 12, 1947 report, the Planning Committee recommended that the status of the Library as the "national library" be officially recognized, that the Library improve its coordination with other organizations and institutions, and overall that its national functions be expanded. Suggested new services included a traveling exhibitions program, a research library for science and technology, contracts with other government agencies to perform bibliographical and reference services, and a national library for the blind. The committee also urged the Library to develop a national acquisitions program by ensuring the acquisition of at least one copy of every current item published worldwide that would be of interest for research, except for the medical and agricultural materials acquired by the Army Medical Library and the Library of the Department of Agriculture. Additional recommendations supported strengthening services to libraries and individual researchers, the Library's own publications program, and the Americana collections. Although Congress never approved this specific set of recommendations, it did begin increasing the Library's budget to support many of the activities outlined in the Planning Committee's report.

1962–1966

In 1962, the Library's collection numbered approximately 12 million volumes and there were about 3,000 employees. In that year, Senator Claiborne Pell (D-R.I.), a member of the Joint Committee on the Library, asked Douglas W. Bryant, associate director of the Harvard University Library, to prepare a memorandum about the role of the Library of Congress and the federal government, particularly in supporting research library activities. Bryant called for new federal programs in several areas and for strengthening the Library of Congress's services to libraries. He also advocated officially recognizing the Library of Congress "as the National

Library (without necessarily changing its name)" and creating an explicit statement of the Library's responsibilities for which Congress would provide support. Because of the range of national services already performed by the institution, Bryant thought that it "logically ought to be attached" to the executive branch of government. However, if it appeared that this move "would encounter serious practical difficulties, it would not be essential to pursue it." He also recommended, as natural extensions of the Library's national role, the formation of both a federal library council and a national library advisory committee—the latter as an executive or independent agency.

Librarian Mumford replied to the Bryant memorandum in the form of a report, dated September 28, 1962, to the Joint Committee on the Library. While he opposed removing the Library from the legislative branch of government and changing its name, he did support the idea of a comprehensive statement of the Library's role as a national library since such statements existed for both the National Library of Medicine (established 1956) and the National Agricultural Library (established 1962). He also promised to consider a Federal Library Council, advocated a national commission for libraries, and noted that, in addition to the Library's advisory groups for specific programs, he was forming three more: one for library association and foundation representatives; one for scholars in the humanities and social sciences; and one for scholars in the sciences. A second review of the Library's national role during the 1960s took place in response to a request from the new (1966) National Advisory Commission on Libraries. A National Commission on Libraries was created as a result of the Advisory Commission's report, but the recommendations regarding the role of the Library of Congress aimed at enhancing its national role rather than changing its governance or functions.

1976–1978

In 1976, the Library's book collection was approximately 15 million volumes and its staff numbered 4,300. After Librarian Mumford retired on December 31, 1974, President Gerald Ford nominated historian Daniel J. Boorstin to be the next Librarian of Congress. Boorstin promised Congress a review of the extent to which the Library was serving all of its constituencies satisfactorily. On January 16, 1976, he created an 11-person staff Task Force on Goals, Organization, and Planning, chaired by John Y. Cole of the Reference Department, to carry out a one-year review. More than 150 staff members served on Task Force subcommittees. The generosity of several private foundations enabled the Library to enlist the help of eight outside advisory groups, chosen to represent the Library's various constituencies. A total of 75 distinguished individuals from the United States, plus four from abroad, served as advisors. The Task Force submitted its 33 major recommendations and the suggestions from the outside advisory groups to the Librarian of Congress in January 1977. A new Office of Planning and Development began reviewing the recommendations and several new offices were established quickly, including the Council of Scholars, a new readers' advisory service, a computer catalog center, and the Center for the Book.

Drawing on the Task Force report and incorporating many of its suggested changes, the Planning Office and the Library's top administrators carried out a major reorganization throughout 1978; it focused on service to four major audiences: Congress (the Congressional Research Service), the nation's artistic-creative sector (the Copyright Office), the nation's libraries (Processing Services), and the public (Research Services). According to the Library's 1978 *Annual Report*, it was the first large-scale reorganization of the Library's administrative structure in 38 years. A proposed reorganization of the Law Library was deferred pending further study, and the Copyright Office reorganization also was affected by new responsibilities it undertook in accordance with the copyright law of 1976.

1987–1990

In 1987, the book collection numbered approximately 15 million volumes and the total collection included approximately 85 million items. There were about 4,600 employees. When Librarian Boorstin stepped down on December 10, 1986, President Reagan nominated James H. Billington, a scholar of Russian culture, to succeed him. Shortly after taking office on September 14, 1987, Billington announced a comprehensive review and planning process to chart the Library's future. The review included four components: an internal staff Management and Planning Committee (MAP), an external National Advisory Committee, regional forums with local library communities, and a review by a management consultant firm. In addition, Billington asked the General Accounting Office to perform an audit, which produced several suggestions for management improvements.

In January 1988, the Librarian gave the 27-person MAP Committee, which was chaired by Ellen Hahn, General Reading Rooms Division, a threefold charge: to find ways to increase the Library's effectiveness in serving the Congress, the federal government, the nation's libraries, scholars, the entire creative community, and all citizens; to review the Library's legislative, national, and international roles and responsibilities; and to recommend broad goals the Library should achieve by the year 2000 and practical steps to implement them.

The MAP committee presented its vision for the Library's future in a 300-page report dated November 1988 that contained 108 separate recommendations. After a senior management retreat in December 1988, a Library-wide Transition Team, working from January 1989 through the end of fiscal year 1989 (September 30, 1989) incorporated the MAP and other recommendations into a strategic planning document that identified the Library's values, mission, goals, objectives, and strategies. The Library's organization was changed in accordance with the strategic plan. Effective October 1, 1989, seven new service units were formed: Congressional Services, Collection Services, Constituent Services, Copyright Services, Cultural Affairs, Library Management Services, and Special Projects. A final decision on the Law Library's organizational structure was postponed; in the end, it remained as a separate service unit. Collections Services and Constituent Services were complicated units. Each included separate directorates but through a joint management team together they administered two directorates: Public Service and Collection Management I (eight divisions) and Public Service and Collection Management II (seven divisions and three program offices).

In November 1995, the Librarian combined the Collections Services, Constituent Services, and Cultural Affairs service units into Library Services, a new service unit. Library Services itself was divided into seven directorates (Acquisitions, Area Studies Collections, Cataloging, National Services, Operations, Preservation, and Public Service Collections) and several unique Library programs, including the American Folklife Center, the Cataloging Distribution Service, the Network Development and MARC Standards Office, and the National Library for the Blind and Physically Handicapped.

Many organizational changes during the next decade led to the development of a strategic plan that identified the Library's objectives and priorities for the first decade of the twenty-first century. A new Planning, Management, and Evaluation Directorate began implementing the plan and developed an annual performance planning process. The Library's mission, as stated in the strategic plan for the fiscal years 2004–2008, is "to make its resources available and useful to the Congress and to the American people and to sustain and preserve a universal collection of knowledge and creativity for future generations." Its priorities are to 1) make information, knowledge, and creativity available to and useful for the Congress of the United States; 2) acquire, organize, preserve, secure and sustain a comprehensive record of American history and creativity and a universal collection of human knowledge; 3) make the Library's collections maximally accessible to the Congress, the U.S. government, and the public; and 4) add interpretive and educational value to the Library's collections and enhance and highlight the Library's contributions to the nation's creative work, scholarly activity, and future progress. (JYC, JA)

See the *Annual Reports of the Librarian of Congress* for 1940 (pp. 20–29); 1947 (pp. 18–20, 101–108); 1962 (pp. 94–111); 1976 (pp. xvii–xviii); 1977 (pp. 1–4); 1988 (pp. 1–6); 1989 (pp. 7–16, 82–87); and 1990 (pp. 6–8).

Cole, John Y., ed. *The Library of Congress in Perspective: A Volume Based on the Reports of the 1976 Librarian's Task Force and Advisory Groups*. New York: R.R. Bowker, 1978.

MacLeish, Archibald. "The Reorganization of the Librarian of Congress, 1939–1944," *Library Quarterly* 14 (October 1944): 277–315.

Rosenberg, Jane A. "Foundation for Service: The 1896 Hearings on the Library of Congress," *Journal of Library History* 21 (1986): 107–130.

LIBRARY OF CONGRESS, STRATEGIC PLAN

On August 28, 2003, Librarian of Congress James H. Billington issued the Library's strategic plan for fiscal years 2004–2008. His cover letter and portions of the plan are reproduced below. The plan is presented in four parts: Part 1, Introduction: (Background and Future Direction for the Library of Congress); Part 2, Overview (Context: Our History and the Library Today); Part 3, Strategic Goals, Objectives, and Measures; Part 4, Moving Forward.

In February 2004, an accompanying document, the Library's Financial Statements for Fiscal Year 2004, was issued. In his cover letter, Librarian Billington points out that for the eighth consecutive year, independent auditors have issued an unqualified "clean" opinion of the Library's Consolidated Financial Statements. He notes that the net cost of the Library's major programs totaled $579.8 million, including $62.8 million in costs in support of the Library's programs incurred by four other agencies (Architect of the Capitol, Government Printing Office, Office of Personnel Management, and the Department of the Treasury) and $97.5 million in earned revenue from copyright registration fees, cataloging distribution sales, and other fee-based and reimbursable programs. (JYC)

The Library of Congress Strategic Plan for Fiscal Years 2004–2008

Letter from Librarian of Congress James H. Billington, August 28, 2003

The Congress of the United States has been the greatest patron of a library in the history of the world – mandating and funding the programs of this unique resource for knowledge on a nonpartisan basis for 203 years. The Library of Congress under its 2004–2008 strategic plan will continue to build on its historic mission, "...to make its resources available and useful to the Congress and the American people and to sustain and preserve a universal collection of knowledge and creativity for future generations." We are faced with the greatest upheaval in the transmission of knowledge since the invention of the printing press: the electronic onslaught of digitized multimedia communication. This strategic plan will guide the Library as it superimposes a new, networked digital universe on top of its traditional artifactual (analog) collections.

"Every day in America is a new beginning," Ronald Reagan used to say. "We are a nation that never becomes, but that is always becoming." The twentieth century saw an enormous expansion of the collections. With the Congress's support, the Library of Congress became the most universal collection of information and knowledge in the history of the world. The Library's superbly qualified staff now directly serves the Congress through public policy research service, and we serve the nation's libraries with cataloging data, material for the blind, and many electronic services.

When I was sworn [in] as Librarian in late 1987, I defined the task ahead as moving the Library "out more broadly and in more deeply." This remains my focus more than 15 years later as we embark on new initiatives and programs of great potential value to the Congress, to America's communities, and to the world. The strategic plan sets forth 18 goals targeted to reach our vision of leading the nation in ensuring access to knowledge and information and in promoting its creative use for the Congress and its constituents. Integrated within our goals are key objectives focused on: our top priority of serving the Congress regardless of time or place; sustaining and preserving our inclusive collections; getting the National Audio-Visual Conservation Center up and running; implementing the Copyright Office's re-engineered processes; completing the development of, and beginning the conversion to, digital talking book technology for blind and physically handicapped persons; strengthening the digital competencies of our knowledge navigator-curators; and making the transition to a networked digital environment.

In reaching the plan's goals, the Library will continue to depend primarily on appropriated support. Supplementing private support—particularly from the James Madison Council, John Kluge through the Kluge Center, and David Woodley Packard through the Packard Humanities Institute—will help in many ways to "get the champagne out of the bottle" with facilities exhibitions, electronic educational enrichment, and special acquisitions for the national collection.

The future of all of the Library's efforts depends on our greatest asset, the expertise, intellect, and dedication of a Library staff that makes our vast collections and services relevant and accessible. Management must seek to train, develop, and renew our staff and add fresh talent to sustain our leadership role in the twenty-first century.

Our strategic plan will help ensure that this Library—the research and information arm of the national legislature and the world's largest storehouse of knowledge—continues its great tradition, which now also includes congressionally mandated leadership in the digital networked environment, in support of the Congress, the public, and the democratic ideal.

James H. Billington
The Librarian of Congress

Part 1. Introduction: Background and Future Direction for the Library of Congress

America has become what no one once thought possible: a dynamic democracy on a continental scale, with a very diverse population, yet unified by a durable constitution and political institutions. It has prospered in good measure because a free people have continuously used human knowledge to create and innovate.

Our United States is the only great world civilization whose basic unifying institutions were created entirely in the age of print. We have more recently led the world in creating a revolutionary new electronic form of communicating knowledge. America, as a knowledge-based democracy, needs to maximize its utilization of the information contained in digital files, the knowledge contained in books, and the wisdom of those who curate and live with both. The Library of Congress can and must play a central role in meeting this national need—particularly at a time when America's pressing economic and security concerns depend increasingly on better knowledge and understanding of the world.

Our founding fathers linked governance to learning—and legislation to libraries—from the very first time the Continental Congress convened in Philadelphia in July 1774—inside a library. Article I, Section 8 of the Constitution was designed to promote "the progress of science and useful arts." The first Joint Committee of the Congress in the new capital of Washington, D.C., was created for its library. The Congress created the world's first nationwide body of library-based public universities when the Morrill Act paved the way for land grant universities at the state level—underscoring the basic Jeffersonian belief that democracy, to be dynamic, had to be based on ever more people using ever more knowledge in ever more ways.

The Congress of the United States has created the largest repository of human knowledge in the history of the world, and has preserved the mint record of American intellectual creativity by placing the Copyright Office in its library. The mission of the Library of Congress is to acquire, preserve, and make accessible the world's knowledge for the Congress and for America's use and to maintain a universal collection for future generations. That mission does not change, but its sweep and its increasing importance for America's future require a comprehensive strategy solidly based on what the Library of Congress has become—and can uniquely do for America in the early twenty-first century. Four central features of the Library point the way:

The unparalleled collections of the Congress's Library are America's strategic reserve of the world's knowledge and information. With more than 126 million items in its collections, the Library is the only institution in the world that comes even close to acquiring everything important for American culture (except for medicine and agriculture, which have their own national libraries) in whatever language and format it is produced. The Library's unique web of exchanges, of overseas offices (Islamabad, Cairo, Jakarta, New Delhi, Nairobi, Rio de Janeiro) and its U.S. copyright deposits generate an inflow of 22,000 items a day, of which we retain 10,000.

Congress's Library is the central hub of two important knowledge networks: America's own national network of libraries, archives, and other repositories and an international network of major research libraries. The Library of Congress is recognized as the leading provider of free, high-quality educational content on the Internet. Just as Congress endorsed the Library of Congress to provide other libraries with its cataloging data for print material in the early twentieth century, so it has now mandated its Library to create, in the early twenty-first century, a plan for a distributed national network for preserving and making accessible digital material.

The Library of Congress provides the principal research support for the Congress.

The Library serves the American people as a filter and source of knowledge navigation for the increasingly chaotic tide of information and knowledge flooding the Internet.

The Library is a knowledge center for accumulating information and helping assemble it into scholarly knowledge and practical wisdom for both the entire Congress and all Americans. It promotes "the progress of science and useful arts" (1) through the Copyright Office by protecting intellectual property rights and preserving past American creativity as a basis for future creativity, and (2) through the Library's leadership role in bringing primary materials of American history as well as basic information about the Congress free of charge electronically to localities throughout the nation.

Additional facilities off Capitol Hill will enable the Library to store more securely its treasures—thanks to congressional support for the Fort Meade, Maryland, modules currently being built and thanks to the prospect of an unprecedentedly generous private donation from the Packard Humanities Institute for the new National Audio-Visual Conservation Center in Culpeper, Virginia.

Thanks to the continuing support of the Congress, its Library is in a position both to sustain its historical mission in the new arena of electronic information and to make major new contributions to the global and domestic needs of the United States in an increasingly competitive and dangerous world. The Library is an information and knowledge-gathering center unique in the world. In the networked world of the Internet, the Library must increasingly perform its historic mission in a new way. It must combine leadership functions that only it can perform with catalytic activities and new, networked relationships with other nonprofit repositories and productive private sector institutions.

The Library will need the trained staff, the flexible structures, and the mission focus to perform those roles that are central to its mission and for which it is uniquely equipped to perform. The Library will have to sustain much of its present operations but at the same time face three major changes that reach across all aspects of the Library in the next decade:

The Library's dedicated workforce must, to a large extent, be retrained or renewed. Facing a disproportionately large number of experienced personnel at or nearing retirement age, we must create a workforce that will in the aggregate provide even greater diversity of both backgrounds and technical skills. The staff for the twenty-first century must include highly skilled and well-trained experts in the new technologies of the information age and the traditional scholarly substantive expertise required by the richness and variety of the collections. Developing a retooled workforce, in many ways, is the most important single task the Library faces in the next decade.

The Library will have to create new structures of sufficient flexibility to enable the Library to deal with the fast-moving, ever-changing electronic universe and to integrate these materials seamlessly into the massive analog collections of the Library. These structures must be set up in such a way that they can (a) work effectively in an increasingly distributed and networked environment; and, at the same time, (b) guarantee fast, full, and secure global coverage for the Congress. The Library largely has been able to provide comprehensive information in the analog universe, but it may have to share this responsibility with others in the digital network. The priority requirement to respond to congressional and Congressional Research Service (CRS) needs will require high standards of dependability in all partners.

The Library must concentrate more of its overall energies and talents on developing the deep substantive scholarly expertise that will enable the staff to filter, navigate, and objectively interpret knowledge for the Congress and the nation. It will be important in the future not only to provide access to the Library's collections, but also to extend and deepen the objective guidance that both the Congress and the scholarly world will need in confronting the inundation of unfiltered information that is appearing on the Internet and will increasingly characterize the global information environment.

The Congress of the United States creates the laws and oversees the governmental functions of America. It has created within its own branch an enormous, but so far only partially realized, knowledge and information asset for sustaining both the intelligent governance of the United States in the twenty-first century and the prosperity of our people. The present management and staff of the Library are suggesting an optimal strategy for sustaining the service mission of this institution—and of responsibly extending it for the health of our republic.

Part 2. Overview: Context: Our History and the Library Today

A. The Library of Congress is a living monument to the remarkable wisdom of the Founding Fathers, who saw access to an ever-expanding body of knowledge as essential to a dynamic democracy. The Library's three buildings are named for Thomas Jefferson, John Adams, and James Madison. With the support of these presidents, the Congress, as soon as it moved to the new capital city of Washington in 1800, established the Library based on an initial collection of law and reference books, and established the Joint Committee on the Library as the first Joint Committee of the Congress in 1802.

B. Jefferson, in particular, took a keen interest in the new institution. After the British burned the Capitol and the Library during the War of 1812, Congress accepted Jefferson's offer to "recommence" the Library and purchased his multilingual 6,487-volume collection (then the finest in America) at a price of $23,950. It contained volumes in many languages on a wide variety of subjects, from architecture to geography and the sciences. Anticipating the argument that his collection might seem too wide-ranging for the

Congress, Jefferson said that "there is in fact, no subject to which a member of Congress may not have occasion to refer."

C. Jefferson's ideals of a "universal" collection and of sharing knowledge as widely as possible still guide the Library. With congressional blessing and support, the Library has grown to serve the Congress and the nation more broadly in ways that no other library has ever done, largely as a result of four milestone laws: (1) the Copyright Law of 1870, which centralized the nation's copyright functions in the Library and stipulated that two copies of every book, pamphlet, map, print, photograph, and piece of music registered for copyright in the United States be deposited in the Library; (2) the 1886 authorization of the first separate Library of Congress building that contained openly accessible reading rooms and exhibition space for the general public; (3) the 1902 law that authorized the Library to sell copies of its cataloging records inexpensively to the nation's libraries and thus massively help to subsidize the entire American library system; and (4) the law in 1931 that established the program in the Library to create and supply free library materials to blind and physically handicapped readers throughout the country. The Congress thus established the basis both for the continued growth of the collections and for the extension of the Library's services to citizens everywhere.

D. In 1832, the Congress established the Law Library as the first separate department of the Library of Congress, reflecting the Library's origins as a collection of law books to support the legislative work of the Congress. The Law Library remains the only source for the Congress for research and reference services in foreign, comparative, and international law.

E. In 1914, the Congress created the Legislative Reference Service (LRS) as a separate entity within the Library to provide specialized services to "Congress and committees and Members thereof." In 1946, the Congress granted LRS further statutory status within the Library and directed it to employ specialists to cover broad subject areas. The Congress renamed LRS as CRS in 1970 and enhanced its analytical capabilities by defining its policy role for the Congress and emphasizing research support to its committees.

F. More recently, a series of congressional statutes have created within the Library of Congress the American Folklife Center (1976), the American Television and Radio Archives (1976), the National Center for the Book (1977), the National Film Preservation Board (1988), the National Film Preservation Foundation (1996), the Cooperative Acquisitions Program Revolving Fund (1997), the Sound Recording Preservation Board and Foundation (2000), and the authorization of three revolving funds for fee services (2000)—further extending the Library of Congress's national role.

G. In December 2000, Congress tasked the Library (P.L. 106-554) to develop a plan and lead an effort to make sure that important digital materials can be preserved for our national information reserve. The new digital technology offers great promise, but it also creates an unprecedented surfeit of data in an unstable and ephemeral environment. The Library's National Digital Information Infrastructure and Preservation Program (NDIIPP) plan was approved by the Congress in December 2002 and envisions the establishment of a national network of committed partners, collaborating in a digital preservation architecture with defined roles and responsibilities. Over the next two to five years, the Library plans to seed practical projects and to sponsor research-advancing development of a national preservation infrastructure.

H. To begin building that infrastructure, the Library is developing (a) a preservation network of partners to preserve and provide long-term access to digital content and (b) the architecture components that will permit digital preservation. By establishing NDIIPP, Congress chose to capitalize on the Library's long history and unique position in analog selection and preservation to become a steward of the digital preservation infrastructure. As a trusted convener, the Library will continue to bring together all the stakeholders in this new digital landscape—creators, distributors, and users—to build a digital preservation infrastructure that fosters creativity, protects the rights of individuals, and balances the claims of creators for protection and of users to access information and the legacy of innovation

Part 3: Strategic Goals, Objectives, and Measures

Goal 1. Build and preserve a comprehensive collection of knowledge and creativity in all formats and languages for use by the Congress and other customers.

Goal 2. Provide maximum access and facilitate effective use of the collections by the Congress and other customers.

Goal 3. Lead, promote, and support the growth and influence of the national and international library and information communities.

Goal 4. Expand, manage, and communicate Library of Congress digital strategies and roles.

Goal 5. Manage and sustain digital content.

Goal 6. Provide high-quality and timely legal research, analysis, and legal reference services to the Congress, the executive branch agencies, courts, the legal community, and other customers.

Goal 7. Acquire, secure, maintain, preserve, and make accessible a comprehensive legal collection, in both analog and digital formats, for use by the Congress, executive branch agencies, courts, the legal community, and other customers.

Goal 8. Expand and enhance the Global Legal Information Network (GLIN).

Goal 9. Carry out the statutory mission of the Copyright Office to administer copyright and related laws embodied in Title 17 to provide benefit to the nation.

Goal 10. Formulate and provide expert advice to the Congress, executive branch agencies, courts, and international entities in the furtherance of maintaining a strong and effective national and international copyright system.

Goal 11. Be an effective voice for the principles of copyright, which benefit the public, by providing information and informing the public debate on copyright issues.

Goal 12. Carry out the statutory mission of the Congressional Research Service to assist the Congress as it undertakes its legislative responsibilities by providing multidisciplinary, nonpartisan, confidential, timely, and objective analysis of public policy problems and their possible solutions.

Goal 13. Ensure that a high-quality, responsive, and free national reading program is available to the nation's blind and physically handicapped people.

Goal 14. Enhance the management and utilization of the Library's Revolving and Reimbursable funds.

Goal 15. Manage Human Capital so the Library is able to attract and maintain an outstanding workforce with the skills, resources, and dedication to deliver a range of high-quality, cutting-edge services, in all the Library's program and support areas.

Goal 16. Create an environment that supports delivery of superior service to the Congress and the American people through effective communication and management of business and supporting processes and financial resources, and that provides a safe and healthy workplace. This goal and its objectives represent cross-cutting activities that "enable" the program organizations of the Library to carry out their missions. While performance of these objectives should be transparent to the Congress and the public, the objectives are vital to serving the Library's customers.

Goal 17. Manage and sustain mission-critical IT programs.

Goal 18. Provide effective security and emergency planning for the Library's staff and visitors, collections, facilities, and other assets.

Part 4: Moving Forward

A. Process

The Library's Planning, Programming, Budgeting, Execution, and Evaluation System (PPBEES) process is a continuing effort driven by the plan's vision, the progress toward achieving its goals and objectives, and management and stakeholder response to evolving program requirements and the needs of our customers and stakeholders. The plan itself is a living document, subject to review and revision.

To convert the plan's broad, strategic goals into executable fiscal year increments, in step 1 of the PPBEES process, the Library drafts Annual Program Performance Plans (AP3s) with program-focused annual goals and targets. Then, after internal review by the Library's Executive Committee, the annual goals are used to develop the Library's budget request. Within 30 days after enactment of the Library's appropriations, the Library is obligated to revise and convert its AP3s into the Operating Plan, which is submitted to the Congress and which links the annual program goals and targets to the financial resources at the program level.

B. Evaluation

Progress toward achieving the goals and objectives of this strategic plan is a continuing process. In addition to its internal review and evaluation process, the Library relies on ideas and comments from the Congress and external stakeholders. Congressional comments and guidance are of particular importance to the planning process. The three major aspects of the evaluation process are:

1. Annual reviews: As the Library executes the Operating Plans supporting this strategic plan, organizations conduct quarterly program reviews to determine and report their progress toward attaining annual goals. As long as deviations from the Operating Plan are minimal, revisions to this Strategic Plan are not necessary. At the end of each fiscal year, the Library conducts a year-end program review–PPBEES step 5. At that time, the Executive Committee and the Librarian may direct appropriate adjustments to the strategic plan. These adjustments will typically be minor unless some aspect of attaining the strategic plan is clearly in jeopardy. In addition to any minor adjustments to the strategic plan, the Librarian issues an annual planning guidance memorandum identifying modifications needed to: the Operating Plan being executed, the AP3s that are the basis for the budget request being reviewed by the Congress, and/or the AP3s about to be created.

2. Mid-plan: A major review of the Strategic Plan will be conducted during fiscal 2006 at the plan's midpoint. This review may entail "mid-course corrections," but will not, typically, involve a major rewrite.

3. Major revision: During the penultimate year of the plan, fiscal 2007, the Library will convene its planning "community" to undertake the next major revision/rewrite covering the next strategic planning period.

C. Integrating the plan into the Library's management efforts.

1. Each Service and Support Unit will use this plan as the basis for developing a Strategic Plan for its organization. The Digital Executive Oversight Group, through OSI, will oversee the development of the Library's Digital Strategic Plan and ensure its consistency with this plan. Each organization's strategic plan will address the same years (2004–2008) as the Library's plan.

2. Managers throughout the Library will use this plan's strategic goals and objectives and their organization's strategic plan to develop measurable annual program goals and targets. The resulting AP3s serve as the basis for detailed planning and coordination of support requirements between organizations, and the annual goals and targets will form the basis for individual annual performance plans wherever such plans are required by management within the organization.

D. Reporting progress to Library stakeholders.

The Library's "Annual Program Performance Plan, End of Year Program Review" will provide the basis for reporting progress to stakeholders. Additionally, changes made to the strategic plan as a result of annual program reviews and the mid-course review will be distributed to the stakeholders. The Library of Congress Strategic Planning Office will maintain the list of stakeholders, distribute the *Annual Report* to them, and provide for wide dissemination of the report among the Library's staff.

LIBRARY OF CONGRESS TRUST FUND BOARD

Created March 3, 1925, the Library of Congress Trust Fund Board provides the legal structure for the administration of gift funds. In the early 1920s, Mrs. Elizabeth Sprague Coolidge, a trained musician and patroness of music, was seeking a new site for a concert series she supported. She offered Librarian Herbert Putnam $60,000 in 1924 to build an auditorium in the Library. Later, she provided an endowment for music festivals and concerts, awards for original compositions, and an annual honorarium for the chief of the Library's Music Division.

The Coolidge funds were administered through a trust company because there was no law permitting the Library to administer endowments. However, Senator George Wharton Pepper soon introduced a bill drafted by Librarian Herbert Putnam to create a Board consisting of the Librarian (as Secretary), the secretary of the Treasury, the chair of Congress's Joint Committee on the Library, and two members of the public appointed by the president. The role of the Board was to "accept, receive, hold, and administer such gifts, bequests, or devises of property for the benefit of, or in connection with the Library, its collections, or its services." Although the role of receiver and administrator of gifts in the public interest was new to the federal government, Congress unanimously approved the bill. Among the most prominent early benefactors were James B. Wilbur, Archer Huntington, John D. Rockefeller, and Gertrude Clarke Whittall. Together with Mrs. Coolidge's gift, Whittall's presentation of five Stradivari instruments and funds for concerts helped establish the Library as a patron of the arts. Gifts also enabled Herbert Putnam to employ scholars as consultants.

The Trust Fund Board accepts endowments subject to the approval of the Joint Committee on the Library and acts as trustee for the purposes of investing and collecting income. The Treasurer of the United States is the custodian of securities and funds. In 1992, Public Law 102-246 expanded the number of public members of the Board to 10: four appointed by the Speaker of the House, four by the Senate majority leader, and two by the president.

From a modest beginning in the 1920s, the fund gradually increased. Support for the National Digital Library Project brought the Trust Fund to $36 million in fiscal 1995, and the rapid increases in market value created the need for an investment subcommittee of the Board to help manage the portfolio.

The Library's uses of private funds have always been strictly limited: "to do for American scholarship and cultivation what is not likely to be done by other agencies." But Herbert Putnam's hopes that the Library might share its collections more widely and employ experts to develop them has been echoed by every Librarian since. The Library's current educational and cultural programs thus result from the generosity of private citizens. (JA)

Rosenberg, Jane Aikin. *The Nation's Great Library: Herbert Putnam and the Library of Congress, 1899–1939.* Urbana, Ill.: University of Illinois Press, 1993.

Library of Congress Trust Fund Board. *Annual Report for the Fiscal Year Ending September 30, 2003.* Washington, D.C.: Library of Congress, 2004.

LIBRARY SERVICES

The largest Library of Congress administrative service unit, Library Services, was formed in November 1995 from divisions and offices in three former service units: Collections Services, Constituent Services, and Cultural Affairs. It is the service unit, which performs most "standard" library functions, including acquisitions, cataloging, classification, reference service, and preservation of the collections. Its mission is "to organize, preserve, secure, and sustain for the present and future use of the Congress and the Nation a comprehensive record of American history and creativity and a universal collection of human knowledge." Under the direction of an Associate Librarian, Library Services initially was organized into seven directorates: Acquisitions, Area Studies Collections, Cataloging, National Services, Operations, Preservation, and Public Services Collections. In September 2004, a realignment of Library Services into five directorates was approved: Acquisitions and Bibliographic Access, Collections and Services, Preservation, Partnerships and Outreach Programs, and Technology Policy. Library Services also administers many unique Library of Congress programs, including the National Film Preservation Board, the American Television and Radio Archives, the Network Development and MARC Standards Office, the Cataloging Distribution Service, the National Library for the Blind and Physically Handicapped, the American Folklife Center, and the Center for the Book.

At the end of fiscal year 2003 (September 30, 2003), 2,088 of the Library's 4,151 permanent, full-time employees were part of Library Services. (JYC)

LINCOLNIANA

The Library of Congress contains one of the largest collections of research materials by and about Abraham Lincoln (1809–1865) in the world. The Lincoln Papers in the Manuscript Division contain approximately 20,000 items, mostly from the 1850s through 1861–1865, his presidential years. Treasures include Lincoln's draft of the Emancipation Proclamation and his March 4, 1865, draft of his second Inaugural Address. The final release of the Lincoln Papers online took place in early 2002. The papers can be accessed at the American Memory Web site. The collection includes 20,000 documents, comprising 61,000 digital images and annotated transcriptions of approximately 11,000 documents provided by the Lincoln Studies Center at Knox College in Galesburg, Illinois.

An ambrotype portrait of Abraham Lincoln ca. 1855-60, from the Library's Anson Conger Goodyear Collection. The Library of Congress has one of the largest and most varied collections of research materials by and about Abraham Lincoln in existence. LC/Prints and Photographs Division. LC-USZ62-7728A.

Alfred Whital Stern (1881–1960) of Chicago deposited his renowned Lincolniana collection of items by and about Lincoln in the Library in 1951, accompanied by an endowment to provide for its future growth, and the promise that it would be converted in time to a gift. It was formally presented to the Library in 1953. Today it comprises more than 10,500 books, as well as pamphlets, broadsides, sheet music, autograph letters, prints, cartoons, maps, drawings, and other memorabilia that offer a unique view of Lincoln's life and times. The "We'll Sing to Abe Our Song!" online collection, drawn from the Stern collection, includes more than 200 sheet music compositions that represent Lincoln, emancipation, and the Civil War as reflected in popular music.

In February 2000, the Illinois Historic Preservation Agency presented to the Library the "Lincoln Legal Papers DVD Edition," a collection of more than 100,000 records associated with Lincoln's legal career from 1836 to 1861. The DVD complements the Lincoln materials in the Library of Congress, many of which are available online in a Web presentation called "Mr. Lincoln's Virtual Library." The Lincoln Papers came to the Library of Congress from Robert Todd Lincoln (1843–1926), who arranged for their organization and care shortly after his father was assassinated. Prior to their deposit in the Library in 1919, they were used by Lincoln's presidential secretaries, John G. Nicolay and John Hay in the research and writing of their 10-volume biography, *Abraham Lincoln: A History* (N.Y., 1890). Robert Todd Lincoln deeded the papers to the Library in 1923 on the condition that they remain closed for 21 years after his own death. On July 26, 1947, the Lincoln papers were officially opened to the public.

Lincoln's relationship to the Library of Congress, while not as vital to the institution as its connection with Jefferson, nonetheless is of close and lasting interest.

The relationship's beginnings were rocky. Ignoring the advice of the Joint Committee on the Library to continue the appointment of the current Librarian, on May 24, 1861, newly elected President Lincoln named a political supporter, Indiana physician John G. Stephenson, as the new Librarian of Congress. However four years later Lincoln appointed a more qualified candidate, bookman Ainsworth Rand Spofford, as Librarian. Between March 1861 and April 1865, when Lincoln was assassinated, approximately 125 books were charged out to the President's account; it appears likely, however, that most of them were used by his family or staff.

The Library's close involvement with Lincoln was reinforced in the middle decades of the twentieth century by the personal interest of two Library of Congress Lincoln enthusiasts and scholars: David C. Mearns and Roy P. Basler. Mearns held many administrative positions at the Library from 1918 until his retirement in 1967. As director of the Reference Department from 1943 to 1949, he presided over the 1947 opening of the Lincoln papers. His books *The Lincoln Papers* (1948) and *Largely Lincoln* (1961) trace the Library of Congress-Lincoln connection and evoke the cultural climate of the 1940s and 1950s. Basler, who edited *The Collected Works of Abraham*

Lincoln (1953), came to the Library in 1952 after serving for five years as the executive secretary of the Abraham Lincoln Association.

Lincoln and the Library of Congress also reinforce each other as symbols of American democracy. Lincoln and his words are depicted several times in the Jefferson Building, which was begun in 1886 and completed in 1897. Librarian of Congress Spofford, for example, chose the words from the Gettysburg Address that are inscribed on the ceiling of the second floor Northeast Pavilion; the same quotation ("government of the people, by the people, for the people. . .) is featured in the central panel of artist Elihu Vedder's mural "Government" above the entrance door to the Main Reading Room. Artist Edwin Blashfield's "Evolution of Civilization" mural in the collar of the dome of the Main Reading Room uses a beardless Lincoln as the model for the face of "Science," which is depicted as America's major contribution to civilization and culture.

Lincoln's influence continues to be felt at the Library of Congress. In 1975 in the closet safe in the Librarian's Office, Librarian of Congress Daniel J. Boorstin discovered a large envelope containing the contents of Lincoln's pockets on the night he was assassinated at Ford's Theater. A donation from Robert Todd Lincoln's daughter to the Library in 1937, the two pairs of eyeglasses, penknife, watch fob, cuff link, monogrammed handkerchief and wallet (which contained newspaper clippings about Lincoln and a Confederate $5 bill) were put on public display on February 12, 1976. Today these items are among the most popular displays in "American Treasures of the Library of Congress," the permanent exhibition in the Library's Jefferson Building. (JYC)

In 1975, in the closet safe in the Librarian's Office, Librarian of Congress Daniel J. Boorstin discovered a large envelope that contained the contents of Lincoln's pockets the night he was assassinated. A twentieth century gift to the Library from Robert Todd Lincoln's daughter, the envelope contained two pairs of eyeglasses, a lens polisher, penknife, watch fob, cufflink, monogrammed handkerchief, a wallet containing nine newspaper clippings about Lincoln, and a Confederate $5 bill. Photograph: Roger Foley.

LOAN SERVICES

In 1905, Librarian of Congress Herbert Putnam, defending his recently inaugurated practice (1901) of lending Congress's books to other libraries, told a critic that he believed it was worth the risk of losing the book in transit because "a book used is, after all, fulfilling a higher mission than a book that is merely being preserved for possible future use." Putnam had reason to be defensive because interlibrary lending was still a novel idea that was viewed with suspicion by the guardians of large libraries, including several members of the congressional committees that oversaw his stewardship of the Library of Congress.

When Congress first established its Library in the Capitol in 1800, the members knew that the books would be a resource in great demand in a muddy, half-built city that lacked cultural institutions. The earliest set of rules (1802) restricted use to members of the House and Senate and the president and vice president of the United States. Even then, some items were non-circulating; according to the rules, "No map shall be permitted to be taken out of said library."

It was not until 1812 that the justices of the Supreme Court, who sat in a courtroom in the Capitol but worked out of their homes, were allowed to borrow books from the Library. For the rest of the century, Congress slowly but gradually approved borrowing privileges for new classes of borrowers: the diplomatic corps, the House and Senate chaplains, the press, ex-presidents (when in the District of Columbia), and Cabinet secretaries. But it rejected some requests, for example, in 1857 when judges of the Court of Claims were refused on the grounds that "The list of those who are entitled to take books from the Library of Congress is very large; and the privilege is often abused by those who are entitled to it, using it for the supply of others than themselves and their own families." Outside of Congress itself, direct loans from the Library of Congress are still restricted, mostly to federal government officials.

By the turn of the century, when Putnam took up the cause of interlibrary loan, the nature of the Library had changed dramatically. Decades earlier in 1866, with its receipt of the transfer of the Smithsonian Institution library, the Library of Congress began to move swiftly towards a new destiny as a national institution. This compass change was fixed by the assignment of the U.S. Copyright Office and function to the Library in 1870, and confirmed by the construction of a new building, which was opened in 1897. On the eve of the Library's move to its own building, the Joint Committee on the Library held hearings on the "condition" and administration of the Library. At those hearings Melvil Dewey, director of the New York State Library, recommended that "the national library ought, under certain circumstances, to lend books all over the country." Putnam, then librarian at the Boston Public Library and also a witness, mentioned that "loaning of books" was a function the Library might undertake.

In March 1901, President McKinley signed a supplemental appropriations act that included the obscure provision that "facilities for study and research in the Government Departments, the Library of Congress, the National Museum, the Zoological Park, the Bureau of Ethnology, the Fish Commission, the Botanic Gardens, and similar institutions ... shall be afforded to scientific investigators and to duly qualified individuals, students and graduates of institutions of learning in the several States and Territories." Already armed with the authority allowing him "to make rules and regulations for the government of the Library of Congress," Putnam recognized the 1901 law as the basis on which to extend loans to libraries outside the District of Columbia and the Library's interlibrary loan service was soon inaugurated.

He was careful to set the stage in an address to the American Library Association in July 1901. "Must the use of this great collection be limited to Washington?" he asked in a talk entitled *What May be Done for Libraries by the Nation*. "How many of the students who need some book in the Library of Congress—perhaps there alone—can come to Washington to consult it at the moment of need? ... If the National Library is to *be* the national library—?" He left the question unanswered, but in December of that year he told the American Historical Association that scholars were welcome to request material from the Library of Congress. "A system of inter-library loan may thus enable the unusual book at Washington to render a service in any part of the United States." Three books were lent in 1901 and 110 in 1902, and in 1907 Putnam reprinted the Library's circular on lending rules in his *Annual Report*. In the circular, he espoused a *noblesse oblige* philosophy that would remain the watchword of American interlending for most of the century: "The loan will rest on the theory of a special service to scholarship which is not within the power or the duty of the local library to render. Its purpose is to aid research calculated to advance the boundaries of knowledge, by the loan of unusual books not readily accessible elsewhere."

Two years later, William Warner Bishop, Superintendent of the Reading Room, described a growing national trend toward lending books among libraries in the cause of scholarship. Writing in the

December 1909 issue of *Library Journal*, Bishop described the beginnings of standardized request forms and analyzed statistics: during the year, the Library had received 919 requests and filled 562. The primary reason for not filling requests was "the fact that the Library of Congress did not own the books desired," but some were not sent because "they did not come within the scope of inter-library loans as defined by this library." Requests had come from 119 institutions in 40 states, Canada, and Cuba. Borrowing institutions were about equally split between public and academic libraries, but college and university libraries requested twice as many items as their public library counterparts.

It should have come as no surprise that librarians were quick to identify and request material in the Library's collections. In the same year that he quietly began lending to other libraries, Putnam more publicly inaugurated one of the most significant works in American bibliography, the National Union Catalog. In his 1901 *Annual Report*, he wrote that, "next in importance to an adequate exhibit of its own resources, comes the ability [of a library] to supply information as to the resources of other libraries." To this end, the Library of Congress would distribute its own cataloging and also compile in Washington an integrated file of cataloging from the major American research libraries. By 1909, the Union Catalog included cards from the Boston Public Library, Harvard University Library, John Crerar Library, and the New York Public Library, and Putnam stated that it gave scholars "the closest approximation now available to a complete record of books in American libraries."

The Union Catalog was an idea perfect for its time. Librarians rushed to contribute their own cataloging. By 1926, the catalog had grown to nearly 3 million cards, but it was inadequate to meet the growing needs of libraries. The American Library Association then convinced John D. Rockefeller Jr. to support the project for five years at $50,000 per year, after which the Library of Congress continued it with appropriated funds.

When Rockefeller committed to support the Union Catalog, it was because interlibrary lending had become the norm among American university libraries and the Library of Congress had become the pre-eminent lender in the country, providing more than 3,000 books a year to libraries outside the District of Columbia and as far away as Canada, Italy, Germany, and Norway. But lending placed both financial and philosophical strains on institutions. As Frederick W. Ashley, then Superintendent of the Reading Room, told members of the American Library Association who were trying to convince him to lend Library of Congress books to graduate students (as opposed only to faculty members): "Scholars resorting to [the national library] from all parts of the country expect to find upon its shelves any book which it is known to have acquired. In meeting that obligation the circulation of books is not a help. A national library that lends books forces some sort of a compromise between the interests of the passing and coming generations."

In 1944, faced with a growing demand for loans, Librarian of Congress Archibald McLeish centralized responsibility for lending in a single division during his massive reorganization of the Library. Up to that time the nine reference divisions and the Law Library had each been responsible for keeping records and establishing policies for lending its own material. Under McLeish's reorganization the new Loan Division "administers all outside loans (including loans of books, periodicals, maps, music, prints, embossed books, sound recordings, etc.) And, as a result of this centralization of responsibility, is enabled to exercise uniform controls and establish uniform procedures governing the Library's lending operations." The division also took control of a "central charge file," which promised to record the whereabouts of every book withdrawn from the stacks for use in the library's buildings or on loan outside the buildings. In its first full year of operation, the new division oversaw the loan of 13,628 items to libraries outside the Washington area.

Loans continued to increase. The post-war years brought students flooding into American universities, creating unprecedented demands for research material and making interlibrary borrowing a critical ingredient of any graduate program. By 1963, George A. Schwegmann Jr., chief of the Union Catalog Division, would tell a gathering of librarians, "we are living in a time when the relatively unrestricted interlibrary use of research materials is considered by many to be a normal function of research libraries." Schwegmann pointed out that "approximately 50 percent of all the different book titles owned by American libraries are held in one copy only and that practically all of these single copies are owned by about 100 major research libraries." He concluded that "library interdependence, including inter-library loan, is changing from a courtesy and privilege to something close to a duty and an obligation in the national interest."

The key to this interdependence, and perhaps its cause, as Schwegmann was uniquely aware, was the growth of local, regional and national union catalogs modeled on the Library's Union Catalog. During the post-war period, the Library began publishing its catalog in book format and its *National Union Catalog of Pre-1956 Imprints* began in 1968 to create one massive location tool for older publications in U.S. libraries. Knowledge of these holdings stimulated requests for loans, and in that year the Loan Division sent 33,971 pieces to other libraries.

The Library of Congress automated its own public catalog at the end of 1980, and the next year the final supplemental volumes of the 755-volume *National Union Catalog of Pre-1956 Imprints* were sent to subscribers. In the same year, the Library reassigned to the Loan Division the staff who had been providing locations to libraries seeking books listed in the thousands of cards that had been the Union Catalog. This organizational change created a single service to provide both "last resort" loans from the Library's collection and referrals to other libraries when the material was not owned by the Library. "The division's work was contained in two wooden boxes, one for traditional loan requests and one filled (and always overflowing) with mimeographed location request forms from libraries asking for assistance in finding some obscure item," wrote the head of the loan service in 1988. Seeking to identify an obscure item, Loan Division staff might search the Library's new computer catalog, its official (paper) catalog, published union catalogs, the Ohio College Library Center (OCLC) or Research Libraries Group (RLG) databases, foreign national library catalogs, and commercial databases.

Unlike the United Kingdom or Canada, both of which created centralized lending collections in their national libraries, the Library filled a unique role, providing a service in Washington that could not be provided in a borrower's home state or region. While large university libraries might actually lend more books, the Library served as the lender of last resort. Foreign lending has never been channeled through Washington, to the confusion of some foreign borrowers who expected the Library of Congress to act as a clearinghouse but were told that they must redirect their request to another U.S. library.

By 1990, and as more and more libraries joined bibliographic networks, the value of a centralized location service diminished. Faced with the enormous riches found on the computerized bibliographic networks, users began to focus more on acquiring known items and to worry less about rounding up the obscure citation. The total number of filled loans among U.S. libraries during this period grew exponentially, thanks to easy identification and ordering through bibliographic networks such as OCLC and RLG. The number of loan requests coming to the Library from U.S. libraries increased only, though not in proportion to the amount of lending going on around the country. Emphasis began to be placed on expediting responses to the outpouring of online requests from libraries using the bibliographic utilities. Searching for alternative locations was quietly abandoned in favor of faster deliveries of what was available from Washington.

The year 2001 marked the centennial of interlibrary lending at the Library of Congress. By then, it had become increasingly clear that new digital technologies were allowing more and more material to be "shipped" over the Internet and delivered directly to the researchers' desk. Moreover, a new integrated library system was beginning to provide borrowers and potential borrowers with far more accurate knowledge of what was available from the Library of Congress than ever before. In 2002, the Library merged its Loan Division and its Collections Management Division into a new unit, the Collections Access, Loan and Management Division. Yet the Library's basic lending policy remains the one defined by Herbert Putnam in his first 1901 circular on the rules for interlibrary loan: "The loan will rest on the theory of a special service to scholarship which it is not within the power or the duty of the local library to render. Its purpose is to aid the research calculated to advance the boundaries of knowledge, by the loan of unusual books not readily accessible elsewhere." (LCW)

LOCAL HISTORY AND GENEALOGY

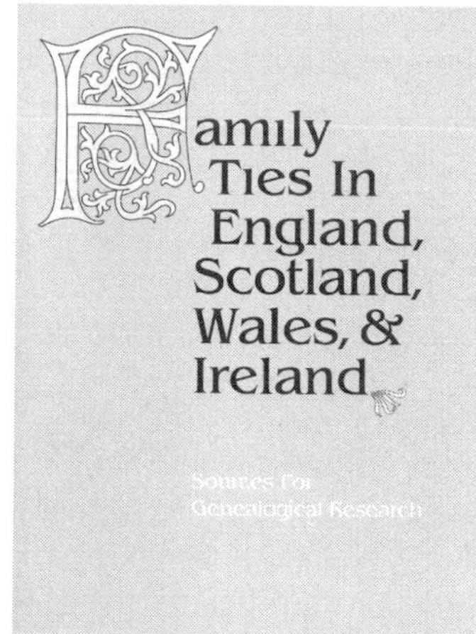

A genealogical reference work published by the Library in 1998.
LC/Publishing Office.

The Library of Congress has one of the world's premier collections of U.S. and foreign genealogical and local historical publications. The Library's genealogy collection began in 1815 when Congress purchased Thomas Jefferson's personal library, which included the *Domesday Book*, Sir William Dugdale's *The Baronetage of England*, and *Peerage of Ireland*.

The collection grew slowly until 1870 when Congress centralized all copyright registration and deposit activity at the Library of Congress. However, immediate space problems in the Capitol prevented the active use of the collection until the Jefferson Building opened in 1897. In 1899, Chief Assistant Librarian of Congress Ainsworth Rand Spofford mentioned the genealogical collections in his essay "The Function of a National Library," which was published in Herbert Small's *Handbook of the New Library of Congress*. To demonstrate how the Library of Congress, as a national library, was "in some degree, the intellectual centre of a great capital," with great flourish Spofford described how "numberless seekers after books and information" used the Library. For example, "here the zealous grubber after facts of genealogy borrows among endless tables of family births, deaths, and marriages, and the ever present investigator of heraldry traces the blazonry of crests and coats of arms."

In August 1935, a "Reading Room for American Local History and Genealogy" was opened on Deck 47 in the stacks of the Thomas Jefferson Building. Its purpose was "to provide a more adequate service for those coming to the Library from all parts of the United States to consult our unusually large and important collections of genealogy, including state and local history, and to throw proper safeguards about these collections, large portions of which are irreplaceable." The genealogy and local history collections were combined on Deck 47, and space was cleared for approximately 50 readers' desks, for a reference collection of about 5,000 volumes, and for the necessary card indexes. The Librarian's 1936 *Annual Report* notes that two assistants were continuously on duty from 9 a.m. to 10 p.m., and during the first year of operation, "between 600 and 700 readers used the collection each week." Since 1935, the Local History and Genealogy Reading Room has been relocated six times; currently, it is on the ground floor of the Jefferson Building. However, wherever it has been located, it always has been one of the Library's busiest reading rooms.

The local history and genealogy collections are especially strong in North American, British Isles and Irish, French, German, and Scandinavian resources. The majority of the genealogies have come as gifts from around the world; the Australians have been particularly generous, and their donations have greatly enhanced British Isles and Australian research at the Library of Congress. These international strengths are further supported and enriched by the Library's incomparable royalty, nobility, and heraldry collection, making it one of a few libraries in America that offer such comprehensive collections.

In addition to the national and international genealogy and local history collections at the Library of Congress, other related material of great significance to these fields is found in the areas of archival resources, biography, church history, city directories, folklore, geography, and history. Important genealogical resources are also found in special collections of manuscripts, maps and atlases, microforms, newspapers, photographs, rare books, and CD-ROMs and other electronic forms, housed in various custodial divisions of the Library.

Fortunately, the Library has a number of outstanding tools to help users gain access to these collections. *The Library of Congress: A Guide to Genealogical and Historical Research* by James Neagles (Salt Lake City, Utah: Ancestry Publishing, 1990) is a comprehensive handbook for the Library's genealogical collections and also contains an inventory of the Library's vast city directories collection. Additionally, the Library has more than a dozen reference guides to assist genealogical researchers.

For remote access, the Library of Congress provides many resources and services via the Internet, all of which are described or available from the Library's Web site. The Local History and Genealogy

Reading Room's homepage provides general information about the reading room, including the collections and their use. Equally important, both the Library's and the Local History and Genealogy Reading Room's homepages provide access to the Library's online catalog. The Library is beginning to link catalog records to digital versions of actual works, offering some digital versions of books in the collections. Currently, no genealogies have been included, but more than 300 local histories have been digitized and are available on the Library's American Memory site.

Aside from digital versions of a few local histories, material in microform for which the Library holds the master negative is available for interlibrary loan. Since the Library has microfilmed all of its holdings in class CS71 (U.S. genealogy) published from 1876 to 1900, a significant part of the genealogical collection has become available through interlibrary loan for use in libraries around the country. To identify genealogy titles on microfilm consult *Genealogies Cataloged by the Library of Congress Since 1986: With a List of Established Forms of Family Names and a List of Genealogies Converted to Microfilm Since 1983* (Washington, D.C. : Library of Congress, 1991). The Library of Congress does not permit its books on genealogy, heraldry, and U.S. local history to circulate on interlibrary loan. The Library's Photoduplication Service can supply photocopies of items located in the Library's collection if there are no copyright restrictions.

Staff members in the Local History and Genealogy Reading Room (LH&G), located on the ground floor of the Jefferson Building, answer questions about heraldry, royalty and nobility, biography, military and naval history, American history, as well as genealogy and local history. Because many genealogies are self-published and have been donated to the Library from around the world for many generations, the Library's collections contain more than 40,000 genealogies and more than 100,000 volumes of local history.

Specialized card catalogs that index genealogy, heraldry, and local history in the collections are kept in the LH&G Reading Room, where public Internet terminals and subscription databases also are available. In addition to its genealogy collection, many of the Library's reading rooms offer essential sources for genealogy, particularly the Main Reading Room, and the Geography and Map, Manuscript, Microform, Newspaper and Current Periodical, and Rare Book and Special Collections Reading Rooms.

The Local History and Genealogy Reading Room on the ground floor of the Jefferson Building. Photograph: LC/Levon Avdoyan.

While the Library of Congress is rich in collections of manuscripts, microfilms, newspapers, photographs, maps, and published material, it is not an archive or repository for unpublished or primary source county, state, or church records. Researchers seeking county records will need to visit the courthouse or a library in the county of interest, the state archives, the Family History Library in Salt Lake City or one of its Family History Centers, all of which might have either the original county records or microform copies. Libraries, archives, and genealogical and historical societies at the national, state, and local levels are all vital resources in this complex puzzle of genealogical research. (JPR)

Library of Congress Information Bulletin 49 (July 30, 1990): 271–273.

MACHINE-READABLE CATALOGING (MARC)

MARC is the acronym for a computer format for bibliographic data. MARC originated at the Library of Congress. It is a structure that can be used to transmit within and between computer systems information about library and other materials. The MARC format helped to make possible the computer-based networks that supply library users worldwide with catalog information in every language. The development of MARC as a standard means for entering bibliographic information helped encourage librarians to computerize their operations beginning in the 1970s.

Early in the 1960s, with the assistance of a grant from the Council on Library Resources, Inc. (CLR), a survey team's report *Automation and the Library of Congress* (1964) urged the conversion of the Library's card catalog and other bibliographic operations to machine-readable form. A study by Inforonics, Inc. yielded a method for producing machine-readable cataloging from perforated tape generated by computer-controlled equipment. At a Conference on MAchine-Readable Catalog Copy held in January 1965, advisors from the library community agreed that the Library of Congress should develop machine-readable catalog records that other libraries could use. A three-member staff team subsequently delivered "A Proposed Format for a Standardized MAchine-Readable Record" in June 1965. At a second conference, held in November 1965, librarians once again expressed support for the work, and the Library obtained funding from CLR for a pilot project.

The MARC pilot project began in February 1966. It was headed by Henriette Avram, who subsequently revised the proposed format and would become the head of the MARC Distribution Service (1969) and the MARC Development Office (1970). With the addition of four more libraries, the project operated until June 1968, distributing 50,000 records. Team members at the Library then revised the format, named it MARC II, and the Library produced a *Subscriber's Guide to the MARC Distribution Service* (August 1968) and other MARC instruction manuals. The first tapes were sent to subscribers in March 1969. A series of MARC institutes sponsored by the Library with the support of the American Library Association (ALA) and held at various locations nationwide drew several thousand library staff members over the next two years. MARC tapes were quickly adopted as the base for a centralized database by not-for-profit bibliographic utilities such as the OCLC Online Computer Library Network, the Research Libraries Information Network, and the Western Library Network, which also incorporated their member libraries' catalog records. By 1969, MARC had also been adopted by the American Library Association, the Special Libraries Association, the Committee on Science and Technical Information, the Federal Library Committee and the National Libraries Task Force on Automation and Other Cooperative Services. The MARC Editorial Office, functioning originally in the Information Systems Office, moved to the Processing Department that same year to work with the Descriptive Cataloging Division, initially handling only the English-language monographs cataloged by the Library of Congress. In the meantime, the British National Bibliography expressed interest in mounting a United Kingdom MARC project and began working with Library staff. Other countries, too, soon started planning their own machine-readable cataloging systems. One feature that encouraged worldwide use of the MARC format was the development during the pilot project of an expanded character set for roman alphabet languages and romanized forms of non-roman alphabets. Another encouraging development was its adoption as an American National Standard for the transmission of bibliographic data in 1971. Both UK MARC and US MARC were submitted to the International Standards Organization and approved in 1973, thus establishing further incentives for international use. The International Federation of Library Associations (IFLA) began distributing a version known as the MARC International Format in 1975, with the first edition published in 1977 under the title UNIMARC. When fully developed, UNIMARC simplified the exchange of different versions of MARC records, meaning that libraries could translate cataloging records into their own versions of MARC.

By the mid-1970s, the Library of Congress staff had extended MARC to include serials, maps, films, manuscripts, and music; had completed a retrospective conversion project for its cataloged English-language monographs for the years 1968–1973; and had used MARC records to produce the Library's book catalogs for the first time. Non-roman alphabet records were first converted to MARC in 1979, and full conversion from UNIMARC to US MARC was implemented by the mid-1980s, facilitating the use of foreign bibliographic records.

When viewed on a computer screen, a MARC record looks much like a traditional catalog card, but its structure is codified, and catalogers had to learn the codes as well as additional formats for name and subject entries. In 1974, at the Library's suggestion, an American Library Association committee began working with the Library on necessary changes to the format, thus involving the library community in its long-term development. This Committee on Representation in MAchine-Readable Form of Bibliographic Information (MARBI) and the Library's US MARC Advisory Committee review proposals for additions and changes to the MARC formats. The Library also maintains an electronic discussion forum for over 800 users of the formats worldwide.

Librarians initially used MARC records to print cards to file in their catalogs. However, by 1971 the Library had begun work on the Multiple Use MARC System (MUMS), an input-update system that relied on disk storage rather than tape and could therefore be accessible online. By the end of 1972, over 289,000 catalog records were available with about 100,000 added each year. The Library of Congress installed the first terminals for public use in 1975, and by 1977 had opened a Computer Catalog Center to assist users. On the last day of 1980, the Library staff ceased to add cards to the card catalog, and a few years later Library officials contracted with Carrollton Press to convert the cataloged holdings to MARC format.

Terminals available throughout the Library provide free access to all catalogs and databases that the Library maintains or for which it has subscriptions, and public use of the catalog is also available through the Library's Web site. Similarly, many other libraries have now mounted their own Web sites and make their catalogs available to remote users. MARC has permanently changed library work by replacing card and book catalogs with standardized computer records that provide information to a wider public than ever before. (JA)

Avram, Henriette D. *MARC: Its History and Implications*. Washington, D.C.: Library of Congress, 1975.

MACLEISH, ARCHIBALD (1892–1982)

Writer and poet Archibald MacLeish was the first well-known figure from outside the library profession to be nominated and confirmed as Librarian of Congress. His achievements at the Library of Congress between 1939 and 1944 were many; he also was an eloquent spokesman on behalf of libraries and librarianship. His chief accomplishments as Librarian

Writer and poet Archibald MacLeish was the first well-known figure from outside the library world to be nominated and confirmed as Librarian of Congress. In choosing MacLeish to be the ninth Librarian in 1939, President Franklin D. Roosevelt followed the advice of Supreme Court Justice Felix Frankfurter who told him that "only a scholarly man of letters can make a great national library a general place of habitation for scholars."
LC/Prints and Photographs Division. LC-USZ62-614321.

of Congress were a thorough reorganization, development of the first explicit statements of the institution's objectives (the "Canons of Selection" and a statement of reference and research objectives), and a concern for procedures and fairness that brought the Library's administration and staff into accord for the first time in many years. Furthermore, he permanently enlarged the role of the Library of Congress as a repository of the American intellectual and cultural tradition. His contribution to the library profession centered on his frequently expressed belief that librarians must play an active role in American life, particularly in educating the American public to the value of the democratic process.

MacLeish entered public life for the first time at age 47 when, on July 10, 1939, the local postmaster at Conway, Massachusetts administered his oath of office as Librarian of Congress. Born in Glencoe, Illinois, on May 7, 1892, he attended Hotchkiss preparatory school in Connecticut before entering Yale in 1911. After graduating from Yale, he was elected to Phi Beta Kappa. After entering Harvard Law School, he served in the U.S. Army in France during World War I, then returned to Harvard, where he served as editor of the *Harvard Law Review* before graduating in 1919. He gave up law practice with a prominent Boston firm in 1923 for Paris, where he established close ties with other American writers living on the Left Bank and published several collections of verse. He returned to the United States in 1929, joining Henry Luce's new *Fortune* magazine, for which he wrote articles on political and cultural subjects for the next nine years. He continued to write verse and drama, the subjects reflecting his liberal social and political views. Such opinions reinforced MacLeish's intellectual sympathy with the New Deal and contributed to his departure from the Luce organization. They also paved the way for his nomination as Librarian of Congress.

From the start President Franklin D. Roosevelt looked outside the library profession for a successor to Librarian of Congress Herbert Putnam. In choosing MacLeish, Roosevelt followed the advice of his friend Supreme Court Justice Felix Frankfurter, who told the president that "only a scholarly man of letters can make a great national library a general place of habitation for scholars." The nomination was announced at a press conference on June 6, 1939, at which Roosevelt proclaimed that the job of Librarian of Congress required not a professional librarian but "a gentleman and a scholar."

The American Library Association, ignored in the nomination process, protested vigorously. At its annual meeting in San Francisco on June 18, the ALA adopted a resolution opposing the nomination because "the Congress and the American people should have as a Librarian. . . one who is not only a gentleman and a scholar but who is also the ablest Library administrator available. The ALA testified unsuccessfully against the nomination in the Senate hearings. On June 29, 1939, by a vote of 63 to 8, the Senate confirmed the president's choice, and MacLeish became the ninth Librarian of Congress.

When the new Librarian officially began work on October 2, the Library had a book collection of about 6 million volumes, a staff of 1,100, and, in fiscal year 1939, an appropriation of approximately $3 million. The new Librarian immediately tackled the Library's most pressing internal problems, launching studies of the Library's cataloging, acquisitions, personnel, and budget policies. The results were distressing, and MacLeish and his senior staff asked for a substantial increase in the Library's appropriations to remedy the many problems: the request was for $4,200,000 and included 287 additional positions. The Appropriations Committee approved 130 of the new positions and encouraged the new Librarian to continue his "industrious and intelligent" beginning. In response to the Appropriations Committee's report and to continue the studies underway, on April 10, 1941, MacLeish appointed a special Librarian's Committee to analyze the Library's operations—especially its processing activities. The report of the committee, headed by Carleton B. Joeckel of the University of Chicago's Graduate Library School, served as a catalyst for MacLeish's reorganization—a functional restructuring that served as the basis of the Library's administrative structure for the next three years.

While the administrative reorganization was probably MacLeish's most important achievement, it was only one of his accomplishments. He also enhanced the Library's reputation as a major cultural institution, not only because of his own prominence as a poet but also by inaugurating a series of public poetry readings. He also brought many prominent writers and poets to the Library, including the war refugees Alexis Saint-Leger Leger (who wrote using the name Saint-John Perse) and Thomas Mann. Distinguished poet Allen Tate came to the Library to occupy the Library's chair of Poetry in English and to serve as the first editor of a new publication, *The Library of Congress Quarterly Journal of Current Acquisitions*. Relationships between the Library and scholarly and literary communities were improved through a new program of resident fellowships for young scholars and the formation of the Fellows of the Library of Congress, a group of prominent writers and poets.

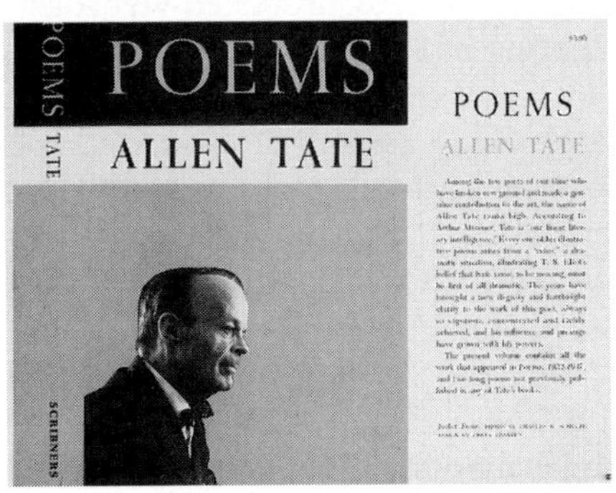

Among his many achievements, MacLeish enhanced the Library's reputation as a major cultural institution. He inaugurated a series of public poetry readings and brought many writers and poets to the Library. He named eminent poet and critic Allen Tate (pictured here) as the Library's Consultant in Poetry in English and as the first editor of the new periodical, The Library of Congress Quarterly Journal of Current Acquisitions. LC Poetry Office.

A wartime librarian, MacLeish quickly became a leading spokesman for the cause of democracy. Speaking before the ALA on May 31, 1940, he asserted that librarians "must become active and not passive agents of the democratic process." People who had bitterly opposed his nomination a year earlier applauded vigorously, and relations between the Library and ALA were on the mend.

MacLeish and Luther H. Evans, his Chief Assistant Librarian, inaugurated a staff *Information Bulletin* and created a staff advisory committee. In April 1942, MacLeish announced the formation of the Librarian's Council, composed of distinguished librarians, scholars, and book collectors who would make recommendations about collection development and reference service. Weekly meetings with department directors were started, and in 1943 the Library administration began holding informal monthly meetings with the professional staff.

During the war, MacLeish helped President Roosevelt in many ways. Those activities meant that he served only part-time as Librarian of Congress, which makes the many achievements of his administration especially remarkable. In October 1941, the president asked him to assume, in addition to his duties as Librarian, supervision of the government's newly established Office of Facts and Figures. In June 1942, the Office of Facts and Figures was combined with other agencies to form the Office of War Information, which MacLeish served part-time as an assistant director. The Librarian also drafted speeches for the president and represented the government at various high-level meetings, as in March 1944 when he went to London as a delegate to the Conference of Allied Ministers of Education, a forerunner of the United Nations. MacLeish apparently indicated a wish to leave the Library of Congress as early as the summer of 1943, but he stayed in office until December 19, 1944, when he resigned to become an Assistant Secretary of State, in charge of public and cultural relations.

MacLeish's relatively brief administration was one of the most fruitful in the history of the Library. The accomplishments were not his alone; the Librarian was the first to acknowledge that his colleagues Luther H. Evans, Verner W. Clapp, and David C. Mearns played major roles. The style, tone, and motivation, however, came directly from MacLeish. He provided the Library and the library profession with inspiration and a sense of historical perspective. His succinct statement of the Library's purpose in the first issue of *The Library of Congress Quarterly*

In September 1944, Librarian MacLeish, center, joins colleagues David C. Mearns, left, and Verner W. Clapp in examining Thomas Jefferson's rough draft of the Declaration of Independence. The document and other Library top treasures had just been returned from wartime safekeeping at Fort Knox, Kentucky.
LC Archives.

Journal of Current Acquisitions (1943) stands today as both a summary and challenge: "The first duty of the Library of Congress is to serve the Congress and the officers and agencies of government. Its second duty is to serve the world of scholarship and letters. Through both it endeavors to serve the American people to whom it belongs and for whom it exists."

Archibald MacLeish died in Boston on April 20, 1982. (JYC)

Benco, Nancy. "Archibald MacLeish: The Poet Librarian," *The Quarterly Journal of the Library of Congress* 33 (July 1976): 233–249.

Goldschmidt, Eva M., comp. *Champion of a Cause: Essays and Addresses on Librarianship by Archibald MacLeish*. Chicago: American Library Association, 1971.

MADISON COUNCIL

Librarian of Congress James H. Billington established the James Madison Council in 1990 to serve as the institution's primary link to the business and philanthropic communities. A private-sector advisory body, the Council consists of approximately 100 public-spirited citizens who provide financial support for specific projects and help the Library raise funds to increase its visibility, enhance its programs, and strengthen its collections. The Madison Council is a major component in Librarian Billington's campaign to increase access to the Library's collections and "to put the Library to work on behalf of American education and international competitiveness."

The National Digital Library Program was one of the Madison Council's early principal projects. As the founding chairman of the Madison Council in 1990 and one of two founding sponsors of the National Digital Library Program, John W. Kluge, president of Metromedia Company, led a successful campaign to raise $45 million from the private sector

John W. Kluge, president of Metromedia and founding chairman of the Madison Council. Created by Librarian Billington in 1990, the Council is a private-sector advisory body that provides and raises funds to increase the Library's visibility, enhance its programs, and strengthen its collections. LC/Development Office.

to digitize one-of-a-kind historic documents at the Library and other repositories across the nation and make them available worldwide via the Internet. Kluge himself gave $10 million, and the campaign exceeded its goal. The $45 million, as agreed with members of Congress, was matched by $15 million in appropriated funds.

Madison Council members also serve as ambassadors for the Library of Congress. In October 1999, for example, Dr. Billington hosted the fourth in a series of Madison Council "Great Libraries of the World" visits. Following successful trips to England, France, and Italy, Spain was the destination. Twenty-nine Council members and their guests accompanied Chairman John Kluge and Vice-Chairman Ed Cox for the tour of Spain's leading libraries and cultural institutions and memorable gatherings with Spanish statesmen, noted librarians and scholars, and members of the royal family. One of the highlights occurred when Congressman Charles Taylor, chairman of the U.S. House of Representatives Legislative Branch Appropriations Subcommittee, bearing greetings from the U.S. Congress, joined Librarian Billington and Council members for a private audience with His Majesty Juan Carlos de Bourbon, the King of Spain, and Her Majesty Queen Sofia.

In Seville, Madison Council members witnessed the signing of a landmark agreement between the Biblioteca Columbina and the Library of Congress for a digital collaboration that will make unique documents from the cultural heritage of both nations widely available. The project was further advanced by the signing of a second agreement with the National Library of Spain on February 24, 2000 in a Great Hall ceremony at the Library of Congress in the presence of King Juan Carlos I and Queen Sofia.

The Spring 2000 issue of the Madison Council Bulletin *featured a description of the Council's trip to Spain in October 1999.* LC/Development Office.

The fifth Great Libraries of the World tour went to Russia in May 2002. Dr. Billington, himself an expert on Russian history and culture, led a group of 37 Madison Council members and their guests. Participants helped strengthen friendship between the Library and their hosts in key cultural institutions, including the Russian State Library in Moscow and the Russian National Library in St. Petersburg.

Congressman Jim Moran, ranking member of the U.S. House of Representatives Legislative Branch Appropriations Subcommittee, joined the group as it reviewed the treasures from these two great institutions, many of which have been digitized and incorporated into the Library's Meeting of Frontiers Web site. A highlight of the visit was a luncheon invitation from Russian First Lady Liudmila Putina for the members of the Madison Council Steering Committee. A direct result of the luncheon was Mrs. Putina's participation in the Library's 2002 National Book Festival and her development of a Russian Book Festival in 2003, in which Librarian Billington and U.S. First Lady Laura Bush participated.

The Madison Council took the lead in celebrating the Library's bicentennial in 2000, providing major funding for the yearlong program, particularly the bicentennial's "Gifts to the Nation" initiative for special acquisitions and projects. The highlight was Chairman Kluge's unprecedented gift of $60 million to establish the John W. Kluge Center in the Library of Congress and the Kluge Prize in the Human Sciences, a program that includes several endowed scholarly chairs.

The first Kluge Prize for Lifetime Achievement in the Human Sciences, created at the financial level of the Nobel awards to recognize the wide range of disciplines not covered by Nobel Prizes, was awarded to Leszek Kolakowski in November 2003. Professor Kolakowski is a scholar, philosopher, and historian, and was a key figure behind the Polish Solidarity movement in the 1980s inside his native Poland.

In 2003, generous gifts from Madison Council members John Hendricks and the Discovery Channel, Gerry and Marguerite Lenfest, and David Koch matched funds provided by Congress to raise the $10 million needed for the Library to acquire the Waldseemüller Map (1507), the first document to use the name "America" for the new lands explored by Columbus, Vespucci, and others. In the same year, Madison Council members John and Teresa Amend from Workplace USA and Jim Parkel from AARP lent financial support to the 2003 National Book Festival, held on the National Mall in a partnership between First Lady Laura Bush and the Library of Congress.

At the April 2004 spring meeting of the Madison Council, Librarian Billington announced that since its founding in 1990, the Madison Council had provided $153 million to support 247 Library of Congress projects. He pointed out that the initiatives supported by the Madison Council greatly enhanced the Library's service to the nation—and that many of the projects would not have happened without the Madison Council. (JYC)

MADISON, JAMES

The Library's third major building on Capitol Hill honors James Madison, the fourth president of the United States and a close friend of Thomas Jefferson. Both men believed that the power of knowledge, acquired mostly through books, was essential for individual liberty and democratic government. In 1783, 17 years before the Library of Congress was established, Madison unsuccessfully proposed that the Continental Congress purchase approximately 1,300 books to begin its own library.
LC/Prints and Photographs Division. LC-USZ62-214061.

The Library of Congress's third major building on Capitol Hill, the James Madison Memorial Building, opened to the public in 1980. The largest of the Library's buildings, it also is the nation's official memorial to James Madison, the "father" of the Constitution and the Bill of Rights and the fourth president of the United States.

That a major Library of Congress building should also become a memorial to James Madison is fitting, for the institution's debt to him is considerable. In 1783, as a member of the Continental Congress he proposed that Congress acquire 307 titles (in approximately 1,300 volumes) that would be useful to legislators, an effort that preceded by 17 years the establishment of the Library of Congress. The proposed list, in Madison's handwriting, included works on international law, history, politics, war, geography, and language. However, at the time, Congress felt it could not spend the money. According to Madison's notes, a majority of the delegates agreed with the argument that it would be cheaper to purchase the books after the Treaty of Paris was ratified.

In 1815, Madison was president of the United States when the library of his personal friend, collaborator, and fellow bibliophile Thomas Jefferson became the foundation of the Library of Congress after the destruction by the British of the U.S. Capitol in 1814. Both were enlightened statesman who believed the power of knowledge, acquired mostly through books, was essential for individual liberty and democratic government.

Two quotations from Madison about knowledge, liberty, and learning, are located on each side of the main entrance of the Madison Building on Independence Avenue.

On the left side of the main entrance:

Knowledge will forever govern ignorance; and a people who mean to be their own governors, must arm themselves with the power which knowledge gives.

—Madison to W. T. Barry, August 4, 1822

On the right side of the entrance:

What spectacle can be more edifying or more seasonable, than that of liberty and learning, each leaning on the other for their mutual and surest support?

—Madison to W. T. Barry, August 4, 1822

James Madison developed a personal library estimated at several thousand volumes. He was more a user of books than a collector; his library was a workshop that provided the knowledge and information he needed as a legislator, presidential advisor, Cabinet member, and finally, president. Madison had hoped to give his library to the University of Virginia, but instead his books and pamphlets had to be sold to settle claims on his estate. Today 587 of his pamphlets survive at his Montpelier, Virginia home.

On March 16, 2001, in cooperation with the James Madison Commemoration Commission, the Library of Congress hosted a symposium to mark the 250th anniversary of Madison's birth: "James Madison: Philosopher and Practitioner of Liberal Democracy." (JYC)

Rutland, Robert A. "Madison's Bookish Habits." *The Quarterly Journal of the Library of Congress* 37 (Spring 1980): 176–192.

MADISON MEMORIAL BUILDING

The Independence Avenue entrance to the Madison Building as seen from gardens beside the Jefferson Building across the street. The Library's Madison Building is the only national memorial to the nation's fourth president. Photograph: LC/Jim Higgins.

The Library's Madison Building is the nation's only memorial to its fourth president. In 1957, Librarian of Congress L. Quincy Mumford initiated studies for a third Library building. Congress appropriated planning funds for that structure, today's James Madison Memorial Building, in 1960. Initially two separate Capitol Hill projects, the creation of the memorial and the construction of a third Library of Congress Building were united in 1965 in what was to become the Library of Congress James Madison Memorial Building. Construction was authorized the same year.

The Madison Building under construction in September 1974. Photograph: Architect of the Capitol.

On May 27, 1971, the U.S. House of Representatives Building Commission, chaired by Representative Carl Albert of Oklahoma, the Speaker of the House, recommended that no further action be taken on the appropriation of funds for a third Library building until the location of a fourth House office building had been determined. On June 4, 1971, in a debate in the House of Representatives on the legislative branch appropriation for fiscal 1972, the House rejected by a vote of 69-48 an amendment that would have deleted the recommended appropriation for the James Madison Memorial Building. The cornerstone was laid on March 8, 1974, and the Madison Building was dedicated as a Library building on April 24, 1980—the Library's 180th anniversary. The next year, on November 20, 1981, President Ronald Reagan, in the company of Librarian of Congress Daniel J. Boorstin, Chief Justice Warren E. Burger and other dignitaries, dedicated Madison Memorial Hall on the building's ground floor.

Modern in style, the Madison Building was designed by the firm of DeWitt, Poor and Shelton, Associated Architects. When it opened, it was one of the three largest public buildings in the Washington, D.C., area (the others being the Pentagon and the F.B.I. buildings), containing 2,100,000 square feet with 1,500,000 square feet of assignable space. It houses administrative offices, including the Office of the Librarian, as well as the Copyright Office, the Congressional Research Service, Library Services, and the Law Library. The building also holds the Library's map, manuscript, music, motion picture, newspaper, and graphic arts collections, and eight of the Library's reading rooms.

Over the main entrance is the four-story relief in bronze, "Falling Books," by Frank Eliscu. Off the entrance hall to the immediate left is the James Madison Memorial Hall, which is decorated in marble and teak. Designed by Alfred Poor of DeWitt, Poor, and Shelton, its walls bear eight quotations from Madison, incised in wood by Constantine L. Seferlis. Walter Hancock carved the heroic 11-feet-tall white Carrara marble statue of Madison at the end of the hall. It depicts Madison at the age of 32, when he

On November 20, 1981, President Ronald Reagan dedicated James Madison Memorial Hall, which is just inside the building's Independence Avenue entrance. In the background is a heroic white Italian marble statue of Madison, carved by sculptor Walter Hancock. Eight quotations from Madison are incised in wood within the hall. LC/Prints and Photographs Division. LC-USP6-9509.

drew up a list of books "proper for the use of Congress." In his right hand, he is holding a volume of the *Encyclopédie Méthodique*, which was published in Paris between 1782 and 1832. Appropriately, it is volume 32, which deals with politics, economics, and diplomacy.

At the end of the entrance hall, above the doorways to the Manuscript Reading Room and the Manuscript Division office, are a pair of bronze medallions by Robert Alexander Weinmann. The one on the left shows the profile of Madison and the one on the right depicts Madison at work. (JYC)

Library of Congress Information Bulletin 39 (April 18, 1980): 129–133.

Library of Congress Information Bulletin 40 (December 11, 1981): 437–439.

MAGRUDER, PATRICK (1768–1819)

Patrick Magruder, a Maryland lawyer and politician, was the second Librarian of Congress, serving from 1807 until 1815. Like his predecessor John Beckley, he served concurrently as Clerk of the House of Representatives and as Librarian of Congress. He resigned from his post in 1815 after an investigation of the accounts under his control.

Patrick Magruder, a one-term member of the House of Representatives from Maryland, was the second Librarian of Congress, serving from 1807 until 1815. Like his predecessor John Beckley, he served concurrently as Clerk of the House of Representatives and as Librarian of Congress.
LC/Prints and Photographs Division. LC-USZ62-6004.

Born in 1768, he was one of the 11 children of Revolutionary War Major and Mrs. Samuel Wade Magruder, all born at the family estate "Locust Grove" in Montgomery County, Maryland. Patrick attended Princeton College, but returned home before graduation and became a lawyer. He became active in politics as a Republican, serving between 1797 and 1807 as a member of the Maryland House of Delegates, an associate judge of the county circuit court, and a one-term member of the House of Representatives during the Ninth Congress (1805–1807).

Magruder's term in Congress ended on March 3, 1807. A month later John Beckley died and in October Magruder was one of eight applicants competing for the vacant post of Clerk of the House. He won the vote on the fifth ballot in the House of Representatives on October 26, 1807. Although Beckley had held the two positions concurrently, Magruder's selection as Librarian was not automatic. After Beckley's death, President Jefferson considered separating the two positions, telling his secretary of war that he was "a little puzzled. . .between doubt and inclination" on the matter. In the end, probably because of potential political problems if he made the change, Jefferson decided to continue the combined post. He so informed Magruder on November 6, 1807, and on the same day explained to one of the disappointed candidates: "Considering it as the surest course for the performance of my duty in appointing a keeper to the library of Congress, I have conceived the election of Mr. Magruder as successor to Mr. Beckley as designating him also as his successor as Librarian."

Magruder, like Beckley before him, spent more time on the clerkship than on Library matters. The decisions regarding book selection and Library finances were in the hands of the Joint Congressional Committee on the Library. It is likely that the 1808 Library catalog and an additional 1809 report were prepared by the committee under the guidance of its learned chairman, Samuel Latham Mitchill of New York. The same is probably true of the rules and regulations for the Library promulgated in the 1808 catalog and included in revised form in another catalog, this one published in 1812. Martin Gordon, who has written about the Magruder period in the Library, finds it "impossible" to state what Magruder's role might have been in the compilation and production of these catalogs. Another factor, Gordon points out, was Magruder's "sporadic ill health."

Patrick Magruder was re-elected Clerk of the House when Congress convened in 1809, 1811, and 1813. On a personal level, he retained his interest in Montgomery County and Washington, D.C. politics and in local Masonic affairs. He and his wife Martha, the daughter of Virginia Congressman Colonel Peterson Goodwyn, had two children. They also maintained an active social life.

The 1812 catalog was the Library's first classified catalog, listing 3,076 volumes and 53 maps, charts, and plans according to 16 subject and two format categories. The rules published in the catalog make clear the clerical and custodial nature of the Librarian's duties. His major tasks were "to label and number the books, place them on shelves, and preserve due lists and catalogues of the same." He also checked books in and out and kept track of circulation and the Library's accounts.

Patrick Magruder's ill health returned in December 1813 and on December 9, 1813, the House of Representatives approved his brother George, his chief clerk in the Office of the Clerk, as acting Clerk of the House. Magruder left Washington toward the end of July in 1814 and went to the Springs of Virginia for his continued recovery. On August 14, 1814, the British army captured the city of Washington and burned the U. S. Capitol Building, including the Library of Congress. Magruder's office records were destroyed along with the Library's collections.

President James Madison called Congress into session, convening it on September 19, 1814. Magruder, who had left the Library in charge of his brother George and two assistants, asked for a congressional investigation into the conduct of his office and the handling of the funds for which he was responsible. The Speaker of the House immediately appointed a select committee, chaired by Joseph Pearson of North Carolina, to carry out the investigation.

The committee reported on December 12, 1814, and while it observed that "due precaution and diligence were not exercised to prevent the destruction and loss which has been sustained," it concentrated on Magruder's financial records. The destruction of the Library, while regretted, was not of paramount importance to the committee or apparently to the Congress itself.

It appears that Magruder's papers were the only government financial records not saved from the British. In attempting to reconstruct the records the committee found several discrepancies involving both Patrick and George Magruder, including an apparent shortage of approximately $20,000. In the accounts concerning Roger Weightman, who held most of the House's printing contracts in this period and had printed the Library's catalog of 1812, the committee found an example of the mixing of governmental and personal accounts.

Patrick Magruder answered these charges five days later, defending his apparent ignorance in certain instances and also asserting that the House Committee on Accounts had approved his expenses. The committee responded on January 16, 1815, claiming that Magruder had provided no new information and reiterating its charges. On January 21, 1815, a resolution was introduced that would remove Magruder from his clerkship, but by a narrow vote its consideration was delayed for a week. It was never debated, however, because on January 28, 1815, Patrick Magruder resigned the office of Clerk of the House and by inference the office of Librarian of Congress.

A new Clerk of the House was elected on January 30, 1815, and in March President James Madison separated the offices of Clerk of the House and Librarian when he named George Watterston as Librarian of Congress. Patrick Magruder left Washington to settle on his wife's family plantation "Sweden" near Petersburg, Virginia, and in February 1816 the federal government filed suit to recover approximately $18,000 from the former Clerk and Librarian of Congress. The case never came to trial and on December 14, 1819, Patrick Magruder died and was buried at "Sweden." (JYC)

Gordon, Martin K. "Patrick Magruder: Citizen, Congressman, Librarian of Congress." *The Quarterly Journal of the Library of Congress* 32 (July 1975): 155–171.

MAIN READING ROOM

The richly decorated Main Reading Room—the heart of the Library's reference service and center of the Thomas Jefferson Building—offers a grand sight for all using it. An architectural wonder, it inspires awe. "Even the brashest tourist speaks in a whisper. What goes on here, he perceives instinctively, matches the majesty of the surroundings." The visitor recognizes that the splendor of the Main Reading Room reflects the importance of the pursuit of learning and scholarship taking place in it.

The Main Reading Room in the 1990s after its renovation from 1987 to 1991. The view is looking toward the west doors, which are located below the clock by sculptor John Flanagan.
Photograph: Anne Day.

The room's lavish and vibrant decorations subtlety suggest learning. Edwin Blashfield's allegorical figure floats in the center of the huge dome, which rises 160 feet above the room. Symbolizing human understanding, she lifts the veil of ignorance. Seated beneath her are 12 brightly painted men and women representing those countries and periods that have contributed to America's cultural heritage. At the top of the room's eight marble pillars stand towering plaster figures depicting the fruits of civilization: religion, commerce, history, art, philosophy, poetry, law, and science. The 16 bronze statues in the gallery of the Main Reading Room are those men who excelled in the above disciplines. John Flanagan's handsome clock crowns the west entrance to the room. Bejeweled and covered with gilt, the clock is set against a mosaic background, and a life-size figure of Father Time looms above it. Light streams into the room through large semicircular windows adorned with stained glass images of the seals of certain of the states. Cherubs and other winged creatures, rosettes, and caryatids embellish the room throughout. Without ever turning the pages of a book, the visitor can look around the Main Reading Room and learn about western civilization.

Opening on November 1, 1897, the Main Reading Room ushered in a new era in the Library's history. Library administrators were now given new scope for developing fresh and progressive reference service for the public. Although earlier Librarians of Congress had supported improved service to readers,

The Main Reading Room in 1898, with graceful table lamps and star-shaped clusters of lights in the balconies.
LC/Prints and Photographs Division. LC-USZ62-47260.

they had been hampered by a small staff and limited space. It was left to Herbert Putnam, eighth Librarian of Congress, and to the Main Reading Room superintendents to define reading room reference service for the coming years.

Putnam was very clear about what he wanted. In the 1901 *Annual Report of the Librarian of Congress*, he strongly stressed that "the Main Reading Room is usually the point first approached by an inquirer. It is the duty of the desk attendants to place at his disposal such information as they have." The policy evolved and by 1939 it had been set. Putnam and his appointed supervisors had decided that assiduous but balanced attention would be the hallmark of Main Reading Room reference service.

Experienced men were chosen to implement the Main Reading Room's service-oriented program. Becoming Main Reading Room superintendent in 1897, David Hutcheson was known for his management skill, knowledge, and public service spirit. William Warner Bishop, his successor in 1907, and one of the "scholar-librarians," was a University of Michigan graduate, a classicist, and linguist. Frederick W. Ashley, the first superintendent to receive a library school degree, served from 1915 until 1926. Martin

Arnold Roberts, a longtime Library administrator, became superintendent in 1927 and held the office until 1937. Selected as superintendent in 1938 and author of *The Story Up to Now: The Library of Congress, 1800–1946* (1947), David C. Mearns was described by Archibald MacLeish as "the rarest treasure in the Library of Congress."

From the beginning, Main Reading Room staff were expected to have broad educational backgrounds and experience in reference work. Applicants not only needed college degrees, but language skills, knowledge of literature, history, and geography, and some knowledge of the various sciences. Such personal attributes as good manners, tact, patience, and a good memory were also required.

The staff of the Main Reading Room at the central desk in 1927. LC/Prints and Photographs Division. LC-USZ62-30515.

Men and women worked in the Main Reading Room, but women were hired with some reservations. Supervisors felt that they lacked the temperament and strength needed for the job. Eight women, according to an 1898 report, were assigned to the room, but none worked at the reference desk. Reference deskwork apparently was not one of the "gentle and useful offices suitable for women."

The Main Reading Room employed African American staff members too. Paul Laurence Dunbar, the celebrated poet, was assigned there. Having charge of one of the decks, he worked from September 1897 until December 1898. Daniel Murray, an ardent bibliophile and Dunbar colleague, was also a reading room staff member. Best known for having assembled a collection of the works of African-American authors, Murray in 1898 worked with the Library's Smithsonian Collection. In 1910, he is listed as an assistant in the Main Reading Room.

The Main Reading Room assistants had many and varied duties. Stationed at the large reference desk in the center of the room, they provided direct assistance to Main Reading Room readers. Telephone reference took place at the desk as well as circulation and interlibrary loan service and study carrel service. Congressional requests were also received in the reading room; members of Congress and their staff either visited the desk with requests or sent written ones.

Reading room assistants were certainly the first contact for many readers, but they did not have the final word in answering queries. The Bibliography Division served as the major backup for the Main Reading Room force. Staff in that unit prepared bibliographies and undertook those complicated searches that could not be answered by the reading room assistants.

The work of the Main Reading Room staff was greatly hampered in that the room lacked the catalogs and indexes that are today considered standard reference tools. In 1897, for example, the assistants relied on a makeshift catalog kept in boxes at the desk. In 1898, the Catalog Division developed a dictionary catalog for the Main Reading Room.

The card catalog in the Main Reading Room was installed in 1898 and grew until additions ceased at the end of 1980. It was removed to a deck area adjacent to the Main Reading Room in 1991. LC/Photographic Section.

Over the years, the growth of the collections, the demands of an "information hungry" public, and the increased competence of the assistants led to an evolution in reading room service. Superintendent Martin Roberts, writing in 1930, noted this transformation. The Main Reading Room "has now grown into something more important than a place set aside for the perusal of books—it has now become a centre of reference work and research."

Archibald MacLeish succeeded Herbert Putnam as Librarian of Congress in 1939. His dynamic leadership and America's entrance into World War

II dramatically changed reference service in the Main Reading Room.

By 1941, the reading room staff had begun surveying portions of the general collections, selecting books and pamphlets for preservation in the event of a national emergency. In an extensive two-month period, reference assistants, aided by volunteers from other divisions, examined more than two million volumes and removed, labeled, and reshelved some 170,000 pieces "without interruption in our service," Robert C. Gooch, Main Reading Room superintendent, noted proudly. The assistants in the Main Reading Room gave expanded and expedited services to the defense agencies and arranged for assignments of personnel to assist defense library operations. This necessary concentration on war work affected service to others.

In 1942, Main Reading Room hours were shortened. The room closed at 6:00 p.m. rather than 10:00 p.m., but a small staff remained to care for the collections and to answer telephone inquiries. Late in 1942, stack access, which had been restricted in 1941, was totally discontinued.

A major change took place in 1944. The duty station of the reference assistants was moved from the center desk to the Main Reading Room alcoves. "The move resulted in a marked increase in the proportion of readers receiving personal attention."

The Main Reading Room, in 1944, ceased to be a department. As part of Librarian MacLeish's reorganization of the Library of Congress, the Reading Room became a unit in the Public Reference Section of the General Reference and Bibliography Division.

On December 19, 1944, MacLeish resigned as Librarian, leaving the Library in the hands of Luther Harris Evans as Acting Librarian. Dr. Evans was nominated as Librarian of Congress by President Truman on June 18 and assumed the office on June 30, 1945. Librarian Evans set about immediately preparing the Library for its new peacetime mission.

A smaller staff, budget constraints, and an aging plant made work in the Main Reading Room somewhat stressful. However, the librarians continued to assist government agencies, private researchers, and the general public with many war related queries. Staff also spent time on collection development in an effort to make up for missed opportunities during the war. In 1952, in an attempt to streamline Main Reading Room service, the telephone reference service was shifted from the alcoves to an area near the entrance to the Main Reading Room. Staff morale was raised considerably by the successful conclusion of a classification review, which led to higher grades for Main Reading Room reference librarians.

In 1954, when Librarian of Congress L. Quincy Mumford took office, the Main Reading Room staff numbered 17 librarians. Although the provision of reference service in the reading room and the Thomas Jefferson Room in the Adams (then Annex) Building was their main duty, these librarians performed library functions across the board. They served too as recommending officers and bibliographic specialists.

Milton Lomask, author of *Odd Destiny: A Life of Alexander Hamilton*, dedicated his book to one of the Main Reading Room librarians. The inscription— "One of the nobler beings, second only to guardian angels and honest mechanics, is a good reference librarian"—could have been the encomium for the work of all the reading room librarians during the first decade of the Mumford years.

The first 10 years of the Mumford administration ended with the closing of the Main Reading Room—for the first time since it opened in 1897—on May 4, 1964, to permit renovation and the installation of air-conditioning. During the renovation period, readers used the Thomas Jefferson and North Reading Rooms in the Library's Annex. On Monday, August 16, 1965, "the room reopened for service. Five minutes later the first call slip was turned in at the great circular desk by Anne Harvey, a candidate for a master's degree in Spanish literature, and business had begun."

Traditional reference practices continued in the Main Reading Room, but the librarians' reference horizons had begun to change. Main Reading Room librarians now realized the compelling effect that automation could have on searching and retrieving material. Staff, in 1966, began working on a computer-produced catalog of the Main Reading Room's reference collection. By 1973, the catalog database contained 11,500 monographic and 2,400 serial titles.

Modernization was also taking place elsewhere in the room. More than 200 signs were installed so that readers could find their way through the reference alcoves more easily. Semimonthly meetings were held for a short time in 1965 to acquaint new readers with the Library's reference services and facilities, and photocopiers were installed in the Main Reading Room in 1972. Readers were pleased to have the labor-saving machines, but were frequently annoyed because they broke down so often.

Daniel J. Boorstin's arrival in 1975 as Librarian of Congress had an immediate effect on service in the Main Reading Room. Responding to his desire to make the readers' introduction to the Library even smoother and more productive, Main Reading Room supervisors and staff introduced a series of changes. Additional librarians were assigned to the room to provide research guidance and assistance, particularly to those using the Library for the first time. A number of new informational brochures were produced, and a cataloger was assigned to a new work station to help readers use the card catalog. During the Boorstin reorganization of the Library in 1978 the Main Reading Room became a section in the new General Reading Rooms Division.

In 1978, a new approach to reference service was tried in the Main Reading Room. The librarians rotated among a number of service points in the room, making them more accessible to the public. By year's end librarians were working at the Research Guidance Office near the entrance to the Reading Room, the center desk, Alcoves 4 and 5, and the new computer Catalog Center.

The first computer terminal was installed in the Main Reading Room in May 1976, changing the nature of public reference work forever. Computer services were expanded in 1977 and made more accessible to both readers and staff. By 1981, the main card catalog was "frozen," leaving the computers as the only searchable book file for items acquired after December 31, 1980.

The Librarian's *Annual Report* for 1981 noted: "With the January closing of the Main Card Catalog, computer terminals have become the preferred means of access to current catalog information. Because of the growing use of computer terminals, the Computer Catalog Center, located behind the Main Reading Room, was expanded in February from six to eighteen terminals, most with associated printers. Two reference librarians are now on duty in the expanded center during the peak hours and provide training for new users and some instruction in advanced techniques for those experienced in computer searching."

The 1980s were a busy time for Main Reading Room reference librarians. They compiled a variety of finding aids, published bibliographies and books in their subject fields, lectured, gave speeches at library schools, and attended professional meetings. Main Reading Room librarians established, in 1984, a new public training program for users of the Library's online systems. More than 1,000 users and staff received training that year. The very popular program continues today.

Dramatic change came to the Main Reading Room in 1987. James H. Billington took the oath of office as the 13th Librarian of Congress on September 14, 1987, and on December 9, 1987, the Main Reading Room closed for renovation. The renovation of the Main Reading Room surely symbolized the new Librarian's desire for a renewed and more accessible Library of Congress.

Reopening on June 3, 1991, the Main Reading Room emerged from the renovation equipped to serve the needs of the public in the 1990s. Restored to its nineteenth-century glory, it presented the latest in information technology. All reader desks were wired for power and data transmission, permitting readers to use their laptop computers easily. Workstations, in the expanded Computer Catalog Center, were set up for searching the Library's computer catalog system, including the main books file. Workstations for searching the Internet and the Main Reading Room CD-Rom network as well as special equipment for researchers with disabilities were made available in the center.

"History," by Daniel Chester French, is one of eight large statues above the giant marble columns that surround the Main Reading Room. They represent eight categories of knowledge, each considered symbolic of civilized life and thought. The others are Philosophy, Art, Commerce, Religion, Science, Law, and Poetry. Photograph: Anne Day.

Herbert Putnam set high standards for Main Reading Room reference service at the beginning of the twentieth century. The same high standards are still maintained at the beginning of this new century. Experienced librarians with an array of book and electronic sources at their disposal continue to offer the public in-depth reference assistance in the beautifully appointed Main Reading Room. The Main Reading Room librarians have certainly remained faithful to the Putnam model of reference librarianship. (JN)

Nelson, Josephus, and Judith Farley. *Full Circle: Ninety Years of Service in the Main Reading Room.* Washington, D.C.: Library of Congress, 1991.

MANUSCRIPT DIVISION AND COLLECTIONS

Administrative History

On May 17, 1950, President Harry S Truman spoke at a program in the Coolidge Auditorium marking the publication by Princeton University Press of the first volume of The Papers of Thomas Jefferson, *edited by Julian Boyd. From left to right: Chief Assistant Librarian Verner W. Clapp, President Truman, Gen. George C. Marshall, Harold W. Dodds, President of Princeton University.* LC Archives.

The Manuscript Division of the Library of Congress ranks as one of the nation's preeminent repositories of original documents relating to American history and culture. Its holdings constituted an integral part of the Library long before the division was formally established in 1897. Records of the Virginia Company of London, for example, were included in separate sales of Thomas Jefferson's books to the federal government in 1815 and 1829. However, it was not until the appointment of Ainsworth Rand Spofford as Librarian of Congress (1864) that the tempo of manuscript acquisitions increased. In 1867, upon the urging of Spofford, Congress appropriated the remarkable sum of $100,000 to purchase the library of collector Peter Force, which included many original manuscripts and transcripts relating to early American history. During the next 30 years, Spofford prevailed upon Congress to accept the gift of the Joseph M. Toner collection of Washingtoniana (1882) and to provide special funds to buy the papers of French Revolutionary War general Marquis de Rochambeau (1883), thereby adding significantly to the Library's manuscript collections. In his 1875 *Annual Report*, Spofford responded with foresight to the rise of professionalism and growing interest in American history by recommending to Congress that historical records in the Library's care receive special attention: "It is very important that every manuscript or written paper in the Library which can throw any light on any portion of American history should be systematically arranged and indexed. The increasing attention that is paid to these memorials of the past, and the new uses that are found for old documents, give force to the suggestion now made . . . that a competent historical scholar should be employed to put all these loose materials for history in order. . . ."

Despite Spofford's advocacy, it was not until 1897 that historical collections received "increasing attention" with the appointment of Herbert Friedenwald as superintendent of the Manuscript Department. Friedenwald was a graduate of The Johns Hopkins University who received his doctorate from the University of Pennsylvania in 1894. Although he resigned in 1900, Friedenwald was able to bring a measure of control to the chaos caused by inadequate staff and storage space. By the end of his tenure, manuscripts had been classified and arranged, a system of restoring damaged items had been introduced, and important additions had been made to the collections.

Following a hiatus of two years, during which chief assistant John C. Fitzpatrick managed the division, Librarian Herbert Putnam appointed Worthington C. Ford chief in 1902. An accomplished scholar, Ford remained with the Library for seven years and presided over a crucial period in the division's history. Originally located in the Northeast Pavilion of the Thomas Jefferson Building, by 1903 the renamed Division of Manuscripts had moved to the northwest curtain of the second floor, where a staff of four cared for a collection of some 63,000 manuscripts. In that same year, the Library began to receive from the Department of State, by executive order of President Theodore Roosevelt, historical papers which had been acquired by the government, including the papers of several early presidents and the voluminous records of the Continental Congress.

Two years later, the division embarked on an ambitious program of copying manuscripts and records relating to American history in foreign archives. The Foreign Copying Program began when Librarian Putnam employed the London firm of B. F. Stevens and Brown to transcribe manuscripts relating to American history in the British Museum Library (now the British Library). Except for brief interruptions during the two World Wars, the Foreign Copying Program carried on with support of gift and trust funds provided by James B. Wilbur in 1925 and John D. Rockefeller Jr., in 1927. In 1965, this work continued with a grant from the Council on Library Resources, which created the Center for Coordination of Foreign Manuscript Copying. The result is a collection of approximately 2,750,000 manuscripts copied from libraries and archives in 24 foreign countries, although most items are reproductions from repositories in Great Britain, Spain, France, and Germany. The earliest copies are in the form of handwritten transcripts made by professional copyists or, in a few instances, glass photographic plates. Technological advances in the 1920s led to the use of photostatic copies and enlargement prints made from negative microfilm. Virtually all reproductions made since 1935 appear on 35mm positive microfilm.

When Ford left the Library in 1909, his successor, Gaillard Hunt, came from the Department of State, the agency that transferred some of the most important historical manuscripts to the Library. An experienced historian, Hunt had written biographies of James Madison and John C. Calhoun and edited the nine-volume edition of the *Writings of James Madison* before coming to the Library. He is primarily recognized as promoting a significant increase in the donation of gifts of personal papers, but he also spearheaded improvements in bibliographic control. As the collections increased in size and number, Hunt concluded that the production of calendars (detailed lists of correspondence) was unrealistic and insufficient as a means of making the resources of the Manuscript Division known. He decided instead to issue a handbook, which would describe "the character and scope" of all the division's collections.

Subjects and correspondents would be listed and indexed, and minor collections, often of considerable historical value, would be described. A major contribution to the growing bibliography on American history, the *Handbook of Manuscripts in the Library of Congress* (Washington, D.C.: Government Printing Office, 1918), was the first comprehensive guide to the division's collections. Supplements to the *Handbook* were issued in 1931 and 1938.

Hunt returned to the State Department in 1917, but maintained close ties with the Library. Once again, John C. Fitzpatrick became acting chief until a replacement was found. In 1919, Librarian Putnam turned to Charles Moore, a Harvard graduate who earned his doctorate at Columbia College, later The George Washington University. Moore had published a history of Michigan and biographies of architects Charles Follen McKim and Daniel Burnham. President William Howard Taft appointed him to the Fine Arts Commission in 1910, a post he retained while serving in the Manuscript Division. His official title in the Manuscript Division, however, was acting chief and would remain so until he resigned in 1926. Moore's numerous civic undertakings and wide acquaintance among authors, artists, business leaders, and politicians made him valuable to the Library in the critical area of gift acquisitions. The most significant event occurred on September 30, 1921, when the Department of State (with the assistance of Hunt) transferred to the Library the original manuscripts of the Declaration of Independence and the U.S. Constitution.

By 1927, the Manuscript Division had acquired a vast array of nationally significant collections and accumulated 30 years experience in administering them. It was the recognized leader in the field. In that year, William Evarts Benjamin endowed a chair in American history in the Library, which carried an honorarium for the chief of the Manuscript Division and gave Librarian Putnam the resources to engage an outstanding historian. His choice was J. Franklin Jameson. This distinguished scholar was the first recipient of a doctorate in history from The Johns Hopkins University. He had participated in the founding of the American Historical Association and had taught at The Johns Hopkins University and the University of Chicago. In 1905, he came to Washington to head the Department of Historical Research at the Carnegie Institution, where he remained until his appointment as chief of the Manuscript Division in 1928. Jameson's vision helped shift the direction of the division's acquisition efforts. The writing of history generally had concentrated on political and military events, with an emphasis on the role of personalities, but Jameson wanted to expand the field to include intellectual, scientific, and social thought.

Thus, he broadened the Library's acquisition interests to include cultural history, the history of science, legal history, African American history, and the archives of non-governmental organizations. When Jameson died in 1937, the result of injuries suffered in a traffic accident, Librarian Putnam appointed as his successor St. George L. Sioussat, a well-known professor of history who taught at several universities and was an active member of the American Historical Association. In 1942, Sioussat oversaw the move of the division to the third floor of the John Adams Building, and during World War II, he supervised the temporary transfer of the division's most treasured documents to Fort Knox, Kentucky, for safekeeping.

Solon J. Buck replaced Sioussat upon the latter's retirement in 1948. Holding a Harvard doctorate in history, Buck had served as United States Archivist at the National Archives from 1941 to 1948. During his brief tenure in the Manuscript Division, negotiations proceeded for the transfer of the Declaration of Independence, Constitution, and papers of the Continental Congress to the National Archives in 1952. Buck also reorganized the division staff and introduced new procedures to establish better intellectual control over recent accessions.

Since 1913, when John C. Fitzpatrick published a treatise entitled *Notes on the Care, Cataloguing, Calendaring and Arranging of Manuscripts* (Washington, D.C.: Government Printing Office, 1913), the division had grappled with issues relating to organization, description, and access to the disparate collections in its custody. Fitzpatrick's brief manual was the first printed guide for the care of manuscripts. It emphasized the use of a device known as a calendar to describe manuscript collections. A calendar is a chronological list of documents, accompanied by annotations and an index. Innovative at the time, calendars were best suited to smaller collections because of the amount of staff time needed to produce the annotations and index. By the late 1940s, however, newly received collections regularly exceeded hundreds of thousands of items, which made the production of calendars impractical. Under the guidance of Katherine Brand, head of the Recent Manuscripts Section, an access tool known as the register became the standard descriptive device for manuscript collections. The development of registers in the division was gradual, but generally they came to include the following information: statement of the collection's provenance; biographical note or organizational history; scope and content note describing the arrangement and topical coverage of the collection; series description outlining the major groups or series of papers; and container list identifying the contents of the papers together with the corresponding container numbers. Currently, the division's Preparation Section, established during a 1961 reorganization, is principally responsible for organizing collections and creating registers. For years, the most popular registers were published in printed form, and now many are made available online and encoded according to an international standard, which division staff helped to develop.

When Buck was promoted to assistant librarian in 1951, David C. Mearns was appointed chief. A self-described "superannuated reference librarian," Mearns presided over a period of increased activity in the division. Among other achievements, he was responsible for four major programs during his 16-year tenure as chief: a broader and more aggressive acquisitions program; creation of the *National Union Catalog of Manuscript Collections (NUCMC)*; initiation of the Presidential Papers Program; and introduction of automation in the intellectual control and description of the collections.

The enhanced acquisitions program began in 1954, when hundreds of American leaders in various fields were invited to donate their papers to the Library of Congress. With this initiative, Mearns continued Jameson's expansion of the division's traditional holdings into cultural history, history of science, and African American history. The *NUCMC* had a long gestation period; the project did not begin until November 1958, when the Library received a $200,000 grant from the Council on Library Resources.

Public Law 85-147, approved August 16, 1957, authorized a program "to arrange, index, and microfilm the papers of the Presidents of the United States in the collections of the Library of Congress." A separate processing and indexing section was established in August of the following year, and two years later the first four microfilm editions were released. The program was completed in the 1970s, with some two million manuscripts filmed and indexed for 23 presidential collections. In developing the Presidential Papers Program, the division pioneered the use of automatic data processing technology for manuscript administration and description. It used IBM punch cards to produce the published indexes for each of the presidential collections, and in 1966 the division introduced IBM cards in the reading room as call slips in order to compile reference statistics. In December 1966, the first printout of the Master Record of Manuscript Collections appeared, and with additional refinements, this information was eventually made accessible through the Library's larger online catalog systems.

An accomplished Lincoln scholar, Mearns was a prolific writer and speaker who represented the Library in numerous publications and events. After a distinguished career, he retired from the Library in December 1967. Roy P. Basler, also a Lincoln scholar and the editor of the multivolume *Collected Works of Abraham Lincoln*, was appointed chief. Serving in different capacities at the Library since 1952, Basler was instrumental in expanding the Gertrude Clarke Whittall Poetry and Lecture Series. During this time, improved automation operations led to the production of the Master Record II format, which provided collection-level description of the division's holdings.

When Basler retired in 1975, he was succeeded by John C. Broderick, who served until 1978, when he was promoted to Assistant Librarian for Research Services. Accessions during these years exceeded one million items per year, with more than 3.1 million items received in fiscal year 1977 alone. To handle the swelling volume, off-site storage space was secured to house unprocessed collections. Increased accessions also brought increased users, and the Manuscript

John C. Broderick served as Assistant Chief of the Manuscript Division, then Chief from 1975–1978, then as Assistant Librarian for Research Services until he retired in 1988. Like Roy P. Basler, his predecessor as head of the Manuscript Division, he was a literary scholar who also directed the Library's poetry and literature programs. LC Archives.

Reading Room expanded services to include self-service, coin-operated photocopiers, and the division's first microfilm reader-printers. In 1978, the Library's American Revolution Bicentennial Office (ARBO) was transferred to the division. Created in 1968 as part of the Library's contribution to the nation's bicentennial, by the close of fiscal year 1969, the Library completed the recruitment of a staff of professional historians who cooperated with Manuscript Division staff to produce scholarly publications that added considerably to the knowledge of the Revolution. A prime example of the ARBO's work is *Manuscript Sources in the Library of Congress for Research on the American Revolution* (Washington, D.C.: Library of Congress, 1975). Another ambitious venture resulted in ARBO project staff (later known as the Historical Publications Office) compiling, editing, and publishing the award-winning, 25-volume *Letters of Delegates to Congress, 1774–1789*. This series assembled 23,000 documents located in repositories across the nation in order to preserve and disseminate a documentary record of America's first national government.

After Broderick's promotion, Paul T. Heffron served briefly as acting chief. His term marked the debut of the publication *Library of Congress Acquisitions: Manuscript Division* (Washington, D.C.: Library of Congress, 1981–1997), which described the division's acquisitions annually beginning with 1979. This information previously had been published in the Library's *Annual Reports* and as part of *The Quarterly Journal of the Library of Congress*, but the new *Acquisitions* reports allowed for more in-depth essays, tables, and lists for describing the division's ever-increasing and valuable holdings. In the summer of 1981, Heffron oversaw the successful transfer of the division's approximately 34 million items from the Adams Building to the first floor of the James Madison Memorial Building.

James H. Hutson, appointed in 1982, is the longest-serving chief in the division's history. One of the division's most pressing concerns during his tenure was the accumulation of large accessions during the 1970s and 1980s, which led to significant backlogs. In 1991, Congress appropriated funds to hire additional staff to process the arrearage. The results of this program have notably reduced the division's unprocessed arrearage by 40 percent from a high of 13 million items in 1991. In 2004, the total number of items in the division was more than 55 million, arranged in 11,300 collections, which occupy 13 miles of shelving space in the Madison Building, and another eight miles in off-site storage. Shelving space in the Madison Building is full, and an increasing number of processed collections are now stored with unprocessed collections in off-site facilities.

Another milestone of the 1990s has been the digitization of historical collections and their dissemination via the Internet. With the development of the Library's American Memory and National Digital Library programs, individual documents and portions of selected collections are made available in digital format. In addition to several presidential collections, the division's digital offerings include the papers of Hannah Arendt, Alexander Graham Bell, Frederick Douglass, Zora Neale Hurston, and Wilbur and Orville Wright, all of which and more are available via the Library's American Memory Web site.

Manuscript Division specialists and archivists contribute support for these digital initiatives. In addition, staff also participated in the development of the Encoded Archival Description (EAD) project, which designed international standards for disseminating collection finding aids in electronic format. These programs continue the strong tradition of the Manuscript Division as one of the outstanding archival repositories of American history and culture in the nation. (JMF)

Manuscript Division Collections

Overview

The Library of Congress Manuscript Division holds what is perhaps the most extensive and comprehensive collection of personal papers and organizational records relating to American history and culture ever assembled. The division's holdings number more than 11,000 collections containing more than 55 million items, including some of the greatest manuscript treasures of American civilization. Among these are Thomas Jefferson's rough draft of the Declaration of Independence, James Madison's notes on the Constitutional Convention, George Washington's first inaugural address, the paper tape of the first telegraphic message, Abraham Lincoln's Gettysburg Address, Alexander Graham Bell's first drawing of the telephone, drafts of Walt Whitman's famous poem "O Captain! My Captain!," and countless other items documenting many of the most dramatic events and people in our nation's history.

Foremost among the division's collections are the papers of 23 presidents of the United States, many Cabinet ministers, and hundreds of members of the United States Senate and House of Representatives. Also preserved are the papers of Supreme Court justices and other members of the federal judiciary, military officers and diplomats, scientists and inventors, artists and writers, and scores of other prominent Americans whose lives reflect our country's evolution. The most interesting of these collections relate not only to individuals' professional or political careers but also reflect their private lives, suggesting how their origins, family relationships, personal experiences, motivations, prejudices, and humor affected their public behavior and activities. As a record of the whole person, these collections contain many different types of manuscripts, including diaries, correspondence (both incoming and copies of outgoing letters), notebooks, accounts, logs, scrapbooks, press clippings, subject files, photographs, and other documents in every conceivable form—handwritten and typewritten, originals, carbons, letterpress copies, microfilm, and computer diskettes. Joining the papers of individuals are the records of various organizations, mainly civil rights and reform associations that have significantly shaped American society. Supplementing the division's original manuscript sources are photostatic and microfilm copies of related collections in other American and foreign repositories.

Manuscripts are normally acquired by the Library of Congress in one of three ways: purchase, gift, or copyright deposit. Many of the earliest acquisitions were purchased by the Library directly or transferred from other government agencies. The institution's first manuscript acquisition, the Records of the Virginia Company of London, was included with the books, maps, and other items that the federal government purchased from Thomas Jefferson in 1815 and 1829 to replace the earlier congressional library burned by British troops during the War of 1812. The company's records document the founding and early government of the oldest English-speaking colony in North America, Jefferson's beloved commonwealth of Virginia. In 1867, Congress appropriated $100,000 to purchase the papers of Peter Force, a printer, mayor of Washington, D.C., and publisher of the massive compilations *Documentary History of the American Revolution and The American Archives*, who had assembled one of the nation's most important private collections relating to the founding of the country and its Revolutionary period. A year earlier, Dolley Madison's papers had been transferred from the Smithsonian Institution, and in 1903 President Theodore Roosevelt signed an executive order directing the transfer to the Manuscript Division of the State Department's historical archives. Roosevelt's action, one of the most significant in the division's history, brought to the Library the major corpus of the papers of George Washington, Thomas Jefferson, James Madison, and James Monroe, as well as large bodies of the papers of Benjamin Franklin and Alexander Hamilton. Funds established by private benefactors also permitted the Library to purchase manuscripts unobtainable within the budget appropriated by Congress, including the papers of poet Walt Whitman, artist James A. McNeill Whistler, and psychoanalyst Sigmund Freud, as well as copies of records in foreign repositories relating to American history.

Notwithstanding these notable purchases, most of the Manuscript Division's acquisitions in the twentieth century have been donated or, in the case of microfilm, acquired through copyright deposit. Many prominent Americans have accepted the division's invitation to donate their papers to the national library during their lifetimes. Other collections have been bequeathed or received as gifts from heirs. Only through the generosity of countless donors has the Manuscript Division amassed one of the world's finest collections of historical manuscripts. As such, its holdings are a testament to the patriotism of the American people, who have followed Thomas Jefferson's charge that it is "the duty of every good citizen to use all the opportunities, which occur to him, for preserving documents relating to the history of our country."

Space does not permit a complete account here of all the division's collections, but short summaries of seven of the division's collection strengths provide a glimpse of many of its major holdings, and a description of its Presidential Papers Collection appears at the end of this article. Moreover, individual descriptions of all division collections are available as part of the Library's online catalog, which is accessible via the Internet.

<u>Congressional Collections</u>

As befits the Library of Congress, the papers of members of Congress occupy a special place in its collections. More than 900 members are represented, from Patrick Henry and George Washington, delegates to the First Continental Congress in 1774, to Patsy Mink, a member of the 107th Congress convened in 2001. This impressive roster includes many of the presidents mentioned in this article as well as hundreds of others whose collections cover the entire sweep of American history, from the dawning of our independent political existence to the space age.

The course of the American Revolution and the creation of the nation that followed may be investigated in the papers of our earliest lawmakers, among them Benjamin Franklin, Alexander Hamilton, James McHenry, Robert Morris, and Roger Sherman. The War of 1812, the war with Mexico, the slavery question, territorial expansion, and the beginnings of a transportation and industrial revolution in the years before the Civil War are topics covered in the papers of Henry Clay, Daniel Webster, and John C. Calhoun—the Great Triumvirate—as well as in those of William Plumer, Samuel Smith, Amasa J. Parker, John J. Crittenden, William C. Rives, Levi Woodbury, Caleb Cushing, Thomas Ewing, Benjamin Tappan, Alexander H. Stephens, and Salmon P. Chase.

Dominant members of Congress who remained in Washington during the Civil War to pass legislation needed to raise armies, fund the war effort, and cope with emergency situations were Benjamin F. Wade, Thaddeus Stevens, and Zachariah Chandler, all of whose papers are in the Manuscript Division. In the aftermath of the war, as the nation attempted to right itself, Congress faced problems involving the freed slaves, the passage of civil rights amendments, Andrew Johnson's impeachment, and the restoration of order in the South. Members whose papers illustrate these and related issues include Nathaniel P. Banks, James G. Blaine, Henry L. Dawes, John Sherman, Benjamin F. Butler, Simon Cameron, John A. Logan, Elihu B. Washburne, Thomas F. Bayard, and Carl Schurz. Some of these individuals continued in office through the end of the century and were joined by other members—William M. Evarts, John Coit Spooner, Matthew S. Quay, Nelson W. Aldrich, and William Jennings Bryan—whose papers show how Congress dealt with legislation concerning monetary policies, the tariff, the rise of great corporations, labor, agriculture, immigration, and natural resources.

The swift conclusion of the Spanish-American War toward the end of the nineteenth century dramatized the elevation of the United States to the status of a world power. Twentieth-century Congresses were required to meet the challenges of this new internationalism while also addressing increasingly complex domestic demands. Trust busting, regulatory legislation, conservation, a world war, and the making of peace are revealed in the papers of Albert J. Beveridge, John Sharp Williams, Nicholas Longworth, Elihu Root, Robert M. La Follette, and Thomas J. Walsh. George W. Norris and William E. Borah were noteworthy as long-term legislators whose papers extend from the early twentieth century into the era of the Great Depression, the New Deal, and the onset of World War II. Sharing in the legislative battles during the Franklin D. Roosevelt and Harry S. Truman administrations were Tom Connally, Emanuel Celler, Theodore Francis Green, Clare Boothe Luce, Robert A. Taft, and James W. Wadsworth.

Collections documenting the Vietnam and Persian Gulf wars, Watergate, women's rights, environmental concerns, welfare, civil rights, and other domestic and international issues of the last quarter of the twentieth century include the papers of John H. Glenn, Daniel Patrick Moynihan, and Patsy Mink. Although the character of congressional collections has changed considerably over the years, notably in terms of intimacy, size, and completeness, they remain invaluable records of the American past and are among the most important papers held by the Manuscript Division.

Legal Collections

Although perhaps best known for its spectacular presidential and congressional collections, the Manuscript Division also holds the nation's largest gathering of papers of chief justices and associate justices of the United States, as well as the papers of many judges of the lower federal courts. Among the chief justices, the division holds the papers of Oliver Ellsworth, John Marshall, Roger Brooke Taney, Salmon P. Chase, Morrison R. Waite, Melville Weston Fuller, William Howard Taft, Charles Evans Hughes, Harlan Fiske Stone, and Earl Warren. The papers of associate justices are too numerous to list here. Suffice it to say that, for the Warren Court (1953–1969) alone, the division holds the papers of Hugo L. Black, William O. Douglas, Felix Frankfurter, Harold H. Burton, Robert H. Jackson, William J. Brennan Jr., Byron R. White, Thurgood Marshall, and Arthur J. Goldberg. It also holds the papers of Sandra Day O'Connor and Ruth Bader Ginsburg, the first two women to serve on the court.

In addition to the papers of Supreme Court justices, the division also collects the papers of many lower-court judges, especially those who played a vanguard role in the modern civil rights movement, such as Simon E. Sobeloff, J. Skelly Wright, and Frank M. Johnson Jr. Modern federal judges have also played leading roles in the fields of administrative law, criminal justice, and legislative reapportionment, and these matters can be explored in the papers of Gerhard A. Gesell, Clement F. Haynsworth Jr., Shirley Hufstedler, Irving R. Kaufman, Harold Leventhal, Carl E.

McGowan, Robert P. Patterson, E. Barrett Prettyman, John J. Sirica, and David S. Tatel.

Complementing the division's judicial collections are the papers of numerous attorneys general spanning from Edmund Randolph through Elliot Richardson as well as the papers of many solicitors general, including Benjamin Bristow, Charles Fahy, and Robert Bork, who argue the government's cases in the Supreme Court and in important litigation elsewhere. The government's pursuit and prosecution of criminal activity is also revealed in the records of such diverse bodies as the New York Society for the Suppression of Vice and Pinkerton's National Detective Agency. Papers of private lawyers also abound in the Manuscript Division and provide excellent information on the country's legal affairs. These include the papers of Daniel Webster, Moorfield Storey, Joseph H. Choate, Clarence S. Darrow, Elihu Root, Thomas G. Corcoran, James M. Landis, Joseph L. Rauh Jr., Elmer Gertz, Edward Bennett Williams, Leonard Garment, Telford Taylor, and others. Furthermore, modern litigation is often undertaken by public interest groups, and the study of recent legal history is greatly enhanced by the records of the National Association for the Advancement of Colored People (NAACP), the NAACP Legal Defense and Educational Fund, and the Center for National Policy Review. Journalists who cover the federal judiciary have also placed papers in the division's care, including keen observers of the judicial process such as Joseph and Stewart Alsop, Fred P. Graham, George Lardner, and Anthony Lewis.

Military Affairs

Military records comprise another important part of the Manuscript Division's holdings. Included are the papers of military heroes from George Washington, commander in chief of the Continental Army, to Gen. Curtis E. LeMay, commanding general of the Strategic Air Command and chief of staff of the United States Air Force after World War II. Interspersed between these two luminaries are the personal papers of numerous career officers, volunteers, and noncommissioned officers and enlisted personnel, as well as defense secretaries, war correspondents, spouses, medical personnel, and private citizens caught in the path of war.

The division's military collections span the entire history of the United States, but they are particularly rich for the eighteenth and nineteenth centuries. The Revolutionary War is the focus of innumerable collections, including the papers of George Washington, John Paul Jones, Nathanael Greene, Jean-Baptiste-Donatien de Vimeur Rochambeau, Robert Morris, and the Shippen family. The War of 1812 is best represented in the papers of Jacob J. Brown, William Henry Harrison, Andrew Jackson, Thomas Macdonough, James Madison, Duncan McArthur, Winfield Scott, and William H. Winder. No military topic is better documented than the Civil War. The division is the principal repository for the papers of President Abraham Lincoln as well as those of generals Nathaniel P. Banks, Pierre G. Beauregard, Benjamin F. Butler, Jubal A. Early, Richard S. Ewell, Charles Ewing, William B. Franklin, James A. Garfield, Ulysses S. Grant, Samuel P. Heintzelman, Henry J. Hunt, Joseph W. Keifer, George B. McClellan, Montgomery C. Meigs, Carl Schurz, Philip H. Sheridan, and William T. Sherman. Admirals Andrew Hill Foote, Louis M. Goldsborough, and Samuel Phillips Lee are also represented, as are hundreds of noncommissioned officers and enlisted personnel. The famous Confederate States of America collection, the papers of war correspondents Sylvanus Cadwallader (*New York Herald*) and Whitelaw Reid (*Cincinnati Gazette*), and the papers of Burton N. Harrison, secretary to Jefferson Davis, are also among the more than 1,000 collections in the division that relate to the war between the states.

One of the chief sources of the division's naval collections has been the Naval Historical Foundation (NHF), which has donated more than 335,000 items in more than 250 separate collections. These touch on naval affairs from the War of 1812 through World War II and include the papers of such notables as Washington Irving Chambers, William Frederick Halsey, Stanford C. Hooper, and the famous Rodgers family.

The division has also acquired a significant amount of material from World War I, World War II, the Korean War, and the Vietnam War. The papers of Woodrow Wilson, Gen. John Joseph Pershing, Maj. Gen. John Archer Lejeune, and Adm. William Sowden Sims document American participation in World War I. For the World War II period, the division has the papers of Adm. Ernest J. King and of generals Henry H. Arnold, Ira C. Eaker, Curtis E. LeMay, George S. Patton, and Carl A. Spaatz. Naval operations during the Vietnam War are highlighted in the papers of Adm. Edwin Bickford Hooper. The Edward L. Rowny Papers cover World War II, the Korean and Vietnam wars, and recent strategic arms negotiations on behalf of the North Atlantic Treaty Organization (NATO). Modern military affairs are also documented in the papers of recent secretaries of defense Harold Brown, Clark M. Clifford, Robert S. McNamara, Elliot Richardson, Donald Rumsfeld, James R. Schlesinger, and Caspar W. Weinberger; former White House chief of staff Donald T. Regan; and national security advisors Zbigniew K. Brzezinski, Morton H. Halperin, Anthony Lake, and Paul H. Nitze.

Diplomacy and Foreign Policy

Only the official records of the State Department surpass the richness of the Manuscript Division's holdings for documenting American foreign policy. Aside from the wealth of information available in the Library's presidential collections, the division houses the papers of more than half of the individuals who have served as secretary of state from the first secretary, Thomas Jefferson, who assumed office in 1789, to Alexander Haig, who resigned in 1982. More than 200 other collections comprise the papers of diplomats or contain significant material relating to American diplomacy. These, too, span American history, from Benjamin Franklin's letters when he was the American colonies' diplomatic representative to France in 1776 to the papers of William Howard Taft IV, who became the United States ambassador to NATO in 1989.

Many of the division's earliest documents relating to American diplomatic history are transcripts, photoreproductions, and other copies of rare materials held in repositories outside the United States. In 1898, within a year of its creation, the Manuscript Division acquired Benjamin Franklin Stevens's collection of facsimiles and transcripts of British manuscripts. Soon thereafter it obtained photoreproductions of additional papers relating to America held in European archives. Donations from two private sources—James B. Wilbur in 1925 and John D. Rockefeller Jr., in 1927—provided funds to expand the division's Foreign Copying Program, which today has grown to include thousands of volumes of transcripts, photostats, microfiche, and microfilm. Supplementing the foreign reproductions were donations from two private collectors—Edward S. Harkness in 1927 and Hans P. Kraus in 1969—of original materials concerning the early Spanish and Portuguese involvement in North America.

American diplomatic affairs from the Revolution through the late nineteenth century are reflected in the papers of presidents, cabinet officers, military figures, diplomats, and members of Congress, many of whose names have already been mentioned elsewhere in this article. Diplomacy during World War I is extensively documented in the papers of President Woodrow Wilson and his cabinet members Robert Lansing, Philander C. Knox, William Jennings Bryan, Newton D. Baker, Josephus Daniels, and others. In the twentieth century no foreign policy relationship has been so fraught with danger as that of the United States and the Soviet Union. The Library's manuscript resources are particularly rich for studying the relations between these two superpowers, as the division's holdings include the papers of several of this country's diplomats to tsarist Russia (George Washington Campbell, Simon Cameron, and George von Lengerke Meyer) and seven of its ambassadors to the Soviet Union (Joseph E. Davies, Laurence A. Steinhardt, William Harrison Standley, W. Averell Harriman, Alan Goodrich Kirk, Charles E. Bohlen, and Malcolm Toon). The Harriman Papers constitute one of the richest collections anywhere on modern American foreign policy. Complementing the papers of ambassadors and other State Department officials are the papers of individuals who promoted the nation's foreign policy through covert means, including Central Intelligence Agency officials Ray S. Cline, Cord Meyer, David Atlee Phillips, Archibald Roosevelt Jr., and others involved in espionage and intelligence operations in the post-World War II period.

Arts and Literature

The Manuscript Division's collections are not confined to the fields of political and military history. All areas of American studies, including our country's rich cultural and literary legacy, are documented. Some of the nation's most influential writers and artists are represented, arguably none more notable than the preeminent poet Walt Whitman, whose papers the Library acquired by purchase and through generous gifts from Thomas Harned and Charles Feinberg. Today, the division holds the world's most extensive collection of Whitman items, including the only surviving manuscript page from the first edition (1855) of *Leaves of Grass* and many drafts of Whitman's famous Lincoln lectures and poems.

The Library holds the world's largest collection of Walt Whitman materials, featuring more than 20,000 manuscript items alone. LC/Prints and Photographs Division. LC-Z62-89949.

Twentieth-century literary papers include representatives of a wide array of movements, forms, and points of view. The collections of Benjamin Holt Ticknor, Hiram Haydn, Oscar Williams, and Ken

McCormick provide the perspective of literary agents and editors. The papers of writers Owen Wister and Zane Grey reflect the country's fascination with the American West. Works by women range from those of the poets Edna St. Vincent Millay and Muriel Rukeyser—who were concerned with women's rights and other liberal and humanitarian causes—to those of novelist-philosopher Ayn Rand—who championed individualism, capitalism, and anticommunism. The recently acquired papers of Ralph Ellison include drafts of his prize-winning novel *Invisible Man* and document the emergence of African American literature of identity. Small but interesting collections exist for the poets Langston Hughes, Robert Frost, John Ciardi, and Louis Simpson, while poet-dramatist Archibald MacLeish, who served as Librarian of Congress during World War II, is represented by a larger collection. Other modern fiction writers represented by major collections are James M. Cain, James A. Michener, Shirley Jackson, Bernard Malamud, Truman Capote, and Philip Roth.

Theatrical papers also have a long history in the division. The papers of Frances "Fanny" Kemble and Charlotte Cushman document the lives of two nineteenth-century actresses, while the papers of John Thompson Ford, owner of the theater where President Lincoln was assassinated, provide a rich source for theatrical history from the manager's point of view. Major twentieth-century theatrical collections include the papers of film star Lillian Gish; stage actress Eva La Gallienne; playwright and diplomat Clare Boothe Luce; film and theatrical directors Joshua Logan and Rouben Mamoulian; television personalities Sid Caesar and Johnny Carson; actor Vincent Price; humorist and actor Groucho Marx; and well-known theatrical couples Ruth Gordon and Garson Kanin, and Jessica Tandy and Hume Cronyn.

The Library of Congress also holds some remarkable fine arts-related collections. The work of amateur and professional artists, such as George R. West, D. M. N. Stouffer, and Charles Reed, may be discovered in collections documenting nineteenth-century scientific explorations, diplomatic missions, and military engagements. More famous artists, like portrait painter and inventor Samuel Finley Breese Morse and painter and etcher James McNeill Whistler, are represented by their own collections. The Whistler Collection, which was gathered by Joseph and Elizabeth Robins Pennell, is one of the finest sources in the world for information on Whistler and his contemporaries as well as on the earlier pre-Raphaelite painters and their patrons. Sculptors Paul Wayland Bartlett, John Gutzon de la Mothe Borglum, Jo Davidson, Daniel Chester French, Vinnie Ream, Adelaide Johnson, Lee Oskar Lawrie, and William Zorach all have collections of papers in the Manuscript Division. Correspondence, client files, designs, drawings, photographs, and other materials (divided by format among the Library's custodial divisions) document the influential careers of industrial designer Raymond Loewy, filmmakers and designers Charles and Ray Eames, cartoonist and dramatist Jules Feiffer, and filmmaker and photographer Gordon Parks. The papers of photographer Frances Benjamin Johnston, celebrated chiefly for her portraits of prominent personalities, include information on her photographs of southern gardens and architecture, while other architectural and engineering achievements are documented in the papers of Montgomery C. Meigs, William Thornton, Charles Follen McKim, Frank Lloyd Wright, Ludwig Mies van der Rohe, Victor Gruen, and I. M. Pei.

Science, Medicine, Exploration, and Invention

Over the years, the Manuscript Division has acquired the papers of outstanding scientists, engineers, explorers, and inventors—collections that illustrate epochs of scientific endeavor ranging from Thomas Jefferson's and Benjamin Franklin's path-breaking experiments in colonial America to Wernher Von Braun's contributions to space exploration. These collections offer glimpses of such diverse technological achievements as John Fitch's 1794 steamboat, Samuel Finley Breese Morse's telegraph, and Herman Hollerith's computer. Also documented are Gifford Pinchot's efforts to save American forests, Luther Burbank's plant breeding experiments, Frederick A. Cook's polar discoveries, and Gregory Pincus's development of the birth control pill.

Researchers can trace the history of communications in the Morse and Alexander Graham Bell collections as well as in the papers of Lee De Forest, inventor of the vacuum tube and other electronic devices essential to the development of radio. The history of aviation is reflected in the archives of the American Institute of Aeronautics and Astronautics, which contain photographs and other materials spanning from Thaddeus Lowe's Civil War ballooning exploits to modern space rocketry. These archives supplement the personal papers of Wilbur and Orville Wright, whose notebooks and diaries cover the brothers' scientific experiments and their celebrated flights at Kitty Hawk, North Carolina. Other aviation collections include the papers of Octave Chanute, Benjamin Delahauf Foulois, Grover Cleveland Loening, Glenn

Luther Martin, George E. Mueller, the Piccard family, Marjorie Claire Stinson, and numerous army and air force pilots and officers.

Insight into the history of nineteenth-century medical practice may be found in the Joseph M. Toner collections and in the papers of Elizabeth Blackwell, considered to be the first American woman to earn a medical degree. The papers of Abraham Flexner are also of major importance, since they provided the basis for his controversial 1910 report, which revolutionized the teaching of medicine and forced more than half of the existing schools to close.

Few repositories can match the Manuscript Division's holdings relating to the history of psychoanalysis, many of which are part of the Sigmund Freud Collection. At the center of this unparalleled collection are the personal papers of the founder of psychoanalysis himself, which contain abundant family correspondence, including letters exchanged between Freud and his wife Martha during the years of their engagement ("Brautbriefe," 1883–1886) and while he traveled ("Reisebriefe," 1900–1930) as well as Freud's correspondence with his boyhood friend Eduard Silberstein, his close friend and fellow psychiatrist Wilhelm Fliess, and members of his ever-changing psychoanalytic inner circle, among them Hanns Sachs, Lou Andreas-Salomé, Max Eitingon, Sándor Ferenczi, and Ernest Jones. Manuscripts of Freud's writings in his spidery and often baffling hand include several chapters of *Totem and Tabu*, his accounts of the Wolf Man and Rat Man cases, his works relating to Moses, his notes on dreams, and the speech delivered on his receipt of the Goethe prize from the city of Frankfurt. Joining the Sigmund Freud Papers are approximately 50 other related collections totaling more than 230,000 items. Most prominent are the papers of Anna Freud, the psychoanalyst's daughter and chief disciple, whose correspondence documents the extension of psychoanalytic techniques to the treatment of childhood psychological disorders. Also notable are the papers of psychoanalysts Karl Abraham, Heinz Hartmann, and Paul Federn and of Freud acolyte Princess Marie Bonaparte, who played a vital role in securing Freud's escape from Vienna after the Nazi takeover in 1938. Freud family history is documented in collections of his brother, Alexander, his sister Rosa Freud Graf, his son Oliver, and his nephew Harry Freud.

Scientific exploration of native and foreign lands and people is another recurring topic in the division's collections. Included are Thomas Jefferson's instructions to Meriwether Lewis and William Clark to explore the land acquired through the Louisiana Purchase; engineer and army officer Frederick West Lander's surveys of the western United States; ethnologist and geologist Henry Rowe Schoolcraft's studies of the Great Lakes and Northwest; and archaeologist and ethnologist Ephraim George Squier's examination of native peoples in New York, Ohio, and the Mississippi Valley. Examples of foreign explorations include Robert Wilson Shufeldt's expeditions to Africa; Lewis Varick Frissell's trips to study and film Newfoundland; Adolphus Washington Greeley's and Frederick A. Cook's expeditions to the polar regions; George Kennan's studies of Russia and Siberia; Thomas Oliver Selfridge's surveys of the Isthmus of Darien (Panama); and Charles Wilkes's journeys to the Antarctic, Hawaii, and other Pacific islands. The latter region also figures prominently in the extensive papers of anthropologist Margaret Mead, which include the "Pacific Ethnographic Archives," a mass of field notes, diaries, photographs, and oral transcripts assembled by Mead and her associates during their many trips to study native peoples of the Pacific.

Beginning with the Second World War, an increasingly close relationship has developed between the government and the scientific community. A vast amount of federal money has been spent on sponsored research, much of it concentrated on the development of atomic energy, as documented in the papers of Vannevar Bush, supervisor of the Manhattan Project; J. Robert Oppenheimer, head of the Los Alamos atomic project; John Von Neumann, longtime consultant to the Los Alamos Scientific Laboratory and member of the United States Atomic Energy Commission; I. I. Rabi, a leading molecular physicist and scientific statesman; and Glenn T. Seaborg, discoverer of plutonium and negotiator of the 1963 Test Ban Treaty with the Soviet Union.

Commanding public attention today are questions about the fate of the earth. Several manuscript collections concern this subject, including the conservation manifestos and other papers of William Hornaday, longtime director of the New York Zoological Park; the papers of Barry Commoner, the "Paul Revere of environmental activists;" and the papers of Pulitzer Prize-winning biologist and environmentalist E. O. Wilson. Other recent acquisitions include the papers of Nobel Prize-winning physicist Charles Townes, one of the inventors of the laser; biologist Lynn Margulis, whose contributions to cell biology and microbial evolution earned her the Presidential Medal of Science; and astronomer Vera Rubin, whose research on spiral galaxies and dark matter has caused scientists to rethink long-accepted theories about the universe.

African American History and Culture

Ethel L. Payne (left) and Alice Dunnigan, the second and first African American women, respectively, to be admitted to the White House press corps. Photograph, 1982.
LC/Ethel L. Payne Papers. Manuscript Division.

The Manuscript Division possesses one of the nation's most valuable collections for the study of African American history and culture. Extensive documentation exists for researching slavery and African American life in the eighteenth and nineteenth centuries and for studying the civil rights movement in the twentieth century. The manuscripts of black and white abolitionists such as Frederick Douglass and Salmon P. Chase describe efforts to alleviate the plight of slaves, and the records of the American Colonization Society detail the saga of African Americans who left the United States to establish the West African nation of Liberia in the mid-nineteenth century. Papers relating to black participation and victimization in the Civil War abound, and African American history during Reconstruction is reflected in collections pertaining to newly elected black officials such as John Mercer Langston, Blanche K. Bruce, Hiram R. Revels, and Francis L. Cardozo. Efforts by African Americans to educate themselves and find meaningful employment can be traced in the papers of historian Carter G. Woodson, lawyer and judge Robert H. Terrell, and educators Mary Church Terrell and Nannie Helen Burroughs. Also available are the papers of the first three presidents of Tuskegee Institute—Booker T. Washington, Robert Russa Moton, and Frederick D. Patterson.

The division's collections are particularly strong for the history of the twentieth-century civil rights movement. The NAACP and the National Urban League (NUL) were founded in the first decade of the twentieth century and became important vehicles for the advancement of civil rights for blacks in the United States. Their records document the battle for equal employment opportunities and the struggle against segregation, discrimination, lynching, and other forms of racial oppression. In addition to the NAACP organizational records, the division holds the personal papers of some of the individuals who worked closely with the group, such as Moorfield Storey, the association's first president; Arthur B. Spingarn, its third president; and Roy Wilkins, longtime administrator and executive director from 1965 to 1977. The division also holds the records of the NAACP Legal Defense and Educational Fund (LDF), which was created by the NAACP just before World War II but eventually became independent of the parent organization. Complementing those records are the personal papers of Supreme Court Justice Thurgood Marshall, who was the special counsel and director of the LDF from its creation until 1961. Other important civil rights activists and organizations include the Brotherhood of Sleeping Car Porters, Asa Philip Randolph, Bayard T. Rustin, Rayford W. Logan, Lorenzo J. Greene, Kenneth Bancroft Clark, Joseph L. Rauh, Harold C. Fleming, Robert Lee Carter, William L. Taylor, Louis Martin, and Clarence Mitchell Jr. and family.

The papers of Patricia Harris, Edward W. Brooke, and Hugh H. and Mabel M. Smythe also illustrate the efforts of African Americans to move into the center of the political arena. Harris, the first black woman to hold a Cabinet position, served as secretary of Housing and Urban Development and secretary of Health, Education, and Welfare (later called Health and Human Services) under President Jimmy Carter. Brooke was the third black United States Senator in the nation's history and the only one elected in the twentieth century until Carol Moseley Braun's victory. The Smythes were two of the first African Americans to break the racial barrier in the State Department's diplomatic corps. All of these pathbreaking achievements followed on the heels of Jackie Robinson's historic admission in 1947 to the ranks of major league baseball. Robinson's recently acquired papers document his pioneering baseball career and his lifelong contributions as a civil rights leader. For more information on the division's holdings in black history, see *The African American Mosaic: A Library of Congress Resource Guide for the*

Study of Black History and Culture (Washington, D.C.: Library of Congress, 1993).

Women's History

The Library of Congress is the principal repository of the writings and the photographs of Frances Benjamin Johnston (1864–1952), one of the first American women to achieve prominence as a photographer. Her personal papers are in the Manuscript Division, her photography in the Prints and Photographs Division. LC/Prints and Photographs Division.

The Library's manuscript sources for the study of women's history are also among the finest and most comprehensive anywhere. Contained in nearly every collection are materials of interest to historians reflecting the full range of women's experiences. In 1903, the same year that President Roosevelt ordered the transfer of the State Department's historical archives, Librarian of Congress Ainsworth Rand Spofford acquired the personal library and manuscripts of his friend Susan B. Anthony, the noted suffragist and reformer. Accompanying Anthony's papers were four portfolios of documents from her mentor, Elizabeth Cady Stanton, one of the founders of the women's rights movement. Throughout the next half-century, the Manuscript Division augmented the Stanton and Anthony collections with the papers of other prominent suffragists—notably Carrie Chapman Catt, Lucy Stone, and the Blackwell family—amassing in the process an unparalleled source of documents relating to American women's fight for the vote. The division supplemented the papers of individual suffragists with the records of two significant organizations, the National American Woman Suffrage Association (NAWSA) and its more militant offshoot, the National Woman's Party. Once suffrage was secured, the NAWSA became the League of Women Voters, and the League's records are also held by the division.

Many of the early suffragists and women's rights leaders came to the movement by way of the abolitionist cause. The division's collections of Julia Ward Howe and Anna E. Dickinson papers are excellent sources for understanding women's involvement in the antislavery movement and the adoption of techniques and strategies from that struggle for use in the woman suffrage campaign. After women secured the right to vote, many former suffragists and their daughters became active in other reform initiatives, which may be traced in the papers of progressive reformers and political wives Belle Case La Follette and Cornelia Bryce Pinchot; social worker and lawyer Sophonisba Breckinridge; Mary Church Terrell, founder of the National Association of Colored Women; Hannah G. Solomon, founder of the National Council of Jewish Women; and birth control advocate Margaret Sanger. Collections of personal papers are supplemented by large and extensive organizational records of the National Women's Trade Union League, National Consumers' League, National Council of Jewish Women, Child Labor Committee, Women's Joint Congressional Committee, and ERAmerica.

In addition to documenting women's political activities, the division's holdings also reflect women's everyday existence and show how gender has shaped cultural affairs and domestic politics in the United States. The daily activities, concerns, and observations of American women from the colonial period through the twentieth century may be seen in the letters, diaries, and other papers of Elizabeth Shaw, Mercy Otis Warren, Anna Maria Thornton, Issa Desha Breckinridge, and Evalyn Walsh McLean as well as in the papers of numerous First Ladies and of hundreds of lesser-known women whose writings were acquired with the papers of a more famous husband, father, brother, or son.

Women's labor outside the home is also well documented, especially for the literate, white middle class. Nineteenth-century work as missionaries, teachers, doctors, and nurses is represented, for example, by the papers of Fidelia Church Coan, Myrtilla Miner, Elizabeth and Emily Blackwell, and Clara Barton, respectively. More recent collections reflect the expansion of women's employment opportunities in the twentieth century. Included are the papers of numerous government officials, such as Congresswomen Ruth Hanna McCormick Simms, Clare Boothe Luce, and Patsy Mink; Cabinet secretaries Oveta Culp Hobby, Shirley Hufstedler, and Patricia Harris; judges Florence E. Allen and Juanita Stout Kidd; Supreme Court Justices Sandra Day O'Connor and Ruth Bader Ginsburg; diplomats Florence Jaffray Harriman, Mabel M. Smythe, and Pamela Digby Churchill Hayward Harriman; economist Alice M. Rivlin; physician and Food and Drug

Administration official Frances O. Kelsey; State Department official Katie S. Louchheim; Defense Department analyst Jeanne S. Mintz; and foreign service officer Mary Vance Trent.

Women's involvement in journalism is particularly well represented in the division's holdings, which include the papers of newspaper editors Elisabeth Mills Reid, Helen Rogers Reid, and Katherine A. Graham as well as reporters Ruby A. Black, Bess Furman, Janet Flanner, May Craig, Dorothy Godfrey Wayman, and Ethel L. Payne. Their papers join those of novelists Shirley Jackson and Ayn Rand and poets Muriel Rukeyser and Edna St. Vincent Millay.

Nearly every field is represented by successful and path-breaking women. The papers of anthropologists Margaret Mead and Anita Newcomb McGee, biologist Lynn Margulis, and astronomer Vera Rubin have found homes in the Manuscript Division. Also available are the papers of actresses Lillian Gish, Minnie Maddern Fiske, Eva La Gallienne, Margaret Webster, Ruth Gordon, and Jessica Tandy; aviator Marjorie Claire Stinson; sociologist Helen Merrell Lynd; political scientist Hannah Arendt; sculptors Vinnie Ream and Adelaide Johnson; and photographer Frances Benjamin Johnston. These and many other collections, documenting the lives of both notable and ordinary women, are described in the recent 456-page publication *American Women: A Library of Congress Guide for the Study of Women's History and Culture in the United States* (Washington, D.C.: Library of Congress, 2001). (JER)

Revised and updated from *Library of Congress Manuscripts: An Illustrated Guide*. Introduction by James H. Hutson. Washington, D. C.: Library of Congress, 1993.

Presidential Papers Collection

Few people know that the Library of Congress Manuscript Division is the nation's oldest and most comprehensive presidential library. While the recently built presidential libraries each hold the papers of a single chief executive, the Manuscript Division has in its custody the papers of 23 presidents, including the men who founded the nation, wrote its fundamental documents, and led it through the greatest crisis of its existence. The Manuscript Division began acquiring presidential papers soon after the Library occupied the imposing, new Thomas Jefferson Building in 1897. The building was "the natural and fitting depository" for presidential papers, declared the descendants of Francis P. Blair, who in 1903 gave the division its first presidential collection, the papers of Andrew Jackson. Shortly after the Jackson Papers arrived, President Theodore Roosevelt issued an executive order transferring from the State Department the papers of George Washington, Thomas Jefferson, James Madison, and James Monroe. In subsequent years, the division acquired other presidential papers, obtaining some by purchase—the papers of John Tyler, James K. Polk, Franklin Pierce, Andrew Johnson, and Chester A. Arthur, for example—and many more by gift—including those of Martin Van Buren, William Henry Harrison, Zachary Taylor, Abraham Lincoln, Ulysses S. Grant, James A. Garfield, Grover Cleveland, Benjamin Harrison, William McKinley, Theodore Roosevelt, William Howard Taft, Woodrow Wilson, and Calvin Coolidge.

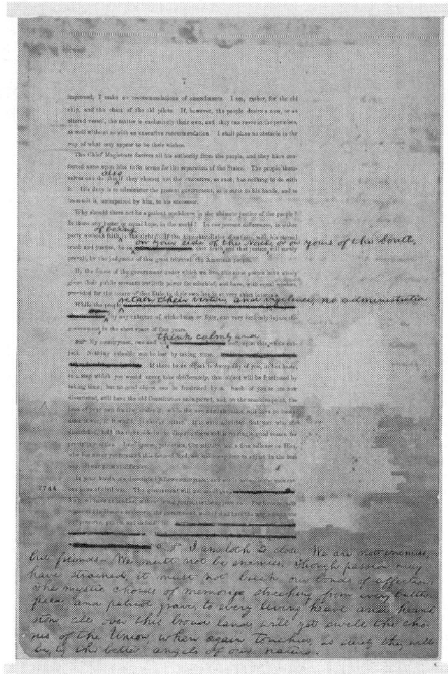

The final page of a draft of President Abraham Lincoln's first Inaugural Address, delivered on March 4, 1861. The handwritten last sentence is one of Lincoln's best known: "The mystic chords of memory, stretching from every battlefield, and patriot grave, to every living heart and hearthstone, all over this broad land, will yet swell the chorus of the Union, when again touched, as surely they will be, by the better angels of our nature.
LC/Abraham Lincoln Papers, Manuscript Division.

Among these collections are more than two million items in the form of diaries and journals, letters (incoming and copies of outgoing correspondence), speeches, scrapbooks, memoranda, notebooks, orderly books, logs, commonplace books, account books, articles, reports, press releases, and various other items that illuminate both the public and personal lives of individuals holding America's highest public office. Most of the documents have been indexed and microfilmed, and they are available in that format in repositories all over the world. Efforts to digitize the presidential papers and make them available over the Internet began during the 1990s, and thus far the papers of George Washington, Thomas Jefferson, and Abraham Lincoln are available electronically.

Laws governing the preservation of presidential papers were not enacted until the latter half of the twentieth century, leaving the disposition of both the public and private papers to each president. While the papers of most of the early presidents from Washington through Coolidge are housed in the Library of Congress, others, such as those of John Adams, John Quincy Adams, Millard Fillmore, James Buchanan, Rutherford B. Hayes, and Warren G. Harding, were deposited in historical societies or special libraries. Beginning with Franklin Delano Roosevelt, presidential libraries became the accepted method for housing presidential papers. As Roosevelt's successors followed suit, a system of presidential libraries administered by the National Archives and Records Administration developed. President Herbert Hoover, who had initially deposited his collection in the Hoover Institute Library on War, Revolution, and Peace at Stanford University, moved his papers in 1962 to a special library built at his birthplace in West Branch, Iowa.

Many priceless presidential collections changed hands during and after the lives of their creators, traveling long and circuitous routes before resting finally in the stacks of the Library of Congress. The history of each presidential collection held by the Library is described in a detailed essay at the beginning of the collection's finding aid. The actual size of the presidential collections vary from 631 items comprising the Zachary Taylor Papers to 675,000 items documenting the life of William Howard Taft.

From the beginning, George Washington, as founding father and first president of the United States, realized the importance of the historical record and made every effort to protect and preserve his papers, particularly those pertaining to the public activities documenting the creation of a new nation. He wrote that he considered his papers "as a species of Public property, sacred in my hands," and he began storing them at Mount Vernon. Those accumulated during his presidency joined papers already preserved from his labors as a farmer and surveyor and as an officer in the Virginia colonial militia and Continental Army. When he took possession of his presidential papers at the close of his second term, Washington established a precedent for those who followed. So concerned was he about the treatment of the papers that he developed a classification scheme and hired a staff to organize, transcribe, and inventory the documents. In 1833, his descendants deposited a portion of his papers in the State Department's historical archives, and Congress agreed to purchase the collection for $35,000. More papers were added in 1849 with an additional payment of $20,000, and these papers, as well as other documents stored at the State Department, were eventually transferred to the Library of Congress by President Roosevelt's 1903 executive order.

Washington's papers are particularly significant for their comprehensive coverage of his life. Among the collection are school copybooks from his teenage years and diaries dating from 1748 to 1799, the year of his death. Two noteworthy items are his commission as commander in chief of the Continental Army, dated June 19, 1775, and the "Articles of Capitulation" signed between Washington and Earl Cornwallis at Yorktown on October 19, 1781. The collection also contains his two inaugural addresses and an early draft of the Constitution drawn up by the Committee of Style of the Constitutional Convention on September 12, 1787.

Thomas Jefferson's Papers were purchased by the U.S. government from his grandson, Thomas Jefferson Randolph, in 1848 for $20,000 and deposited in the Department of State. Among these papers are many of the documents that trace the intellectual foundation of the new republic, such as Jefferson's rough draft of the Declaration of Independence, which bears emendations by John Adams and Benjamin Franklin. The collection also includes early records of the Virginia Company of London dating from 1619 to 1625.

The State Department's historical archives also became the repository for papers of James Madison purchased by the government from Dolley Madison in 1838 for $30,000; another portion was acquired for $25,000 in 1848. Dolley Madison's son from a previous marriage, John Payne Todd, also had access to Madison's papers and, unbeknownst to his mother, sold documents to the well-known department store owner, Marshall Field of Chicago, who later gave them to the Chicago Historical Society. These, too, were later purchased by the government and placed in the historical archives at the State Department. Included in Madison's papers are his notes on the debates in the Federal Convention, believed to be the most accurate account of the creation of the Constitution. The papers of Madison's successor, James Monroe, also found a home in the State Department's historical archives.

In his 1897 *Annual Report*, Librarian of Congress John Russell Young advocated the transfer of the State Department's historical archives to the newly completed Thomas Jefferson Building, in which a separate Department of Manuscripts had been created. In 1903, this relocation was accomplished through Roosevelt's executive order, which stated that the papers should be "preserved and rendered accessible" for historical and "other legitimate uses."

Many other presidential papers came directly to the Library of Congress from heirs, executors, friends, or historians entrusted with the documents for the purpose of writing biographies. Andrew Jackson left his papers first to biographer Amos Kendall and later appointed his friend, Francis P. Blair, as the keeper of the historical record; it was Blair's descendants who eventually donated the collection to the Library of Congress. Of particular interest in this collection is Jackson's account of the Battle of New Orleans written in his own hand. Although the Jackson Papers was the first presidential collection acquired by the division, the papers most persistently sought by the Library of Congress were those of President Abraham Lincoln. In 1916, two drafts of Lincoln's Gettysburg Address were presented to the Library of Congress by descendants of his secretary, John Hay. Lincoln's son, Robert Todd Lincoln, controlled the major collection of his father's papers and moved them numerous times before agreeing in 1919 to deposit them in the Library of Congress. The collection was donated to the Library in 1923 with the provision that it would not be opened to the public until 21 years after the death of Robert Todd Lincoln, which occurred in 1926. The Abraham Lincoln Papers were duly opened to the public on July 26, 1947. In addition to the Gettysburg Address, the collection includes other famous writings, such as Lincoln's draft of the Emancipation Proclamation, his two inaugural addresses, and his farewell to the people of Springfield, Illinois.

The first president to give his papers directly to the Library of Congress was Theodore Roosevelt, who as an author and historian was keenly aware of the importance of preserving the historical record. In 1917, the Library received the first installment of his papers, with many subsequent additions to follow, including one of Roosevelt's diaries donated by his daughter Alice Roosevelt Longworth in 1958. Roosevelt's successor, William Howard Taft, also chose the Library of Congress as the repository for his papers, and his files began arriving in 1919. Taft was always well-organized, and his collection is the

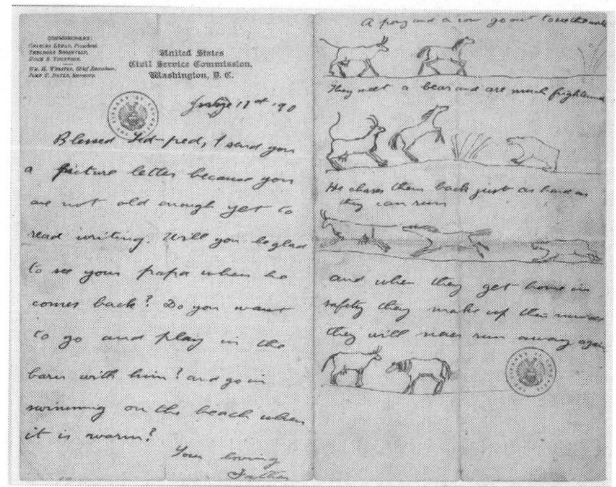
United States
Civil Service Commission,
Washington, D. C.

July 11th '90

Blessed ... I send you a picture letter because you are not old enough yet to read writing. Will you be glad to see your papa when he comes back? Do you want to go and play in the barn with him? and go in swimming on the beach when it is warm!

Your loving
Father

They meet a bear and are much frightened
He chases them back just as hard as they can run
and when they get home in safety they make up their minds they will never run away again

Theodore Roosevelt's letter to his son, July 11, 1890, written while Roosevelt was a Civil Service Commissioner. The illustrated letter was to be shown and read aloud to his three-year-old boy, who could not yet read.

LC/Theodore Roosevelt Papers, Manuscript Division.

largest and most complete of the presidential papers. Woodrow Wilson's Papers came to the Library through his second wife, Edith Bolling Galt Wilson, who prepared a confidential memorandum in 1929, in which she stipulated that the donation would become official in 1935 under specific circumstances. The collection began arriving in 1939 and was made available the following year to those receiving Mrs. Wilson's permission, a practice that continued until her death in 1961. Particularly significant is Woodrow Wilson's draft of the Fourteen Points for the establishment of lasting peace throughout the world. The last presidential collection to be donated to the Library of Congress was that of Calvin Coolidge, who began corresponding with Manuscript Division officials in 1929 shortly after leaving office. In 1953, the Coolidge Papers, which had previously been deposited in the Library of Congress, were officially converted to a gift.

In 1957, Representative Paul Jones of Missouri introduced a bill to give the Librarian of Congress the authority and funds to index and microfilm the presidential papers. Public Law 85-147 (71 Stat. 368) enacted August 16, 1957, established the Presidential Papers Program, a project to microfilm the presidential papers and sell positive copies at cost to libraries throughout the nation. The project commenced in August 1958, with an initial portion of the

$720,000 appropriation funded by Congress. The Library undertook the processing or organization of the papers into a precise arrangement, verifying the writer or recipient of each document and creating an index entry for each item containing the appropriate name or title, date, length of document, and supplemental information necessary for its identification. The collections were microfilmed on 35mm film stock and marketed widely, the major purchasers being colleges and universities.

The Library agreed to publish the indexes to the papers and to make the microfilm editions of the collections widely available for interlibrary loan. Most government depository libraries acquired copies of the Library of Congress *Presidential Papers Index Series*, as it was titled. A record of the location of many of the repositories holding the microfilm editions of these presidential papers is kept in the Manuscript Division to direct interested scholars to the nearest library holding a copy of the microfilm. By 1976, indexes were produced for all presidential collections with the exception of the Martin Van Buren Papers, for which the original calendar was deemed a satisfactory guide to the microfilm. To date, the Presidential Papers Program has produced approximately 3,000 reels of microfilm.

To provide the most complete record of each presidency, the Manuscript Division has continued to acquire additional papers, primarily through gift and purchase of both original documents and reproductions, for each of its 23 presidential collections. (MMW)

MEEHAN, JOHN SILVA (1790–1863)

John Silva Meehan, a printer, was the fourth Librarian of Congress, serving from 1829 until 1861. A democrat, he was appointed by President Andrew Jackson, and he served no less than nine U.S. presidents. A passive "gentleman of amiable manners," he

The fourth Librarian of Congress, John Silva Meehan, held the office from 1829 until 1861, serving under nine presidents. Appointed as a political supporter of President Andrew Jackson, he lost his job to a political supporter of President Abraham Lincoln. LC/Prints and Photographs Division. LC-USZ62-43063.

loyally and efficiently carried out the duties expected of him by a Congress that viewed the Library primarily as its own reference library. In particular, from 1846 until he was replaced in 1861, Librarian Meehan carried out the wishes of a strong-willed chairman of the Joint Committee on the Library, Senator James A. Pearce of Maryland, a man who felt that the Library of Congress had a limited role to play and who resisted all efforts to make the Library a more national institution.

John Silva Meehan was born in New York City on February 6, 1790, where he was educated and became a printer. In his biographical article about Meehan, historian John McDonough points out that early records relating to Meehan are "few and unreliable." It is known, however, that in 1811 or 1812, he was in Burlington, N.J. to help with the printing of Richard S. Coxe's *New Critical Pronouncing Dictionary of the English Language*. After a brief period as a midshipman in the U.S. Navy, he returned to his career as a printer. He was married in 1814 to Margaret Jones Monington of Burlington, and after the birth of their daughter the next year, the family moved to Philadelphia. In partnership with Robert Anderson, in 1818 he began publishing a Baptist journal, the *Latter Day Luminary*. The firm of Anderson and Meehan moved to Washington in 1822 and, under Baptist auspices, also began publishing a weekly newspaper, *The Columbia Star*.

In 1826, Meehan turned to the publication of a political journal, the *Washington Gazette*, an anti-President John Quincy Adams newspaper supported by pro-Andrew Jackson forces, particularly Senator John Henry Eaton of Tennessee. The newspaper was soon renamed *The United States' Telegraph*. Meehan, however, apparently was not aggressive enough for the Jacksonians; by the end of the year he had been replaced by a new and more dynamic editor, Duff Green, who began assailing the Adams administration.

During this difficult period, Meehan's wife of 12 years died just after the birth of their seventh child. The child also died and Meehan remained a widower until October 27, 1827, when he married Rachel T. Monington, his wife's sister. Two children were born of this second marriage.

Meehan served as secretary of the board of trustees of Washington's Columbian College (later The George Washington University) and continued to support Andrew Jackson, who was elected president in 1828. Meehan's political loyalty was rewarded on May 28, 1829, when President Jackson named him as the fourth Librarian of Congress.

Meehan replaced George Watterston, an outspoken Whig and friend of Henry Clay, one of Jackson's political opponents. Watterston immediately began a long but unsuccessful campaign of threats and flattery to regain his job.

By contrast, Meehan was gentlemanly, polite, of cheerful disposition, and decidedly nonpartisan. The Library of Congress in his charge, located in the central portion of the Capitol's west front, contained about 16,000 volumes. The new Librarian had only one assistant. He soon added a messenger and eventually two more assistants, one of whom was his son, Charles Henry Wharton Meehan.

In 1832, Congress strengthened the Library's law department, creating in effect a separate Law Library that was controlled largely by the justices of the Supreme Court. Meehan's son became the custodian of the Law Library and was the only survivor of the political changes made in the Library during the first days of the Lincoln administration in 1861. C.H.W. Meehan remained at his post until his death on July 5, 1872.

The chairman of the Joint Committee on the Library, not the Librarian of Congress, selected the books for the Library's collection during the entire period of Meehan's librarianship. A precise man, Meehan kept the various committee chairmen fully informed about the Library's affairs, deferring to their wishes at all times. In 1836 and 1844, Congress rejected the purchase of valuable private libraries that would have greatly enriched the Library of Congress and strengthened its national role. Meehan, whose major jobs were to lend the books, prepare and publish Library catalogs (which he issued in 1830, 1839, 1849, and 1861), and keep the accounts for the Joint Library Committee, played no role in the congressional rejection of these collections.

Between 1845 and 1861, Meehan developed a close working relationship with Senator James Alfred Pearce of Maryland, who served as chairman of the Joint Library Committee during the entire period. A conservative, cultured man, Pearce had great influence over the Library. He felt it was inappropriate for a government-funded institution to become a large national library and, with fellow congressmen such as Rufus Choate and George Perkins Marsh, in the 1840s he looked to the new Smithsonian Institution as a possible home for a national collection of books. Smithsonian Secretary Joseph Henry, however, blocked such development and instead looked to the Library of Congress as the future home of a national library.

Senator James A. Pearce, the conservative and scholarly chairman of the Joint Library Committee from 1846 until 1862, and Librarian Meehan developed a close working relationship. After the disastrous fire in the Library in 1851, Pearce took the lead in obtaining generous appropriations to replace the lost books and to repair, enlarge, and fireproof the Library.

LC/Prints and Photographs Division. LC-USZ62-109962.

A disastrous fire in the Library on December 24, 1851, destroyed two-thirds of the institution's 55,000 books, including about two-thirds of Thomas Jefferson's personal library. The cause was a faulty chimney flue and, to the relief of both Meehan and Pearce, the Architect of the Capitol reported that "no human forethought or vigilance could, under the circumstances, have prevented the catastrophe." Pearce took the lead in obtaining generous appropriations to repair and enlarge the Library and to replace the lost books. The Library's handsome new fireproof quarters, "the largest room made of iron in the world," opened in the Capitol's west front on August 23, 1853.

Viewed from today's perspective, the Library of Congress lost many opportunities—as well as important functions such as copyright repository, and central agent for the international exchange of books and documents and for the distribution of public documents—during John Silva Meehan's librarianship. However, Meehan's view of the Library as primarily an institution that served Congress reflected the wishes of most members of Congress—and certainly echoed the opinion of chairman Pearce. Moreover, the Meehan-Pearce partnership served to protect the Library as an institution during what might have been difficult times, especially after the fire of 1851.

The election of Abraham Lincoln as president in November 1860 meant the end of Meehan's long career as Librarian. Pearce wrote Lincoln on March 8, 1861, informing him about the Library and recommending that "no change" be made in the librarianship, trusting that the Library staff would be "safe from the influence of political partisanship which has heretofore had no influence in the republic of letters." There is no record of a response to this letter, and on May 24, 1861, President Lincoln rewarded a political supporter, John G. Stephenson, a physician from Terre Haute, Indiana, with the job of Librarian of Congress.

Meehan, a gentleman to the end, took his dismissal calmly. He and Senator Pearce died within a few months of each other, Pearce on December 20, 1862, and Meehan in his home on Capitol Hill on April 24, 1863. Meehan died suddenly, of apoplexy, and an obituary in a local newspaper described his work at the Library and his characteristics: "He was remarkably punctual and assiduous in his duties, unobtrusive, moral, and domestic in his habits, and of sterling integrity as a man." (JYC)

McDonough, John. "John Silva Meehan: A Gentleman of Amiable Manners." *The Quarterly Journal of the Library of Congress* 33 (January 1976): 3–28.

MOTION PICTURE, BROADCASTING, AND RECORDED SOUND DIVISION AND COLLECTIONS

Administrative History

Collecting, preserving, and providing public access to the Library's audio-visual collections is the responsibility of the Motion Picture, Broadcasting, and Recorded Sound Division (MBRS). Though the division was officially established in 1978, the Library's efforts to acquire motion pictures and sound recordings dates to ad hoc collecting initiatives undertaken by different organizational units, beginning with the deposit of the world's first motion picture copyright registration on October 6, 1893.

Motion pictures, acquired as legal deposits through the activities of the Copyright Office, were the first type of audio-visual materials routinely collected by the Library. Between 1893 and 1915, nearly 3,000 complete films and related documentation were received by the Copyright Office, forming the basis of what is recognized today as the most complete collection of surviving early American films in the world. However, due to concern over the flammable nature of early film stocks and the lack of proper storage facilities, the Library stopped collecting motion picture film prints after 1912. It was not until the mid-1930s that the Library began actively collecting audio-visual items.

The Library's first sound recording was acquired in 1904, as a gift: a specially recorded greeting on cylinder of Emperor Wilhelm II of Germany. As sound recordings were not to be eligible for federal copyright protection until 1972, Library collections did not benefit from mandatory copyright deposits of recordings as they did from deposits of books, maps, photographs, musical scores, and other materials. However, player piano rolls often included songs lyrics and other textual content and were deposited for copyright in the early years of the twentieth century; they could be considered the first sound recordings regularly received by the Library of Congress. It was not until 1925 that the Library began regularly acquiring sound recordings. In that year, the Victor Talking Machine Company offered the Music Division a selection of its new releases on 78 rpm disc as well as a machine on which to play the recordings. The company and Library officials agreed that the Library would not accept popular music releases and that the regular gifts would focus on releases from Victor's Red Seal (classical music) catalog. Upon solicitation by the Music Division, other record companies followed Victor's lead and made regular gifts to the Library of new record releases. The establishment of the Archive of American Folk Song in the Music Division in 1928 and consequent field recording projects of the 1930s resulted in the acquisition of hundreds of disc recordings of indigenous music and speech. Folk song specialists also made certain that the Library purchased a number of important commercial folk recordings for the collections.

In 1939, Librarian Archibald MacLeish established an Archive of Radio Recordings in the Library. Though short-lived as a named collection, the radio archive effort resulted in the acquisition of hundreds of unpublished radio broadcast recordings, a program that continues into the twenty-first century. In 1940, MacLeish obtained funding from the Carnegie Corporation to establish a Recording Laboratory in the Music Division. The purpose of the laboratory was to disseminate copies of the field recordings in the Archive of American Folk Song, in the words of MacLeish, "to educate and inform the American people as to the value of their culture and national civi-

In 1940, Librarian of Congress Archibald MacLeish obtained funding from the Carnegie Foundation to establish a Recording Laboratory in the Music Division. This 1941 photograph shows staff members Alan Lomax and Jerome B. Weisner at work on the Library's one-year Radio Research Project, which MacLeish funded through a grant from the Rockefeller Foundation.
LC Archives.

lization." In addition to duplicating Library audio holdings, the laboratory supported several World War II Washington-based Allied propaganda and troop morale programs. MacLeish helped establish the U.S. Office of War Information (OWI) at the beginning of the war; after it ended, the Library obtained over 30,000 OWI Voice of America radio broadcast recordings of Allied propaganda in over a dozen languages. The Library's World War II-era radio collection was further strengthened in the 1960s, when, upon rumors of the imminent destruction of a large group of recordings, Senator Robert F. Kennedy intervened to make the Library the chief repository of radio broadcasts distributed by the Armed Forces Radio Service.

The Library's re-entry into the archival realm of motion picture acquisition and preservation began in 1939, with the acquisition of a 35 mm print of *Sierra de Teruel*, an anti-fascist film produced by the poet Andre Malraux and smuggled to America after the Nazis confiscated and burned the original negative. Soon thereafter, Librarian MacLeish became aware of the large collection of early films in the Copyright Office archives that had been received as copyright deposits prior to 1912. Recognizing their historical importance, MacLeish broadened the Library's collection policies to include films. In 1942, the Library received a Rockefeller Foundation grant to establish a national motion picture collection. The Motion Picture Section was formed to administer the selection of motion pictures for the Library's permanent collection, seek additional important acquisitions, and develop a method for preserving the motion picture copyright registrations received prior to 1912. Congress directed the dissolution of the section as an administrative unit in 1947, however, its basic functions were transferred to the Reference Department and eventually to the Prints and Photographs Division in 1961.

During the 1940s, the Library established itself as a major force in the field of film preservation with the acquisition of the personal collections of fabled film star Mary Pickford and George Kleine, a Chicago-based pioneer of international film distribution. Along with the Paper Print collection of early silent films, the Pickford and Kleine collections form the cornerstone of the largest collection of American-produced films in the world. In 1967, the Library took another important step in its development as a motion picture archive by supporting the effort of government and private sector grant-making organizations to create the American Film Institute and by establishing its own film preservation laboratory. Motion picture acquisitions increased substantially after that date as specialists recognized how many movies of the silent and sound eras had been lost or were in need of serious attention from trained conservators. Today, the Library of Congress Motion Picture Conservation Center remains the nation's only full-time, publicly funded film preservation laboratory, and it has conserved more than 15,000 feature films and short subjects during the past 30 years.

The division's audio preservation program began in the 1950s when a Rockefeller Foundation grant made possible the reformatting of the instantaneous discs in the then-named Archive of Folk Song.

In 1990, the Library began a project to preserve and restore all of Frank Capra's films, using funding provided by the David and Lucile Packard Foundation. Only 60 percent of the original negative of the 1939 film Mr. Smith Goes to Washington *survives.* Courtesy of Columbia Pictures.

A concerted program to reformat unpublished sound recordings in danger of deterioration began in 1966. Since that time, tens of thousands of hours of radio broadcast recordings, ethnographic recordings, and other unpublished audio treasures have been copied to more durable media in the Library's Recording Laboratory. Because nearly all instantaneous recording media, such as tape recordings and lacquer discs, are in danger of disintegration, the Library's audio preservation program, successful as it has been, faces enormous challenges. Some forms of polyester tape, the target medium in most audio preservation efforts, have proven themselves to be prone to rapid deterioration through binder breakdown. Recently, the division's Recording Laboratory has taken national leadership in the field of digital preservation, creating digital files to be stored and periodically refreshed in a digital repository.

A Recorded Sound Section was established in the Library's Music Division in 1963, about the same time that annual audio acquisitions exceeded 10,000 items. Today, annual acquisitions of recordings average about 100,000 per year; approximately half are obtained as copyright deposits. A substantial number of recordings are acquired each year in an effort to fill the gaps in holdings created by the lack of a mandatory copyright deposit requirement prior to 1972. In 1978, the Recorded Sound Section and the Motion Picture Section, which had been part of the Prints and Photographs Division, were combined to create the Motion Picture, Broadcasting, and Recorded Sound Division (MBRS). The chiefs of the division have been Erik Barnouw (1978–1981), Robert Saudek

(1983-1991), David Francis (1991-2001), and Gregory A. Lukow (2003–). By 2003, its collections contained more than 650,000 film titles (35 mm, 16 mm, and other formats), more than 350,000 television broadcasts in various film and video formats, and more than 2.5 million sound recordings, including 500,000 radio broadcasts.

The collections cover the broad history of American entertainment over the past 100 years and are especially rich in the music, motion pictures, sound recordings, radio broadcasts, and videos that document the performing arts. The motion picture collection alone includes the original camera negatives for many Warner Bros., RKO, and Columbia features of the 1930s and 1940s, plus Paramount titles of the mid-1910s and 1920s. Major personal collections in the Library include those of Leonard Bernstein, George and Ira Gershwin, Gordon Parks, Danny Kaye and Sylvia Fine, Bob Hope, and the Gwen Verdon/Bob Fosse Collection.

The comprehensive personal collection of comedian Bob Hope was donated to the Library in 1999, and, with support from the Hope family, the Bob Hope Gallery of American Entertainment opened in the Jefferson Building in 2000. Hope's files include this photograph of the reconstruction of the Seven Foys' vaudeville act for his 1955 film biography of Eddie Foy. LC/Motion Picture, Broadcasting, and Recorded Sound Division.

The Library is noted for its leading role in preserving films by African Americans, particularly those of the pioneer producer/director Oscar Micheaux. The diverse collections also include the ethnographic films of Margaret Mead and Gregory Bateson, the early exploration films of Osa and Martin Johnson, and movies made for Yiddish-language audiences. Particular strengths include German, Japanese, and Italian feature films and newsreels of the 1930s and 1940s, British films of the post-WWII era, and Chinese-language features distributed in American since 1978.

In recognition of its long history in the acquisition of moving image and sound recording materials on behalf of the American people, Congress has confirmed the Library's mandate in this field in three major pieces of legislation. The first was part of the Copyright Reform Act of 1976, which created the American Television and Radio Archive (ATRA) of the Library of Congress. The charge to the Library under ATRA is to develop and maintain an ongoing collection of television and radio broadcasts that document the history of those media since their inception. As a result, MBRS has become the nation's focal point for collecting, preserving, and providing research access to the historical broadcasts and records of America's radio and television media.

The second major legislative mandate is the National Film Preservation Act of 1988, which established the National Film Preservation Board (NFPB), a group consisting of representatives from the major Hollywood guilds, film critics, scholars, and film archivists. The NFPB was created after Congress became aware that more than one half of all films produced in America before 1951 had been lost due to neglect and deterioration, including over 80 percent of those produced before 1920. The main role of the board is to advise the Librarian of Congress about preservation issues affecting those films that survive and consult on the selection of 25 films per year for the Library of Congress National Film Registry. Owners of films selected for the Registry are encouraged by Congress to cooperate with the Library and other film archives in their long-term preservation. Criteria for choosing films for the Registry require that they be historically, aesthetically, or culturally important and that they be American in origin and at least 10 years old at the time of their selection. Films chosen for the Registry include a broad range of works that represent not only the Hollywood classics, but also films from less well known areas of cinema history such as documentaries, avant garde, newsreels, home movies, and movies made for ethnic audiences in the pre-WWII era. The third mandate is the National Recording Preservation Act of 2000, which was modeled on the National Film Preservation Act. The law directs the Librarian each year to add "culturally, historically, or aesthetically significant" sound recordings to a National Recording Registry. The National Recording Preservation Board, created by the Act, was directed by Congress to conduct a study on the state of audio preservation and access to historical recordings. Utilizing the study's findings, the Librarian of Congress is directed to create a national plan for the preservation of sound.

MBRS research, storage, and laboratory facilities are located in Ohio, Virginia, Maryland, Pennsylvania, and the District of Columbia. The division's plans for the first decade of the twenty-first century centered on developing a property in Culpeper, Virginia, purchased in 1998 with a grant from the David and Lucile Packard Foundation. This new facility, being built by the Packard Humanities Institute, will allow the division to centralize its operations and to create a state-of-the-art facility, the National Audio-Visual Conservation Center. (PL, SB)

Newsom, Iris, ed. *Wonderful Inventions: Motion Pictures, Broadcasting, and Recorded Sound at the Library of Congress.* Washington, D.C.: Library of Congress, 1985.

Library of Congress Motion Pictures, Broadcasting, and Recorded Sound: An Illustrated Guide. Washington, D.C.: Library of Congress, 2002.

The Development of the Motion Picture, Broadcasting, and Recorded Sound Collections

A resident of Washington, D.C., around the turn of the twentieth century would not be at all surprised to learn that 100 years later, the nation's greatest collection of films, radio and television programs, and sound recordings would reside at the Library of Congress. Between the 1870s and the 1920s, the nation's capital supported almost as many inventors as politicians. They flooded to the U.S. Patent and Trademark Office to see what their colleagues were attempting and to protect their own achievements. It was in Washington, D.C. that Charles Sumner Tainter and Chichester Bell experimented with the first wax phonograph cylinder and Emile Berliner, the flat disc recording, which would eventually dominate the record industry. Berliner also invented the microphone, the mainstay of the broadcasting industry. Washingtonian Thomas Armat showed films to paying audiences on his Phantoscope projector at the Cotton States Exposition in Atlanta, Georgia in October 1895, one month before the Lumiere Brothers held their first public screening in Paris on December 28, 1895. His co-inventor, C. Francis Jenkins, gave the first demonstration of television—he actually called it "radio-vision"—in 1923.

Washington was also one of the first cities to market these inventions. The Columbia Phonograph Company, later known as Columbia Records, was named after the District of Columbia and was first established there in 1889. The company also opened one of the nation's first kinetoscope parlors on the ground floor of its headquarters, now the site of the FBI Headquarters. The Victor Talking Machine Company also had its origins in the nation's capital. It evolved from Emile Berliner's Gramophone Company.

The Library could be considered the world's first film archive because W.K.L. Dickson, Thomas Edison's assistant, had deposited in October 1893 several films under the collective title "Kinetoscopic Records" with the Copyright Office. Dickson actually made the deposit in the form of multiple still photos printed on paper because at the time, there was no specific copyright legislation that applied to motion picture pictures. This practice resulted in one of the

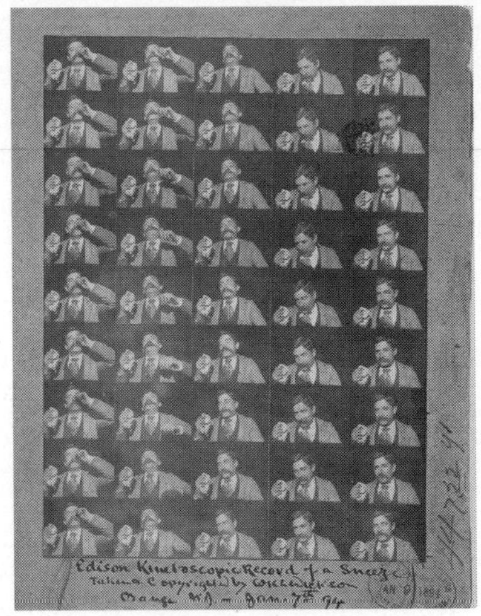

The Edison Kinetoscopic Record of a Sneeze *is one of a series of short films made in 1894 by W.K.L. Dickson, a young Englishman who was one of Thomas Edison's best assistants.* LC/Motion Picture, Broadcasting, and Recorded Sound Division.

Library's best known audio-visual collections—the Paper Print Collection. Between 1893 and about 1915, some 3,000 virtually complete movies were deposited in the form of contact paper prints made directly from the original 35 mm camera negatives. Fragments, usually one or more frames from more than 5,000 other titles, are also included in the collection. These paper prints form a unique record of life in America around the turn of the century as well as charting the early development of the cinema as a medium of entertainment and public information.

There was a great deal of cinematic activity abroad during the first two decades of the cinema, particularly in Italy, France, Germany, Sweden, and the United Kingdom. George Kleine, whose collection of films, stills, pressbooks, and papers is held by the Library, made his fortune importing the best "film d'art" and spectacle films from Europe. Later, he co-founded the Kalem film production company with Samuel Long and Frank Marion. Their historic five-reel production *From the Manger to the Cross*, filmed in the Holy Land in 1913, was greatly influenced by Cines' *Quo Vadis and The Last Days of Pompeii*, which he had earlier imported from Italy.

One of the names associated with the development of television in this country is David Sarnoff, who in 1926 set up the National Broadcasting Company, Inc. (NBC). In 1978, NBC made the first in a series of gifts to the Library, a collection that by the early 1990s had become the largest archive of an American broadcasting network or station available to the public. Later, some 9,000 kinescopes of NBC television programs were received and even more recently, the company donated to the Library their correspondence files and programs dating back to 1922.

On March 11, 1956, 22 years before it began donating its own archive to the Library, NBC donated kinescopes of its television series "Wide, Wide World." The presentation was televised by a local NBC station. Librarian of Congress L. Quincy Mumford (right) prepares to accept the gift in the presence of representatives from the network and General Motors, the program's sponsor.
LC/Mark English Collection.
Prints and Photographs Division.

As early as 1939 NBC's rival, the Columbia Broadcasting System (CBS), presented the Library with copies of some of its most important musical performances. Soon after, the Library acquired about 500 transcription discs produced by the Federal Music Project of the Work Progress Administration for broadcast by non-network radio stations. Later, the Library received a selection of the programs broadcast by CBS under the "Columbia Workshop" title. This included "The Fall of the City," written by Librarian of Congress Archibald MacLeish, and featuring Orson Welles. Other original radio dramas such as the Mercury Theater production of H. G. Wells's "War of the Worlds," which depicted a Martian invasion of New York City and caused panic among the city's residents, are prominent in the Library's holdings.

Not all the Library's collections are in Washington. Nitrate 35 mm motion picture film, which was in use by the commercial film industry until 1951, is highly flammable and must be stored in specially designed vaults outside urban areas. The Library's Motion Picture Conservation Center holds the original negatives and best surviving film elements to a diverse array of productions, including *The Great Train Robbery* and *Casablanca*, the home movies of Marion Davies, and the Vitaphone early commercial sound films, which were originally screened with synchronized 33 1/3 shellac discs on specially designed projectors.

The revised Copyright Act of 1912, the first to formally recognize theatrical motion pictures as a unique category of creative enterprise, obligated producers to deposit an actual 35 mm print of the title being registered. However, the Library could not safely retain these highly flammable nitrate copies, and returned the prints to the owners after recording the relevant legal information. The decision was not reconsidered until 1942 when Librarian MacLeish established the national film collection and inaugurated the Library's first administrative unit for collecting motion pictures. Funding for this operation was obtained from the Rockefeller Foundation and the annual selection of films was undertaken in cooperation with a team led by Iris Barry, Curator of the Film Department at the Museum of Modern Art in New York City. Since the 1940s, the Library's selection policy for moving image materials has been greatly expanded to include a broad sample of all types and genres of film, television, and other broadcast media. Gradually, the staff selected more and more of the titles registered. Today, it retains all American-produced feature films and a significant number of all other titles registered.

To fill the existing gap between 1911 and 1942, the Library entered into an agreement with the American Film Institute (AFI) of Los Angeles, California, under which the AFI agreed to negotiate with the studios on the Library's behalf, on condition that all material so acquired be known as the AFI Collection at the Library of Congress. In this way, the Library acquired a majority of the sound films made by Columbia Pictures before 1951 and large collections of Universal, Paramount, Warner Bros., and Metro-Goldwyn-Mayer (MGM) titles.

However, the collections do not only represent mainstream entertainment. They also record technical changes like the coming of sound; they include the work of explorers and anthropologists, films made for black audiences, newsreels and documentaries, and the work of independent filmmakers. The coming of sound had a significant impact on cinema. Silent films were discarded because they were thought to have no commercial value; only around 10 percent of the titles produced in the teens of the twentieth century still survive. However, the early sound processes, like the Lee de Forest Phonofilms and the Vitaphone shorts in which the picture was synchronized with a 16-inch shellac disc recorded at 33 1/3 rpm, are well represented in the vaults. The Vitaphone shorts provide fascinating glimpses of the popular entertainers of the day from the great tenor, Benjamino Gigli, to Al Jolson before *The Jazz Singer,* and a very young comedy team called "Burns and Allen." Explorers Osa and Martin Johnson are represented by nearly 700 reels of film used in their lectures throughout the world. They utilized very sophisticated equipment; Carl Akeley invented a special gyroscopic camera for them, which would give movement-free images even while filming from a vehicle moving across rough terrain. They achieved synchronized sound by linking a wire recorder mechanically to their camera and they produced the first extensive movies of African wildlife recorded from aircraft. The Library's most famous anthropological collection contains the films of Margaret Mead and Gregory Bateson shot in Bali, the Admiralty Islands, and elsewhere. In her film collection was discovered several rolls of film recorded in the 1930s by Zora Neale Hurston including footage of the oldest known surviving former slave in South Carolina. The Library has as well Oscar Micheaux's first surviving feature, *Within Our Gates*, which was discovered by a researcher in the Spanish national film archive.

The Library's motion picture collection is especially rich in its holdings of German, Japanese, and Italian films of the 1930s and 1940s. At the end of World War II, virtually all of the feature films and newsreels produced in these countries during the fascist era were confiscated and brought to the United States for study. In the 1960s, the original film elements were repatriated but 16mm copies were kept by the Library to maintain a permanent research record of these important cultural and historical documents open to scholars from around the world.

During the war, the U.S. Office of War Information's Voice of America beamed propaganda to other continents. The Armed Forces Radio Service, which broadcast to the troops during the war, created documentary and entertainment programming and also culled existing programming from the commercial networks. Many of the original commercial programs have long since disappeared but transcription discs recovered from all corners of the world ensure that these programs exist for future generations to enjoy. Entertainers donated their services to the Armed Forces Radio Service, making subsequent commercial distribution very difficult. The Motion Picture, Broadcasting, and Recorded Sound Division is the largest repository of these unique and significant performances by comedians and popular musicians preserved on these disc pressings.

The Library began to collect television broadcasts actively in the 1950s. During the early years, before the introduction of videotape, television programs were recorded primarily on 16 mm black-and-white motion picture film directly from a television tube while the live broadcast was in progress. Again, copyright deposits have been the principal source of television acquisitions over the years, nevertheless significant gifts have also been received from producers and artists. A principal benefactor is Robert Saudek, a pioneering producer and former chief of the MBRS, who donated copies of his groundbreaking series *Omnibus* and original production materials for the equally important *Profiles in Courage* series, based on the book by President John F. Kennedy. Major collections also document the careers of Danny Kaye and Sylvia Fine, Gwen Verdon and Bob Fosse, broadcast journalist Irving R. Levine, actor Lew Ayres, independent filmmaker Fred Wiseman, Ed Sullivan, and, perhaps the greatest all-around American entertainer of the twentieth century, Bob Hope.

Important collections documenting the history of audio-visual media from the nineteenth century to the present abound in the MBRS. One of the most unusual in terms of its precarious journey to being preserved by the Library is the Dawson City film collection, which consists of hundreds of movies from the 1910s that had lain for 50 or more years at the bottom of a swimming pool in the far north of Canada. They survived because of the accidental environmentally favorable storage conditions created by the permafrost of the Arctic region, which largely preserved the films from deterioration while there counterparts in warmer climates around the world disintegrated. Other important collections of lost American films from the silent era have also been repatriated and preserved by the Library from lost collections found in Australia, New Zealand, and Finland.

The division's most important collections in all media consist of copyright deposits. However, there was no copyright legislation governing sound recordings until 1972. Since then, the Library has received two copies of every long-playing record, cassette, and compact disc produced in America. As is the case with film, the Library has made strenuous efforts to fill the gap before copyright legislation and to build a comprehensive collection of American music. The holdings of jazz 78 rpms have become nearly comprehensive due to the acquisition of the Robert Altshuler Collection in 1992. The Jerry Valburn Collection, also a very valuable acquisition, includes every known record (except one) made by Washington-born jazz great, Duke Ellington. The collection also contains Ellington performances in every other audio-visual medium.

Copyright legislation pertaining to radio and television is not so helpful for collecting purposes as that for film and sound recordings. The act of transmission does not constitute publication, so many producers only register programs when they rent or sell them to the public. Because the deposit format is generally the one most widely distributed, the Library often receives television programs on VHS and other non-archival videocassette formats. Ensuring the long-term preservation of America's television heritage remains a matter of great concern to audiovisual archivists because the broadcast industry has not yet met the challenge of developing long-lived recording formats. The optimum method is to record programs at the time of transmission on a preservation format of choice. The Library's American Television and Radio Archive strives to meet that goal by preserving the historic record of America's broadcast news, public affairs, and entertainment history for posterity. (PL, SB)

The Paper Print Collection

When motion pictures were introduced by the Thomas Edison Company into the public entertainment market place in 1893, they represented a new form of creative work that the U.S. Copyright Law of the time did not recognize. Edison and other film producers who needed protection from infringement of their rights therefore established the practice of registering movies as "photographs"—an established copyrightable format—based on the idea that "motion pictures" represented an extension of the same underlying technical process. Between 1893 and 1915, when the last complete paper prints were received, between 8,000 and 9,000 movies were deposited by American and European film producers as photographic registrations.

In August 1912, the U.S. Copyright Law was amended by Congress to recognize motion pictures as a creative entity distinct from any that had gone before, that is, books, music scores, lithographs, photographs, and so forth. Prior to that date, the Copyright Office allowed filmmakers to establish their claims by depositing positive image copies of their movies printed on photographic paper. Most producers simply deposited short photographic strips containing fragmentary scenes and images. Some producers, primarily the Edison and Biograph companies, went to extraordinary lengths to protect their works by depositing complete copies of their films contact printed from the original camera negatives on long, thin strips of photographic paper. Before 1900, motion pictures were brief and most of the films on paper were received on rolls no more than 50 feet in length. One effect of the rapid growth of the industry after 1905 was the increased length of movies to several hundred feet and, by 1912, to 1,000 feet. When the copyright law changed in 1912, allowing the registration and deposit of actual 35 mm film prints instead of paper copies, the Library decided against collecting motion pictures because of the danger posed by the flammable nature of the nitrate film stock used by the industry. Film acquisition activities thus became dormant at the Library for the next 30 years, until the Library founded its first Motion Picture Section and re-established the practice of accepting motion picture copyright deposits in 1942.

One of the major reasons why the new section was created was the discovery of more than 3,000 complete pre-1912 motion pictures on paper rolls, totaling more than one million feet, in the basement storage vaults of the Jefferson Building. Librarian of Congress MacLeish recognized their importance as artifacts that documented an important lost period of American film history and arranged the first steps in the long conservation process of photocopying the paper rolls and restoring the viewable projection prints. After much effort and a special appropriation from Congress in 1956, the copying of the paper print collection to 16 mm was finally completed in 1962.

In January 1986, film historian and restoration expert Kemp R. Niver (right) presented a program about his work in restoring the Library's Paper Print Collection of early motion pictures. He is pictured with Paul C. Spehr, Assistant Chief of the Motion Picture, Broadcasting, and Recorded Sound Division.
LC Archives.

For the first time, modern film scholars were able to study comedy, drama and actuality films that had not been seen in over 60 years. Among the many important discoveries were virtually all the movies made by Edwin S. Porter and D.W. Griffith from their earliest days in the industry, including Porter's *The Great Train Robbery* (1903) and Griffith's first effort as a director, *The Adventures of Dollie* (1908). Today, the Paper Print Collection is recognized by historians as the largest representative sample of surviving films from the earliest period of American cinema history in the world.

Major revisions to modern historical interpretations of the early years of cinema have resulted from discoveries in the Paper Print Collection and many more remain to be found. The MBRS division has launched a long-term program to raise the level of restoration for the paper prints and improve image quality by re-copying the entire collection to 35 mm film stock, allowing researchers to better see and understand the historical riches they contain. (PL)

Library of Congress Information Bulletin 51 (April 20, 1992): 169–175.

Niver, Kemp R. *Early Motion Pictures: The Paper Print Collection in the Library of Congress*. Washington, D.C.: Library of Congress, 1985.

The American Television and Radio Archive (ATRA)

The American Television and Radio Archive (ATRA) was established in the Library of Congress as part of the Copyright Reform Act of 1976 to preserve a permanent and accessible public record of the television and radio programs that are the heritage of the people of the United States.

Conservation of these materials takes place in the Library's own state-of-the-art laboratory for historic broadcast formats, where obsolete equipment is maintained to preserve historic recordings of the pre-magnetic and magnetic eras, such as acetate disk transcriptions of vintage radio broadcasts, wire recordings, and TV programs recorded on two-inch videotapes. Thousands of items each year are acquired, preserved, cataloged, and added to the ATRA collection, making the Library of Congress the largest and most comprehensive research archive of historical American broadcast programming.

Noteworthy acquisitions include the NBC transcription collection of approximately 175,000 radio broadcasts from the early 1930s to the late 1960s, and nearly 18,000 16 mm television kinescope picture and sound track elements of NBC television broadcasts, covering the period 1948–1972. The history of public television is preserved in the Library through the National Educational Television (NET) and the Public Broadcasting Service (PBS) collections. Together, these collections total more than 70,000 programs with additional PBS items being added on a yearly basis. TV network news broadcasts form a particularly rich part of the ATRA collection and contain virtually a complete record of evening news and special broadcasts by ABC, NBC, and CBS dating from the mid-1970s to the present. A notable example is the three-day coverage by NBC of the events surrounding the assassination and funeral of President John F. Kennedy from November 22–25, 1963, consisting of 122 reels of 16 mm kinescope recordings. The Library also collects an archival video record of all floor proceedings of the Senate and the House of Representatives.

The Library's history of national leadership under ATRA authority in the preservation of broadcast media was enhanced in 1997 with its publication of a four-volume report, *Television and Video Preservation 1997: A Study of the Current State of American Television and Video Preservation*. This landmark study of the condition and survival rates of American radio and television media since the 1940s is the first nationwide survey of its kind. It documents lost segments of broadcast history and the lack of archival conditions in which many important private collections are held. Much has been lost and much remains to be done. It points the way for future MBRS staff activities in seeking lost and important radio and television items and preserving them for posterity. (PL)

The NBC Collection

The National Broadcasting Company (NBC) Collection is considered the largest archive of an American broadcasting network or station available to the public. The collection comprises several discrete segments donated to the Library from 1978 to 1992.

Materials relating to the 1926 founding and early history of NBC were set aside by NBC employees in a corporate archive termed the "History Files," an extraordinary, but seemingly haphazardly compiled collection of memoranda, official publications, executives' speeches, and a small amount of audience mail. The History Files are particularly strong in documenting the founding of the network and the late-1940s competition with CBS over color television standards. However, they offer little documentation on such important subjects as program development, relations with advertising agencies, or the network's news operations. (An NBC manuscript collection at the State Historical Society of Wisconsin includes a more formal corporate archive, emphasizing the period 1948–1958.)

The first major collection received by the Library from NBC was 150,000 16-inch lacquer-coated instantaneous discs, transcriptions of radio broadcasts made between 1934 and 1972. The Library transferred to tape and cataloged most of the disc collection, including all of the broadcast recordings dating before 1955. The broadcast recording collection includes all genres of network radio programming, including comedy, drama, news, educational broadcasts, public affairs programs, soap operas, sports, and music. A particular strength of the collection is World War II-era programs. Many broadcast days during the war are represented by recordings of every NBC radio network program aired.

The NBC Collection also includes approximately 18,000 separate picture and sound track elements for television programs produced and broadcast by NBC through the early 1970s. The programs date from the beginning of network television in the United States in 1948 through 1972, and include performances by major actors and musical talents, sports, game shows, children's programs, and daytime television. Kinescopes comprise most of the NBC Television Collection. The rest are programs produced on film prior to broadcast. The division holds mostly separate picture and sound track negatives, which must be combined to produce accessible viewing copies. Viewing copies are available for only a few titles. The NBC Television Collection does not include NBC's news archives nor any post-1977 material. However, a significant number of NBC television programs of all genres have also been acquired through the copyright registration process.

The NBC transcription disc and kinescope collections represent about 75,000 hours of programming, only a fraction of the thousands of hours the network aired each year. The collection, however, provides extensive written documentation of the network, which enables a researcher to "reconstruct" a wide range of radio and television productions not recorded in any audio-visual format. Indexes maintained by the network and now held by the Library list all New York-based program titles, many by subject; thousands of entertainers' appearances on the network; listings of non-entertainer appearances; lists of World War II-related programs; and daily broadcast logbooks from 1922 to 1960.

Another major component is the microfilm of each television and radio broadcast day's Master Book, wire clip-bound daily compilations of print materials relating to its broadcasts. The Master Books contain program scripts, advertising copy, news copy, and the so-called master music sheets, which list the musical contents of the programs. The original paper copies of these documents were destroyed by NBC after they were microfilmed. These collections of scripts comprise what is likely to be the largest single collection of American radio scripts in existence. The nearly complete bound set of press releases written by NBC and its predecessors between 1922 and 1980 also complement the audio and kinescope recording collections represented at the Library by providing a record of organizational announcements as well as advance cast and production details of broadcasts. Since its founding in 1926, the network has made many special efforts to document and preserve its history. As preserved and cataloged by the Library, most of the fruits of these efforts are now available for public study. (SB)

The Mary Pickford Collection

Mary Pickford was one of the true founders of the modern film industry in America. Her career in movies began in 1909 with the Biograph Company under the tutelage of famed director D. W. Griffith. Soon, she established herself as a popular film actress and by the early teens was the most famous and highly paid star in the business. Her popularity with audiences throughout the world helped establish American dominance of the international film market that continues to this day. Pickford was famous within the industry for her shrewdness and ability to make business deals and in 1919 she joined Griffith, Charlie Chaplin, and Douglas Fairbanks in forming the United Artists Corporation. Pickford's stardom continued throughout the 1920s and in 1929, she received the Academy Award for Best Actress for her performance in "Coquette." Pickford starred in more than 120 short films and 52 feature length films during her career, which ended in 1933 with "Secrets."

The Mary Pickford Collection was acquired in 1946 and is one of the crown jewels of MBRS. It was the first major acquisition of a privately held film collection after the Motion Picture Section was established in 1942. A brief note in the Library's *Annual Report* for 1947 states, "One of the principal acquisitions of the [previous] year was the gift by Miss Mary Pickford of her personal collection, in 1,121 reels consisting for most subjects of both positive and negatives, of most of the pictures in which she appeared."

Silent film star Mary Pickford, shown on location in 1916, gave the Library its first major gift of motion pictures following its decision in 1945 to become a major film repository. She also provided funds for preservation efforts and for a film theater, which opened in the Madison Building in 1983.
LC/Prints and Photographs Division.

The Pickford Collection is important because it not only documents the career of the genuinely important filmmaker of the silent era, but it also covers the historical period when movies developed from short one-reel productions to features of multi-reel length that are now the industry standard.

Mary Pickford's legacy in the Library of Congress extends beyond the acquisitions and preservation of her films. In 1983, the Library announced that the 64-seat movie theater in the James Madison Building would be known henceforth as the Mary Pickford Theater and the Mary Pickford Foundation donated $500,000 to fund free public film programs. The movies preserved in the Mary Pickford Collection are among the most frequently requested items in the MBRS Film and Television Reading Room. (PL)

The American Film Institute Collection

In 1967, the movement to preserve America's film history led to a cooperative effort by the Library of Congress and the National Endowment for the Arts to join with concerned preservationists in forming the American Film Institute (AFI). The Library, which had been actively collecting motion pictures since the 1940s, agreed to take on the preservation responsibilities and establish a motion picture conservation laboratory, with a mission to collect, preserve, and catalog historically and culturally important theatrical films in danger of being lost to deterioration and neglect. The nitrate film stock used by the movie industry between 1893 and 1951 was highly flammable, chemically unstable, and subject to rapid deterioration when improperly stored. The Library's commitment to the effort was based on the realization that by the 1960s much of the classical era of Hollywood cinema had been lost and the remainder was at serious risk. The Library's film archivists estimated in the mid-1980s that more than one half of the movies made in America before 1951 have been lost and the loss rate for the silent film era before 1927 exceeded 80 percent. The role of the American Film Institute then and now is to contact the major studios and search movie theaters, garages, attics, and basements across the country for surviving nitrate films and donate them to the Library and other archives for preservation.

The Library's AFI Collection today includes nearly 30,000 feature films and short subjects of the nitrate film era. Major segments of important Hollywood studio nitrate film libraries survive in the AFI Collection and are being preserved by the Library's Motion Picture Conservation Center including for example, Columbia Pictures features and cartoons from the early 1930s to 1951, which include the original camera negative for "Mr. Smith Goes to Washington" and 16 other films directed by Frank Capra. United Artists, Universal, Paramount, Hal Roach, Monogram, and other studio productions of the silent and sound eras are also well represented in the AFI Collection. A major part of the Library's AFI Collection consists of less well known independent productions from the early silent era by such early pioneering studios as Vitagraph, Edison, and Thanhouser. The collection is also a major source of rare surviving movies produced for pre-WWII African-American and foreign-language audiences that are now recognized as equally important to the development and understanding of America's film heritage as those made by the major studios.

The AFI collection makes up fully one tenth of the Library's theatrical motion picture collection and is the single most important source of surviving original production elements for movies of the mainstream Hollywood era. (PL)

The Recorded Sound Section Collections—An Overview

The Library of Congress holds the nation's largest public collection of sound recordings, totaling over two and one-half million items, comprising music of all kinds, radio broadcasts, and the spoken word. The collection covers over 100 years of sound recordings and includes a number of collections of unusual and historic significance. The holdings consist of nearly every audio medium ever used, from wax cylinders to DVD-Audio and SACD compact discs. Although international in scope, the commercially published sound recordings are predominantly American in origin and contain an outstanding collection of pre-1900 recordings, operatic recordings, and extensive holdings of twentieth century American music of all types: classical, jazz, folk, rock, musical theater, and popular song. The collection is particularly strong in recordings made since 1972 when the copyright law was amended to cover sound recordings.

Unpublished recordings include radio broadcasts from the major American networks: ABC, CBS, NBC, Mutual, and NPR. The holdings also include special collections donated by scholars, organizations, political figures, and such performing artists and composers as Aaron Copland, George Gershwin, Leonard Bernstein, Serge Rachmaninoff, and Rosa Ponselle. A selective list of the unpublished collections held by the Recorded Sound Section follows:

- *The Brander Matthews Dramatic Museum Collection* consists of over 500 recordings representing major figures in world politics and cultural life. Included are recordings of twentieth century poets such as Robert Frost, Gertrude Stein, W. H. Auden, and Edgar Lee Masters as are recordings of English-language dialects and American Indian and African American folk music.

- *The Armed Forces Radio and Television Service Collection* contains over 300,000 transcription discs and cassettes of broadcasts to the armed services from 1942 to 1997. The programming encompasses both original programs and re-broadcasts of network programs.

- *The Office of War Information* recordings are housed in the Division and provide researchers access to the U.S. government's ideological campaign broadcast in all major Western European and many Asian languages during World War II.

The Library holds a major collection of recordings and films produced during World War II by the U.S. Government's Office of War Information (OWI). An OWI film about the Library included the Budapest String Quartet (above) performing in the Coolidge Auditorium. The Library itself has recorded Music Division concerts for its permanent collections since 1940.
LC/Motion Picture, Broadcasting, and Recorded Sound Division.

- *Cynthia Lowry Collection of Mary Margaret McBride Broadcast Recordings* contains several thousand daily broadcasts of radio host Mary Margaret McBride. The bulk of the collection dates from 1935 to 1956 and includes interviews with such figures as Eleanor Roosevelt, Frank Lloyd Wright, Bob Hope, H.V. Kaltenborn, Margaret Bourke-White, Arthur Miller, and Joe DiMaggio.

- *The Voice of America Collection* contains over 65,000 broadcasts on disc and open reel tape of classical, folk, and jazz performances. Symphonic performances by the New York Philharmonic, the Philadelphia Orchestra, the Louisville Philharmonic, and the Oklahoma Symphony Orchestra are well represented in the collection. In addition, Voice of America broadcasts the yearly Newport Jazz Festival featuring such performers as John Coltrane, Miles Davis, Coleman Hawkins, and Sonny Rollins.

- *The Recorded Sound Section* houses a large collection of cultural events recorded at the Library of Congress. Not only are the many scholarly talks given at the Library represented in these collections, but they also include recordings from the *Music Division Concert Series*, the Library's *Archive of Recorded Poetry and Literature* and the *Archive of Hispanic Literature on Tape*. The latter collections include readings by most major twentieth century poets from the Western Hemisphere. The concerts have been recorded since 1937 and feature chamber music by such notable ensembles as the Juilliard String Quartet, The Beaux Arts trio, and Budapest String Quartet.

- *BBC Sound Archive Collection* comprises 6,000 long-playing discs of the BBC's most significant broadcasts. Researchers can hear nearly every significant political figure of the twentieth century in addition to a large sampling of musical programming.

- *National Public Radio's The Recorded Sound Section* holds the cultural programming from NPR, a collection that includes some 32,000 programs of jazz, folk, and classical music in addition to some of the only dramatic productions in radio today. The Library's NPR holdings span the period from 1971 to 1990. (SB)

The 78 RPM Recordings Collection

With the words, "Famous voices . . . for the enlightenment of future generations," written in a 1925 letter from John G. Paine, the Victor Talking Machine Company sent a Victrola and 412 discs to Carl Engel, Chief of the Music Division. The foresight of these two men gave birth to the Library's recorded sound collection. During the intervening 75 years, the Library's 78 rpm collection has grown to some half million discs spanning the years 1888 to 1960.

The Library's collection of 78 rpm discs is itself a fascinating artifact of early twentieth century life. It illustrates the technological history of the first 70 years of recorded sound on disc, ranging from Emile Berliner's pioneering efforts, through the acoustical era and the advent of electrical recording in the mid 1920s, to the eventual phase-out of 78s in the 1950s. These "pre-editing era" 78s are real-time performances from start to finish—a concept foreign to most of today's artists and studios. Due to the nature of the recording process at that time, musicians had one opportunity to present their performances. If the performance was found to be lacking, the "take" was not used and the musicians would commence again from the beginning. The process of piecing together the best portions of multiple takes was not possible. Recordings on 78s not infrequently include minor mistakes, and represent unique single performances.

The aural contents of the recordings themselves are also of paramount interest. Whether music or spoken word, the discs present famous voices that many have never heard. From William Jennings Bryan and Robert E. Peary, the Carter Family and Enrico Caruso, Bessie Smith and Len Spencer, to bebop and the birth of rock 'n roll, 78 rpm discs capture the essence of a bygone era.

The vast majority of 78 rpm discs at the Library of Congress came as gifts or purchases from numerous private record collectors. While differing in

The Manuscript score of "Jelly Roll" Morton's "Frog-I-More Rag," shown with a 78-rpm Paramount recording of the work and a tinted photograph of Morton. The Nesuhi Ertegun Collection includes Morton's 78-rpm commercial releases.
LC/Motion Picture, Broadcasting, and Recorded Sound Division.

their tastes, these collectors shared an indefatigable passion for seeking out, acquiring, and safeguarding recordings, and then passing on the results of their lifelong efforts to future generations through the Library. The foci of their collections include specific performer(s), musical genres, geographical areas, technological processes, and manufacturer labels.

The Library holds a collection of recordings dated 1888 to 1900 from the company of Emile Berliner, the inventor and founder of the disc recording industry. Through the generosity of his descendants and other collectors such as John R. Adams and Isabelle Sayers, the Library has an impressive sampling of this Washingtonian's recording legacy—foreign and domestic, published and unpublished—as well as his notebooks, correspondence, photographs, and business records. Included are musical performances by the Sousa Band and individual musicians, Native American music, and voice recordings of Berliner and his family.

In addition to the Berliner, Adams, and Sayers Collections, other acoustically recorded materials are included in the John Secrist Collection, which contains nearly complete sets of the commercial releases of Enrico Caruso and Rosa Ponselle, as well as acoustic recordings of Suzanne Adams, Ernestine Schumann-Heink, Giovanni Zenatello, and others; and the Joel Berger Collection of over 40 Imperial Russian Opera singers. The Victor Talking Machine Company/RCA-Victor generously continued to supply the Library with recordings (Red Seals, jazz, popular, folk, and ethnic) through the 1930s.

Popular music recordings of the acoustic era are strongly represented by some 40,000 discs in the Ulysses "Jim" Walsh Collection (highlighted by many Edison Diamond discs and recordings by the first generation of commercial recording artists) and the Fairleigh Dickinson/George Moss Collections. The largest collection received to date, that of Robert Altshuler, contains some 220,000 recordings (1917–1950) of most classic blues and jazz artists recorded during the 78 rpm era. The collections of Jerry Valburn, Karl Bambach, and the Maud Powell Foundation provide Library users with comprehensive archives of recordings by jazz great Duke Ellington, tenor John McCormack, and violinist Maud Powell, and there is also the Nesuhi Ertegun Collection of "Jelly Roll" Morton, donated by Time-Warner. A.F.R. Lawrence's collection of test pressings offers researchers a rare cache of otherwise-unknown materials, including experimental electrical recordings, rehearsals, and performances by the Philadelphia Orchestra in the 1920s and 1930s, as well as opera and recital performances by Friedrich Schorr, Lawrence Tibbet, and others.

These notable complementary collections provide an unparalleled body of 78 rpm recordings. While the Library and listeners benefit from the work and expertise of collectors named and unnamed, Recorded Sound staff continue to shape and refine the collection as a whole by seeking out the many recordings not yet represented. (MRB)

MUMFORD, L. QUINCY (1903–1982)

L. Quincy Mumford, Librarian of Congress from 1954 to 1974, was born on a farm near Ayden in Pitt County, North Carolina, the son of Jacob Edward Mumford and Emma Luvenia Stocks. Quincy Mumford worked on the family tobacco farm while attending grammar and high school. He attended Duke University, receiving his A.B. in 1925. The 1925 Duke yearbook reported, "He doesn't make much noise, but he is always doing something." In 1928, he received an M.A. in English from Duke. As an undergraduate, Mumford was a student assistant in the Duke University Library. He worked full-time in the library from 1926 to 1928 while pursuing his graduate studies. In the fall of 1928, he enrolled in Columbia University's School of Library Science, receiving his B.S. degree in 1929.

L. Quincy Mumford, Librarian of Congress from 1954 to 1974, was the first Librarian to hold a degree in Library Science. He was the director of the Cleveland Public Library and president of the American Library Association when he was nominated to the post by President Dwight D. Eisenhower. The Library's annual appropriation grew tenfold during his 20-year tenure.
Photograph: Harris and Ewing. LC Archives.

Mumford then accepted a job offer from Keyes D. Metcalf at the New York Public Library, beginning a career and a personal relationship that lasted a lifetime. Mumford spent 16 years in positions of increasing responsibility at the New York Public Library. Soon after he joined the staff, he met Permelia Catherine (Pam) Stevens, a children's librarian. Permelia Mumford died in 1961, and in 1969 Mumford married Betsy Perrin Fox.

Mumford's career at the New York Public Library was interrupted between September 1940 and August 1941, when he was asked to analyze the Library of Congress's cataloging operations and make recommendations for their improvement. After the committee report was issued, Librarian Archibald MacLeish persuaded Mumford to take a leave of absence from the New York Public Library to organize the new Processing Department at the Library of Congress and serve as its director. In his 1941 *Annual Report*, MacLeish said Mumford performed "a minor—perhaps a major—miracle" during his year there.

In 1945, Mumford became assistant director at the Cleveland Public Library and director in 1950. At Cleveland, Mumford won consistent gains in the library's budget, skillfully dealing with city officials and business leaders. He served as president of the Ohio Library Association (1947–1948), and chaired several committees of the American Library Association (ALA) between 1944 and 1953. He was elected president of ALA for 1954–1955.

On April 22, 1954, President Dwight D. Eisenhower nominated Mumford to become Librarian of Congress; when confirmed by the Senate on July 24, 1954, he became the first Librarian of Congress to hold a degree in Library Science. In 1939, the ALA had opposed President Franklin D. Roosevelt's nomination of writer and poet Archibald MacLeish because he was not a trained librarian. Luther H. Evans, Mumford's immediate predecessor, was a political scientist.

Relations between the Congress and the Library had deteriorated during the Evans administration, and Congress refused to approve the Librarian's requests for a greatly increased budget. Speaking in the U.S. House of Representatives in favor of Mumford's nomination, Congresswoman Frances P. Bolton of Ohio said the Library of Congress was "in need of a very real housecleaning... (it) has fallen into patterns of inefficient and unwise operations."

Mumford immediately learned about congressional unhappiness with his predecessors. At the Library's 1954 budget hearings he was told "The Librarian should be mindful that the Library is the instrument and the creature of Congress." At his confirmation hearings that July, he heard complaints about Evans's frequent absences from Washington and learned that some members of Congress felt the Library should consider "withdrawing" or at least "de-emphasizing" many of its national services. Mumford promised to be a full-time librarian, to strengthen the Library's services to Congress, and to consider all the questions raised by members of Congress and their staffs. But he stood his ground against the diminution of the Library's national role, maintaining that its vast resources should be available both to Congress and to the nation at large.

Working to overcome the atmosphere of distrust he had inherited, Mumford politely explained and justified each budget request. Consultation with Congress was frequent and the Library's budget slowly increased, as did its staff and the size of its collections. Further expansion was on the horizon: in 1957 Mumford initiated planning for a third major Library of Congress Building. The James Madison Memorial Building, the largest library building in the world, was authorized in 1965. Construction began in 1971 and was completed in 1980. Mumford shared this accomplishment with an important ally in Congress, Senator B. Everett Jordan of North Carolina.

In 1957, Librarian Mumford initiated planning for the third major Library building on Capitol Hill. The James Madison Memorial Building was authorized in 1965. Construction began in 1971, and when it was completed in 1980 it was the largest library building in the world. The exterior of the new building is shown near completion in this 1974 photograph.
Photograph: Architect of the Capitol.

While Mumford's cautious philosophy worked with Congress, it made others impatient and uncomfortable. Research and academic librarians felt that Mumford, whose experience was largely in public libraries, was not exercising the national leadership that research libraries expected from the Library of Congress. In 1962, at the request of Senator Claiborne Pell of the Joint Committee on the Library, Harvard University director Douglas W. Bryant prepared a memorandum on "what the Library of Congress does and ought to do for the Government and the Nation generally." Bryant urged expansion of the Library's national activities and services, recommending that the Library of Congress be officially recognized as the national library and that it be transferred to the executive branch of government where, he felt, it would receive more generous funding.

Mumford and his senior advisors, Chief Assistant Librarian Rutherford B. Rogers and Assistant Librarian for Public Affairs Elizabeth Hamer, decided to rebut the "Bryant memorandum," and Senator Jordan inserted Mumford's reply in the *Congressional Record* for October 2, 1962. The Librarian strongly defended the Library's position in the legislative branch of government, asserting that it performed "more national functions than any other national library in the world."

The Bryant memorandum and Mumford's reply were published in the Library's 1962 *Annual Report*. The Library's forceful response signaled a new confidence. The Madison Building had been authorized and more federal funds for education were becoming available. For the Library of Congress, this translated immediately into new acquisitions and cataloging programs.

The expansion during the Mumford era of the Library's overseas acquisitions and cataloging programs was in part an extension of earlier international initiatives taken by Librarian of Congress Luther H. Evans. In 1958, the Library was authorized to use U.S.-owned foreign currencies (under the Agricultural Trade Development and Assistance Act, PL-480) to acquire books for itself and other U.S. libraries and to establish acquisitions offices in foreign countries. The Higher Education Act of 1965, through Title II-C, had great significance for the Library of Congress and for academic and research libraries, providing funds to the Library for the ambitious purpose of acquiring and cataloging, insofar as possible, all current library materials of value to scholarship published throughout the world.

The successful introduction of automation to the Library's cataloging procedures in the mid-1960s was an achievement of great importance for libraries and scholarship, particularly through the 1965 inauguration of the MARC system for distributing cataloging information in machine-readable form. Other

Verner W. Clapp, President of the Council on Library Resources, and Librarian Mumford in 1957 proudly displaying a copy of the newly published facsimile of Captain John Smith's Map of Virginia, the first item to be funded by the Library's new Verner W. Clapp Publication Fund. After a long and fruitful career at the Library, Clapp retired in 1956 to become the council's first president. LC Archives.

expansions of the Library's national role during the Mumford administration included the publication of bibliographic tools such as the *National Union Catalog of Manuscript Collections* and the *National Union Catalog, Pre-1956 Imprints*, and the expansion of the National Books for the Blind program to include the physically handicapped.

The Legislative Reorganization Act of 1970 redesignated the Legislative Reference Service, the department that works directly for the Congress, as the Congressional Research Service (CRS), broadened its responsibilities, and provided for the rapid expansion of its staff. It also gave the CRS a new independence within the Library's administrative structure. There was an internal cost, however: a split between CRS and the rest of the Library that became increasingly difficult for Mumford and his senior officers to bridge.

The last years of the Mumford administration were troublesome for other reasons as well. Final approval from Congress for the use of the Madison Building as a Library of Congress Building did not occur until 1971; in the meantime, the Library's two other buildings became badly overcrowded. The Library was accused by employee groups of "discrimination on racial grounds in recruitment, training, and promotion practices," beginning more than two decades of controversy and lawsuits. A shy man, Librarian Mumford became increasingly remote. His health suffered. He retired on December 31, 1974.

Although his 20-year administration may have ended unhappily for him personally, Mumford's librarianship was one of the most productive in the Library's history. The growth of the institution under his leadership was unprecedented. In two decades, the size of the Library's annual appropriation increased tenfold, from $9,400,000 to $96,696,000; the number of staff members nearly tripled, from 1,564 to 4,250; and the number of items in the collections more than doubled from approximately 33 million to 74 million.

Mumford was fortunate to head the Library of Congress during a period of economic growth and, as part of President Lyndon B. Johnson's "Great Society," increased federal expenditure and involvement in education and research. But Mumford also created his own opportunities. The rapprochement he reached with Congress between 1954 and the early 1960s was his most important accomplishment. (JYC)

Nomination of Lawrence Quincy Mumford of the District of Columbia To Be Librarian of Congress. Committee on Rules and Administration of the United States Senate. 83rd Congress, 2nd Sess. July 26, 1974, p. 147.

Powell, Benjamin E. "Lawrence Quincy Mumford: Twenty Years of Progress." *The Quarterly Journal of the Library of Congress* 33 (July 1976): 269–287.

MUSIC DIVISION AND COLLECTIONS

General Overview

The Music Division holds the world's largest collection of material supporting research in the areas of music, theater, and dance. In addition to facilitating access to these resources, the division's outreach activities involve support of the Library's public concert series by the efforts of the Concert Office, of community and national cultural programs, and of an increasing online presence of research material from the division's collections. The nearly 13 million items that comprise the division's collections include the classified music and book collections; music and literary manuscripts and related artifacts included in general and archival collections; microforms; periodicals related to the performing arts; copyright deposits; and musical instruments, reflecting a span of over 800 years of cultural and creative activity.

While the division holds substantial musical material from European and other sources from all over the world, its collections—adhering to the vision of the division's second chief, Oscar George Theodore Sonneck, to create a "national library"—are particularly strong in the area of American music. The general collections of the Music Division are unique in that their already comprehensive holdings have been continually enriched by the steady influx of music and music-related material published in this country and submitted for copyright deposit with the Library. This published material complements the primary research resources contained in the division's special collections. The division currently holds over 500 named collections, which vary in size from a handful of items to over a million distinct items. Most of these collections were acquired directly by bequest or donated to the Library. The diversity alone of the material contained in these special collections is remarkable, containing literally millions of items in an incredible variety of formats: music manuscripts; printed music; correspondence and other literary manuscripts; books; pamphlets; concert programs; posters; playbills; newspaper and magazine clippings; business records; scrapbooks; photographs; drawings; etchings; paintings; bronze and plaster busts; certificates; citations; medals and honors. The realia held in the division's collections range from the Library's Stradivari stringed instruments to a lock of Ludwig van Beethoven's hair, and from self-portraits painted by both George and Ira Gershwin to Victor Herbert's death mask.

Many of the collections consist of personal papers of such eminent figures as composers Irving Berlin, Aaron Copland, Leonard Bernstein, Charles Mingus, and Sergei Rachmaninoff; violinists Jascha Heifetz, Fritz Kreisler, and Henryk Szeryng; singers Geraldine Farrar, Beverly Sills, and Helen Traubel; pianists Artur Rubenstein, Leopold Godowsky, and Harold Bauer; conductors Serge Koussevitzky, André Kostelanetz, and Otto Klemperer; musicologist Nicolas Slonimsky; and dancers/choreographers Franziska Boas, Martha Graham, and Bronislava Nijinska. Other collections document the collaboration of two or more individuals, such as George and Ira Gershwin, Richard Rodgers and Lorenz Hart, composers and educators Charles and Ruth Crawford Seeger, choreographer/director Bob Fosse and dancer/singer Gwen Verdon, the members of the Budapest String Quartet, or the National Negro Opera Company. Several collections contain business records of important American music publishers such as the Arthur P. Schmidt Company Archive, the *Modern Music* Archive, and the Theodore Presser Collection.

Other collections represent the work of a scholar or collector, such as the Dayton C. Miller Flute Collection, containing more than 1,600 wind instruments and thousands of other items related to the flute, and the Albert Schatz Collection of over 12,500 opera libretti from the seventeenth through the nineteenth centuries, purchased by the Library in 1909. The Moldenhauer Archives contain an extraordinary and diverse collection of autograph music manuscripts and correspondence dating from medieval times to the present. While the collection is particularly strong in material related to Johannes Brahms and Anton Webern, it also contains individual treasures such as the autograph scores of Ernest Bloch's *Schelomo*, the famed "Coronation Scene" from

Giacomo Puccini. Detail from a leaf (Act II) of the composer's holograph score for La Boheme *(1896). Moldenhauer Archives.* LC/Music Division.

over the previous year's purchases. In 1908, Sonneck arranged for the purchase of an important collection of over 12,500 opera librettos and related documentation from Albert Schatz of Rostock, Germany, for which he and Putnam persuaded Congress to authorize a special appropriation. The acquisition of the Schatz Collection was one of the first instances in the division's history where an entire collection of material was purchased outright, helping to establish a precedent for future acquisitions. At Putnam's suggestion, Sonneck also began to create a system of classifying music, first implemented in 1904. It is a tribute to Sonneck's skill and foresight that his original classification system forms the basis of the system still in use today at the Library and in many music libraries throughout the nation.

Perhaps Sonneck's greatest legacy, however, is his devotion to the cause of American music, and in his conviction that as a part of "our National Library," the Music Division must cultivate a "National Music Collection." This fundamental idea of a collection emphasizing what Sonneck termed "American music and music in America" has determined the course of the development of the division and its holdings since that time. Sonneck's appreciation of the value of American music was as pioneering as it was unrecognized. Not until decades later did the academic community begin to accept as a subject of legitimate study the legacy that Sonneck strove to preserve.

Sonneck eventually left the division in 1917, under strained circumstances. The years of the first World War witnessed the growth of a profound nationalist sentiment in America, and Sonneck, born of German parents, fell under official suspicion of being a German sympathizer. He resigned from the Library and accepted the post as director of publications for the music publisher G. Schirmer in New York; he subsequently became vice president of that firm in 1921. Despite repeated offers by Librarian of Congress Putnam to return to the Music Division and to a post to which, by Sonneck's own admission, he was greatly attached, Sonneck continually refused, preferring instead to use the advantages of his professional position to promote the publication and performance of the works of American composers.

Carl Engel (1883–1944), who, like Sonneck, was a musicologist and composer by training, became chief of the Music Division in 1922, a position he held until 1934. Besides perpetuating the ideals of his predecessor in his efforts to expand the music collections, it was Engel who first established both the Library's collection of sound recordings and the Archive of American Folk Song, which eventually became part of the collections of the Library's Motion Picture, Broadcasting, and Recorded Sound Division, as well as forming the basis for what is now known as the Library's American Folklife Center. Engel, like Sonneck, eventually also accepted a position with the G. Schirmer music publishing firm (he became its president in 1929), where he, too, was able to encourage the cause of both the American composer and American musical culture.

Carl Engel, Chief of the Music Division from 1922 to 1934, expanded the division and its scope, establishing both the collection of sound recordings and the Archive of American Folk Song. He also worked closely and successfully with Elizabeth Sprague Coolidge, a great benefactor of the Music Division and the Library. LC Archives.

Engel's influential collaboration with American music patron Elizabeth Sprague Coolidge (1864–1953) substantially enlarged the scope of the Music Division, and in a larger sense, advanced the

Elizabeth Sprague Coolidge (1864–1953), who in 1925 donated funds to build an auditorium for the performance of chamber music and established an endowment to aid in the "study, composition, and appreciation of music." Her endowment led to the creation of the Library of Congress Trust Fund Board.
Portrait: John Sargent. LC/Prints and Photographs Division. LC-USP6-1532A.

cause of Western musical culture. Mrs. Coolidge, who among her many philanthropic activities had established an internationally renowned series of chamber music concerts at South Mountain in Pittsfield, Massachusetts in 1918 (for which she built a concert hall and performers' accommodations, assumed responsibility for all administrative and artistic fees, and commissioned original musical works), wished to make her enterprise permanent by entrusting it to a major institution. She found in the Library of Congress the ideal situation, one, which also appealed to her vision of involving the federal government in the support of musical activities. As early as 1921, Mrs. Coolidge began to present her ideas through correspondence with Oscar George Theodore Sonneck, and subsequently with Engel and Putnam. Their diplomatic advice, combined with Mrs. Coolidge's own unwavering ambition to realize her goals resulted, in 1924, in a bold and original proposal by Coolidge to establish an endowment for the construction of a concert hall at the Library, and for commissioning new musical works. Such an offer to the federal government from a private citizen was unprecedented. But despite the complexity of the issues involved, legislation allowing the acceptance of Mrs. Coolidge's generosity was quickly approved by both House and Senate, and the bill was signed into law by President Calvin Coolidge (no close relation) on January 23, 1925—only three months to the day after Mrs. Coolidge's original letter of intent had been submitted to Putnam.

The establishment of the Elizabeth Sprague Coolidge Foundation at the Library, as well as a Library of Congress Trust Fund Board to administer the Foundation's assets and future endowments—not to mention the construction of the Coolidge Auditorium itself—had a tremendous effect on the Music Division. As part of Mrs. Coolidge's desire to build the twentieth-century chamber music repertoire, commissions for new chamber works were awarded by the Foundation, and the manuscripts were deposited in the Music Division. Many of these commissions are among the most important chamber works of this century. The manuscripts of nearly 300 works by the major composers of this century, along with Mrs. Coolidge's voluminous correspondence with each of these composers, performers, and other colleagues, not only enriches Western music and music scholarship as a whole, but also established the Library as a major repository and research center for musical studies. The Coolidge Auditorium, which seats approximately 500, was constructed in the northwest courtyard of the Library's Jefferson Building in 1925, providing an ideal venue for concerts and lectures.

Although as chief of the Music Division Carl Engel held the responsibility for the administration of the Coolidge Foundation, Mrs. Coolidge retained at least an equal influence in the Foundation's administration. What began as a unique collaboration of government and private concerns to promote a common interest resulted in a close friendship, documented in their voluminous correspondence. Their mutual respect is best illustrated by a single fact: Mrs. Coolidge eventually permitted Engel to offer many commissions himself, without her prior approval. On one important point, however, they disagreed. Engel felt that the Coolidge Foundation should support American music exclusively. But Coolidge insisted that the scope of her philanthropy be international. Without so enlightened a view, many of the greatest composers of the twentieth-century could not have received her support at the time of their greatest need, including Stravinsky, Schoenberg, Hindemith, Bartók, and Prokofiev, some of whom became American citizens and all of whom made substantial contributions to music in America, as well as to Western music in general.

Mrs. Coolidge's philanthropy inspired further endowments for the Music Division. In 1935 and

Gertrude Clarke Whittall (1867–1965), who from 1935 to 1937 donated five Stradivari instruments to the Library, also established a foundation to support concerts in which the instruments were to be used and donated funds to build a pavilion in which they were to be housed. She established a Poetry Fund in 1950. LC Archives.

1936, Gertrude Clarke Whittall (1867–1965) donated five stringed instruments to the Library made by famed Cremonese master Antonio Stradivari: the "Castelbarco" cello (1697), the "Cassavetti" viola (1727), and three violins, the "Ward" (1700), the "Castelbarco" (1699), and the "Betts" (1704), all named for former owners. A gift of five bows by distinguished French bowmaker François Tourte accompanied these instruments. In addition, Mrs. Whittall also established an endowment in 1936 to maintain these instruments through their use in Library concerts, thus establishing the "string quartet in residence" program, which continues even today. From 1940 to 1962, the Budapest String Quartet held this distinction; it was succeeded by the Juilliard String Quartet. This endowment also provided for the construction (1938) of a pavilion adjoining the Coolidge Auditorium to house these instruments. With the purchase of portions of the Stonborough-Wittgenstein Collection in 1941, Mrs. Whittall expanded the activities of her Foundation to include the acquisition of original musical manuscript scores and sketches of European masters, among them Bach, Beethoven, Brahms, Haydn, and Mozart. In 1944, the Foundation purchased a large amount of important and varied material relating to the Italian violin virtuoso and composer Nicolò Paganini, as well as a significant collection of Felix Mendelssohn material, including correspondence and the autograph score to the composer's *Octet*, the latter from Walter Hinrichsen, heir to the Leipzig music publishing firm of C.F. Peters.

The stringed instruments presented to the Music Division by Mrs. Whittall, otherwise known as the Cremonese Collection, form the basis of the division's present collection of musical instruments from around the world. In 1937, Dr. H. Blaikston Wilkins, former Honorary Curator of the Cremonese Collection, donated six early stringed instruments to the Library. The Wilkins Collection includes a 1749 pardessus de viole (five-string treble viol), a 14-string viola d'amore from the late eighteenth century, a 12-string viola d'amore (1763), a seven-string bass viol (early eighteenth century), a five-string quinton (1760), and the remains of a late seventeenth-century bass viol, which had been subsequently converted into a cello.

The third and largest collection of musical instruments to be donated to the Library was included in a 1941 bequest from physicist Dr. Dayton C. Miller. Miller was an avid amateur flutist, and during his lifetime assembled the world's largest collection of wind instruments (most of which are flutes) and related material. In addition to over 1,600 instruments, the Miller Collection also contains nearly 10,000 pieces of music, 3,000 rare books, extensive documentation on wind instrument manufacturers active in his lifetime, portraits, photographs, and extensive personal correspondence. Three-dimensional objects in the collection include nearly 60 statuettes and three bronzes, as well as over 600 prints and engravings; almost all of these objects feature representations of flute or pipe players. The instruments in this collection (including those acquired since Miller's original bequest) represent nearly every world culture, dating from about 1100 B.C. to the 1980s. They include simple folk instruments as well as complex mechanical specimens, and the materials used in their construction range from clay, bone, and bamboo to jade, ivory, crystal, silver, and gold. The Miller Collection is strong in Native American instruments.

The fourth musical instrument collection received by the Library came in 1960 from King Bhumibol Adulyadej of Thailand. It consists of 10 finely crafted Siamese-style folk instruments, including a pair of finger cymbals, small hand drums, two vertical flutes, and several two- and three-stringed instruments.

As the musical instrument collections in the Music Division were developed through the generosity of donors, and based on the pioneering efforts of Mrs. Coolidge and Mrs. Whittall, so have the division's philanthropic foundations, following the legacy of these two remarkable women, enriched the division's activities, collections, and history. Each of these foundations supports this country's musical culture in various ways, among them by encouraging the composition, performance, recording, dissemination, and collection of new or existing works, and by doing so help to assure the continued development of music in a world society. (KL)

Anderson, Gillian B. "Putting the Experience of the World at the Nation's Command: Music at the Library of Congress, 1800–1917," *Journal of the American Musicological Society*, 42 (1989): 108–149.

Barr, Cyrilla. *Elizabeth Sprague Coolidge: American Patron of Music*. New York: Schirmer Books, 1998.

Library of Congress Music, Theater, Dance: An Illustrated Guide. Washington, D.C.: Library of Congress, 1993.

NATIONAL BOOK FESTIVAL

On September 8, 2001, three days before the terrorist attacks on the World Trade Center and the Pentagon, the Library of Congress and First Lady Laura Bush hosted the first National Book Festival. On this warm and sunny day, approximately 25,000 people enjoyed listening to more than 60 award-winning authors, illustrators, storytellers, and poets on the east lawn of the U.S. Capitol and in the Library's Jefferson and Madison Buildings. A celebration of the joy of books and reading, the National Book Festival was organized by the Library of Congress and supported by donations from private sector sponsors. Security became a prime concern on Capitol Hill after September 11, 2001. The 2002 National Book Festival was held outdoors on the west Capitol grounds and the National Mall on October 12, 2002. In spite of poor weather and the ongoing sniper threat in the Washington, D.C. area, the Festival attracted a crowd of more than 45,000 and its place as an annual event was assured. The 2003 National Book Festival took place entirely on the National Mall and approximately 70,000 people attended, listening to 85 authors, illustrators, poets, and storytellers, getting their books signed, and visiting the Festival's reading and literacy promotion pavilions. The fourth Festival, on October 9, 2004, presented 76 well-known authors, illustrators, and poets and drew a crowd of approximately 85,000.

A Dixieland band plays in front of the Thomas Jefferson Building to a happy crowd enjoying the first National Book Festival. Photograph: LC/Christina Wenks.

The idea of a National Book Festival came from First Lady Laura Bush, who established the Texas Book Festival in 1995, when she was the First Lady of Texas. A former schoolteacher and librarian, Mrs. Bush dedicated the Texas Book Festival to the public libraries of Texas, and proceeds from the Festival go to the state's public libraries. After George W. Bush was elected president of the United States in 2000, Mrs. Bush invited Librarian of Congress James H. Billington and the Library of Congress to join her in creating and hosting the National Book Festival. Planning for the first Festival began in March 2001, six months before it took place.

The National Book Festival is sponsored and organized by the Library of Congress and hosted by First Lady Laura Bush. Here, at the first festival, Mrs. Bush stands in front of the Festival banner on the Jefferson Building's Neptune Plaza. Photograph: LC/Michaela McNichol.

From the beginning, Festival planners focused on promoting the joys of reading and the need to attract popular authors and illustrators who would appeal to a wide variety of children and adults. It was to be a family event that would include book signings—an opportunity for members of the public to meet and be inspired by award-winning writers. It would be nonpartisan and non-commercial, supported by contributions and not by the sale of exhibit space

The commemorative program for the second National Book Festival. Photograph: LC/Clarke Allen.

to publishers, booksellers, or vendors; all sales of books for author signings would be handled by the Library. The national and unique nature of the Festival would be highlighted by a Pavilion of the States, at which each state would promote its own literary heritage and writers, including libraries and statewide book and reading-promoting activities such as book festivals and book awards and literacy programs. The Pavilion of the States was inaugurated at the second National Festival. A second unique feature was a pavilion highlighting the activities of national nonprofit organizations that promote books, reading, literacy, and libraries. Further information about the National Book Festival, including the presentations of most of the authors, illustrators, storytellers, and poets at the first four Festivals, can be found on the Library's Web site. (JYC)

Library of Congress Information Bulletin 62 (November 2003).

NATIONAL SERIALS DATA PROGRAM

The Library of Congress, the National Library of Medicine, and the National Agricultural Library announced on June 26, 1967 the formation of the U.S. National Libraries Task Force on Automation and Other Cooperative Services. The Task Force's first project, a National Serials Pilot Project, began in January 1968, sponsored by the Association of Research Libraries with the support of the Council on Library Resources, Inc., and the National Science Foundation. In the first phase, project staff identified the data elements needed for complete cataloging of serials and incorporated them into a MARC format for serials. In the second phase, staff began creating a machine-readable file of the science and technology serials of the three national libraries. For phase three, they planned to develop a central database of catalog information for all serials.

At the same time, the United Nations Educational, Scientific, and Cultural Organization (UNESCO) and the International Council of Scientific Unions were planning a worldwide science information system. As part of this system, they established an International Serials Data System (ISDS) that would employ the international identification code for serial publications devised by the American National Standards Institute (ANSI) and approved in draft form by the International Standards Organization in October 1972. Representatives from all three U.S. national libraries served on the ANSI committee that prepared the code, a unique identifier that would allow librarians to distinguish among serials having the same or similar names and would help them track the many name changes that serials undergo. The resulting ISSN is an eight-digit number that uniquely identifies any serial publication, regardless of place of publication, language, frequency, or format.

The National Serials Pilot Project became the National Serials Data Program (NSDP) on April 17, 1972, when an office was established at the Library of Congress to handle U.S. contributions to the international center. As the American national center, the NSDP assigns data elements, including the identification code, called the International Standard Serial Number (ISSN) to serial titles originating in the United States. The NSDP records are sent to the ISSN International Centre in Paris where they are added to the international file and made available worldwide. The other tasks of the NSDP are to obtain any ISSN data needed by librarians in this country and to encourage publishers and bibliographic agencies to use the ISSN to identify their publications. The program was moved into the Library's Processing Department in 1975 and remained a part of the succeeding administrative units of Processing Services (1978), Collections Services (1990), and Library Services (1995).

From the outset, librarians nationwide wanted the ISSN added to computerized catalog records for serial publications. There was some difficulty in fulfilling that wish because while Library of Congress catalogers began to create computerized catalog records for serials on February 1, 1973, and these were distributed to subscribers beginning in June 1973, the Library could produce only 8,000 to 10,000 records annually. This small number was not sufficient for the comprehensive database that librarians needed as they sought to convert all their serial cataloging to electronic format. Ultimately a cooperative database building effort named Conversion of Serials (CONSER) filled the gap, with the NSDP staff contributing the ISSN data and playing a role in reviewing and revising records contributed to the CONSER database.

In addition to being used for library cataloging, the ISSN has been useful to other agencies and businesses worldwide. Libraries and subscription agencies use it for the management of claims and orders. Copyright centers employ it for the collection and dissemination of royalties. The U. S. Postal Service uses it as an official registration number for serials mailed second class. In interlibrary loan transactions, union catalogs, and automated systems it facilitates exact identification, and it can be used in bar codes to optically identify serial publications. The NSDP provides instructions for applying for an ISSN and application forms on its Web site. (JA)

Sauer, Mary. "National Serials Data Program," *The Bowker Annual* (1979): 66–71.

______."How to Obtain an ISSN," *The Bowker Annual* (2004): 551–556.

NATIONAL UNION CATALOG

In 1901, Herbert Putnam asked the Card Section staff to send one copy of each Library of Congress catalog card to selected libraries scattered throughout the country. These so-called depository libraries created their own catalogs of Library of Congress cards, which they agreed to maintain. Putnam also began exchanging cards with other libraries that were producing printed cards and had the staff interfile the other libraries' cards with Library of Congress cards to begin a Union Catalog of library holdings. The Union Catalog became, as Putnam described it, "the closest approximation now available to a complete record of books in American libraries."

Initially only Library of Congress staff used the Union Catalog, but in the mid-1920s, at the request of the American Library Association (ALA), John D. Rockefeller provided $250,000 for a five-year expansion project. The project began in September 1927, with the goal of recording the locations of all important research materials in American libraries. Under the direction of Ernest Cushing Richardson, 31 staff members recorded books held by more than 500 U.S. libraries and many important foreign libraries and listed over 4,800 special collections. Thus, the Union Catalog grew from approximately 1.5 million titles on 1.96 million cards to seven million titles with nine million locations recorded on 13 million cards. The Library also established union catalogs for non-Roman languages, including Chinese, Hebraic, Japanese, Korean, and Slavic.

After the Rockefeller funding was exhausted, Putnam established a Union Catalog Division in the Library in September 1932 and asked librarians to continue to contribute their holdings. Directed by Ernest Kletsch, the 11-member staff filed cards from more than 600 contributing libraries, made photostat copies of library holdings from records loaned by major research libraries, and answered librarians' mail inquiries about the locations of specific titles. In 1936, the Library, the ALA's Committee on Resources of American Libraries, and the Carnegie Corporation sponsored an invitational conference to consider the future of the Union Catalog as a cooperative project. There was no immediate result other than some improvements in the reporting system, but eight years later an increased appropriation allowed the staff to begin comparing entries from the Cleveland and Philadelphia catalogs with the Union Catalog and to add titles previously unlisted. In 1948 the catalog was renamed the National Union Catalog, and in 1954 the ALA's Board on Resources of American Libraries established a Subcommittee on the National Union Catalog—two developments that reflected the rapid increases in interlibrary loan traffic in the post-war period and the library community's consequent need to make location information more readily available.

By the 1930s, some librarians also wanted to exchange their voluminous depository catalogs for a less expensive alternative. Members of the Association of Research Libraries, in cooperation with Edward Brothers of Ann Arbor, Michigan, proposed printing a book catalog from the Library of Congress's card catalog. While Putnam refused their proposal, early in the 1940s Librarian Archibald MacLeish agreed, and Edwards Brothers issued the 167-volume *Catalog of Books Represented by Library of Congress Printed Cards* between 1942 and 1946, with a 42-volume supplement in 1948–1949. The Library began publishing and selling by subscription its own book catalogs with the *Books: Authors Catalog* in 1947 and *Books: Subjects* beginning in 1950. Separate volumes for maps and atlases, films, and music and phonograph records began appearing in 1953.

But the National Union Catalog still served as the sole record of publications held by all American libraries, and the Subcommittee on the National Union Catalog asked the Library to expand its book catalogs to include other libraries' current acquisitions. With the January 1956 issue, the *Cumulative Catalog of Library of Congress Cards* arranged by author became the *National Union Catalog: A Cumulative Author List* (NUC), including catalog information and locations for printed publications issued in 1956 and thereafter, as reported by the Library of Congress and by other North American libraries. Supplementary volumes for motion pictures and filmstrips and music and phonorecords appeared in 1958, and location reports received after publication appeared in a *Register of Additional Locations* beginning in 1965.

In 1958, the Council on Library Resources, Inc. (CLR) provided funding to enable the Library to compile the *National Union Catalog of Manuscript Collections* (NUCMC). Based on reports received from archival and manuscript repositories, the first volume appeared in 1962. NUCMC enabled scholars and researchers for the first time to find manuscripts written by or to particular people, or manuscripts dealing with particular historical periods, places, topics, and events. Meanwhile the National Union Catalog Division's Microfilm Clearing House maintained extensive records of filming projects and at intervals issued bulletins or union lists and bibliographies, such as *Newspapers on Microfilm*. Having

them promptly. This program became the National Program for Acquisitions and Cataloging (NPAC). Both Regional Acquisitions Centers and Shared Cataloging offices were established. Under it, additional offices were created. Two Regional Acquisitions Centers, one in Rio de Janeiro, and the other in Nairobi, were set up in 1966. Somewhat later, in 1970, the Jakarta office was converted to an NPAC center, PL-480 funds there having been depleted.

The first Shared Cataloging Office, in London, was opened in 1966. Others opened in 1966 were those in Vienna, Wiesbaden, and Oslo. Subsequently Shared Cataloging offices were opened in The Hague (1967), Tokyo (1968), Barcelona (1973), and Florence (1973).These offices operated in close cooperation with the national bibliographic agencies of their host countries, receiving cataloging data from them and selectively acquiring publications from these countries. Where bibliographic data was lacking, preliminary cataloging was done in the offices, the resulting cataloging being supplied with the publications. Fiscal constraints caused the closing of these offices between 1979 and 1981.

Thus, during the 1960s and early 1970s, an extensive network of overseas offices emerged, under these two distinct legislative acts. A total of 21 field offices and sub offices have been in operation, although not all at one time. The following table summarizes the history of these offices, first listing those currently active.

As PL-480 funds were used up, existing SFC and NPAC offices obtained additional funding through the Cooperative Acquisition Program (CAP), under which participating libraries contributed funds for the acquisition of their materials, plus an administrative charge. The CAP has attracted continuing support from the research library community since 1970. In recent years, acquisitions for participants have totaled roughly 400,000–600,000 pieces per year. Since 1962, millions of pieces have been acquired for participating libraries, in addition to those for the Library of Congress.

A byproduct of the acquisitions and cataloging work done by the PL-480 offices and the NPAC regional offices has been the regular issuance of *Accessions Lists*. These quickly became essential acquisitions tools, especially for non-participant libraries, and achieved a wide distribution both in the United States and abroad. Indeed, in the absence of up-to-date national bibliographies, for example, in Eastern Africa, the *Accessions Lists* functioned as essential bibliographical tools for librarians and researchers. They were never national bibliographies, however. In the absence of the latter, they did contribute an invaluable current bibliography of local publications. In the mid-1990s, publication of most of the lists was halted, on budgetary and technological grounds. The South Asia list was commercially published from 1998 to 2002 and then ceased. The African list continues.

Field office staffs typically consist of an American field director and local staff who are librarians, library clerks, and general office staff. The number varies in each office, but a staff of 20–30 is

	Years active	Office/program status
Offices Currently Active		
New Delhi, India	1961–present	Cooperative Acquisitions Program
Karachi, Pakistan (now in Islamabad)	1962–present	Cooperative Acquisitions Program
Cairo, Egypt	1962–present	Cooperative Acquisitions Program
Jakarta, Indonesia	1963–present	Cooperative Acquisitions Program
Nairobi, Kenya	1966–present	Cooperative Acquisitions Program
Rio de Janeiro, Brazil	1966–present	Cooperative Acquisitions Program
Offices Formerly Active		
Dhaka, Pakistan (later Bangladesh)	1962–1974	Cooperative Acquisitions Program operated out of the New Delhi office since 1974
Tel Aviv, Israel	1963–1973	Special Foreign Currency
Bangalore, India	1966–1967	Sub-office of New Delhi office
Colombo, Ceylon (later Sri Lanka)	1967–1973	Cooperative Acquisitions Program operated out of the New Delhi office since 1973
London, England	1966–1981	Shared Cataloging Office
Paris, France	1966–1979	Shared Cataloging Office
Wiesbaden, W. Germany	1966–1981	Shared Cataloging Office
Oslo, Norway	1966–1969	Shared Cataloging Office
Vienna, Australia	1966–1980	Shared Cataloging Office
Belgrade, Yugoslavia	1966–1973	Shared Cataloging Office
The Hague, Netherlands	1967–1980	Shared Cataloging Office
Tokyo, Japan	1968–1985	Shared Cataloging Office
Warsaw, Poland	1972–1978	Funded but never established
Barcelona, Spain	1973–1979	Shared Cataloging Office
Florence, Italy	1973–1980	Shared Cataloging Office

typical. New Delhi's and Jakarta's staffs are larger, reflecting the scale and complexity of their operations. From time to time, selected local staff members have been brought to Washington for training, which has also been done at the field offices by Library of Congress–Washington staffers. The contribution of these expert local staff members to the overall achievement of the offices cannot be overstated. It is their knowledge of local publishing, their linguistic skills, and their cataloging know-how that keeps the offices abreast of the ceaseless flow of publications. Individual staff members are themselves often well-known members in their local library communities.

Field directors have been recruited from the Washington staff of the Library, as well as from outside the Library. Directors have had varied library backgrounds, from cataloging, acquisitions, and area studies. Rotation from post to post has been a feature of the program, with many directors serving at more than a single post. The benefits of this have been considerable, with experience gained at one post then being transferred to another. Prior foreign-language training has not been a feature of the program, but most directors have known, or subsequently acquired, relevant local languages.

Field directors' conferences have proved themselves a useful means of addressing the many complex issues facing the offices. Initially held rarely, in recent years they have become more frequent. Venues have switched from overseas to the Washington area, with the 14th such conference held in 2003. The patchwork regional coverage of the field offices was at times puzzling to purists, who wondered for example why there was no office in Hong Kong to cover China, or why there was no office in Spanish-speaking Latin America. But setting up new offices, although mooted from time to time, proved difficult in the 1980s and 1990s. An attempt to establish an office in Mexico City ran into opposition from U.S. and Mexican book-dealers and their client libraries; a proposed West African office, long sought by the Library to balance the successful Nairobi office, foundered for lack of congressional funding. Expansion of the Rio office to cover other countries in Latin America did not advance beyond Uruguay. The Jakarta office was successful in establishing sub offices in Bangkok (1990), Kuala Lumpur (1990), and Manila (1991).

Over the years, there was a distinct thrust to give more scope, more responsibility, to the field offices. This was most apparent in the New Delhi office,where a series of initiatives were undertaken. Preservation microfilming was inaugurated in the New Delhi office in 1966, and has become increasingly important. While Indian publications have, of course, predominated, microfilming and microfiching of materials coming from the Cairo, Nairobi, and

Librarian of Congress Mumford, front row center with leis around his neck, on a visit to the Library's American Libraries Book Procurement Center in New Delhi, India, on November 4, 1963. The New Delhi office opened in 1961 and is one of six overseas offices still in operation.

Jakarta offices has been done as well. In 1991, the Library and the government of India undertook a collaborative project to retrospectively film the titles listed in *The National Bibliography of Indian Literature.* Some 22,686 titles in 15 languages were filmed by 2002. New Delhi has also filmed some 1,500 pamphlet collections with more than 22,000 items. The South Asian Literary Recordings Project was started in 2000, to preserve and disseminate, via a Web site, the voices of prominent authors from the region.

Another major initiative in the New Delhi office was the Overseas Data Entry program, which after extensive preparation, began in March 1984. Using (for the period) state-of-the-art Terak hardware, 96,153 monographic records were sent to the Library of Congress in machine-readable form by October 1993. By the late 1980s, however, all the offices were using conventional desktop computers to prepare cataloging records, which were initially sent to Washington on diskettes, and later online.

The Nairobi office has, since 1990, published a *Quarterly Index to Periodical Literature, Eastern and Southern Africa*, which provides unrivaled access to this literature. A notable project undertaken by the Rio office was the collection and organization of materials for "Brazil's Popular Groups: a Microfilm Collection of Materials Issued by Socio-political, Religious, Labor and Minority Grass-roots Organizations, 1966–1986," available from the Library's Photoduplication Service. Annual supplements have been subsequently issued.

Historically, there has been an increase in the field offices' geographical scope (countries covered). The Nairobi office grew from 14 countries to 23 in 1978–1990, and has since expanded coverage, on a trial basis, to four countries in West Africa. The Rio office now addresses the acquisitions of publications

The Library's office in Jakarta, Indonesia, opened in 1963. Here books are loaded on a betjak for delivery to the bindery.
LC/Prints and Photographs Division. LC-USP6-5168A.

from the three Guineas; the Islamabad office now obtains exchange publications from the five Central Asian countries of the Commonwealth of Independent States.

The technological revolution wrought by improved telecommunications and desktop computers has had a profound effect on the operations of the field offices, enabling them to undertake far more ambitious tasks in acquisitions, cataloging, participant programs, cost accounting, and reporting. Although this changeover has been gradual, the results have been dramatic. All of the offices now have very informative Web sites.

In the 1960s and through much of the 1970s, the typewriter ruled, and communications went by air-mail. Telephone calls were rare and costly. The telex machine changed things, as later did desktop computers and their new word processing and accounting software, the fax machine, and especially, email. The offices are now much closer to Washington—only minutes or a few hours away—than they were in the first years of the program, when a routine query might get an answer in a month, or longer. True, time zone differences remain, as do uncertain power supplies and telephone services in the countries where the offices operate, but the norm now is for prompt and frequent communication, with interruptions exceptional. The result, in operational terms, is that management in Washington is now much more involved in the daily conduct of business, than was the case in the early years of the program.

The threat of terrorist attacks on official U.S. installations abroad has been a significant factor for the Library's overseas offices since the attack on the American Embassy in Nairobi on August 7, 1998. Although the office, being located away from the Embassy, was not directly affected, there were many secondary consequences for the Nairobi office and indeed for the entire program, as U.S. embassies worldwide strove to increase their security preparedness and readiness. A number of measures affecting the offices were taken, ranging from training of local staff to strengthening gates, and installing improved alarm systems and surveillance cameras. Another unfortunate consequence of these global threats has been the disruptive evacuation from threatened posts of field directors and their families, typically for long periods. This has placed an added burden on local office staff, to which they have responded well.

The Department of State's program to build numerous new embassies worldwide and to assess agencies for their capital costs presented a budgetary dilemma to the Library, which is still pending. (JCA)

PHOTODUPLICATION SERVICE

Photographer Jim Higgins prepares to photograph a rare book in the Photoduplication Service's Photographic Section.
LC/Photoduplication Service.

Before the turn of the twentieth century, Library of Congress materials could be used only in Washington, D.C. Librarian Herbert Putnam initiated interlibrary loan services in 1901, but during his administration there was no appropriation for reproduction services, and statutory provisions barred the use of receipts to finance such services.

In 1938, a $35,000 gift from the Rockefeller Foundation enabled the Library to purchase equipment and establish a revolving fund to finance the reproduction of items from the collections. All salary, supply, and equipment costs were to be paid from income. The Photoduplication Service, which began operating on March 1, 1938, moved to the subbasement of the Adams Building in June 1939. There, it was equipped with state-of-the-art machines, three technicians began producing photostats, microfilm, photographic negatives, contact prints, enlargement prints, and lantern slides. Since there were no funds for a full-time director, Union Catalog Division chief George A. Schwegmann Jr. supervised the Service in addition to his other duties.

The Photoduplication Service became part of the Reference Department when Archibald MacLeish reorganized the Library in 1940, but it was transferred in 1944 to the Department of Administrative Services. Almost from the outset, photoduplication was recognized as one of the Library's most important services. As the number of orders climbed from 932 in 1938 to 8,391 by 1945 and the staff grew to 36, Librarian Luther Evans obtained an appropriation for administrative funds and named Donald C. Holmes as chief.

The Service received most orders by mail in its business office, originally located in the Jefferson Building basement, but moved in 1947 to the Adams Building. The research staff provided complete bibliographical information, checked copyright restrictions, and prepared estimates. Searchers located the material, and technicians copied and mailed it. When an order was for an entire book or a set, the Service retained the archival negative. The preservation of master negatives, which are not made available to readers, allows not only duplication for sale but also the replacement of lost or damaged microfilm.

In addition to handling readers' requests and taking over office duplication from the Chief Clerk's office, the Service began a program to microfilm the Library's deteriorating nineteenth-century newspapers. Also, in cooperation with the University of North Carolina, between 1941 and 1950 the staff filmed a collection of early state records. A Publication Board Reports Unit was established July 1, 1948 as the custodian of the reports of special post-war missions to occupied countries, and until 1961 that unit acquired and reproduced declassified federal scientific and technical reports. Before 1968, the unit also had custody of the Auxiliary Publications Program of the American Documentation Institute (later the American Society for Information Science). This unpublished research documentation supporting articles printed in the Institute's journal was duplicated for users upon request.

By 1950, the Photoduplication Service staff included more than 60 employees, and its output had grown to nearly 13 million items annually, with receipts of around $400,000. Under a program of continuous modernization, machines were replaced every few years, keeping the Service technology abreast of the latest developments in the field. The laboratory cooperated with commercial firms by testing new processes and equipment, and as the result of discussions with the State Department, took over the duplication laboratory of the Benjamin Franklin Library in Mexico City between 1949 and 1951. The facility was used to film Mexican governmental and legal records and other archival material. Through other post-war diplomatic, military, and Library initiatives, microfilming equipment was sent to other countries to continue the Library's long-standing program of foreign manuscript copying. Increasingly, the Service filmed collections of research material that were not available from commercial vendors but much needed—not only for the Library's collections, but also those of other research libraries. With subscribing libraries sharing the costs, foreign newspapers and government documents, in particular, have been filmed continuously as well as other series such as the Voice of America scripts and the Daily Reports of the Foreign Broadcast Information Service.

The Photoduplication Service has been an active partner in the Library's preservation microfilming activities. To the extent possible, the Service has microfilmed important items in the collections, including books that were deteriorating due to poor paper quality and other library materials in poor physical condition. As the holdings of archival quality microfilm increased, in 1955 all negative microfilm was moved to the Photoduplication Service archive to establish a Permanent Record Microfilm Collection. The Service also established a facility to test its own

Shirley Ball cuts positive film strips for microfilm reels. LC/Photoduplication Service.

microfilm and film acquired from commercial vendors to ensure that the quality met accepted standards. Eventually the *Specifications for Library of Congress Microfilming* appeared in 1964, which described the standard of quality that the Library required and outlined the Photoduplication Service's procedures. After this initial publication, more specialized instructions regarding the filming of particular types of materials—books, pamphlets, newspapers, and manuscripts—were subsequently issued. At the request of

Adam Rosenberg irons newspapers so they can be photographed perfectly flat. LC/Photoduplication Service.

the Association of Research Libraries, the Library accepted responsibility in 1965 for compiling and issuing the *National Register of Microform Masters* to record the locations of high-quality master microforms in the Library of Congress and other repositories.

Xerography entered the Library in January 1958 with the arrival of the Haliod Xerox Copyflo No. 1, and electrostatic prints thereafter took the place of facsimile and enlargement printing equipment for most orders. The introduction of xerography made it possible to photograph catalog cards for duplication on a Xerox printer, producing cards of acceptable strength and quality for the card catalog

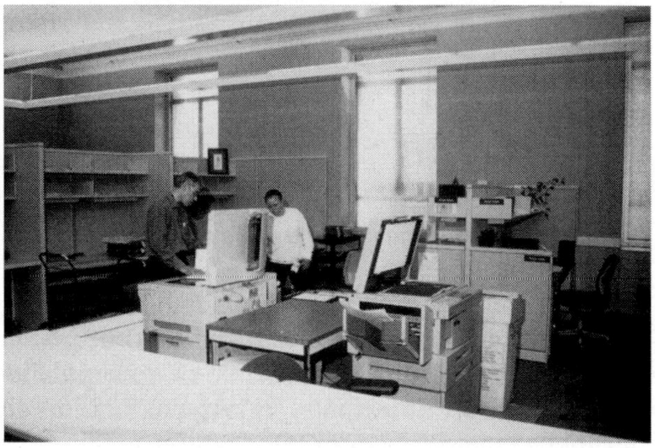

Bonnie Coles and Art Hodges copy books for Photoduplication Service customers. LC/Photoduplication Service.

and for sale by the Card Division. Major microfilming projects continued to appear during the 1950s; for example, Public Law 85-147 passed in August 1957 directed the microfilming of the Library's collections of papers of the presidents of the United States. By the mid-1960s, the Service had begun filming all congressional bills and resolutions and cooperated with the Library's Public Law 480 program to establish work stations abroad so that official gazettes, newspapers, and other materials acquired through that program could be filmed as they were issued. Libraries that lacked portions of the *United States Statutes at Large*, volumes 1 through 76-A (1962) were able to obtain them through another microfilming project, while a $30,000 grant from the Carnegie Corporation financed completing the files of 150 mainland Chinese periodicals and microfilming them.

Increased appropriations supported these projects and allowed the Service to expand the microfilming of deteriorating books and long runs of serials. Many of the Library's most important and valuable manuscripts, rare books, music, and maps were filmed to save handling the originals. With significant increases in its activities, the Service required more space, which became available in 1964. A temperature- and humidity-controlled vault was constructed for the master negative microfilm collection, which had grown to nearly 55,000 reels, and all microfilming was consolidated in the Adams Building's southeast sub-basement. By the end of the decade, the staff was filming over 1,000 newspapers, periodicals, and government publications annually as well as many back files of serials.

The introduction of the coin-operated copiers that soon became familiar to library users also occurred in the 1960s. In July 1963, a "Quick Copy" machine appeared at the Service's customer counter, followed by self-service installations in the six reading rooms in 1972. Self-service copying increased dramatically over the next several years; and as copiers improved, the Service upgraded the machines, added more, installed bill changers (and later the copy card system) and obtained microform reader-printers to assist patrons who needed to copy from those media. Servicing the variety of copying machines and associated devices remains a large part of the daily work of the staff.

Large projects to preserve both the complete records of copyright applications and all printed cards for the years 1898–1939 began in 1969, and a revised version of the microfilming specifications titled *Specifications for the Microfilming of Newspapers in the Library of Congress* appeared in 1972, with a companion volume, *Specifications for the Microfilming of Books and Pamphlets in the Library of Congress,* published the following year. Specialized Library card files were filmed for the G.K. Hall Company, a publisher of book catalogs, which subsequently issued them under its imprint—for example, *Catalog of Broadsides in the Rare Book Division*; *Africa South of the Sahara: Index to Periodical Literature*; and the Geography and Map Division's *Bibliography of Cartography*. The 17-year-old project of microfilming the presidential papers held by the Library was completed in 1975, while the staff continued to film brittle books and serials and Latin American and Southern Asian gazettes.

© The Cartoon Bank. Alan Dunn, 1966.

A full-scale renovation of the laboratories during the early 1970s included installation of a linear diffusion air distribution system, improved lighting, acoustical ceilings, and enclosed work areas for camera operators. In 1971, when sales passed the $2 million mark for the first time, the staff numbered 163, of which about half were engaged in microfilming. Deck 1 South in the Adams Building became available to the Service, allowing the expansion of the Reference, Special Services, Microphotographic and Photographic operations. A Technical Services Section was established in 1978 to handle equipment maintenance and supplies as the Library's copying needs grew.

With the storage vault overcrowded by the early 1980s, the Library leased underground space in Boyers, Pennsylvania to provide temperature- and humidity-controlled space for part of the collection of over 270,000 master negatives. In 1991, as part of a general Library reorganization and following a full review of its operations, administration, accounting procedures and organization, the Photoduplication Service was transferred from Library Management Services to the Constituent Services directorate, and in 1995 it became part of the Preservation Office within the new Library Services directorate. Its functions remained the same—to provide copies of material in the collections to scholars, the public, the media, other libraries, institutions and organizations; and to preserve collection material by converting it to

Erica Kelly assists a customer with a purchase at the Photoduplication Service desk in the Adams Building.
LC/Photoduplication Service.

other formats such as microfilm. Overseas microfilming projects continued, assisted by the Library's overseas centers and the Department of Defense, which late in the decade assisted with initiating projects with research and government institutions in Russia, Lithuania, Poland, and Rumania, bringing important materials from these areas to American scholars. Contractors were increasingly used for special microfilming projects by the late 1990s, as well as for preservation microfilming, and a vendor handled a new "Film to Paper" process to scan microfilm to create an electronic document that would then produce paper from diskette or CD-ROM. By 2001, the Service was filming only items that had to be filmed on site. Because security and preservation-related concerns had by that time led to restrictions on public photocopying in the Rare Book and Special Collections Division and on the use of photographic equipment in most of the Library's new reading rooms, readers who needed copies of such materials were referred to the Photoduplication Service, as were readers who wanted scan-on-demand and digital print-on-demand services for items on the American Memory Web site or from the Prints and Photographs online catalog.

Moved from the Preservation directorate to the National Services directorate within the Library Services service unit in 2002, the Photoduplication Service includes customer services and marketing, public and administrative photocopying, preservation microfilming, commercial microfilming, and photographic services. It remains the largest library copying service worldwide, providing scholars and researchers with black/white and color photocopies, color slides, photographs, exhibit-quality reproductions of prints and photographs, copies of digitized materials, and archival quality microfilm. (JA)

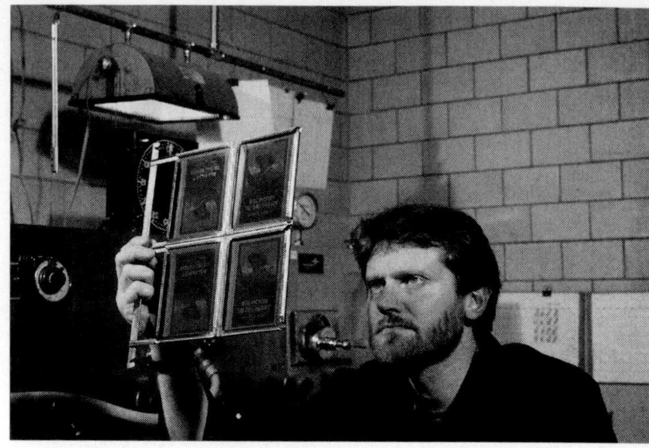

Photographer Yusef El-Amin inspects a frame with four inch by five inch color transparencies for quality control.
LC/Photoduplication Service.

U.S. Library of Congress. *Photoduplication Service.* Washington, D.C.: Library of Congress, 1950.

POETRY PROGRAM AND POETS LAUREATE

Poetry and Literature Center

On February 19, 1872, meeting in the U.S. Capitol not far from the Library of Congress itself, the Joint Congressional Committee on the Library considered a petition from T. N. Hornsby, a citizen of Kentucky, asking Congress to establish a "bureau of poets and poesy," but no action was taken. More than half a century later, in 1936, Archer M. Huntington endowed a Chair of Poetry at the Library of Congress, creating what in the 1940s became the Library's Poetry and Literature Center. Librarian Archibald MacLeish (1939–1944) reshaped the nature of the poetry consultant's job, and also brought to the institution a new emphasis on literary events and personalities. He appointed, for example, French diplomat-poet Alexis Saint-Leger (St.-John Perse) as Consultant in French Literature and Thomas Mann as Consultant in Germanic Literature.

The Library of Congress actively promotes poetry and literature through many programs, including those of the Poetry and Literature Center. In 1949, however, Librarian Luther Evans had to overcome a controversy that threatened the Library's emerging role in poetry and literature. In February, the Fellows of the Library of Congress, a group of 13 poets and writers who served the Library as honorary consultants, awarded the Library's new Bollingen Prize in Poetry to Ezra Pound for his book *The Pisan Cantos*. At the time Pound, who had been indicted for treason, was in an institution for the insane. Because of the ensuing controversy, in August the Joint Committee on the Library unanimously recommended that the Library cancel all arrangements it had made for giving prizes and making awards, and Librarian Evans immediately complied.

Since 1951, the Center has been almost exclusively supported by a gift from the late Gertrude Clark Whittall, who wanted to bring the appreciation of good literature to a larger audience. Mrs. Whittall, one of the Library's most generous donors, also provided funds for the decoration and furnishing of the Library's Poetry Room, which is located in the northwest corner of the third floor of the Jefferson Building. She was the guest of honor when it opened on April 23, 1951—the birthday of William Shakespeare. Roy P. Basler of the Library's Reference Department and later chief of the Manuscript Division, managed the Library's literary and poetry programs from 1954 until he retired in 1974. His successor as Manuscript Division Chief, John C. Broderick, managed the programs until he retired in 1988.

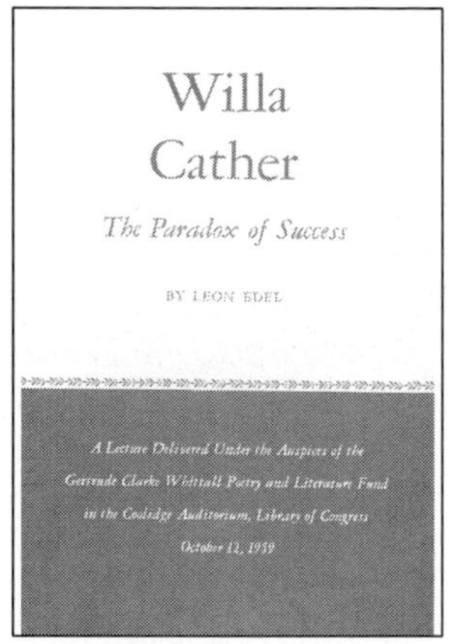

Willa Cather: The Paradox of Success, *by biographer Leon Edel, a lecture and publication supported by the Whittall Poetry and Literature Fund.* LC/Publishing Office.

Today, the Poetry and Literature Center is the home of the Poet Laureate Consultant in Poetry at the Library of Congress. In addition to supporting the Poet Laureate's activities and interests, it sponsors an annual series of public poetry and fiction readings, lectures, symposia, occasional dramatic performances, and other literary events. As a unit of the Library of Congress, the Center functions within the Library's Office of Scholarly Programs.

The Center administers the Rebekah Johnson Bobbitt National Prize for Poetry, a biennial, privately funded $10,000 award for the best book of poetry published by a living U.S. author during the two years preceding the year of the award. The prize is donated by the family of the late Mrs. Bobbitt of Austin, Texas,

Roy P. Basler in the Library's Recording Laboratory in February 1961. A Lincoln scholar, Basler joined the Library's staff in 1952 and served in several capacities. From 1954 to 1974, he developed and directed the Library's literary and poetry programs. LC Archives.

in her memory and established by the Library of Congress. Bobbitt was the late President Lyndon B. Johnson's sister. While a graduate student in Washington, D.C. during the 1930s, Rebekah Johnson met college student O.P. Bobbitt when they worked in the cataloging department of the Library of Congress. They married and returned to Texas.

The first Bobbitt Prize was awarded in 1990 to James Merrill for *The Inner Room*. Subsequent winners have been: Louise Gluck for *Ararat* and Mark Strand for *The Continuous Life* (1992); A.R. Ammons for *Garbage* (1994); Kenneth Koch for *One Train* (1996); Frank Bidart for *Desire* (1998); David Ferry for *Of No Country I Know: New and Selected Poems and Translations* (2000); and Alice Fulton for *Felt* (2002).

The Center also coordinates the Witter Bynner Fellowships for newer poets, a five-year program to recognize emerging poetic talent. An initiative of Poet Laureate Robert Hass, the fellowships are funded by the Witter Bynner Foundation for Poetry, which was incorporated in New Mexico—the home of poet and translator Witter Bynner (1881–1968)—to provide grant support for programs in poetry through nonprofit organizations. The fellows are chosen by the Poet Laureate in cooperation with the Library, and awards may go to two or more poets a year. The fellowships are to be used to support the writing of poetry; they provide both a remarkable opportunity for the participants and a wonderful enrichment of the Library's poetry presentations.

The fellows have only two obligations: to organize a local poetry reading and to participate in a poetry program at the Library of Congress.

The first Witter Bynner Fellows, appointed by Poet Laureate Robert Pinsky in 1998, were Carl Phillips of St. Louis and Carole Muskie of Los Angeles. Subsequent fellows have been: 1999–David Gewanter (Washington, D.C.), Campbell McGrath (Miami, Florida), and Heather McHugh (Seattle, Washington and Swannanoa, North Carolina); 2000–Naomi Shihab Nye (San Antonio, Texas) and Joshua Weiner (Chicago, Illinois); 2001–Tory Dent (New York City) and Nick Flynn (Provincetown, Massachusetts); 2002–George Bilgere (Cleveland, Ohio) and Katia Kapovich (Cambridge, Massachusetts); 2003–Major Jackson (Philadelphia, Pennsylvania) and Rebecca Wee (Rock Island, Illinois) and 2004–Dana Levin (San Antonio, Texas) and Spencer Reese (Palm Beach, Florida).

Begun in 1943, when Allen Tate was Consultant in Poetry to the Library, the Archive of Recorded Poetry and Literature now contains records of more than 2,000 poets reading their own work. It includes recordings of poetry readings and other literary events held at the Library, tapes of poets reading their poems in the Library's Recording Laboratory or elsewhere for the Archive, and recordings received through occasional gifts, exchanges, or purchases.

The Gertrude Clarke Whittall Poetry and Literature Series, begun in 1951, has taken many forms. Hundreds of literary recordings have been added to the Archive of Recorded Poetry and Literature and distributed to the public through National Public Radio. A series of publications have been issued, including lectures presented by the Consultants in Poetry and others and proceedings of conferences on literary topics. The heart of the literary series, however, has been poetry readings, lectures, and dramatic performances open to the public and presented from the stage of the Coolidge Auditorium and, since the 1980s, in the Library's Madison Building. Highlights from the early years of the Whittall series include: the first program, May 1, 1951, which featured Burgess Meredith reading from the poems of Edwin Arlington Robinson; a poetry reading by Carl Sandberg (1954), who also presented a lecture in 1959; Thornton Wilder reading his play *The Alcestiad* (1955); a poetry reading by Robert Frost (1955), the first of several through the years; performances by the *Canadian Players of Man and Superman* (1957) and *As You Like It* (1958); a performance of *Love's Labour's Lost* (1959) by Arnold Moss and the Shakespeare Festival Players; a performance of Lorraine Hansberry's *To Be Young, Gifted, and Black* (1971); a national poetry festival (1962); an international poetry festival (1970); a conference on teaching creative writing (1973); a poetry reading by Gary Snyder (1973); a conference on publishing poetry and fiction (1975); and performances of plays from the Federal Theatre Project (1977). (JYC)

Poetry Consultants and Poets Laureate

In 1936, Archer M. Huntington, son of the railroad magnate Collis P. Huntington, established an endowment that made possible the position of Poetry Consultant in the Library of Congress. The first appointment, of Joseph Auslander, was made in 1937 by Librarian Herbert Putnam. Archibald MacLeish, who in October 1939 succeeded Putnam as Librarian, was a poet of considerable distinction, and he soon moved Auslander to another position and converted the Consultantship into a visiting appointment. As he explained in a letter (April 19, 1943), MacLeish believed the position "should be filled from year to year by distinguished men of letters who will bring to the Library a contact with the living world of creative writing." This decision enabled the Library to include among its 30 Consultants and nine Poets Laureates a range and variety of American poetic voices and styles. The Huntington gift, supplemented by the gifts of Gertrude Clarke Whittall in 1951, embedded a privately funded position and poetry program within the Library. The Whittall gift of monies for programming required, in turn, an office to plan and administer these programs, consolidating the position originally begun by Phyllis Armstrong in 1946 as the first Special Assistant for Poetry.

Librarian Mumford, Randall Jarrell, and former Librarian of Congress Archibald MacLeish in the Poetry Room, December 4, 1956. LC Archives.

The first of MacLeish's appointments was Allen Tate (1943–1944), followed by Robert Penn Warren (1944–1945). Although MacLeish left the Library to become Assistant Secretary of State in 1944, this pattern of appointments continued under Luther Evans. The poets appointed during the 1940s and 1950s include many now recognized as having written enduring American poetry: Louise Bogan, Karl Shapiro, Robert Lowell, Elizabeth Bishop, Conrad Aiken, Randall Jarrell, and Robert Frost. Conrad Aiken, appointed in 1950, served a second year, and since his time 10 other Consultants and four Poets Laureate have, with mutual agreement, renewed their annual appointments to serve a second year in office.

The change in title from Poetry Consultant in the Library of Congress to Poet Laureate Consultant in Poetry to the Library of Congress occurred on December 20, 1985 (Public Law 99-194) as the result of persistent advocacy by Congressman (1964), then Senator (1976) Spark M. Matsunaga of Hawaii. At first little change was noticeable with the change of title. No appropriated money was added to the Laureate's stipend drawn from the Huntington and Whittall endowments, and despite the great distinc-

The Library of Congress Fellows in American Letters, in the Whittall Pavilion, February 29, 1948. Standing from left to right: Conrad Aiken, Cleanth Brooks, and Robert Penn Warren. Seated, from left to right: W.H. Auden, Katherine Garrison Chapin, Librarian of Congress Luther Evans, Leonie Adams, and R.P. Blackmur. LC Archives. LC-USP6-2082-C.

tion of the first two Poets Laureate—Robert Penn Warren 1986–1987 and Richard Wilbur 1987–1988—the expectations for the position did not change significantly.

By design, the annual terms of appointment for both Consultants and Poets Laureate require minimal formal duties; they are specified as one lecture and one reading, advice and assistance in selecting the poets to read at the Library during the year, and answering such inquiries as they come to the office. Over the past decade, however, the energy and quality of the Poets Laureate and the increased attention accorded by the media to the title "Laureate" have changed public expectations—and hence the responsibilities—of the position. The volume of correspondence and telephone calls, requests for personal appearances and readings, television and radio opportunities, and appeals for help with literacy and educational programs across the country have grown exponentially. Technology has made possible video interviews and live national coverage of events by *C-SPAN*, "The NewsHour," and others; the Internet has made possible the combining of text, voice, and image for 24-hour accessibility.

That is not to imply that earlier Consultants were hidden away in the Library. Robert Frost (1958–1959) sought and received national attention, renewed when he took part in John F. Kennedy's inauguration. James Dickey (1966–1968) made several appearances as President Jimmy Carter's favorite poet. In April 1970, an International Poetry Festival brought eight foreign poets and five translators to the

Library. A complementary event, arranged by the National Endowment for the Arts, welcomed the foreign poets by bringing together for a reading a group of American poets: Maxine Kumin, Stanley Kunitz, Denise Levertov, Howard Nemerov, Anne Sexton, Louis Simpson, William Jay Smith, A.B. Spellman, and Mark Strand.

The Consultants in Poetry at a March 6, 1978 reunion at the Library. Standing, left to right: Reed Whittemore, Richard Eberhart, Robert Hayden, William Jay Smith, Stephen Spender, Stanley Kunitz, Karl Shapiro, and Howard Nemerov. Seated, left to right: William Stafford, James Dickey, Josephine Jacobsen, Elizabeth Bishop, and Daniel Hoffman.
LC Archives. USP6-7901-27C.

In addition to short tours to read their own poetry and inviting other poets to read at the Library, the Consultants often took on special projects with the USIA and other agencies. For instance, William Stafford visited cultural centers in Egypt, Iran, Pakistan, India, Nepal, and Bangladesh in 1971. In January 1973, Josephine Jacobsen chaired a two-day Conference on Teaching Creative Writing attended by 500 people. Consultants also paid attention to the local Washington scene. Gwendolyn Brooks (1985–1986) worked with teachers and students in the District of Columbia's school system. Howard Nemerov, who had been a Consultant in 1963–1964, and a Laureate (1988–1990), wrote several poems for public purposes, such as "To The Congress of the United States, Entering Its Third Century," and "Witnessing the Launch of the Shuttle Atlantis."

In March 1987, a Consultants' Reunion (the second since there had been an initial one in 1978) celebrated the 50th anniversary of the Consultantship. It brought together all the living Consultants and the first Poet Laureate, Robert Penn Warren (1986–1987), who had been the third Consultant in 1944–1945. The 50th anniversary was also the occasion for commissioning *Poetry's Catbird Seat* by William McGuire, a history of the Consultantship.

Joseph Brodsky, already a Nobel Prize winner when he became Poet Laureate in 1991, altered the office when he conceived and publicized the idea that inexpensive American poetry should be available in public places—hospitals, motels, shopping malls, airline clubs, hotels—where people unfamiliar with poetry could encounter it. Coming from a society where the power of poetry was acknowledged by the imprisonment and banishment of poets, he knew that a dispirited, restless, lonely, exhausted people could find in poetry an affirmation of life, a realization that even painful emotions are an assertion of vitality, and comfort in the tightly wrought expression of feelings. With initial support from the Book-of-the-Month Club and other donors, his idea has spread, assisted principally by Andrew Carroll, and thousands of inexpensive editions of poetry have been distributed at and in public spaces since 1992.

During her two years as Poet Laureate (1993–1995), Rita Dove sustained a staggering schedule of appearances, readings, talks, and interviews for the sake of poetry—at sites ranging from the White House to elementary school classrooms. She participated in an hour-long interview with Bill Moyers that was widely shown on National Public Television; she worked through the Dodge Foundation with a special group of schoolteachers in New Jersey, and in a similar venture with closed circuit television in Virginia schools. She was featured in a program in Dallas, Texas that combined a celebration for the Texas Center for the Book with evening readings by regional Texas poets. She brought together at the Library poets Michael Harper and Quincy Troupe with a jazz combo that improvised as the poets read. She organized readings by Crow Indian children from Montana and by school children from Washington, D.C. She sponsored and hosted a conference of poets, essayists, musicians, and novelists focused on "The Black Diaspora," particularly the multiple cultural varieties of the Caribbean.

Robert Hass (1995–1997) also pursued the idea of increased popular access to poetry; he believed that poetry should be brought back into newspapers, where it had regularly appeared in the nineteenth century. He developed a weekly Sunday column for *The Washington Post*, selecting a poem and writing brief commentary about it. This proved immensely popular, and was syndicated, first in *The San Francisco Examiner*, and later in other newspapers. Giving considerable attention to the west coast as a Californian, Hass spoke to Rotary Clubs and school teachers, at library celebrations and literacy promotions, on the radio and TV. He gave a frequently repeated hour-long interview to *C-SPAN*. He helped to organize (with the Academy of American Poets in New York) the first National Poetry Month event in Washington early in April 1996 where six distinguished poets from the Baltimore–Charlottesville region read to a packed audience at the Library. Later the same month, Hass led a weeklong series of readings, seminars, and musical events entitled "Watershed" supported by the Orion Society. The "Watershed" conference brought 26 of the country's best nature writers—poets, short story writers, folklorists, ecologists—to the Library for a round of events. During the week, thousands of people participated, and a national contest—"River of Words"—involving poems and posters created by elementary school students, started originally for "Watershed," has now become a project and annual event hosted by the Library's Center for the Book.

During the second year of Hass's tenure as Poet Laureate, the Poetry Office organized in April the 60th anniversary of the creation of the Poetry Consultant's position in 1937: "Poetry's 'Catbird Seat' at Sixty." Of the 16 Consultants and Laureates then living, 11 were able to attend and read. Gwendolyn Brooks and Richard Wilbur had prior conflicting engagements that they could not avoid; Josephine Jacobsen, Karl Shapiro, and Richard Eberhardt were not in sufficiently good health to be able to participate. The others read for 15 minutes each, in a program divided by time for a buffet dinner. Robert Hass, Reed Whittmore, Mark Strand, Mona Van Duyn, and Anthony Hecht read in the afternoon; Rita Dove, William Jay Smith Maxine Kumin, Daniel Hoffman, William Meredith, and Stanley Kunitz read in the evening. The packed audience in the northwest curtain of the Jefferson Building appreciated that the occasion was indeed a tribute to the quality of American poetry in the second half of the twentieth century.

Robert Hass's final lecture at the end of the spring season was a masterful delineation of several of the poetic traditions within the United States. Amplified and combined with his first lecture, they were published as a book by Counterpoint in 1999. *Poets Choice*, a book made from the weekly columns written by Hass in *The Washington Post* was published by Ecco Press in the summer of 1998.

When Robert Pinsky arrived as Poet Laureate in the fall of 1997, he conceived the idea of having a variety of American citizens read their favorite poems aloud in various public fora and recording these readings as a indication of the public state of poetry at the end of the century. Pinsky was deeply interested in the physical art of reading poetry, as demonstrated by his little book *The Sounds of Poetry: A Brief Guide* that appeared from Farrar, Straus, and Giroux in the summer of 1998. He was also, as the poetry editor of the online magazine *Slate,* well aware of the electronic developments that would put audio broadcasting on the Internet. The "Favorite Poem Project" took off, and with collaboration and a variety of sponsors led to readings in New York, Boston, Washington, St. Louis, and Los Angeles, at which a wide variety of citizens—from eminent to unknown, of all ages and great diversity of race and ethnic backgrounds—read their favorite poems to large audiences. The project became integrated into the Library's bicentennial celebrations for the year 2000, with the expectation that the archive of favorite poems would be presented to the Library during Poetry Month (April) of 2000.

Following the unusual extension of a third year as Poet Laureate for Robert Pinsky, related directly to the completion of the filming of selected readings from the "Favorite Poem Project," the Librarian appointed Stanley Kunitz as Poet Laureate. Kunitz had served as the Library's Consultant in Poetry from 1974–1976; his appointment, at age 95 as Poet Laureate, honored his life-long commitment to writing and teaching poetry. Nobody else could match his 70 years of creative work, which continued with a new volume of *Collected Poems*, published by W.W. Norton in 2000. Kunitz gave two readings to overflow audiences in the 500-seat Coolidge Auditorium at the beginning and the end of his term, celebrating the vigor and continuing insights of his ninth decade of dedication to American poetry.

Billy Collins, who served as Poet Laureate for the two years (2001–2003), brought humor, a positive spirit, and great energy to the position. He traveled widely, both within the United States and abroad, carrying his message: "I am convinced that for every nonreader of poetry there is a poem waiting to reconnect them to poetry." Practicing and believing in the accessibility of poetry to everybody, and especially to the young, he designed at the Library POETRY 180, a Web site containing 180 poems—one for each day for the high school year. The idea "was to assemble a generous selection of short, clear poems which any listener could basically "get" on first hearing—poems whose injection of pleasure is immediate." These were poems to be heard, not analyzed. The Web site is refreshed, changing, but one version has now been published as a paperback, *Poetry 180: A Turning Back to Poetry* (Random House, 2003). Thus, the inventiveness of the Poet Laureates continues as they reach out to bring poetry to the public.

In 2003, Librarian of Congress James H. Billington, named Louise Gluck as Poet Laureate. Louise Gluck has written a series of major books, each a complex series of inter-related, sustaining poems, a coherent narrative made up of many poems. Yet each of her books is a separate telling of growing up, of love, of divorce, of loss, of persistence, of the nature of memory. "The poem," she wrote in 1993, "may embody perception so luminous it seems truth; but what keeps it alive is not fixed discovery but the means to discovery; what keeps it alive is intelligence." As Poet Laureate, in February 2004 she brought together five younger poets, each of who had just published his or her first book. They read their poems and spoke to each other and to the public about how they became poets and what sustained them as poets.

In August 2004, Librarian Billington named Ted Kooser to be the 13th Poet Laureate Consultant in Poetry to the Library of Congress. On making the appointment, Billington said "Ted Kooser is a major poetic voice for rural and small town America and the first Poet Laureate chosen from the Great Plains. His verse reaches beyond his native region to touch on universal themes in accessible ways."

The ultimate justification for the Poet Laureate's position is that it calls attention to the rich variety of American poetry, demonstrating through the quality of the Laureate's collective writing that poetry speaks to all conditions. These are characteristic American voices, and it has been fortunate for the Library that during the second half of the twentieth century a number of distinguished American poets have been willing to lend their efforts to giving poetry a public face. (PG)

Basler, Roy P. *The Muse and the Librarian*. N.Y.: Greenwood Press, 1974.

McGuire, William. *Poetry's Catbird Seat: The Consultantship in Poetry in the English Language at the Library of Congress, 1937–1987*. Washington, D.C.: Library of Congress, 1988.

Poets Who Have Held the Library of Congress Poetry Position, 1937–present

-Joseph Auslander, 1937–1941
(Auslander's appointment to the Poetry chair had no fixed term)
-Allen Tate, 1943–1944
-Robert Penn Warren, 1944–1945
-Louise Bogan, 1945–1946
-Karl Shapiro, 1946–1947
-Robert Lowell, 1947–1948
-Leonie Adams, 1948–1949
-Elizabeth Bishop, 1949–1950
-Conrad Aiken, 1950–1952
(First to serve two terms)
-William Carlos Williams
(Appointed in 1952 but did not serve)
-Randall Jarrell, 1956–1958
-Robert Frost, 1958–1959
-Richard Eberhart, 1959–1961
-Louis Untermeyer, 1961–1963
-Howard Nemerov, 1963–1964
-Reed Whittemore, 1964–1965
-Stephen Spender, 1965–1966
-James Dickey, 1966–1968
-William Jay Smith, 1968–1970
-William Stafford, 1970–1971
-Josephine Jacobsen, 1971–1973
-Daniel Hoffman, 1973–1974
-Stanley Kunitz, 1974–1976
-Robert Hayden, 1976–1978
-William Meredith, 1978–1980
-Maxine Kumin, 1980–1982
-Anthony Hecht, 1982–1984
-Robert Fitzgerald, 1984–1985
(Appointed and served in a health-limited capacity, but did not come to the Library)
-Reed Whittemore, 1984–1985
(Interim Consultant in Poetry)
-Gwendolyn Brooks, 1985–1986

Gwendolyn Brooks, Consultant in Poetry, 1985–1986
Photograph: Bill Tague.

-Robert Penn Warren, 1986–1987
(First to be designated Poet Laureate Consultant in Poetry)
-Richard Wilbur, 1987–1988
-Howard Nemerov, 1988–1990
-Mark Strand, 1990–1991
-Joseph Brodsky, 1991–1992
-Mona Van Duyn, 1992–1993
-Rita Dove, 1993–1995

Rita Dove, Poet Laureate Consultant in Poetry, 1993–1995
Photograph: LC/Jim Higgins.

-Robert Hass, 1995–1997
-Robert Pinsky, 1997–2000
(First to serve three consecutive terms)
-Special Library of Congress Bicentennial Consultants, 1999–2000: Rita Dove, Louise Gluck and W.S. Merwin
-Stanley Kunitz, 2000–2001
-Billy Collins, 2001–2003
-Louise Gluck, 2003–2004
-Ted Kooser, 2004–

PRESERVATION AND CONSERVATION

Introduction

In the United States, "preservation" is a term that describes all of the activities that minimize chemical and physical deterioration and damage and that prevent loss of informational content. The primary goal of preservation is to prolong the existence of library and archival material for use, either in their original physical form or in other ways. Preservation has broader implications than "conservation" (which it includes), encompassing binding, reformatting, rehousing, physical support, cleaning, environmental stabilization, and related technical and facility issues that provide for longevity of an institution's collections. "Conservation" describes examination, documentation, and treatment of important artifacts such as manuscripts, rare books, works of art, or museum objects. It includes stabilization, strengthening, restoration, or housing of materials to ensure survival of the objects as long as possible in their original form. Conservation is the individual treatment of single objects of great intrinsic or cultural value. In some other cultures, however, the connotations of the terms are reversed, with derivatives of the word "preservation" being used to describe activities that we characterize in this country as "conservation," and vice versa.

Although the Library has a tradition of concern for minimizing the deterioration of printed matter by improving handling and care procedures, preservation activities have been centralized only relatively recently. In 1967, the Library consolidated preservation activities into an organizational unit responsible for protecting the collections and extending their useful life. A concerted program is now carried out by components of the Preservation Directorate—the Office of the Director for Preservation (which includes the Mass Deacidification and U.S. Newspaper programs) plus five divisions: the Binding and Collections Care Division; the Conservation Division; the Preservation Research and Testing Division; and the Preservation Reformatting Division. The Library's holdings cover more than 530 miles of shelf space and include research materials in approximately 460 languages and almost all media and materials through which knowledge and creativity are preserved and communicated, including leather, vellum, palm leaves, papyrus, paper, nitrate film, CD-ROM, wax cylinders, vinyl discs, and magnetic tape. The vast quantity of the holdings, along with the tremendous variety of formats and materials and the uniqueness of many items, makes tackling the Library of Congress's preservation needs a highly challenging proposition.

Early Years to 1967

One of the first noted concerns about preservation can be found in the 1898 *Annual Report of Librarian of Congress* John Russell Young, who commented on the "questionable quality of the paper upon which so much of the Library material is printed"—the papers that were then being mass produced from wood pulp being far less permanent than the papers made prior to the 1840s, which utilized rags. Decrying the use of this cheap, nondurable paper by publishers, Young warned that many of the works coming into the Library "threaten in a few years to crumble into a waste heap, with no value as record."

Not only has the quality of paper been of continuing concern to the Library, but also the effect of the environment upon the Library's holdings. One of the first steps to minimize deterioration induced by the environment was taken in the early 1900s by Herbert Putnam, Young's successor. The final *Report of the Committee of the Society of Arts on Leather for Bookbinding* had confirmed the view that bookbinding leathers being used then were inferior to those used 50 years earlier; degradation was attributed not only to mechanical causes (changes in methods of manufacture and tanning) but also to the "injurious effect of light and gas fumes which at that time were common in many libraries." Learning of this British study, Putnam sought a system for controlling sunlight in rooms. He directed the Superintendent of the Buildings and Grounds to devise a "system of blinds which will protect the . . . west windows" of the stack areas, which were normally flooded by sunlight. But coping with the oppressively hot and humid summer climate of Washington awaited the development several decades later of suitable air conditioning and dehumidification systems and controls.

Putnam was instrumental in having the Government Printing Office (GPO) establish a branch bindery and print shop within the Library in 1900; the staffs' preservation responsibilities included binding, repair, and other collection maintenance activities. The "binding and repair shop," as it was generally called, remained under the control of GPO from 1900 to 1968. By 1923, it employed 60 persons "rebinding of thousands of library books" for the Library. The 1923 report of the Public Printer stated that the "most important work of the branch bindery is the repair and preservation of the treasured books and manuscripts in the Library. . . . Even the original manuscript of the Declaration of Independence was intrusted to the branch bindery for some preservation touches. . . ."

In the early years, this office did very little that could be called book restoration; but, through the years, it gradually undertook a greater variety of restoration operations: treating manuscripts and other documents by silking or laminating them, cleaning and matting prints and photographs, and performing similar tasks. Armed with knowledge of currently acceptable preservation practices, some of this early work now appears less than desirable, such as silking and cellulose acetate lamination of documents.

In June 1940, Librarian of Congress Archibald MacLeish appointed Alvin W. Kremer as the Library's first Keeper of the Collections. His first assignment was "custodial care" of the collections, however, his office eventually also began supervision of the binding and repair work carried out at the Library by Government Printing Office staff. In this May 16, 1951, photograph, he is removing a valuable Guatemalan manuscript from the closet safe in the office of the Librarian of Congress.
LC/Prints and Photographs Division. LC-USP6-1843C.

The next major advance came in June 1940 when Librarian of Congress Archibald MacLeish created the position of Keeper of the Collections. At first the responsibilities of Alvin W. Kremer, the person appointed to this position, encompassed only "custodial care of the collections of the Reading Rooms." But gradually, over the next 23 years of his tenure, the custodial duties for all of the collections were centralized and brought under the administrative control of the Keeper's Office. His office also undertook administrative responsibility for the binding and repair activities staffed by GPO.

Document restorers were engaged to preserve some of the Library's precious documents, while a new crew of workers was instructed in maintenance procedures such as cleaning books and stack areas. Stack inspections were undertaken to evaluate (and subsequently try to remedy) existing and potential fire hazards. Investigations of commercial binding methods were undertaken in cooperation with the GPO in order to upgrade binding specifications. In addition, research programs into methods of document lamination were co-sponsored with other government agencies. The first significant effort at independent research into the preservation of audiovisual materials was carried out in the 1950s when the Library commissioned a study into the preservation of sound recordings. This resulted in the 1959 publication *Preservation and Storage of Sound Recordings*.

Upon Kremer's retirement in 1963, the Keeper's Office was reorganized and renamed the Office of Collections Maintenance and Preservation, with Paul Edlund appointed as principal officer. One of the first problems he encountered was the need to relocate 1.5 million books in the Jefferson Building so that ductwork for a new ventilation system could be installed. Solving this portion of the environmental control problem presented another difficulty—the loss of about 5 percent of the total stack area in this building. Other preservation activities of the Library during the early-to-mid-1960s included pH testing of books, artificial aging tests on motion picture films, and studies of environmental control equipment such as humidifiers and of laboratory devices, including pH meters and ultrasonic cleaners. Binding and much of the restoration activity, however, stayed under the supervision of the GPO.

A 1965 joint conference of the Library of Congress and the Association of Research Libraries focused on the need for a national preservation program. This led the Library to re-examine its preservation activities to determine how well they fulfilled Library requirements and how the Library might assume a leadership role for library preservation throughout the United States and elsewhere. In addition, the Library recognized "the need for greater emphasis on the application of scientific principles and sound administrative methods to an effective preservation program." As a result, plans were formulated to centralize most of the preservation activities into one office, and to establish a research and testing operation and a modern conservation facility under direct Library control.

Preservation Office and Directorate

On May 15, 1967, the position of the Assistant Director for Preservation was established, and the name of the Office of Collections Maintenance and Preservation was changed to the Preservation Office, located within the Administrative Department. This new unit was given the responsibility of comprehensively dealing with the Library's preservation programs. Led by Frazer G. Poole, the Office created a preservation microfilming section, a research and testing laboratory, and a restoration group, and brought

Between 1967 and 1978, Frazer G. Poole spearheaded a new, centralized Library preservation program. He also was instrumental in the interior design of the James Madison Memorial Building.
LC/Prints and Photographs Division. LC-USP6-6912C.

these together with the Binding Office (which came from Processing Services) and the collections maintenance function (which was transferred from the Stack and Reader Division). By a 1968 agreement, the GPO relinquished control of matters fundamental to preservation, such as staffing, development of technical standards, and procedures for treatments and specifications for materials used in the preservation of Library collections; the only exception was that the GPO retained oversight on binding contracts. Poole was succeeded by Norman Shaffer as Assistant Director for Preservation in 1978, when the Preservation Office was transferred to Research Services. The preservation administrator's title became Director for Preservation when Peter Sparks was appointed to that position in the Preservation Office in 1981.

In 1989, the Preservation Office became the Preservation Directorate, under the Associate Librarian for Collections Services. The Directorate consisted of five offices, each having a specific area of preservation responsibility but cooperating closely with each other. In a 1995 Library reorganization, Collections Services was abolished; the Preservation Directorate became one of seven directorates in Library Services, a new service unit that brought together all national library functions.

The Directorate was reorganized the same year, and the preservation offices were redesignated as divisions. The National Preservation Program Office, where preservation informational and reference services as well as coordination of many domestic and international preservation activities had been handled since 1977, was integrated into the Office of the Director; and the Photoduplication Service became an organizational unit of the Preservation Directorate. For the past two decades, the Director for Preservation position has been held, successively, by Peter G. Sparks, 1981–1989; Kenneth E. Harris, 1990–1994; Diane Nester Kresh, 1994–2000; Mark S. Roosa, 2000–2004, and Dianne L. van der Reyden, acting director, 2004–.

The Preservation Directorate Today

The Library's Preservation Directorate is the largest library preservation and conservation facility in the world. It is the most extensive and oldest operation of its kind in the United States, has the largest conservation laboratory, and was the first program to include a materials science research and testing component. The program is administered by the Director for Preservation, who is responsible for planning, coordinating, and directing all activities.

The Directorate coordinates and oversees all activities throughout the Library relating to the preservation and physical protection of Library materials. It works actively with other national and international research institutions and organizations in developing and implementing immediate and long-range library preservation initiatives; plans and coordinates preservation education and information programs for Library staff and patrons that will raise preservation awareness; provides reference and information services as well as emergency response and recovery assistance to other libraries, outside agencies, institutions, and individuals on matters involving preservation, conservation, and physical custody and care of library materials, including materials affected by vandalism and theft or damaged by fire, flood, or other catastrophes; and provides technical liaison between the Library and other government agencies and scientific and professional organizations.

The mission of the Preservation Directorate is to assure long-term access to the intellectual content of the Library's collections, either in original or reformatted form. This mission is accomplished directly through the provision of conservation, binding and repair, housing, reformatting, materials science and preservation research and development, and staff and user education; and indirectly through coordinating and overseeing all Library-wide activities relating to the preservation and physical protection of Library materials.

The Library of Congress uses the full range of traditional methods of conservation and binding as well as newer technologies such as the deacidification of paper and the digitization of original materials to preserve its collections and make them more accessible to users. These measures include maintaining materials in the proper environment, being prepared for emergencies such as water leaks, ensuring the proper care and handling of the collections by both staff and researchers, and stabilizing fragile and rare materials by placing them in alkaline buffered or pH-neutral containers to significantly retard deterioration and thus prolong their useful life.

The Preservation Directorate has a strong national and international educational outreach program and provides information about preservation to the Congress, government agencies, other libraries, institutions, and the general public. The office has

A book conservator demonstrating gold-tooling on the spine of a rare book at the Library's 2002 Preservation Awareness Day. LC/Preservation Office.

played a key role in organizing and hosting preservation planning meetings for U.S. institutions as well as preservation science symposia that have been both national and global in scope. The Directorate's Conservation Division administers an active professional internship program through which it provides advanced training in specialized conservation skills to interns who come to the Library from around the world.

Following the 1986 creation of the Preservation and Conservation Core Program (PAC) of the International Federation of Library Associations and Institutions (IFLA), the Directorate served as the organizing and coordinating focal point, managing the organization's preservation activities during the initial five years of PAC's existence. Since 1992, the Library has continued to serve as the PAC Regional Center for the United States and Canada, one of five such centers that serves preservation interests in a particular global geographic area. In both capacities, the Directorate has supported cooperation with the other PAC regions through specific preservation activities involving seminars, conferences, education and training, publications such as *International Preservation News* (the IFLA/PAC newsletter), the creation of various types of preservation standards, and through hosting Robert Vosper IFLA Fellows to produce preservation publications of interest to the library community at large. Along with several other leading U.S. libraries, the Library has also sponsored Mellon Fellows, who have received advanced training in preservation administration through assignments in various divisions of the Preservation Directorate.

The Directorate provides programs for Library staff and patrons that raise preservation awareness and increase the level of knowledge about the Library's preservation policies and practices. For example, a daylong Preservation Awareness Workshop, usually held in the Library each year in conjunction with National Library Week, provides general information services about preservation and conservation to the public.

The staff of the Preservation Directorate at the Library of Congress has made noteworthy contributions to the literature of library, archival, and cultural preservation. In leaflets, annuals, scholarly and scientific articles, proceedings, bulletins, newsletters, books, and slide presentations, authors from A (Albro) to Z (Zimmermann) have taken a close look at the challenges of the preservation, conservation, and materials science professions and have sought to lend practical advice, and share their knowledge and experience. Some of these written accomplishments are reflected in a bibliography that can be obtained from the office of the Director for Preservation. Many relevant publications are available on the Preservation Directorate's Web site.

Preservation Directorate staff have participated actively in the recent development of a Preservation Security Plan that provides a framework for identifying the Library of Congress's minimum standards for preservation controls that are essential for securing the collections for future generations. Incorporating preservation needs into the Library's security plan acknowledges risks posed by a failure to protect collections. Control measures depicted in this framework provide an integrated, comprehensive preservation approach, addressing the needs of Library materials on both the collections and individual item levels.

The Preservation Directorate has five divisions and two special programs that are administered from the Office of the Director.

Binding and Collections Care Division

Established in 1900 as a branch bindery of the Government Printing Office under the Chief Clerk with Arthur Kimball in charge, the binding program was the first unit created by the Library to support preservation activities. Mr. Kimball retired in 1932 and was succeeded by George Morgan as head of the GPO-operated Binding Division.

When the Administrative Department was created in the Library in 1940, the Binding Division became the Binding Records Section of the Supply Office. The Reading Room Binding Unit and approximately 20 other binding units of the Reference Department prepared and transmitted material to the Binding Division. In 1941, David Wahl conducted a survey of all binding activities in the Library. As a result, in 1942 the Binding Office was created, absorbing the Reading Room Binding Unit and the Binding Records Section of the Supply Office. Wahl was named Binding Officer, and the office was transferred to the Reference Department under the direction of the Keeper of the Collections.

To coordinate binding activities more closely with other processing units, the Binding Office was transferred to the Processing Department in 1943. Ruth Kline was designated Binding Officer under the Director of Processing. Concurrently, the binding activities that had been operating more-or-less independently in 20 or more units were transferred at this time to the Binding Office.

From 1950 until 1969, there was a transition away from an onsite (GPO) bindery to the use of contract services provided by commercial library binders. The GPO, however, continued its relationship with the Library in the role of contract management. For a brief time, the Binding Office reported to the Subject Cataloging Division in the Library's Processing Department, then it was incorporated into the new Preservation Office in 1967.

The Binding and Collections Care Division (BCCD) is responsible for the care of the Library's permanent research collections that are in bound formats, performing treatment on a large scale in a cost-effective manner. In fiscal year 1999, the division processed (bound on contract, labeled, repaired, or boxed) about 30,000 items per month. Responsibilities include binding preparation and contract management; book repair; in-house binding, such as pamphlet binding; housing; and shelf preparation. The division supports the care of special collections through the construction of custom-fit protective enclosures, using an automated box-making machine. Rare books that require treatment of their bindings, however, are handled by the Conservation Division.

There are two organizational units within the BCCD: the Library Binding Section and the Collections Care Section. Staff work closely with, in particular, the collections maintenance staff in the custodial divisions who identify retrospective collection materials in need of treatment and the cataloging staff who indicate when items require special attention.

<u>The Library Binding Section</u> is responsible for binding and labeling. Formed as a branch bindery under GPO in 1900, it provided the foundation for the Library's future preservation program. The Library has always required that general collections materials acquired as paperbacks receive library binding as a way to safeguard them. The only exceptions to this policy are multiple copies, items that receive minimal level cataloging, or those that are unsuitable for binding due to their format. This has been particularly important as publishers' use of hot-melt adhesives, cross-grain paper (that is paper with grain running at right angles to the spine), and burst binding has increased, causing many text blocks to fail before cataloging is completed. Further, all original signatures are retained either by sewing through the fold or recasing (providing a new buckram cover for an intact text block). This improves openability and enhances the longevity of the book.

The Library has been closely involved in standards setting for library binding, through the efforts of successive Binding Officers working with the Library Binding Institute (LBI) and the American Library Association (ALA). In 1997, the Library sponsored binding research to support the work of the National Information Standards Organization (NISO)/LBI Standards Committee ZZ to set performance specifications for library binding. This work is included in the American National Standards Institute/NISO Z39.78 Standard for Library Binding.

Currently, the binding program relies upon three binding contracts to handle the nearly 240,000 volumes commercially library-bound annually at a cost of approximately $1.4 million. The focus of the program in recent years has been on the installation of automation equipment and software to speed up the work of the section and improve accuracy of data entry. Until 1994, Library staff used typewriters to process materials for binding. Now it is possible to download author, title, and call number information from the Library's catalog directly to BCCD's binding automation system, LARS (Library Automated Retrieval System). BCCD has expanded use of the LARS system to the Serial and Government Publications Division, the European Division, the Law Library, the Hebraic Section of the African and Middle Eastern Division, and the Geography and Map Division for decentralized binding preparation. It is particularly helpful to decentralize in cases where the custodial division has resident expertise in vernacular languages or format. The Serial and Government Publications Division, which began using LARS in 1996, has built up a LARS database of over 30,000 serial binding records to date.

The Library Binding Section also has responsibility for shelf preparation—the labeling and property stamping of publisher-bound volumes. The labeling program has changed dramatically over the years. First, the Library used labels that were preprinted with classification letters (e.g., "AP"); then a staff member would write the rest of the call number in ink below. These were affixed to the spine with wheat paste. Then for many years the Library used Se-Lin® heat-activated labels, which required ironing to set the adhesive, making it very labor-intensive.

In 1996, BCCD began using a laser-printed, pressure-sensitive label based on specifications developed by the Preservation Research and Testing Division (PR&TD). At the same time, BCCD implemented a new software program that allows author, title, and call number information to be extracted from the Library's catalog and formatted for a spine label. A portion of the labeling activity is now done in the Cataloging Directorate using these new procedures, thereby reducing the time an item takes to reach the shelf. In fiscal year 1998, over 155,000 volumes were labeled in BCCD.

The spine label specification is just one of many collaborative efforts between BCCD and PR&TD to improve the quality of products used in processing materials for the shelf. Others include testing of security devices, bar codes, labels, book plates, and marking inks.

The Collections Care Section provides in-house repair and binding for items in the general and reference collections and produces custom-fitted boxes for general and special collections materials. Repair may include tip-ins, recasing, new covers, page mending, consolidation of text blocks, or spine repair. In-house binding may include pamphlet binding or stiffening. By having these capabilities in-house, BCCD is able to serve the reading rooms that cannot afford to be without materials for the five weeks required for commercial library binding.

Rehousing fragile materials in custom-fitted archival books.
LC/Preservation Office.

Housing provides custom-fitted protective enclosures for materials that require physical support or cannot be bound, repaired, or otherwise physically treated. Examples include protective enclosures for Bernstein scrapbooks in the Music Division, unbound serials in the American Folklife Center, and books with accompanying CDs in the Humanities and Social Sciences Division.

The Collections Care Section was created in 1995 to expand the range of treatment options for preservation of original materials. Previously, there was a Book Repair Unit, created in 1983, but staffed with only one technician. Thus, for many years, there was only one choice for materials from the general or reference collections—the Binding Office could rebind the item in ruby buckram.

Today, instead, the collections care program aims to (1) get materials back in circulation as soon as possible, (2) perform the minimal amount of treatment necessary to stabilize the item, (3) retain components of nineteenth and twentieth century books with potential artifactual value, and (4) provide options such as constructing protective enclosures where binding or reformatting is inappropriate or costly. Staff from the Collections Care Section serve as members of liaison teams to the Library's custodial divisions. They work closely with other preservation staff, especially with the key professional conservators from the Conservation Division, who serve as the primary preservation liaisons with the special collections divisions, to provide the full range of treatment options for the collections.

Conservation Division

The Library of Congress was the first library in the United States to establish a conservation office (originally titled the Restoration Office) staffed by professional book and paper conservators. The Conservation Division is responsible for examination, documentation, treatment, and preventive care of intrinsically valuable manuscripts, prints, drawings, photographs, maps, and rare books that must be retained in their original format. This work requires the skill of book, paper, collection level, and photograph conservators whose special abilities are developed through academic and intern training. In specially equipped laboratories, conservators treat (stabilize and restore) rare and special collections materials, to minimize further deterioration. In addition to treatment, conservators advise custodial divisions on the care of library materials.

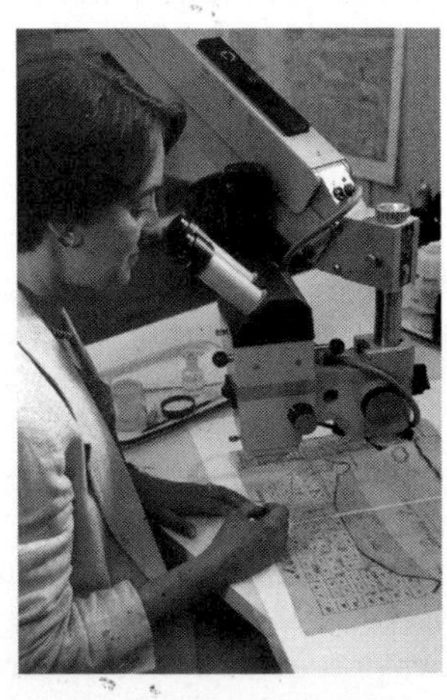

Library of Congress conservator Heather Wanser treats George Washington's 1749 map of Alexandria, Virginia.
Photograph: Roger Foley © 1996.

Traditional restoration activities had been performed since the early 1900s by the original GPO restorer staff (called bindery workers). In the late 1960s, Frazer G. Poole convinced Librarian of Congress L. Quincy Mumford that it was important to professionalize the approach to conservation management and practice. Unable to recruit a qualified U.S. citizen to head the new Restoration Office, he obtained permission to secure a laboratory manager and other experienced conservators from other countries. Poole hired Peter Waters from England on contract in 1969 and worked closely with him for two years to plan the development and staffing of the new office. Waters moved to Washington to accept the full-time position as the Library's Restoration Officer in 1971. On Waters' advice, Poole hired two other British conservators who were also critical to the early development of this program—Donald Etherington, who joined the office in 1970 and served as training specialist for 10 years, and Chris Clarkson, who for five years was head of the Rare Book Conservation Section. Poole hired this team of conservation managers due to the reputations they had earned, in part, through their professional involvement and experiences in disaster recovery operations following the Florence Flood of 1966, as well as their book conservation training experience under Roger Powell and Sydney Cockerell, two well-known English book conservators.

Because of the dearth of qualified artisans and conservation training schools in the United States at that time, Poole decided to attempt to recruit conservators by hiring individuals with a good education and then seek specialized training for them. Margaret Brown, the first conservator, already possessed both education and experience in art restoration. The Library arranged for her to receive specialized training for several months in the paper restoration shop of the Museum of Modern Art in New York. Later, she learned relevant paper testing techniques at the Barrow Research Laboratory in Richmond and studied fiber microscopy at the Institute of Paper Chemistry. Poole also hired Marilyn Weidner, a highly skilled paper conservator, as a consultant to provide advanced conservation training to Ms. Brown and advice on difficult treatment problems. Thus, the Library developed its first conservator largely through apprentice training.

During the 1970s and later, the professional staff of paper and rare book conservators, and eventually "phased conservators," was built up, partly by hiring experienced personnel from other institutions and from the new conservation training schools in the United States, with the result that a full complement of conservators eventually consisted of both apprentice-trained and program-trained (that is with graduate degrees) personnel.

The Conservation Division has provided leadership in the development of the profession of library conservation as we know it today. Many innovative treatments have been developed in its laboratory over the years. The division is known worldwide for its development of new concepts, products, techniques, and procedures for the conservation and preservation of library and archival materials. Working with the Preservation Research and Testing Division, and in coordination with other offices as appropriate, the Conservation Division establishes criteria and standards for supplies and techniques used in the Library's conservation, housing, and storage activities. The division works to ensure that all collection materials are displayed, housed, and stored under appropriate environmental conditions. It oversees the preservation needs of all Library materials that are exhibited by the Library or by borrowing institutions, domestic or international.

Rebacking the cover of a book with new support materials.
LC/Preservation Office.

Since the 1980s, the division has offered internship opportunities to third-year conservation students from the conservation graduate programs in the United States, as well as foreign advanced or mid-career students. These internships, traditionally in book or paper conservation, have now been expanded to include advanced training in photograph conservation and preventive conservation.

The division functions in a manner similar to that of a museum operation where preservation priorities are determined by custodial division managers and subject-matter experts in collaboration with professional staff of the Conservation Division, who prepare treatment proposals and condition reports and, in their capacity as "conservation liaisons," advise the division about conservation options that can be properly carried out within manpower constraints. Conservators advise the divisions on a broad range of collection issues, such as the selection of housing during processing, proper handling guidelines, environmental concerns, and staff training.

In order to better plan the treatment schedule for the various special collections in the Library, a time management system called the "point system" was initiated in the Conservation Office in the 1980s. The Library's custodial divisions are assigned a "budget" of a specified number of points in a given year, one point being equivalent to one hour of conservation work. With the custodial units receiving roughly equivalent numbers of hours in their allotted annual points budgets for conservation treatment, custodial division personnel exercise great care in nominating and selecting important Library materials for which either collection level or single item treatment is requested.

In 1995, the Conservation Office became the Conservation Division and was reorganized from three sections (Rare Book; Paper; and Phased) into two: the Book and Paper Conservation Section and the Preventive Conservation Section.

The Book and Paper Conservation Section is responsible for the examination, documentation, and treatment of rare, intrinsically valuable, bound and unbound items in the Library's collections. These include, but are not limited to, incunabula and other rare books, unbound maps, atlases, globes, manuscripts, prints and drawings, posters, photographs, and related materials.

Treatment options are diverse. By performing thorough examinations and carefully documenting the existing condition of items, and taking into account their future use, conservators can make decisions about appropriate treatments ranging from minor surface cleaning and physical stabilization to interventive, complex restoration activities. The types of treatment are selected to be compatible with the period of the artifact, and optimal quality materials are always used for repair and rehabilitation measures.

The necessity for full treatment varies for bound materials; but book leaves may be washed and cleaned, and rare book bindings may be repaired or replaced with new materials sympathetic to the original period and style of binding. Flat or unbound paper-based materials may be chemically stabilized and mended; poor quality adhesives and coatings or previous repairs and treatments may be removed; individual leaves may be washed or cleaned; and media may be consolidated to avoid future loss.

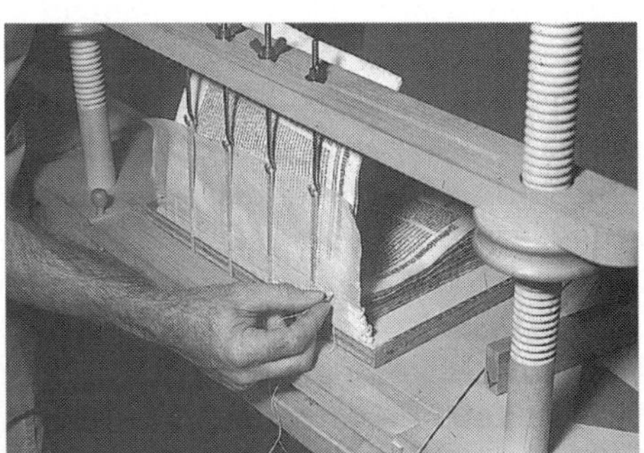

Sewing an early binding using a sewing frame. LC/Preservation Office.

Materials may also be conserved by such means as leafcasting, which repairs documents by filling in voids and missing margins with pulp that is compatible with the original; and they may be physically supported in boxes, folders, mats, or by enclosure (encapsulation) in clear, chemically inert polyester film. Section staff provide advisory and consulting services to the Library's curatorial and custodial divisions. Conservators are also responsible for serving as liaisons to custodial and curatorial divisions in the selection of materials for treatment each fiscal year.

The Preventive Conservation Section develops and applies conservation strategies, which is treatment and housing solutions, for collections or portions of collections in the Library. Section staff carry out individual and batch treatments of rare and special collections materials, as identified in consultation with the curatorial divisions and in collaboration with other units of the Preservation Directorate. Staff are also responsible for coordinating the selection of materials to receive conservation treatment for the coming fiscal year. An important theme in the work of the Section is the prevention of damage and methods that will enhance preservation through the selection of materials for housing that provide appropriate physical support and chemical stability, correct handling in use and storage, optimal environment, early conservation treatment, and preparedness to minimize the impact of disasters.

The Section has primary responsibility for developing and maintaining the preservation components in the Library's overall disaster plan. This role is a natural outgrowth of the work performed over the years by the Library's conservation staff in support of recovery from fire and water disasters at other cultural institutions throughout the world. These efforts stemmed largely from experiences following the noted Florence Flood in the 1960s and the Library's sustained assistance to the Library of the Russian Academy of Sciences in St. Petersburg after the tragic fire that occurred there in 1988.

"Phased conservation" was a concept first introduced by Conservation Officer Peter Waters in the mid-1970s. The idea behind "phased" work was a focused conservation strategy whereby collections or single items were treated in stages, that is, phases, over a period of time according to a planned and logical sequence of priorities and procedures. The main emphasis was on large treatment and rehousing projects that could achieve economies of scale. In the present program, this concept has evolved into collection level treatment, which includes the mitigation of deterioration and damage to collections materials through the formulation and implementation of policies and procedures for the following: appropriate environmental conditions; handling and maintenance procedures for storage, exhibition, packing, transportation, and use; and emergency preparedness and response.

The Preventive Conservation Section utilizes many creative collection stabilization techniques based on the type of use the collection receives or will receive, its inherent value, and its physical vulnerability. Its activities include providing protective care and preventive activities such as environmental control, improved housekeeping, cleaning, single item deacidification and mending, encapsulation, boxing, and construction of custom-designed enclosures. This unit manages the Library's program to monitor and optimize environmental conditions for the full range of collections at various Library sites. Section staff work with curatorial units and with the Library's facilities staff as well as with the office of the Architect of the Capitol to monitor and effect changes as needed.

Specifications based on American Society for Testing of Materials and International Standards Organization standards are developed and used by staff to facilitate the purchase of materials to house collections. Conservation Division liaisons work with curators and specialists in Library custodial divisions to determine the most appropriate housing solutions. Procurement of these materials is then carried out by the Conservation Division to insure that all housing supplies meet rigid Library of Congress specifications.

In addition, this Section responds as needed to emergency incidents in the Library that require conservation intervention, and assists in training other staff in disaster response techniques, according to procedures developed in conjunction with the Security Office and Library policy. Emergency supplies are stocked and strategically located in Library stack areas and in other key locations in all three buildings on Capitol Hill as well as in off-site locations.

Preservation Research and Testing Division

In 1965, Librarian L. Quincy Mumford committed the Library to establishing a preservation program "which would specifically include a research laboratory." The Preservation Research and Testing Office, a unique and distinctive feature of the newly created Preservation Office, was established in 1971 to begin a rigorous in-house research effort designed to develop lasting solutions to problems that had long confronted librarians and archivists.

Its essential mission is to provide scientific and technical support for the Library's preservation program and to seek solutions to complex technical problems for the benefit of the entire library and archival community. As a result, the Library of Congress is the only research library in the country that has an in-house scientific research laboratory dedicated to the support of its preservation activities. Today's Preservation Research and Testing Division (PR&TD) evaluates existing and future preservation strategies. Staffed with a dozen research scientists and other technical experts, the PR&TD facility consists of a spacious main laboratory and three smaller, specialized laboratories equipped with state-of-the-art scientific equipment.

The division's scientists initiate and conduct fundamental research, testing, and technology assessment to establish preservation practices and specifications for a variety of materials, including paper as well as non-paper-based media such as motion picture film, still photographic materials, magnetic tape, wax cylinders, cellulose acetate discs, and CD-ROMs. The PR&TD staff also participates extensively in standards setting bodies to safeguard the long-term preservation interests of the Library of Congress and the library community. The unit's work has a significant impact on the general practice of preservation in libraries and archives throughout the world.

While the Binding and Collections Care Division helps preserve library materials by what is essentially a preventive maintenance operation and the Preservation Reformatting Division transforms information from a deteriorated material to a more stable medium, the Preservation Research and Testing Division focuses on developing and evaluating new materials and methods that could extend the lifetime of our intellectual heritage. Thus, the Preservation Research and Testing Division undertakes scientific and technical research to advance and support Library preservation. For example, studies in deacidification techniques aim at preserving materials in their original format. Research also is directed toward gaining a better understanding of deterioration mechanisms. This knowledge, in turn, may enable more appropriate treatments for degraded items to be formulated.

Topics for study include paper permanence; longevity of digital, photographic, magnetic, CD-ROM, and other contemporary media; adhesives behavior; storage conditions; binding methods; deacidification; preservation of digital collections over time; and other problems affecting the preservation of the diverse materials in the Library's collections. The division also tests supplies and materials to ensure that items purchased for use in conservation treatment, binding, housing, and storage of Library materials meet appropriate standards of quality.

The Preservation Research and Testing Division works closely with the Conservation Division in establishing criteria and specifications for supplies and techniques used in the Library's conservation, housing, and storage activities, in coordination with other offices as appropriate. The two divisions collaborated, for example, in extending earlier research on the effects of cellulose acetate lamination (created in the 1930s by scientists at the National Bureau of Standards as a method of reinforcing brittle paper) and subsequent development and adoption at the Library of an alternative, now widely accepted method of providing physical support to fragile paper artifacts—that is, polyester encapsulation. The scientific division also works with the Conservation Division, with other offices of the Library, and with the Architect of the Capitol's office to assure that all collection materials are displayed, housed, and stored under appropriate environmental conditions.

PR&TD communicates the results of its research to other research facilities that conduct similar or related investigations (both in government and private agencies) and to the preservation community of libraries, archives, and museums. Some recent research and development initiatives are an accelerated aging test for paper, preservation of digital media, and the security labeling of CDs. Additional recent research developments include completing risk assessment studies on motion picture film and magnetic tape; developing of new chromatographic techniques for quantitative measurement of aging of paper that are much more sensitive than other available techniques; demonstrating that the rate of aging of acidic paper accelerates with time, which shows the urgency of preservation actions such as deacidification and reformatting; and refining quantitative methods to optimize the storage environments for preservation of library collections.

Mass Deacidification Program

An important outgrowth of the Library's materials science activities is its Mass Deacidification Program to save books and other paper-based materials on a large scale and extend their useful life. The primary reason modern books and other paper artifacts often deteriorate significantly within 50 to 100 years is that they are acidic—a condition brought about largely by the introduction in the mid-nineteenth century of alum-rosin compounds that were used as sizing agents in the paper.

Since the late nineteenth century, paper deterioration has been further hastened by the introduction of mechanically produced ground wood pulp in

An example of a treatment option for book deacidification.
LC/Preservation Office.

the papermaking process. These products, frequently not chemically purified, resulted in weaker paper and in additional formation of acids and peroxides that promoted the aging process. Other factors contributing to the deterioration of paper include atmospheric pollutants, high temperature and humidity levels, light exposure, insects and rodents that feed on paper and book bindings, and microorganisms such as mold and bacteria.

Acidity in paper undermines the use and long-term preservation of library collections and archival materials. Chemists now know that acid deterioration can be minimized by deacidification and simultaneous impregnation with alkaline buffering agents. Millions of deteriorating books and documents in libraries and archives throughout the world attest to this problem. Mass deacidification retards embrittlement of paper and is, therefore, a preservation treatment appropriate for books that are acidic and at risk of irreversible deterioration if no action is taken.

The Library has provided leadership over several decades in research and development efforts that have encouraged the success of mass deacidification technologies that are being used in several countries to ensure the long-term useful life of paper-based materials. A Mass Deacidification Action Plan approved by Congress is making it possible for the Library to mass deacidify significant quantities of acidic books each year from the general and special collections.

Deacidification has been an important area of research and development. Several approaches involving aqueous and non-aqueous systems were developed for single-sheet deacidification. Vapor phase (gaseous) mass deacidification using the diethyl zinc (DEZ) process received major research and engineering emphasis after the Library's scientists patented this technology in the mid-1970s. By 1978, the first series of tests were carried out on 1,600 disposable volumes, using a vacuum chamber at General Electric's Valley Forge, Pennsylvania facility.

Beginning in 1981, tests of the DEZ process were conducted in a vacuum chamber at NASA's Goddard Space Flight Center in Greenbelt, Maryland with the assistance of Northrup Services, Inc., a NASA contractor.

A testing program in late 1985 and early 1986 that resulted in two DEZ-related fires caused a temporary setback for development of this technology. At a pilot test facility subsequently built near Houston and operated for the Library by Texas Alkyls and its successor Akzo Chemicals, Inc., the Library conducted 31 small-scale DEZ tests to perfect the process. After completion of 12 more experimental DEZ runs in 1993 and 1994, which resulted in resolving two remaining problems with the DEZ process, Akzo chemicals announced that it was getting out of deacidification for business reasons and subsequently closed down the Texas DEZ plant. Fortunately, a technical evaluation committee reported almost simultaneously to the Library, encouraging the institution to work with Preservation Technologies, Inc., to enhance and hopefully utilize its promising Bookkeeper mass deacidification technology.

The Bookkeeper method deacidifies paper when it is immersed in a dispersion of extremely fine magnesium oxide suspended in a fluid. The process takes two hours from the time books are placed in the treatment cylinders until the volumes are ready to be packed for return to their home library. All steps in the process, from selection to reshelving, are monitored to ensure that the intended results are achieved. The process meets the Library's basic preservation requirements by (1) raising the pH level of treated paper to the acceptable range of 6.8 pH to 10.4 pH, (2) achieving a minimum alkaline reserve of 1.5 percent, and (3) extending the useful life of acidic paper (measured by fold endurance after accelerated aging) by at least 300 percent.

Early in 1995, Congress approved a two-year action plan in which the Library proposed using this new book deacidification technology. As a result, the Library awarded a limited production contract in 1995 to utilize the Bookkeeper deacidification process to neutralize the acid in books. The primary focus of this initiative was to ensure uniform, effective deacidification treatment of processed books and to enhance work flow, including book handling, storage, packing, and transportation procedures.

Through a competitive process, the Library in 1997 negotiated a second contract for mass deacidification. The contract was again awarded to Preservation Technologies, Limited Partnership (PTLP) of Pennsylvania, which is providing book preservation services to the Library with their Bookkeeper mass deacidification process for four more years. By the end of fiscal year 2003, the Library had deacidified more than 775,000 books from its general and law collections.

Deacidification treatment is reserved for books that are acidic and at risk of loss if no action is taken. The Library is focusing primarily on selection of "Americana" for early treatment under the mass deacidification program, emphasizing the selection of endangered volumes from collections that are central to the Library's mission.

In the summer of 2000, Congress approved a Library proposal to establish mass deacidification as a permanent preservation program activity and to commence work on a one-generation deacidification program. The plan calls for scaling up deacidification over the next few years in order to save and greatly extend the longevity of a large volume of unbound paper-based materials as well as all retrospective (existing) and prospective (to be acquired) books that will benefit from mass deacidification treatment.

Preservation Reformatting Division

The Preservation Reformatting Division (PRD) preserves materials that are on unstable media, such as groundwood paper, so their content will be accessible and usable. In 1967, the Council on Library Resources funded a "Brittle Books Project" at the Library through the Association of Research Libraries. Although the Library began microfilming materials in the late 1930s, the Preservation Microfilming Office was not established until 1968, as a result of the pilot Brittle Books Project. The unit establishes internal microfilming requirements for the Library. Brittle book replacement is still part of the Library's preservation program.

This unit ensures adherence to national standards and recognized guidelines for reformatting and conversion, such as those promulgated by the Association for Information and Image Management International and the Research Libraries Group. Along with these technical and bibliographic standards, the reformatting program collaborates with other preservation staff in developing a coordinated array of preservation services to assist custodians of the collections in making informed decisions for preserving individual items and discrete collections.

The Preservation Reformatting Division staff assist custodians and curators of paper-based collections in making condition assessments of library materials and in determining the most appropriate reformatting method—microfilming, preservation photocopying, or digitizing. The staff conduct searches to identify replacement copies in paper or other formats of items that must be replaced because they are on fragile media that will not remain usable. They evaluate the quality of replacements in microform available from other sources. The division compiles and delivers this information to collection custodians and advises them on options to preserve the content of materials through replacement or provision of surrogates.

If custodial and preservation staff decide to reformat fragile items, staff or contractors determine the completeness of the originals based on an inventory and a page-by-page collation. The staff orders missing materials through interlibrary loan or otherwise arranges to borrow it from other institutions. Once a complete job is assembled for reformatting, the staff or contractors create finding aids and other internal information to facilitate use of the works that are being reproduced. Librarians provide catalogers with the information about a title or collection that is ready for the cameras so that the Library will have an accurate bibliographic record of the newly created work.

Library staff inspect newly created microfilm to assure that it is readable, represents as complete and as accurate a version of the original as possible, and meets technical preservation standards. The division tightened these standards to generate microfilm that can be digitally scanned at high quality in the future to facilitate improved access.

For 25 years, the preservation reformatting staff could provide only one option—microfilming – to replace fragile materials without great intrinsic value as artifacts (such as telephone directories) or to create surrogates for valuable original items that would be damaged by use (such as George Washington's papers). Preservation microfilming matured during this period, not only through the development of stringent preservation microfilming standards, but also with improvements in equipment. Library clients became more accepting, if reluctantly, of microfilm as a useful medium that facilitated long-term access and preservation, in part because of improvements in reader-printers and due to interlibrary loan programs.

In 1992, the Library began creating paper-to-paper replacements by contracting for preservation photocopies of items such as reference works that were not suited for microfilming. Illustrations with gray-scale images are captured digitally and printed out on preservation quality paper. All volumes are bound according to Library Binding Institute standards.

In the late 1990s, the Preservation Reformatting Division began to establish a program using digitization as a method of reformatting. The preservation community responded to end-user enthusiasm for digital images due to accessibility of images when distributed on the World Wide Web, rapid improvements in scanning and delivery equipment, and the ability to capture and deliver materials in color. Though the Library has not fully accepted any existing digital format as a preservation medium, it acknowledges the value of providing highly accessible digital surrogates for fragile materials. The initial work selected for digitization in this program was the first full run of a serial to be distributed on the World Wide Web—*Garden & Forest*, a horticultural newsletter, which was published weekly from February 29, 1888 through December 29, 1897. The project includes establishment of guidelines for selection, preparation, indexing, search and retrieval, as well as presentation and archiving of digital images for preservation and access purposes.

U.S. Newspaper Program

The United States Newspaper Program (USNP), which is managed by the Library's Preservation Directorate, marked its 20th anniversary in fiscal year 2003. During the past 20 years, access to U.S. newspapers has been greatly enhanced through the program's effort to catalog more than 167,000 titles and to preserve on microfilm more than 65 million newspaper pages. The program is funded by the National Endowment for the Humanities (NEH). It is jointly coordinated by NEH and the Library, with the goal of locating, inventorying, cataloging, and selectively preserving all newspapers published in the United States and its territories since colonial times. Project teams are established in each state to survey collections in libraries, archives, historical societies, and publishers' offices; inventory and catalog those collections; and preserve on microfilm important newspaper collections discovered as a result of project activity. Initiated in 1983, it is expected that this comprehensive newspaper preservation work will be completed by 2007.

State-of-the-Art Storage and Special Media Conservation Activities

Many preservation activities concerning special media (largely non-paper-based materials) within the Library's collections are funded through the preservation budget that is managed by the Director for Preservation. Technical support as required is provided by the staff of the Preservation Directorate, although day-to-day program activities concerning these media are managed by other Library organizational units such as the Geography and Map Division; the Motion Picture, Broadcasting and Recorded Sound Division; and the Prints and Photographs Division.

National Audio-Visual Conservation Center at Culpeper, Virginia

In 1998, the David and Lucile Packard Foundation gave the Library a grant of $10 million to begin development of a state-of-the-art National

Audio-Visual Conservation Center on a site near Culpeper, Virginia. The grant included funds for the Foundation to acquire, on behalf of the Library and the Architect of the Capitol, a 140,078-square-foot building on a 41-acre tract of land.

The Culpeper acquisition, authorized by Congress, will enable the Library to develop a central storage and conservation facility that will accommodate all of the Library's audio-visual collections. It will feature specialized, newly designed preservation laboratories for all of its audio-visual media. The Library of Congress holds the world's largest collection of films, as well as massive collections of video and audio recordings. In many cases, audio-video materials in the Library's collections are the only extant copies. With the new center, the Library will continue its important work as the major conservator of the nation's critical, world-renowned film, television, and audio heritage.

High Density Collections Storage Facility at Fort Meade, Maryland

On a 100-acre site on the grounds of Ft. George G. Meade, Anne Arundel County, Maryland, located approximately 30 miles north of Capitol Hill, construction is under way for the first of a series of new storage modules for the Library of Congress to be erected on that site. These modules will provide a cool, safe environment for both paper-based and non-paper-based Library materials. The facility, which will focus on storing the overflow collections from Library buildings on Capitol Hill, will be built in modular fashion. Construction of the first module, which has been designed specifically for paper-based collections, will include, in addition to the module itself, an office area, loading docks, mechanical rooms, vestibule, and circulation corridors. Subsequent modules will be attached to Module 1 and will share the loading dock, mechanical room, and office area. The state-of-the-art facility will house materials in an environment that will help preserve the materials for generations.

Improved environmental storage conditions employed in the design of this facility make it a preservation tool aimed at reducing deterioration of the collections stored there. Preservation Directorate staff worked closely with other Library units, contractors, and the office of the Architect of the Capitol on specifications for the environmental systems, the selection of preservation-compatible materials for use in the building's construction, and the design and components of storage enclosures that will house books and other materials that will be transferred to the new site. (KEH, SES)

Harris, Kenneth E. and Susan E. Schur. *Caring for America's Library: A Brief History of Preservation and Conservation at the Library of Congress.* Washington, D.C.: Library of Congress, 2000.

Library of Congress Information Bulletin 50 (July 1, 1991): 247–253; 256 (April 21, 1997): 148–151.

PRINTS AND PHOTOGRAPHS DIVISION AND COLLECTIONS

Administrative History

The Library of Congress is unusual among research libraries for having pictorial collections so extensive that an entire division is devoted to their ongoing acquisition, processing, cataloging, preservation, reference, and outreach services. The Prints and Photographs Division (P&P), early conceived as a department devoted to the fine arts, has come to assume a leading role in the visual documentation of politics, society, and daily culture. Today, P&P's collections, numbering almost 14 million pieces, form an impressive visual record of the history of the United States, the lives, concerns, and achievements of its people, and of countries throughout the world.

The Library's Division of Prints was originally located on the second floor of the south side of the Jefferson Building.
LC/Prints and Photographs Division. LC-BH836-266.

The administrative history of P&P falls into three broad eras as the division evolved from an accumulation of visual copyright deposits into an art and architecture library and finally into an organization that combines the roles of subject-based picture library, vast photographic archives, and museum emphasizing image creators.

- 1802–1896: Antecedents in the acquisition, chiefly through copyright deposit, of commercial graphic art prints, posters, and photographs. Managed as part of the general collections.
- 1897–1944: Emphasis on fine art prints and art reproductions, with services geared to the study of the history of art and architecture, including books and periodicals in that subject area. Managed through the Department of Graphic Arts (1897–1898), the Division of Prints (1899–1929), and the Division of Fine Arts (1929–1944).
- 1943/1944–present: Massive additions of documentary photographs; architecture, design, and engineering archives; and political and cartoon drawings, with services geared to picture researchers, cultural historians, mass media producers, collectors, and general students. Managed through the Prints and Photographs Division (1944–).

Thomas Jefferson's personal library, acquired by the Library of Congress in 1815, was rich in books about architecture and the fine arts. The beginning of the Library's graphic arts collections can be traced to this acquisition, which was housed in Blodget's Hotel before the Library of Congress moved back into the U.S. Capitol in 1818.

On September 15, 1815, perhaps inspired by the Jefferson purchase, Librarian of Congress George Watterston published a notice in the Washington, D.C. newspaper *National Intelligencer* asking that "American authors, engravers, and painters" transmit copies of their work to the Library of Congress to serve "not only as a literary history of this now interesting country, but [also] to exhibit the progress and the improvement of the arts." There is no record of a response to Watterston's request, but the expansion of the Library's interest to include the promotion of the arts was permanent. By 1866, interest in visual materials had reached the point that the Library Committee approved a new rule: "all engravings and works of art will be constantly protected and used only with special permission from the Librarian."

When the Smithsonian Institution was established by an act of Congress on August 10, 1846, one section of the law authorized the Library of Congress, along with the Smithsonian Institution, to receive as a deposit for its collections one copy of every copyrighted "book, map, chart, musical composition, print, cut, or engraving." This provision was repealed on February 5, 1859, but reinstated on March 3, 1865, at the urging of Librarian of Congress Ainsworth Rand Spofford. Moreover, the 1865 law granted copyright protection to photographs, thus requiring not only the deposit of every "print, cut, or engraving," but also every photograph. Spofford was unhappy, however, with the lack of enforcement power in the law, and in

1870 he arranged for an amendment that centralized all U.S. copyright activities at the Library of Congress. The Library was now entitled to two copies of copyrighted works, and the law included paintings, drawings, sculpture, and models or designs for works of the fine arts.

Although copyright dominated as an acquisitions source, certain collections and individual items came to the Library's graphic arts collection in the nineteenth century through purchase and exchange or as part of larger acquisitions. The primary examples are: 1) the 1865 purchase of more than 850 photographic views of California and Nevada published by Lawrence & Houseworth; 2) the transfer, in 1866, of the Smithsonian Institution Library to the Library of Congress, which included 1,300 prints the Smithsonian had purchased in 1850 from George P. Marsh and copyright deposits gathered by the Smithsonian between 1846 and 1859; and 3) the 1867 purchase by the Library of Congress of the Peter Force Library, which contained nearly 400 engraved portraits by Charles Balthazar Julien Fevret de Saint-Mémin.

In a report to Congress in late 1895, as the Library of Congress was preparing to move across the Capitol's east plaza into its own building, Librarian Spofford described the Library's "works of graphic art" as an "important class, demanding special treatment." The Librarian estimated that this collection embraced "nearly a quarter of a million engravings, photographs, chromos, photogravures, etchings, and pictorial illustrations of every kind, many of them of great beauty and value, acquired without a dollar of expense to the Government through the steady operation of the copyright law for twenty-five years." He noted that once these collections were properly arranged, they would "present a most instructive illustration of the progress of the arts of design," and that one of the large galleries in the new building "is specially adapted for the arrangement and display of these treasures, so long buried from view and so interesting both to art students and to the general public."

In the reorganization and expansion of the Library approved by Congress on February 19, 1897, a separate department for "arts" was approved, even though it soon was referred to as the "graphic arts" administrative unit. A new Librarian of Congress, John Russell Young, took office on July 1, 1897, just prior to the move into the new building. Young recognized the value of pictorial collections, noting that "Whatever comes as graphic art, however trivial or even questionable, will be preserved as elucidating the manners and customs of our day." When the new building opened on November 1, 1897, the south gallery on its second floor had indeed been set aside for "a series of graphic-art exhibitions." Thomas Alvord, the first superintendent of the Department of Graphic Arts and the Library's chief clerk, described three challenges that became constant themes as acquisitions continue to outpace available resources: a vast quantity of uncataloged material, smallness of staff, and lack of storage facilities.

In 1898, Gertrude M. Hubbard gave the Library the distinguished collection of European and American prints formed by her late husband, American industrialist Gardiner Greene Hubbard.

In 1898, Mrs. Gardiner Greene Hubbard donated to the Library its first major collection of fine prints, assembled by her husband Gardiner Greene Hubbard, who was a pioneer in the telephone industry. Among the 2,700 prints was The Expulsion from Paradise, *or* The Fall of Man *by Albrecht Durer. Woodcut, 1510.* LC/Prints and Photographs Division. LC-USZ62-17353.

Librarian of Congress John Russell Young died on January 17, 1899, and his successor Herbert Putnam, recognizing the significance of the Hubbard Collection, changed the name of the department from "graphic arts" to "prints."

In 1900, Putnam changed the Library's nomenclature: "department" became "division" and "superintendent" became "chief." For the first chief of the Prints Division, Putnam named a scholar thoroughly acquainted with fine prints, Arthur Jeffrey Parsons. He targeted three audiences: tourists who benefited from fine prints displayed in art exhibits; art students who could borrow photographic art reproductions; and art history scholars who studied original prints and consulted reference books and periodicals. The 1901 Library *Annual Report* describes a division of five employees plus a "repairer and mounter" from the Government Printing Office. The division was located in the second floor south curtain, the southeast pavilion, and the southeast attic above the pavilion. It also had responsibility for the exhibitions located in the second floor southwest pavilion or curtain and the southwest gallery. The collection in 1901 numbered more than 106,000 items, consisting mostly of copyright deposits. The 1901 *Annual Report* notes that more than half of the collection consisted of photographs, and that a large percentage of the photographs were portraits. The report also describes valuable prints that had been loaned by collectors for exhibit in the Library's gallery. The division's fine arts and architecture book collection was immediately accessible in the neighboring stack area. Librarian Putnam notes in his report that it consisted of "7,458 volumes classified as fine arts, and but 2,642 as architecture."

Parsons prepared an elegant catalog of the Hubbard Collection of prints, which the Library published on handmade paper in 1905. The Library also recognized the subject value of pictures by publishing in 1906 an index to more than 100,000 portraits available in illustrated books, compiled for an American Library Association project. When Parsons resigned because of ill health in 1911, the collections numbered more than 340,000 pieces. In his obituary four years later, Putnam saluted Parsons's achievement: "When he took charge of thc Division, it was without distinction in material, service, or repute. It has now a certain distinction in all three."

The next division chief, Richard A. Rice, served the Library from 1915 until his death in 1925. He continued the emphasis on fine arts established by his predecessor, although significant documentary collections arrived during his tenure, including Civil War drawings, daguerreotypes from Mathew Brady's studio, and British cartoons purchased from Windsor Castle. In 1917, American printmaker, illustrator, and critic Joseph Pennell donated to the Library his extensive collection of the prints, drawings, and letters of the American artist James McNeill Whistler. Pennell made the Library the primary beneficiary of his substantial estate, with instructions to use funds from the estate to purchase modern prints. Since 1938, the Pennell Fund has supported a program of acquisitions, the prints selected by a committee composed of artists and the division chief. From 1943 to 1976, the fund also supported the National Print Exhibition, a juried show organized by division staff from which purchases were also made. The division formally incorporated photography into its fine art mission in 1926 by purchasing more than 50 artistic photographic prints by Clarence H. White and Gertrude Käsebier.

In 1927, the Carnegie Corporation endowed a Chair of Fine Arts at the Library, and in 1929, Leicester B. Holland became the first incumbent with the title Chair of Fine Arts and Chief of the Division. The name of the division was changed to the Division of Fine Arts in recognition of the Carnegie gift, and the Library launched major programs to record American architecture. With the financial assistance of the Carnegie Corporation, Holland was instrumental in 1930 in the creation of the Pictorial Archives of Early American Architecture, and the Library commissioned pioneer woman photographer Frances Benjamin Johnston to document historic buildings in the South. Another significant achievement was the Cabinet of American Illustration, which Holland created with the help of William Patten, art editor for *Harper's Magazine* during the 1880s and 1890s. The collection consists of several thousand original drawings made by more than 200 American illustrators active in the period 1870 through World War I.

In 1933, largely through the efforts of Charles E. Peterson of the National Park Service, the Historic American Buildings Survey (HABS) was founded to help provide work for unemployed architects and draftsmen during the Depression. The Library of Congress became a partner in this project to document diverse types of American architecture and the repository for the resulting photographs, measured drawings, and written descriptions. Joined in 1969 by the Historic American Engineering Record (HAER), HABS has recorded more than 30,000 sites, structures, and artifacts. Since its inception, with new materials transferred annually, it has remained one of the division's most popular collections. The Rockefeller Foundation's funding of an in-house Photoduplication Service in 1938 significantly simplified the division's ability to print negatives and copy other photographs.

Writer and poet Archibald MacLeish succeeded Herbert Putnam as Librarian of Congress in 1939, and soon undertook a major reorganization. Among the changes was a "reorientation" of the Fine Arts Division towards a new emphasis on the photographic documentation of the American experience. Extensive consultation with sister institutions and library staff as well as advocates of photography confirmed the national need for a depository of documentary photographs. An internal library report had noted the importance of rescuing and arranging an estimated 772,000 copyrighted photographs of immediate interest as a record of American life. A strong proponent of the division's role in art research, chief Holland disagreed with the expanded mission based on the physical format of visual materials rather than the subject area of art and architecture. Holland resigned in 1943. The *Annual Report* for 1943 already reflected the new orientation in three pages devoted to photographic acquisitions.

In 1944, the combined archives of two landmark photographic documentation projects carried out successively within two federal agencies, the Farm Security Administration (FSA) and the Office of War

Information (OWI), were placed by executive order under the Library's administration. To the Library's already extensive pictorial backlog of American buildings, cities, and news events, the FSA-OWI archive added an unparalleled contemporary record of the everyday experience of a broad spectrum of Americans in the period 1935–1945. New collections of photography flooded the division in the 1940s, many transferred from other government agencies, others purchased, for example the first of many extensive photojournalism archives: 100,000 glass plate negatives and prints from the Bain News Service.

Appropriately, in 1944, the name of the division was once again changed, this time to its current name—the Prints and Photographs Division—and a specialist in photography was appointed. MacLeish also restored the principle of the undivided general book collection, which led, in 1947, to the transfer of custodial responsibility for the books on art and architecture to the Stack and Reader Division. As a result, the number of patrons visiting the reading room in the Southeast Pavilion dropped by over a half. Luther Evans, appointed Librarian of Congress in 1945, summarized the value of a new approach to still pictures in his first *Annual Report*. "For more than a century we have collected prints, but these have been collected as works of this or that engraver, lithographer, etcher, or photographer rather than as factual representations of a place or a person, an episodc or a time. This is not for a moment to disparage a point of view, nor to asperse a method, for certainly both are important to us. On the contrary it is intended to point up an opportunity to build our picture collection along other lines as well. . . . After all, this is a generation grown more facile, more adept at seeing, than at reading. . . . For us this means that we must as assiduously collect the national record as visually presented by the printmaker and the photographer and the cinematographer, as we have sought it in books and scores and maps and manuscripts." The division quickly issued its first subject-based guide: *Pictorial Americana: A Select List of Photographic Negatives in the Prints and Photographs Division of the Library of Congress* (1945).

Paul Vanderbilt, the chief of the Prints and Photographs Division from 1947 through 1950, made a major contribution through the compilation of *Guide to the Special Collections of Prints and Photographs in the Library of Congress*, which the Library published in 1955. Its descriptions of the individual collections, combined with those contained in the 1980 Library publication compiled by Annette Melville, *Special Collections in the Library of Congress*, are of great use to researchers and Library staff alike. Vanderbilt, a librarian, had supervised the organization of the vast FSA collection and at the Library introduced the system of organizing large pictorial collections into "lots," or related groups of items. Since that time, it has been an important means of gaining bibliographic control over the division's immense holdings. Vanderbilt also brought a new technology, microfilming photographs and prints, into the division's daily work. Staff soon developed visual catalogs by filing large prints from microfilm frames in subject-browsing files and pasting small prints on 3" x 5" catalog cards describing individual historical prints.

In 1954, the year L. Quincy Mumford was named Librarian, the seven-person division, headed by acting chief and fine prints curator Alice Lee Parker, moved from the Southeast Pavilion to the south curtain of the main building. Two years later, when art historian Edgar Breitenbach became chief, the collection of 2.9 million photographs was cited as "an unmatched store of graphic materials by which the past can be recreated for the eyes of the present." During Breitenbach's 17-year tenure, the Library began actively to preserve deteriorating photographs by making copy negatives and service prints and, with an increase in division staff to 15, to process the backlog of important, uncataloged collections, including that of William Henry Jackson and the Detroit Publishing Company.

The 1960 meeting of the Pennell Fund committee to select prints for the Library's collections. Standing are (left to right) lithographer Benton Spruance and Prints and Photographs Division Chief Edgar Breitenbach; seated are Assistant Chief Alice Lee Parker and etcher Arthur Heintzelman. LC Archives.

In 1961, the Motion Picture Section was transferred from Stack and Reader Services to the Prints and Photographs Division to consolidate the care of original visual materials. Under Breitenbach's direction, the film collections grew rapidly and the Motion Picture Section expanded to become a national center for film preservation and cinema scholarship. The films moved again in 1978 when the Library created a Motion Picture, Broadcasting, and Recorded Sound Division to promote attention for radio and television programs as well as films.

In 1964, to further the cataloging of a backlog of unprocessed collections, the Processing and Curatorial Section was established. An active solicitation of gifts that year resulted in Ansel Adams's donation of his photographs of Japanese-American internment at Manzanar. Other outstanding acquisitions prior to Breitenbach's retirement in 1973 included the one million images in the *New York World-Telegram and the Sun* Newspaper Photograph Collection (1967), 300,000 images by photojournalist and fashion photographer Toni Frissell (1970), and the five million photographs in the *Look* Magazine Photograph Collection (1971). The division's holdings of American fine prints, described as "the greatest repository of American prints in the country," were given prominent coverage in *American Prints in the Library of Congress: A Catalog of the Collection* (1970), recording some 12,000 works.

In 1971, the division moved from the Jefferson Building to the first floor of the Adams Building, where it had stored some collections for many years. Several collections were also held off site in Library-leased warehouses in Middle River, Maryland; Alexandria, Virginia; and then Landover, Maryland. Nitrate negatives were stored in a special facility in Suitland, Maryland, until space became available in 2002 at Wright-Patterson Air Force Base in Dayton, Ohio.

Alan Fern, curator of fine prints since 1961 and assistant chief since 1964, was made chief in 1973, prior to becoming director of the Library's new Research Department in 1976. He was instrumental in acquiring the Caroline and Erwin Swann Collection of Caricature and Cartoon, comprising more than 2,000 original American and European cartoons that came to the Library in 1974 and 1977 with a special fund to maintain, preserve, and develop the collection, and to support the display of cartoon, political satire, and illustration art. Augmenting similar holdings, including the finest assembly of British satires outside the United Kingdom, it helped establish the Library as an important research center for cartoon and caricature. In 1995, The Swann Foundation was transferred to the Library. Fern also acquired six early daguerreotypes by John Plumbe Jr., made circa 1846, that included the earliest photographs of the U.S. Capitol and the White House.

As chief, Fern also oversaw the publication of *Viewpoints: A Selection from the Pictorial Collections of the Library of Congress* (1975), the first illustrated volume to reveal the breadth of the division's pictorial holdings. Articles published in *The Quarterly Journal of the Library of Congress* were gathered together in *Graphic Sampler* (1979), a compilation of essays by staff members on fine prints and popular graphic arts, and *A Century of Photographs, 1846–1946* (1980), a similar collection of essays covering the photography holdings. Book-length staff publications treating specific collections also flourished, for example, *Historic America: Buildings, Structures and Sites* (1983), *Documenting America, 1935–1943* (1988), focusing on the FSA/OWI collections, *Washingtoniana Photographs* (1989), and *American Political Prints, 1766–1876* (1991).

Alan Fern, formerly Curator of Fine Prints and Assistant Chief (1964–1973), was Chief of the Prints and Photographs Division from 1973 until he became director of the Library's new Research Department in 1976. LC Archives.

Several acting chiefs oversaw the division until the 1981–1982 appointment of chief Oliver Jensen, a co-founder of the American Heritage Publishing Company and author of *America's Yesterdays: Images of Our Lost Past Discovered in the Photographic Archives of the Library of Congress* (1978). In 1982, the Prints and Photographs Division moved from temporary quarters on the fourth deck and south side of the Adams [Annex] Building to its present location on the third floor of the James Madison Memorial Building. At the time, the collections numbered more than eight million items but they soon swelled with the addition of 600,000 news photos from the archives of *U.S. News & World Report*. In mid-1984, when the staff numbered 35, art historian and administrator Stephen E. Ostrow was appointed chief. During his 12-year tenure, as a result of several important, Library-wide programs as well as local initiatives, the division underwent a period of rapid growth and transformation.

In 1984, the division's work with the Optical Disk Pilot Program introduced to the reading room the first videodiscs containing 50,000 images from 13 collections for display on a television monitor. The images were soon connected interactively to P&P's first microcomputer database to create a local online catalog. It proved the beginning of a revolution in electronic access to the division's collections. The ground-breaking application of automated technologies to retrieving linked images and catalog records resulted not only in the speedier delivery of selected items but also, with reduced need for handling, assisted in the overall preservation of the collections. However, automation necessitated increased standardization of bibliographic controls for graphic materials, including brief access records. Cataloging specialist and later assistant chief Elisabeth Betz Parker lead the development of national standards through such Library publications as *Graphic Materials: Rules for Describing Original Items and Historical Collections* (1982), followed by thesauri for indexing pictures by subject and by form, genre, and physical characteristics. Division staff continue to maintain these tools for international users in libraries and archives as well as commercial collections.

In 1987, a division reorganization separated the Curatorial and Processing Section. By 1989, three projects supported by Congress, began to dominate the division's activities. To fulfill its new obligations, by 1991 the staff of the Prints and Photographs division had expanded to 51. The Deteriorating Negative Project (1989–2002) preserved more than 200,000 inherently fragile nitrate and diacetate photographic negatives through rehousing the originals, and creating preservation copies, and increasing cold storage facilities. The ongoing Library-wide Arrearage Reduction Program aimed at eliminating huge backlogs of unprocessed collections encompassed approximately 10 million pictures in P&P. By 1995, some 2.7 million pictorial items had been cataloged by processing several large news photo morgues as well as many smaller collections of high-demand items such as daguerreotypes. By 2002, the backlog had shrunk to four million items, despite large new acquisitions, with almost 10 million items available for public use. As a result, demands for reference service increased, raising security concerns in the crowded reading room.

In the early 1990s, the Library explored the use of digital images on CD-ROM and in June 1994, the release of American Memory on the World Wide Web (WWW) comprised three collections of digitized pictures from the Prints and Photographs Division. Still pictures suited the new Web environment so well that by 2000, P&P had scanned more than 500,000 items and contributed more than 40 percent of the content to an expanded National Digital Library program. Four criteria drove selection of collections to digitize: enduring public demand (e.g., Civil War photos); risks in serving a fragile original format (e.g., negatives); previous lack of cataloging (e.g., Panoramic photographs), and absence of restrictions on reproduction (e.g., WPA posters).

In 1996, the division's first home page appeared on the WWW providing information on how to use the collections, and the searchable analog videodiscs were replaced in the reading room by a local (intranet) online catalog dubbed the "digital one-box." It allowed patrons to browse more than 130,000 records and almost 95,000 images.

In 1998, the Prints and Photographs Online Catalog (PPOC) was launched on the WWW, making some 355,000 images accessible worldwide via the Internet and redefining the division's role as a research resource. By 2003, digital scanning of collections had become a mainstream activity in the division and the number of digital images available in PPOC had increased to almost one million, ensuring the Library's leadership role in the digital revolution in visual collections. In 2002, more than 250,000 users conducted some 1.7 million searches on the online catalog. To facilitate remote access to reference services, in 2002 the division's specialists also began to reply electronically to patrons' e-mailed queries via the QuestionPoint pilot program, extending the reading room's reach to a global audience.

Under Ostrow, the Curatorial Section focused acquisitions on specific subjects, themes, and geographic areas. As a result of this selective collecting process, growth slowed from over 500,000 items a year to an average of under 50,000, helping stem the tide of new unprocessed collections and assisting the division to meet its arrearage reduction goals. The 1990s featured major acquisitions under the leadership of Librarian of Congress James H. Billington and curatorial section head Bernard Reilly. Among many outstanding additions was the Marian S. Carson Collection, which included the first American photographic record of a human face—a self-portrait by Robert Cornelius made in 1839. The brief tenure of American art specialist Linda Ayres as chief (1997–1999) emphasized preservation of the collections and lead to the hiring of a full-time photograph conservator.

After moving into the Madison Building, the Prints and Photographs Division continued its long-established exhibit program, not only by contributing materials to Library exhibitions, such as "The American Cowboy" (1983) and "The Pennell Legacy" (1985), but also by organizing cartoon and caricature shows in the Oval Gallery on the sixth floor. In February 1998, after the renovation of the Jefferson Building, these regular displays were relocated to the new Swann Gallery on the ground floor of the

Jefferson Building. In 2001, the year art historian Jeremy Adamson was appointed chief, the division assisted with the organization of the Library's exhibition "The Empire that was Russia." Utilizing recent advances in digital technology, it recreated the unique color photographic record of the Russian Empire made by S. M. Prokudin-Gorskii on the eve of the Revolution.

The following year, Adamson and division curators built a special archive of pictorial materials, both documentary and creative, and including architecture, related to the September 11, 2001 terrorist attacks. In November 2002, the Library of Congress Center for Architecture, Design, and Engineering was established through a bequest from the distinguished American architect Paul Rudolph, whose collection recently had been given to the Library, and other contributors. Integral to the Center's educational program is the publication of the series *Norton/Library of Congress Sourcebooks in Architecture, Design, and Engineering* drawn on the division's wide-ranging architectural holdings, a significant component of its collection.

For more than a century the Prints and Photographs Division has acquired, cared for, and made available to a growing public the Library's largest concentration of photographs, prints, drawings, posters, and architectural records. Images in P&P support the vast range of scholarly resources in the Library, including the history of science, the arts and literature of all countries, as well as the geographically focused research collections in African and Latin American area studies and the cultures of Asia and the Middle East. In considering pictorial resources throughout the Library of Congress, it is important to mention the valuable illustrations in the Rare Book, Manuscript, and general collection divisions as well as the large photographic holdings acquired and maintained in the American Folklife Center and Music Division as part of multi-media archives. Two recent popular publications exemplify the benefits for visual history of weaving together resources from the full sweep of the Library's pictorial holdings: *Eyes of the Nation: A Visual History of the United States* (1997) and *American Women: A Library of Congress Guide for the Study of Women's History and Culture in the United States* (2001). (JYC, JAD, HZ)

Arms, Caroline R. "Getting the Picture: Observations from the Library of Congress on Providing Online Access to Pictorial Images," *Library Trends* 48:2 (Fall 1999): 379–409. <http://memory.loc.gov/ammem/techdocs/libt1999/libt1999.html>

Breitenbach, Edgar. "Picture Research at the Library of Congress," *Special Libraries* 51 (July 1960): 281–287.

Kusnerz, Peggy Ann. "Picturing the Past: Photographs at the Library of Congress, 1865–1964." Ph.D. dissertation., University of Michigan, Department of Communications, 1992.

Library of Congress Prints and Photographs: An Illustrated Guide. Preface by Stephen E. Ostrow. Washington, D.C.: Library of Congress, 1995.

Shaw, Renata V., comp. *A Century of Photographs 1846–1946. Selected from the Library of Congress. Washington,* D.C., Library of Congress, 1980.

Collections

The Prints and Photographs Division holds some 14 million images documenting the history of the United States, the lives, interests, and achievements of its diverse peoples, and the nation's impact on world affairs—and vice versa. Nearly every pictorial means of documentary and artistic communication from the fifteenth century to the present is represented within the divisional holdings: historical and contemporary prints and drawings, posters, cartoons and caricatures, architectural renderings, design and engineering drawings, and photographic prints and negatives.

These pictorial collections represent an immense fund of human experience, knowledge and accomplishment and touch upon almost every realm of endeavor. The division's holdings reveal that the varied arts of drawing, printmaking, and photography have served a multitude of purposes, as bearers of information, vehicles of commentary, and means of artistic expression.

Photography

Documentary photographs, from the invention of the medium in 1839 through today's high-tech digital photography, predominate. Aside from abundant documentation of the United States, the photography collections include often unique photo-documentation of Central and Latin America, the Middle East, Eastern Europe, Mexico, and Russia from the 1840s through World War II.

The first photographs entered the Library's collections in the early 1850s. Since that time, the collections have grown continually, through gifts, purchases, transfers from other government agencies, and copyright deposits, and now include some 12 million photographic prints, negatives, and digital files.

The photography collections associated with social documentation include works by the most significant creators during critical eras in American history. Among them are approximately 5,000 photographs by Lewis Hine taken for the National Child Labor Committee (1904–1953) and more than 164,000 photographs from the Farm Security Administration/Office of War Information (1935–1945), which employed such noted photographers as Dorothea Lange, Walker Evans, and Gordon Parks to chronicle the lives of ordinary Americans during the Great Depression and World War II. The collections also include remarkable archives assembled by influential social agencies including the American Red Cross, the National Association for the Advancement of Colored People, and the National Urban League.

The division's Civil War-related holdings are among the most comprehensive in existence, featuring seminal work by the studio of Mathew Brady, as well as the work of such contemporaries as Alexander Gardner, Timothy O'Sullivan, and A. J. Russell. The collections also represent the post-war work of cameramen and their colleagues who participated in the numerous landscape surveys of the American West carried out in the 1860s and 1870s. Among the highlights are spectacular, large-format views of Western landscapes by Carleton Watkins and William Henry Jackson. In addition, the division has custody of the largest collection of American panoramic photographs (1860–1930). Numerous unique daguerreotypes by the earliest American photographers, including John Plumbe Jr.'s views of the United States Capitol and other federal buildings (circa 1846), reveal the fresh-hewn look of the young Republic.

An unidentified Union soldier of the U.S. Civil War. Ambrotype, circa 1863–1865. The Library's photographic holdings on the Civil War are particularly rich. LC/Prints and Photographs Division. LC-USZC4-4608.

Famous Americans, as well as anonymous citizens, are portrayed in every photographic format, including the first American photographic portrait ever taken (a self-portrait daguerreotype by Philadelphian Robert Cornelius in 1839). The collection of 725 daguerreotypes taken in 1839–1864 include the earliest known photograph of Abraham Lincoln (circa 1846), as well as anonymous occupational portraits including that of an anonymous fireman (1840s) and seamstress (circa 1853). The collections of portrait photography also comprise thousands of mounted silver and albumen prints from the studios of Mathew Brady and his rivals, Edward Curtis's original gelatin silver photographs of Native Americans, and Toni Frissell's portraits of prominent Americans in the second half of the twentieth century.

Native American Child. Photographer Edward S. Curtis (1868–1952) spent 30 years traveling among the Indian peoples of North America. The Library has approximately 1,700 first-generation Curtis photoprints in its collections. LC/Prints and Photographs Division.

American achievements in science, technology, and engineering are well recorded and include extended coverage of the history of aeronautics from the Wright Brothers through World War II. Photo albums donated by the family of Thomas Edison document his extraordinary inventive genius, while early twentieth-century American buildings and gardens are reflected in the work of pioneering female photographer Frances Benjamin Johnston.

Johnston served as President Theodore Roosevelt's official White House photographer and contributed to the early history of American photojournalism, for which the Library is a leading national study center. Among the division's vast archives devoted to photojournalism are the Bain News Service Collection (1890s to 1930s), the earliest news picture agency in the country; *New York World-Telegram and the Sun* Newspaper Photograph

Collection (chiefly 1920–1967); *U.S. News & World Report* Magazine Collection (1952–1986); and *Look* Magazine Photograph Collection (approximately five million images from 1937 to 1971). Additionally, more than 25,000 photographs from the Detroit Publishing Company, one of the country's largest publishers of postcards and souvenir views, provide additional views of scenery and life in the United States in the early twentieth century.

The Library's non-U.S. holdings are particularly strong. The Prints and Photographs Division houses one of the most extensive collections of nineteenth-century photographs of the Middle East, including the 51-volume photographic survey of the Ottoman Empire (circa 1880–1893) from the collection of Sultan Abdul Hamid II; the Matson Photo Service Collection (1898–1946); and photographs by Francis Frith, as well as other major photography firms catering to the international market. Images of Germany under the Third Reich, gathered by American forces during World War II, are another strength, with work ranging from the 47 personal photo albums of Hermann Goering to an album of photographs of the 1936 Olympics in Berlin from the Nazi perspective, personally inscribed and presented to Hitler by photographer and filmmaker Leni Riefenstahl.

The Library also holds outstanding collections of photographs documenting Eastern Europe, the Russian Empire, and the former Soviet Union. These works include the landmark portfolio of 263 Crimean War photographs by Roger Fenton (1855), unique, three-color photographs of Imperial Russia taken by Sergei Prokudin-Gorskii (1905–1915) and commissioned by Czar Nicholas II, and the work of numerous American Red Cross photographers who recorded the aftermath of World War I in Eastern Europe. Latin America art and architecture from the colonial period to the 1960s is documented in the Archive of Hispanic Culture.

Since the 1920s, the Library has collected photographs as fine art and now holds thousands of works by the most influential American master photographers. The collection is particularly strong in photographs by turn-of-the-nineteenth-century American Pictorialists. Works by Alfred Stieglitz, Edward Steichen, Gertrude Käsebier, and the largest extant body of work by F. Holland Day, their British predecessors and contemporaries, notably Julia Margaret Cameron, Peter Henry Emerson, and Alvin Langdon Coburn, are represented. Clarence H. White and his influential school of photography is also well-represented, while representative works by artists active later in the twentieth century such as Imogen Cunningham, Edward Steichen, Diane Arbus, Paul Outerbridge, Aaron Siskind, Danny Lyon, Nicholas Nixon, Richard Avedon, Mark Klett, and Edward Burtynsky, to name just a few, round out examples of twentieth-century work. Other notable holdings include the largest single collection of the work of Arnold Genthe (1898–1930s), and Ansel Adams's photographs of Japanese-American internees at the Manzanar War Relocation Center (1943).

<u>Architecture, Design, and Engineering</u>

The Architecture, Design, and Engineering collections include more than two million items—drawings, photographs, fine prints, blueprints, specifications, and related material. Unmatched in scope and richness, they document the development and contributions of architects, engineers, and designers, and of the related disciplines of landscape, interior, and industrial architecture and design. The greatest strength of these collections lie in their documentation of American forms from the late eighteenth century to the present. Indeed, the division has pioneered the documentation of America's historic architecture since the 1920s and 1930s, when it was instrumental in the creation of the Pictorial Archives of Early American Architecture (1930), the Carnegie Survey of the Architecture of the South (1933–1940), and the Historic American Buildings Survey (HABS; 1933–). In 1969, the division joined in the creation of the Historic American Engineering Record (HAER), and in 1980 it received the photographic survey of United States county courthouses commissioned from 24 photographers by Joseph E. Seagram & Company in celebration of the nation's bicentennial.

American architectural photography is a particular strength. Related collections range from the beginnings of American architectural photography to the present and include substantial bodies of work by William Henry Jackson, Frances Benjamin Johnston, Irving Underhill, F. S. Lincoln, Ansel Adams, Sigurd Fischer, David Plowden, and Carol Highsmith. Spanning more than five decades, nearly 30,000 images in the Gottscho-Schleisner Collection feature the work of many of the early twentieth-century's outstanding architects, landscape architects, and interior and industrial designers. The Detroit Photographic Company archive provides an incomparably rich portrait of turn-of-the-century American cities, parks, resorts, buildings, monuments, transportation, and industry. A large collection of photographs by Theodor Horydczak depict Washington, D.C., architecture and daily life between 1923 and 1959. Carol Highsmith, a contemporary Washington, D.C.-based photographer inspired by the career of Frances Benjamin Johnston, has spent her own career photographing American cities and towns in an effort to create a legacy of recent architectural images for future generations to consult. Her complete archives are promised to the Library, rights free, along with funds to support a project to document the continuing development of the building and sites in which the American people live and work.

In many formats, the division also holds collections of nineteenth- and early twentieth-century photographs of architecture in other countries. These works range from the large photographic prints of the Königliche Preussischen Messbildanstalt, perhaps the first photogrammetric survey of architectural monuments, to Thomas Annan's volumes of carbon prints depicting the old buildings of Glasgow. The work of many of the finest nineteenth-century architectural photographers and agencies are represented in these collections, including Roger Fenton, Édouard-Denis Baldus, Carlo Ponti, Francis Frith, Giraudon, Bonfils, the French Service des Monuments Historiques, and Service des Ponts et Chaussées, among others. In addition, there is an exceptional body of material representing the architectural, engineering, and planning projects of Germany's Third Reich.

The division's collections are particularly notable for the qualitative and chronological breadth of architectural drawings by individuals and firms whose contributions have significantly influenced or defined developments in American architecture, design, and engineering. Architects ranging from Richard Upjohn, Cass Gilbert, and Frank Lloyd Wright to Frederick Kiesler, Richard Neutra, Ludwig Mies van der Rohe, Louis Skidmore, and Nathaniel Owings are well represented. The division is the principal repository for the architectural drawings of Charles Bulfinch, B. Henry Latrobe, and William Thornton. The work of engineers, such as Montgomery Meigs, and formative designers including Victor Gruen, Raymond Loewy, and Winold Reiss are also well represented.

The division is the repository of the comprehensive archive of designers Charles and Ray Eames, numbering about 750,000 items and spanning the couple's working career. More recently, the Library has acquired the archives of Paul Rudolph, as well as original drawings and sketchbooks from the office of I. M. Pei. Other contemporary architects represented in the collection include Cesar Pelli, Robert A. M. Stern, Michael Graves, Allan Greenberg, Hardy Holzman Pfeiffer, Maya Ying Lin, and Mark Mack, among others. The collection of Kenneth Walker, acquired in 1999, contains outstanding original drawings by the leading architects of the past three centuries.

Drawings in the Library's architecture, design, and engineering collections document a wide range of methods of representation, media and formats, and include both original drawings and examples of reproduction and dissemination. The Library has also acquired student drawings by Americans trained under the apprentice system at the École des Beaux-Arts and at the Bauhaus. Indeed, the development of the perspective drawing in America can be traced from Bulfinch's treatise on the subject to the influential conventions introduced by Frank Lloyd Wright and John Hedjuk. Media innovations are represented by B. H. Latrobe's watercolor renderings, Frederick Kiesler's use of the airbrush, Richard Neutra's pastels, Ray Eames's collages, and Robert Venturi's fluid marker on yellow trace drawings.

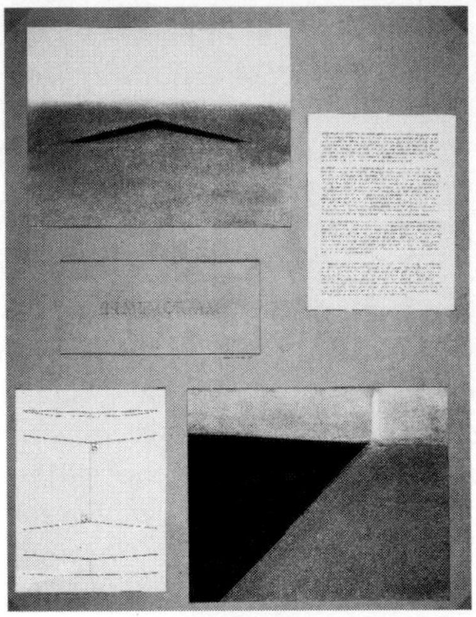

Maya Ying Lin. Vietnam Veterans Memorial Competition. Presentation panel in mixed media on paper. 1981. The memorial, originally designed as a student project by Maya Lin at Yale University Architectural School, has become a profound national symbol. LC/Prints and Photographs Division.

In addition, the division's popular and applied graphic art, poster, and fine print collections also contain rich documentation of American architecture, design, and engineering. In those collections are works by architects as diverse as William Thornton, Charles Bulfinch, William Strickland, Alexander Jackson Davis, Frank Lloyd Wright, Louis Skidmore, and Charles and Ray Eames, who often depicted architectural subjects as printmakers, illustrators, and graphic designers.

Posters

The Library's holdings of more than 100,000 posters form the most comprehensive collection of its kind. Originally formed by copyright deposits and subsequently augmented by gifts and purchases, this international collection covers the entire history of the genre, from large hand-colored woodblock posters of the 1840s to recent digital work. It includes posters designed for a myriad of purposes, including political propaganda and war recruitment, travel, advertising, cultural events, performing arts, and films. More than two-thirds of the posters were produced in countries other than the United States. Posters from the Hispanic world are particularly strong, with fine examples of Latin American posters from the 1930s and 1940s, travel posters from the 1950s through the 1980s, Spanish Civil War posters, Cuban film posters of the 1960s and 1970s, and Nicaraguan propaganda posters of the 1970s and 1980s. Political posters from around the world are well represented, with significant holdings from Africa, the Middle East, and Asia—including a large group of Japanese posters dating from the 1920s through the 1980s, 1930s tourism posters from India, and hand-cut images from 1960s China supporting the Cultural Revolution.

From Western Europe, the collection includes major works by the great European masters of the genre, who pioneered the development of the poster as an art form in the 1880s–1890s. Works by Jules Cheret, Henri Toulouse-Lautrec, and Theophile Steinlen, as well as other posters designed within the principles of the Art Nouveau and Jugendstil movements are numerous. Posters documenting the major political movements of the twentieth century are also in abundance, especially those created during World War I and World War II in Austria, Canada, Germany, Great Britain, and Italy. Three thousand posters from Germany, dating 1941 to 1945, depict Nazi propaganda. The collection also is strong in travel posters from all English-speaking countries, work by the early masters of the British poster, and London Underground and British Railway posters from the early part of the twentieth century to the present. The collection's Eastern European posters, especially notable for their design, include work by Czech, Hungarian, Polish, and Soviet artists. The Soviet collection features more than 1,200 images produced by the TASS news agency between 1941 and 1945.

The Library's collection of U.S. posters is particularly strong in the performing arts. Numbering about 10,000 and ranging from the 1840s to the present, the performing arts posters include nineteenth-century theater posters (legitimate and variety stage, burlesque, and vaudeville) and the McManus-Young Collection of posters, handbills, and broadsides depicting famous magicians (1900s–1940s). Also in this area are minstrel and circus posters and several thousand film posters from the 1900s to the present that record the transition from silent film to sound, the rise of the movie star, and the emergence of the major Hollywood studios. Posters relating to American product advertising from 1840 to World War I document advertising strategies for such commodities as patent medicines, tobacco, gas lighting, and sewing machines. The collection's strengths also include twentieth-century posters by significant American artists, designers, and illustrators whose

Newport Jazz Festival, 1954–1978. Signed by artist Milton Glaser. At the end of fiscal year 2003, the Library's poster collection included more than 88,000 items.
LC/Poster Collection. Prints and Photographs Division.

work has influenced and defined new directions in the medium, such as Milton Glaser, Seymour Chwast, Ben Shahn, Paul Rand, and Ivan Chermayeff.

The division also houses a substantial group of posters from American political campaigns from 1848 to the present, including the first known presidential campaign poster depicting Mexican War hero and presidential candidate Zachary Taylor. The collection of nearly 1,000 posters from the Works Progress Administration is believed to be the largest WPA poster collection in existence. The collections also include propaganda and protest art documenting a broad spectrum of political ideology and social and economic change; the Yanker Collection comprises more than 3,500 propaganda posters issued from the late 1950s to the 1980s. The collection also includes approximately 3,000 posters documenting the major publicity campaigns related to World War I and World War II, including James Montgomery Flagg's iconic "I Want You for the US Army."

Fine Prints and Drawings

The division's collections of graphic art are divided into two areas: fine prints and drawings, and popular and applied graphic arts. The fine print collection is international in scope. Chronicling the history of printmaking, it includes some 75,000 engravings, etchings, woodcuts, lithographs, and silkscreens from the fifteenth century to the present. Chronicles of the history of printmaking, they were acquired through copyright deposit, purchase, and gift. Notable early gifts by such collectors as former National

Geographic Society president Gardiner Greene Hubbard and Justice Oliver Wendell Holmes laid the foundation for the Library's substantial holdings of Old Master prints.

Among the highlights are exemplary prints by artists such as Mantegna, Durer, and Rembrandt, an important album of sixteenth-century chiaroscuro woodcuts by Italian masters, and an outstanding collection of Japanese wood block prints, works by German Expressionists, and rich holdings in nineteenth century French prints, including the work of Mary Cassatt and other Impressionists. The voluminous bequest of Joseph and Elizabeth Robins Pennell brought to the Library a significant collection of prints, drawings, and manuscripts by James Abbott McNeill Whistler, a nearly complete set of Joseph Pennell's prints and drawings, and a fund for the purchase of fine prints created within the past 100 years.

Researchers studying American printmaking between 1880 and 1940 will find broad and comprehensive holdings, including works by such artists as Winslow Homer, Childe Hassam, J. Alden Weir, John Sloan, George Bellows, Arthur B. Davies, Frank Benson, Ernest Haskell, John Taylor Arms, Thomas Hart Benton, Raphael Soyer, Reginald Marsh, and many others. In addition, the Library has substantial holdings of prints by artists employed by the Works Progress Administration, by Artists For Victory (during World War II), and by African-American artists collected by the Harmon Foundation. Recent acquisitions include the Ben and Beatrice Goldstein Foundation Collection, a comprehensive group of social realist and political prints and drawings dating from about 1910 to 1970.

In terms of drawings, the division also holds examples by sixteenth- and seventeenth-century German, Swiss, and Netherlandic artists, as well as seventeenth- and eighteenth-century works by French, Italian, and British draftsmen, including sketchbooks of George Romney and Thomas Stothard. Numerous works by James Abbott McNeill Whistler (including a much-celebrated pen-and-ink self-portrait), Charles Keene, Joseph Pennell, and William Zorach form a strength in the Library's collection of American fine art drawings.

In 1945, political cartoonist Clifford K. Berryman presented one of his cartoons to Librarian of Congress Luther Evans and Alice Lee Parker, Acting Chief of the Prints and Photographs Division. LC/Prints and Photographs Division. LC-USP6-303C.

Popular and Applied Graphic Art

The second major area of prints and drawings in the division is the popular and applied graphic art collection (PAGA). It contains historical and documentary prints and drawings, political and social cartoons and caricatures, illustrators' drawings, American and European graphic design, advertising prints, and ephemera, and reflects popular values and public concerns as well as detailing the development of graphic technology and design. PAGA includes the largest extant group of eyewitness Civil War drawings—some 1,600 sheets by Alfred Waud, William Waud, and Edwin Forbes, among others. In these drawings, produced for contemporary periodicals, are recorded camp life, marches, and other important events.

PAGA also includes political prints ranging from seventeenth- and eighteenth-century British and Dutch prints to eighteenth- and nineteenth-century French, German, and American work. A significant group of French political prints (1789–1871) record the events of the French Revolution and the reign of Napoleon Bonaparte, while 10,000 British cartoons (primarily for the period 1780–1820) comprise one of the finest assemblages of British satirical prints outside Great Britain.

The division houses the largest collection of American political prints and drawings in existence, plus more than 50,000 original cartoon drawings by several generations of leading American cartoonists and illustrators. The latter include works by Charles Dana Gibson, Walt Kelly, Jules Feiffer, Pat Oliphant, and Garry Trudeau, as well as drawings for cartoons and cover illustrations for *The New Yorker* magazine from 1933–1970. In spring 2003, the Library received as a gift the entire personal archives of celebrated *Washington Post* editorial cartoonist Herbert L. Block, better known as "Herblock." The Herblock Foundation Collection contains an estimated 20,000 original drawings and sketches by the most influential political cartoonist in American history.

The Caroline and Erwin Swann Collection of Caricature and Cartoon forms the core of the Library's cartoon studies program while the Cabinet of American Illustration, created during the Depression by a former art director for *Harper's*

Magazine, contains more than 4,000 original drawings by most of the leading artists of the golden age of American illustration, 1880–1920. The Cabinet includes outstanding works by some 200 American book, magazine, and newspaper illustrators, including Charles Dana Gibson, Jessie Wilcox Smith, and Arthur B. Frost. In 2002, the Library completed an agreement to acquire the Art Wood Collection of Cartoon and Caricature, the largest private collection of its kind. Composed of 32,000 items, it represents the best work by American and European cartoonists of the past 300 years.

European and American popular prints within the division date from 1600 to the present; they include portraits, views, certificates, charts, advertising trade cards, printed signs, and the nation's largest collection of historical lithographs printed by the firm of Currier & Ives. American city views, depicting cities, towns, and settlements from the colonial period to the end of the nineteenth century, are especially well represented, as is a major group of nearly 750 prints, drawings, and watercolors of Jacksonian-era America by John Rubens Smith.

The graphic design collection, both European and American in scope, includes a wide variety of material—calendars, menus, postage stamps, seed envelopes, illustrated book and sheet music covers, architectural and environmental graphics, banknote engravings, and a significant group of packaging labels for tobacco, patent medicines, and other American products dating from 1850 to the present. These reveal regional and international trends in graphic design and printing techniques.

The Prints and Photographs Division continues to collect actively in all areas in its purview, as demonstrated by the recent acquisition of the Marian S. Carson Collection, considered to have been the finest private collection of Americana. Composed of more than 10,000 manuscripts, photographs, prints, drawings, books, and broadsides, the Carson Collection focuses on the development of the United States from an English colony to a burgeoning, autonomous republic. It strengthens the Prints and Photographs Division's holdings by adding more than 150 daguerreotypes, photographs on glass, and early paper negatives and salted-paper prints dating from the early years of photography. The Carson Collection also brings such rarities as a memorial portrait drawing of George Washington by Charles Saint-Memin, Thomas Birch's view of Master Commandant Oliver Hazard Perry's victory at the Battle of Lake Erie during the War of 1812, a watercolor depicting the Liberian Senate in 1856, and Robert Cornelius's 1839 self-portrait, believed to be the first photograph of the human face made in America. (LAY, HLK, JAD)

The Caroline and Erwin Swann Collection of Caricature and Cartoon

During the 1960s and early 1970s, New York advertising executive Erwin Swann (1906–1973) assembled, with the support of his wife Caroline, an extraordinarily diverse collection of political prints and drawings, caricatures, cartoon strips and panels, and magazine illustrations. He conceived and assembled the collection specifically to promote the preservation and connoisseurship of original cartoon and illustration drawings. Composed of works by 400 artists from a dozen countries and spanning two centuries, the collection was given to the Library in 1974 by the Swann estate as a bequest following his death, along with a fund supporting its preservation and further development. The bequest established the Caroline and Erwin Swann Collection of Caricature and Cartoon and also provided for the creation and maintenance of a permanent gallery within the Library to promote the study and appreciation of original cartoon drawings as works of art and vehicles for social and political commentary. The Swann Gallery of Caricature and Cartoon in the Jefferson Building offers rotating exhibitions reflecting recent acquisitions and historical themes and issues, and a permanent display of facsimiles drawn from the Swann Collection and related holdings. These ongoing presentations demonstrate the great depth and diversity of the Library's collections of original cartoons, caricatures, and illustrators' drawings.

Erwin Swann believed that original caricatures and cartoons should be studied within the same context as fine art drawings, and along with cartoon art his collection included European master prints and drawings, including works by Bonnard, Degas, Henry Moore, and Picasso. Drawings in the collection by such European artists as Camille Pissarro, Guillaume Chevalier Gavarni, Constantin Guys, John Leech, and Richard Doyle in fact blur the line between fine and popular art.

The true glory of the collection resides, however, in the rich diversity of twentieth-century American and European cartoon drawings. American cartoonists and illustrators of the 1920s and 1930s are particularly well represented through works by John Held Jr., Ralph Barton, Rea Irvin, Anne Harriet Fish, Russell Patterson, and Peggy Bacon. The collection includes a fine group of watercolor and gouache covers for *Vanity Fair* and cartoon drawings for *The New Yorker* by Peter Arno, Whitney Darrow, and others. The Swann Collection also presents a distinguished selection of early twentieth-century political and social caricatures, including works by Homer Davenport, Luther Bradley, Max Beerbohm, Oliver Herford, and Miguel Covarrubias. From the 1950s,

1960s, and early 1970s, Swann collected works by contemporary American and European cartoonists and illustrators, including Robert Osborn, Edward Sorel, Anita Siegel, David Levine, Jean-Claude Suarez, Jose Luis Cuevas, Jean-Michel Folon, Andre Francois, and Eugene Mihaesco. Historically strong Mexican traditions in caricature are dramatically represented in the collection by the largest surviving group of printing blocks by popular printmaker Jose Guadalupe Posada and numerous original caricatures by Miguel Covarrubias.

In addition to these political and social caricatures and cartoons, the Swann Collection amply records the early history of the American newspaper cartoon strip. Works by R. F. Outcault, Frederick Opper, Winsor McCay, George McManus, George Herriman, and others document the early growth of the genre. Its further development may be traced through drawings by pioneering women cartoonists such as Grace Drayton and Virginia Huget, and by later comic art legends including Hal Foster, Chester Gould, Milton Caniff, Burne Hogarth, and Dale Messick.

In 1968, seeking to harness the scholarly and popular potential of his collection, Erwin Swann created the Swann Foundation, a non-profit tax-exempt institution guided by an advisory board composed of prominent art historians, curators, and cartoonists. For almost 30 years, the New York-based Swann Foundation provided funding for numerous influential scholarly and popular exhibitions, publications, artist's awards, and research grants related to the art of caricature and cartoons. In 1996, the Swann Foundation endowment was transferred to the Library of Congress and reunited with the Swann Collection. Administered by the Prints and Photographs Division, the Swann Foundation at the Library of Congress offers lectures, symposia, and an annual fellowship for graduate students pursuing projects related to cartoon, caricature, and illustration. In conjunction with the division's other related holdings, the Swann Collection and Swann Foundation activities thus offer unparalleled resources for the study of cartoon and caricature within the broader realms of human experience, intellectual activity, and artistic creativity. (HLK, SD)

PROTECTING THE LIBRARY'S COLLECTIONS

In 1896, two Library employees stole valuable manuscripts–including George Washington's diary–from Librarian of Congress Ainsworth Rand Spofford's office, then in the U.S. Capitol. Spofford was not aware of the loss until a New York manuscript dealer contacted the Washington police.

From the time the Library of Congress was established in 1800, it has had to be concerned about threats to the collections, including the occasional serious theft. And again, it has often been the honest book dealer who has reported the discovery. Such thefts are painful reminders that the Library's collections are vulnerable, all the more so when the theft is perpetrated by an insider.

Throughout its history, the Library has developed increasingly sophisticated security controls to combat theft and mutilation of the collections—from locks and keys in the earliest days to state-of-the-art electronic security systems two centuries later. The Library also safeguards its collections by protecting them from environmental damage and securing them through bibliographic, inventory, and preservation controls. These controls improve as technology evolves.

During the nineteenth century, the main threat to the security of the collections was fire. In 1814, when the British burned the Capitol, the Library, located in the north wing of the Capitol, was burned and all 3,000 volumes destroyed. In order to "recommence" the Library, Thomas Jefferson sold his personal library—6,487 volumes—to the government for the sum of $23,950. This new collection was housed at the site of the temporary Capitol, at Blodget's Hotel, 7th and E Streets NW, until it was returned to the Capitol Building in 1818, this time to a room in the west front of the building. Another fire, on December 22, 1825, caused by a candle left burning in the gallery, was controlled before it could cause serious damage. Investigations into fireproofing the Library room concluded that the expense would be too great.

But this decision would have disastrous results. On December 24, 1851, the most serious fire in the Library's history took place. Caused by faulty chimney flues in the Library's principal room in the Capitol, the fire destroyed some 35,000 of the 55,000 volumes, including two-thirds of Jefferson's library. A new, fireproof Library room opened August 23, 1853. Called by the press the "largest room made of iron in the world," it was also referred to by one admirer as "the most beautiful room in the world"—a happy marriage of function and aesthetics. When the new Library of Congress Building—today known as the Thomas Jefferson Building—opened in 1897, it too was fireproof and the "largest, costliest, and safest" library building in the world. "All parts of the building [were constructed] of fireproof materials, no wood being employed in any part of the structure."

Fire was not the only problem, however. In 1861, an inventory of the Library's 70,000 volumes revealed more than 1,300 missing or "drawn out and unreturned books." Of these, 856 were charged to "persons no longer members of Congress or of the Government" and 276 "to persons belonging to the so-called seceded states." After the 1896 theft of the manuscripts from Librarian Spofford's office, safeguards were expanded from locks and keys and fireproof materials to increased compartmentalization and controlled access, particularly for manuscripts and rare books. Fire controls improved with the installation of fire alarm boxes and automatic sprinklers in 1920 and, in 1923, with construction of a fireproof vault with steel shelving in the cellar of the Library, intended for motion pictures. In 1934, the east front of the Library was extended, providing specially designed quarters for the Rare Book Room and sequestered stacks for the rare book collections.

Opened to the public in 1939, the Annex Building—now known as the John Adams Building—was designed with a central portion containing book stacks that would accommodate some 10.2 million books. For protection against fire, the deck floors were built solid from wall to wall instead of the usual installation of tier stacks and were further divided in half by vertical walls. All stairways and elevator shafts were enclosed. The potential for fire to spread was thus reduced to less than 5 percent of the risk associated with the usual tiered construction of stacks.

In 1940, Librarian of Congress Archibald MacLeish established the position of Keeper of the Collections to centralize responsibility for the protection, care, and preservation of the collections. The immediate concern was the threat of war. Nations already at war had sent some of their most priceless items to the Library for safekeeping, among them Britain's Lincoln Cathedral copy of Magna Carta (1939). Library officials drew up evacuation plans to remove the most valuable materials, and in December 1941 approximately 26 freight cars of material were removed for safekeeping. For the duration, the Constitution and Declaration of Independence were sheltered at Fort Knox, Kentucky, a military secret revealed only after their return in September 1944.

After the war, Library operations resumed on a normal basis. The collections now numbered more than seven million items and were growing rapidly.

The Library's Guard Force was given police powers in 1950 to clarify its authority and was renamed the Special Police Force. In the years following, fire alarm and burglar systems were installed. The 1950s and 1960s saw continuing expansion of the collections, and with both buildings overcrowded, Library operations spread to a number of other sites in the Washington, D.C., area, raising further security concerns. Authorized in 1965 and opened in 1980, the James Madison Memorial Building was constructed with advanced security controls. Installation of a sophisticated electronic security system in the Library's three main buildings provided for more comprehensive security for the exhibits and collections in the Library's Capitol Hill complex.

In 1974, the Library issued a management report addressing collections security, and four years later began an inventory of the general book collections to identify missing items and vulnerable areas. A number of physical security controls were introduced in the next decade and a half: stack access identification cards; closed-circuit television monitors in principal exhibit areas and high-risk collections areas; the Automated Fire Protection and Security system; sprinkler systems in the book stacks; intrusion detection systems; and electromagnetic security devices at entrance and exit doors in the Madison Building. The name of the police force changed in 1987 from the Special Police Force to the Library of Congress Police, becoming analogous in rank structure and pay with the U.S. Capitol Police.

The much-publicized thefts of manuscript material by the scholar Charles Merrill Mount in 1987 resulted in intensified security efforts—audits, reports, and enhanced technology. Librarian James H. Billington, taking office in 1987, pledged further scrutiny of the security of the Library's collections. His Management and Planning Committee (MAP) produced a 1988 report suggesting a number of improvements. An additional internal study on protecting the collections (1989) led to further collections security planning. In response to the Persian Gulf War, in January 1991, entrance inspections began—in addition to the existing exit inspections—for all visitors and readers, and Library staff members were required to wear identification badges visibly.

Despite improved security controls, in the early 1990s the Library discovered serious losses, including volumes gutted of their rare plates, volumes missing from the general collections, and thefts of rare maps and manuscripts. These losses led to numerous actions undertaken in 1992, which marked a watershed in collections security activities and planning. On March 30, 1992, Librarian Billington closed the stacks to the general public and shortly thereafter greatly reduced staff access to the stacks. Electronic theft detection gates were installed in April 1992.

Also in 1992, the Collections Security Oversight Committee (CSOC) was established, a Library-wide organization composed of security professionals, senior librarians, and support services managers charged with making recommendations for improving collections security and for overseeing their implementation. The CSOC's Plan for Enhancing Collections Security (October 1992) contained 46 initiatives for improving security in reading rooms and elsewhere, expanding electronic security systems, and strengthening the security of collections storage areas. Reader registration was implemented in 1996. Since its inception, the CSOC has continued to play an active and critical role in planning and implementing the Library's collections security program.

In the mid-1990s, the Library engaged outside experts and consultants to assess security and accepted recommendations to appoint a permanent director of security (1997); establish an Office of Security to centralize authority and responsibility within the Library's security structure (1997); develop a comprehensive security plan; define the threat to the collections; establish a priority order for protecting the collections; and expand security awareness. In addition, security improvements recommended in a 1996 comprehensive physical security survey of the Library were put in place.

In October 1997, the Library published the first Library of Congress Security Plan. Developed by the Office of Security and the CSOC working in close collaboration, the Plan provides the framework for security planning and budgeting Library-wide, and its actions are updated annually. The Security Plan defined the threat to the collections and focused on creating a planning framework of physical security controls to protect the Library's collections, and it also established parameters for the Library to protect its facilities, staff, visitors, and other assets.

The 1997 Security Plan categorized the Library's collections into a hierarchy of five risk levels, with the strongest protection accorded the Library's "Treasures" and other rare items and with lesser degrees of security controls for general and other collections. The Plan identified the four cycles that collections items go through in the Library: in process, in storage, in use, and in transit. Using the five risk levels and the four cycles, the plan established a priority order for baseline protection standards for each item category in each Library cycle. The Office of Security and the CSOC subsequently expanded the collections security planning framework to include a fifth cycle (on exhibit). In 1998 and 1999, the Library developed a preservation security framework, now integrated in the overall collections planning framework. The preservation controls address environment, emergency preparedness, storage, handling, needs assessment, physical treatment, and reformatting and are organized in a protection prioritization framework modeled on the physical security framework.

Three Library-wide initiatives in the late 1990s directly support the collections security planning framework: risk assessments, random sampling projects, and the Integrated Library System (ILS). In 1997, the Library began a multiyear program to conduct risk assessments within individual custodial and processing divisions. The findings of these risk assessments, conducted by an outside auditor, are integrated into the Security Plan to enhance controls within the divisions. In early 1999, the Library began to contract random sampling projects to provide the Library's first credible baselines of theft and mutilation to measure the effectiveness of security controls. Later in 1999, the ILS went into effect, significantly strengthening inventory controls by tracking incoming books and other materials at the item level.

As the Library's overall security program has expanded, so too has its security awareness program. The Office of Security and the CSOC have expanded publicity, with articles in the Library's weekly and quarterly publications and with creation of security Web sites for the public and staff (2001 and 2002, respectively). The Site Assistance Visit (SAV) program, launched in April 2002, focuses on reinforcing staff members' commitment to the Library's collections security program. Office of Security experts and senior librarians visit all the Library's divisions on a two-year cycle. The SAVs have had a noticeably positive impact, improving security practices while strengthening relationships between the Office of Security and the divisions visited.

A major undertaking for the Office of Security and the CSOC in expanding security awareness was collaboration on the Library's bicentennial symposium "To Preserve and Protect: The Strategic Stewardship of Cultural Resources," held at the Library in October 2000. The symposium attracted some 200 participants from the United States and abroad. The papers given by the 22 speakers—recognized scholars, experts, and professionals in the fields of preservation and security—were published by the Library in 2002.

In addition to the Library's ever-expanding collections security program, the Library has steadily improved its facilities security. The major security enhancements improve protection of the facilities, staff, visitors, and collections. Facilities security improvements were accelerated in 1995 under federal guidelines established after the Oklahoma City bombing. In 1998, the Library's security program intensified in the wake of the July 1998 shootings of two U.S. Capitol Police officers at the Capitol and the August 1998 U.S. embassy bombings in East Africa. Visitors were required to be screened with metal detectors beginning in August 1998 and with x-ray machines beginning in May 1999. Congress authorized additional emergency supplemental funding to upgrade security in the Capitol Complex.

The facilities upgrades are described in the 1999 Library of Congress Security Enhancement Implementation Plan. The plan, coordinated by the Office of Security, is a multiyear program of security upgrades to strengthen the Library's established minimum standards (as articulated in the October 1997 Library of Congress Security Plan) for police command and control, entry and perimeter security, and related law enforcement enhancements, including substantially increasing the size of the Library of Congress Police force. The enhancements at the Library are coordinated with the rest of the Capitol Complex to conform with the overall Capitol Complex security objectives.

The harrowing events of September 11, 2001, heightened security dramatically. Security planning already under way received new urgency and was expanded further. Congress approved an additional emergency supplemental appropriation to fund emergency communications, including construction of an Emergency Management Center for the Library. Full-entry security screening began in December 2001, so that staff members—like the public—are also required to be screened with magnetometers and x-ray machines. In January 2003, the Office of Security assumed the responsibility for oversight of emergency management and was renamed the Office of Security and Emergency Preparedness.

Integral to the Library's security program are the Personnel Security Office and the Office of Investigations within the Office of Security and Emergency Preparedness. The Personnel Security Office manages the Library's background investigations program to determine the suitability of employees, contractors and volunteers, and employee security clearance eligibility when appropriate. The Office of Investigations acts on allegations involving violations of law or regulations that affect Library programs and operations. Both offices help prevent or curtail insider and other threats to the collections.

As the Library of Congress enters its third century, it can point to a security program that continues to evolve with changing requirements and changing technology. New challenges include protecting digitized materials, for which the Library has developed a planning framework to protect digitized collections.

From the Library's 3,000 volumes in 1800 to some 125 million items more than 200 years later, from one room in the Capitol Building to a three-building complex on Capitol Hill and numerous other facilities, from locks and keys to sophisticated state-of-the-art electronic and other security controls, the Library offers some of the most advanced security anywhere. Protection ranges from internal collections management controls (reader registration, personal belongings restrictions, controlled service, marking and tagging, transit accountability, and reading room configuration) to external physical controls (entrance and exit electronic screening, intrusion detection systems, closed-circuit television, electronic access controls, theft-detection devices, vaults and cages, and key control). The Office of Security and Emergency Preparedness shares its collections security knowledge with other institutions and continues to provide leadership to U.S. and foreign libraries and comparable institutions on collections security planning.

As the nation's "library of last resort," the Library of Congress is committed to safeguarding its collections so that they will be available for the use of current and future generations. The Library shares with other U.S. public institutions the responsibility for protecting its facilities, staff, visitors, and other assets. In addition, the Library has the unique obligation of preserving and securing–for the present and future use of Congress and the nation–the largest, richest, and most diverse collections of recorded knowledge in the world. The Library, in cooperation with law enforcement agencies and book dealers around the globe, is able to bring all its resources to bear on those who would pose threats to the collections. Libraries, museums, and other cultural institutions continue to share information—the good and the bad—so that security controls can be improved and so that lost items can be found.

Today, George Washington's diary is well protected. Under the Library's collections security program, this "Treasure," and indeed all the Library's vast collections, is safeguarded to the highest extent possible, to ensure that the nation's heritage is protected as the Library enters the new millennium. (AM)

PUBLISHING AND PUBLICATIONS

Publishing at the Library of Congress began in 1801 with the Library's first booklist, which described 728 books and three maps acquired from a bookseller in London. Approximately 80 publications, mostly catalogs and annual reports, were issued before 1897, when the Library moved from the U.S. Capitol into its own building. In the twentieth century, the Library produced many thousands of publications, including cataloging manuals, technical bulletins, specialized bibliographies, pamphlets, serials, books in Braille, catalogs, indexes, union lists, descriptive guides, and scholarly monographs, most of which contain detailed information about the institution, its services, and its collections.

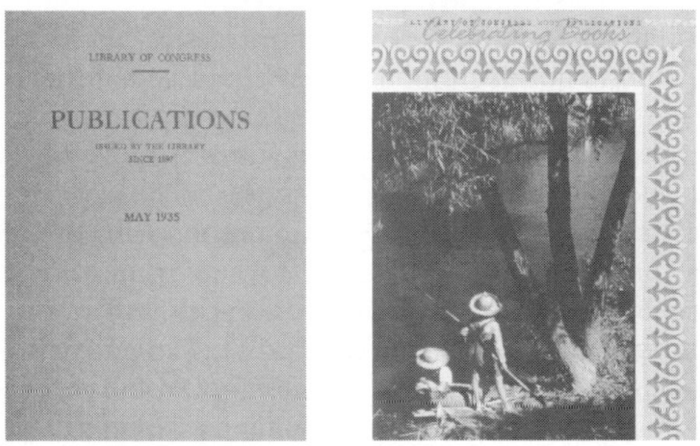

Two Library of Congress publication lists: a 1935 compilation of all the Library's publications since 1897, and the most recent list of titles produced by the Library's Publishing Office (2004).
LC/Publishing Office.

Since the administration of Librarian of Congress Herbert Putnam (1899–1939), the Library's publications have reflected the institution's gradual change, first from a legislative library into a national institution, and then into a complex government entity that serves many different constituencies nationally and worldwide. In the process, not surprisingly, publishing at the Library of Congress has become a decentralized and extremely diverse enterprise.

Putnam's extensive publishing program, inaugurated in 1900–1901, was a practical demonstration of his belief that the Library of Congress, as a national library, should actively serve other libraries. He outlined both his plan and his progress in his 1901 *Annual Report*. Notable achievements included the completion and publication of the first volume of a completely new classification scheme, based on the Library's own collections, and the sale and distribution of Library of Congress printed catalog cards. The decision to begin printing and distributing the Library's printed cards to other libraries—an enormous publishing project in itself—spelled the end of the printed book catalog in American libraries, at least for the next half century. Putnam established a branch of the Government Printing Office in the Library to print the cards. To justify his bold statement that "the publications of the Library since July 1, 1900, have been the most important within its history," he described four substantial new publications and pointed the way to future projects and publications. The new items were a 315-page *Union List of Periodicals, Transactions, and Allied Publications Currently Received in the Principal Libraries of the District of Columbia* (1901); a 293-page *Checklist of American Newspapers in the Library of Congress* (1901); the 1,137-page *A List of Maps of America in the Library of Congress* (1901); and a calendar of the George Washington manuscripts in the Library (1901), presented as an early example of Putnam's belief that the Library should aid historical research by publishing original source material about American history.

One of the Library's earliest and most significant historical publications appeared in 1904: the first volume of the *Journals of the Continental Congress 1774–1789*, edited from the original records in the Library by Worthington Chauncey Ford, Chief of the Manuscript Division. The edition eventually required 34 volumes, the last published in 1937. This was the first publication of the journals in full, supplemented by relevant original sources of the period. Another pioneering Library publication, *Guide to the Diplomatic History of the United States, 1775–1921* (1935) by Samuel Flagg Bemis and Grace Gardner Griffin, helped stimulate scholarly interest in America's role in world affairs, and proved so valuable that it was reprinted in 1951.

One of the few publishing projects that Putnam could not complete was a projected 12-volume *Contributions to American Library History* series that was to cover libraries and librarianship in America's regions and major cities. The only volume published was William Dawson Johnston's valuable 535-page *History of the Library of Congress, Volume I, 1800–1864* (1904).

In 1944, the Library announced a grant from the Rockefeller Foundation to support a series of books about the history and civilization of the United States "at the midpoint of the twentieth century." Published by Harvard University Press under the editorship of Ralph Henry Gabriel, the Library of Congress Series in American Civilization produced 11 volumes, each written by a prominent scholar. The final volume, *American Perspectives: The National Self-Image in the Twentieth Century*, a book of essays, was published in 1961. The great strength of the

Library's general collections was made abundantly clear by the publication of the 1,193-page *A Guide to the Study of The United States of America: Representative Books Reflecting the Development of American Life and Thought* (1960) and its 526-page supplement (1976).

Beginning with the 1980s, the computer revolution, cost restraints, and a new emphasis on national outreach services brought changes to the traditional, print-based publishing programs of the Library of Congress. In 1983, the Cataloging Distribution Service started producing and distributing its products on microfiche. The same year, searching for a new magazine with a broader readership, in 1983 the Library stopped publishing its *Quarterly Journal*, which had been produced since 1943 by the Government Printing Office. The 1980s also saw the first steps toward co-publishing books with university presses and trade publishers. In 1993, the Library obtained congressional approval to make an online version of its bibliographic data available on the Internet.

During the 1990s, publishing remained a vital—if rapidly changing—part of the Library's activities. An extensive Library-wide publishing survey completed in 1994 concluded that the institution's various departments and specialized divisions currently produced approximately 1,100 publications and that the combined annual cost of its different publishing programs was at least $12 million.

In 1994, Arundel Press/Arundel Antiquarian Books in Los Angeles, California organized "A Century of Library Publications, 1893–1993," a juried traveling exhibition featuring notable publications from major libraries during the previous century. Six Library of Congress publications were chosen for the exhibition, which was seen at major college and university libraries between 1994 and 1996. They were: *Report of the Librarian of Congress for the Fiscal Year 1901* (1901); *History of the Library of Congress, 1800–1864* (1904); *A List of Geographical Atlases in the Library of Congress* (nine volumes, 1909–1992); *Catalogue of the Library of Thomas Jefferson* (five volumes, 1952–1959); *The National Union Catalog* (1958–1983); and *The Printer & The Pardoner* (1986).

Private sector support for publishing at the Library of Congress increased dramatically in the mid-1990s. In October 1994, Librarian of Congress James H. Billington announced private gifts of $13 million to help the Library digitize its Americana collections, the beginning of a large-scale effort to make many of the Library's original historical documents, personal papers, films, maps, graphic materials, music, and photographs available in electronic form. Second, after several years of development, the first issue of *Civilization: The Magazine of the Library of Congress* was published. A bimonthly membership magazine for a general audience, *Civilization*—which ceased publication in 2000—was published under license by a partnership controlled by L.O.C. Management Corporation of New York.

While the Library's new online National Digital Library Project and the new magazine appeared in different media, each was a form of publishing that drew on the vast riches of the Library of Congress to illuminate both the past and the present. There are other similarities. Both were public-private partnerships that reached, at least by previous Library of Congress standards, huge general interest audiences. Both also were major efforts to adapt to the new fiscal and technological environment of the 1990s.

For the Library's publishing programs, the fiscal restraints of the 1990s meant a decline in the appropriated funds available for traditional, print-based publishing and a shrinking market for the technical publications and products (in all formats) produced primarily for the library market by the Cataloging Distribution Service. On the positive side, the computer revolution—from the MARC project of the late 1960s to the National Digital Library Project—gave the Library enormous opportunities for sharing its collections and the knowledge of its specialists with Congress, scholars, librarians, and people worldwide.

Increasing accessibility to the Library's collections through publishing remains the core of the Library's publishing efforts. Since the mid-1990s, publishing at the Library has been characterized by the development of new cooperative publishing partnerships, frequently with university presses or commercial houses, and a corresponding decline in reliance on the U.S. Government Printing Office. Today, the Library publishes trade titles based on its historical collections, topical reference books aimed at a general audience, and calendars. All of these products are "branded" with the Library's name and distributed nationally, and some internationally. Increasing accessibility to the Library's collections through publications remains the core of the mission of the Publishing Office.

Brief histories of the Library's principal print publications and the publishing activities of several different Library offices are presented below.

The Annual Report of the Librarian of Congress, 1866–

Librarian of Congress Ainsworth Rand Spofford (1864–1897) used the Library's first printed annual report in 1866 to argue the case for transforming the Library into "a great and truly national library," and his successors as Librarian often have used their reports for similar purposes. Until 1938, when the word "Annual" was permanently added, the

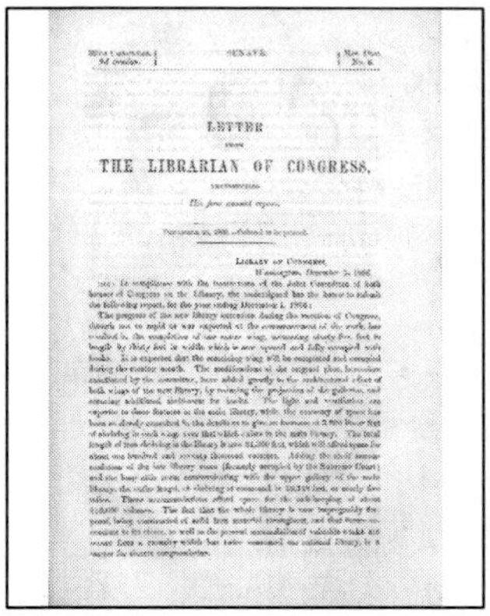

The first (1866) and latest (2003) Annual Reports of the Librarian of Congress. LC/Publishing Office.

publication was titled *Report of the Librarian of Congress*. The annual reports for the years 1897 through 1946 also are especially rich in historical materials. Three volumes are of special interest: Librarian Putnam's comprehensive "state of the art" 1901 report; the 1940 report of Librarian Archibald MacLeish, which describes MacLeish's objectives for the Library and his impending reorganization; and the 1946 report of Librarian Luther Evans, which includes a sweeping budget request and justification for the Library's expansion and David C. Mearns's delightful history of the Library's national role, *The Story Up To Now: A Brief History of the Library of Congress*.

The Library of Congress Information Bulletin, 1943– and *The Gazette*, 1990–

Under Librarian MacLeish's leadership, the Library published the first issue of its *Information Bulletin* in July 1943. A monthly publication, it combined and superseded the *Staff Information Bulletin* and the *Monthly Public Information Bulletin*, both started by MacLeish in 1942. From 1943 to 1990, the *Bulletin* contained news for the public and staff news in various combinations. In 1990, Librarian James H. Billington established a separate weekly publication, *The Gazette*, for staff news, and changed the *Information Bulletin* to a biweekly that described the Library's activities and collections for an outside audience. The *Bulletin* became a monthly publication in July 1997.

The Quarterly Journal of the Library of Congress, 1943–1983

Created by Librarian MacLeish under the title *The Library of Congress Quarterly Journal of Current Acquisitions*, this publication featured articles about the Library's collections and its current acquisitions written by the Library's specialists. The first issue, reporting acquisitions from July to September

Issues of The Quarterly Journal of the Library of Congress *(1943–1983)*. LC/Publishing Office.

1943, was edited by poetry consultant Allen Tate, who remained editor for one year until he was succeeded by Robert Penn Warren, poetry consultant for 1944–1945. In 1964, the name was changed to *The Quarterly Journal of the Library of Congress*, and acquisitions reports began to be published in a separate series in 1979. The Winter 1979 issue of *The Quarterly Journal* contains a brief history by its editor, Frederick Mohr. *The Quarterly Journal* ceased publication in 1983 during the administration of Librarian Daniel J. Boorstin who began to negotiate with groups outside the Library to publish a commercially produced magazine that would reach a general audience. Negotiations with the private sector for a new magazine, however, did not succeed until the administration of Librarian Billington.

Civilization: The Magazine of the Library of Congress, 1994–2000

An independent bimonthly magazine published under a licensing agreement with the Library, *Civilization: The Magazine of the Library of Congress* was a significant publishing departure for the Library of Congress. A commercial venture inspired by the Library and its collections, it was not an official Library publication.

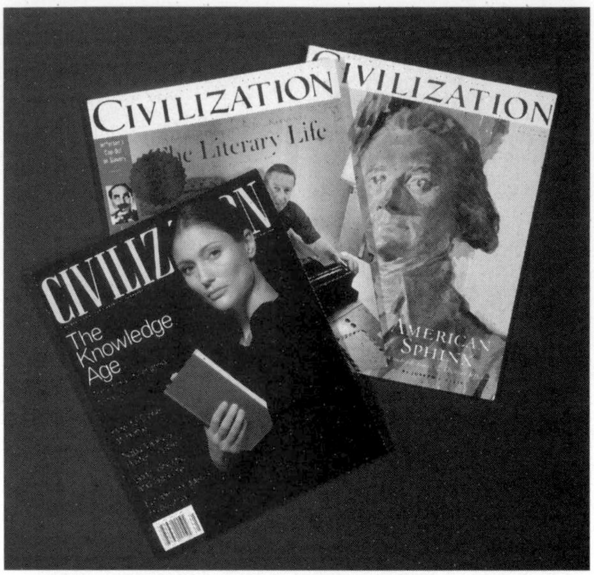

A selection of issues of Civilization: The Magazine of the Library of Congress *(1994–2000).* LC/Publishing Office.

The premiere issue was dated November–December 1994. The magazine won the 1996 National Magazine Award, and paid circulation eventually reached approximately 250,000. However in 1997, the group of private investors formed to publish *Civilization* (L.O.C. Management Corporation) sold it to Worth Media, which changed its emphasis and soon encountered a decline in circulation and advertising revenues. In 2000, the Library's agreement with Worth Media was terminated. In a letter to subscribers, Librarian Billington expressed his regret that the arrangement had come to an end, "because it did give the Library a chance to reach out to a national audience in a way that we could not do on our own."

Congressional Research Service

A list of books about banking and finance compiled and published in 1892 by Librarian Spofford set a precedent of published bibliographies and research papers for Congress that continues to this day under the jurisdiction of the Library's Congressional Research Service (CRS). Prior to the creation in 1914 of CRS's predecessor, the Legislative Reference Service, the Library's Division of Bibliography provided Congress with timely bibliographies on topics such as Hawaii (1898), Cuba (1898), interoceanic canals and railway routes (1900), child labor (1906), income tax (1907), and natural resources (1912). Occasionally, the Library has published reference books based primarily on CRS activities, for example *Respectfully Quoted: A Dictionary of Quotations Requested from the Congressional Research Service* (1989). Today, two of the Congressional Research Service's major publications are available to the public: *The Digest of Public General Bills* and *The U.S. Constitution Annotated.*

The Publishing Office: Scholarly Publications, Collection Guides, and General Books

Librarian Putnam established the policy of sharing the Library's unparalleled resources through publishing. Today, this goal is aggressively pursued through both print and electronic publishing by Librarian of Congress James H. Billington. Publication of most of the scholarly books, exhibition catalogs, and collection guides is the responsibility of the Library's Publishing Office, which also develops and produces books, calendars, and other products aimed at a general audience. Publications are produced using appropriated funds, gift funds, and

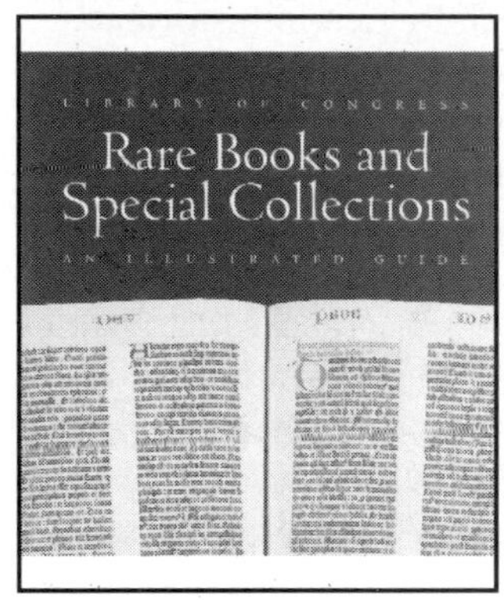

In 1992, the Library launched two new publication series: illustrated guides to specialized research collections and resource guides to subjects in which the Library's holdings were especially strong and wide-ranging. LC/Publishing Office.

increasingly through cooperative arrangements with commercial publishers. A colorful new series of illustrated guides to the collections, supported by gift funds and aimed at a general audience, was launched in 1992 with the publication of *Rare Books and Special Collections: An Illustrated Guide.* A second series of guides, this one for resources found throughout the collections of the Library for the study of a specific subject, began the same year with the publication of *The Largest Event: A Library of Congress Resource Guide for the Study of World War II* (1994). A handsome series of large format and scholarly exhibition catalogs first appeared in 1993 with the publication of *Rome Reborn: The Vatican Library and Renaissance Culture*, a volume co-published with Yale University Press. In 1997, the Library released a major trade title, *Eyes of the Nation: A Visual History of the United States.*

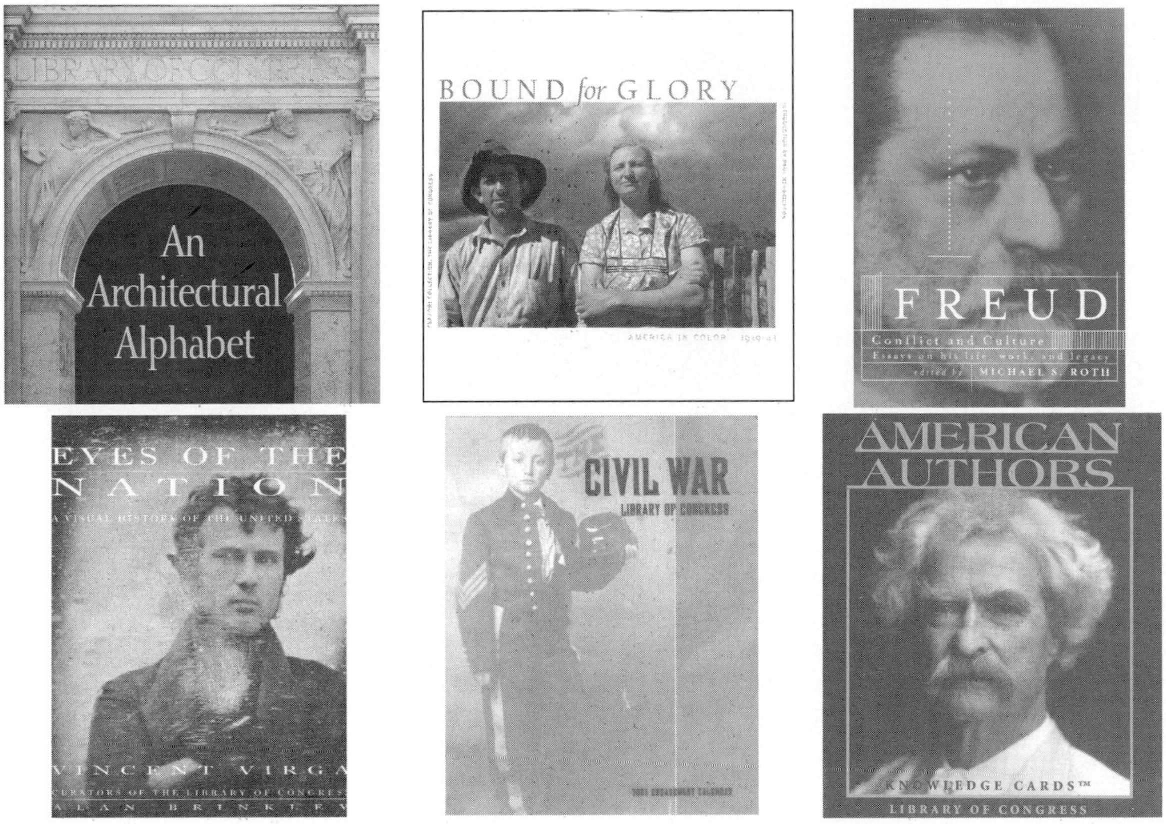

The Publishing Office produces a variety of general titles as well as calendars and knowledge cards.
LC/Publishing Office.

As the Publishing Office's collection guide and exhibit catalog series indicate, the Library of Congress will continue to use print publishing as an important means of reaching and developing a wider audience for its collections and services. However, new technologies for electronic publishing—interactive CD-ROM and optical disk products, online search and retrieval systems, and electronic dissemination of publications using the Internet—are rapidly changing the concept of publishing both inside and outside the Library. The Cataloging Distribution Service and the American Memory Project have created successful CD-ROM products for professional librarians as well as for targeted public use. The digitized information in some of these products is now being designed for distribution over the Internet via the National Digital Library Program. More than 50 major Library of Congress exhibits also are available on the Internet, and the Publishing Office is now making use of some of the content from the exhibition catalogs that are part of these electronic exhibits. (JYC)

Cole, John Y. "Publishing at the Library of Congress: A Brief History," *Publishing Research Quarterly* 12 (Summer 1996): 38–49.

"List of Publications of the Library of Congress, 1800–1901," *Report of the Librarian of Congress for the Fiscal Year Ending June 30, 1901*. Washington, D.C.: Government Printing Office, 1901, pp. 362–367.

PUTNAM, HERBERT (1861–1955)

George Herbert Putnam, Librarian of the Minneapolis Athenaeum (1884–1887), the Minneapolis Public Library (1887–1891), and the Boston Public Library (1895–1899) and Librarian of Congress (1899–1939), was a leading figure of the American library movement. He was the first experienced librarian to hold the post of Librarian of

Herbert Putnam served as Librarian of Congress for 40 years, from 1899 to 1939—longer than any other Librarian. He established and defined the Library's pattern of national services to its major constituencies—Congress, other libraries, and the world of scholarship.

LC/Prints and Photographs Division. LC-USZ62-6012A.

Congress. His major contribution to the Library came directly from his previous experience: he linked the Library's policies firmly with the broader interests of American librarianship. To do so, he sought and obtained the support of the U.S. Congress, professional librarians, and especially the American Library Association (ALA) and the American scholarly community. As a result, Putnam established and defined the Library's pattern of national library services to its major constituencies—the Congress, the nation's libraries, and the world of scholarship.

Putnam was born in New York City on September 20, 1861, the 10th child of Victorine Putnam and George Palmer Putnam, the founder of the Putnam publishing house. Herbert attended private schools and received his bachelor's degree from Harvard in 1883, graduating magna cum laude. The next year he attended Columbia University Law School, but he was soon enticed by friends to become head of the library of the Minneapolis Athenaeum. Simultaneously he pursued his legal studies and was admitted to the Minnesota bar. On October 5, 1886, he married Charlotte Elizabeth Monroe of Cambridge, Massachusetts. They had two daughters, Shirley and Brenda.

In 1887, Herbert Putnam became Librarian of the new Minneapolis Public Library, which had absorbed the Athenaeum. After vigorously leading the library through its fledgling years, Putnam resigned in 1891 and returned to Massachusetts to be near his wife's ailing mother. He practiced law until he was persuaded to return to librarianship as Superintendent of the Boston Public Library, the nation's largest public library. He assumed his duties in February 1895.

Putnam's leadership abilities and his new position quickly involved him in the activities of the American Library Association. In late 1896, the Congressional Joint Committee on the Library held hearings on the "condition" of the Library on the eve of its move into its new building, and Putnam was one of the six ALA witnesses. He and Melvil Dewey were the dominant witnesses, and each advocated an expanded national role for the Library—a role that extended far beyond the concept or accomplishments of Ainsworth Rand Spofford, who had served as Librarian since 1864.

The 1896 hearings marked a turning point in relations between the Library and the American library movement. For the first time, the ALA offered advice to Congress, albeit cautiously, about the Library's purpose and functions. Moreover, Congress listened, and a restructuring and expansion of the Library became effective on July 1, 1897. On the same day, a new Librarian of Congress took office: John Russell Young, a journalist and former diplomat, had been nominated by President William McKinley and confirmed by the U.S. Senate.

Young presided over the move of the collection from the Capitol into the new building, which opened to public acclaim on November 1, 1897. The new Librarian's major concerns were organizational, particularly the hiring of a staff that had increased from 42 to 108. Never a healthy man, Young did not recover from two severe falls during the winter of 1898–1899, and he died on January 17, 1899. This time, the ALA took the lead in recommending candidates for Librarian of Congress to President McKinley. Boston librarian Putnam was its candidate and it appears that ALA President William Coolidge

Lane not only persuaded McKinley to make the nomination but that Lane and his colleagues, in the end, also persuaded Putnam to take the job. He was appointed as eighth Librarian of Congress on March 13, 1899, during the congressional recess, took the oath of office on April 5, and was confirmed by the U.S. Senate on December 12, 1899.

As Librarian of Congress, Putnam moved quickly to expand the Library into the type of national library he advocated in his 1896 testimony before the Joint Committee on the Library. Service to other libraries was a key component. He continued the development of a new classification scheme, which was soon shared with the rest of the nation, started the sale and distribution of printed catalog cards, interlibrary loan, and a national union catalog. In an appendix to his 1901 *Annual Report*, he described the organization and collections of the Library in a "manual" that came to be regarded as a model of contemporary library practice.

Other Putnam accomplishments during the first two decades of his librarianship included obtaining the support of President Theodore Roosevelt for the expansion of the Library's activities, most dramatically through an executive order transferring presidential and other state papers to the Library; revision of the 1870 Copyright Law in 1909; the acquisition, in 1907, of important collections of Russian and Japanese books, establishing the foundations of the Library's Slavic and Asian collections; and direction of the ALA's Library War Service Committee (1917–1919), which was a model of efficiency and a triumph of American librarianship.

Librarian Putnam with young readers in the Main Reading Room of the Library of Congress about 1910.
LC/Prints and Photographs Division. LC-USZ62-4541.

During the first half of Putnam's administration, lasting roughly through World War I, the Librarian had, by and large, the full support of professional librarians and the ALA. The next 20 years were not so harmonious, and the Library and the American library community drifted apart.

One reason was that Putnam gave increasing attention to matters that did not directly concern the library community. A separate Legislative Reference Service was created in 1914. In 1921, the Declaration of Independence and the Constitution of the United States were transferred from the State Department to the Library enhancing the image of the Library as a symbol of American democracy. Through Putnam's efforts in the 1920s, the Library became a national patron of the arts; a gift from Elizabeth Sprague Coolidge provided an auditorium for the performance of chamber music, and a generous endowment from Mrs. Coolidge shortly thereafter led to the creation in

Putnam at his desk in the Jefferson Building early in his career as the eighth Librarian of Congress. This richly decorated office is still used for ceremonial purposes.
LC/Prints and Photographs Division. LC-BH833332.

1925 of the Library of Congress Trust Fund Board, an instrument that enabled the Library, for the first time, to accept, hold, and invest gifts and bequests.

Furthermore, Putnam's personal interest in library cooperation and related technical matters diminished as he became concerned about the "interpretation" of the collections. He had always viewed the use of the Library's collections as the prime object of his administration; in the 1896 hearings, for example, he described the national library as, ideally, the library "which stands foremost as a model and example of assisting forward the work of scholarship in the United States." After the creation of the Library of Congress Trust Fund Board, he began to obtain private funds to support "chairs" and consultantships for subject specialists who could both advance scholarship through their own work and assist others in the use of the collections.

As he focused on other activities, Putnam's interest in the role of the Library of Congress as a leader among American libraries lessened. His authoritarian style presented further difficulties. He was a stern administrator, both venerated and feared. Apparently no associate ever called him by his first name, and it appears that there was no one, inside or outside the Library, who was able to influence him to any significant degree.

By the mid-1930s, the Library was suffering from administrative stagnation, intensified by low staff salaries and morale and operational problems such as a large cataloging and card-printing backlog. These problems were compounded by Putnam's refusal, or inability, to delegate responsibility. By 1939, there were 35 divisions, each reporting directly to the Librarian, compared with the 16 listed in his 1901 *Annual Report*. Even Putnam, a talented administrator, could not successfully oversee 35 diverse units and 1,100 employees. By the late 1930s, there were many librarians and politicians who were waiting for him to decide to retire. Apparently even President Franklin D. Roosevelt chose to wait.

Such difficulties aside, Herbert Putnam was enormously respected by scholars and librarians alike. When he did decide to retire to become, on October 1, 1939, Librarian Emeritus of Congress, the American Library Association paid him tribute as "dean of our profession" who had led the Library of Congress to "its present proud position as the world's largest bibliographical institution." He continued to contribute to the Library, keeping regular office hours for the next 15 years. He died at Woods Hole, Massachusetts, on August 14, 1955.

Herbert Putnam wrote no memoirs; his 40 substantial annual reports between 1899 and 1939 record his achievements at the Library of Congress and serve, as he intended, as his "autobiography." (JYC)

Herbert Putnam, 1861–1955, A Memorial Tribute. Washington, D.C.: Library of Congress, 1956.

Rosenberg, Jane Aikin. *The Nation's Great Library: Herbert Putnam and the Library of Congress, 1899–1939.* Urbana, Ill.: University of Illinois Press, 1993.

RARE BOOK AND SPECIAL COLLECTIONS DIVISION AND COLLECTIONS

Administrative History

As an administrative unit, the Library's Rare Book and Special Collections Division is relatively young—it was established in 1927. However, the Library of Congress's rare book collections and its interest in rare materials date back to the nineteenth century. The collections developed gradually.

Reading Room of the Rare Book and Special Collections Division in the Library's Jefferson Building. Photograph: LC/Reid Baker.

Jefferson's library of 6,487 volumes contained no fifteenth century books; his interest was primarily in modern and scholarly editions, especially those he could find in "handy formats." In 1836, the U.S. Senate narrowly rejected the purchase of a collection that would have put the Library in the forefront of North American research institutions, the 25,000-volume personal library of Dimitrii Buturlin of Florence, an Italian count whose collection was rich in incunabula and early printed books. In 1840, bookseller Obidiah Rich presented to the Library of Congress, one of his customers, a book printed in 1478, and it is the earliest book with a recorded acquisition date.

Ainsworth Rand Spofford, Librarian of Congress from 1864 until 1897, was a former Cincinnati bookseller and knowledgeable about the antiquarian book trade. As he built the Library of Congress, then located in the U.S. Capitol Building, into a national institution, he developed the foundations of the Library's rare book and specialized research collections. Three collections stand out: the 40,000-volume Smithsonian Institution collection (1866), which included about 60 fifteenth-century books; Peter Force's collection of approximately 60,000 books and pamphlets (1867), especially strong in Americana and also containing 161 early books; and Joseph M. Toner's 40,000-item collection of American history and medicine (1882). Many of the Library's early treasures were separated from their larger collections and kept by Spofford under lock and key in his office in the Capitol. Such items were listed as "Office" in the Library's catalogs.

Spofford's centralization in 1870 of U.S. copyright registration and deposit activities at the Library created a strong base for future special collections. The flood of copyright deposits—maps, music, prints, and photographs as well as books—made a separate Library building necessary. In a special report in 1895 on the eve of the move into the new building, Librarian Spofford recommended the creation of a department of printed books as one of the several Library departments, but no special administrative department for rare books.

He did advocate, however, that the rare books be kept separately from the other collections. On September 13, 1897, after having been replaced as Librarian of Congress two months earlier by John Russell Young, Assistant Librarian Spofford recommended to Young that rare printed books not be placed in the custody of the newly created Manuscript Department. He pointed out that "in all great National Libraries," manuscripts were separated from rare books. In his view, the "department of rare books and Americana should be in direct charge of the one in the Library who knows their pecuniary and comparative and intrinsic value, and who also could discriminate from the great mass for special care and treatment." The rare book collection, he felt, should consist primarily of early Americana, incunabula, and first or very rare editions of notable writers.

Spofford prevailed, and in 1897 the Library's rare books were housed in a separate room on the east side of the second floor in the new building; they were served to readers through the Main Reading Room. In 1910, the books were moved to special stack space in the north curtain. Two other early "special collections," Jefferson's library and the Toner Collection, also were housed in "locked-off" stack space and available through the Main Reading Room.

In 1906, Librarian of Congress Herbert Putnam expanded the Library's rare book collection beyond Americana when he placed 4,000 rare Russian books in the collection. They were purchased for the Library as part of the 80,000-volume Russian literature collection of G.V. Yudin. In 1925, the Library received the John Boyd Thacher Collection consisting of rare examples of early printing, autographs of notable Europeans, and a sizable gathering of material on the French Revolution. The momentum continued with gifts and bequests and, in 1926, with the publication of a desiderata list, *The Library of Congress: Some Notable Items That It Has, Some Examples of Many Others That It Needs*. In this 113-page booklet, which marked a new aggressiveness on the part of the Library in soliciting acquisitions, Librarian Putnam said that he hoped "collectors who have had the relish of collecting, and a sufficient satisfaction in the possession, may come to consider the permanent disposition of their collections and may turn to the National Library as inevitably as the British collector turns to the British Museum."

By 1927, the collection was large enough to warrant its own quarters, which were established on Deck 37 in a new bookstack in the former northeast courtyard. The "Office" books were transferred into small rooms in the central section of the deck, and a separate reading room was established in an adjacent area. The new Rare Book Room, with its collection of approximately 30,000 volumes, opened for business in July 1927. Putnam also appointed the Library's first rare book curator, V. Valta Parma, who systematically combed the Library's general collections for candidates for the rare book collections.

In 1930, the Library attracted attention in the rare book world with the purchase, through a special congressional appropriation of $1.5 million, of the 3,000-volume Vollbehr Collection fifteenth century books. Moreover, included in the purchase was a copy of the Gutenberg Bible printed on vellum—one of three perfect copies. The Vollbehr purchase forced a new consideration of rare books at the Library of Congress; the Rare Book Room as it then existed was unable to handle such a large and valuable collection. A new room was needed, and it was included in an addition to the east side of the Library, begun in 1932. It provided a second story reading room and shelving area for the rapidly growing collection of rare books, and much needed space for catalogs near the Main Reading Room on the first floor, plus bookshelves for the general collections, and study facilities for visiting researchers.

When it opened in June 1934, the new Rare Book Reading Room was recognized as one of the most beautiful rooms in the Library of Congress. Its elegant Georgian simplicity is in striking contrast to the ornate architecture of the Jefferson Building itself, which was completed in 1897. Considering the strong holdings of the division in early American history, it is fitting that many of the reading room's architectural details were inspired by rooms in Philadelphia's Independence Hall, a building that played such a prominent role in the formation of the nation. The designs of the three panels on each of the two massive bronze doors at the entrance are symbolic testimonies to the importance of the history of printing to civilization.

With the Vollbehr purchase, the collection now numbered approximately 60,000 volumes. In February 1939, the Rare Book Collection became a separate administrative unit, no longer part of the Reading Rooms Division. It was placed under the administrative supervision of the director of the Reference Department.

Archibald MacLeish became Librarian of Congress in July 1939. On April 1, 1940, he appointed Arthur A. Houghton Jr., "one of the most distinguished American collectors of rare books," to replace Parma as the Library's rare book curator. Houghton brought his assistant, Frederick R. Goff, with him to the Library. Goff became acting division chief in 1941 and Houghton, by then only working part-time as curator, resigned in March 1942. By then the collections had grown to 127,000 volumes.

In 1943, MacLeish asked Lawrence Wroth, librarian of the John Carter Brown Library, to help give direction to the Library's rare book acquisitions and activities. In his report, Wroth urged a broad view, one that would move the Rare Book Collection in a more scholarly direction. For example, the Library should choose rare books "without regard to form" and in anticipation of possible future trends of scholarly interest. Particular attention, he felt, should be paid to Americana before 1860 and to "the history of ideas," for example significant books in the development of literature and the fine arts, science, economics, politics, and industry." But in addition to individual rarities, emphasis also should be placed on developing "special collections" in these and other subjects. Writing in the middle of World War II, Wroth also recommended that the Library build book collections about Russia, the Pacific, and eastern Asia. In his *Annual Report* for fiscal year 1945, MacLeish noted that Wroth's "many recommendations for carrying out the policy for collecting rare books" had been accepted by the Library's administration.

In 1943, the Library announced the gift of one of its most magnificent acquisitions, the Lessing J. Rosenwald Collection of illustrated books. It contained approximately 500 volumes in 1943, but the final total, after Rosenwald's death in 1979, came to 2,653 books and 588 incunabules. On March 25, 1944, the Rare Book Collection became a full-fledged division as part of the Public Reference Service in the newly reorganized Reference Department. On March 1, 1945, acting chief Frederick R. Goff, who was working closely with Lessing J. Rosenwald, became chief of the new Rare Book Division.

Frederick R. Goff retired on June 30, 1972. Additional collection highlights during his long and fruitful career as division chief included: the publication

Between 1943 and 1979, Lessing J. Rosenwald (1891–1979) gave the Library more than 2,600 rare illustrated books. It is the most valuable collection ever donated to the Library by a single individual. LC/Prints and Photographs Division. LC-USP6-4884.

of a bibliographical reconstruction of the library of Thomas Jefferson by Millicent Sowerby, culminating a project begun in 1942; the acquisition of the Alfred Whital Stern Collection of Lincolniana in 1951; Lessing J. Rosenwald's 1952 donation to the Library, as a "gift to the nation," of the Giant Bible of Mainz; the publication of Goff's census of fifteenth century books, *Incunabula in American Libraries* (1964); and the acquisition, in 1966, of a copy of the famed *Bay Psalm Book* of 1640, the first extant book known to

Frederick R. Goff was acting chief of the Rare Book Division from 1941 to 1945. He was promoted to chief in 1945 and headed the division until 1972. This photograph was taken on March 27, 1950. LC/Prints and Photographs Division. LC-USP6-1314C.

be published in English-speaking America.

Goff's successor in 1972 was William Matheson, former head of rare books and special collections at Washington University in St. Louis. His achievements included a considerable expansion of the division's staff and greatly strengthening its modern American and British literature, fine printing, and private press collections. He also stressed the development of scholarly specialized collections; in 1975, the Rare Book Division was renamed the Rare Book and Special Collections Division. In the same year, with the Library's Center for the Book, he organized a significant symposium and publication, *The Early Illustrated Book: Essays in Honor of Lessing J. Rosenwald,* ed. by Sandra Hindman (1982).

Matheson retired in 1987, and in 1989, Larry Sullivan became the division's fifth chief. In 1991, Sullivan helped organize the Library's commemoration of Lessing J. Rosenwald's birth. A major element was the dedication in September 1991 of a Memorial Room, which was designed to replicate in some ways Rosenwald's book room at the Alverthorpe Gallery near Philadelphia. Sullivan also supervised the development of *Rare Book and Special Collections* (1992), the first in a series of illustrated guides to the Library's collections. Sullivan left in 1995, and in 1998 Mark Dimunation, formerly curator of rare books and exhibitions at Cornell University, was named to the post. One of his first undertakings was the development of a project for the Library's forthcoming bicentennial that would reconstruct Thomas Jefferson's original library, which is part of the collections of the Rare Book and Special Collections Division.

Since the late 1990s, the Rare Book and Special Collections Division has played an increasingly active role in identifying and organizing materials from its collections for digitization as part of the Library's National Digital Library. Three of the earliest digital files were composed of images and texts from the Alfred Whital Stern Collection of Lincolniana, and collections of American song sheets and printed ephemera. Since then, the division has contributed significantly to more than a dozen American Memory collections as varied as *African American Perspectives: Pamphlets from the Daniel A.P. Murray Collection, 1818–1900*; *The Evolution of the Conservation Movement, 1850–1920*; *Documents from the Continental Congress and the Constitutional Convention, 1774–1789*; and *Slaves and the Courts, 1740–1860*.

In 1999, the division began a project with the Octavo Corporation in Oakland, California, to produce high-quality, low-cost CD-ROMs of individual titles from the Rosenwald Collection. In 2003, the division and Octavo announced the completion of the digitization of the Library's copy of the Gutenberg Bible, which became available on a two-CD facsimile. (JYC)

The Collections

Today, the division's collections number approximately 800,000 books, broadsides, pamphlets, theater playbills, title pages, prints, posters, photographs, and medieval and Renaissance manuscripts. Although the materials in the collections have come into its custody for a variety of reasons—their monetary value, their importance in the history of printing; or their binding, association interest, or fragility—they have one point in common: they provide scholarly and often unique documentation about the traditions of life and learning in Western civilization and especially in the United States of America.

A broadside advertising an award of $100,000 for the capture of John Wilkes Booth, murderer of President Abraham Lincoln, is one of many thousands of items that make up the Library's unparalleled collections about the American Civil War. LC/Rare Book and Special Collections Division. LC-USZ62-11193.

The division's holdings encompass nearly all eras and subjects, and contain a multitude of strengths. The collection of nearly 5,700 incunabula (fifteenth century imprints) is the richest such grouping in the Western Hemisphere. The Americana collections date from a letter by Columbus (1493) to the present and include more than 16,000 imprints from 1640 to 1800; extensive holdings of Western Americana; publications of the Confederate States of America; and thousands of nineteenth century pamphlets.

The division maintains more than 100 separate, specialized collections. The examples that follow are grouped by category.

<u>Personal Libraries</u>:

Thomas Jefferson (2,375 titles). Thomas Jefferson's personal library, which was purchased by Congress in 1815.

Woodrow Wilson (9,186 items). Books and personal mementos from Woodrow Wilson's personal library.

Theodore Roosevelt (254 titles). Roosevelt family books on hunting, natural history, and exploration.

Susan B. Anthony (272 titles). The personal library of Susan B. Anthony, which contains inscribed and autographed volumes of feminist and anti-slavery literature.

Oliver Wendell Holmes (12,126 items). The Holmes family library.

Frederic W. Goudy (2,499 items). The personal library, papers, and publications of type designer Frederic W. Goudy.

Harry Houdini (10,355 items). Publications, scrapbooks, and other materials relating to spiritualism and magic from the library of Harry Houdini.

<u>Comprehensive Author Collections</u>

Early editions of the works of Walt Whitman (516 titles), Henry James (132 titles), and Sigmund Freud (187 titles); the Rudyard Kipling Collection (5,089 items), consisting of early editions of Kipling's works, manuscripts, notebooks, photographs, and memorabilia from the Carpenter, Chandler, and Colt estates; and the Benjamin Franklin Collection (850 titles), consisting of publications written, printed, edited, or published by Franklin.

<u>Subject Collections—A Selection</u>

African-American History. The African-American Pamphlet Collection, consisting of 274 nineteenth century pamphlets (some by African authors) relating to issues such as slavery, Reconstruction, colonization, and emigration to Liberia; the Daniel Murray Pamphlet Collection, consisting of 384 pamphlets on all aspects of African-American life, primarily from the second half of the nineteenth century.

Magic. The McManus-Young Collection of 673 items, consisting of publications, scrapbooks, and paraphernalia relating to magic and slight of hand.

Gastronomy. The Katherine Golden Bitting Collection of 4,346 titles, including publications and manuscripts on gastronomy from the fifteenth to twentieth centuries; the Elizabeth Robins Pennell Collection of 732 cookbooks.

Radical Literature. The Radical Pamphlets Collection of 2,000 pamphlets, broadsides, and memorabilia concerning American communism, anarchism, and socialism, 1870–1980 (especially 1930–1949); the Anarchism Collection of 341 books relating to the study of anarchy between 1850 and 1970.

Aeronautics. The Baston and Albert Tissandier Collection of 1,800 publications relating to aeronautics.

Papermaking. The Harrison Elliott Collection of 4,500 specimens, personal papers, and research materials relating to the history of papermaking.

Russian History and Literature. The Yudin Collection, consisting of 4,173 titles relating to eighteenth and nineteenth century Russian history, bibliography, and literature.

Sir Francis Drake. The Hans P. and Hanni Kraus Collection of 60 items, including early books, manuscripts, maps, and memorabilia related to the explorations of Sir Francis Drake.

Abraham Lincoln. Alfred Whital Stern Collection of Lincolniana, an 11,100-item collection of publications, manuscripts, prints, and other material relating to Lincoln; 64 publications presented to the Library by Lincoln's descendants.

Woman's Suffrage. National American Woman Suffrage Association Collection, consisting of 575 book relating to the women's suffrage movement from the library of Carrie Chapman Catt, president of the National Woman Suffrage Association.

Collections with Unusual Provenance. The Russian Imperial Collection of 2,600 books from the libraries of the Russian imperial family; the Third Reich Collection, consisting of photographs and 1,019 books from the libraries of Nazi leaders.

Generic Collections—A Selection

American Almanacs; American Children's Books; Armed Services Editions, an archival set of 1,319 paperback titles published for the American armed forces, 1943–1947; American children's books; Bibles; Big Little Books, 534 titles of popular children's books from the mid-twentieth century; Broadsides; Broadside songs (a 4,525-item collection of nineteenth-century musical lyrics in English); congressional speech collection, consisting of 3,750 speeches delivered by members of Congress between 1825 and 1940; Dell paperback collection, an archival set of 6,501 titles published from the 1930s to the 1970s; Documents of the First Fourteen Congresses, consisting of 12,922 titles, 1789–1817, consisting of 12,922 titles; Dime Novels, 40,000 titles of popular paperback fiction from the nineteenth century to the early twentieth century; Manuscript Plays, consisting of more than 3,000 typescripts of American plays submitted for copyright deposit in the nineteenth and twentieth centuries; Medieval and Renaissance Manuscripts; Miniature Books; National Endowment for the Arts Small Press Collection; Pulp Fiction Collection; the Theater Playbills Collection, consisting of 3,253 nineteenth-century, English-language playbills; and the World War II Propaganda Collection. (JYC)

One of the unusual items came to the Library in 1999 with the Marian S. Carson Collection is this "peepshow book," published in London in the 1840s. Photograph: Edward Owen. LC/Rare Book and Special Collections Division.

Evans, Clark. "Librarian in Disguise: V. Valta Parma and the Development of Popular Culture Collections at the Library of Congress," *Pioneers, Passionate Ladies, and Private Eyes*. N.Y.; Haworth Press, 1996, pp. 23–38.

Library of Congress Rare Books and Special Collections: An Illustrated Guide. Introduction by Larry E. Sullivan. Washington, D.C.: Library of Congress, 1992.

Matheson, William. "Seeking the Rare, the Important, the Valuable: The Rare Book Division," *The Quarterly Journal of the Library of Congress* 30 (July 1973): 211–227.

Van Wingen, Peter M. "The Incunabula Collections at the Library of Congress," *Rare Books & Manuscripts Librarianship* 4 (Fall 1989): 85–100.

The Vollbehr Collection

On December 3, 1929, Representative Ross Collins (D-Mississippi) proposed to the House of

Representatives that Congress acquire for $1.5 million the 3,000-volume collection of fifteenth-century books assembled by Otto H. F. Vollbehr. Vollbehr had acquired the collection after World War I, investing nearly his entire fortune in rare books as owners sold them to recoup war losses. He exhibited the books in Chicago, New York, and at the Library of Congress in 1926, hoping that an American philanthropist would present them to a U.S. library. At that time, he gave two other collections—one of printers' marks, the other of woodcuts—to the Library of Congress. When no buyer appeared, in November 1929 he announced that he would auction the collection the following spring. At that point, Collins introduced his bill.

Despite the collapse of the stock market in October 1929, Congress remained optimistic that the American commercial establishment would speedily recover, and members seemed receptive when on February 7, 1930, Collins addressed the House, reminding them of the many times that Congress had failed to take advantage of important opportunities to build the Library's collections. The Vollbehr Collection, he emphasized, was a "well-balanced library of the fifteenth century; a cross section of the thought and culture of the people of that period, a history of those times, the great Renaissance, the period contemporaneous with the discovery of America and with the beginning of the Reformation." The richness of the collection became evident as he described its contents: books of Aesop, Aristophanes, Cicero, Euripides, Herodotus, Homer, Horace, Livy, Ovid, Plutarch, Seneca, and Virgil; the humanists Dante, Petrarch, Boccaccio, and Erasmus; the scientists Albertus Magnus, Galen, Hippocrates, Ptolemy, Strabo, and Alfonso X of Spain; and the great religious figures Aquinas, St. Augustine, Savonarola, Duns Scotus, and Pliny. He noted that "knowledge is the best asset in peace and war, and educated nations are the only formidable ones in commerce and warfare," and concluded that the purchase provided a unique opportunity to honor Herbert Putnam's 30 years of service as Librarian. Moreover, he even proposed that the collection be named for Putnam.

The House Committee on the Library held hearings on March 10. Experts on fifteenth-century printing and the book arts reinforced Collins' plea, declaring that the collection was a bargain and a gift that Congress should give to America, and an outpouring of popular support and editorials and stories in newspapers and magazines reinforced their appeal.

Librarian Herbert Putnam made no public comment for two reasons—first, because Collins proposed to honor him, and second, because he feared that the purchase might imperil other Library projects—especially a much-needed second building. The House Library Committee chairman, Rep. Robert Luce, strongly supported the purchase, but the Committee's report presented arguments both pro and con and made no recommendation. Recognizing that the purchase would set a modern precedent for using taxpayer's money for purchasing rare materials for cultural institutions, the committee members felt that responsibility should rest with Congress as a whole.

Nevertheless, on June 9, 1930, a revised bill that omitted any reference to Putnam passed the House and so did the bill for the new building. As Representative Albert Johnson (R-Washington) expressed it, the House had decided that although times were hard "it is all for the United States of America which is going to live for we hope thousands of years."

The Senate Committee on the Library held hearings on June 16, calling Putnam to testify. The Librarian stated that he thought the purchase wise, and certainly it would place the Library of Congress in quite a different class—the same class as the national libraries of Great Britain and France. Agreeing that the Library had become much more than a reference library for Congress—as Senator Frederick Gillett (R-Massachusetts) put it, "a great center of education as well as an assemblage of books, and . . . of great value to the culture of the nation"—the Senate passed the bill, and President Hoover approved it on July 3, 1930.

The 3,000 items for which the United States paid $1.5 million include magnificent specimens of the first 50 years following the invention of printing. The books came from 635 different presses in 100 cities and towns in Germany, Switzerland, Italy, France, Spain, Holland, Belgium, Austria, and England. Moreover, they cover the whole range of fifteenth-century thought: classical literature, theology, law, history, medicine, natural history, music, painting astrono-

In 1930, Congress appropriated $1.5 million for the purchase of the Otto H.F. Vollbehr Collection of incunabula, which included a perfect vellum copy of the Gutenberg Bible. Here, Librarian Herbert Putnam and Dr. Vollbehr pose with several of the volumes.
LC/Prints and Photographs Division. LC-USZ62-57287.

my, logic, zoology, philosophy, and many other subjects. In sum, the collection represents the culture of the early Renaissance.

The Vollbehr Collection quadrupled the number of incunabula in the Library and placed the Library of Congress's collection among the top 10 collections of incunabula worldwide. About 40 percent of the books were not in any other U.S. library. The great treasure of the collection—a perfect copy of the Gutenberg Bible printed on vellum—is one of only three perfect copies in the world. When the collection arrived at the Library between July 15 and September 3, 1931, an exhibit was immediately launched.

Today, the Rare Books and Special Collections Division houses the bulk of the Vollbehr Collection but approximately 450 legal incunabula are in the Law Library's rare book collection. As Herbert Putnam stated, the purchase of this important collection "strikingly demonstrated that Congress earnestly desires to make its Library one of the greatest reference libraries in the world and a center for scholarly research." (JA)

Goff, Frederick R., "Uncle Sam Has a Book," *The Quarterly Journal of the Library of Congress 38* (Summer 1981): 123–133.

U.S. Library of Congress. *Loan Exhibition of Incunabula from the Vollbehr Collection, Books Printed Before 1501 A.D., and Manuscripts of the Fifteenth Century Selected From the Private Library of Dr. Otto H. F. Vollbehr, Berlin, Germany; Spring, 1928.* Washington, D.C.: Government Printing Office, 1928.

U.S. House of Representatives. Committee on the Library. *Vollbehr Collection of Incunabula; Hearing . . . H.R. 6147.* Washington, D.C.: Government Printing Office, 1930.

U.S. Library of Congress. *Exhibit of Books Printed During the XVth Century and Known as Incunabula, Selected from the Vollbehr Collection Purchased by Act of Congress, 1930.* Washington, D.C.: Government Printing Office, 1930.

The Lessing J. Rosenwald Collection of Illustrated Books

Lessing J. Rosenwald, chairman of Sears, Roebuck and Company, formed his collection over a period of nearly 40 years. The collection was given to the Library of Congress in a series of gifts, beginning in 1943 with the final installment coming after his death at age 87 in 1979. It is considered the greatest single gift of books ever donated to the Library and the premier collection of its kind in the United States. It consists of 2,653 titles documenting the history of book illustration over six centuries. Many of the books in the collection are bound in magnificent bindings and have distinguished provenance. The collection contains several excellent examples of Medieval and Renaissance illuminated manuscripts, and 10 fifteenth century block books, the most in any collection in the United States.

This newly published book about the woodcut in early printed books is based on the Rosenwald Collection and documents an exhibition at the Grolier Club in New York City in December 2004 and at the Library of Congress in April 2005.
LC/Publishing Office.

The Rosenwald Collection's 588 illustrated incunables, dating from the invention of printing by Gutenberg to 1501, are a major strength. Most of the illustrations in these books are woodcuts and they represent some of the finest examples of the art as executed by German, Italian, French, and Dutch designers and woodcutters during the incunable period. The collection also contains fine examples of seventeenth century science and architecture books; eighteenth century French illustrated books; illuminated books by William Blake, one of Rosenwald's passions and a unique collection, second only to the collection in the British Library; nineteenth century illustrated books and lithographs; and twentieth century French livres d'artistes, including 16 books illustrated by Pablo Picasso. The focus of the collection is Western Europe, with emphasis on Germany, France, Italy, Spain, Great Britain, and the Low Countries. A catalog of the entire collection was published in 1954, and a second, enlarged edition titled *A Catalog of the Gifts of Lessing J. Rosenwald to the Library of Congress, 1943 to 1975*, was issued in 1977. In 1991, the 100th anniversary of Rosenwald's birth, the Library organized an exhibition of 100 of the collection's most precious books. To accompany the exhibition, the Library published *Vision of a Collector*, a tribute to Rosenwald, which contained a series of short essays describing each book and written by a prominent bibliographer, librarian, art historian, or private collector.

The "Giant Bible of Mainz" is by all accounts the most important individual gift given to the Library of Congress by Mr. Rosenwald. This beautifully written manuscript Bible is illustrated with gold initial letters and illuminated border designs of acanthus leaves, flowers, birds, mammals, and human figures. It measures 575 mm x 404 mm and is bound in full contemporary pigskin over wooden boards. The unknown scribe who worked on the Bible dated his work and we know that he began on April 4, 1452, and completed the manuscript on July 9, 1453. Although it has yet to be proven, it is believed that the "Giant Bible" was created in the city of Mainz at the same time that Johann Gutenberg was printing his 42-line Bible with moveable type.

One example of the collection's many strengths is in the field of early science. It contains a beautifully hand-colored copy of the first edition of Petrus Apianus's privately printed *Astronomicum caesareum*, Ingolstadt, 1540. This lavish production is one of the last astronomical works based on the Ptolemaic system of the universe to be published, as it appeared just three years before Copernicus published his observations that challenged that theory by placing the sun at the center of our solar system. Other highlights representing the beginnings of modern science include: Andreas Veslius's *De humani corporis fabrica*, a monument in the history of astronomy, illustrated with more than 200 woodcuts; Galileo's *Dialogo*, Florence, 1632, from the de Medici Library; and Agostino Ramelli's *Le diverse et artificiose* machine, Paris, 1588, a class in engineering illustrated with 194 engraved plates.

In 1956, Rosenwald purchased a collection of fifteenth and sixteenth century Dutch books from the Duke of Arenberg. Many of these books were known in only a few copies and in a number of cases they were unique. He promptly helped organize an exhibition of these books in Washington, D.C. and Philadelphia in 1958, and allowed the collection to travel to Brussels and The Hague in 1960. Other exhibitions of his collection at the Library of Congress were held in 1973, in honor of his 82nd birthday, 1978 when his final gift of 180 items was announced, and in 1991 to celebrate the 100th anniversary of his birth. By exhibiting his books so generously, Mr. Rosenwald informed the world of the important books in his collection and encouraged museum and library curators to request individual loans for other exhibition venues outside the Washington area. This commitment to lending rare and unique books from the Rosenwald Collection continues today.

Making facsimiles of important books in his collection was another way Rosenwald helped scholars. After having built the most important collection of William Blake's illuminated books outside of Great Britain, he allowed the Blake Trust in London to use his original copies as the source for its series of facsimiles. This series received nearly universal acclaim for the high quality of its color reproductions and as a resource for Blake scholarship that blossomed in the last quarter of the twentieth century. Other examples of facsimile editions based on rare and unique copies of Rosenwald books are the *Le chevalier delibere*, Paris, 1488, by Olivier de la Marche, considered by some to be the finest illustrated French book printed in the fifteenth century; *Danse Macabre*, Paris, 1490, at the time of its purchase the only copy in an American library; *Doctrina Christiana*, Manila, 1593, an unknown Philippine imprint until this copy was discovered; and Giovanni Battista Braccelli's *Bizzarie di varie figure*, Livorno, 1624, at the time of its purchase the only complete copy known. Braccelli's work has been hailed by members of the Surrealist movement as one of the most important series of etchings created in the seventeenth century.

The Library of Congress has continued these traditions established by Mr. Rosenwald by working closely with visiting scholars, encouraging loan requests, creating exhibitions, and digitizing important examples from his collection and making them available to the public on the Rare Book and Special Collection Division's Web site. The Library is also working in cooperation with the Octavo Company of Oakland, California, to produce high quality digital facsimiles in a disk format to make available some of the greatest Rosenwald treasures. The Octavo series encompasses more than a dozen books from the Rosenwald Collection, including two important editions of William Blake's *Songs of Innocence and Experience*, 1794 and 1815; Blake's *The Book of Urizen*, 1815; a fully colored copy of Gerard Mercator's *Atlas sive Cosmographicae*, Duisburg, 1595; an illuminated *Book of Hours* from the workshop of Geoffrey Tory, Paris, 1524; and the three folio volumes of Redoute's *Roses*, considered one of the most beautiful botanical books ever produced. All of the digital facsimiles include essays by prominent scholars describing the importance of the book, the context in which it was produced, a discussion about the method in which the illustrations were made, and information about the binding and provenance of the Rosenwald copy. Many more digital facsimiles are scheduled to be produced in future years. (DD)

DeSimone, Daniel. *A Heavenly Craft: The Woodcut in Early Printed Books, Illustrated Books Purchased by Lessing J. Rosenwald at the Sale of the Library of C.W. Dyson*. Washington, D.C.: Library of Congress, 2004.

Library of Congress Information Bulletin 62 (October 2003): 223–229.

REFERENCE AND RESEARCH SERVICES

The story of reference and research services at the Library of Congress can be divided into the gradual expansion of the Library's use and the development of the Library's reference and research services as its collections continued to grow and its national role continued to expand.

The Use of the Library

When the Library was established in 1800, it was for the use of Congress only. However, the 1802 law that set up the Library's organization granted use privileges to the president and vice president of the United States. Next, in 1812 the justices of the Supreme Court were authorized to use the Library. Members of the public began using the Library's collections in the Capitol—without statutory provision—soon after 1818 when the Library reopened in the Capitol Building after the disastrous fire of 1814. Because of the overall lack of books and libraries in the new city of Washington, another informal practice developed as well: the occasional lending of books to persons who were not members of Congress provided a deposit covering the value of the books was left.

Throughout the rest of the nineteenth century, a series of congressional acts gradually but specifically granted the official use of the Library's collections to federal executive agencies, the diplomatic corps, various officers of the courts, and several special categories, for example, the staff of the Smithsonian Institution by virtue of the transfer of its library to the Library of Congress in 1866, and "former presidents while in the District of Columbia." For a brief period, approximately 1884–1894, as the District of Columbia gradually developed its own public library (founded in 1896), Librarian of Congress Spofford allowed District of Columbia residents to borrow books providing they left an adequate financial deposit that would cover the book's potential loss. In 1892, Congress approved access to the "scientific and literary" collections of government institutions, including the Library of Congress, "the scientific investigators and to students of any institution of higher education now incorporated or hereafter to be incorporated under the laws of Congress or of the District of Columbia." All previous laws and practices were considered to have been repealed by the act of 1897, which vested in the Librarian of Congress the authority to make rules and regulations for administering the Library.

After 1824, when it moved into a spacious new room on the Capitol's west front with a fine view of the mall, the Library became a popular "gathering place." In the post-Civil War years, persons under 16 years old were not allowed to use the Library.

In 1824, the Library moved into new quarters in the west front of the refurbished U.S. Capitol, overlooking the Mall. Seriously damaged by fire in 1851, it was rebuilt with fireproof materials and reopened in 1853. From the collections of the New York Public Library.

However, after the Copyright Law of 1870 began flooding the Library with new acquisitions, the increasingly crowded conditions in the Capitol made use of the Library difficult for everyone.

The 1897 opening of the Jefferson Building was a public event that highlighted the building's dramatic architecture and impressive reading rooms and exhibition halls, which were all open to the public. The Library was affirmed as an important public institution—and major new tourist attraction. This attention naturally greatly increased the Library's use.

With new authority conveyed by the 1897 appropriations act, Librarian of Congress John Russell Young decided that the Library's collections could be consulted by an adult without the necessity of presenting credentials or requesting permission. The Library opened in the evening for the first time on October 1, 1898; Sunday hours (from 2:00 p.m. to 10:00 p.m.) began on September 14, 1902. When in 1901 Congress formally extended access to government libraries to all scholars and students, Librarian of Congress Herbert Putnam interpreted the law as conveying the authority to inaugurate an important new service: interlibrary loan service to other libraries. Putnam had to defend to Congress his decision to begin "sharing" the Library's books to users outside Washington, D.C. He did so successfully, giving a new emphasis to both service and access.

Later in the century, in one area the Library returned to a more restrictive policy, one that had been effective in the Capitol Building prior to the Civil War. In September 1958, with the concurrence

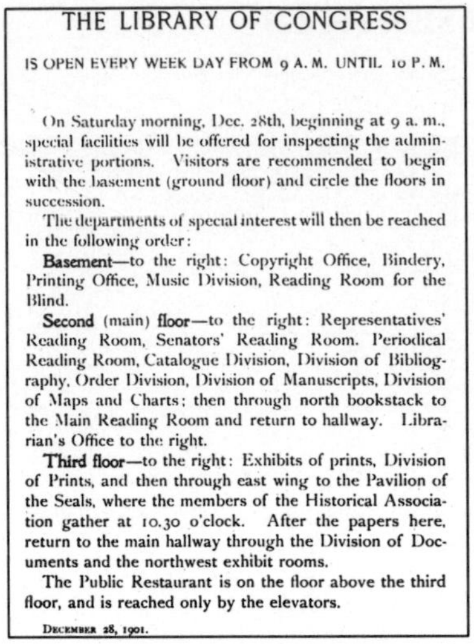
THE LIBRARY OF CONGRESS

IS OPEN EVERY WEEK DAY FROM 9 A. M. UNTIL 10 P. M.

On Saturday morning, Dec. 28th, beginning at 9 a. m., special facilities will be offered for inspecting the administrative portions. Visitors are recommended to begin with the basement (ground floor) and circle the floors in succession.

The departments of special interest will then be reached in the following order:

Basement—to the right: Copyright Office, Bindery, Printing Office, Music Division, Reading Room for the Blind.

Second (main) **floor**—to the right: Representatives' Reading Room, Senators' Reading Room. Periodical Reading Room, Catalogue Division, Division of Bibliography, Order Division, Division of Manuscripts, Division of Maps and Charts; then through north bookstack to the Main Reading Room and return to hallway. Librarian's Office to the right.

Third floor—to the right: Exhibits of prints, Division of Prints, and then through east wing to the Pavilion of the Seals, where the members of the Historical Association gather at 10.30 o'clock. After the papers here, return to the main hallway through the Division of Documents and the northwest exhibit rooms.

The Public Restaurant is on the floor above the third floor, and is reached only by the elevators.

December 28, 1901.

The Library moved into the Jefferson Building in 1897. By 1901, the Main Reading Room and separate reading rooms for members of Congress were in operation, as well as separate reading rooms for the blind, manuscripts, maps and charts, music, periodicals, and prints and graphic arts. This card, prepared for a meeting of a local historical society, invited members of the public to visit several of the reading rooms.
LC Archives.

of the Joint Committee on the Library, Librarian of Congress L. Quincy Mumford curtailed the use of the Library by high school students, requiring certification by the school principal of a student's need to use the Library's research resources.

The Development of Reference and Research Services

The Librarian of Congress himself had to provide any advice or help that readers obtained in the Library of Congress when it was in the Capitol. Such help was limited and passive until the arrival in September 1861 of Ainsworth Rand Spofford. First as Assistant Librarian and then as Librarian of Congress from the last day of 1864 until July 1, 1897, Spofford willingly provided authoritative reference service and research advice to members of Congress, federal agencies, and the public at large. He became known for his prodigious memory and willingness to help. For example, in 1887 Congressman James G. Blaine sent him a reference question from Bar Harbor, Maine: "Can you tell me the origin and application of the phrase 'wood & water?' I bother you because I know no other place to apply—Too great acquisition of knowledge pays a penalty." Another congressman said, "I don't read books—I read Spofford!"

After the Copyright Law of 1870 began flooding the small Library in the Capitol with books, pamphlets, newspapers, maps, music, prints, and photographs, Spofford's time increasingly was taken up by the political and administrative struggle to obtain a new building. The space problem soon dominated all Library activities. Thus, most researchers and scholars did not find the Library's collections generally useful until 1897 when the Jefferson Building opened. The acquisition of the Smithsonian Institution's library in 1866 and Peter Force's personal library of Americana in 1867 gathered in unique research materials, but they could not be made fully available until the new building opened. The same is true of the comprehensive book, map, music, and graphic arts that began to accumulate after the Copyright Law of 1870 became effective.

The opening of the spacious new building with its impressive Main Reading Room and several specialized reading rooms in November 1897 gave researchers and scholars new and ample space. The Library was open to the public generally from 9:00 a.m. until 4:00 p.m., six days a week, and the reading room staff kept careful statistics regarding use and the number of books loaned out. In 1898, Librarian of Congress John Russell Young noted with pleasure that the Library was becoming a "bureau of information," consulted by a wide variety of people who not only sought specific books, but also asked "advice as to reading" or requested "special information." He stated that it was the policy of the Library "to encourage this spirit of inquiry." Desk attendants in the Main Reading Room helped members of the public directly. They also served members of Congress, sending books to the Capitol through a pneumatic tube system connected though a tunnel between the Jefferson Building and the Capitol.

Verner W. Clapp, who served as Assistant Chief Librarian of Congress from 1947 to 1956, worked in the Main Reading Room from 1923 to 1940. Here, he is pictured in the mid-1930s delivering a book to Charles Martel, chief architect of the Library's classification system and a Library consultant when the photo was taken.
LC/Prints and Photographs Division. LC-USP6-56A.

"Hey, look! A congressman!"

© The Cartoon Bank. Mischa Richter, 1976.

It was Herbert Putnam, Librarian of Congress from 1899 to 1939, who defined the Library's reference and research policies. In a memo in 1899, he explained that the "trained librarian" who supervised the Main Reading Room was expected, with help from assistants, "to answer questions as to the best literature on any topic." In his 1901 *Annual Report*, Putnam stressed that it was the duty of the desk attendants in the Main Reading Room to put at the disposal of all inquirers "such information as they may have." When he served as superintendent of the Main Room from 1907 to 1915, William Warner Bishop took a more measured approach, reminding the librarians that they should "guide" readers but should never actually do the reader's work. The 1939 pamphlet, *Information for Readers in the Reading Room*, spells out this "balanced" approach in greater detail: reference desk assistants, "so far as is compatible with the needs of others," could aid a reader in securing information. The Library could not, however, "undertake to conduct research for readers, but must content itself with suggesting material that may bear on the subject."

In the first decade of the twentieth century, Putnam took major steps in developing the collections and "scholarly apparatus" upon which reference and research service were based. In 1903, the Library of Congress became a leading center for historical research after the transfer of many historical and presidential papers from the Department of State. The Library's extensive program of preparing and publishing bibliographies—about current topics for Congress and scholarly topics for researchers—was fully established during the same decade. In his 1907 *Annual Report*, Putnam described with some pride the range of services offered readers at the Library of Congress: "the consideration which investigators meet here, the freedom of access and comfort they enjoy, which seem often to surprise them, are therefore but a natural result of our opportunities not merely as a 'research library,' but as a library exceptional in its equipment and unique in its obligations. In the same report, he described a rapidly growing service: answering inquiries through correspondence, noting that the Library was receiving perhaps as many as 10,000 inquiries a year. The Librarian expressed his overall satisfaction with programs to date in the Library's 1914 *Annual Report*, asserting that the Library of Congress surpassed all other American institutions in making its collections freely available and in aiding in their "interpretation."

In 1914, the Library's foremost mission, service to Congress, was formalized by the establishment of the Legislative Reference Service (LRS) as a separate Library of Congress administrative unit. In addition to reference service and the preparation of bibliographies on specialized topics of legislative interest to Congress, the creation of LRS meant that the Library would begin a formal research service for Congress as well.

In 1939, President Franklin D. Roosevelt named poet and writer Archibald MacLeish as Librarian of Congress and MacLeish quickly took steps that led to a complete administrative reorganization. Functions were redefined, new custodial arrangements established for the collections, and new departments were created. Reference and research services, including the Legislative Reference Service, were placed in a new Reference Department. The Librarian outlined the Library's new reference and research objectives in the Library's 1940 *Annual Report*. First, he restated the priority of reference and research service for the Congress. Next, the Library would undertake government research projects

David C. Mearns, Superintendent of the Reading Room 1928–1943, also served as director of the Reference Department, Assistant Librarian of Congress, and chief of the Manuscript Division. A Lincoln scholar, he also was a historian of the Library.
LC/Manuscript Division.

Students studying in March 1943 in the South (Jefferson) Reading Room of the Adams Building, with one of Ezra Winter's Jefferson murals—this one including Jefferson's quotation about the importance of the "living generation"—above them.
LC/Prints and Photographs Division. LC-USZ62-90458.

"appropriate to the Library." Finally, the Library's reference staff and facilities were "available to members of the public, universities, learned societies, and other libraries requiring service that the Library staff is equipped to give."

Implicit in MacLeish's statement was an assumption that went further than those of his predecessors as Librarian, that the Library of Congress was an active "people's reference library." This concept, influenced by the widening war in Europe, and after 1941, by America's entry into World War II, also was explicitly articulated in the Librarian's 1940 *Annual Report.* Noting that the Library had become what Thomas Jefferson had once called it, "the Library of the United States—the library of the People's representatives in Congress," Librarian MacLeish emphasized that the Library was "a people's library not in the usual sense of the term, the sense familiar in the so-called public libraries, but in a very special and significant sense. As a consequence of the fact that the Congress extended to the people the use, not of the collections only, but of the services of scholarship which had been created to make the collections more usefully available to the Congress, the Library became a reference library to the people—a People's Library of Reference.

Luther H. Evans, Librarian of Congress from 1945 to 1953, was more specific in outlining how "the reference library of the people" should operate. It needed to offer "a highly responsive service at all points where programs are developed and policies decided." There was a need "not only for more builders of bibliographic apparatus but for expositors who will translate (the apparatus) into action and result. For this, specialists of great competence must be found." Such specialists were found, and the Library's reference staff expanded and grew more specialized in the middle decades of the twentieth century.

The Library's traditional policy of making its collections as useful as possible through personal service—as well as, in later years, through the use of the computer and the Internet—has been continued through the administrations of Librarians of Congress L. Quincy Mumford (1954–1974), Daniel J. Boorstin (1975–1987), and James H. Billington (1987–present). Special challenges had to be met, however, beginning with the closing of the Main Reading Room for renovation and the installation of air conditioning in 1964–1965. However, the pervasive change, just beginning in the late 1960 was "mechanization" or, as it soon was called, automation.

The first project was the development, beginning in 1967, of a computer-produced catalog of the Main Reading Room's reference collection. Not only did the computer help with the control of reference and other collections, more significantly it made available to librarians and the general public alike a powerful new service—online bibliographic searches. In April 1975, the first computer terminal for public use in the Library of Congress was installed in the Science Reading Room. In May 1976, the first terminals for public and staff use were installed in the Main Reading Room, and in 1977 computer services were expanded and made more accessible to both readers and staff. The Library's main card catalog was "frozen" on December 31, 1980. No new catalog cards were to be added, thus the computer became the only searchable book file for items acquired after December 31, 1980. Because computer terminals became the preferred means of access to current catalog information (even though the "frozen" card catalog was retained), the Library greatly expanded its new public Computer Catalog Center and reference librarians provided constant training for new users and instruction in advanced techniques for those experienced in computer searching. When the newly renovated Main Reading Room reopened in June 1991, the center offered 40 work stations; by 1998 the number was 58, each with its own printer. In June 1993, the Newspaper and Current Periodical Reading Room opened the Library's first public work station with access to the Internet.

In the mid-1980s, budget cuts began to affect public service, and hours of opening were cut back. In early 1986, the Library was forced to close the Main Reading Room on Sundays and on every evening except Wednesday. For three days in March, an unhappy group of readers, calling itself "Books Not Bombs," staged the first-ever "sit-down" in the Library's Main Reading Room to protest the reduced hours. The Library took no action on the first two nights, but on the third day, 18 protestors who refused to leave were arrested. By July, funds available from a supplemental appropriations bill allowed the Library to restore reading room hours. In his 1986 *Annual Report*, Librarian of Congress Boorstin, who had immediately (and ultimately successfully) appealed the budget reduction, mused: "According to Kierkegaard, life can only be understood backwards, but it must be lived forwards. Library staff members, coping with exasperated and disruptive readers in mid-March did not know that within four months this particular problem would be solved, though it might have made things easier if they did. Nevertheless, there was permanent damage done in 1986 to the department programs, and permanent scars remain."

By 1991, as Josephus Nelson and Judith Farley, the authors of *Full Circle*, a history of reference service in the Main Reading Room have pointed out, the "scars" inflicted in 1986 had faded. They also point out an important lesson: the Library's readers "had spoken decisively about how important their reading room and its complement of services were to them."

During this same period, however, the Library was investigating a series of losses of books and valuable manuscripts and other research materials. Librarian of Congress Billington, taking office in September 1987, promised further investigation and, if necessary, heightened security. In 1991, a general reader registration system was implemented. On March 30, 1992, Librarian Billington closed the stacks to researchers and shortly thereafter to all staff members not directly involved in servicing research materials. In the next few years, division reading rooms began registering readers and implementing appropriate security measures.

Recognizing that more and more users and potential users were turning to resources available on the Internet for information, between 1998 and 2000 the Library developed a cooperative Web-based networked reference service with 16 other libraries to take advantage of the opportunities the Internet presented for improving reference work on both the national and international levels. The resulting cooperative pilot project, the Collaborative Digital Reference Service (CDRS), inaugurated in June 2000, soon created a "virtual reference desk" that spanned three continents and 15 time zones.

CDRS was a precursor to another digital reference project. In early 2001, the Library signed an agreement with OCLC to develop, in consultation with reference librarians, a prototype virtual reference service, which was named QuestionPoint in March 2002. QuestionPoint provides subscribing libraries with online access to the skills and knowledge of a growing collaborative network of reference librarians around the world. Users at a participating library submit questions to the service through the library's Web site at any time of day or night. The questions are answered online either by qualified staff at the user's library or by staff at another participating library around the world.

Another reference service soon developed within the Library of Congress. Through the years, the Library's reference librarians have responded to requests from users outside the Library via surface mail, fax, telephone, e-mail, and "live reference" (or "chat reference") technology pilot projects. In 2002, the Library developed a new "Ask a Librarian" service, designed to lead patrons to various online resources and reference links. The new service allows users to submit questions directly to Library of Congress reading rooms, using World Wide Web forms tailored to each division's collections.

To further the Library's research and reference programs in the digital environment, in 2001 the Library organized a Digital Reference Team within Library Services. The team organizes workshops and interactive programs about using the Library's American Memory, the digital collections, and resources accessed by the Library's Web site; provides information about reference sources available to scholars, educators, and students; compiles subject guides to Web resources; and answers questions directly as part of the Library's "Ask a Librarian" service. (JYC)

Annual Report of the Librarian of Congress for the Fiscal Year Ending June 30, 1907. Washington, D.C.: Government Printing Office, 1907, pp. 70–78, 153–159.

Library of Congress Information Bulletin 51 (November 16, 1992): 487–489.

Nelson, Josephus and Judith Farley. *Full Circle: Ninety Years of Service in the Main Reading Room.* Washington, D.C.: Library of Congress, 1991.

SCIENCE, TECHNOLOGY, AND BUSINESS DIVISION AND COLLECTIONS

Administrative History

The Science, Technology, and Business Division of the Library of Congress has responsibility for recommending acquisitions and providing reference and bibliographic services for the collections in these subject areas. Science and business have been well-represented in Library of Congress collections since the acquisition of Thomas Jefferson's personal library in 1815. Jefferson's books included approximately 500 items in such fields as natural philosophy, agriculture, chemistry, zoology, technical arts, economics, and commerce. Additions to the collection over the next 50 years benefited from international exchange activities and the growing number of federal government agencies engaged in scientific endeavors. With the transfer of about 40,000 volumes of scientific works from the Smithsonian Institution in 1866, the importance of science in the collections of the library was firmly established. The Smithsonian Deposit provided a complete collection of the memoirs and transactions of learned scientific societies throughout the world and sets of the most important science periodicals. A Smithsonian Division was created in 1900 with custodial, acquisition, and reference responsibilities for the Deposit, and in 1929 an Aeronautics Division was established with a grant from the David Guggenheim Fund. Albert F. Zahm became the first chief and holder of the Guggenheim Chair of Aeronautics.

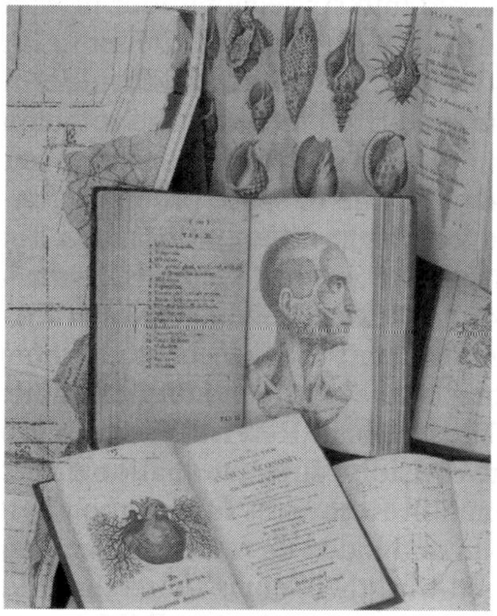

Books in various scientific disciplines from Thomas Jefferson's personal library. Photograph: LC/Reid Baker and Jim Higgins, Photographic Section.

When the Adams Building was completed in 1938, its Thomas Jefferson Room was intended to serve as a Science-Technology Room. However, in the 1944 reorganization of the Library, the Smithsonian Division was discontinued and a consultantship in the history of science was established in the Reference Department's General Reference and Bibliography Division. The first occupant of this consultantship was Frederick E. Brasch, who had administered the Deposit for 20 years. The 1945 *Annual Report of the Librarian of Congress* stated that "plans for the future anticipate the creation of a science division which will include not only this consultantship but also the aeronautics division and other scientific reference services, existing or projected." Budget estimates presented to the Congress for fiscal 1947 included a request for a Science and Technology Division with 46 staff, but when Congress decided not to increase the Library's budget, plans for the division had to be set aside.

But the heightened awareness in the United States of the increased needs for current, reliable scientific and technical information was a strong influence for continued development of the Library's collections and capabilities in these areas. Other driving forces were the federal government's continuing and acute need for scientific information and the defense industry's greatly enlarged presence within the government. Sponsored by the Office of Naval Research, a Science and Technology Project was established at the Library in 1947. The Project was chiefly concerned with the bibliographic control of technical report literature of interest to the Navy and its research and development contractors. One of the initial charges to the Project was to catalog the collection of 30,000 World War II Office of Scientific Research and Development (OSRD) technical reports deposited at the Library when the OSRD was abolished in 1946.

A Science Division was finally established within the Reference Department in 1949 and given responsibility for planning and conducting reference service for the Library's scientific and technological collections, making recommendations for the acquisition of scientific and technological literature, suggesting techniques for the cataloging and other bibliographical control of such literature, and maintaining liaison between the Library of Congress and other government agencies, learned societies, institutions, and organizations interested in the bibliographical control and use of scientific and technological literature. Since the staff was limited to two, the work went slowly. The Science and Technology Project, renamed the Navy Research Section, became part of the Science Division in June 1949.

and technology information services of other government agencies and commercial firms, team members made plans for enhancing the Library's reference resources, achieving better bibliographic control and more rapid availability of foreign technical materials and creating new services, including a referral and reference service. With the submission of a report to the Library's Management team, their work was completed but the following year, Librarian Billington appointed William W. Ellis to a one-year term as Associate Librarian for Science and Technology Information.

By the mid-1990s, the juxtaposition of two service units led to plans to coordinate their functions in a Business/Economics and Science & Technology information service. Likewise, the Business/Economics Reference Section, originally established as part of the Library's Humanities and Social Sciences Division, merged in 1998 with the division, which was renamed the Science, Technology and Business Division. The new division's primary responsibilities became reference and bibliographical services and collection development in all areas of science, technology, business, and economics, with the exceptions of clinical medicine and technical agriculture, which are the specialties of the National Library of Medicine and the National Library of Agriculture, respectively. The division continues to hold special collections of technical reports, standards, and other gray literature, and the materials for which it has responsibility amount to roughly 40 percent of the Library's book and journal collections. Direct reference service is provided through a desk for Science Reference Services and one for Business Reference Services, through bibliographic guides and reports prepared by division specialists, by telephone, by mail, and electronically via the Internet. The division has also since 1997 maintained Science and Business home pages on the Library's Web site, both of which include a number of its publications such as the *Tracer Bullet* series and guides to business and science information. (KRG, JA)

Science and Technology Collections

As broad and encompassing as the Library's holdings in science and technology have become by the end of the twentieth century, the origins of these vast and diverse materials can be traced to a singular, seminal, and very concrete event—the purchase of Thomas Jefferson's private library by the United States government. Jefferson had spent a lifetime, not to mention a small fortune, assembling what was by far the best private library in America. Throughout his life, he was constantly in search of books that would assist his "grand plan" of creating a library that would have utility that went beyond the specific use he would give to it. With the sale of some 6,700 books to the United States government in 1815 for $23,950, Jefferson not only bequeathed a legacy of learning to a new nation, but also left as formative a mark on its national library as he did on its founding documents.

The deliberately universal character of Jefferson's library meant that it would necessarily include science and technology or, in late eighteenth century terms, "natural philosophy and the technical arts." In his own words, Jefferson said his library included "what is chiefly valuable in science and literature generally," and sagely suggested to legislators that "I do not know that it contains any branch of science which Congress would wish to exclude from their collection...."

Considered solely from the aspect of its contents, Jefferson's selections in the field of science and technology reveal him to be a discerning and highly informed collector. Among the titles in his catalog are found many of the landmarks of Western science written by men whose names often form entire chapters in the history of science. Beginning with the classical knowledge of Aristotle, Hippocrates, Archimedes, Theophrastus, and Diophantus through later writers like Pliny, Dioscorides, and Celsus, each field of scientific inquiry is represented by names that will resonate as long as books are written: Lavoisier, Scheele, and Priestly in chemistry; Harvey, Sydenham, and Jenner in medicine; Woodward, Humboldt, and Buffon in geology; Cuvier, Bell, and Hunter in anatomy; Estienne, Tull, and Hales in agriculture; Catesby, Redi, and Spallanzani in zoology; Boerhaave, Tournefort, and Erasmus Darwin in botany; Maclaurin, Euler, and Lagrange in mathematics; Brahe, Huygens, and LaPlace in astronomy; and Digges, Fulton, and Berthollet in technical arts. Besides this pantheon of science and technology, even greater stars like Euclid, Galileo, Newton, Linnaeus, Boyle, and Descartes abound in the Jeffersonian galaxy of books. Taken together, the scientific portion of Jefferson's library offered the new nation the intellectual bedrock upon which today's massive collection would be erected.

In the five decades that followed, little special effort was made for science collecting by the Library of Congress, which, in effect, was living off the richness of Jefferson's materials. However, during this time, many scientific and technical publications of the growing federal bureaucracy did become part of the Library's collections. This included the published works of the National Bureau of Standards, the Geological Survey, and the Coast and Geodetic Survey among others. This relatively unremarkable collecting period for science came to a sudden end in 1866 however, when Joseph Henry, dean of American physics and the first secretary of the Smithsonian Institution, decided, with the encouragement from

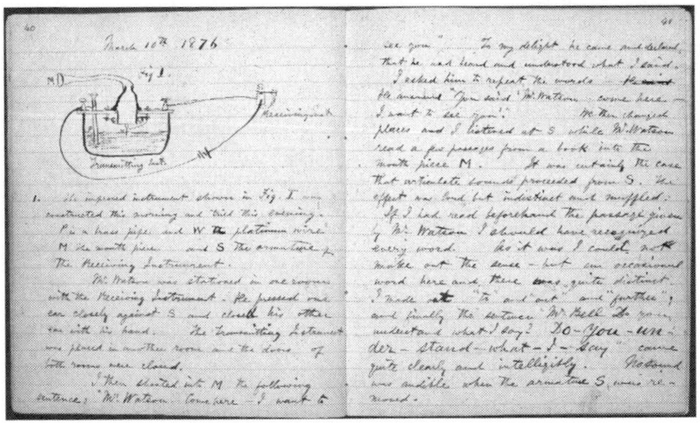

March 10th 1876

Fig 1.

Receiving inst.

Transmitting Inst.

1. The improved instrument shown in Fig. I was constructed this morning and tried this evening. P is a brass pipe and W the platinum wire M the mouth piece and S the armature of the Receiving Instrument.

Mr. Watson was stationed in one room with the Receiving Instrument. He pressed one ear closely against S and closed his other ear with his hand. The Transmitting Instrument was placed in another room and the doors of both rooms were closed.

I then shouted into M the following sentence: "Mr. Watson — Come here — I want to see you." To my delight he came and declared that he had heard and understood what I said.

I asked him to repeat the words. He answered "You said 'Mr. Watson — come here — I want to see you.'" We then changed places and I listened at S while Mr. Watson read a few passages from a book into the mouth piece M. It was certainly the case that articulate sounds proceeded from S. The effect was loud but indistinct and muffled.

If I had read beforehand the passage given by Mr. Watson I should have recognized every word. As it was I could not make out the sense — but an occasional word here and there was quite distinct. I made out "to" and "out" and "further"; and finally the sentence "Mr. Bell Do you understand what I say? Do — you — un — der — stand — what — I — say" came quite clearly and intelligibly. No sound was audible when the armature S was removed.

Alexander Graham Bell's notebook entry of March 10, 1876, describing the first successful experiment with the telephone.
LC/Manuscript Division.

Librarian of Congress Ainsworth Rand Spofford, to transfer the Smithsonian's library to the Library of Congress. The Smithsonian's library was formed originally to obtain "a complete collection of the memoirs and transactions of learned societies throughout the world and an entire series of the most important scientific and literary periodicals." Consisting roughly of 40,000 volumes, this collection was offered by Joseph Henry to the Library of Congress both to insure its physical preservation (and thus relieve the Smithsonian of its upkeep) and to increase its availability to scholars. Henry knew well the importance of this transfer, saying in his *Annual Report* to the Smithsonian regents that "the collection of books owned by the Congress would not be worthy of the name of a national library were it not for the Smithsonian Deposit." He went on to underscore the point that his deposit would also bring the Library's holdings into the mid-nineteenth century since they were "emphatically those essential to the contemporaneous advance of our country in the higher science of the day."

A key factor that assured the permanent growth of the Smithsonian Deposit was the continuation by the Library of Congress of the myriad exchange agreements the Smithsonian had established with foreign academies and universities. In fact, the Library not only continued but also actually expanded this foreign exchange program, which continues even today. These agreements, combined with the passage of the 1870 Copyright Law, assured the Library that it could steadily and rationally build its science collections on its own. Through the operation of that copyright law, the Library regularly receives new scientific and technical material, since it receives two copies of all American publications (and many foreign ones in the scientific field) that are registered for copyright.

In 1882, the Library's science holdings received another external stimulus in the tradition of the Jefferson purchase and the Smithsonian Deposit, but one that was also unique and unprecedented. In March of that year, Washington physician and medical historian Joseph Meredith Toner offered his entire research collection to the Library of Congress as a gift. Within two months, Congress passed a Joint Resolution of Congress to accept this large and valuable personal medical library. In recommending acceptance, the Librarian of Congress, Ainsworth Spofford, wrote hopefully "that this first example of the gift of a library to the nation will be the precursor of many in the future...." Including approximately 40,000 books and assorted pamphlets and periodicals, as well as personal papers totaling some 75,000 items, Toner's collection became a benchmark for the Library since it was the first instance of a large, personal library being given freely to the people of the United States. As Spofford had hoped, Toner's generous gift to the nation became the first of many.

After Toner, science collecting by the Library consisted primarily of the everyday business of acquisition by exchange and copyright until 1901, when the Librarian indicated in his *Annual Report* that "the science section of the Library was very deficient in modern works of reference for advanced study...." To remedy this apparent deficiency, the Library made a conscious effort "to obtain a representative collection of recent and standard works in mathematics, physics, astronomy, and chemistry." After three years of studied and deliberate purchasing, the Librarian's 1904 *Annual Report* included 38 pages of newly acquired titles and further suggested that the purchase of new titles in the geological and biological sciences would

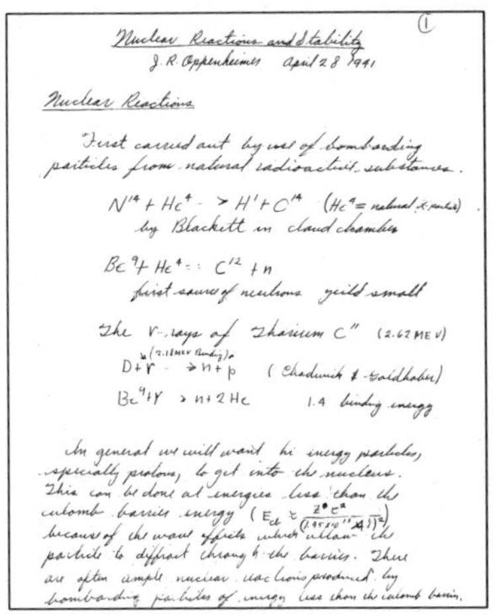

1

Nuclear Reactions and Stability
J. R. Oppenheimer April 28 1941

Nuclear Reactions

First carried out by use of bombarding particles from natural radioactive substances.

$N^{14} + He^4 \rightarrow H^1 + C^{14}$ (He^4 = natural α-particles)
by Blackett in cloud chamber

$Be^9 + He^4 \rightarrow C^{12} + n$
first source of neutrons yield small

The γ-rays of Thorium C″ (2.62 MEV)
$D + \gamma \rightarrow n + p$ (2.18 MEV Binding) (Chadwick & Goldhaber)
$Be^9 + \gamma \rightarrow n + 2He$ 1.4 binding energy

In general we will want hi energy particles, specially protons, to get into the nucleus. This can be done at energies less than the coulomb barrier energy $\left(E_{cb} \approx \frac{Z e^2}{(1.45 \times 10^{-13} A^{1/3})^2}\right)$ because of the wave effects which allow the particle to diffract through the barrier. There are often ample nuclear reactions produced by bombarding particles of energy less than the coulomb barrier.

J. Robert Oppenheimer. Nuclear Reactions and Stability. April 28, 1941. Equations on this page refer to English physicist Patrick M. Blackett's cloud chamber experiments of the 1920s and to the 1932 discovery of neutrons—which would prove to be the most useful particles for initiating nuclear reactions.
LC/Manuscript Division.

soon follow. This type of periodic evaluation and gap-filling would prove essential to the maintenance of a useful and relevant collection of science materials.

The period from the turn of the century to World War II was generally unremarkable for science collecting at the Library, but that situation changed quickly as global conflict underscored the critical importance of science and technology to the nation. By the end of the war, the Smithsonian Deposit—which had existed as a library within a library—was subsumed into the general collections and several years later science was given a new organizational focus in the Library with the creation of a Science Division. The creation of a new divisional focus for science meant that for the first time, a Library unit would have full responsibility for both reference and bibliographical services and for advising on the acquisition of all pertinent scientific and technological materials. It was not a curatorial division however, since a separate science collection no longer existed as a discrete physical entity.

While these organizational changes were important and necessary for the Library to cope with the burgeoning field of post-war science and technology, perhaps the most significant and long-lasting event during those years was again the result of private generosity. When Lessing J. Rosenwald signed a deed of gift in 1943 to give early illustrated books to the Library, he initiated four decades of unsurpassed and distinguished giving. As a collector whose singular focus was the illustrated book and who was able to purchase the most magnificent examples of early printing and finely illustrated books from the fifteenth to the twentieth centuries, Rosenwald also obtained many of the finest examples of early scientific and technical illustration. His gifts to the Library, for example, include, Roberto Valturio's *De Re Militari*, (1472); a revolutionary and highly influential medical textbook; *De Humani Corporis Fabrica* (1543) by Andreas Vesalius, considered a classic of both science and art; and Robert Hooke's 1665 monument to microscopy, *Micrographia*, with its highly detailed, folio-size engravings.

The dispersion of the Smithsonian Deposit established a Library policy that continues to the end of this century—there is no single, separate science and technology collection in the Library of Congress. This wisely reflects the boundless, almost irrepressible nature of the disciplines themselves, not to mention the impossibility of attempting to house in one place a field whose growth is at times exponential. A telling example of this phenomenon is the description of the "vastness of the Library's resources in science," which is found in the Librarian's *Annual Report* for 1953: "If one were to read three books a day for a thousand years, one would not have exhausted these resources...." Nearly 50 years hence, this "vastness" has almost quadrupled, raising the books-per-day ratio considerably higher.

The Library manages this material in roughly two ways, via the general collection and the special collections. In the former, the Library collects books comprehensively but selectively in all the subject classes—for example, QA (Mathematics); QB (Physics); QC (Astronomy), etc. In the latter, it collects both by format and by subject. Thus, while the general collections are composed solely of books and journals, the special collections are organized primarily by the physical nature of the material. Therefore, all prints and photographs are housed together, all manuscripts or personal papers are similarly organized, all rare books together, all maps together, and so on for all other formats. Organized in this manner, science and technology is represented in each special collection in the same dispersed manner as the general collections. For scholars then, science in the Library of Congress is where he or she finds it.

The dispersion of scientific and technical materials by book class and format does not mean that the Library has not built up specialties over the years. Certain strengths and areas stand out as being particularly noteworthy, and one of these is the field of aeronautics. It is safe to say that the Library's holdings of aeronautical books, journals, and technical reports, combined with its special collections of personal papers and prints and photographs, make it the paramount location for any historical treatment of that subject.(LB)

Bruno, Leonard C. *The Tradition of Science: Landmarks of Western Science in the Collections of the Library of Congress*. Washington, D.C.: Library of Congress, 1987.

_________. *The Tradition of Technology: Landmarks of Western Technology in the Collections of the Library of Congress*. Washington, D.C.: Library of Congress, 1995.

Business Collections

Unlike the history of the science and technology collections at the Library of Congress, the business and economics collections developed in a more indirect and complex way. This, however, is consistent with the development of business collections in American libraries generally. Business in particular is a practical field; entrepreneurs and business people are much less interested in historical themes or theoretical works, and much more driven by current trends and future opportunities. In addition, financial elements are part and parcel of most subject fields. In this environment, then, there are difficulties in clearly separating or distinguishing business sources from other subject areas. Standard business bibliographies of the 1920s, for example, contained a great number of ephemeral materials that reflected the diversity and almost transient nature of business resources. However, over time a core group of reference materials—directories, commercial and investment literature, and statistical sources (to name just a few)—became prominent.

Still, there were no seminal events, such as Russia's launching of Sputnik in 1957, that would propel the field of business into the public's imagination or lead to an administrative reorganization at the Library of Congress. Nonetheless, even though the Library's business reference collections continued to be built based on a source's timeliness and practicality, the depth of the Library of Congress's general collection of business works remained unique in the country. The Library's collections in business are especially strong in their historical research value, both for tracing the development of particular industries and in analyzing past financial and economic conditions. Included are a number of key serial titles, U.S. and foreign, in finance and other areas virtually complete back to the mid-nineteenth century. Examples include *Moody's Handbook of Dividend Achievers*; *Dun and Bradstreet Reference Book*; and the *Moody's Stock Survey*. The Library also holds a selective list of trade periodicals covering the various industrial sectors, with preference being given to titles indexed by major indexing services. For investment research, the Library has the annual reports of all companies listed on the New York Stock Exchange and the American Stock Exchange published since 1955. Long runs of directories of companies, stock price records, public budgets, and other long-standing periodical publications incorporate a wealth of information on the history of corporate and public finance in the United States and the rest of the world. The Library also holds a broadly representative collection of published conference papers in economics and business, as well as an in-depth collection of business and economics textbooks that are intended for use in U.S. colleges and universities.

Additionally, the business and economics collections contain a wide-range of statistical resources, including all available U.S. statistical abstracts and many publications from federal, state, and foreign governments. These major runs of publications yield extensive national and international economic statistics over a large span of time; for example, U.S. census data from the first (1790) census to the present and many state censuses are available. And the Library has a unique collection of statistical and other information published by associations on businesses and industries. Furthermore, the reference collection houses a lengthy list of standard business and economic resources, such as *Standard and Poor's Register of Corporations*; *Dun and Bradstreet's Million Dollar Directory*; *Gale's Encyclopedia of Associations*; and *Value Line*, as well as hundreds of national and international industrial directories and several business ratio studies. Also available is a comprehensive biographical reference collection devoted to individuals in all fields of business and economics.

Long-standing exchange programs with foreign governments and academic institutions over the years have resulted in the acquisition of sizable collections of foreign government documents and other publications providing statistical and other data of interest for the study of the economy of those areas. The Library holds runs of country profiles concentrating on foreign post-war economic data, including publications of the Economist Intelligence Unit (EIU) and the Organization for Economic Cooperation and Development (OECD). Moreover, the Library of Congress also has a substantial collection of technical reports published by foreign academic and research institutions in the areas of business and economics. A few examples include materials from the Swedish School of Economics and Business Administration; the Helsinki School of Economics and Business Administration; the Rotterdam Institute for Business Economic Studies (RIBES); and the University of South Africa Bureau of Market Research.

Business materials are also dispersed throughout the special collections of the Library. Among the notable special collections that include business information are *The New York World Telegram and Sun* collection of news photographs in the Prints and Photographs Division, which includes material on business leaders, transportation and labor problems; the National Child Labor Committee Collection of manuscripts and photographs from 1904 to 1953 in the Manuscript and Prints and Photographs Divisions, which includes labor material relating to various U.S. industries; the NAACP collection of manuscripts and photographs in the Manuscript and Prints and Photographs Divisions, which includes material on segregation in business and labor disputes; and the Works Projects Administration collection of recordings and photographs in the AFC's Archive of Folk Culture and the Prints and Photographs Division, which includes material relating to economic conditions and various government work projects organized to give unemployed artists work during the Great Depression. There also are large microfilm collections, such as the Goldsmiths' Library of Economic Literature (emphasizing pre-1850 European and American economic, political, and social history), the

Pandette dei notai antich (commercial records from the Middle Ages), and several series of U.S. corporate annual reports.

In 1983, the Business and Social Science materials that had formerly been part of the general reference collections in the Main Reading Room were removed from that collection and became the foundation of the reference collection for the newly formed Social Science Reading Room in the Adams Building. Nine years later, in turn, selected materials from this collection formed the basis of the reference collection for a new section, Business Reference Services (BRS). BRS itself had been established in response to the recognized need for a special focus on business as an important and growing subject area. Now part of the freshly named Humanities and Social Sciences Division, Business Reference Services managed and provided its services through the Business Reading Room on the fifth floor of the Adams Building. Soon, the reference collection would grow to approximately 20,000 volumes, representing about 9,000 titles.

In March 1993, the Edward Lowe Foundation provided a $1 million gift to the Library of Congress to establish a Business Research Fund. The money was designed to facilitate the creation and distribution in the United States "of a variety of business information tools and services to assist the nation's entrepreneurs and small businesses." From this came the Business Research Project, which sponsored a series of lectures by successful entrepreneurs and funded a widely distributed publication compiled by the staff of Business Reference Services entitled *The Entrepreneur's Reference Guide To Small Business Information*. Also supported by the Fund was the creation of the LC Bibliographic Enrichment Advisory Team (BEAT), designed both to enrich the content of Library of Congress bibliographic records and improve access to the data. As a result of this initiative, many Library of Congress catalog records now contain links to the electronic versions of the table of contents for business books, and increasingly, for books in other subjects as well. Also created was a *Directory of Selected Small Business Information Providers*, which identified peer-recommended low- or no-cost information services available to the small business community.

In 1995, the Library undertook a study to facilitate the delivery of business reference services to the public. The Business and Economics Case Study Team, chaired by the Head of Business Reference Services, James Stewart, concluded that although the Library of Congress business collections were "marked by geographic and historical comprehensiveness and depth," organizational and resource constraints limited the effectiveness of Library services. Specifically, attention was drawn to the dispersal of business-related materials throughout the library and the restrictions on offering commercial online services and databases to the public. In the aftermath of this report, numerous changes were implemented. For example, print subscriptions to current business journals were added to the business reference area, the number of online business databases available to the public increased dramatically, and new initiatives were begun to develop increased coordination of services and sharing of collections among the Library's far-flung specialized reading rooms.

In 1998, a new division, the Science, Technology and Business Division, was created by combining the Science and Technology Division and Business Reference Services. Business Reference Services then became the Business Reference Section. The purpose was to reflect the escalating importance to the Library of the fields of business and economics by stressing reference service in these areas and the great strength and value of the Library's business and economics collections. By the year 2004, the Library of Congress's core business and economics works in the general collections had reached over one million titles, and continues to grow. And currently, approximately one-third of the new serial titles received in the Library belong to the economics and business classes. Reference services have also been enhanced through the Business Reference Section's Web site, with its numerous business and economics guides and bibliographies and links to business resources on the Internet. (LM, CL)

SERIAL AND GOVERNMENT PUBLICATIONS DIVISION AND COLLECTIONS

Serials, periodicals, government publications, and newspapers have had a complicated history at the Library of Congress. Today, the Serial and Government Publications Division has custody of the Library's government publications, serial publications, periodicals, and newspapers, and provides service for these collections in its Newspaper and Current Periodical Room. Bound periodicals (including many newspaper-format publications), however, are classified and placed in the Library's general collections, in the Microform Reading Room, or, if appropriate in the Rare Book and Special Collections Division. Newspapers printed in Asian and Middle Eastern scripts are held in either the Asian Division or the African and Middle Eastern Division. Current issues and microform copies of Slavic- and Baltic-language newspapers are held by the European Division.

The Periodicals Division

In 1897, when the Library was divided into departments, Librarian John Russell Young established a separate Periodical Department with a four-person staff. Located on the first floor, south side of the Jefferson Building, the Periodical Reading Room opened January 22, 1900. It included space for 250 readers, 600 newspapers, and 2,500 periodicals, with an additional 4,000 titles stored in adjacent stacks. Librarian Herbert Putnam renamed this unit the Periodicals Division and increased the staff to 11 to handle the 400,000 issues of periodicals, serials, magazines, and newspapers received annually.

A postcard illustration of the Current Newspaper and Periodical Reading Room on the first floor, south side of the Jefferson Building, in the early years of the twentieth century. LC Archives.

The Periodicals Division ceased to exist when Librarian Archibald MacLeish reorganized the Library in the early 1940s. MacLeish separated the functions of recording serials and reader service, establishing a central Serial Record as a processing unit while placing the reading room under the Reference Department.

The Division of Documents and the Serial and Government Publications Division

In July 1900, Putnam established the Division of Documents to acquire and process official and quasi-official publications—especially those of the federal, state, local, and municipal governments. There was no separate reading area; the staff received inquiries through the Main Reading Room. In the first decade, a period of rapid collection expansion, the number of items received annually in the division rose from 20,000 to 40,000.

James Bennett Childs became acting chief of the division in 1925 and chief in 1926. His encyclopedic knowledge of government structures and government publications worldwide enabled him to mount an aggressive acquisitions program and to prepare a number of important bibliographic aids. While serving as chief of the Catalog Division during the early 1930s, he developed cataloging rules for government publications, and on returning to his position as Chief of the Documents Division in 1934, he encouraged the staff to produce bibliographies about official publications.

The Serial and Government Publications Division's offices and collections have occupied different areas in the Library's three buildings. In 1939, the bound newspaper collection was moved to a newly established Newspaper Reading Room in the Adams Building, and in 1940 the Documents Division moved from its original Northeast Attic location to the east curtain south on the main floor of the Jefferson Building, where a Government Publications Reading Room was established. As part of Librarian Archibald MacLeish's reorganization of the Library, the Division of Documents ceased to exist in June 1943, and its acquisitions functions were transferred to the new Serial Record and Exchange and Gift Divisions. The reference services and custodial responsibilities of the Documents and Serials Division were combined in the Serials Division of the new Reference Department created in 1944. The serials staff moved from the second floor of the Jefferson Building to a location adjacent to the Government Publications Reading Room.

During the 1950s, the overcrowded Jefferson Building required numerous changes in space allocations, and in 1957 the Government Publications and Periodicals Reading Rooms moved to the ground floor, south curtain. When the two reading rooms were combined in 1965, the division was realigned to

James B. Childs, a specialist in government documents bibliography, helped build the Library's government documents collection from 1925 until 1977.
LC/Prints and Photographs Division. US-P6 6169C.

British burned the Capitol in 1814. In 1931, Childs obtained 225 items from the University of Michigan, additional items from the Army War College Library, and promises from the New York Public Library and the Government Printing Office to check their collections for needed items. When a decade later the American Antiquarian Society provided photostats of many documents that were still lacking, the Library's collection finally became the most complete in the nation. The staff also worked to complete the collection of Indian treaties and tried to expand the municipal documents collection by appealing to city clerks to send publications. By 1940, the documents collection that Herbert Putnam had labeled "incomplete" in 1900 had become the largest and most important in the country.

As the Library's documents collection grew, experts began to use it as the base for compiling authoritative bibliographies. Winifred Gregory completed a union *List of the Serial Publications of Foreign Governments, 1815–1931* (1932) at the Library, and with funding from the Carnegie Corporation and the cooperation of the Bureau of the Census and Princeton University, a Census Library Project was organized in 1940 in accordance with a resolution of the Eighth American Scientific Congress to establish a comprehensive collection of population censuses and vital statistics. The project staff acquired material for the Library's collection, published a bibliography in the *Population Index*, provided reference and consultant services, and produced several special studies.

MacLeish's "Canons of Selection," the Library's first written selection policy, stated that the Library's objective was to secure "all of the official publications of all governments of the world." But World War II seemed likely to have a disastrous effect on government publications collections. When MacLeish emphasized to the Roosevelt administration the need to obtain foreign material, however, an Interdepartmental Committee for the Acquisition of Foreign Publications was established, assisted by the Office of Strategic Services, to collect wartime publications. When the war ended, the Library's European Mission succeeded in obtaining material confiscated from the German armed forces and the Nazi Party and other organizations. Simultaneously, federal agencies began clearing wartime collections from their offices and sending them to the Library. Among the most important materials were the Office of War Information's photographs of American subjects and 300,000 Japanese items collected for intelligence purposes.

During the Depression and World War II, government agencies trimmed their printing expenditures by issuing publications in mimeograph or other processed formats. But mimeographed and declassified items did not enter the depository library system for federal publications, and the Library of Congress and other libraries across the country had no means of acquiring them. In 1946, the Library provided space for a foundation-funded Documents Expediting Project, a cooperative effort by several national library associations to acquire and distribute nonclassified and nondepository federal documents, with an initial emphasis on wartime publications. Librarian Luther Evans's appeal to agency heads secured their cooperation in providing up to 150 copies of unclassified documents, ranging in the first year from Office of Strategic Services maps and Petroleum Administration reports on German oil technology to Office of War Information recordings, films, and books originally produced for overseas distribution. For 44 subscribers, the number eventually grew to 125 libraries by the 1990s. "Doc Ex," as it was dubbed, issued its own bibliography beginning in 1951, and in 1968 the Library assumed full responsibility for the work. Such important documents as Congressional Committee prints (generally unavailable to depository libraries until the 1970s), the Central Intelligence Agency's Reference Aids, and the microfilmed Voice of America scripts and Daily Reports of the Foreign Broadcast Information Service appeared in libraries via Doc Ex.

Another means of adding to the collection was microfilming, an activity that increased in importance from the 1940s onward. By mid-century, the Photoduplication Service had completed an eight-year project to microfilm early state records. The Service also filmed the archives of the Japanese Ministry of Foreign Affairs (1868–1945) and Mexican official gazettes. Before captured archives were returned to Japan, grant funds supported the filming of selected Army, Navy, and other records. And when the United Nations was established, the Library arranged to receive its processed documents in addition to the depository documents available to libraries generally. Efforts were made in the mid-1950s, through state-by-state visits with state librarians and other officials, to encourage the enactment of state laws stipulating deposit of all official publications at the Library of Congress. By the 1990s, 43 states had passed such laws, and the number of entries in the *Monthly Checklist* exceeded 26,000 annually.

The material received under the provisions of Public Law 480 and the National Program for Acquisitions and Cataloging beginning in the 1960s included government documents, particularly periodicals and official gazettes. Under these programs, the Library was able to establish offices overseas to facilitate the receipt of currently published materials that otherwise would have been difficult to obtain. At the Librarian's request, the Bureau of the Budget issued a bulletin to federal agencies on June 5, 1967, calling attention to the statutory provisions requiring that copies of all unclassified government publications not published through the Government Printing Office be supplied to the Library for official use and exchange. This effort was aimed at securing the increasing number of items produced in department field offices or printed on contract. A U.S. Government Publications Bibliographic Project, established to handle the receipts, processed around 10,000 items received from agencies.

The next step was the creation of a Federal Documents Section in the Library's Gift and Exchange Division in March 1970, bringing together all activities associated with federal publications, including Doc Ex. The section issued *Non-GPO Imprints Received in the Library of Congress* between 1970 and 1976, until the *Monthly Catalog* expanded to cover these items. A State Documents Section continued to compile the *Monthly Checklist*, and a fourth enlarged edition of Childs's early work appeared in 1976 under the title *Government Publications: A Guide to Bibliographic Tools*, prepared by Vladimir M. Palic, along with a companion volume, *Government Organization Manuals: A Bibliography* (1975). The Division's *Popular Names of U.S. Government Reports: A Catalog*, first published in 1966, was in its sixth edition by 1984. But as automation caught up with the publication of these tools, demand for print products diminished. With a 48 percent decrease in subscribers between 1989 and 1994, the *Monthly Checklist* ceased publication in its 85th year.

As James B. Childs observed, "Government publications are of such importance for the Library of Congress that it is not a matter of selection but of ascertaining what has been and is being issued, of taking any necessary steps to secure copies, and of assisting in making them available." The steady and relentless collecting of hundreds of thousands of these often-obscure publications, day by day and year by year, is one of the Library's most important contributions to preserving the records of government of all nations. (JA, JYC)

Newspapers

Today, the Library of Congress nurtures what has become one of the largest and most comprehensive newspaper collections in the world. The collection includes not only the major titles published in all 50 states and territories of the United States, but also titles from most independent countries and many dependent states that have existed during the past three centuries, and newspapers published in almost all modern languages. The general newspaper collection in the custody of the Serial and Government Publications Division comprises more than 1,000,000 current issues, 30,000 bound volumes, and 600,000

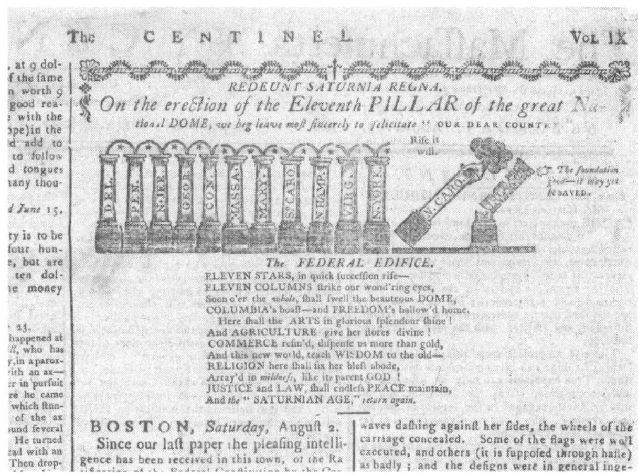
The CENTINEL. VOL IX

REDEUNT SATURNIA REGNA.

On the erection of the Eleventh PILLAR of the great National DOME, we beg leave most sincerely to felicitate "OUR DEAR COUNTRY."

The FEDERAL EDIFICE.

ELEVEN STARS, in quick ſucceſſion riſe—
ELEVEN COLUMNS ſtrike our wond'ring eyes,
Soon o'er the *whole*, ſhall ſwell the beauteous DOME,
COLUMBIA's boaſt—and FREEDOM's hallow'd home.
Here ſhall the ARTS in glorious ſplendour ſhine!
And AGRICULTURE give her ſtores divine!
COMMERCE refin'd, diſpenſe us more than gold,
And this new world, teach WISDOM to the old—
RELIGION here ſhall fix her bleſt abode,
Array'd in *mildneſs*, like its parent GOD!
JUSTICE and LAW, ſhall endleſs PEACE maintain,
And *the* "SATURNIAN AGE," *return again.*

BOSTON, *Saturday*, Auguſt 2.

Since our laſt paper the pleaſing intelligence has been received in this town, of the Ra

waves daſhing againſt her ſides, the wheels of the carriage concealed. Some of the flags were well executed, and others (it is ſuppoſed through haſte) as badly; and the deſigns were in general inge-

"The Federal Edifice" woodcut from The (Massachusetts) Centinel, *August 2, 1788, a rare eighteenth century newspaper cartoon.* LC/Serial and Government Publications Division.

reels of microfilm. The Library receives and retains on a permanent basis approximately 400 U.S. titles and 650 foreign titles. This includes approximately 3,000 current newspapers received each day of the week, and 13,000 reels of microfilm added each year. While most of the collection is in microfilm format, the Library also holds a large collection of original eighteenth century newspapers and many original single issues documenting major historical events of the last 200 years. Also available are specialized microfilm runs such as American Colonial Press, Early English Newspapers (1603–1818), underground newspapers, early African American newspapers, German and Japanese prisoner of war camp newspapers, and the Russian Revolution Newspaper collection.

In his article, "Newspapers and the Library of Congress," S. Branson Marley Jr. divides the history of the collection into three major periods, the first characterized by initial growing pains, followed by a period of development and consolidation, in turn followed by what he then called—without realizing how drastic the change would be—the technological revolution.

The first hundred years, 1801–1901, included very modest growth of the collection in the early years; loss of the entire newspaper collection in the burning of the Capitol Building in 1814, and the subsequent addition of approximately 50 titles, including two foreign titles, through acquisition of the Jefferson library in 1815; and, once again, loss of nearly the entire newspaper collection in the December 24, 1851 fire in the Capitol. Gradually, through continuing subscription and occasional purchase, the collection of newspapers was rebuilt, though most of the Library's U.S. titles dated only from the 1850s.

Credit for the growth of the collection in the last 35 years of the century goes to Librarian Ainsworth Rand Spofford, himself a former newspaperman. Librarian Spofford not only expanded the acquisition of current titles, but also was instrumental in building the excellent eighteenth and early nineteenth century holdings available at the Library today. At his urging, an amendment to the 1865 appropriation act authorized the purchase of files of leading American newspapers to add breadth to the collection. The effort to rebuild the pre-1801 collection was boosted in 1867 with the purchase of the Peter Force collection of materials relating to American history, which included nearly 250 bound volumes of newspapers. That collection was further strengthened in 1882 with the addition of volumes of the *Pennsylvania Gazette*, acquired as part of the Henry Stevens collection of Benjamin Franklin material.

Librarian Spofford also took the creative step of initiating exchanges with other libraries to strengthen holdings and fill gaps in the collection. In 1872, Spofford successfully negotiated with the American Antiquarian Society the exchange of duplicate issues of the *National Intelligencer* for a file of the *Boston Daily Advertiser*. In 1877, Spofford wrote to the State Historical Society of Wisconsin, offering to exchange duplicate issues held by the Library for western newspapers, as well as portions of eastern newspapers held at the society, beginning an exchange partnership with that institution that has continued to the present.

It was during Spofford's term that the outline of an overall policy for acquisition of newspapers was first formulated. In 1874, the Joint Committee on the Library authorized the Librarian to subscribe to at least two newspapers from each state, representing different political points of view, for the Library's collections. That policy has served as the core principle, somewhat modified, for the collection policy for domestic newspapers since that time. Finally, though there was strong resistance to extending copyright protection to newspapers through the end of the nineteenth century, several newspaper publishers nonetheless sought protection, and deposit became another source for acquisition. In 1909, "periodicals, including newspapers" were finally referred to in copyright legislation as among the classes of works eligible for copyright protection.

While actively building the collection, which included transfers of newspapers collections from various government departments that were only too glad to free valuable space in their own facilities, Librarian Spofford used the growing collections and the need to maintain them to lobby Congress for more space. In 1876, the Joint Committee on the Library, writing in support of a bill to erect the new building, specifically highlighted the valuable newspaper collection as "one of the most important features of the Library." The campaign for the new building was successful, and the newspaper collection quickly filled up seven of the nine decks of the south stack, presenting an immediate challenge to the small staff charged with organizing the collection.

The "middle period," 1900–1939, is characterized by efforts to better organize and house the collection, and by the addition of a growing number of foreign titles as political events forced the country and its government to look outward. By 1901, about 22,000 volumes of newspapers, most published domestically, were in the Library. In May of that year, the Library published *A Check List of American Newspapers in the Library of Congress*, followed in 1904 by *A Check List of Foreign Newspapers in the Library of Congress*, the first two of a continuing effort to disseminate bibliographic information about the collection.

As early as the turn of the century, the problem of deterioration of recently received newspapers was recognized. Prior to the mid-1800s, newspapers were printed on paper made using cotton rag fiber. Many of these newspapers, even dating from the early eighteenth century, survive in excellent condition and will, if properly handled and cared for, survive for generations to come. Production of rag papers was a relatively expensive process, however, and as the nineteenth century progressed, paper-making technology and the demands of increasing literacy combined to encourage cheaper production of paper.

By the 1880s, most newspapers and other mass market publications were being published on paper that was produced using a manufacturing technique that substituted untreated ground wood fibers for the more expensive rag content previously used and included additional substances to prevent discoloration and decrease porosity. Paper made using this process carries within itself reactive agents that speed its deterioration. While the use of wood pulp allowed production of a more economical medium for publication, it also guaranteed the instability of that medium over time. The cheapest and least stable form of this paper is newsprint. For those producing newspapers, deterioration was not an issue. After all, the daily paper is meant to be read and discarded. For those who hoped to preserve the daily record for research well into the future, a solution to the problem would prove to be elusive.

In his 1898 *Annual Report*, Librarian John Russell Young, like his predecessor Spofford a former newspaperman, proposed that publishers print copies on more permanent paper for copyright deposit. The proposal was not adopted at the time, and, except for a short trial that was cut short by World War II, was never implemented. Problems of deterioration and a growing backlog awaiting binding impeded management of the collection. Less than a decade after the move to the new building the collection was already overflowing its space, a problem that continued until construction of new book stacks was completed in 1910. The collection by that time included 40,000 volumes.

Following the collection policies originated by Librarian Spofford, the collection grew steadily during the next few decades. By the time of the Copyright Act of 1909, which specifically referred for the first time to "periodicals, including newspapers," as classes of works that may be copyrighted, the basic scope of the Library's newspaper collection policy and acquisition methods were in place. In 1915, the Library received 849 U.S. titles and 116 foreign titles. Of these, the Library retained for binding only 218 U.S. and 94 foreign titles; the rest were kept as current issues for a few months and were then discarded. This policy was a change from the earlier practice of adding those not bound to an arrearage that it was hoped might be one day bound, but instead had continued to grow unchecked.

During World War I, the War Industries Board had ordered newspaper to suspend free distribution of copies. Alarmed at this potential loss of its primary source for newspaper acquisition, the Library pleaded with publishers and the Board to make an exception. The campaign, though finally supported by the Board, was only partially successful, and the number of titles declined through 1920. The period between the wars saw a gradual reversal of that trend, and by 1939, the last year before the disruption of World War II, the number of titles received exceeded 900.

Significant additions to the collection during the early part of the twentieth century included the acquisition in 1905 of about 300 papers published in London during the period 1711–1729, and a collection of early California newspapers that barely escaped the 1906 earthquake and still survived due to their acquisition by the Library. In 1906, John Peter Zenger's *New-York Weekly Journal* for the period 1772–1773 was acquired, as well as John Holt's *New York Journal*; or, the *General Advertiser* for the period 1772–1773. In 1914, the War Department transferred 26 volumes and 1,671 unbound issues of Civil War newspapers, nearly all printed in the South. In 1918, the publisher of the *Baltimore Sun* gave the Library a nearly complete file of that paper, covering the years 1837–1918. The latter gift was heralded as indicative of the importance accorded the Library by newspaper publishers as a potential depository for their publishing legacy. During the several years following, acquisition efforts focused on files of newspapers from Germany and its allies for the 1914–1919 period, from which receipts had been interrupted by the war, and on collecting camp and trench newspapers. A collection of Mexican papers for the 1911–1920 period was accessioned in 1921, and in 1927 the Library acquired issues of 289 Russian newspapers documenting the Civil War, 1917–1920.

An important acquisition, and the precursor of the next era for the newspaper collection, was the acquisition in 1914 of photostat copies of issues of the *Newport Mercury* 1773–1776, from the John Carter Brown Library. This is the first mention in the Library's records of the acquisition of photostat or other photocopied newspapers. In 1915, the Library purchased a "photographic copying machine" that produced a photographic print the full size of a newspaper page. In subsequent years, prints of pages from the collection were made at the request of a number of institutions around the country.

Research use of the collection increased dramatically during this period. The Librarian's *Annual Report for 1915* notes that readers requested a total of 7,641 newspaper volumes during that year. The total collection at that time numbered about 52,000 volumes. During 1940, when the collection had reached over 100,000 volumes, 63,000 volumes and 186,000 unbound issues were served to readers.

The successful acquisitions program once again created space problems, and issues of selection and retention were forced. In 1905 and 1906, the record reports that an accumulation of "worthless and unimportant" papers were destroyed. Again in 1925,

3,127 duplicate volumes were checked against holdings and, as a result, 157 volumes were added to the permanent collection, 1,170 volumes were reserved for a future decision, and 1,800 volumes were disposed of. These attempts at weeding were only expedients, however, for space was becoming a problem for the entire Library. The bound newspaper collection and an adjacent Newspaper Reference Room were relocated in 1939 to the newly completed Adams (then Annex) Building.

Additional space, though, could not ease the growing concern about deterioration of the newspaper collection. The use of microfilm in reducing the bulk of banking and business records had been noted by Library staff and followed with great interest. The project carried out by Recordak in 1935 to film the *New York Times* was an immediate success, and opened a new avenue for preservation of the collections. On March 1, 1938, the Library announced the establishment of the Photoduplication Service, with the assistance of a grant from the Rockefeller Foundation, for the purpose of developing and applying microphotography in documentary reproduction and as an aid to research. It was recognized from the beginning that one of the primary applications would be the preservation of newspapers.

The first newspaper microfilming effort at the Library, funded in 1940 with an appropriation of $1,000, resulted in 129 reels of the *Washington Post*, covering the period December 1877 through March 1905. In 1941, an additional $1,000 was appropriated to film the *Evening Star*, 1815–1918, through a cost-sharing arrangement with the publisher and the District of Columbia Public Library. This was the Library's first truly cooperative newspaper microfilming project.

So successful were these efforts that Congress included in its 1942 appropriation $15,000 for filming old newspaper files and for acquiring microfilm of current titles in lieu of binding. By 1945, the newspaper microfilm collection had grown to nearly 15,000 reels. During that same year, a project was initiated to film, in lieu of binding, 7,409 titles of foreign-language domestic newspapers for the years 1941–1944; and, in cooperation with the Committee on Negro Studies of the American Council of Learned Societies, the filming of a collection of early African American newspapers.

The newspaper preservation microfilming program was rapidly established as a key part of the Library's operational structure. In order to take advantage of the opportunities for distribution of user copies of microfilm and to avoid duplication of effort, in 1948 the Library, at the request of the Association of Research Libraries, established in its Union Catalog Division a Microfilm Clearing House as a centralized source of information about long-running newspaper microfilming projects. The initiative resulted in the publication of *Newspapers on Microfilm: A Union Checklist*, eventually to run to eight editions, the last published by the Library in 1984.

Foreign newspaper holdings at the Library grew rapidly during this period. Increasing attention to global affairs and the events leading up to and including World War II created an increased demand for foreign newspapers, and the numbers of foreign newspapers received by the Library quickly exceeded those from the United States. Transfer of foreign newspapers from other government agencies, acquisition through diplomatic missions, and exchange and purchase agreements all contributed to expanded coverage. In 1946, the Library received the newspaper collection of the Deutsch Auslaender Institut, Stuttart, consisting of 9,014 bound volumes and 80,040 issues of 891 titles published in 43 countries.

Once again, as a result of increased acquisition activity, and in spite of preservation microfilming efforts, the collection of bound volumes had increased nearly 30 percent only 10 years after the move to the Adams Building, and by 1950 space for only one more year's acquisitions remained. In 1951, Librarian Luther Evans authorized the disposal of short runs of newspapers on an *ad hoc* basis, and the reserve set of the *Washington Post* was moved to remote storage. The next year, the Librarian formalized the policy of permitting the disposal of wood pulp bound newspapers to other libraries once newspapers were replaced by microfilm. The increase of acquisition outpaced replacement by microfilm, however, and the storage crisis worsened.

Concurrent with efforts to control the size of the collection, attention was refocused in the early 1950s on acquisition policies for both foreign and domestic newspapers. The establishment of the Microfilm Clearing House was part of a larger effort to relate the microfilm program to collection development activities, and to develop and encourage cooperative acquisition relationships. In 1952, working with the Committee on National Needs of the Association of Research Libraries, the Library sought to refine its internal policies for acquisition of newspapers within the context of a broader cooperative effort to improve the representation of foreign newspapers in American research libraries.

Building on the outline first laid out more than 75 years earlier by Librarian Spofford, the Library formally stated its acquisition policy for domestic newspapers in February 1952. This statement rephrased the Spofford formula, stating that papers for the permanent collection would be limited to those published in the state capitals and those urban centers of population most characteristic of varied phases of local life, with additional titles to be acquired when representative of distinguished journalism or other import. The policy statement noted that the Library would attempt by whatever means are practical to encourage every locality to collect, preserve, and make available the newspapers published in it. In addition, the Library adopted that year a policy limiting its domestic newspaper microfilming activities to metropolitan dailies not filmed elsewhere and urging a division of responsibility for microfilming local and regional newspapers.

In September 1955, the policy governing foreign newspapers was issued, stating that the Library would acquire for its permanent collections current newspapers from each politically independent foreign area and from the more important politically dependent foreign territories. Foreign titles were to be selected to provide the most comprehensive coverage of events and to represent principal political, economic, and social viewpoints. Both policy statements carried the caveat that the decision to retain files would be reviewed periodically in light of the availability of these newspapers in other libraries in the United States.

An effort coordinated by the American Library Association Committee on Cooperative Microfilm Projects to develop a program to preserve American newspapers led to the compilation of a list of important newspapers in each state not yet preserved on microfilm. The list was published by the Microfilm Clearing House in 1953, and distributed to state library associations, historical societies, and other state agencies with an appeal that they direct resources to microfilming the papers in their states.

A similar effort directed toward microfilming of foreign newspapers was also initiated that same year by the Association of Research Libraries through its Committee on Cooperative Access to Newspapers and Other Periodicals, with the Library of Congress as a representative. Working within a much larger context, the committee prepared a selected list of titles for microfilming, and initiated discussion of the possibility for cooperative purchase arrangements with deposit in a central repository. During the following year, the Library prepared and distributed a working paper, "Current Foreign Newspapers Recommended for Microfilming: A Preliminary List." The list included 1,219 titles in priority order, and provided rough cost estimates for a plan that would guarantee availability in the United States of at least one microfilm copy of each title.

This work, and similar work done by other groups such as the Joint Committee on Slavic Studies of the American Council of Learned Societies, led to the formation of the Association of Research Libraries Foreign Newspaper Microfilming Project, in which the Library of Congress played a key role. The project was established to maintain a representative collection of current foreign newspapers on microfilm for research use. Administration of the project was placed at the Midwest Inter-Library Center, now the Center for Research Libraries, in 1956, and work has continued to the present through the activities of the Center's Area Studies Cooperative Microfilming Programs.

By the mid-1960s, the Library had established a cooperative program to microfilm foreign newspapers obtained through its overseas offices in Asia and the Middle East under the Public Law 480 acquisitions program. As the PL-480 program expanded and contracted, the arrangements for filming varied, with some newspaper titles filmed in the countries of origin and some accumulated in the overseas office and shipped to the Photoduplication Service or the Center for Research Libraries for filming. In addition to its filming efforts, the Library maintained a leading role in disseminating bibliographic information and information about microfilming projects. Through a series of publications, including the *Newspaper and Gazette Report*, the *Foreign Newspaper Report*, and the expanded *Newspapers in Microform*, the Library reported holdings of reporting libraries and provided updates on microfilming projects, including lists of titles scheduled for filming. The publications have not only served as finding aids, but also have aided other libraries in attempts to reduce duplicative effort. Cataloging of the Library's vast newspaper collection began in the late 1970s, with the creation of full MARC bibliographic records that are made available in electronic format through the Library's MARC Distribution Service for loading into library catalogs and databases throughout the world.

The Library's newspaper collection policies were revised in 1996. The policy for U.S. newspapers continues to emphasize the broad geographic coverage goal by selecting for the collection major metropolitan dailies and at least one newspaper from each state and territorial capital. For foreign newspapers, broad geographic coverage is maintained through acquisition of current newspapers from each politically independent foreign nation.

Much of the cooperative preservation microfilming effort that was so successful during the previous two decades was redirected in the early 1980s to the United States Newspaper Program (USNP). The need for better access to files of U.S. newspapers throughout the country had long been recognized as a priority by the American Council of Learned Societies, and that need was communicated to the National Endowment for the Humanities. Winifred Gregory's *American Newspapers, 1821–1936: A Union List of Files Available in the United States and Canada* had been published in 1937, with no subsequent update. What began in the mid-1960s as "the Gregory Project" remained in planning stages until the late 1970s, when the wide availability of a national library computer utility, OCLC, Inc., made a national bibliographic and preservation project possible.

Jointly managed by the National Endowment for the Humanities (NEH) and the Library of Congress, the United States Newspaper Program is a coordinated nationwide effort to locate, catalog, preserve on microfilm, and make available to researchers collections of U.S. newspapers repositories throughout the country. Supported by funds from the Endowment's Division of Preservation and Access, and with technical support and project management provided by the Library of Congress Preservation Directorate, projects in each of the 50 states and the U.S. Trust Territories seek out and survey newspaper collections, preparing detailed holdings and condition reports. State project staff members catalog the collections and contribute machine-readable bibliographic and holdings records to the USNP National Union List, which is available throughout the world via the OCLC Online Computer Library Center's WorldCat service. Project staff also organize, select, and prepare appropriate files for preservation microfilming, which is carried out in accordance with national and international preservation standards and procedures.

U.S. Newspaper Program state projects are organized as cooperative efforts within each state, generally with one agency serving as the lead. Project staff survey libraries, courthouses, newspaper offices, historical agencies, archives, and private collections to locate and inventory newspaper files. To support this activity, NEH expects to continue its funding for the program into the first decade of the twenty-first century, at which time it is estimated that projects will have cataloged some 200,000 newspaper titles found in more than 500,000 locations. As of 2001, USNP project teams have cataloged approximately 146,000 newspaper titles, created more than 450,000 holdings records, and preserved on microfilm the content of approximately 62 million pages of newsprint. Bibliographic and holdings information collected through the national program is used by the general public, librarians, and researchers.

A complementary program exists for the preservation and access to foreign newspapers. Initiated in 1997 at the Symposium on Access to and Preservation of Global Newspapers, the International Coalition of Newspapers (iCON) was established in 1999 and is housed at the Center for Research Libraries. The Library of Congress is one of 13 charter members dedicated to preservation, bibliographic access, indexing, and copyright resolution of foreign newspapers. The Newspaper Section contributes to iCON by participating in the selection of titles for project filming and by providing missing print issues for microfilming. As with the USNP, iCON is supported by a grant from the NEH through its Division of Preservation and Access. (RBH)

<u>Special Collections</u>

Comic Books

The largest collection of comic books in the United States is housed in the Serial and Government Publications Division. The collection includes U.S. and foreign comic books—over 5,000 titles in all, totaling more than 100,000 issues. Primarily composed of the original print books, the collection includes color microfiche of selected early comic book titles (such as *Wonder Woman*, *Superman,* and *Action Comics*) and special reprints. Although the collection is most comprehensive from 1950, scattered issues from numerous titles date back to the 1930s. The collection includes a small number of Underground Comic Books "recommended for mature readers." The Library acquires comic books published and distributed in the United States almost exclusively through copyright deposit. Titles are added to the collection on the basis of quality of text and graphic depiction; significance of the artist, writer, or publisher; originality of story or main character; the title's popularity as reflected in circulation statistics or media attention; representation of new ideas or social trends; or availability through copyright.

Through the copyright law, the Serial and Government Publications Division has acquired a special collection of more than 100,000 comic books, many of them now quite rare. LC/Serial and Government Publications Division.

The fragile nature of the collection requires special handling and conservation treatment. Since fall 2002, the Serial and Government Publications Division has participated in the Library's Mass Deacidification Program, which is intended to save endangered ("at risk") paper-based material. To date, over half of the comic book collection has received mass deacidification treatment, a treatment that neutralizes the acid content of comic books to prevent further deterioration and extends the life of the paper.

In part because of their fragility, comic books are available to researchers for use under special conditions only. Access is limited to serious collectors examining specific titles and those doing research of a specific nature, leading toward a publicly available work (a publication, a dissertation, a radio, film or television production, or a public performance).

Historic Events Newspaper Collection

Over the years, the Newspaper Section identified a number of unique newspaper issues representing milestones in journalism history or historic events. Collected as the Historic Events Newspaper Collection, they are intended primarily for exhibit purposes but also to preserve the newspaper as artifact. The collection documents American history through politics, technology, sports, entertainment, and war, and in several cases represents the only extant print copies in existence. The largest recent accession is a collection of several thousand U.S. and foreign newspapers reporting on the tragic events of September 11, 2001, and the subsequent war on terrorism.

Federal Advisory Committee Collection

With the passage of the Federal Advisory Committee (Public Law 92-463) on October 6, 1972, the Library of Congress became the official public repository for reports from committees, board, commissions, councils, conferences, panels, task forces, or any similar groups appointed to obtain advice or recommendations for the president or agencies or officers of the federal government. Charters, annual reports, minutes of meetings, and membership rosters are deposited with the Library; organized, filed, and made available to Congress, researchers, and members of the general public on request in the Newspaper and Current Periodical Room.

Cole, John Y. "Developing a National Foreign Newspaper Microfilming Program," *Library Resources and Technical Services* 18 (Winter 1974): 5–17.

Library of Congress Information Bulletin 50 (November 4, 1991): 413–418.

Marley, S. Branson. "Newspapers and the Library of Congress," *The Quarterly Journal of the Library of Congress* 32 (July 1975): 207–237.

SERIAL RECORD DIVISION

Serials are continuing publications issued at intervals. They include weekly and monthly periodicals such as *Newsweek*, *Vogue* and *Punch*; quarterly publications such as professional journals; and annual reports, yearbooks, and almanacs. Monographs in series, directories, and books issued in parts, even if they are issued irregularly, are considered to be serial items as well. Serials constitute by far the largest number of items published worldwide, and the current information they offer is always in demand. In most libraries, serials have been recorded separately because they need special attention; for example, subscriptions must be placed and monitored, and issues have to be bound together at prescribed intervals.

In 1897, when the Library was first divided into departments, Librarian John Russell Young established a Periodical Department with a four-person staff. Located on the first floor, south side of the Jefferson Building, the Periodical Reading Room opened January 22, 1900. Librarian Herbert Putnam renamed this unit the Periodicals Division and increased the staff to 11 to handle the 400,000 issues of periodicals, serials, magazines, and newspapers received annually. All had to be recorded on check-in cards and prepared for the shelves—a labor-intensive task because "a large percentage of the periodicals received daily must be cut and many sewed, before they can be put out for readers." When an issue failed to appear, the staff had to "claim" the issue—that is, ask the publisher or vendor that supplied the subscription to send the missing item. At the end of a year or when a volume was complete, the staff retrieved and collated the issues for binding. However, the Periodicals Division did not record all of the serials the Library received. Government serials went to the Documents Division and legal serials to the Law Library, while the Smithsonian Division kept scientific journals received on exchange. All these units had their own methods of administering serials work, and by the 1930s there were as many as 32 separate places where serials were recorded.

To save duplication of periodicals in federal libraries, Librarian Putnam in 1901 offered to assist a cooperative effort to compile a union list—a listing, with holdings, of all the periodicals and serials in federal libraries in the District of Columbia. As this list and others appeared, and as librarians discovered the value of union lists for tasks as diverse as exchanging duplicate issues or deciding whether subscriptions were needed, the American Library Association (ALA) asked Putnam whether the Library staff could compile a list of all the serials in U.S. libraries. Citing a shortage of staff, the Librarian refused. The ALA and H.W. Wilson Company ultimately completed the project with the aid of 41 libraries, producing the *Union List of Serials* in 1927.

The Periodicals Division ceased to exist when Librarian Archibald MacLeish reorganized the Library in the early 1940s. Following the recommendation of his Librarian's Committee to establish a separate serial record, MacLeish first placed it in the Processing Department, but in 1943 it was moved into the newly established Accessions Department. The serials records that had been maintained by various divisions (except the Law Library) were reorganized into two files: a Serial Catalog for bound volumes and a Visible File for current issues. But during the 1940s the staff was too small to fully achieve the hoped-for integration, and by 1948 the annual workload of 1.3 million items swamped the staff. Transferred to the Order Division in 1949, the Serial Record remained incomplete but procedures slowly improved, and a separate Serial Record Division was created in 1953. Until the age of automation arrived, the central Serial Record remained the Library's organizing mechanism for recording current periodicals and serials printed in the Roman, Greek, Cyrillic, and Hebraic alphabets.

By January 1951, the staff was able to begin publishing a monthly accessions list called *Serial Titles Newly Received*. With titles listed on 80-column punched cards, they intended to speed processing and move toward an improved serials listing. The accessions list did not provide full cataloging, but librarians elsewhere immediately became interested in the venture, and before the end of the fiscal year, planning had begun for including other libraries' holdings.

Serial Titles Newly Received became New Serial Titles in January 1953, when it was converted to a union list of library holdings to supplement the *Union List of Serials*. It was immediately popular—so much so that by 1955 most major U.S. research libraries were contributing reports of their serial holdings. Since current holdings coverage had never been available before, NST (as it was dubbed) immediately became a valuable tool for both librarians and researchers. The listing included new titles listed by subject as well as alphabetically, with information about serials that had ceased, been suspended, changed title or issuing agency, or merged with other serials.

Beginning with the publication of NST, the Library's serials staff cooperated with other librarians in virtually all national and international activities relating to the bibliographic control of serial publications. "We now find ourselves in an era of serial rather than book publication," stated the *Annual Report of the Librarian of Congress* in 1952, when the Library was receiving over 100,000 titles annually and adding new ones at the rate of 10,000 each year. The rapid growth of contributions to NST showed that other librarians were also expanding serials work. By the early 1950s a revision of the 1943 second edition of the ULS and its two supplements (1945 and 1949) seemed essential, and the Council on Library Resources, Inc. (CLR) provided support in 1959 for a project organized by the Joint Committee on the *Union List of Serials*, Inc., a group representing many library-related groups. The Committee contracted with the Library of Congress's Processing Department to direct the work, and the new ULS appeared in 1966.

The Library's leadership role in serials work seemed natural to many librarians because the Serial Record Division was the largest operation of the type worldwide, receiving over 2.7 million items annually by the 1960s. Whereas in 1941, 8,000 items were recorded, the Serial Record of the 1960s contained over 350,000. As the number of titles in all fields continued to increase and as advances in science and technology, in particular, promoted the publication of journals, technical serials, and documents, in 1967 the Library of Congress, the National Library of Medicine, and the National Agricultural Library agreed to build a database to provide what the ULS and NST did not: complete cataloging for all serial titles. The Joint Committee on the *Union List of Serials* was asked to obtain financial support and serve as an advisory group.

With assistance from the CLR and the National Science Foundation, the first phase of the project began in July 1967 with the compilation of a MARC format for serials, and a few years later all cataloging of serials moved from the Descriptive Cataloging Division to the Serial Record Division. A National Serials Pilot Project began in May 1969 conducted by the Association of Research Libraries (ARL) drew on the national libraries' holdings of scientific and technical serials to investigate the problems of automated serials control.

The automation of serials cataloging provided an opportunity to assign a unique identifier to each title. Because different serials often have similar names, they are easily confused; and when name changes occur, the old and new must be linked. A single, unambiguous number, however, can identify a continuing publication forever. The Library worked with the American National Standards Institute (ANSI) to design a standard numbering system, which was accepted as the American National Standard for Identification Numbers for Serial Publications. Eventually it became the International Standard Serial Number (ISSN). The Library of Congress's National Serials Data Program, established in January 1973, became the agency responsible for assigning the ISSN to U.S. serials.

The third phase of the National Serials Pilot Project was the development of a standardized database. Work began in April 1972, using current cataloging records from the three national libraries as the base file. However, it soon became apparent that using the current cataloging would not build the database quickly enough to be useful to librarians ready to convert all their serial cataloging records to electronic format. Thus in an "Ad Hoc Discussion Group on Serials" (also known as the Toronto Group) meeting convened at the ALA's annual conference in June 1973, U.S. and Canadian librarians considered various methods for establishing a comprehensive database of serials cataloging. Many felt that they could wait no longer; nevertheless, they wanted the ISSN, which was considered extremely important to future serials handling and which could come only from the Library of Congress. Ultimately they asked that the Library conduct a study of its serials processing with a view to coordinating the NSDP, the MARC serials cataloging, and the publication of *New Serial Titles*, and to join a comprehensive database building effort.

With funding and technical support from the CLR, the Ohio College Library Center (OCLC) was selected to mount the database, which would be assembled via tape loads. Named Conversion of Serials (CONSER), the project began in 1974 with the Library as one of the members. In May 1975, the National Serials Pilot Project provided the OCLC with a computer tape of records to be combined with electronic records from the Minnesota Union List of Serials. The responsibility for contributing cataloging to the database rested with the member libraries, but each catalog record would receive quality review by the Library of Congress.

After the first phase, CONSER membership broadened to include other libraries, and the database grew quickly during the 1970s and 1980s as grant-funded projects supported the addition of large numbers of catalog records. In late 1975, the Library made an agreement with the National Library of Canada to exchange machine-readable records so that the Canadian records could be added to CONSER. The National Endowment for the Humanities provided funds in 1976 to add humanities serials. As libraries joined CONSER, they forwarded their cataloging (excluding Canadian imprints) to the Library of

Congress, where the staff reviewed contributed records for conformity to CONSER guidelines and added them to the database. To better coordinate the related activities of MARC serials cataloging, the NSDP, and ongoing automation, the NSDP moved to the Processing Department in 1974. While the Library planned during the mid-1970s to assume responsibility for the CONSER database, by 1978 continuing financial constraints led to the decision to have the OCLC manage the project.

The failure of library budgets to keep pace with inflation during the 1970s forced many libraries to abandon subscriptions to many serials, but the Library of Congress was still acquiring nearly 1.5 current serial titles annually in 1977, and it benefited significantly from CONSER cataloging records. "As the result of participation in CONSER," noted the *Annual Report of the Librarian of Congress*, "LC's current serials cataloging is coming increasingly to represent the equivalent of national bibliographic source records, rather than cataloging uniquely tailored to LC's own collections." To speed processing, the Library adopted as much of one-fourth of its own cataloging from CONSER records, adopted minimal level cataloging for serials of lesser research value, began planning to automate the Serial Record itself in the early 1980s, and began using CONSER records to produce *New Serial Titles*.

In cooperation with the ALA, the Library planned and held several Serials Cataloging Regional Institutes in 1986–1987 that provided opportunities for nearly 600 librarians to learn more about serials cataloging in the electronic environment and about CONSER and NSDP. After a program review in 1987, CONSER was renamed the Cooperative Online Serials Program. The Serial Record Division's bibliographic activities remain closely tied to CONSER since it provides the secretariat. The program has a Web site, a training program for member libraries' staff members, an electronic journal called *CONSERline*, and its own *CONSER Cataloging Manual* and *CONSER Editing Guide*. Member libraries now have the authority to contribute and modify records in conformity with the cataloging manual and editing guide. On October 1, 1997, CONSER became part of the Library's Program for Cooperative Cataloging. Although *New Serial Titles* ceased publication in 1999, a printed catalog of NST records created 1971–1999 is still available.

The Serial Record Division handles serial titles in all languages and all formats. It records newly received issues and volumes, routes them to the appropriate shelving area, catalogs new titles in the OCLC database, contributes to CONSER, and assigns International Standard Serial Numbers to titles published in the United States. Approximately 1.2 million items are received annually, and the Library maintains information for about 900,000 serial entries. (JA)

Livingston, Lawrence G. "A Composite Effort to Build an On-line National Serials Data Base," *Library of Congress Information Bulletin* 35 (February 1, 1974): A35–38.

"Serial Record Division," *Library of Congress Information Bulletin* 51 (July 13, 1992): 309–313, 318–319.

SPOFFORD, AINSWORTH RAND (1825–1908)

The modern history of the Library of Congress began when Ainsworth Rand Spofford became Librarian of Congress, for it was Spofford who transformed the small reference library that served the U.S. Congress into a national institution that also served the American public. Spofford permanently joined the legislative and national functions of the Library, first in practice and then in law through

Ainsworth Rand Spofford, who served as Assistant Librarian from 1861 to 1864, as Librarian of Congress from 1864 to 1897, and as Chief Assistant Librarian from 1897 until his death in 1908. More than any other individual, Spofford was responsible for transforming the Library of Congress from a small library that served the Congress into an institution of national significance. LC/Prints and Photographs Division. LC-BH826-452-A.

the reorganization of 1897. He provided his successors as Librarian with four essential prerequisites for the development of an American national library: 1) firm congressional support for the idea of the Library of Congress as both a legislative and a national library; 2) the beginning of a comprehensive collection of Americana; 3) a magnificent new building, itself a national monument; and 4) a strong and independent Librarian of Congress. Each Librarian of Congress since Spofford has shaped the institution in a different manner, but none has ever wavered from Spofford's fundamental assertion that the Library was both a legislative and a national institution.

Spofford was born in Gilmanton, New Hampshire, on September 12, 1825. He was tutored at home and developed into an avid reader and student. In 1845, he moved west to Cincinnati and soon found congenial employment as a bookstore clerk in the firm of E.D. Truman, bookseller and publisher; thanks to his efforts the store soon became the city's leading importer of the books of the New England transcendentalists—his favorite authors. He was one of the founders of the Literary Club of Cincinnati. In 1852, he married Sarah Partridge, a schoolteacher formerly from Franklin, Massachusetts, and they had three children: Charles, Henry, and Florence.

Spofford began a new career in 1859 as Associate Editor of Cincinnati's leading newspaper, the *Daily Commercial*; in his first editorial, titled "A Bibliologist," he attacked the naive book-buying practices of the city librarian. Two years later the newspaper sent him to Washington, D.C. to report on the opening of the Thirty-Seventh Congress and the inauguration of President Abraham Lincoln, a trip that led

The Capitol and its unfinished dome on March 4, 1861, as Abraham Lincoln is inaugurated as the sixteenth president of the United States. As a correspondent for the Cincinnati Daily Commercial, *Spofford reported on the inaugural and the opening of the 37th Congress. He returned to Washington, D.C. in the summer of 1861 and visited Lincoln's appointee as Librarian of Congress, John G. Stephenson—the brother of a Cincinnati friend. Stephenson offered him the job of Assistant Librarian, and when Stephenson resigned on the last day of 1864, Lincoln appointed Spofford to replace him.* LC/Prints and Photographs Division. LC-USZ62-48564.

to his acceptance, in September 1861, of the position of Assistant Librarian of Congress. Knowledgeable, industrious, and ambitious, he garnered support from many members of Congress when the post of Librarian of Congress became vacant in late 1864. On December 31, 1864, President Lincoln named him to the post. Located in the west front of the U.S. Capitol, the Library had a staff of seven and a book collection of approximately 82,000 volumes.

Spofford immediately set to work establishing the Library's national role, and he pursued this cause with energy and political skill. Congressmen liked him and with help from his friends from Ohio, particularly Rutherford B. Hayes and James A. Garfield, he obtained support for several legislative acts between

1865 and 1870 that ensured the growth of the collections and made the Library of Congress the largest library in the United States. The new laws included the transfer of the Smithsonian Institution's library to the Library of Congress, the purchase for $100,000 of the private library of Americana collector Peter Force, and the use of international exchange to build the Library's collections. The most important new measure was the Copyright Law of 1870, which centralized all U.S. copyright registration and deposit activities at the Library. The new law brought books, pamphlets, maps, prints, photographs, and music into the institution without cost, thus assuring the future growth of the Americana collections and providing the Library with an essential and unique national function.

In his annual reports to Congress, Spofford continually emphasized that a national library should be a permanent, comprehensive collection of national literature that represented "the complete product of the American mind in every department of science and literature." Comprehensiveness was essential, for in his view the American national library should serve both the American citizenry and its elected representatives. Books and information were needed about all subjects and, as the library of the American government, the Library was the natural site for such a comprehensive collection.

In 1874, for the first time, the copyright law brought in more books than were obtained through purchase, and three years later Spofford's already cramped library was out of space and more than 70,000 books, he noted, were "piled on the floor in all directions." His struggle for a separate building, which began in 1871, was a crucial part of his national library effort. A new structure would ensure the unique status of the Library of Congress among American libraries—and would give the United States a national library that would equal and someday surpass the great national libraries of Europe. The latter argument was especially popular with Congress. Spofford proposed a large structure that would also serve as an efficient, well-functioning building. The new building, however, was not authorized until 1886 and not completed for another decade. Spofford's dream was fulfilled in 1897 when the doors to the monumental and ornate new structure across the east plaza from the Capitol, at the time the "largest, costliest, and safest" library building in the world, were finally opened to an admiring public.

In the Library's rooms in the Capitol, Spofford's desk and table are weighted down from above and pushed up by books, an eloquent symbol of the Library's lack of space. Spofford campaigned tirelessly for a new and separate building for the Library.
LC/Prints and Photographs Division. LC-USZ-603.

The Jefferson Building in 1898, a year after it opened to widespread acclaim from Congress, librarians, and the public. The building was suggested by Spofford shortly after the approval of the Copyright Law of 1870, but not authorized until 1886.
LC/Public Affairs Office.

For the most part, Spofford operated independently of the American library movement and the American Library Association (ALA). By 1876, when ALA was founded, the Library of Congress was already the leading library in the country, and Spofford was completely absorbed in the struggle for a new building. His independence from other libraries and librarians was accentuated by his idea of a national library as well as by his personal temperament. The national library was a single, enormous accumulation of the nation's literature. He did not view it as a focal point for cooperative library activities and was not inclined to exert leadership in that direction.

From November 16 to December 7, 1896, the Joint Committee on the Library held hearings about the Library of Congress, its "condition," and its organization. Although Spofford was the principal witness, the ALA sent six librarians to testify. The testimony of Melvil Dewey and Herbert Putnam on the desirable future role of the Library of Congress as a "national" library was of special interest; both men avoided direct criticism of Spofford, but it was obvious that their view of the proper functions of the Library differed from that of the aging Librarian. Putnam wholeheartedly endorsed Dewey's description of the proper and necessary role of a national library: "a center to which the libraries of the whole country can turn for inspiration, guidance, and practical help." Centralized cataloging, interlibrary loan, and a national union catalog were among the services they advocated.

The hearings resulted in a major reorganization and expansion, effective July 1, 1897. Spofford became Chief Assistant Librarian under a new Librarian of Congress, John Russell Young, and he continued as Chief Assistant Librarian under Herbert Putnam, who became Librarian of Congress in April 1899. Spofford died in Holderness, New Hampshire, on August 11, 1908.

Spofford's professional and personal interests were accurately described in the formidable title of his *A Book for All Readers, Designed as an Aid to the Collection, Use, and Preservation of Books and Formation of Public and Private Libraries* (1900). He was respected by librarians, politicians, and the general public, not only because of his accomplishments at the Library, but also because of his fair-mindedness and enthusiasm for sharing his views about his favorite subjects—reading, bibliography, and collection building. Librarian of Congress Putnam paid his friend Ainsworth Rand Spofford a final official tribute in the Library's 1908 *Annual Report*: "His most enduring service—the increase of (the Library's) collections—continued to the last few weeks of his life, and continued with the enthusiasm, the devotion, the simple, patient, and arduous concentration that had always distinguished it. The history of it during its most influential period will be the history of the Library from 1861 to 1897. This will in due course . . .appear." (JYC)

Ainsworth Rand Spofford, 1825–1908, A Memorial Service at the Library of Congress on Thursday, November 12, 1908. New York: Webster Press, 1909.

Cole, John Y., ed. *Ainsworth Rand Spofford: Bookman and Librarian*. Littleton, Colo.: Libraries Unlimited, 1975.

STEPHENSON, JOHN G. (1828–1883)

John Gould Stephenson served as the fifth Librarian of Congress from May 21, 1861, until his resignation, which was effective December 31, 1864. A political appointee of President Abraham Lincoln, Stephenson was a physician and Republican partisan from Terre Haute, Indiana. As Librarian of Congress, Stephenson apparently spent as much time serving as a physician for the Union Army as he did supervising the Library. He could do so because in September 1861, he had hired Cincinnati bookseller and journalist Ainsworth Rand Spofford as his assistant librarian. For all practical purposes the eager and well-qualified Spofford ran the Library during the rest of Stephenson's term of office, and on December 31, 1864, Lincoln appointed Spofford as Librarian. Stephenson's appointment by Lincoln in 1861 appears to be the most blatantly political appointment of a Librarian of Congress ever made by a president. Nevertheless, there is truth in the conclusion by Library of Congress historian David C. Mearns that on the whole John G. Stephenson "did the Library of Congress neither harm nor good during his administration." It also is clear, however, that Stephenson's single most important accomplishment was hiring Spofford as his assistant.

John G. Stephenson served as the fifth Librarian of Congress from May 1861 until his resignation in December 1864. When Stephenson was appointed by President Lincoln, the Library had a staff of five employees. Four months after taking office he hired Ainsworth Rand Spofford as Assistant Librarian, and Spofford soon became the dominant force in the Library. In his 1883 front-page obituary in the Washington Post, *Stephenson was characterized as "largely known and much liked."*
LC/Prints and Photographs Division. LC-USZ62-614319.

John Gould Stephenson was born in Lancaster, New Hampshire, on March 1, 1828, the sixth child of Reuben and Mary King Stephenson. Reuben Stephenson was a prominent Lancaster citizen and one of the incorporators of the Lancaster Academy, where John attended school. From the Academy, Stephenson went to the New Hampshire Medical Institution and then to Castleton Medical College, where he received a doctorate in medicine on November 23, 1849.

About 1851, the young Dr. Stephenson migrated west to Terre Haute and, a few years later, became active in the newly formed Republican Party. He was one of Lincoln's earliest supporters for the presidential nomination, and after Lincoln's nomination and election, Stephenson launched a determined campaign to become Librarian of Congress. Why he chose this particular job to pursue is unclear, but one can speculate that he knew about libraries because his brother, Reuben had served as head of the Cincinnati Mercantile Library since the 1850s—where, in fact, he was a close friend of Ainsworth Spofford.

Stephenson obtained the political support he needed, particularly from Indiana Senator Henry S. Smith and the soon-to-be-Secretary of the Interior Caleb B. Smith. On May 7, 1861, the candidate himself was in Washington and wrote to Lincoln, reminding the president that he had been "an earnest and continuous supporter in the Cause that triumphed in your election." After listing his political endorsements, Stephenson noted that his "pecuniary condition" would be "greatly relieved by you granting the application." A letter from Indiana Republican leader William P. Dole to a friend in Washington, dated May 14, 1861, says that Lincoln is about to appoint Stephenson, which suited Dole just fine even though "the Dr. is not heavy mettal," because "he has worked hard for us & is poor and can hand down books from a shelf to (Members of Congress) as well & as gracefully as any one." Moreover, Dole concluded "he is a Wabash man & I am for home." Lincoln made the appointment a week after the letter was written.

Stephenson hired Spofford in September 1861 and then left the Library for three weeks to serve on the battlefield. Describing Stephenson to a friend in May 1862, Spofford characterized the Librarian as "a thorough good fellow, liberal, high-minded, & active, but with no special knowledge of books." By September 1862, however, relations between the two men had fractured. Upset by the Librarian's dismissal of another assistant, Spofford threatened to quit unless he received a promise of full support from

Stephenson for the future. As Spofford described the situation to his friend Henry B. Blackwell: "I have made it a condition of retaining my post that I am to be subjected to no hasty deprivation of support. . . his readiness to repair the past by doing whatever I should advise, leaves me willing to continue association with him."

The headstrong assistant librarian was responsible for the major accomplishments of the Library of Congress during Stephenson's term of office. These included: the compilation of two lengthy manuscript reports critical of the Library's condition and urging Congress to authorize funds for improvements; successful lobbying for a $160,000 appropriation to expand the Library's room in the Capitol; the inauguration of more comprehensive and efficient book-buying procedures; and, in September 1864, publication of the 1,200 *Alphabetical Catalogue of the Library of Congress: Authors*, the first complete author catalog in the Library's history. Stephenson, however, lent his support and approval to Spofford's efforts.

There is still much to be learned about the motives and the career of John G. Stephenson as Librarian of Congress. In the summer of 1861, shortly after assuming the post, he served as a volunteer surgeon for members of the 19th Indiana Regiment, who were in a temporary hospital set up in the Patent Office Building. For the rest of his Civil War military career, however, his jobs apparently were more political than medical in their nature. According to his own account, in 1863 he served with the Army of the Potomac, not as a surgeon, but "as a volunteer aide-de-camp with my militia rank of Colonel, participating in the battles of Fitzhugh Crossing, Chancellorsville, and Gettysburg." He received a commendation for his performance at Gettysburg.

Nor are the circumstances surrounding Stephenson's resignation fully known. In his *History of the Library of Congress 1800–1864* (1904), William Dawson Johnston implies that Stephenson left the Library under a cloud because of his involvement in "speculations created by the war." He cites as evidence a June 8, 1872 congressional resolution paying the Library's London book agent $1,480 "of which sum he was unjustly defrauded by the conduct of the Librarian in 1863." Despite the harsh wording of the resolution, it is not clear whether war speculations or technical problems involving methods of payment prompted the congressional action.

A 1863 drawing of the charge of the Louisiana brigade at Gettysburg by Alfred R. Waud. A physician, Librarian of Congress John G. Stephenson left for three weeks of volunteer service on the battlefield in September 1861. In Stephenson's words, in 1863 he served with the Army of the Potomac "as a volunteer aide-de-camp with my militia rank of Colonel, participating in the battles of Fitzhugh Crossing, Chancellorsville, and Gettysburg." He received a commendation for his work at Gettysburg. LC/Prints and Photographs Division. LC-USZ62-15837.

Following his resignation as Librarian on December 31, 1864, Stephenson kept his legal residence in Washington and apparently held several political jobs. On November 16, 1881, nearly 17 years after he left the Library, he was appointed as a medical reviewer at the Pension Office. At the age of 55, on November 11, 1883, he died. He is buried in the Congressional Cemetery in Washington, D.C. (JYC)

Carter, Constance. "John Gould Stephenson: Largely Known and Much Liked." *The Quarterly Journal of the Library of Congress* 33 (April 1976): 71–91.

STRATEGIC INITIATIVES, OFFICE OF

The Office of Strategic Initiatives provides oversight for Library-wide digital initiatives and is responsible for developing and implementing a congressionally mandated National Digital Information Infrastructure and Preservation Program (NDIIPP). The office also administers two key Library of Congress programs and administration units: the National Digital Library (NDL) and the Office of Information Technology Services (ITS). The Library created the Office of Strategic Initiatives on October 2, 2000, in response to recommendations in the National Research Council's study, *LC21: A Digital Strategy for the Library of Congress* (July 2000), including the recommendation that the Library, working with other institutions, take the lead in preservation and archiving of digital materials. In December 2000, Congress appropriated $99.8 million to develop and implement a congressionally approved strategic plan for NDIIPP. With certain adjustments, Congress approved the plan, and in September 2004, after a two-year competition, awards totaling $15 million were announced for projects from eight institutions and their partners. (JYC)

WATTERSTON, GEORGE (1783–1854)

George Watterston served as Librarian of Congress from March 21, 1815 until May 28, 1829. Appointed by President James Madison, he was the first Librarian who did not also serve simultaneously as Clerk of the House of Representatives; thus, even though he followed John Beckley and Patrick Magruder in the position, he is sometimes called the first Librarian of Congress.

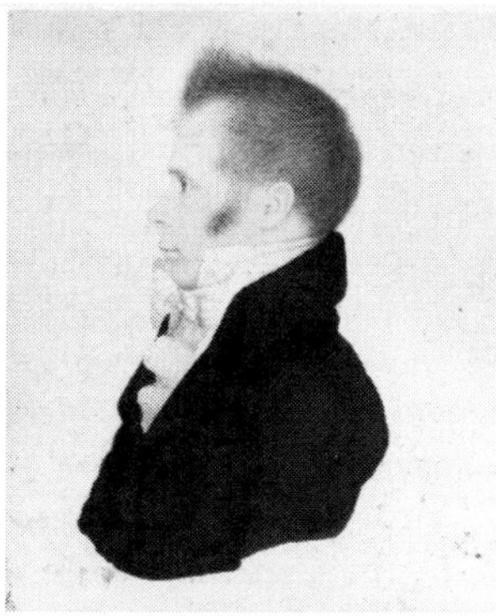

George Watterston, the third Librarian of Congress, served from 1815 until 1829 and was the first full-time Librarian. A lawyer turned literary man, he wrote novels, poetry, and was also considered Washington, D.C.'s first full-time man of letters.
LC Archives.

Like his predecessors, Watterston was a political partisan. He was also controversial, thin-skinned, and outspoken, never passing up an opportunity to lambast one of his many enemies. A lawyer turned literary man, he wrote novels, a play, and poetry, and was Washington's first full-time man of letters. An oft-repeated but unconfirmed story attributes his appointment as Librarian of Congress by President Madison to Watterston's flattering dedication of his 1810 poem "The Wanderer in Jamaica" to Dolley Madison. He was the Librarian of Congress who received and organized Jefferson's library and published its catalog. He also raised for the first time serious arguments on behalf of the Library of Congress as a national library.

Watterston's colorful life began on October 23, 1783, on a ship in New York Harbor. He was the son of David Watterston, a master builder who had left Scotland with his family to start a new life in New York City. Attracted by the construction opportunities in the new federal capital, David Watterston brought his family to Washington in 1791. All of his life, George Watterston retained a strong interest in the city of Washington and its history, promoting the city through his activities, particularly the building of the Washington Monument. He was secretary of the Washington Monument Society from its creation in the 1830s until his death.

Young George was sent to school at Charlotte Hall School, in St. Mary's County, Maryland, where he received a classical education. Next he studied law, and began practicing in Hagerstown, Maryland. He soon developed a distaste for law and began the literary career that continued for the rest of his life. His unhappiness with law and lawyers, which also lasted throughout his lifetime, was at the root of his first novel, *The Lawyer, or Man as He Ought Not to Be*, published anonymously in 1808. An inheritance from a wealthy uncle enabled him to travel to Jamaica, where he wrote the poem dedicated to Mrs. Madison. On his return, he married Maria Shanley, and established a residence on Capitol Hill, where he and his wife eventually raised eight children. He soon published another novel, *Glencarn; or, The Disappointments of Youth* (1810); a play, *The Child of Feeling* (1809); and another poem, "The Scenes of Youth" (1813).

In this period, Watterston began his long involvement in Washington's civic affairs. In 1813, he unsuccessfully petitioned President Madison for the position of "collector of the District of Columbia." The same year, he became editor of the *Washington Civic Gazette*, a Republican paper. This was one of four newspaper editorships he was to hold throughout his life. When the British attacked Washington in 1814, he marched with a local military company to meet the enemy at nearby Bladensburg. He returned to find his own Capitol Hill house pillaged and, of course, the Capitol itself and the nascent Library of Congress destroyed.

Prior to his appointment of Patrick Magruder as Clerk of the House of Representatives and Librarian of Congress in 1807, President Thomas Jefferson considered separating the positions of Clerk and Librarian. In March 1815, the pending arrival of Jefferson's 6,000-volume library, purchased by Congress to "reconstitute" the Library after its destruction by the British, made the appointment of a new Librarian an urgent piece of business, and this time the position was separated from the Clerkship. Watterston was appointed on March 21, 1815 and immediately made preparations to receive Jefferson's books in the "temporary" Capitol Building: Blodget's Hotel and 7th and E Streets NW. The new Librarian, who was to operate without an assistant until 1828, began correspondence with Jefferson regarding the transport and eventual arrangement of his books, which arrived in May. Watterston decided to keep Jefferson's arrangement, based on Sir Francis Bacon's classification of knowledge, intact and it served as the basis of the Library's arrangement until the move into the Library's separate building in 1897.

Without informing the Joint Committee on the Library, to whom he reported, in late 1815 Watterston published a catalog of the Jefferson purchase. Its title, *Catalogue of the Library of the United States*, accurately described the Librarian's ambition for the institution. The committee immediately criticized Watterston, particularly with regard to the catalog's cost, and Watterston haughtily informed Jefferson: "The Library Committee are dissatisfied with me for having the catalogue printed without having consulted their superior judgment, but the members generally speak very highly of your arrangement and the disposition of the books."

In spite of its unhappiness with Watterston himself, in 1816 Congress increased the Librarian's salary and appropriated additional sums for the purchase of books and maps. Moreover, during the first two years of his librarianship, Watterston planted seeds for the expansion of the Library into a national institution. While he never succeeded in furthering his ideas, their public presentation was a first step towards their fulfillment decades later.

On July 31, 1815, in a statement influenced if not written by Watterston, the daily *National Intelligencer* of Washington proclaimed the need for the congressional (or "National Library of the United States") to become "the great repository of the literature of the world." In the same newspaper on September 15, 1815, Watterston signed his name to a notice asking that "American authors, engravers, and painters" transmit copies of their works to the Library to serve "not only as a literary history of this now interesting country, but [also] to exhibit the progress and improvement of the arts." On January 9, 1817, the Senate approved a bill authorizing the selection of copyright deposits sent to the Department of State for the Library's collections, but the House did not take it up. On February 18, Library Committee chairman, Senator Eligius Fromentin of Louisiana, introduced a bill advocating a separate building for the Library. Four days later, the resolution was "determined in the negative," an action deplored in a March 25 letter to the *National Intelligencer* from Librarian Watterston, who noted that "in all other countries" such a structure would be "an object of national pride."

In December 1818, the Library moved, not into a separate building, but back into the reconstructed Capitol Building. Its quarters, however, were in an attic in the Capitol's north wing, where it remained for the next six years. Watterston continued his literary career in the 1820s, and was one of the first novelists to use Washington as a setting. The Library of Congress itself formed part of the background for his *The L. . .Family at Washington* (1822). It was followed by his final novel, *The Wanderer in Washington* (1827), in which Watterston's commentator speaks very favorably about Henry Clay, the author's favorite politician.

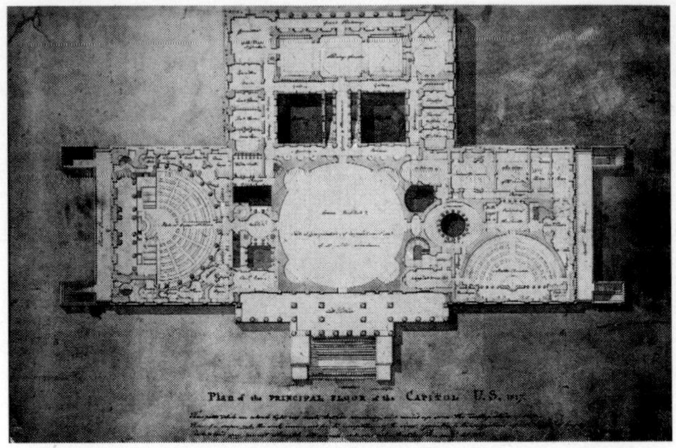

In 1815, Librarian Watterston received and organized Jefferson's recently arrived library and published its catalog, giving it the title Catalogue of the Library of the United States. *In August 1824, the Library moved into new and spacious quarters in the center of the west front of the Capitol. The "Plan of the Principal Floor of the Capitol" that was followed was prepared by architect Benjamin Latrobe in 1817.*
LC/Prints and Photographs Division. LC-USZ62-11125.

Watterston's combative personality and obvious Whig leanings continued to make his librarianship somewhat rocky, and there are indications that his hold on the job of Librarian at times was threatened. Yet substantial milestones occurred; the $2,000 approved by Congress for the purchase of books in 1820 was the first separate annual appropriation for this purpose. In 1824, the princely sum of $5,000 was appropriated for the purchase of books. And in August 1824, the Library moved into spacious and elegant new quarters in the center of the Capitol. The *National Journal* even described the Library's room as "decidedly the most beautiful, and in the best taste of any in this country." The new Library room became a popular social center, but its glory received a setback when a fire on December 22, 1825, damaged the gallery. It was started by a candle left burning in the gallery and controlled before serious damage occurred. A congressional inquiry was unable to fix blame, but the mishap opened the door to Watterston's political enemies. In July 1826, the Librarian complained to a friend about the "greedy & hungry expectants of office" who were hounding him, particularly one unnamed man "who was laboring to undermine me."

The scholarly Edward Everett became chairman of the Joint Committee on the Library in late

1825. The committee, not the Librarian, selected books for the Library, and Watterston's correspondence with Everett is polite and even at times deferential. Moreover, in 1828—retroactive to March 1827, the Librarian of Congress was authorized to employ an assistant. Watterston named Edward B. Stelle to the new position of Assistant Librarian.

In 1827, Watterston had started writing regularly for the *National Journal*, openly advocating the Whig cause—and continuing his praise of Henry Clay. It therefore is hard to believe that he was surprised on May 28, 1829, when newly elected President Andrew Jackson, a Democrat, replaced him as Librarian with a fellow Democrat, John Silva Meehan, a local printer and publisher. But Watterston was furious, and when he left the office he took with him the Library's record books and the manuscript catalog of Jefferson's library. Using the pages of the *National Journal*, which he began editing in 1830, Watterston launched a 20-year campaign to regain his position as Librarian, but even new Whig Presidents in 1841 and 1849 ignored him. As a result, according to his daughter, Watterston himself left the Whig party in 1850.

While battling for his former position, Watterston continued a productive literary and journalistic life. In addition to his work with the Washington Monument Society, he was the longtime secretary of the Washington Botanical Society and wrote about landscape gardening, tobacco, and varied horticultural topics. He also began producing guidebooks about Washington, statistical compendiums, and biographical sketches relating to the Nation's Capitol. *The Southern Literary Messenger*, to which he had contributed many articles, even dubbed him the "Metropolitan Author" after the appearance of the second of his Washington guidebooks (*A New Guide to Washington*) in 1842.

In addition to serving as the first full-time Librarian of Congress, George Watterston was important because he was the first Librarian to advocate a national role for the institution. He took the Library of Congress—still a fledgling institution—seriously and, because of his own personality, forced others to take it seriously as well. (JYC)

Matheson, William. "George Watterston." *The Quarterly Journal of the Library of Congress* 32 (October 1975): 370–388.

YOUNG, JOHN RUSSELL (1840–1899)

Journalist John Russell Young, the seventh Librarian of Congress, did not serve long in the office: from his confirmation by the Senate on June 30, 1897 until his death on January 17, 1899. In this short period, he conscientiously undertook the formidable tasks of overseeing the move of the Library from the U.S. Capitol Building into its own building and of expanding and reorganizing the institution as it took on new responsibilities and faced new expectations.

Librarian John Russell Young, the seventh Librarian of Congress, served from July 1, 1897 until his death on January 17, 1899. During this brief period, he supervised the Library's move from the Capitol into its own building and began developing a professional staff. He also used his diplomatic skills, acquired as a minister to China, in requesting diplomatic and consular representatives around the world to send to the "National Library" newspapers, serials, pamphlets, documents, manuscripts, or reports, or "whatever, in a word, would add to the sum of human knowledge."
Photograph: Dunwiddie. LC Archives.

Young was born on November 20, 1840, in County Tyrone, Ireland, the son of George and Eliza Rankin Young. Brought to the United States when he was less than a year old, he began his formal schooling in Philadelphia, then became a ward of an uncle in New Orleans, where he continued his public schooling. He returned to Philadelphia at age 15, apprenticed himself to another relative who was a printer, and it was then, as his biographer John C. Broderick relates, that his "real education" began. In August 1857, he secured a position as copyboy on the *Philadelphia Press*, beginning a long and fruitful association with its editor John W. Forney, who founded the *Washington Chronicle* in 1861. Through Forney, who also served as Clerk of the House of Representatives at various periods between 1851 and 1868, Young learned about politics and developed his strong pro-Union and antislavery sentiments.

Following the Civil War, at the age of 25, Young became the managing editor of Horace Greeley's *New York Tribune*. Young resigned from the *Tribune* in 1869, in part because he differed with Greeley about the 1868 Republican nominee: Young favored Ulysses S. Grant, Greeley promoted Salmon P. Chase.

Throughout much of the 1870s, Young served as the *New York Herald's* European representative. After Grant left office, he urged Young to accompany him on a well-publicized trip around the world. Young agreed, and the result was the two-volume compilation, *Around the World with General Grant* (1879), an expansion of Young's dispatches to the *Herald*. Grant became Young's advocate, and recommended to President James Garfield in 1881 that Young become American's minister to Japan. Instead, it was President Chester A. Arthur who made Young an ambassador, appointing him as minister to China in 1882, a post in which Young served with distinction until 1885.

Young decided to return to his career in journalism and business in Philadelphia. There he was active in the Union League, which he had helped found in 1862, edited the city's *Memorial History*, and continued to take part in Republican party politics. He was president of the Union League for two years in the 1890s, during which time he arranged for a meeting of Confederate and Union military heroes at Gettysburg in April 1893.

Young's strong Republican connections, buttressed by his administrative capabilities, soon brought him the job of Librarian of Congress. He and president-elect William McKinley became close after McKinley's election in 1896, and while others felt that Young's appointment to another diplomatic post might be best, it was the job of Librarian of Congress that loomed. The Joint Committee on the Library's late 1896 hearings about the "condition" of the Library on the eve of its move into its new building made it clear that a new Librarian of Congress was needed to replace the 72-year old Ainsworth Rand Spofford. McKinley nominated Young on June 30, and he was confirmed by the Senate on the same day. *The Washington Evening Star* reported "a thorough and amicable understanding" between Young and Spofford, who indeed became Chief Assistant Librarian.

Young's business and political skills served him well during his brief term as Librarian of Congress. So did his broader intellectual interests and experience as a diplomat. He used his diplomatic ties, for example, to enlarge the Library's collections. In

February 1898, he sent a letter to U.S. diplomatic and consular representatives throughout the world, asking them to send "to the national library" newspapers, journals, pamphlets, manuscripts, broadsides, "documents illustrative of the history of those various nationalities now coming to our shores to blend into our national life," and other categories of research materials, broadly summarized as "whatever, in a word, would add to the sum of human knowledge." By the end of 1898, books and other materials had been obtained from 11 legations and seven consulates.

The new Librarian skillfully guided the institution's administrative reorganization and expansion. He made many important professional appointments. While himself a political appointee, Young was nonpartisan in his selections and successfully distanced the Library from world of partisan politics. His appointees included Thorvald Solberg, the first register of copyrights, and catalogers J.C.M. Hanson and Charles Martel, who began reclassifying the collections after nearly a century of reliance on the classification scheme Thomas Jefferson provided to the Library along with his books.

Many of Young's administrative innovations were apt and farsighted. Through a program of daily readings in a special "pavilion for the blind" in November of 1897, Young inaugurated what today is one of the Library's best known national activities: library service for the blind and physically handicapped. He contemplated but did not establish a separate children's department. In his 1897 *Annual Report,* he advocated the transfer of historical manuscripts from the Department of State to the Library and decried the use of cheap, nondurable paper by publishers, warning that many of the works coming into the Library "threaten in a few years to crumble into a waste heap, with no value as record."

Young also was sensitive to Spofford's struggles on behalf of the national library prior to the Library of Congress's occupancy of its own separate building. Moreover, he shared Spofford's vision of the Library's future, commenting in his diary on June 12, 1898: "I am trying to build the library far into the future, to make it a true library of research."

Librarian Young's *Annual Report* for 1898 demonstrates the broad range of his interests and his vision for the Library of Congress. Its appendices include reports on special collections, for example the newly acquired Gardiner Greene Hubbard collection of engravings and art books, the "Jefferson Library," and the "Chinese collection;" an historical report on the "close relations" between the Library and the Smithsonian Institution; a list of the books received through the diplomatic and consular service; and his

Begun by Young in 1897, a series of daily readings in a "pavilion for the blind" evolved into what today is one of the Library's best known activities: national library service for the blind and physically handicapped. This photograph of blind and sighted librarians working in the Jefferson Building was probably taken in the 1930s.
LC/Prints and Photographs Division. LC-USP6-116-A.

report on "the durability of paper." It ends with what became Young's valedictory statement about the institution, which he did so much to shape during his brief librarianship: "With the considerate care of Congress and a due appreciation of what has been done and what may so readily be done by the American people, there is no reason why the Library of Congress should not rival those noble establishments of the Old World, whose treasures are a people's pride and whose growth is the highest achievement of modern civilization."

John Russell Young suffered a severe fall on Christmas Eve, 1898, and never fully recovered. He died on January 17, 1899, after only 19 months in office.

Young was married three times. His first two marriages were marked by sadness. He married Rose Fitzpatrick in 1864, but she was frequently ill until her death in 1881 and all three children of the marriage died in childhood. He remarried in 1882, but second wife Julia died in Paris in October 1883, two months after giving birth to their son, who was placed in the care of his mother's family, since Young was in Peking as minister to China. Young and his third wife Mary, whom he married in 1890, were the parents of Gordon Russell Young, who was born in 1891 and became a prominent military engineer and a commissioner of the District of Columbia. (JYC)

Broderick, John C. "John Russell Young: The Internationalist as Librarian," *The Quarterly Journal of the Library of Congress* 33 (April 1976): 116–149.

APPENDICES

Part III.1. Senior Library Officials, 1802–2004: A Selective List

Detailed information about the history of most of the Library's organizational units and the names of most of the Library's senior officials down to the division chief level may be found in the *Annual Reports of the Library of Congress*, particularly between 1901 and 1987. Additional information is available in the unpublished departmental and divisional reports in the Library of Congress Archives in the Manuscript Division.

Librarian of Congress
Established in 1802 as a joint position, combined with the Clerk of the House of Representatives; the positions were separated in 1815.
John James Beckley, 1802–1807
Patrick Magruder, 1807–1815
George Watterston, 1815–1829
John Silva Meehan, 1829–1861
John G. Stephenson, 1861–1864
Ainsworth Rand Spofford, 1864–1897
John Russell Young, 1897–1899
Ainsworth Rand Spofford, Acting, 1899
Herbert Putnam, 1899–1939; Librarian of Congress Emeritus, 1939–1955
Archibald MacLeish, 1939–1944
Luther H. Evans, 1945–1953
Verner W. Clapp, Acting, 1953–1954
Lawrence Quincy Mumford, 1954–1974
John G. Lorenz, Acting, 1975
Daniel J. Boorstin, 1975–1987; Librarian of Congress Emeritus, 1987–2004
James H. Billington, 1987–

Deputy Librarian of Congress
Established as Chief Assistant Librarian 1897, renamed Deputy Librarian of Congress 1962.
Ainsworth Rand Spofford, 1897–1908
Appleton Prentiss Clark Griffin, 1908–1926
Frederick William Ashley, 1927–1936
Martin Arnold Roberts, 1937–1939
Luther H. Evans, 1940–1945
Verner W. Clapp, 1947–1956
Rutherford D. Rogers, 1957–1964
John G. Lorenz, 1965–1975
William J. Welsh, 1976–1988
Winston Tabb, Acting, 1989–1991
Daniel P. Mulhollan, Acting, 1992–1993
Hiram L. Davis, 1994–1995
Thomas P. Carney, Acting, 1996
Donald L. Scott, 1996–

Deputy Chief Assistant Librarian
Established 1950, abolished 1962.
Dan M. Lacy, 1950–1951
Frederick W. Wagman, Acting, 1951–1953
Lucile M. Morsch, 1953–1962

Assistant Librarian of Congress
Established 1949; abolished 1954; re-established 1960; title changed to Assistant Librarian for Public Affairs, 1960; to Assistant Librarian, 1963; to Assistant Librarian for American and Library Studies, 1976.
David C. Mearns, Assistant Librarian, 1949–1951
Solon J. Buck, Assistant Librarian, 1951–1954
Elizabeth Hamer Kegan, Assistant Librarian for Public Affairs, 1960–1962; Assistant Librarian, 1963–1975; Assistant Librarian for American and Library Studies, 1976–1978

The Assistant Librarian of Congress
Established 1976, abolished 1978.
Donald C. Curran, 1976–1978

The Associate Librarian of Congress
Established 1978, renamed Associate Librarian for Operations, 1989.
Donald C. Curran, The Associate Librarian of Congress, 1978–1989; Associate Librarian for Operations, 1989–1990

Associate Librarian for Science and Technology Information
Established 1991 as a one-year office.
William W. Ellis, 1991–1992

Associate Librarian for Management
Established 1978, abolished 1993.
Edmond L. Applebaum, 1978–1980
Glen A. Zimmerman, 1980–1988
Donald C. Curran, Acting, 1988–1989
Rhoda W. Canter, 1989–1993

Associate Librarian for Special Projects
Established 1989, abolished 1993.
Rhoda W. Canter, Acting, 1989–1993

Associate Librarian for Human Resources
Established 1993, became Associate Librarian for Human Resources Services, 1993; became Director, Human Resources Services, 1999.
Lloyd A. Pauls, Acting, 1992–1993, Associate Librarian, 1993–1998

Associate Librarian for Strategic Initiatives
Established 2000.
Laura E. Campbell, 2000–

Associate Librarian for Library Services
Established 1995, by merging divisions and offices from three service units: Collections Services, Constituent Services, and Cultural Affairs; realigned 2004 to comprise Acquisitions & Bibliographic Access, Collections & Services, Partnerships & Outreach Programs, Preservation, and Technology Policy.
Winston Tabb, Associate Librarian, 1995–2002
Beacher J.E. Wiggins, Acting Associate Librarian, 2002–2003
Deanna Marcum, Associate Librarian 2003–

National Library Service for the Blind and Physically Handicapped
Established as a service in 1897 with the creation of a special reading room for the blind in the Jefferson Building; established as an administrative unit as the Division for the Blind, 1946; transferred to the Reference Department, 1951; renamed the Division for the Blind and Physically Handicapped, 1966; transferred to the Reader Services Department, 1976; renamed the National Library Service for the Blind and Physically Handicapped and transferred to the Office of the Associate Librarian for National Programs, 1978; transferred to Constituent Services, 1989; transferred into the Office of Associate Librarian for Library Services, 1995.
Xenophon P. Smith, Director, Division for the Blind, 1946–1948
George A. Schwegmann Jr., Chief, 1948–1951
Donald G. Patterson, 1951–1957
Robert S. Bray, 1957–1972
Frank Kurt Cylke, Chief, 1973–1978, Director, 1978–

Associate Librarian for Collections Services
Established 1989, merged into Office of Associate Librarian for Library Services, 1995.
Henriette D. Avram, Associate Librarian for Collections Services, 1989–1991
Winston Tabb, Associate Librarian of Collections Services, 1992–1995

Assistant Librarian for Processing Services
Established in 1940 as the Processing Department; Director of the Processing Department became the Assistant Librarian for Processing Services, 1978; reorganized into Collections Services, 1989.
Lawrence Quincy Mumford, Director, Processing Department, 1940–1941
Herman H. Henkle, 1942–1947
Frederick H. Wagman, 1947–1951
John W. Cronin, 1951–1968
Joseph H. Howard, 1976; Assistant Librarian for Processing Services, 1978–1982
Henriette D. Avram, 1984–1989

Associate Librarian for Constituent Services
Established 1989, merged into Office of Associate Librarian for Library Services, 1995.
Donald C. Curran, Acting Associate Librarian for Constituent Services, 1989–1990
Donald C. Curran, Associate Librarian for Constituent Services, 1990–1995

Assistant Librarian for Research Services
Established in 1940 as the Reference Department; divided into the Reader Services Department and the Research Department, 1976; combined into the Research Services Department, 1978; reorganized into Collections Services, 1989.
Luther Harris Evans, Director, Reference Department, 1940–1942
David C. Mearns, 1943–1949
Burton W. Atkinson, 1949–1957
Roy P. Basler, 1958–1968
John Lester Nolan, 1968–1969
Paul L. Berry, 1969–1975
Fred E. Croxton, Director, Reader Services Department, 1976–1978
Alan M. Fern, Director, Research Department, 1976–1978
Donald C. Curran, Acting Assistant Librarian for Research Services, 1978
John C. Broderick, Assistant Librarian for Research Services, 1979–1988

Associate Librarian for Cultural Affairs
Established 1989, merged into Office of Associate Librarian for Library Services, 1995.
Alan Jabbour, Acting Associate Librarian, 1989–1990
John Y. Cole, Acting Associate Librarian, 1990–1992
Carolyn T. Brown, Associate Librarian for Cultural Affairs, 1992–1995

Assistant Librarian for Public Education
Established 1976, merged into Office of Assistant Librarian for National Programs, 1978; merged into Office of Associate Librarian for Cultural Affairs, 1989
James Parton, Assistant Librarian for Public Education, 1976–1977
Carol A. Nemeyer, Assistant Librarian for Public Education, 1977
Ruth Ann Stewart, Assistant Librarian for National Programs, 1986–1989

Congressional Research Service

Established 1915 as the Legislative Reference Service; merged into the Reference Department, 1940; became a separate and independent department, 1946; renamed Congressional Research Service, 1971; the Director also became the Associate Librarian for Congressional Services, 1990; reverted to title of Director in 1994.

James David Thompson, in charge, 1914–1919
Gilbert Hirsch, in charge, 1919–1920
Charles Warren Collins Jr., in charge, 1920–1921
Hermann H. B. Meyer, in charge, 1921–1923, Acting Director, 1923–1927, Director 1928–1935
George J. Schulz, 1936–1937
John T. Vance, in charge, 1937–1939
Luther H. Evans, Director, 1939–1940
Ernest S. Griffith, 1940–1958
Hugh L. Elsbree, 1958–1966
Lester S. Jayson, Director, Legislative Reference Service, 1966–1970, Director, Congressional Research Service, 1971–1975
Norman Beckman, Acting, 1975–1976
Gilbert Gude, 1977–1985
Joseph E. Ross, Director, 1986–1989; Director and Acting Associate Librarian for Congressional Services, 1990–1992; Director and Associate Librarian for Congressional Services, 1993
Daniel P. Mulhollan, Director, Congressional Research Service 1994–

Law Library

Established as a separate department of the Library in 1832; was known as the Law Library from 1900 until 1936; called the Law Division between 1936 and 1939, reverted to the Law Library in 1940.

Charles H.W. Meehan, Assistant in Law, 1833–1872
Charles W. Hoffman, 1872–1886
George F. Curtis, 1886–1897
Thomas Harvey Clark, Custodian, 1897–1902,
George Winfield Scott, Custodian, 1903–1906, Law Librarian, 1907
Middleton Goldsmith Beaman, Law Librarian, 1908–1910
Edwin Montefiore Borchard, Law Librarian, 1911–1913; 1914–1916
James David Thompson, Acting Law Librarian, 1913–1914 and Law Librarian and in charge, Legislative Reference Service, 1916–1919
Gilbert Hirsch, Acting Law Librarian and in charge, Legislative Reference Service, 1919–1920
Charles Warren Collins Jr., 1920–1921
Walter H. McClenon, Acting, 1921
Roger Boutell, 1921–1924
John T. Vance Jr., 1924–1943
Eldon R. James, 1943–1946
Francis X. Dwyer, Acting, 1947–1949; 1963–1964
William Lawrence Keitt, Law Librarian and General Counsel for the Library of Congress, 1949–1963
Lewis C. Coffin, Law Librarian and General Counsel for the Library of Congress, 1964–1971
Carleton W. Kenyon, Law Librarian, 1971–1988
Charles Doyle, Acting, 1989–1990
M. Kathleen Price, 1990–1993
Rubens Medina, 1994–

Copyright Office

Established 1897 as Copyright Department; Register of Copyrights became Register and Assistant Librarian for Copyright Services, 1980; became Register and Associate Librarian for Copyright Services, 1990; reverted to Register of Copyrights, 1997.

Thorvald Solberg, Register of Copyrights, 1897–1930
William Lincoln Brown, 1930–1936
Clement Lincoln Bouvé, 1936–1943
Richard C. DeWolf, Acting, 1944–1945
Sam Bass Warner, 1945–1951
Arthur Fisher, 1951–1960
Abraham L. Kaminstein, 1960–1971
George D. Cary, 1971–1973
Abe A. Goldman, Acting, 1973
Barbara Ringer, 1973–1980
David Ladd, Register of Copyrights and Assistant Librarian for Copyright Services, 1980–1984
Ralph M. Oman, Register of Copyrights and Assistant Librarian for Copyright Services, 1985–1990; Register and Associate Librarian for Copyright Services, 1990–1994
Marybeth Peters, Register of Copyrights and Associate Librarian for Copyright Services, 1994–1997; Register of Copyrights, 1997–

PART III.2. Table 1. Library of Congress Legislative Appropriations, 1800–1850

(Figures are rounded to the nearest dollar.)

Year	Salaries	Books	Law books	Exchanges	Contingent expenses [1]	Publication of catalogue	Construction and repair	Furniture
1800	-	5 000	-	-	-	-	-	-
1805	-	-	-	-	900	-	700	-
1806	-	5 000	-	-	450	-	-	-
1807	-	-	-	-	800	-	-	-
1808	-	-	-	-	800	-	-	-
1809	-	-	-	-	800	-	5 000	-
1810	-	-	-	-	800	-	-	-
1811	-	5 000	-	-	800	-	600	-
1812	-	-	-	-	800	-	-	-
1813	-	-	-	-	800	-	-	-
1814	-	-	-	-	800	-	-	-
1815	-	[2]23 950	-	-	800	-	-	972
1816	-	-	-	-	6 263	-	-	1 521
1817	900	-	-	-	450	-	-	-
1818	1 500	2 000	-	-	450	-	-	537
1819	1 500	-	-	-	450	-	-	376
1820	1 500	2 000	-	-	450	-	-	-
1821	1 500	1 000	-	-	450	-	-	-
1822	1 500	1 000	-	-	450	-	-	-
1823	1 500	2 000	-	-	450	-	-	-
1824	1 500	5 000	-	-	450	-	-	1 546
1825	1 500	5 000	-	-	450	-	-	339
1826	1 500	5 000	-	-	450	-	-	295
1827	2 300	3 000	-	-	450	-	-	-
1828	2 961	5 000	-	-	-	-	-	-
1829	2 300	5 000	-	-	450	-	-	-
1830	2 300	5 000	-	-	450	-	-	-
1831	2 300	5 000	-	-	800	-	-	-
1832	2 300	5 000	5 000	-	800	-	-	3 000
1833	2 650	5 000	1 000	-	900	-	-	-
1834	2 650	5 000	1 000	-	1 100	-	-	-
1835	2 650	5 000	1 000	-	1 100	-	-	1 500
1836	3 048	5 000	1 000	-	1 200	-	-	-
1837	4 148	5 000	5 000	-	500	-	-	-
1838	3 922	5 000	-	-	500	1 400	-	-
1839	3 350	5 000	-	-	600	-	-	-
1840	3 788	5 000	-	-	600	-	-	-
1841	4 579	5 000	-	-	600	273	-	-
1842	5 300	5 000	1 000	-	1 800	-	-	-
1843 [3]	2 250	2 500	500	-	400	-	-	-
1843–1844	4 500	5 000	1 000	-	800	-	-	225
1844–1845	4 500	2 500	1 000	-	600	-	-	-
1845–1846	4 500	5 000	1 000	-	600	-	-	-
1846–1847	4 500	5 000	1 000	500	800	-	-	-
1847–1848	4 500	5 000	1 000	-	1 400	-	2 412	-
1848–1849	4 500	5 000	1 000	2 000	1 400	-	-	-
1849–1850	4 500	5 000	1 000	-	800	2 000	-	-

Source: William Dawson Johnston, *History of the Library of Congress, 1800–1864* (Washington, D.C.: Library of Congress, 1904), p. 515.

[1] 1805–1815: includes Librarian's allowance of $2 per day. The first Librarian was appointed in 1802, but until 1805 his allowance was paid out of the Senate and House Contingent Fund. "Contingent expenses" included stationery and other supplies, travel, postage, transportation, and communications costs. The category also occasionally included repairs and labor costs.

[2] Congress appropriated $23,950 for the purchase of Thomas Jefferson's Library.

[3] Figures are for January–June only. For 1843–1844 and succeeding years, appropriations were made on a fiscal year basis, that is, July 1, 1843 through June 30, 1844.

- = Quantity zero.

PART III.2. Table 2. Library of Congress Legislative Appropriations, 1850–1897

(Figures are rounded to the nearest dollar.)

Year	Salaries	Copyright office salaries	Books	Law books	Newspapers and periodicals	Exchanges	Contingent expenses	Copyright expenses	Printing and binding	Construction and repair	Furniture, fuel and equipment	Total	Other appropri-ations
1850–1851	4 500	-	5 000	2 000	-	2 000	1 800	-	-	-	-	15 300	-
1851–1852	4 500	-	5 000	2 000	-	-	800	-	-	-	-	12 300	-
1852–1853	5 273	-	[1]85 000	2 000	-	1 000	800	-	-	[2]78 700	-	172 773	-
1853–1854	4 500	-	5 000	3 700	-	-	1 000	-	3 000	[2]20 500	-	37 700	-
1854–1855	6 714	-	5 000	2 000	-	-	1 000	-	5 000	[2]3 500	-	23 214	-
1855–1856	10 417	-	5 000	2 000	-	-	1 000	-	-		-	18 417	-
1856–1857	9 000	-	5 000	2 000	-	-	1 000	-	-	-	400	17 400	-
1857–1858	9 000	-	5 000	2 000	-	-	1 000	-	4 000	-	270	21 270	-
1858–1859	9 000	-	5 000	2 000	-	-	1 000	-	-	-	600	17 600	-
1859–1860	9 000	-	5 000	2 000	-	-	1 000	-	-	-	-	17 000	-
1860–1861	9 000	-	5 000	2 000	-	-	1 000	-	-	-	-	17 000	-
1861–1862	9 000	-	5 000	2 000	-	-	1 000	-	-	-	-	17 000	-
1862–1863	10 000	-	5 000	2 000	-	-	1 000	-	-	-	-	18 000	-
1863–1864	10 208	-	5 000	2 000	-	-	1 000	-	-	7 500	-	25 708	-
1864–1865	10 500	-	5 000	2 000	-	-	2 000	-	-	1 700	-	21 200	[3]4 000
1865–1866	10 800	-	8 000	2 000	1 500	-	2 000	-	-	[4]160 000	1 500	185 800	-
1866–1867	16 000	-	8 000	4 000	-	-	2 000	-	-	5 260	-	35 260	[5]105 000
1867–1868	16 416	-	8 000	2 000	1 500	-	2 000	-	-	-	-	29 916	-
1868–1869	20 064	-	8 000	2 000	1 500	1 500	2 000	-	-	-	-	35 064	-
1869–1870	19 872	-	8 000	2 000	1 500	1 500	2 000	-	-	-	-	34 872	-
1870–1871	21 280	-	8 000	2 000	1 500	1 500	2 000	-	-	-	-	36 280	-
1871–1872	26 140	-	8 000	2 000	1 500	1 500	2 000	500	-	1 000	-	42 640	257
1872–1873	26 140	-	8 000	2 000	1 500	1 500	2 000	-	-	-	2 000	43 140	[6]5 000
1873–1874	26 140	-	8 000	2 000	1 500	1 500	2 000	500	-	-	-	41 640	[7]5 000
1874–1875	29 340	-	9 000	2 000	2 500	1 500	2 000	500	-	-	-	46 840	[7]2 000
1875–1876	29 340	-	9 000	2 000	2 500	1 500	2 000	500	-	-	-	46 840	-
1876–1877	30 040	-	7 000	2 000	2 500	1 000	1 000	1 200	-	-	-	44 740	-
1877–1878	30 440	-	5 000	2 000	2 500	1 000	1 000	500	[8]35 000	-	-	77 440	-
1878–1879	33 240	-	5 000	2 000	2 500	1 000	1 000	500	10 000	-	-	55 240	-
1879–1880	33 240	-	5 000	2 000	2 500	1 000	1 000	500	19 000	-	-	64 240	-
1880–1881	36 840	-	5 000	2 000	2 500	1 000	1 000	500	19 000	-	1 500	69 340	-
1881–1882	36 840	-	5 000	2 000	2 500	1 000	1 000	500	19 000	-	-	67 840	-
1882–1883	36 640	-	5 000	2 000	2 500	1 000	1 000	500	19 000	-	3 500	71 140	-
1883–1884	36 640	-	5 000	2 000	2 500	1 000	1 000	500	19 000	10 000	-	77 640	[9]28 000
1884–1885	38 320	-	5 000	2 000	2 500	1 000	1 000	500	13 680	-	-	64 000	-
1885–1886	38 320	-	3 000	2 000	2 500	1 000	1 000	500	10 238	1 000 500	-	1 059 058	[10]4 000
1886–1887	38 560	-	3 000	1 500	2 500	1 500	1 000	500	12 000	35 000	-	95 560	[10]2 500
1887–1888	38 560	-	3 000	1 500	2 500	1 500	1 000	500	15 000	-	-	63 560	-
1888–1889	39 000	-	4 000	1 500	2 500	1 500	1 000	500	15 000	500 000	-	565 000	-
1889–1890	41 500	-	4 000	1 500	2 500	1 500	1 000	500	15 000	500 000	-	567 500	-
1890–1891	43 050	-	4 000	1 500	2 500	1 500	1 000	500	15 000	850 000	-	919 050	-
1891–1892	45 100	-	4 000	1 500	2 500	1 500	1 000	500	15 000	600 000	-	671 100	-
1892–1893	45 100	-	4 000	1 500	2 500	1 500	1 000	500	12 000	450 000	-	518 100	-
1893–1894	46 375	-	4 000	1 500	2 500	1 500	500	500	12 000	950 000	-	1 018 875	-
1894–1895	53 820	-	4 000	1 500	2 500	1 500	500	500	12 000	900 000	-	976 320	-
1895–1896	52 620	-	4 000	1 500	2 500	1 500	500	500	12 000	480 000	-	555 120	-
1896–1897	55 320	-	4 000	1 500	2 500	1 500	500	500	12 000	-	-	77 820	-

Source: William Dawson Johnston, *History of the Library of Congress, 1800–1864* (Washington, D.C.: Library of Congress, 1904); *Statutes at Large.*

[1] Includes contingent funds and furniture.
[2] Includes funds for fighting the fire of December 1851, repairing the damage, and replacing books and other materials.
[3] For "selections from European periodicals" relating to the Civil War.
[4] For building two fireproof wings onto the Library.
[5] For the purchase of the law library of James L. Petigru and for the purchase of the Peter Force Library.
[6] For the purchase of a collection of English county histories.
[7] For plans for the new Library building.
[8] Beginning this fiscal year, the Library received a printing and binding allocation from the legislative appropriation for government printing needs.
[9] For the purchase of the Marquis de Rochambeau's papers and the purchase of Supreme Court records from the estate of Matthew Carpenter.
[10] For the compilation of volumes in the *American Archives* series.
- = Quantity zero.

PART III.2. Table 3. Library of Congress Legislative Appropriations, 1897–1940

(Figures are rounded to the nearest dollar; except as noted, "Other appropriations" were made to supplement several budget lines.)

Year	Library salaries	Copyright salaries	Legislative Reference Service salaries and expenses	Card service salaries and expenses	Union catalog salaries and expenses	Index to state legislative salaries and expenses	Books for the Blind	Books	Law books	Newspapers and periodicals
1897–1898	92 020	36 440	-	-	-	-	-	4 000	1 500	2 500
1898–1899	105 785	36 840	-	-	-	-	-	15 000	2 500	2 500
1899–1900	126 905	36 840	-	-	-	-	-	25 000	2 500	2 500
1900–1901	180 780	51 080	-	-	-	-	-	50 000	3 000	5 000
1901–1902	200 320	55 480	-	-	-	-	-	60 000	3 000	5 000
1902–1903	243 560	66 750	-	1 225	-	-	-	80 000	3 000	5 000
1903–1904	247 660	70 440	-	4 900	-	-	-	90 000	3 000	5 000
1904–1905	248 660	74 700	-	6 800	-	-	-	90 000	3 000	5 000
1905–1906	248 660	74 700	-	7 800	-	-	-	90 000	3 000	5 000
1906–1907	260 600	75 300	-	10 800	-	-	-	90 000	3 000	5 000
1907–1908	256 900	75 300	-	12 300	-	-	-	100 000	3 000	5 000
1908–1909	257 212	77 800	-	16 800	-	-	-	100 000	3 000	5 000
1909–1910	264 460	87 860	-	16 800	-	-	-	100 000	3 000	5 000
1910–1911	263 040	92 900	-	18 800	-	-	-	100 000	3 000	5 000
1911–1912	259 380	95 180	-	21 800	-	-	-	90 000	3 000	5 000
1912–1913	262 140	96 980	-	24 500	-	-	-	90 000	3 000	5 000
1913–1914	267 680	102 580	-	30 000	-	-	-	90 000	3 000	5 000
1914–1915	277 080	102 580	25 000	33 500	-	-	-	90 000	3 000	5 000
1915–1916	277 080	102 580	25 000	39 500	-	-	-	90 000	3 000	5 000
1916–1917	283 620	104 440	25 000	43 000	-	-	-	90 000	3 000	5 000
1917–1918	285 820	104 740	27 000	46 900	-	-	-	90 000	3 000	5 000
1918–1919	289 420	104 740	30 000	49 042	-	-	-	90 000	3 000	5 000
1919–1920	292 320	104 740	45 000	52 100	-	-	-	90 000	3 000	5 000
1920–1921	296 340	104 740	25 000	53 600	-	-	-	90 000	3 000	5 000
1921–1922	296 840	104 740	25 000	50 900	-	-	-	90 000	3 000	5 000
1922–1923	307 300	104 740	35 000	53 900	-	-	-	90 000	3 000	5 000
1923–1924	316 665	112 400	40 000	57 400	-	-	-	90 000	3 000	5 000
1924–1925	473 145	147 320	56 000	85 634	-	-	-	90 000	3 000	5 000
1925–1926	500 905	159 800	58 660	95 414	-	-	-	90 000	3 000	5 000
1926–1927	534 710	165 640	61 530	102 364	-	-	-	95 000	3 000	-
1927–1928	581 930	175 100	63 650	118 010	-	15 000	-	105 000	3 000	-
1928–1929	707 665	224 940	69 390	141 830	-	32 500	-	105 000	3 000	-
1929–1930	740 345	228 740	70 950	149 050	-	33 280	-	105 000	3 000	-
1930–1931	799 665	233 140	71 410	157 740	-	38 280	-	130 000	50 000	-
1931–1932	855 165	247 940	73 990	170 500	-	33 460	100 000	130 000	50 000	-
1932–1933	863 045	249 380	67 500	170 000	20 000	25 000	90 000	100 000	25 000	-
1933–1934	794 110	228 600	68 365	165 265	18 335	30 915	90 000	100 000	50 000	-
1934–1935	793 241	224 442	66 662	162 260	18 100	36 420	99 620	100 000	50 000	-
1935–1936	910 245	249 620	87 990	181 830	22 000	39 700	175 000	115 000	90 000	-
1936–1937	933 665	251 420	92 990	182 190	22 000	33 000	175 000	115 000	50 000	-
1937–1938	960 485	251 900	100 490	197 190	24 000	39 700	275 000	100 000	70 000	-
1938–1939	1 076 550	255 400	99 500	210 000	23 300	32 000	275 000	112 000	70 000	-
1939–1940	1 096 457	284 160	99 500	224 560	26 180	39 200	[1]275 000	118 000	85 000	-

[1]Began to include personal services and travel.
- = Quantity zero.

PART III.2. Table 3. Library of Congress Legislative Appropriations, 1897–1940—*Continued*

(Figures are rounded to the nearest dollar; except as noted, "Other appropriations" were made to supplement several budget lines.)

Year	Exchanges	Contingent expenses	Copyright expenses	Printing and binding	Trust fund board	Building and grounds salaries	Total	Building and grounds expense	Furniture and equipment	Construction	Other appro-priations
1897–1898	1 500	500	500	12 000	-	51 440	202 400	35 000	400	-	-
1898–1899	1 500	1 500	-	25 000	-	61 395	252 020	25 000	20 000	-	-
1899–1900	1 680	4 170	-	35 000	-	64 655	299 250	25 000	15 000	-	-
1900–1901	1 680	8 500	-	75 000	-	67 065	442 105	25 000	45 000	-	-
1901–1902	1 800	7 300	-	93 000	-	70 945	496 845	25 000	60 000	-	-
1902–1903	1 800	7 300	-	95 000	-	75 105	578 740	30 000	45 000	-	15 000
1903–1904	1 800	7 300	-	185 000	-	77 245	692 345	36 000	45 000	-	-
1904–1905	1 800	7 300	-	185 000	-	79 585	701 845	32 500	40 000	-	-
1905–1906	-	7 300	-	185 000	-	80 305	701 765	33 500	40 000	-	-
1906–1907	-	7 300	-	205 000	-	80 305	737 305	33 500	20 000	2 500	-
1907–1908	-	7 300	-	205 000	-	79 585	744 385	33 500	40 000	-	-
1908–1909	-	7 300	-	202 000	-	79 705	748 817	33 500	40 000	100 000	-
1909–1910	-	7 300	-	202 000	-	79 705	766 125	33 500	25 000	200 000	-
1910–1911	-	7 300	-	202 000	-	79 705	771 745	33 500	25 000	10 000	-
1911–1912	-	6 800	-	202 000	-	74 505	757 665	19 000	20 000	-	-
1912–1913	-	6 800	-	202 000	-	75 485	765 905	15 000	10 000	-	-
1913–1914	-	6 800	-	200 000	-	77 325	782 385	15 000	10 000	-	500
1914–1915	-	7 300	-	200 000	-	80 205	823 665	17 000	10 000	-	-
1915–1916	-	7 300	-	209 000	-	79 645	838 105	15 000	17 000	-	-
1916–1917	-	7 300	-	200 000	-	83 245	844 605	27 500	10 000	-	-
1917–1918	-	7 300	-	200 000	-	86 005	855 765	34 000	10 000	-	-
1918–1919	-	8 671	-	200 000	-	88 065	867 938	22 500	12 000	10 000	[2]58 766
1919–1920	-	7 300	-	263 000	-	89 065	951 525	17 000	12 000	10 000	[2]125 003
1920–1921	-	9 000	-	250 000	-	94 545	931 225	29 000	12 000	-	[2]126 211
1921–1922	-	8 000	-	250 000	-	95 265	928 745	17 000	12 000	5 000	[2]128 111
1922–1923	-	9 000	-	212 250	-	95 985	916 175	17 000	12 000	6 000	[2,3]135 636
1923–1924	-	10 000	-	212 250	-	75 195	921 910	[4]7 000	-	([4])	136 596
1924–1925	-	10 000	-	250 000	-	103 638	1 223 737	7 000	-	-	-
1925–1926	-	10 000	-	325 000	-	108 448	1 356 227	7 000	-	-	-
1926–1927	-	10 000	-	305 000	500	111 752	1 389 496	7 000	-	-	-
1927–1928	-	10 000	-	337 000	500	124 142	1 533 332	7 000	-	-	-
1928–1929	-	10 500	-	336 000	500	147 467	1 778 792	8 900	-	-	-
1929–1930	-	13 000	-	356 000	500	153 447	1 853 312	7 000	-	[5]600 000	-
1930–1931	-	13 000	-	379 500	500	153 447	2 026 682	8 900	-	[5]10 000	[6]1 500 000
1931–1932	-	14 000	-	426 400	500	166 622	2 268 577	7 000	-	[5]1 321 202	[7]50 000
1932–1933	-	14 000	-	360 000	-	166 822	2 150 747	8 900	-	[5]475 000	-
1933–1934	-	14 000	-	365 000	500	155 645	2 080 735	7 000	-	[5]2 800 000	-
1934–1935	-	14 000	-	365 000	500	149 690	2 079 935	8 900	-	([5])	-
1935–1936	-	14 000	-	434 300	500	169 206	2 489 391	7 000	-	([5])	-
1936–1937	-	14 000	-	464 200	500	169 860	2 503 825	8 900	-	2 225 000	-
1937–1938	-	14 000	-	464 000	500	173 400	2 670 665	7 000	-	-	-
1938–1939	-	14 000	-	463 500	500	277 600	2 909 350	16 700	-	-	[8]37 500
1939–1940	-	17 000	-	538 300	500	291 350	3 095 207	12 500	-	-	-

Source: Statutes at Large; Annual Report of the Librarian of Congress.

2"Other appropriations" provided increased compensation to employees pending the revision of the federal salary structure.
3Includes funds "for a safe, permanent repository" for the originals of the *Declaration of Independence* and the *Constitution of the United States.*
4Funding for construction, repair, and other work relating to the building and grounds was transferred to the Architect of the Capitol.
5Construction appropriations were made to the Architect of the Capitol for the construction of the John Adams Building.
6Funded the purchase of the Vollbehr collection of incunabula.
7Funded the preparation of an Index to Federal Statutes.
8For the purchase of the Pinckney Papers and other constitutional documents.
\- = Quantity zero.

PART III.2. Table 4. Library of Congress Legislative Appropriations, 1940–1960

(Figures are rounded to the nearest dollar.)

Year	Library salaries	Copyright salaries	Legislative Reference Service salaries and expenses	Card service salaries and expenses	Index to state legislative salaries and expenses	Union catalog salaries and expenses	Books for the blind salaries and expenses	Presidential papers salaries and expenses	Books
1940–1941	1 281 952	293 240	122 080	246 760	32 500	26 180	325 000	-	148 000
1941–1942	1 347 883	289 740	131 220	260 345	39 785	26 645	350 000	-	248 000
1942–1943	1 485 917	295 670	153 440	265 487	39 356	27 541	370 000	-	173 000
1943–1944	1 736 256	325 759	176 371	273 953	43 380	57 773	370 000	-	198 000
1944–1945	1 760 000	348 000	178 000	271 605	35 000	46 925	500 000	-	198 000
1945–1946	2 053 717	350 700	234 034	282 100	41 242	53 266	500 000	-	525 000
1946–1947	2 325 000	591 925	469 300	344 000	94 100	98 000	500 000	-	370 000
1947–1948	2 350 000	591 925	455 000	376 000	50 000	61 000	1 000 000	-	300 000
1948–1949	2 705 571	742 300	[1]514 700	448 900	26 800	70 200	979 400	-	300 000
1949–1950	2 912 260	819 728	716 598	507 736	-	72 561	1 000 000	-	300 000
1950–1951	3 044 000	890 000	790 000	552 100	-	77 000	1 000 000	-	270 000
1951–1952	3 417 838	987 510	866 300	622 250	-	80 660	1 000 000	-	270 000
1952–1953	3 470 000	1 008 409	891 159	648 607	-	85 492	1 000 000	-	270 000
1953–1954	[2]4 810 272	[2]1 100 000	901 721	1 264 800	-	-	1 000 000	-	270 000
1954–1955	4 815 636	1 123 900	897 300	1 349 100	-	-	1 000 000	-	260 000
1955–1956	5 143 064	1 238 475	1 054 932	1 402 359	-	-	1 006 678	-	300 000
1956–1957	5 310 593	1 287 547	1 067 387	1 487 100	-	-	1 067 481	-	300 000
1957–1958	6 100 000	1 447 000	1 267 000	1 715 000	-	-	1 206 000	-	320 000
1958–1959	6 748 300	1 397 256	1 390 300	1 878 635	-	-	1 367 900	106 800	320 000
1959–1960	7 159 890	1 450 000	1 455 400	1 981 300	-	-	1 619 400	106 800	350 000

Year	Law books	Motion picture preservation	Printing and binding	Contingent expenses	Trust fund board	Library building salaries	Library building maintenance	Other appropriations
1940–1941	85 000	-	657 100	17 000	500	298 286	16 700	-
1941–1942	90 000	-	605 000	50 630	500	283 719	13 500	[3]164 500
1942–1943	90 000	-	505 000	47 635	500	327 613	18 200	21 673
1943–1944	95 000	-	560 000	47 500	100	369 633	16 600	[4]16 000
1944–1945	85 000	-	580 000	44 900	500	358 000	18 000	[4]13 000
1945–1946	150 000	12 296	599 000	50 700	500	402 626	22 800	-
1946–1947	125 000	100 000	827 882	80 700	500	495 460	34 000	-
1947–1948	95 000	12 000	790 500	84 700	500	495 000	30 000	-
1948–1949	95 000	-	869 475	60 700	500	571 800	30 000	-
1949–1950	95 000	-	1 000 500	76 000	500	624 799	34 000	[5]35 000
1950–1951	85 000	-	1 040 000	85 000	500	[6]698 680	-	-
1951–1952	85 500	-	1 040 000	80 000	500	786 485	-	-
1952–1953	85 500	-	1 081 000	80 000	500	794 820	-	-
1953–1954	90 000	-	-	-	-	-	-	-
1954–1955	90 000	-	-	-	-	-	-	-
1955–1956	90 000	-	-	-	-	-	-	-
1956–1957	90 000	-	-	-	-	-	-	-
1957–1958	90 000	-	-	-	-	-	-	-
1958–1959	90 000	60 000	-	-	-	-	-	-
1959–1960	90 000	60 000	-	-	-	-	-	-

Source: Statutes at Large; Annual Report of the Librarian of Congress.

[1]Began to include both salaries and expenses.
[2]Began to include both salaries and expenses; "Printing and binding," "contingent expenses," "trust fund board," and "library building expenses" were included in the "salaries and expenses" categories.
[3]"Other appropriations" were "to assure security of the collections" in wartime ($100,000) and for "furniture and labor-saving devices" ($64,500).
[4]"Other appropriations" were for "furniture and labor-saving devices."
[5]For revising the Annotated *Constitution of the United States.*
[6]Began to include building expenses.
- = Quantity zero.

PART III.2. Table 5. Library of Congress Legislative Appropriations, 1960–2004

(Figures are rounded to the nearest dollar.)

Year	Library salaries and expenses	Copyright salaries and expenses	Congressional Research Service salaries and expenses [1]	Card service salaries and expenses	Blind and Physically Handicapped salaries and expenses [2]	Presidential papers salaries and expenses	Books
1960–1961	8 122 800	1 588 800	1 780 200	2 172 700	1 723 200	112 800	400 000
1961–1962	8 455 000	1 600 000	1 809 200	2 347 000	1 786 100	112 800	470 000
1962–1963	10 074 380	1 673 560	1 960 820	2 754 370	1 893 910	112 800	570 000
1963–1964	9 726 000	1 781 000	2 119 000	3 042 000	1 900 000	112 800	670 000
1964–1965	11 001 800	1 914 200	2 412 800	3 810 100	2 458 600	112 800	670 000
1965–1966[3]	12 994 700	2 072 500	2 586 200	4 100 300	2 681 600	112 800	780 000
1966–1967	13 524 100	2 329 000	3 010 500	4 648 600	4 603 100	112 800	800 000
1967–1968	15 810 968	2 532 832	3 349 323	6 422 800	5 968 234	112 800	590 000
1968–1969	18 019 300	2 987 800	3 870 000	7 250 000	6 668 000	118 800	665 000
1969–1970	20 881 000	3 496 006	4 683 000	8 025 000	7 030 000	136 000	750 000
1970–1971[3]	23 183 000	3 906 000	5 653 000	9 000 000	7 647 000	150 500	800 000
1971–1972	33 931 000	4 622 000	7 238 000	9 548 750	8 572 000	-	973 000
1972–1973	37 181 000	4 911 500	9 155 000	10 193 000	8 905 500	-	1 118 650
1973–1974	42 531 800	5 432 700	11 391 000	11 161 200	9 894 600	-	1 194 650
1974–1975	49 825 000	5 992 000	13 722 000	10 780 000	11 416 900	-	1 458 000
1975–1976[4]	74 751 800	8 961 500	21 818 000	14 598 500	19 672 000	-	2 151 000
1976–1977	69 260 000	9 642 300	20 484 200	12 311 000	21 818 000	-	1 760 000
1977–1978	92 139 689	12 056 182	23 041 000	-	28 853 700	-	-
1978–1979	100 682 000	13 221 500	25 553 000	-	34 735 700	-	-
1979–1980	110 350 345	14 332 000	27 890 000	-	34 500 000	-	-
1980–1981	113 113 183	14 701 000	29 689 000	-	32 890 650	-	-
1981–1982	121 503 204	14 627 000	31 605 000	-	33 221 000	-	-
1982–1983	129 054 409	15 657 000	35 240 000	-	33 384 000	-	-
1983–1984	144 676 000	16 322 000	37 632 000	-	35 099 000	-	-
1984–1985	139 325 000	17 301 000	40 333 000	-	36 592 000	-	-
1985–1986	132 985 000	16 905 000	37 288 000	-	32 309 000	-	-
1986–1987	193 186 484	17 767 456	40 448 647	-	36 099 000	-	-
1987–1988	245 357 914	19 222 313	43 164 342	-	36 187 118	-	-
1988–1989	215 936 029	19 653 985	44 709 658	-	36 474 472	-	-
1989–1990	223 722 678	20 054 506	45 836 945	-	37 113 960	-	-
1990–1991	247 199 670	22 925 223	51 910 877	-	40 130 548	-	-
1991–1992	262 019 365	26 059 306	56 959 124	-	42 186 055	-	-
1992–1993	263 877 039	25 997 810	58 852 122	-	43 145 416	-	-
1993–1994	262 569 716	26 381 500	58 160 459	-	42 615 803	-	-
1994–1995	210 014 000	27 456 000	60 084 000	-	44 851 000	-	-
1995–1996	211 664 000	30 818 000	60 084 000	-	44 951 000	-	-
1996–1997	216 007 000	33 402 000	62 641 000	-	44 964 000	-	-
1997–1998	227 504 000	34 361 000	64 603 000	-	46 561 000	-	-
1998–1999	238 373 000	34 891 000	67 124 000	-	46 824 000	-	-
1999–2000	256 779 000	37 628 000	71 244 000	-	47 984 000	-	-
2000–2001	385 095 756	38 438 249	73 430 098	-	48 502 060	-	-
2001–2002	338 267 000	48 396 000	81 454 000	-	49 788 000	-	-
2002–2003	361 644 000	38 971 000	88 250 000	-	50 632 000	-	-
2003–2004	370 897 000	48 290 000	91 726 000	-	51 706 000	-	-

[1] In January 1971, the Legislative Reference Service became the Congressional Research Service.
[2] Books for the Blind becomes Books for the Blind and Physically Handicapped.
[3] Funds for the National Program for Acquisitions and Cataloging were initially appropriated to the Commissioner of Education, who transferred them to the Library. This arrangement ceased in 1971–1972 when the funds became a part of the Library's appropriation.
[4] The fiscal year changed from beginning in July to beginning October 1. Appropriations reflect an additional amount for July–October 1976.
- = Quantity zero.

PART III.2. Table 5. Library of Congress Legislative Appropriations, 1960–2004—*Continued*

(Figures are rounded to the nearest dollar.)

Year	Law books	Motion picture preservation	PL-480 U.S. currency	Pl-480 foreign currency	Furniture and furnishings	Building plans and construction	Other appropriations
1960–1961	125 000	60 600	-	-	-	75 000	-
1961–1962	128 000	60 600	36 500	363 500	-	-	[5]25 000
1962–1963	110 000	60 600	49 900	630 000	-	-	[6]15 000
1963–1964	110 000	50 000	80 000	898 000	-	-	-
1964–1965	110 000	50 000	124 500	1 417 000	-	-	-
1965–1966[3]	125 000	50 000	154 500	1 694 000	-	500 000	-
1966–1967	125 000	50 000	180 000	2 088 000	-	-	-
1967–1968	125 000	-	220 000	2 003 000	-	-	-
1968–1969	125 000	-	201 400	1 807 600	-	-	-
1969–1970	140 000	-	213 000	1 603 000	-	2 800 000	-
1970–1971[3]	140 000	-	241 000	2 148 000	350 000	15 610 000	[7]140 709
1971–1972	156 500	-	266 000	2 625 000	454 000	71 090 000	[8]76 000
1972–1973	181 500	-	276 000	2 627 000	4 435 300	-	[9]120 000
1973–1974	208 500	-	295 600	1 971 400	868 000	-	[10]175 300
1974–1975	229 000	-	295 600	1 718 500	3 319 000	-	[11]34 000
1975–1976[4]	326 000	312 800	367 600	2 144 500	4 223 300	33 000 000	[12]498 000
1976–1977	286 000	-	230 000	2 680 200	2 942 000	-	[4]595 500
1977–1978	-	-	256 600	3 184 600	7 030 700	7 675 000	-
1978–1979	-	-	256 600	3 603 500	12 493 535	-	[13]559 500
1979–1980	-	-	375 900	3 187 100	70 000	-	[14]1 182 000
1980–1981	-	-	3 479 000	-	1 686 250	-	-
1981–1982	-	-	4 405 000	-	1 089 000	-	-
1982–1983	-	-	4 438 000	-	1 226 000	-	-
1983–1984	-	-	2 962 000	-	1 524 000	-	-
1984–1985	-	-	3 318 000	-	1 673 000	-	-
1985–1986	-	-	796 000	-	853 000	-	-
1986–1987	-	-	390 000	-	5 120 000	-	-
1987–1988	-	-	-	-	5 816 000	-	-
1988–1989	-	-	-	-	3 381 000	-	[15]250 000
1989–1990	-	-	-	-	2 568 000	-	-
1990–1991	-	-	-	-	3 744 951	-	-
1991–1992	-	-	-	-	4 490 000	-	-
1992–1993	-	-	-	-	4 490 000	-	-
1993–1994	-	-	-	-	3 346 000	-	-
1994–1995	-	-	-	-	5 825 000	-	-
1995–1996	-	-	-	-	4 882 000	-	-
1996–1997	-	-	-	-	4 882 000	-	-
1997–1998	-	-	-	-	4 178 000	-	-
1998–1999	-	-	-	-	4 448 000	-	-
1999–2000	-	-	-	-	5 415 000	-	-
2000–2001	-	-	-	-	4 881 238	-	-
2001–2002	-	-	-	-	7 932 000	-	-
2002–2003	-	-	-	-	-	-	-
2003–2004	-	-	-	-	-	-	-

Source: Statutes at Large; Annual Report of the Librarian of Congress.

[3]Funds for the National Program for Acquisitions and Cataloging were initially appropriated to the Commissioner of Education, who transferred them to the Library. This arrangement ceased in 1971–1972 when the funds became a part of the Library's appropriation.
[4]The fiscal year changed from beginning in July to beginning October 1. Appropriations reflect an additional amount for July–October 1976.
[5]For revision of the *Constitution of the United States—Analysis and Interpretation.*
[6]For microfilming the records of the Russian Orthodox Greek Catholic Church of Alaska.
[7]For revision of the *Constitution of the United States*, $110,709, and for preparing a supplement to *Hinds' Precedents of the House of Representatives* and *Cannon's Precedents of the House of Representatives*, $30,000.
[8]For the supplement to *Hinds'* and *Cannon's Precedents*, $76,000.
[9]For the supplement to *Hinds'* and *Cannon's Precedents*, $120,000.
[10]For preparing the supplement to *Hinds'* and *Cannon's Precedents*, $143,400, and for revision of the *Constitution of the United States*, $31,900.
[11]To cover revision of the *Constitution of the United States*, $34,000.
[12]To cover revision of the *Constitution of the United States*, $43,000 and the work of the National Commission on New Technological Uses of Copyrighted Works (CONTU), $455,000.
[13]To cover the work of the National Commission on New Technological Uses of Copyrighted Works (CONTU), $559,500.
[14]To cover a lump sum for increased pay costs.
[15]For the National Film Preservation Board.
- = Quantity zero.

PART III.3. Table 1. Growth of the Library's Collections, 1801–1896

(Round numbers represent estimates. 1891–1896 figures are all estimated. Through 1874, the report year is December 1–November 30. The 1875 report covers December 1, 1874–December 31, 1875.)

Year	Volumes	Pamphlets	Maps and charts
1801	740	-	3
1802	[1]964	-	9
1812	3 076	-	[2]53
1815	[3]6 487	-	-
1822	12 000	-	-
1825	14 000	-	-
1829	16 000	-	-
1836	24 000	-	-
1840	30 000	-	-
1845	40 000	-	-
1847	42 000	-	-
1849	45 000	-	-
1850	50 000	-	-
1851	55 000	-	-
1852	[4]20 000	-	-
1853	35 000	-	-
1854	40 000	-	-
1860	63 000	-	-
1861	70 000	-	-
1863	79 214	-	-
1864	82 000	-	-
1866	99 650	-	-
1867	[5]165 467	-	-
1868	173 965	-	-
1869	185 227	-	-
1870	197 668	30 000	-
1871	236 846	40 000	-
1872	246 345	45 000	-
1873	258 752	48 000	-
1874	274 157	53 000	-
1875	293 507	60 000	-
1876	311 097	100 000	-
1877	331 118	110 000	-
1878	352 655	120 000	-
1879	374 022	[6]120 000	-
1880	396 788	133 000	-
1881	420 092	145 000	-
1882	480 076	160 000	-
1883	513 441	170 000	-
1884	544 687	185 000	-
1885	565 134	191 000	-
1886	581 678	193 000	-
1887	596 957	194 000	-
1888	615 781	200 000	-
1889	633 717	206 000	-
1890	648 928	207 000	-
1891	659 843	210 000	-
1892	677 286	220 000	-
1893	695 880	223 000	-
1894	710 470	225 000	-
1895	731 441	230 000	-
1896	748 115	245 000	-

Source: William Dawson Johnston, *History of the Library of Congress, 1800–1864* (Washington, D.C.: Library of Congress, 1904); *Annual Report of the Librarian of Congress.*

[1]Before the Library was established in 1800, Congress acquired 243 volumes. These were added to the Library's holdings in 1802.
[2]After 1812, maps and charts were not reported again until 1897.
[3]British troops burned the Capitol on August 24, 1814, and the entire Library was destroyed. Congress purchased Thomas Jefferson's private library of 6,487 volumes to replace the lost books.
[4]Much of the Library's collection was destroyed in a December 1851 fire in the Capitol.
[5]The Smithsonian collection and part of the Peter Force Library are added to the Library of Congress's collections.
[6]Librarian Answorth Rand Spofford reported the same number of pamphlets in 1878 and 1879.
- = Quantity zero.

PART III.3. Table 2. Growth of the Library's Collections, 1897–1939

(Report is for the fiscal year ending June 30. Statistics indicate the number of volumes or physical pieces rather than titles.)

Year	Books	Pamphlets	Manuscripts	Maps and charts	Music	Prints
1897	787 715	218 340	-	27 700	189 046	54 233
1898	[1]705 122	226 972	24 933	50 195	199 894	59 908
1899	[2]957 056	-	26 500	52 181	277 465	70 823
1900	995 166	-	27 278	55 717	294 070	84 871
1901	1 071 647	-	36 619	60 025	311 020	106 326
1902	1 114 111	-	99 532	64 921	345 511	127 002
1903	1 195 531	-	103 115	69 814	366 616	142 337
1904	1 275 667	-	121 266	76 129	384 418	158 451
1905	1 344 618	-	-	82 476	410 352	183 724
1906	1 379 244	-	-	89 869	437 510	214 276
1907	1 433 848	-	-	98 483	464 618	253 822
1908	1 535 008	-	-	105 118	483 411	279 567
1909	1 702 685	-	-	111 343	501 293	303 036
1910	1 793 158	-	-	118 165	517 806	320 251
1911	1 891 729	-	-	123 946	557 010	339 014
1912	2 012 393	-	-	129 123	591 632	349 745
1913	2 128 255	-	-	135 223	630 799	360 494
1914	2 253 309	-	-	141 712	663 474	376 812
1915	2 363 873	-	-	147 553	727 808	385 757
1916	2 451 974	-	-	154 200	770 248	392 905
1917	2 537 922	-	-	158 480	795 749	397 945
1918	2 614 523	-	-	160 090	822 009	402 291
1919	2 710 556	-	-	163 484	848 292	409 029
1920	2 831 333	-	-	166 448	884 227	418 976
1921	2 918 256	-	-	170 005	919 041	424 783
1922	3 000 408	-	-	174 093	954 304	428 745
1923	3 089 341	-	-	177 905	972 130	436 802
1924	3 179 104	-	-	182 233	986 354	442 977
1925	3 285 765	-	-	[3]939 992	1 001 645	449 418
1926	3 420 345	-	-	985 390	1 007 007	458 132
1927	3 556 767	-	-	1 028 257	1 022 057	462 860
1928	3 726 502	-	-	1 068 874	1 033 513	469 062
1929	3 907 304	-	-	1 117 211	1 045 481	494 991
1930	4 103 936	-	-	1 161 478	1 062 194	498 715
1931	4 292 288	-	-	1 206 408	1 074 714	512 046
1932	4 477 431	-	-	1 265 116	1 087 607	520 828
1933	4 633 476	-	-	1 281 228	1 100 428	524 321
1934	4 805 646	-	-	1 319 697	1 116 895	528 256
1935	4 992 510	-	-	1 337 415	1 131 747	534 642
1936	5 220 794	-	-	1 358 479	1 150 044	538 629
1937	5 395 044	-	-	1 376 801	1 168 584	540 851
1938	5 591 710	-	-	1 402 658	1 194 697	542 074
1939	5 828 126	-	-	1 421 285	1 221 333	548 622

Source: Annual Report of the Librarian of Congress.

[1]The 1897 figures are estimates. Librarian John Russell Young ordered an actual count of the book collection, which was completed in 1898.
[2]From 1899 onward the "Books" figure includes pamphlets.
[3]Category expanded to include insurance, ordinance, and duplicate maps previously excluded from the statistics.
- = Quantity zero.

PART III.3. Table 3. Growth of the Library's Collections, 1940–1982

(Except as noted below, decreases reflect either disposal of duplicates and other unneeded material or totals adjusted to reflect the collections more accurately.)

Year	Books and pamphlets	Bound newspaper vols.	Manuscripts	Maps	Music	Prints	Microforms
1940	6 102 259	-	-	1 441 719	1 399 357	552 514	-
1941	6 353 516	-	-	1 459 995	1 598 776	558 101	-
1942	6 609 387	-	-	1 472 251	1 619 280	561 779	6 917
1943	6 822 448	-	[1]7 500 000	1 503 819	1 641 654	564 814	[2]24 657
1944	7 304 181	-	[1]7 790 616	1 537 168	1 664 730	572 461	32 214
1945	7 877 002	-	[1]7 929 903	1 639 505	1 703 599	575 083	43 343
1946	7 946 460	118 159	8 121 913	1 711 292	1 719 610	576 946	59 001
1947	8 187 064	121 251	8 620 162	1 810 810	1 743 394	578 527	66 181
1948	8 387 385	124 619	[1]10 500 000	1 868 911	1 788 449	578 765	71 060
1949	8 689 639	128 055	11 320 000	1 928 574	1 819 609	579 298	76 609
1950	8 956 993	131 176	11 970 000	1 981 608	1 849 513	579 669	81 322
1951	9 241 765	136 717	12 163 121	2 004 334	1 881 840	580 017	95 863
1952	9 578 701	140 573	12 855 870	2 138 698	1 917 191	580 451	118 687
1953	9 846 561	143 860	13 239 450	2 242 210	1 960 030	580 904	143 054
1954	10 155 307	147 090	14 282 594	2 307 534	2 002 277	582 212	162 653
1955	10 513 048	151 623	14 578 313	2 362 581	1 883 405	582 888	186 445
1956	10 776 013	155 921	15 107 865	2 289 137	1 925 620	583 261	211 924
1957	11 057 773	159 015	15 469 572	2 317 388	1 958 186	583 591	243 922
1958	11 411 475	161 389	15 687 836	2 387 286	1 988 572	582 879	291 076
1959	11 779 894	165 941	16 185 209	2 469 085	2 018 017	583 738	[3]274 517
1960	12 075 447	167 654	16 531 145	2 563 362	2 049 723	584 163	296 808
1961	12 329 678	169 993	17 731 181	2 622 105	2 076 834	586 256	324 075
1962	12 534 351	160 466	17 989 445	2 684 076	2 110 660	587 345	325 060
1963	12 752 792	156 766	18 610 876	2 746 879	2 140 991	588 641	369 829
1964	13 139 494	150 530	18 970 817	2 797 715	3 176 433	[4]174 378	406 308
1965	13 453 168	149 509	27 959 731	2 886 455	3 214 974	175 604	445 061
1966	13 767 403	145 721	28 117 882	3 003 049	3 247 923	176 524	514 862
1967	14 107 259	139 184	28 415 370	3 083 265	3 275 207	175 436	574 554
1968	14 479 171	132 113	29 145 621	3 208 892	3 296 829	176 227	653 658
1969	14 846 317	130 227	29 572 093	3 277 665	3 316 628	176 443	747 543
1970	15 258 327	125 466	29 936 636	3 315 210	3 335 348	176 926	[5]1 270 459
1971	15 660 523	121 362	30 338 713	3 371 628	3 366 026	175 298	1 471 726
1972	16 064 837	115 933	30 618 658	3 444 234	3 373 825	176 482	1 731 946
1973	16 466 899	111 014	31 031 504	3 502 101	3 384 178	174 412	1 944 136
1974	16 761 198	106 027	31 498 669	3 531 304	3 415 128	174 610	2 125 169
1975	17 454 995	87 331	31 722 263	3 533 598	3 488 933	177 921	2 335 074
1976[6]	18 013 089	78 838	32 516 931	3 571 934	3 631 666	179 136	2 634 415
1977	18 320 256	74 677	32 672 753	3 590 395	3 646 457	179 501	2 936 326
1978	18 638 633	70 585	32 757 891	3 605 789	3 662 265	179 816	3 226 532
1979	18 930 905	67 423	33 391 320	3 624 347	3 668 063	180 327	3 477 685
1980	19 155 165	62 394	33 873 879	3 643 703	3 684 485	180 569	3 873 981
1981	19 578 334	55 402	34 627 783	3 726 919	3 687 764	205 797	4 228 586
1982	19 721 066	50 910	34 881 616	3 755 745	3 690 395	208 796	[7]4 573 577

[1]Figures are estimates.
[2]An inventory of "microforms" was taken in 1942–1943.
[3]"Microforms" is adjusted to exclude microfilmed newspapers.
[4]Figures reflect a number of changes in categories and adjustments in totals. "Prints" is redefined to include drawings. Photographic "negatives, prints, and slides" was redefined.
[5]Figures for "books" and for "microforms" include technical reports and other material not previously reported.
[6]The report year changed from July 1–June 30 to October 1–September 30. Figures reflect increases from July 1, 1976 to September 30, 1976.
[7]"Microforms" began to include newspapers and technical reports.
- = Quantity zero.

PART III.3. Table 3. Growth of the Library's Collections, 1940–1982—*Continued*

(Except as noted below, decreases reflect either disposal of duplicates and other unneeded material or totals adjusted to reflect the collections more accurately.)

Year	Recordings	Books for the Blind	Motion pictures	Posters and other material	Negatives, prints, and slides	Newspapers	Reports
1940	-	42 120	-	-	-	-	-
1941	-	44 509	-	-	-	-	-
1942	[8]72 753	-	-	-	-	-	-
1943	88 451	-	5 129	-	-	-	-
1944	105 574	-	9 127	[1]137 424	[1]881 631	-	-
1945	123 134	-	11 955	[1]231 965	[1]936 412	-	-
1946	260 588	-	43 555	287 237	950 834	-	-
1947	274 092	-	61 100	[9]560 188	1 063 879	-	-
1948	[10]287 414	-	64 451	624 163	1 708 247	-	-
1949	305 848	-	81 278	668 732	1 963 231	-	-
1950	326 889	-	84 193	689 604	2 038 960	-	-
1951	354 536	-	90 591	694 457	2 076 362	-	-
1952	387 396	-	98 314	704 965	2 225 926	-	-
1953	411 993	-	106 873	717 678	2 233 938	-	-
1954	438 881	-	110 116	726 129	2 238 059	-	-
1955	92 686	366 073	112 150	752 429	2 619 773	-	-
1956	97 937	379 801	115 816	761 383	2 926 979	-	-
1957	101 490	395 494	118 832	766 522	2 946 854	-	-
1958	104 271	414 868	121 883	784 541	2 969 843	-	-
1959	107 927	429 056	124 418	951 300	2 981 017	56 122	-
1960	109 376	445 877	126 756	[11]893 144	3 024 890	63 025	-
1961	116 751	[12]1 039 389	133 577	1 023 056	3 060 524	69 600	-
1962	114 756	1 076 626	[13]68 738	1 033 746	3 088 167	94 058	-
1963	125 164	1 266 978	75 378	1 060 124	3 124 741	112 320	-
1964	154 059	1 516 376	78 817	1 000 414	[5]1 794 068	130 576	-
1965	165 203	1 799 543	82 124	998 519	1 800 808	141 771	-
1966	183 801	2 078 956	86 124	990 932	1 782 714	155 081	-
1967	220 931	2 364 263	89 056	991 618	1 812 867	169 275	-
1968	245 862	2 750 377	92 450	991 772	3 066 963	184 065	-
1969	266 564	3 167 696	96 999	984 690	3 070 232	197 256	-
1970	285 164	[14]3 477 370	121 789	984 540	3 136 473	213 726	-
1971	322 767	3 821 126	158 665	1 026 483	3 137 297	228 970	1 264 517
1972	344 003	4 084 503	167 753	1 027 457	8 446 394	242 826	1 267 306
1973	383 742	4 270 488	183 202	1 025 072	8 448 707	259 868	1 281 603
1974	428 784	[15]47 861	202 552	1 020 698	8 450 287	275 754	1 294 811
1975	467 554	51 991	219 784	965 978	8 452 896	294 025	1 270 531
1976[6]	641 022	58 098	238 964	971 915	8 484 043	326 592	1 259 266
1977	711 654	66 469	252 157	973 788	8 516 171	347 810	1 275 465
1978	748 948	70 241	268 147	975 892	8 522 797	368 096	1 291 942
1979	791 656	75 318	279 910	977 978	8 538 964	384 613	1 295 185
1980	865 053	82 201	291 236	979 524	8 567 684	414 112	1 271 374
1981	892 080	86 428	299 711	1 105 653	8 625 727	437 740	1 283 166
1982	937 081	91 188	310 754	1 107 133	8 660 636	459 644	1 294 465

Source: *Annual Report of the Librarian of Congress.*

[1]Figures are estimates.
[5]Figures for "books" and for "microforms" include technical reports and other material not previously reported.
[6]The report year changed from July 1–June 30 to October 1–September 30. Figures reflect increases from July 1, 1976 to September 30, 1976.
[8]The "recordings" figure is an estimate covering collections in the Music Division and the service for the blind.
[9]Broadsides, posters, and other material adds photostats.
[10]"Recordings" excludes talking books, which were moved to the "Books for the Blind" category.
[11]Broadsides, posters and other material excludes books in raised characters, which were added to Books for the Blind.
[12]"Books for the Blind" includes books in regional libraries for the blind.
[13]Motion pictures reflects discards of surplus and deteriorated films.
[14]"Books for the Blind" became "Books for the Blind and Physically Handicapped."
[15]"Books for the Blind and Physically Handicapped" excludes books deposited in regional libraries for the blind and physically handicapped.
- = Quantity zero.

PART III.3. Table 4. Growth of the Library's Collections, 1983–2003

(The count represents items, not titles. Decreases reflect either disposal of duplicates and other unneeded material or totals adjusted to reflect the collections more accurately.)

Year	Classified book collections	Music	Bound newspapers	Technical reports	Other printed works	Audio material	Manuscripts	Maps	Microforms	Motion pictures	Other visual material	Machine readable material
1983	13 247 804	3 691 377	47 721	1 320 750	6 864 405	1 003 531	35 041 305	3 801 247	5 378 694	314 651	10 086 967	-
1984	13 474 783	3 693 666	44 947	1 379 240	6 911 749	1 053 058	35 282 878	3 805 176	5 801 068	321 410	10 137 941	-
1985	13 757 631	3 694 256	41 281	1 398 679	6 948 858	1 091 732	36 154 097	3 830 566	6 297 601	325 127	10 230 875	-
1986	14 045 520	3 699 260	40 130	1 414 076	7 018 335	1 149 065	36 175 568	3 862 328	6 653 286	331 008	10 306 243	-
1987	14 324 945	3 704 498	39 271	1 443 344	7 084 728	1 214 136	36 138 986	3 889 778	7 012 227	339 418	11 043 922	-
1988	14 581 944	3 710 366	37 617	1 453 345	7 148 496	1 302 800	36 563 392	3 919 000	7 343 209	345 234	11 910 131	-
1989	14 829 080	3 716 577	37 120	1 458 658	7 213 783	1 350 165	36 992 230	3 945 770	7 686 396	339 539	12 968 916	-
1990	15 095 645	3 729 417	36 886	1 455 298	7 280 397	1 809 683	39 413 936	3 976 778	8 160 285	525 589	15 780 323	-
1991	15 374 079	3 751 129	36 231	1 426 746	7 366 740	1 870 190	39 693 433	4 098 486	8 690 174	532 609	15 797 137	-
1992	15 700 905	3 757 296	36 136	1 364 440	7 468 350	1 859 247	41 467 185	4 156 896	9 350 504	691 459	15 542 839	-
1993	16 055 353	3 768 733	35 825	1 375 647	7 572 778	2 161 976	43 226 412	4 247 049	9 793 544	994 188	15 603 147	-
1994	16 448 469	3 774 153	35 786	1 386 310	7 673 744	2 198 467	45 300 615	4 345 837	10 315 270	1 026 935	15 318 923	-
1995	16 764 805	3 774 600	35 777	1 397 481	7 736 645	2 223 066	46 623 436	4 346 337	10 842 392	715 763	13 949 241	23 827
1996	17 079 138	3 825 735	35 759	1 402 929	7 817 054	2 298 982	47 911 077	4 408 464	11 339 461	742 699	14 188 865	30 503
1997	17 402 100	4 110 025	34 792	1 409 434	7 863 875	2 390 167	49 147 855	4 451 790	11 767 481	772 104	13 640 922	36 197
1998	17 772 400	4 127 568	30 570	1 419 156	7 929 665	2 374 011	50 682 161	4 481 334	12 171 496	803 077	13 671 835	42 422
1999	18 024 002	4 206 449	[1]30 570	1 424 039	7 974 575	2 452 699	53 120 327	4 523 049	12 555 509	821 527	13 808 914	51 969
2000	18 306 178	4 234 234	30 710	1 434 658	8 015 143	2 551 305	54 143 744	4 562 267	12 915 487	844 328	13 878 769	59 516
2001	18 631 989	5 051 611	30 860	1 444 425	8 152 680	2 612 336	55 204 250	4 908 085	13 339 537	877 591	13 924 464	69 774
2002	18 993 274	5 108 553	30 874	1 450 791	8 214 220	2 676 572	56 107 162	4 863 681	13 532 501	899 561	14 103 741	80 050
2003	19 367 655	5 107 852	[1]30 874	1 453 733	8 257 219	2 715 554	57 033 626	4 793 399	13 733 491	924 804	14 197 925	104 748

Source: *Annual Report of the Librarian of Congress.*

Note: "Books" represent only books in the classified book collections. "Other printed works" includes books in large type and books in raised characters (previously included in Books for the Blind and Physically Handicapped), incunabula, minimal-level cataloged monographs, and pamphlets. "Audio" includes talking books and other recorded formats previously included in Books for the Blind and Physically Handicapped. "Manuscripts" includes manuscripts in the Manuscripts and Music Divisions. "Visual material" includes photographs (negatives, prints, and slides), posters, prints and drawings, videotape and videodisc, broadsides, photocopies, photostats and nonpictorial material.

[1]No bound newspapers were added or withdrawn.

\- = Quantity zero.

Part III.4. MAJOR GIFTS AND ENDOWMENTS FOR THE LIBRARY'S COLLECTIONS, 1869–2004: A SELECTIVE LIST

1869 *Chinese Collection*
The emperor of China sent a gift of 934 volumes to the U.S. government in 1869, which formed the nucleus of the Library's Chinese collection.

1882 *Joseph M. Toner Collection*
On May 19, 1882, President Chester A. Arthur approved a joint resolution of Congress authorizing the Librarian of Congress to accept the donation by Joseph M. Toner of his medical research library. It included approximately 40,000 books and pamphlets and 75,000 items of personal papers.

1884 *Turkish Collection*
Through the efforts of Representative Abram S. Hewitt of New York, the Library received in 1884 a gift of 284 volumes from Sultan Abdul Hamid II of Turkey, which provided the foundation of the Library's Turkish collection.

1898 *Gardiner Greene Hubbard Collection*
On July 7, 1898, President William McKinley approved a joint resolution of Congress authorizing the Librarian to accept the Gardiner Greene Hubbard's collection of European and American prints, the gift of his widow, Gertrude M. Hubbard. In 1912, Mrs. Hubbard provided a bequest to support the future growth of the collection.

1903 *Andrew Jackson Papers*
The first presidential papers given to the Library were those of Andrew Jackson, presented by the Francis P. Blair family in 1903.

1910 *John Boyd Thacher Collection*
Mrs. John Boyd Thacher, widow of a former mayor of Albany, New York, on April 27, 1910 placed her husband's 840-volume collection of fifteenth-century books, autographs, early printing, works on American exploration and the French Revolution, and manuscripts on deposit at the Library. On her death on February 18, 1927, the collection was bequeathed to the Library.

1910 *Henry Harrisse Collection*
Henry Harrisse, a bibliographer and historian, died in 1910, bequeathing to the Library his personal collection of maps, manuscripts, rare books, and a complete file of his own writings.

1912 *Joseph H. Schiff Collection*
Ephraim Deinard gathered a collection of nearly 10,000 volumes and pamphlets of Hebraica, which was donated to the Library beginning in 1912 by Jacob H. Schiff of New York City. It provided the foundation of the Judaica collection.

1912 *Signers of the Declaration of Independence*
J. Pierpont Morgan presented to the nation in 1912, for placement in the Library of Congress, "a complete bound set of letters and documents" of the Signers of the Declaration of Independence.

1917 *Drafts of the Gettysburg Address*
In January 1917, descendants of John Hay gave the United States government the original and second drafts of the Gettysburg Address, to be placed in the custody of the Library of Congress.

1917 *Theodore R. Roosevelt Papers*
The first installment of Theodore Roosevelt's papers arrived in January 1917; they were the first group of presidential papers to be received directly from a former president.

1917 *Joseph Pennell Collection*
Mr. and Mrs. Joseph Pennell, the authorized biographers of James Whistler, on May 24, 1917 presented a collection of Whistler prints and sketches together with their collection of books and research materials relating to the artist and his times. Joseph Pennell died April 23, 1926, leaving most of his estate to the U.S. government to be used for collections and services in the Library's Division of Prints.

1919 *Abraham Lincoln Papers*
Robert Todd Lincoln, the son of President Abraham Lincoln, deposited a major collection of his father's papers in the Library, May 7, 1919, and donated them formally on January 23, 1923 on the condition that they be kept sealed until 21 years after his own death. He died in 1926, and accordingly the papers were opened to the public on July 26, 1947.

1924–1925 *Gifts of Elizabeth Sprague Coolidge*
Mrs. Coolidge in 1924 donated the original scores of musical compositions that received awards at her Pittsfield, Massachusetts Festival. A separate gift of $60,000 supported the construction of an auditorium within the Library for the performance of chamber

music. In 1925 she established an endowment to aid the Library's Music Division to mount concerts and festivals, and award prizes for original compositions, with an additional amount as an honorarium for the chief of the division. The first Library of Congress chamber music festival was held in the newly completed Coolidge Auditorium on October 28–30, 1925.

1925, 1933 *James B. Wilbur Gifts and Chair*
James B. Wilbur, of Manchester, Vermont, provided funds for reproducing by photostat manuscript material on American history held in European archives, with the copies to be retained in the Library's collections In 1933, Mr. Wilbur endowed a chair of geography and provided funds for the additional development of source materials in American history.

1925 *Victor Recordings*
The Victor Talking Machine Company of Camden, New Jersey donated a Victrola and a selection of 412 recordings, December 7, 1925.

1927–1932 *John D. Rockefeller Jr. Gift*
In 1927, John D. Rockefeller Jr. provided $700,000 over a five-year period (1927–1932) to allow the Library (1) to acquire facsimiles and copies of source materials in foreign archives for the study of American history, and (2) to develop the bibliographical apparatus, particularly the Union Catalog.

1927–1936 *Huntington Endowments and Gifts*
In 1927, Archer M. Huntington of New York City gave an endowment for the purchase of books relating "to Spanish, Portuguese, and South American arts, crafts, literature, and history." In 1928, he donated funds to establish a chair of Spanish and Portuguese literature. In 1936, he gave he gave the Library funds to "equip and maintain" a room to be known as the Hispanic Society Room and to establish and maintain a chair of poetry of the English language.

1928 *Archive of American Folk Song*
In May 1928, with funding from several individuals, Librarian Herbert Putnam established the "Archive of the American Folk Song" project in the Music Division.

1929 *Oscar G. T. Sonneck Memorial Fund*
On September 10, 1929, the Beethoven Association of New York established the Sonneck Memorial Fund, named for Oscar G. T. Sonneck, the first chief of the Music Division, and intended to assist the Library to support music research.

1929 *Guggenheim Chair*
On October 29, 1929, Harry F. Guggenheim, president of the Daniel Guggenheim Fund for the Promotion of Aeronautics, endowed a chair of aeronautics and provided funds for the purchase of aeronautics materials.

1930 *Early American Architecture*
The Carnegie Corporation in 1930 provided funds to support a collection of pictorial images of early American architecture.

1935 *Oliver Wendell Holmes Jr. Collection*
Former Supreme Court Justice Oliver Wendell Holmes Jr., who died on March 6, 1935, bequeathed his private library to the Library of Congress.

1935–1938 *Gifts of Gertrude Clarke Whittall*
In 1935, the Library received, as a gift from Gertrude Clarke Whittall, four stringed instruments made by Antonio Stradivari. In 1936, she established a foundation to support concerts in which the instruments were used, and in the next year she added a fifth instrument to her gift. In 1938, she donated funds to build an elegant pavilion in which the instruments were to be housed and displayed. The Whittall Pavilion, adjacent to the Coolidge Auditorium in the Jefferson Building, opened March 6, 1939.

1939 *The George and Ira Gershwin Collection*
The Gershwin family presented the first Gershwin gift to the Library in 1939, and additional music manuscripts, papers, and pictorial materials have been added through the years. Support is through the Ira and Leonore S. Gershwin Fund (1992). The George and Ira Gershwin Room, in the Jefferson Building, opened March 17, 1998.

1941 *Dayton C. Miller Flute Collection*
Dayton C. Miller, a physicist by profession, bequeathed to the Library in 1941 his collection of more than 1,600 flute instruments, his library of flute music and literature, and funds to support and expand the collection.

1942 *Netherlands Collection*
The Trust Fund for Netherlands-American Cultural Activities provided funding in 1942 to enable the Library to organize a Netherlands study unit to evaluate and expand the collection of material relating to that country.

1943 *Lessing J. Rosenwald Collection*
On March 17, 1943, the Library announced that Lessing J. Rosenwald of Jenkintown, Pennsylvania, a

well-known collector, had given more than 500 rare illustrated books to the Library, including 200 incunabula. The gifts, which continued until Mr. Rosenwald's death in 1979, resulted in a collection of 2,653 titles, including 588 incunables.

1945 *Bill of Rights*
One of 13 engrossed copies of the proposed amendments to the Constitution, sent on October 2, 1789 to the 11 states and Rhode Island and North Carolina, was presented to the Library by Barney Balaban, president of Paramount Pictures, Inc., on February 21, 1945.

1945–1948 *Leonard Kebler Collection*
Between 1945 and 1948, Leonard Kebler gave the Library his collection of first editions of Cervantes, Dickens, Washington Irving, and other authors.

1946 *Woodrow Wilson Library*
In 1946, Edith Bolling Galt Wilson, the widow of the former president, donated Wilson's 9,000-volume personal library to the Library of Congress.

1946 *Mary Pickford Collection*
Actress Mary Pickford gave the Library her personal collection of motion pictures in 1946. With support from the Mary Pickford Foundation, on May 10, 1983, the Mary Pickford Theater opened in the Library's Madison Building.

1949 *Wright Brothers Collection*
The papers of Orville and Wilbur Wright, a 30,000-item collection that includes 303 glass-plate negatives documenting their flights, were donated to the Library in 1949.

1951–1953 *Stern Collection of Lincolniana*
In 1951, Chicago businessman Alfred Whital Stern began depositing in the Library portions of his extensive collection of publications, manuscripts, prints, and other materials relating to Abraham Lincoln. On September 29, 1953, the entire collection was donated to the Library.

1950–1954 *G.C. Whittall Literary Gifts*
Whittall established the Whittall Poetry Fund in 1950 to support poetry readings and public programs and to furnish a room in the Jefferson Building to be known as the Poetry Room. The literary series began in 1951 and the Poetry Room opened on April 23, 1951. In 1952 and 1954, she donated additional funds to support literary programming.

1952 *Giant Bible of Mainz*
On April 4, 1952, philanthropist and book collector Lessing J. Rosenwald presented the nation with a copy of the Giant Bible of Mainz, the illuminated manuscript Bible written in Mainz, Germany in 1452–1453. The Library placed it in a special exhibit case in the Great Hall, across from its contemporary, the Gutenberg Bible.

1952 *Sigmund Freud Archives*
On July 23, 1952, the Library received the first installment of the Freud collection, deposited by the Sigmund Freud Archives, Inc., of New York.

1954 *Mathew Brady Photographs*
Over 3,000 negatives by Civil War photographer Mathew B. Brady plus several thousand plates made by his nephew, Levin C. Handy, were donated to the Library on September 13, 1954. The collection was the gift of the Handy family.

1964 *NAACP Records*
In November 1964 the Library received the first containers of the records of the National Association for the Advancement of Colored People, an archive of over one million items.

1965 *Louchheim Broadcasting Gifts*
Mr. and Mrs. Walter C. Louchheim Jr., of Washington, D.C., provided funds in 1965 to distribute tapes of Library of Congress concerts to educational and commercial broadcasters nationwide. Three years later they established the Katie and Walter Louchheim Fund to support musical performances and poetry readings, preparation of audio and videotapes to broadcast concerts and literary presentations and the production of sound recordings and videotapes for the public and for educational institutions.

1966 *Bay Psalm Book*
The last copy of the Bay Psalm Book remaining in private hands was deposited in the Library by Mrs. Adrian Van Sinderen, Washington, Connecticut, on May 2, 1966, with the promise that title would be transferred upon her death.

1966 *Folk Music Recordings Preservation*
The Martha Baird Rockefeller Fund for Music, Inc., provided funding in 1966 to transfer the earliest field recordings of American folk music to magnetic tape, as a preservation measure.

1967 *Engelhard Publications Fund*
Mrs. Charles William Engelhard Jr., of Far Hills, New Jersey, established a revolving fund in 1967 to support publications describing the Library's collections and services.

1969 *Spanish American Manuscripts*
Hans P. Kraus, New York City, an antiquarian book dealer, donated his collection of 162 manuscripts relating to the history and culture of colonial Spanish America in 1969.

1969 *Walt Whitman Collection*
Gifts from anonymous donors enabled the Library to purchase Charles E. Feinberg's Walt Whitman collection, numbering over 20,000 items, in 1969. Whitman's manuscripts were the gift of Thomas Harned in 1918, and Carolyn Wells Houghton bequeathed a collection of Whitman publications in 1922.

1970 *McKim Chamber Music Fund*
Through an endowment from Mrs. W. Duncan McKim, the Library established in 1970 a fund for the support of compositions and performances of chamber music for violin and piano.

1974–1979 *Swann Collection*
The Caroline and Erwin Swann Collection of Caricature and Cartoon came to the Library in installments, in the 1970s. The Swann Gallery in the Jefferson Building opened on February 25, 1998.

1975 *Alexander Graham Bell Collection*
In 1975, the heirs of Alexander Graham Bell presented his manuscripts to the Library, a collection of 130,000 items.

1978 *NBC Collection*
The National Broadcasting Company in 1978 made the first in a series of gifts of its archive to the Library, a collection that by the early 1990s had become the largest archive of an American broadcasting network or station available to the public.

1987 *Hans Moldenhauer Archives*
The Moldenhauer collection of autograph music, manuscripts, letters, and documents—one of the most significant collections of primary sources in music—was donated to the Library in 1987. The Archives span the history of western music. The bequest also provided funds for a guide to the collection.

1988 *Charles and Ray Eames Collection*
Noted California designers Charles and Ray Eames donated their studio collections to the Library in 1988. It included original papers, office records, drawings, photographs and transparencies, graphics, and motion pictures.

1993 *Public Broadcasting Service Collection*
In 1993, the Public Broadcasting Service (PBS) donated its vast collection of video holdings covering more than four decades of programming.

1999 *Bob Hope Collection*
In 1999, the family of Bob Hope donated to the Library his personal papers, radio and television broadcasts, scripts, joke files, films, and other material. The gift included endowment of the Bob Hope Gallery of American Entertainment, which opened in the Jefferson Building on May 9, 2000.

1999 *Reconstruction of Jefferson's Library*
Jerral and Gene Jones, members of the Madison Council, and James and Margaret Elkins provided a gift in 1999 to reassemble works included in Thomas Jefferson's personal collection, which was purchased after the Library of Congress was burned by the British during the War of 1812.

2004 *Alan Lomax Collection*
Through an agreement with the Association for Cultural Equity at Hunters College and the generosity of an anonymous donor, the Library in March 2004 acquired folklorist Alan Lomax's ethnographic documentation, which joins the collection Lomax and his father, John, amassed for the Library during the 1930s and early 1940s.

2004 *Early Americas Collection*
The Jay I. Kislak Foundation of Miami Lakes, Florida donated in April 2004 Mr. Kislak's collection of rare books, manuscripts, historic documents, maps and art of the Southeastern United States, the Caribbean and Mesoamerica. The collection of more than 4,000 items contains some of the earliest records of indigenous peoples of North America.

PART III.5. Table 1. Chairmen of the Congressional Committees on the Library, 1805–2004

Year	Chairman	Congress
1805–1807	Senator Samuel Latham Mitchill (NY) Representative Joseph Clay (PA)	9th
1807–1808	Senator Samuel Latham Mitchill (NY) Representative Samuel W. Dana (CT)	10th, 1st session
1808–1809	Senator William B. Giles (VA) Representative Wilson C. Nicholas (VA)	10th, 2nd session–11th, 1st session
1809–1810	Senator James Lloyd (MA) Representative Samuel W. Dana (CT)	11th, 2nd session
1810–1812	Senator Michael Leib (PA) Representative Adam Seybert (PA)	11th, 3rd session–12th, 1st session
1812–1813	Senator Michael Leib (PA) Representative Samuel Latham Mitchill (NY)	12th, 2nd session
1813–1814	Senator Michael Leib (PA) Representative Adam Seybert (PA)	13th, 1st–2nd sessions
1814–1815	Senator Robert H. Goldsborough (MD) Representative Adam Seybert (PA)	13th, 3rd session
1815–1817	Senator Eligius Fromentin (LA) Representative John W. Taylor (NY)	14th
1817–1819	Senator Mahlon Dickerson (NJ) Representative Adam Seybert (PA)	15th
1819–1820	Senator Mahlon Dickerson (NJ) Representative Charles Pinckney (SC)	16th, 1st session
1820–1821	Senator Mahlon Dickerson (NJ) Representative Rollin C. Mallary (VT)	16th, 2nd session
1821–1822	Senator Mahlon Dickerson (NJ) Representative Joel R. Poinsett (SC)	17th, 1st session
1822–1824	Senator Mahlon Dickerson (NJ) Representative Alexander Smyth (VA)	17th, 2nd session–18th, 1st session
1824–1825	Senator Mahlon Dickerson (NJ) Representative William C. Rives (VA)	18th, 2nd session
1825–1828	Senator Mahlon Dickerson (NJ) Representative Edward Everett (MA)	19th–20th, 1st session
1828–1829	Senator Nathan Sanford (NY) Representative Edward Everett (MA)	20th, 2nd session
1829–1835	Senator Asher Robbins (RI) Representative Edward Everett (MA)	21st–23rd
1835–1836	Senator William C. Preston (SC) Representative George Loyall (VA)	24th, 1st session
1836–1838	Senator Asher Robbins (RI) Representative John M. Patton (VA)	24th, 2nd session–25th, 2nd session
1838–1839	Senator Asher Robbins (RI) Representative John Pope (KY)	25th, 3rd session
1839–1840	Senator Benjamin Tappan (OH) Representative Dixon H. Lewis (AL)	26th, 1st session
1840–1841	Senator Garret Dorset Wall (NJ) Representative Joseph L. Tillinghast (RI)	26th, 2nd session
1841	Senator Thomas Clayton (DE) Representative Joseph L. Tillinghast (RI)	27th, 1st session
1841–1842	Senator William C. Preston (SC) Representative Joseph L. Tillinghast (RI)	27th, 2nd session
1842–1843	Senator William Woodbridge (MI) Representative Joseph L. Tillinghast (RI)	27th, 3rd session
1843–1845	Senator Rufus Choate (MA) Representative Edmund Burke (NH)	28th
1845–1847	Senator James A. Pearce (MD) Representative Richard Brodhead (PA)	29th
1847–1848	Senator James A. Pearce (MD) Representative John Quincy Adams (MA)	30th, 1st session
1848–1849	Senator James A. Pearce (MD) Representative William B. Preston (VA)	30th, 2nd session
1849–1851	Senator James A. Pearce (MD) Representative Isaac E. Holmes (SC)	31st
1851–1855	Senator James A. Pearce (MD) Representative Joseph R. Chandler (PA)	32nd–33rd
1855–1857	Senator James A. Pearce (MD) Representative William Aiken (SC)	34th
1857–1859	Senator James A. Pearce (MD) Representative William H. Dimmick (PA)	35th
1859–1861	Senator James A. Pearce (MD) Representative John U. Pettit (IN)	36th
1861–1863	Senator James A. Pearce (MD) Representative Edward McPherson (PA)	37th
1863–1865	Senator Jacob Collamer (VT) Representative Augustus Frank (NY)	38th
1865–1866	Senator Timothy O. Howe (WI) Representative Rutherford B. Hayes (OH)	39th, 1st session
1866–1867	Senator John A. Creswell (MD) Representative Rutherford B. Hayes (OH)	39th, 2nd session
1867–1869	Senator Edwin D. Morgan (NY) Representative John D. Baldwin (MA)[1]	40th
1869–1871	Senator Alexander G. Cattell (NJ) Representative John A. Peters (ME)	41st
1871–1873	Senator Lot M. Morrill (ME) Representative John A. Peters (ME)	42nd
1873–1875	Senator Timothy O. Howe (WI) Representative William P. Frye (ME)	43rd
1875–1877	Senator Timothy O. Howe (WI) Representative Hiester Clymer (PA)	44th
1877–1879	Senator Timothy O. Howe (WI) Representative Samuel S. Cox (NY)	45th

[1]There is no listing in the *Congressional Directory* for the Joint Committee on the Library under the House Committees for the 40th Congress, First Session. Baldwin appears in the Second Session *Directory*.

PART III.5. Table 1. Chairmen of the Congressional Committees on the Library, 1805–2004—*Continued*

Year	Chairman	Congress
1879–1881	Senator Daniel W. Voorhees (IN) Representative George W. Geddes (OH)	46th
1881–1883	Senator John Sherman (OH) Representative Anson G. McCook (NY)	47th
1883–1885	Senator John Sherman (OH) Representative Otho R. Singleton (MS)	48th
1885–1887	Senator William J. Sewell (NJ) Representative Otho R. Singleton (MS)	49th
1887–1889	Senator William M. Evarts (NY) Representative William G. Stahlnecker (NY)	50th
1889–1891	Senator William M. Evarts (NY) Representative Charles O'Neill (PA)	51st
1891–1892	Senator George F. Hoar (MA)[2]	52nd, 1st session
1892–1893	Senator Matthew S. Quay (PA)[3] Representative Amos J. Cummings (NY)	52nd
1893–1895	Senator Roger Q. Mills (TX) Representative John R. Fellows (NY)[4] Representative Barnes Compton (MD) Representative Franklin Bartlett (NY)	53rd
1895–1897	Senator Henry C. Hansbrough (ND) Representative Alfred C. Harmer (PA)	54th
1897	Senator Henry C. Hansbrough (ND)[5]	55th, 1st session
1897–1900	Senator George P. Wetmore (RI)[6] Representative Alfred C. Harmer (PA)	55th, 1st session–56th, 1st session
1900–1907	Senator George P. Wetmore (RI) Representative James T. McCleary (MN)	56th, 2nd session–59th
1907–1911	Senator George P. Wetmore (RI) Representative Samuel W. McCall (MA)	60th–61st
1911–	Senator George P. Wetmore (RI) Representative James L. Slayden (TX)	62nd
1913–1916	Senator Luke Lea (TN) Representative James L. Slayden (TX)	63rd–64th, 1st session
1916–1919	Senator John Sharp Williams (MS)[7] *Representative James L. Slayden (TX)*[8]	
1919–1923	Senator Frank B. Brandegee (CT) *Representative Norman J. Gould (NY)*	64th, 2nd session–65th
1924–1925	Senator George W. Pepper (PA) *Representative Robert Luce (MA)*	66th–67th
1925–1931	Senator Simeon D. Fess (OH) *Representative Robert Luce (MA)*	68th
1931–1933	Senator Simeon D. Fess (OH) *Representative Ralph Gilbert (KY)*	69th–71st
1933–1941	Senator Alben W. Barkley (KY) *Representative Kent E. Keller (IL)*	72nd
1941–1943	Senator Alben W. Barkley (KY) *Representative Robert T. Secrest (OH)*	73rd–76th
1943	Senator Alben W. Barkley (KY) *Representative Graham A. Barden (NC)*	77th
1943	Senator Alben W. Barkley (KY) *Representative Donald L. O'Toole*	78th, 1st session
1947–1949	Senator C. Wayland Brooks (IL) *Representative Karl M. LeCompte (IA)*	78th, 1st session–79th
1949–1951	Senator Theodore F. Green (RI) *Representative Mary T. Norton (NJ)*	80th
1951–1952	Senator Theodore F. Green (RI) *Representative Thomas B. Stanley (VA)*	81st
1952–1953	Senator Theodore F. Green (RI) *Representative Ken Regan (TX)*	82nd, 1st session
1953–1954	Senator William A. Purtell (CT) Representative Karl M. LeCompte (IA)	82nd, 2nd session
1954–1955	Senator Joseph R. McCarthy (WI) Representative Karl M. LeCompte (IA)	83rd,[9] 1st session
1955–1956	Representative Omar T. Burleson (D-TX)	83rd, 2nd session
1956–1957	Senator Theodore F. Green (D-RI)	
1957–1958	Representative Omar T. Burleson (D-TX)	84th, 1st session[10]
1958–1959	Senator Theodore F. Green (D-RI)	84th, 2nd session
1959–1960	Senator Theodore F. Green (D-RI)	85th, 1st session
1960–1961	Representative Omar T. Burleson (D-TX)	85th, 2nd session
1961–1963	Representative Omar T. Burleson (D-TX)	86th, 1st session
1963–1964	Representative Omar T. Burleson (D-TX)	86th, 2nd session
1964–1965	Senator B. Everett Jordan (D-NC)	87th[11]
1965–1966	Representative Omar T. Burleson (D-TX)	88th, 1st session
1966–1967	Senator B. Everett Jordan (D-NC)	88th, 2nd session
1967–1968	Representative Omar T. Burleson (D-TX)	89th, 1st session
1968–1969	Senator B. Everett Jordan (D-NC)	89th, 2nd session
1969–1970	Representative Samuel N. Friedel (D-MD)	90th, 1st session

[2]Hoar is listed under the Senate Committee on the Library in the *Congressional Directory*, 52nd Congress, First Session, First Edition. There are no House Committees listed in this edition.
[3]Quay is listed under the Senate Committee on the Library in the *Congressional Directory*, 52nd Congress, First Session, Second Edition, which is corrected to January 29, 1892.
[4]Fellows is listed under the House Committee on the Library in the *Congressional Directory*, 53rd Congress, Second Session, First Edition. (No House committees are listed in the First Session *Directory*.) Compton is listed in the Second Session, Second Edition, corrected to February 1, 1894, and Bartlett is listed in the *Congressional Directory*, 53rd Congress, Third Session.
[5]Hansbrough is listed under the Senate Library Committee in the *Congressional Directory*, 55th Congress, Extra (1st) Session, First Edition. The House Library Committee is not listed in this session.
[6]Wetmore is listed under the Senate Library Committee in the *Congressional Directory*, 55th Congress, Extra (1st) Session, Second Edition. The House Library Committee members are listed in the Directory, 55th Congress, Second Session.
[7]Beginning with the *Congressional Directory* for the 64th Congress, First Session, Second Edition, the Joint Committee on the Library was listed under Congressional Commissions and Joint Committees, with the chairman always listed as the ranking senator. Prior to this, the Senate and House each listed a separate Committee on the Library under their standing committees, each with its own chairman.
[8]Italics designates the ranking House member of the committee.
[9]No committee chair is listed in either session of the *Congressional Directory* for the 83rd Congress.
[10]Beginning with the 84th Congress, the committee began designating a vice chairman and alternated the chairmanship and vice chairmanship between the House and Senate members each session.
[11]During the 87th Congress, Representative Burleson served as chairman of the committee and Senator Mike Mansfield (MT) served as vice chairman during the whole Congress. They did not alternate each session.

PART III.5. Table 1. Chairmen of the Congressional Committees on the Library, 1805–2004—*Continued*

Year	Chairman	Congress
1970–1971	Senator B. Everett Jordan (D-NC)	90th, 2nd session
1971–1972	Representative Wayne L. Hays (D-OH)	91st, 1st session
1972–1973	Senator B. Everett Jordan (D-NC)	91st, 2nd session
1973–1974	Representative Lucien N. Nedzi (D-MI)	92nd, 1st session
1974–1975	Senator Howard W. Cannon (D-NV)	92nd, 2nd session
1975–1976	Representative Lucien N. Nedzi (D-MI)	93rd, 1st session
1976–1977	Senator Howard W. Cannon (D-NV)	93rd, 2nd session
1977–1979	Representative Lucien N. Nedzi (D-MI)	94th, 1st session
1979–1981	Senator Claiborne D. Pell (D-RI)	94th, 2nd session
1981–1983	Representative Augustus F. Hawkins (D-CA)	95th[12]
1983–1985	Senator Charles McC Mathias (R-MD)	96th
1985–1987	Representative Frank Annunzio (D-IL)	97th
1987–1989	Senator Claiborne D. Pell (D-RI)	98th
1989–1991	Representative Frank Annunzio (D-IL)	99th
1991–1993	Senator Claiborne D. Pell (D-RI)	100th
1993–1995	Representative Charles G. Rose III (D-NC)	101st
1995–1997	Senator Mark O. Hatfield (R-OR)	102nd
1997–1999	Representative William M. Thomas (R-CA)	103rd
1999–2001	Senator Theodore F. Stevens (R-AK)	104th
2001–2003	Representative Vernon J. Ehlers (R-MI)	105th
2003–2004	Senator Theodore F. Stevens (R-AK)	106th

Source: Congressional Directory; Johnston, William Dawson, *History of the Library of Congress Volume I, 1800–1864.* Washington, D.C.: GPO, 1904.

[12]Starting with the 95th Congress, the chairmanship and vice chairmanship of the committee alternated between the House and Senate members every Congress, rather than every session.

Part IV. FURTHER RESEARCH AND READING

Thousands of articles, reports, and documents about the Library of Congress and its activities have been published through the years, along with dozens of books. The selective list below highlights historical treatments and articles of a general nature. Citations to more specific items follow many of the individual essays and articles in this volume.

The most valuable published resources for the study of the history and development of the Library of Congress are the *Annual Report of the Librarian of Congress* (1866–) and the *Library of Congress Information Bulletin* (1943–). From 1943 to 1983, the Library published *The Quarterly Journal of the Library of Congress*, which focused on new acquisitions and the Library's collections. *Civilization: The Magazine of the Library of Congress*, published commercially from 1994 to 2000, broadened the Library's audience.

The Library also publishes guides to its collections, technical specifications and standards, exhibition catalogs, recordings, calendars, and related materials. The Library's Web site <www.loc.gov> is the best source for information about its publications and about the current activities of its administrative units.

Since 1899, the Library of Congress has maintained an archive of its own historically valuable records. Since the 1940s, these unpublished records, now encompassing more than three million items, have been housed in the Library's Manuscript Division.

Early records in the Library of Congress Archives include the correspondence of the Librarians of Congress from 1843 until 1973. This correspondence is complemented by the Central File, which spans the administrations of John Russell Young, Herbert Putnam, Archibald MacLeish, and Luther H. Evans. The Central File documents the Library's major administrative policies and programs from 1897 through 1953. The personal papers of several Librarians of Congress and senior Library officials can also be found in the Library of Congress Archives.

Other items of special interest are the ledgers, receipts, and correspondence describing the construction of the Library's Thomas Jefferson Building. The Archives also contain the Library's general and special orders, which are the official statements of Library policies and procedures. Annual accountings of the Library's acquisitions, services, and other activities are found in the reports of the divisions and departments of the Library. These form the basis for the *Annual Reports of the Librarian of Congress*. Frederick B. Ashley's unpublished "History of the Library of Congress, 1897–1939" a description of the Library's development into a national institution, is a rich, first-hand resource. A large collection of newspaper clippings (1814–1950), as well as photographs, illustrations, and selected objects that portray Library events, staff, buildings, and ceremonial occasions are also included in the Archives.

Aikin, Jane. "Foundation for Service: The 1896 Hearings on the Library of Congress." *The Journal of Library History*, 21 (Winter 1986): 107–130.

______. "High Culture, Low Culture: The Singular Diversity of the Library of Congress." *American Studies*, 42 (Fall 2001): 43–61.

Bisbort, Alan and Linda Barnett Osborne. *The Library of Congress: The Nation's Library*. Washington, D.C.: Library of Congress in cooperation with Scala Publisher, 2000.

Cole, John Y. *For Congress and the Nation: A Chronological History of the Library of Congress*. Washington, D.C.: Library of Congress, 1979.

______. *Jefferson's Legacy: A Brief History of the Library of Congress*. Washington, D.C.: Library of Congress, 1993.

______. ed., with Henry Hope Reed. *The Library of Congress: The Art and Architecture of the Thomas Jefferson Building*. N.Y. : W.W. Norton & Company, 1997.

______. ed. *The Library of Congress: A Documentary History. Guide to the Microfiche Edition*. Bethesda, Md.: Congressional Information Service, Inc., 1987.

______. ed. *The Library of Congress in Perspective: A Volume Based on the Reports of the 1976 Librarian's Task Force and Advisory Groups*. N.Y.: R. R. Bowker Company, 1978.

Conaway, James. *America's Library: The Story of the Library of Congress, 1800–2000*. New Haven, Conn.: Yale University Press, 2000.

Dawson, William Johnston. *History of the Library of Congress, 1800–1864*. Washington, D.C.: Government Printing Office, 1904.

Goodrum, Charles A. *Treasures of the Library of Congress, revised and expanded edition.* N.Y.: Harry N. Abrams, Inc., 1991.

Librarians of Congress, 1802–1974. Washington, D.C.: Library of Congress, 1977.

McGuire, William. *Poetry's Catbird Seat: The Consultantship in Poetry in the English Language at the Library of Congress, 1937–1987.* Washington, D.C.: Library of Congress, 1988.

Mearns, David C. *The Story Up to Now: The Library of Congress, 1800–1946.* Washington, D.C.: Library of Congress, 1947.

Melville, Annette, comp. *Special Collections in the Library of Congress.* Washington, D.C.: Library of Congress, 1980.

Ostrowski, Carl. *Books, Maps, and Politics: A Cultural History of the Library of Congress, 1783–1861.* Amherst, MA: University of Massachusetts, 2004.

Rosenberg, Jane Aikin. *The Nation's Great Library: Herbert Putnam and the Library of Congress, 1899–1939.* Urbana, Ill.: University of Illinois Press, 1993.

Salamanca, Lucy. *Fortress of Freedom: The Story of the Library of Congress.* With a Foreword by Archibald MacLeish. Philadelphia: J. B. Lippincott Company, 1942.

Small, Herbert. *The Library of Congress: Its Architecture and Decoration.* New York: W. W. Norton & Company, 1982. A revised edition of Small's 1897 guidebook.

Illustrated Guides to the Collections of the Library of Congress

Library of Congress Africana Collections: An Illustrated Guide. Foreword by Beverly Gray. Introduction by Joanne M. Zellers. Washington, D.C.: Library of Congress, 2001.

Library of Congress American Folklife Center: An Illustrated Guide. Foreword by Peggy A. Bulger. Preface by James Hardin. Washington, D.C.: Library of Congress, 2004.

Library of Congress Asian Collections: An Illustrated Guide. Introduction by Mya Thanda Poe. Washington, D.C.: Library of Congress, 2000.

Library of Congress European Collections: An Illustrated Guide. Introduction by Michael H. Haltzel. Washington, D.C.: Library of Congress, 1995.

Library of Congress Geography and Maps: An Illustrated Guide. Introduction by Ralph E. Ehrenberg. Washington, D.C.: Library of Congress, 1996.

Library of Congress Hebraic Collections: An Illustrated Guide. Foreword by Beverly Gray. Washington, D.C.: Library of Congress, 2001.

Library of Congress Hispanic and Portuguese Collections: An Illustrated Guide. Introduction by John R. Hébert. Washington, D.C.: Library of Congress, 1996.

Library of Congress Manuscripts: An Illustrated Guide. Introduction by James H. Hutson. Washington, D.C.: Library of Congress, 1993.

Library of Congress Motion Pictures, Broadcasting, Recorded Sound: An Illustrated Guide. Introduction by David J. Francis. Washington, D.C.: Library of Congress, 2002.

Library of Congress Music, Theater, Dance: An Illustrated Guide. Introduction by James W. Pruett. Washington, D.C.: Library of Congress, 1993.

Library of Congress Near East Collections: An Illustrated Guide. Foreword by Beverly Gray. Introduction by Levon Avdoyan. Washington, D.C.: Library of Congress, 2001.

Library of Congress Prints and Photographs: An Illustrated Guide. Preface by Stephen E. Ostrow. Washington, D.C.: Library of Congress, 1995.

Library of Congress Rare Books and Special Collections: An Illustrated Guide. Introduction by Larry E. Sullivan. Washington, D.C.: Library of Congress, 1992.

Library of Congress Resource Guides

The African-American Mosaic: A Library of Congress Resource Guide for the Study of Black History and Culture, edited by Debra Newman Ham. Washington, D.C.: Library of Congress, 1993.

American Women: A Library of Congress Guide for the Study of Women's History and Culture in the United States, edited by Sheridan Harvey, Janice E. Ruth, Barbara Orbach Natanson, Sara Day, and Evelyn Sinclair. Introduction by Susan Ware. Washington, D.C.: Library of Congress, 2001.

Keys to the Encounter: A Library of Congress Resource Guide for the Study of the Age of Discovery, by Louis De Vorsey Jr. Washington, D.C.: Library of Congress, 1992.

The Largest Event: A Library of Congress Resource Guide for the Study of World War II, by Peter T. Rohrbach. Washington, D.C.: Library of Congress, 1994.

Many Nations: A Library of Congress Resource Guide for the Study of Indian and Alaska Native Peoples of the United States, edited by Patrick Frazier and the Publishing Office. Washington, D.C.: Library of Congress, 1996.

CONTRIBUTORS

A list of the authors of signed essays and articles follows. Special thanks go to these authors and to the following Library of Congress staff members and former staff members who submitted ideas and preliminary drafts in the early stages of the project or helped review articles: James Agenbroad, Linda Arret, Frederick W. Bauman, Audrey Fischer, David Francis, John Kaldahl, Victoria Hill, Mary Levering, Daniel P. Mulhollan, Harriet L. Oler, Margaret Wagner, Beacher Wiggins, and Robert Zich. We also are grateful to Richard A. Baker of the U.S. Senate Historical Office and his colleagues for preparing the list of the chairmen of the Congressional Committees on the Library that appears in Part III. Several of the individuals listed below have retired from the Library since completing their essays or articles.

Editors and Contributors:

John Y. Cole (JYC), Director, Center for the Book, Library of Congress
Jane Aikin (JA), Senior Academic Advisor, Division of Research Programs, National Endowment for the Humanities

Contributors:

Jeremy Adamson (JAD), Prints and Photographs Division
Carol Armbruster (CA), European Division
James C. Armstrong (JCA), Overseas Operations Division
Levon Avdoyan (LA), African and Middle Eastern Division
Linda Ayers (LAY), Prints and Photographs Division

John C. Broderick, Assistant Librarian for Research Services
Leonard C. Bruno (LCB), Science, Technology and Business Division
Samuel Brylawski (SB), Motion Picture, Broadcasting, and Recorded Sound Division
Mary R. Bucknum (MRB), Motion Picture, Broadcasting, and Recorded Sound Division

Laura E. Campbell, Associate Librarian for Strategic Initiatives
Margaret Coughlan (MC), Children's Literature Center

Donald R. DeGlopper, Law Library
Daniel DeSimone (DD), Rare Book and Special Collections Division
Georgette Dorn (GD), Hispanic Division
Sarah Duke (SD), Prints and Photographs Division

Ralph E. Ehrenberg (REE), Geography and Map Division

Jeffery M. Flannery (JMF), Manuscript Division
Amy Friedlander, consultant, Office of Strategic Initiatives

Prosser Gifford (PG), Office of Scholarly Programs
Beverly Gray (BG), African and Middle Eastern Division
Karl R. Green (KRG), Science, Technology and Business Division
Ronald E. Grim (REG), Geography and Map Division
Michael Grunberger (MG), African and Middle Eastern Division
Nancy E. Gwinn, Smithsonian Institution Libraries

James Hardin (JH), American Folklife Center
Robert B. Harriman Jr. (RBH), Preservation Office
Kenneth E. Harris (KEH), Preservation Office
Steven J. Herman (SJH), Collections Access, Loan, and Management Division

Alan Jabbour (AJ), American Folklife Center
Sybille A. Jagusch (SAJ), Children's Literature Center

Harry L. Katz (HLK), Prints and Photographs Division

Guy Lamolinara, Office of Strategic Initiatives
Carolyn Larson (CL), Science, Technology and Business Division
Kevin LaVine (KL), Music Division
Hwa-Wei Lee (HWL), Asian Division
Patrick Loughney (PL), Motion Picture, Broadcasting, and Recorded Sound Division

Lawrence Marcus (LM), Science, Technology and Business Division
Harold E. Meinheit (HEM), consultant, Asian Division
Andrea Merrill (AM), Office of Personnel Security

Josephus Nelson (JN), Manuscript Division

Mya Thanda Poe (MTP), Asian Collection
Stephen Prine, National Library Service for the Blind and Physically Handicapped
Joseph Puccio (JP), Library Services

Judith P. Roach (JPR), Local History and Genealogy Section
Janice E. Ruth (JER), Manuscript Division

Susan E. Schur (SES), consultant, Preservation Office

George F. Thuronyi, Copyright Office

Mary Wolfskill (MMW), Manuscript Division
Robert Worden (RW), Federal Research Division
L. Christopher Wright (LCW), Loan Division

Abby L. Yochelson, Humanities and Social Science Division

Joanne Zellers (JZ), African and Middle Eastern Division

Helena Zinkham (HZ), Prints and Photographs Division

INDEX

Q